8TH EDITION

SOCIAL PSYCHOLOGY

ALFRED R. LINDESMITH
ANSELM L. STRAUSS
NORMAN K. DENZIN

SAGE Publications
International Educational and Professional Publisher
Thousand Oaks London New Delhi

For information:

SAGE Publications, Inc.
2455 Teller Road
Thousand Oaks, California 91320
E-mail: order@sagepub.com

SAGE Publications Ltd.
6 Bonhill Street
London EC2A 4PU
United Kingdom

SAGE Publications India Pvt. Ltd.
M-32 Market
Greater Kailash I
New Delhi 110 048 India

Printed in the United States of America

Library of Congress Cataloging-in-Publication Data

Lindesmith, Alfred Ray, 1905-
Social psychology / by Alfred R. Lindesmith, Anselm L. Strauss, and Norman K. Denzin. — 8th ed.
p. cm.
Includes bibliographical references.
ISBN 0-7619-0745-9 (cloth: alk. paper)
ISBN 0-7619-0746-7 (pbk.: alk. paper)
1. Social psychology. I. Strauss, Anselm L. II. Denzin, Norman K. III. Title.—
HM251.L477 1999
302—dc21 98-48146

This book is printed on acid-free paper.

04 10 9 8 7 6 5 4

Acquiring Editor: Peter Labella
Editorial Assistant: Renée Piernot
Production Editor: Astrid Virding
Editorial Assistant: Nevair Kabakian
Designer/Typesetter: Janelle LeMaster
Cover Designer: Candice Harman

8TH EDITION

SOCIAL PSYCHOL

To Anselm Strauss
(1916-1996)

Contents

PART II
SOCIAL STRUCTURE AND LANGUAGE

PART III
CHILDHOOD SOCIALIZATION

Preface

This eighth edition of *Social Psychology* significantly updates the previous edition. Virtually a third of the text is new. Chapter 1 introduces a long, new section on cultural studies and the narrative turn in social psychology. Chapter 2 offers a critical examination of the field of primatology, drawing on Donna Haraway's analysis of primate visions. The four chapters that make up Part II have been revised and condensed. Chapter 3 contains new material on speech as narrative discourse, and Chapter 4 includes new material concerning Jung's theory of dreams. Chapter 6 introduces activity theory as an important addition to the literature on perception, memory, and planning. The three chapters in Part III introduce several recent literatures into our analysis of childhood socialization. In Chapter 7 we argue that speech act theory sheds important light on the learning and use of language in early childhood. Drawing on the work of Judith Butler, we also argue that gender is best seen as a performance. In Chapter 8 we give considerable attention to recent arguments concerning social constructionism, essentialism, and identity politics. Chapter 9 expands our earlier treatment of gender performances, and also presents discussion of recent extensions and criticisms of G. H. Mead's theory of the self and the generalized other.

The greatest number of revisions and changes are found in Part IV. Chapter 10 introduces the notions of the cinematic society, the everyday gaze, the cinematic imagination, and the cultural logics of postmodernism. It situates the interaction order within the public places that define civil society. In Chapter 11 we compare and contrast modern and postmodern theories of the self and outline Lonnie Athens's theory of dramatic self-change. Chapter 12 presents discussion of recent histories and theories of sexuality, bisexuality, transgendered persons, the AIDS crisis, queer theory, and queer nation. In Chapter 13 we apply social constructionism and the medicalization model to the understanding of deviance, deviant bodies, and deviant worlds. Finally, in Chapter 14 we give special attention to the technologies of power that are contained within the medical establishment. We examine the medical body and chronic illness, and offer criticisms of the risk society and the central place of the medicalization process in these social structures.

Like the previous edition, this edition is written in the spirit of C. W. Mills's *The Sociological Imagination.* We ask how a sociological imagination, sensitive to power, gender, language, subjective experience, the media, and the circuits of culture, can speak to our collective lives in the last years of the 20th century. We hope that this revision continues to convey the excitement and fulfillment that comes from the application of symbolic interactionism to the study of human group life. We regard this perspective as the most sociological of all social psychologies. When placed within an interpretive cultural framework, symbolic interactionism offers the social sciences the most sensible theory of mind, self, and reflexive conduct.

It is our hope that interested readers will be motivated to read more deeply in this perspective and to perhaps examine the journals *Symbolic Interaction* and *Studies in Symbolic Interaction,* which present the latest research and theoretical work in this tradition.

The first edition of this book was published in 1949. With this edition, *Social Psychology* becomes the oldest social psychology text in the United States. It is an honor to be with Sage Publications for this edition. At Sage we thank Peter Labella, who graciously took this project on and has provided continuous support throughout every stage in the process. At Sage we also thank Astrid Virding and Judy Selhorst for their patience, consideration, and assistance. We also thank Sylvia Allegretto, Shawn Miklaucic, Jack Bratich, and Michael Elavsky for their excellent assistance in preparing this revision, including indexing and proofreading.

It is with great regret that I record the death of Anselm Strauss on September 5, 1996. This book is dedicated to the memory of Lindy and Anselm. They started it all, and somewhere in the mid-1970s they allowed me to become a part of it. I thank them.

—Norman K. Denzin

PART I

THE SOCIAL PSYCHOLOGICAL IMAGINATION

1

The Field of Social Psychology

The chapters in Part I offer an overview of our conception of the field of social psychology. In this chapter we have two major goals. The first is to define and locate the field of social psychology within the human disciplines. The second is to make a statement concerning our position as social psychologists. We call our point of view *critical symbolic interactionism* and connect it to cultural studies and pragmatic, feminist social philosophy (see Denzin, 1992, 1997; Seigfried, 1996; Strauss, 1993; West, 1989).

A Definition of the Field

Social psychology is an interdisciplinary field located midway between sociology and psychology. It also occupies central places on the borderlines that separate anthropology, history, and literature (Benson, 1993). Sociologists study the economic, political, and cultural processes that shape social structure and contemporary cultural life (Fine, House, & Cook, 1995, p. xi; Hall, 1996a, p. 9). Psychologists study the processes of mental life: memory, perception, reasoning, cognition, and emotion.

Sociological social psychologists study how interacting individuals, in today's advanced, late-capitalist societies, do things together (Becker, 1986, p. 11; Giddens, 1989, p. 520)—how people do collective protests, cook meals, play games, make love, have family dinners, go to the movies, attend and give lectures, and so on. Social psychologists examine how humans use language and develop conceptions of social and personal identity (Hall, 1996b, p. 597), including how these identities are shaped by such factors as race, ethnicity, gender, nationality, sexual orientation, and age.

Following C. Wright Mills (1963), it is understood that individuals live in a secondhand world, a world shaped and defined, in large part, by the mass media. Human existence is not determined solely by interaction, or by social acts. Mills puts this forcefully: "The consciousness of human beings does not determine their existence; nor does their existence determine their consciousness. Between the human consciousness and material existence stand communications, and designs, patterns, and values which influence decisively such consciousness as they have" (p. 375). The information technologies (the mass media) of late-modern societies mediate and define everyday social life.

American social psychology is deeply embedded in world culture. The social psychological project has changed because the world that social psychology confronts has changed. Disjuncture, disruption, and difference define the global, cultural economy in which we all live (Appadurai, 1996). National boundaries and identities blur. Today many people are tourists, immigrants, refugees, exiles, or guest workers, moving from one part of the world to another. The global cultural economy is shaped by new information technologies, shifting systems of money, and media images that flow across old national borders. Cultural narratives still entangled in the Enlightenment worldview circulate between the First and Third Worlds (see Fischer, 1994; Geertz, 1995, pp. 128-131). The periphery has been electronically transported into the center of these First World stories. Old master images and values —from freedom to welfare, human rights, sovereignty, representation, and "the master-term 'democracy' " (Appadurai, 1990, p. 10)—are part of this global system.

Because we live today in a postcolonial world, it is necessary to think beyond the nation or the local group as the focus of social psychological inquiry (Appadurai, 1993, p. 411; see also Appadurai, 1990, 1996). This is the age of electronic capitalism. Postnational social formations compete for resources to serve the needs of refugees, exiles, and victims of ethnic and cultural genocide. The United States has become "a federation of diasporas, American-Indians, American-Haitians, American-Irish, American-Africans . . . the hyphenated American might have to be twice hyphenated (Asian-American-Japanese, or . . . Hispanic-American-Bolivian)" (Appadurai, 1993, p. 424).

These worldwide changes are challenging traditional understandings surrounding gender, sexuality, family, nationality, and personhood. The meanings of these changes are amplified by the electronic media. As a consequence of this complex international situation, many individuals now experience crises of identity. Some social theorists argue that contemporary identities are breaking up and becoming fractured (Gergen, 1991; Hall, 1996b, p. 596). Paraphrasing Hall's (1996b, p. 597) quote of Mercer (1990, p. 43), for many individuals, something that was previously assumed to be stable, fixed, and coherent is now defined by experiences of uncertainty and doubt.

The Existential Focus

This crisis leads to an existential focus on how humans experience freedom and constraint in their daily lives. That is, how do individuals bring purpose and meaning into their lives when doubt, uncertainty, and personal responsibility are in flux and change? Of course, humans define and create their own experiences, but the situations in which experiences occur, and the meanings of those experiences, are often given in advance by the social, cultural, political, and economic institutions of society. Social psychologists study the interplay between gendered lives and social structures as well as the interplay among biographies, personal and social constraints, and the social order.

This focus leads to an examination of two key issues: how humans are created and transformed by the social order and, in turn, how humans create and shape the social situations that mold their behavior. These two issues can be broken down into four basic problems pertaining to (a) stability and change in gendered human interaction; (b) the emergence of new forms and patterns of interaction in daily life; (c) conformity, conventionality, deviance, and power; and (d) social order, constraint, and personal freedom.

The following example should help make our point. The United States is a drug-taking society. Not only do Americans use and abuse prescription drugs at a high rate, but alcohol, cocaine, marijuana, heroin, and other "street drugs" are regularly consumed by more than half of the adult American population. Some 22 million Americans—1 out of every 10—report having used cocaine at least once. In fact, a decade ago, middle-class America's drug of choice was cocaine, for everyone from athletes and doctors to rock musicians and railroad employees. In the late 1980s, crack cocaine became the drug of choice for many (Reeves & Campbell, 1994); more recently, many Americans have been drawn back to a drug that was very popular at midcentury—heroin.

In the past decade, the commissioners of the National Football League, the National Basketball Association, and Major League Baseball have ruled that all athletes in their organizations must submit to regular drug tests to determine if they are free of illegal drugs, including cocaine. Drug testing is also now required for all federal employees. Some see these measures as an invasion of personal freedom.

As society reaches out through its laws and legal agencies into the workplace and the home, it creates social situations that constrain human experience. Although on the one hand American society encourages drug taking, on the other it argues that taking certain drugs is illegal.

We have, with this example, an illustration of the four concerns of the social psychologist. Drug-taking experiences are changing as a result of these controversies. At the same time, new drugs are appearing, and perhaps some will replace crack cocaine and alcohol. Some people will conform to the new laws, others will deviate and not conform. As this occurs, society through its laws exercises power and constraint over those who deviate. Hence new forms of constraint will come into existence as the freedom to take drugs is challenged, if not removed.

The Narrative Turn in Social Psychology

Symbolic interactionists emphasize the reflexive, situated nature of human experience. They examine the place of language and multiple meanings in interactional contexts. This reflexive concern is also evidenced in other points of view, including phenomenology (the study of meaningful inner experience); hermeneutics (the study of texts and their meanings); semiotics (the science of language); psychoanalysis; feminism (Nicolson, 1995); narratology (Murray, 1995); cultural (Much, 1995), discursive (Harré, 1995; Perinbanayagam, 1991), and dialogical psychologies (Shotter, 1995); interpretive sociology; and cultural studies (see Hall, 1996a, p. 14).

The concern for these issues has been called the narrative, or discursive, turn in the human disciplines. This implies greater interest in language, discourse, and discursive practices, and the argument that meaning is contextual (Hall, 1996a, p. 14). This narrative turn moves in two directions at the same time. First, social psychologists formulate and offer various narrative versions, or stories, about how the social world operates. This form of narrative is usually called a *theory*—for example, Freud's theory of psychosexual development.

Second, social psychologists study narratives and systems of discourse, arguing that these structures give coherence and meaning to the world. A system of *discourse* is a way of representing the world. A complex set of discourses is called a *discursive formation* (Hall, 1996c, p. 201). The traditional gender belief system in U.S. culture, with its focus on patriarchy and woman's place being in the home, is an instance of a discursive formation. Discursive formations are implemented through discursive practices, such as patriarchy and the traditional etiquette system.

Systems of discourse both summarize and produce knowledge about the world (Foucault, 1980b, p. 27). These discursive systems are seldom just true or false. In the world of human affairs, truth and facts can be constructed in different ways. Consider this question: "Are those Palestinians who are fighting to regain a home on the West Bank of Israel freedom fighters, or terrorists?" (Hall, 1996c, p. 203). The very words that are used to describe individuals prejudge and evaluate their activities. *Freedom fighter* and *terrorist* are not neutral terms. They are embedded in competing discourses. As such, they are connected to struggles over power —that is, who has the power to determine which term will be used? As Hall (1996c) notes, "It is the outcome of this struggle which will define the 'truth' of the situation." Often it is power, "rather than facts about reality, which makes things 'true' " (p. 203).

Power produces knowledge (Foucault, 1980b, p. 27). Regimes of truth can be said to operate when discursive systems regulate relations of power and knowledge (Hall, 1996c, p. 205). The traditional gender belief system, which regulates the power relations between men and women in this culture, is such a regime. In these ways discursive systems affect lives.

Experience and Its Representations

Of course, it is not possible to study experience directly, so social psychologists study representations of experience—interviews, stories, performances, myth, ritual, and drama. These representations, as systems of discourse, are social texts, or narrative, discursive constructions. Bruner (1984) clarifies this situation, making needed distinctions among three terms: reality, experience, and expressions of experience.

Reality refers to "what is really out there" (Bruner, 1984, p. 7). *Experience* refers to "how that reality presents itself to consciousness" (p. 7). *Expressions* describe "how individual experience is framed" (p. 7). A "life experience consists of the images, feelings, sentiments . . . and meanings known to the person whose life it is. . . . A life as told . . . is a narrative" (p. 7). The meanings and forms of experience are always given in narrative representations. These representations are texts that are performed, stories told to others. Bruner is explicit on this point: Representations must "be performed to be experienced" (p. 7). In these ways, social psychologists deal with performed texts, rituals, stories told, songs sung, novels read, dramas performed. To paraphrase Bruner: Experience is a performance. Social psychologists study how people perform meaningful experience.

The politics of representation is basic to the study of experience. As indicated above, how a thing is represented often involves a struggle over power and meaning. Although social psychologists have traditionally privileged experience itself, it is now understood that no life, no experience, can be lived outside of some system of representation (Hall, 1996d, p. 473). Indeed, "there is no escaping from the politics of representation" (Hall, 1996d, p. 473).

This narrative turn suggests that social psychologists are constantly constructing interpretations about the world, giving shape and meaning to what they describe. Still, all accounts, "however carefully tested and supported, are, in the end 'authored' " (Hall, 1996a, p. 14). Social psychological explanations reflect the points of view of their authors. They do not carry the guarantee of truth and objectivity. For example, feminist scholars have repeatedly argued (rightly, we believe) that the methods and aims of positivistic social psychology are gender biased, that they reflect patriarchal beliefs and practices. In addition, the traditional experimental methods of social psychological inquiry reproduce these biases (Nicolson, 1995, pp. 122-125).

Assessing Interpretations

The narrative turn and the feminist critique have led social psychologists to be much more tentative in terms of the arguments and positions they put forward. It is now understood that there is no final, or authorized, version of the truth. Still, there are criteria of assessment that should be used. Social psychologists are "committed to providing systematic, rigorous, coherent, comprehensive, conceptually clear, well-evidenced accounts, which make their underlying theoretical structure and value assumptions clear to readers. . . . [Still] we cannot deny the ultimately interpretive character of the social science enterprise" (Hall, 1996a, p. 14).

Charles Lemert (1995) reminds us that sociology is an act of the imagination, that the various sociologies are "stories people tell about what they have figured out about their experiences in social life" (p. 14). This is how we can understand social psychology: various stories about the social world, stories people tell themselves about their lives and the worlds they live in, stories that may or may not work.

Basic Social Processes

Four fundamental processes structure human experience. The first is material reality itself, which includes human needs, money, wealth, health, housing, work, and labor. The second process involves the interconnections among race, ethnicity, gender, and sexuality. A gender- and race-based system of stratification organizes the relations between men and women in any society (Clough, 1994). Language is the third process; it defines and mediates human experience. Language, in the form of laws, visual representations, and printed texts, has a material presence in everyday life. It regulates social experience. Subjective experience is the fourth major process that gives meaning to human experience. Subjective experience is mediated by language. In this subjective realm struggles over race, gender, sexuality, and material reality occur.

Race and Gender

All of human experience is influenced by race and gender—that is, filtered through the socially constructed categories of race and of male and female. In U.S. society, the system privileges whiteness over blackness. It reproduces racial and ethnic stereotypes about dark-skinned persons. It regulates interracial, interethnic sexual relationships. Through most of the 20th century, miscegenation laws prohibited sexual relations between whites and nonwhites, until these laws were ruled unconstitutional by the U.S. Supreme Court in the late 1960s (Healey, 1995, p. 16).

Of race and the self, W. E. B. Du Bois (1903/1989), writing at the turn of the 20th century, observed, "The Negro is . . . born with a veil, and gifted with second-sight in this American world—a world which yields him no true self-consciousness, but only lets him see himself through the revelation of the other world" (p. 4). Du Bois argues that the color line in the United States creates a sense of double-consciousness for the African American. This is a racial self that is always looking at itself "through the eyes of others" (p. 4). It is always measuring itself "by the tape of a world that looks on in amused contempt and pity" (p. 4). Of this feeling, Du Bois notes, "One feels his twoness—an American, a Negro; two souls . . . two warring ideals in one dark body" (p. 4). At the time he wrote, Du Bois felt that race was the greatest problem facing the United States—that white America had yet to learn how to accord respect and dignity to the black self. This observation holds to the present day.

The gendered categories (male and female) of the racial self are enacted in performances in daily life: in the conversations between males and females (West & Zimmerman, 1987) and in dating situations, when males open doors for females and women fix dinners for men. A feminist sociological imagination (Balsamo, 1990; Deegan & Hill, 1987), which draws upon symbolic interactionism, examines how contemporary culture recruits and creates sexually gendered subjects. It asks how deviant labels are applied to men and women who do not fit the "heterosexual" norms of the culture (gays and lesbians) and studies the current AIDS crisis as an instance of the homophobia that permeates much of Western culture. In later chapters, we take up the topics of gender socialization in early childhood and the worlds of gay men and women. For the moment, we note only that gender and race, commonly ignored categories in social psychological theory, greatly influence subjective experience, one of the four basic processes that structure all of human experience.

Language

Ferdinand de Saussure (1959), the Swiss linguist, applies the term *langue* to the system of language that exists for any speech community (e.g., English for Americans). He uses the term *parole* to refer to the speaking side of language. Language is "the norm of all other manifestations of speech" (Saussure, 1959, p. 9). Languages are social institutions; they have their own systems of organization and their own history, and they are external to any given speaker. Speech is particular to each user of a language. However, the way any speaker uses a term will not alter its meaning within *langue,* or the larger language system.

Language refers to (a) a system of signs or words; (b) a set of rules that combines those signs into meaningful utterances (syntax); (c) a system of meanings attached to those words that arises out of use and speech; (d) speech behavior itself; (e) the institution of speaking and thinking for any group, culture, or society; and (f) the culture of a group (see Hymes, 1972). Language exists over and above speech and can be studied separately from speaking. The science that "*studies the life of signs within a society*" (Saussure, 1959, p. 16) is called *semiology* or *semiotics,* from the Greek word *semeto,* or sign. Semiotics is a part of the field of social psychology.

A sign has two parts: the *signifier* and the *signified.* These two terms refer, respectively, to the *sound-image* that is heard and seen when a word is spoken (e.g., tree) and the concept that is seen as lying behind the sound-image. When I say the word *tree,* you hear the sound of the word and can imagine the picture of a tree in your mind. You have a concept that gives meaning to that word. Saussure (1959, pp. 66-67) calls the sound-image the signifier and the concept the signified.

Language is a system of interdependent terms in which the value of each term results from the simultaneous presence of the others. Imagine language as a sheet of paper, where thought is the "front and the sound is the back" (Saussure, 1959, p. 114). We cannot divide thought and sound; each depends on the other. The process of using signs, which are like words but mean more than words, is called *signification.*

Robert Perinbanayagam (1985) uses the term "signifying act" to describe the act of articulating "a symbol by the initiator of a message" (p. 9). Humans communicate and interact through signifying acts, which rest on signs and their meanings.

According to Saussure (1959), signs are arbitrary and are understood as social facts that exist within the system of language of any social group. However, groups assign values to their terms, so that a sign not only signifies (points to) something in reality, it gives a value to what is signified. Saussure offers an example:

> Modern French *mouton* can have the same signification as English *sheep* but not the same value, and this for several reasons, particularly because in speaking of a piece of

> meat to be served on the table, English uses *mutton* and not *sheep*. The difference in value between *sheep* and *mouton* is due to the fact that *sheep* has beside it a second term while the French word does not. (pp. 115-116)

We could offer additional examples. The English word *madam*, although the equivalent of the French word *madame*, which refers to a married woman, can signify a woman who runs a house of prostitution. The English term carries at least two meanings. Many observers have noted that the English language is sexist and trivializes women (for a review, see Nash, 1985, pp. 234-236). An adult woman can be called a girl, a hussy, a spinster, a broad, a mistress, a wife, a mother, a whore, and so on. As Nash (1985) notes, English contains thousands of words and phrases that are used to describe women in sexually derogatory ways, but not nearly so many for men. Signs, then, signify reality and give a value, or meaning, to the unit of reality that is signified.

The language system of a society interacts with and reflects the race and gender stratifications of the society, and this system in turn rests on the economic division of labor that exists in the society. Hence language, gender, race, and labor, together with subjective experience, constitute the fundamental processes that order social experience.

The Social Psychological Imagination

C. Wright Mills (1959) coined the term *sociological imagination* to refer to a form of sociological thought that attempts to speak to the promise of the social sciences. Borrowing Mills's term, we can call the "social psychological imagination" that perspective that attempts to grasp the larger historical context that shapes lived experiences. This view tries to come to terms with the personal and public problems of any given generation. It studies inner and outer lives, locating each person as a *universal singular* (Sartre, 1981) in his or her historical time. Each person's life is seen as having universal themes that are articulated in his or her experiences with self and others. Social psychology examines the dominant themes of each historical epoch. Strauss, Fagerhaugh, Suczek, and Wiener (1985) studied medical technology and the influence of current medical practices on the experiences of the chronically ill. Lindesmith (1968) studied the process of drug addiction. Denzin (1987a, 1987b, 1987c) studied the American alcoholic. These kinds of investigations attempt to take common human experiences and reveal how they are given meaning by interacting individuals. They locate these experiences within their historical moment.

The person with social psychological imagination makes an effort to understand how the broader historical scene creates false consciousness, indifference, and insecurity for particular groups of individuals. This imagination promotes self-reflectiveness. It calls for a critical attitude toward the interpretations of history and the world situation that enter one's life on a daily basis through the mass media. This perspective assumes that humans can influence how their histories are made. The social psychological imagination also attempts to identify the dominant themes and problems of any given generation; it then examines those problems as they enter into people's lives. If the 1960s focused on civil rights and the Vietnam War, the 1970s focused on women's rights, the Equal Rights Amendment, and the like. The 1990s have taken on the threat of nuclear war, personal freedoms, health and medical care, worldwide terrorism, protection of the natural environment, family violence and child abuse, and alcohol and drug abuse as central problems. We address these issues throughout this book, and in so doing attempt to promote a sense of the social psychological imagination in our readers.

Symbolic Interactionism

The term *symbolic interaction* refers to a sociological and social psychological approach to the study of human group life and human interaction (Blumer, 1969, p. 1). Within American sociology, the work of Herbert Blumer (1969) has been most commonly associated with this perspective.

Symbolic interactionism is that unique American sociological and social psychological perspective that traces its roots to the early American pragmatists—James, Dewey, Peirce, and Mead. Symbolic interactionists have been called the loyal opposition in American sociology (Mullins, 1973, p. 98), and symbolic interactionism has been described as the most sociological of social psychologies (Manis & Meltzer, 1972, p. 557). Only recently has this perspective entered the field of psychology, where the works of Mead have joined with the theories of Wittgenstein and Vygotsky (see Gergen, 1991; Harré, 1995). Harré (1992), for example, places "symbolic interactions" at the heart of psychology, showing how selves, attitudes, motives, genders, and emotions are "discursive productions, attributes of conversations rather than mental entities" (p. 526). Other psychologists are adopting an interactionist-informed narrative approach to the study of lives, identities, and social relationships (see Josselson & Lieblich, 1993). A relatively new journal, *Mind, Culture, and Activity*, publishes work that connects the symbolic interactionist tradition with science studies, cultural psychology, and the Soviet tradition represented by the works of Vygotsky and others. The journal *Symbolic Interaction* and the research annual *Studies in Symbolic Interaction* routinely publish work by symbolic interactionists, including members of the Society for the Study of Symbolic Interaction.

Basic Principles of Symbolic Interactionism

In its canonical form (Blumer, 1969), symbolic interactionism rests on the following root assumptions. First, "human beings act toward things on the basis of the meanings that the things have for them" (Blumer, 1969, p. 2). Second, the meanings of things arise out of the process of social interaction. Third, meanings are modified through an interpretive process that involves self-reflective individuals symbolically interacting with one another (Blumer, 1969, p. 2). Fourth, human beings create the worlds of experience in which they live. Fifth, the meanings of these worlds come from interaction, and they are shaped by the self-reflections individuals bring to their situations. Sixth, such self-interaction is "interwoven with social interaction and influences that social interaction" (Blumer, 1981,

p. 153). Seventh, joint acts, their formation, dissolution, conflict, and merger, constitute what Blumer calls the "social life of a human society." A society consists of the joint or social acts that "are formed and carried out by [its] members" (Blumer, 1981, p. 153). Eighth, a complex interpretive process shapes the meanings things have for human beings. This process is anchored in the cultural world, in the "circuit of culture" (du Gay, Hall, Janes, Mackay, & Negus, 1997, p. 3) where meanings are defined by the mass media, including advertising, cinema, and television. This process is based on the *articulation* or interconnection of several distinct and contingent processes (du Gay et al., 1997, p. 3).

In the circuits of cultural meaning, five interconnected processes—representation, identification, production, consumption, and regulation—mutually influence one another (du Gay et al., 1997, p. 3). Objects and experiences are *represented* in terms of salient cultural categories. These categories are directly connected to social and personal *identities.* These identities are attached to representations of family, race, age, gender, nationality, and social class. These objects and identities are in turn located in an ongoing political economy, which is a complex, interconnected system. The political economy structures the *production, distribution,* and *consumption* of wealth in a society. It determines the "who, what, when, where, why, and how" of wealth and power in everyday life—that is, who gets what income, at what time, in what places, for what labor, and why. This economy *regulates* the production, distribution, and consumption of cultural objects. It does so by repeatedly forging links that connect cultural objects (cars, clothing, food, houses), their material representations, and the personal identities of consumers as gendered human beings (see the discussion below).

To summarize, an understanding of these five processes leads the social psychologist to examine how cultural objects are represented in the media. Social psychologists then move from this level of analysis to the study of those social identities that are attached to the cultural object, asking, at the same time, How is this object "produced and consumed, and what mechanisms regulate its distribution and use" (du Gay et al., 1997, p. 3)? An instance occurs in the moment when a cultural fad—a style of dress, a particular possession, a hairstyle—seemingly sweeps across an age or gender group. An object is given new meaning—the Sony Walkman, the personal computer, the mountain bike, a pair of torn blue jeans, a baseball hat worn backward. New and old identities are attached to the use of the object, which is produced for consumption by a small number of manufacturers who regulate price and distribution.

People interact with and interpret the objects they act toward. As a consequence, the meanings of objects change in and through the course of action. Meanings are not fixed; they are constantly being transformed in and through the circuits of culture discussed above. For example, an American might well be attracted to a meal that features roast leg of lamb with young potatoes and garden salad. Few Americans would be attracted to a meal of "roast leg of sheep." The meaning of the term and the object lies in the interpretive process and in the meanings brought to the object and the word. Or take another example, one that reveals how meanings change: The acronym *PC* (for personal computer) has little meaning to a person who knows nothing about computers or word processing. Only a decade ago, personal computers were part of the daily lives of relatively few people; today, however, PCs are commonplace. Computers have become personal possessions, the proliferation of laptops being a recent example.

Key Terms

A brief discussion of some of the terms we have used above, and their implications, is necessary. Language, as we have indicated, is the means for interaction and the medium through which it occurs. The term *symbolic* in the phrase *symbolic interaction* refers to the underlying linguistic foundations of human life, just as the word *interaction* refers to the fact that people do not *act toward* one another but *interact with* each other. Language, as a system of signs, symbols, oppositions, and meanings, permits people to enter into their own and others' activities and to make those activities objects of meaning and action. Through language, people enter into one another's ongoing lines of conduct. The study of language lies at the core of social psychology, and symbolic interactionism makes language a fundamental point of departure in the study of human interaction (Saussure, 1959).

By using the term *interaction,* symbolic interactionists commit themselves to the study and analysis of the developmental course of action that occurs when two or more persons join their individual lines of action together into joint action, or into interactional sequences. Goffman's studies of encounters (1961a), frame analysis (1974), and forms of talk (1981) have at times emphasized this interactive feature of human conduct. Hence the study of symbolic interaction requires constant attention to the study of a process—the process of interaction. This emphasis on process sets symbolic interaction apart from other points of view that stress the fixed, static, structural, and attributelike properties of persons and their actions (Strauss, 1977, pp. 282-284).

The central object with whom one must deal is oneself. Persons are both objects and subjects to themselves. The division between subjective and objective worlds of experience is removed in symbolic interactionist thought. The world is in the person, just as the person is in the world. The two are connected through the "circuit of selfness" (Sartre, 1943/1956, pp. 155-158), wherein the person, the world, the situation, and self-consciousness interact, interpenetrate, and plunge through one another in a synthesis of being, action, meaning, and consciousness.

The self of the person, which is connected, in part, to the individual's identities (see below), is a multilayered phenomenon and comes in several forms. The *phenomenological self* constitutes the inner stream of consciousness of the person in the social situation. The *interactional self* is the self that is presented and displayed to others in concrete sequences of action (e.g., customer). The self is also a linguistic, emotional, and symbolic process. The *linguistic self* is the self that fills in the empty personal pronouns (*I, me*) with personal, biographical, and emotional meanings. The self also involves material possessions. The *material self,* or the self-as-a-material-object, consists of all the person calls his or hers at a particular moment in time. The material self is also commodified in the exchange relations that the person enters into. The *ideological self* comprises the broader cultural and historical meanings that surround the definition of the individual in particular group or social situations (e.g., tourist, husband, wife). (*Ideology* here refers to the "imaginary relations of individuals to the real relations in which they 'live' and which govern their existence"; "Ideology constitutes concrete individuals as subjects"; Althusser, 1971, pp. 165, 171.) The *self-as-desire* joins with the *gendered and racialized self* to form the erotic, gendered self-experience that connects the person to others. These forms of the self (phenomenological, interactional, linguistic, material, ideological, as desire) are enacted in the interactional situation and become part of the biography of the person.

The interaction order (Goffman, 1983) is shaped by negotiated, situated, temporal, biographical, emergent, and taken-for-granted processes (Garfinkel, 1967b). The central object to be negotiated in interaction is personal identity, or the self-meanings of the person. These identities, which are personal (names), circumstantial (age, gender), and social or structural (professor, student), range across the modes of self-identification just described (Stone, 1962). The meanings of identity lie in the interaction process; they emerge and shift as persons establish and negotiate the tasks at hand (Couch, Saxton, & Katovich, 1986, p. xxiii).

The situations of interaction may be routinized, ritualized, or highly problematic. In them, consequential experience occurs. Epiphanic experiences rupture routines and lives and provoke radical redefinitions of the self. In moments of epiphany, people redefine themselves. Epiphanies are connected to turning-point experiences (Strauss, 1959). Interpretive interactionists study epiphanic experiences. The interactionist locates epiphanies and personal crises in those interactional situations where personal troubles become public issues (Denzin, 1989, p. 18). In this way the personal is connected to the mass media, social structure, and culture through biographical and interactional experiences.

Exposure to the mass media often structures these crises and their meanings for individuals. A good example is found in this statement of a 38-year-old male alcoholic; he is standing outside the door of a building in which an Alcoholics Anonymous meeting is about to be held:

> How to get into one of those A.A. meetings? What do I say? I seen them in the movies. That Michael Keaton in *Clean and Sober.* He went to one of them. He just stood up and said he was an alcoholic. Do I have to do that? I ain't even sure I am one, but I drank a fifth of Beam last night and I started up agin this mornin'. I'm scared.

This man experiences a crisis in his life that is connected to his use of alcohol. Here is a story waiting to be told, already partially told through the figure of Michael Keaton, an actor, playing a fictional character (Daryl) who goes to a fictional A.A. meeting in a Hollywood film (*Clean and Sober*). Texts within texts, movies, everyday life, a man down on his luck, A.A., a door into a building where meetings are held, anxiety, fear. Here the everyday existential world connects to the cinematic apparatus, and this drunk on the street hopes to begin a story that will have a happy ending, like Michael Keaton's. He may well become the story he sees in this film.

The existential nature of human group life is connected to the larger institutional, mass-media apparatuses that provide specific epiphanic narratives for specific groups or local cultures.

Communication as Culture

Personal experience and social structure are mediated through the process of communication. This process is connected to the world of cultural meanings. These meanings are defined, in part, by the systems of ideology and power in a particular social order. They circulate through specific communication systems (oral, print, electronic). The messages they convey are structured and contained within a narrative code that invests all "newsworthy" events with an aura of political, social, and historical meaning. This code short-circuits receivers and interlocutors. The messages come already interpreted; they overflow with meaning (see Baudrillard, 1972/1981, pp. 175-179). They enter into and define the structures of everyday life (Lefebvre, 1971/1984). In the contemporary, postmodern world (post-World War II), these communication systems display a preoccupation with the real and its representations in video images.

The basic task of the mass media is to make this secondhand world we all live in appear to be natural and invisible. Barthes (1957/1972) elaborates, noting that the media dress up reality, giving it a sense of naturalness, so that "Nature and History [are] confused at every turn" (p. 11). This is how the circuits of culture operate.

These circuits connect people to the media. The prime goals of the mass-media complex are fourfold. The mass media seek to create audiences that (a) become consumers of the products advertised in the media while (b) engaging in consumption practices that conform to the norms of possessive individualism endorsed by the capitalist political system and (c) adhering to a public opinion that is supportive of the strategic polices of the state (Smythe, 1994, p. 285). At this level, the information technologies of late capitalism function to create audiences who use the income from their own labor to buy the products that their labor produces (Smythe, 1994, p. 285). The primary commodity produced by information technologies is not information, messages, images, meaning, or education; the commodity "form of mass-produced, advertiser-supported communications [under monopoly capitalism] . . . is audiences" (Smythe, 1994, p. 268).

The fourth goal of the mass-media complex is clear: to do everything it can to make consumers as audience members think they are not commodities. Herein lies the importance of cultural narratives and stories that reinforce the epiphanic nature of human existence under late-20th-century capitalism. These stories give us the illusion of a soul, of structural freedom and free will.

The circuits of culture (production, distribution, representation) help to implement this system. That is, a dual commodity form structures the work of the communication industries: The consumer as a commodity form must be connected to a cultural object, which is a media and cultural artifact. This cultural object is a social text and a commodity. Consumers as commodities and media artifacts cannot be separated from the larger institutional spheres and cultural codes that organize everyday life (Price, 1993, p. 133).

As a text, the object is first presented within an advertisement format. This format connects the consumer to the product in an informational, image, personalized, or lifestyle format (see Price, 1993, p. 131). The ad creates a need and a desire for the need to be met, and offers a product (brand) that will meet that need. The ad's format shows the person how to use the object and how to associate its use with valued, emotional cultural experiences. Once the consumer purchases the commodity, his or her needs and desires quickly decline in relevance.

In order for an ad to work, a specific audience for the product must be created. Audiences are market categories created by the media and the advertising industry. Emotional needs specific to market categories—such as youth, men, women, and children—are then created. Potential users are targeted for media campaigns that focus on new cultural commodities. Thus does the institution of advertising use the information technologies of the culture.

The phrase *communication as culture* points to the complex relationships among information structures, systems of communication, the popular cultures of particular times, and the lived experiences of interacting individuals. Communication is indispensable to the processes that articulate cultural meanings (Carey, 1989, pp. 64-65). These meanings are symbolic, never singular, always multiple, always carried through the processes of direct and mediated communication (Carey, 1989, pp. 64-65).

Gendered Identities

As we argue in later chapters, every human being in American culture belongs to a specific sex class, male or female, and this assignment is made immediately upon birth (Cahill, 1989, p. 282). *Femininity* and *masculinity* are socially defined terms that are added to the biologically determined sex class of the individual (Garfinkel, 1967a, pp. 16-17, 122-124; Mitchell, 1983, p. 2). Gender defines the social and cultural meanings brought to each anatomical sex class; that is, children learn how to "pass as" and "act as" members of their assigned sexual categories.

Gender, however, is more than learning masculine and feminine behavior (Deegan, 1987, p. 4). Gender also involves sexuality, sexual desire, and being sexual—that, is enacting a gendered sexual identity with another. As Mitchell (1983) argues, people are "formed through their sexuality" and their sexual desires, which become part of their personal sexual identities (p. 2). Sexuality (being sexual) is culturally shaped (e.g., being sexually alluring or sexually dominant), and these cultural understandings are fitted to the sexual biography of the individual.

Emotional codes specific to each gender are learned as language is acquired. These codes interact with the sexual selves and sexual identities that circulate in the various arenas of popular culture in everyday life. The masculine code in U.S. society represses emotionality, whereas the feminine code encourages vulnerability and nurturant forms of emotionality. Each code speaks to a body culture that stresses health, beauty, and erotic attraction. Two gender-specific sexual and emotional cultures thus exist side by side, with females taught to do the emotional work (Hochschild, 1983) that males avoid, yet expect females to do.

The gendered identity is an interactional production. It is embedded in those interactional places (home, work) that give recurring meaning to ordinary experience. These are sites where emotional experiences, including sexual practices, occur. In them, concrete individuals are constituted as gendered subjects who have emotions, beliefs, and social relationships with others. In these sites, ideology—beliefs about the way the world is and ought to be—intertwines with taken-for-granted cultural understandings about love, intimacy, sexuality, the value of work and family, money, prestige, status, and the meaning of the "good life."

Ideology, which works at the level of language and the symbolic (e.g., everyday conversation), also exists as a set of material (economic), interactional practices (inscriptions by social sciences, popular music and film, and so on) that "*hail or interpellate concrete individuals as concrete subjects*" (Althusser, 1971, p. 173). Ideology consists of the myths, beliefs, desires, and ideas people have in their heads about the way things are and should be. At the material level, ideology works through the interactional structures that bring persons together. In this way ideology recruits sexually gendered subjects. Through this process of interpellation, or hailing ("Hey, girl, come here!"), individuals are called to their sexual-gendered identities. In Althusser's (1971) words, "The hailed individual [when called] will turn around. By this mere one-hundred-and-eighty-degree physical conversion, he becomes a *subject*. Why? Because he has recognized that the hail was 'really' to him, and that 'it was *really him* who was hailed' " (p. 174). Daily greetings, requests, and conversational exchanges ("Honey, I need a cup of coffee"; "Hey, big fella, give me a hand here") cast individuals in gendered identities. These activities constitute individuals as concrete gendered subjects in the gender stratification order.

It must be understood that an interactional, dialectical relationship connects these material practices to the worlds of experience where gendered identities are produced. Specific systems of discourse and meaning operate within specific sites to create particular sexually gendered versions of the human being. These systems cohere during particular periods of time (e.g., the Victorian era, immediate post-World War II America) to create coherent, consistent images of the gender stratification order (e.g., the return of women to the home after their introduction to the world of work outside the home during World War II). During other historical moments these systems fall apart or enter interregnums during which there are conflicting images of sexuality, gender, family, marriage, and work (e.g., the 1970s and 1980s in the United States), only to be brought back together again during other historical moments (e.g., the 1990s return of the "traditional" mother and woman as promoted by such magazines as *Good Housekeeping*).

The terms defined above and their meanings are culturally and historically specific. The sexually gendered human being in the late-20th-century United States is a social, economic, and historical construction, built up out of the patriarchal cultural myths that have been articulated in American popular culture for the past 200 years.

What Symbolic Interactionists Do Not Like

We can clarify the special features of symbolic interactionism as a perspective by outlining the empirical and theoretical practices that interactionists value as well as those they do not value.

Interpretive (and symbolic) interactionists do not write grand or global theories of societies (Blumer, 1981, p. 162; 1990, pp. 113-114). They understand society to be something that is lived in the here and now, in the face-to-face and mediated interactions that connect persons to one another. Society, as it is lived, known, felt, and written about, goes on behind people's backs (Marx, 1844/1983). Interactionists believe that they should write about how people are constrained by the constructions they build and inherit from the past.

Society, like interaction, is an emergent phenomenon (Blumer, 1981, p. 153), a framework for the construction of diverse forms of social action (Blumer, 1990, p. 133). Interactionists study how people produce their situated versions of society. They see these situated versions of the social everywhere, from encounters to friendships, to interactions in small groups, to economic exchanges in the marketplace, to the interactions that occur when a television viewer argues with the president during a televised speech.

Rejecting totalizing, grand theories of the social, interactionists, like many poststructural (Foucault, 1980b) and postmodern theorists (Lyotard, 1979/1984) believe in writing local narratives about how people do things together (Becker, 1986; Richardson, 1997). These narratives take the form of small-scale ethnographies, life stories, in-depth interviews, laboratory studies, historical analyses, and textual readings of bits and pieces of popular culture as given in films, novels, and popular music.

Interactionists do not believe in *Sociology* with a capital *S*. Sociology for them simply means studying how social things hang together. They do not believe in using complex sociological terms that refer to things that cannot be immediately observable in the interactions of individuals. This means that they rework concepts like culture and institution to describe the recurring meanings and practices individuals produce when they do things together. Interactionists like to use the ordinary language and interpretive theories that everyday people use. They do not like to use theories that make sense only to other sociologists.

Interactionists don't like theories that are imported from other disciplines, such as the natural sciences, psychology, or economics (Blumer, 1981, p. 155). Such models have not been fitted to the actual lived, emotional experiences of interacting human beings. Aligning themselves more with the humanities than the natural sciences, interactionists approach their materials from a narrative, textual position, understanding that their texts create the subject matter they write about. They don't like overly rational, cognitive theories of human behavior. They don't like monocausal theories, which stress single factors like exchange, reward, or sexual desire as the causes of human behavior. They believe that the human being is active, from the moment of birth to death. The important question becomes one of understanding how humans develop their own accounts and motives for explaining their actions to one another. Interactionists reject monocausal, motivational theories.

Interactionists don't like theories that ignore history, but they are not historical determinists. They believe that persons, not history, make history, but they understand that the histories that individuals make may not always be of their own making. In that case any individual's or group's history becomes the history of other people. Symbolic and interpretive interactionists attempt to speak to the nuances, realities, and fabrics of these two forms of history that shape one another. This is how they study power, which they also call force or violence. This means they study the micro power relations that structure the daily performances of race, ethnicity, gender, and class in interactional situations.

Interpretive interactionists are skeptical of those who call themselves scientists. They believe that science too often gets confused with ideology and the powers of the state (Foucault, 1980b). They think that the findings of science are often used to manipulate people in the name of some societal good or goal, which is always defined in political terms. They are fearful of those who would build a totalizing science of the social. They are antiscience, or at least they like to see themselves as cultural subversives who undermine the repressive workings of science in everyday life.

Interactionists don't like theories that ignore the biographies and lived experiences of interacting individuals. They believe that the biographies of individuals articulate specific historical moments. Each individual is a universal singular (Sartre, 1981), expressing in his or her lifetime the general and specific features of a historical epoch. Hence interactionists don't like Sociologies that ignore the stories people tell one another about their life experiences.

Interactionists don't believe in asking "why" questions. They ask, instead, "how" questions. How, for example is a given strip of experience structured, lived, and given meaning?

Interactionists don't like theories that objectify and quantify human experience (Blumer, 1969, p. 57). They assume that the important human processes cannot be quantified: Mind cannot be measured, and the human body is not a behavioral machine whose actions can be meaningfully understood through procedures that count activity. Interactionists don't like theorists who pontificate about human conduct, who write as if they understand what a given experience means to an individual or the members of a group. They prefer, instead, to write texts that remain close to the actual experiences of the people they are writing about. They like texts that do not place a wedge between themselves and what they are writing about. They like texts that express an immediacy of experience, unmediated by the sociologists' interpretations (see Richardson, 1997). This means that interactionist narratives often convey pathos, sentimentalism, and romantic identification with the persons being written about. Interactionists write about people who struggle to make sense of themselves and their life experiences. But all too often, these people find that personal, biographical, and structural factors make them and their lives less than they could be. Interactionists study the marked, deviant, stigmatized, lonely, unhappy, alienated, powerful, and powerless people in everyday life.

Because of all these things that interactionists don't like and don't like to do, they are often criticized for not doing what other people think they should. They are criticized for not conducting macrostudies of power structures, for not having clearly defined concepts and terms, for being overly cognitive, for having emergent theories, and for being ahistorical and astructural (see Reynolds, 1990, pp. 135-157). Too often these criticisms reflect the failure of the critics either to understand what the interactionist agenda is or to read what interactionists have written.

We can summarize the material in this section by enumerating the key assertions that define symbolic interactionism:

1. Biological variables do not determine behavior; they only influence it.
2. Interactional experience is based on self-indications and reasons for acting, called motives, that persons learn from others.
3. Motives explain past behavior and are used to predict future behavior.
4. Humans live in symbolic environments that are mediated by language and culture.
5. Self-reflectiveness is basic to human experience; it is learned through the socialization process and is influenced by gender and language.
6. Interaction involves the ability to take the attitudes of others and to know how to define situations.
7. Interactional rituals contribute to the maintenance of the interactional order; rituals are ways of acting that confer status on self and others, and rules of etiquette are interactional rituals.
8. Everyday life is situated; it occurs in social situations.
9. Social situations are created through interaction.
10. Power and force are basic features of everyday life. Power is relational—it exists in social relationships and in social interaction. "Power is force or interpersonal dominance actualized in human relationships through the manipulation, control, and often destruction (both physical and mental) of one human by another human" (Denzin, 1985, p. 40).
11. Human experience is dialectical; that is, it rests on a logic that is conflictual, interactional, and emergent.
12. The self, defined as all that a person calls his or her own at a particular moment, stands at the center of human existence. The self is a social process; it consists of the "self-as-knower" and the "self-as-known" to others (James, 1890/1950). The self rests on self-feelings, which involve feelings of moral worth. The self is in the world of social interaction; it is not in the person.
13. Emotionality, the process of being emotional, is a central feature of social interaction (Denzin, 1984a).
14. Intersubjectivity is basic to shared, human group life; it refers to the shared knowledge that exists between two persons re-

garding each other's conscious mental states. Intersubjectivity produces an intersection or intertwining of two fields of experience into a single shared experience. *Subjectivity,* in contrast, refers to a subject's knowledge of his or her own mental state (see Denzin, 1984a, p. 283).

15. Time and how it is experienced is an integral part of human experience (Heidegger, 1927/1962).
16. Much of human experience involves careers, or movements through social positions. A career has two sides, one objective and the other subjective. The objective feature of the career involves the individual's movement from one position to another; the subjective side references the changes in self, self-feeling, and social relationships that follow objective career movements (Strauss, 1977, pp. 291-292).

It is our position that a truly sociological social psychology is one that builds on the following basic propositions concerning human behavior:

1. There is a psychic unity to human experience; that is, human behavior involves minded, symbolic, self-reflective conduct.
2. There is extreme cultural variability to human experience.
3. Human experience is based on the creative ability of individuals to change and modify their behaviors continually to fit new historical circumstances.
4. Human beings are able to "feed back complex correctives" to their behavior, without engaging in trial and error, conditioning, or new learning (Kuhn, 1964, p. 82).
5. The ability of humans to produce and use symbols sets them apart from non-symbol-using organisms. Hence findings from the study of lower animals will have only limited usefulness for the field of social psychology.
6. Human experience is relational and influenced by the presence of other individuals.
7. Social psychology must be built up through the careful study of human experience. The methods of social psychology must be fitted to the lived experiences of human beings. Social psychology must be an interactional, interpretive field of study.

These assertions point to the multifaceted nature of the features of human social experience that are of concern to the social psychologist. Thus no social psychologist should ignore the interactive relations among biology, physiology, genetics, self-indications, motives, language, culture, self-reflectiveness, ritual, social situations, power, self, emotionality, shared experiences, temporality, and objective and subjective moral careers in the study of any interactional problematic. Sartre (1981) summarizes our position well:

> In each particular case each individual must be seen like a man of *chance* . . . and yet the player acts, he casts his dice in a certain way, he reacts in one fashion or another to the numbers that turn up and afterwards tries to parlay his good or bad fortune. This is to . . . integrate it (chance) into praxis as its indelible mark. . . . I apprehend myself as a man of chance and at the same time as the son of my works. . . . soon the truth of my praxis appears to me in the obscurity of the accidents that make me what I must be to live. . . . We see this in lovers: for them, the object of their love is chance itself; they try to

> reduce it to their first chance encounter and at the same time claim that this product of an encounter was always theirs. (pp. 49-50)

Sartre goes on to argue that the only way to make sense of a person's life is to reconstruct objectively that person's history; this will also involve understanding his or her family. The social psychologist must work forward through the person's life, finding the conditions and events that set basic turning points, the contingencies that turned the person one way and not another.

Sartre is saying that every person has a moral career through life. This life is a product of chance from the outset, and is conditioned by the individual's family. We integrate our pasts into our lives, making who we have been into projects to be pursued in the present and in the future. Whereas Sartre brings our analysis down to the level of individual biography and life history, his general perspective can be applied to the analysis of interactional experiences that pertain to social relationships, groups, and larger social structures.

With the foregoing assumptions in mind, the following considerations remain to be discussed.

Behaviorism and Mind-Body Dualism

We assume that human behavior provides the primary data with which social psychology deals, and that the explanation of any particular form of behavior requires that its relation to other types be traced and demonstrated. Thus a given behavior is explained in terms of its interrelationships with other behaviors and not in terms of forces, drives, or anything else that lies outside the behavioral field or that is inferred from behavior. In accordance with this principle, we reject the idea that behavior is "caused" by psychological states, desires, motives, states of consciousness, or unconscious motives when these are taken to refer to forces that "make" things happen. Such terms are only ways of naming various kinds of activities; they have no special explanatory value. We believe that it is entirely fallacious to explain the existence of science in terms of a "rational faculty" or innate "reason." It is much more plausible to look at reason not as a force or faculty, but as a complex and highly evolved form of symbolic activity that has emerged gradually as a historical product from other, simpler types of behavior. Similarly, "conscience" should not be thought of as a psychic force mysteriously implanted in humans, but as a special form of regulatory behavior by means of which other activities are inhibited or facilitated.

This implies that in order to understand how and why people do what they do, we must know how they think. The chief source of information about how people think is what they say. These conclusions, however, are not of the type that behaviorist psychologists endorse. In addition to the usual tendency to ignore language, they also avoid dealing with behavior that cannot be directly observed. Internal symbolic processes admittedly are not accessible to direct observation, and for this reason, among others, behaviorists neglect them. Evidence of mental activity in human beings is usually secured through introspection or verbal testimony (and the lower animals most often utilized in experimental work do not give verbal reports or engage in introspection). Moreover, evidence so obtained is difficult to interpret. Nevertheless, if we agree that human thought is a vital feature of human behavior, no evidence concerning it should be passed over (see Ericsson & Simon, 1984).

The behaviorists have been reacting against a tradition going back to the ancient Greeks, which has been termed *mind-body dualism.* Body and mind are viewed as separate and radically different kinds of reality. The body is physically real and tangible; the mind is intangible, nonmaterial, and separate from the body. Once this separation is made, two distinct vocabularies evolve to deal with the two realms, and nonsensical questions (e.g., "Which is more important, the mind or the body?" or "How can the mind influence the body?") arise. Our view of this position is also strongly negative: Mental activity is simply that activity of the human organism in which the central nervous system plays a leading role. On this problem we agree with the French phenomenologist Merleau-Ponty (1963): The structure of human behavior is such that mind and body are intertwined processes whose meaning is given in the perceptual field that connects the individual to the direct world of lived experience.

Reductionism and Atomism

Some scholars seek explanations of behavior in the biological mechanisms involved. A common expression of this tendency is to refer to the nervous system or neural mechanisms to explain certain acts or kinds of behavior. Laypersons may say that their nerves are "on edge" or "frayed." Neurologists and physiologists sometimes account for observed behavior by reference to some supposed neural or physiological process. Explanations of this type are called *reductionist,* because they tend to reduce behavioral problems to the biological level.

The term *atomism,* which is closely related to *reductionism,* refers to the attempt to discover what things are like by taking them apart. The assumption is that "the whole is equal to the sum of its parts." The Greeks proposed the idea that all matter consists of tiny, indivisible particles. The history of physicists' attempts to unravel the nature of matter is the prime example of the fruitfulness of this conception. The search for those ultimate "atoms" or building blocks of the universe has not turned out as anticipated, but it has given us modern nuclear physics.

Sociologists ordinarily oppose both the reductionist and atomist positions. They oppose the reductionist contention that human behavior can be understood and explained in terms of physiological, neurological, anatomic, chemical, or physical concepts, and assume instead that at each level of scientific concern, phenomena are and must be explained by reference to other phenomena at the same level. Chemical phenomena are explainable by reference to other chemical phenomena, and so on. Social behavior similarly must be analyzed and explained on its own level.

Sociologists ordinarily also reject the atomistic approach. A whole, they argue, is definitely more than the sum of its parts. For example, a group may act as a unit, and this involves, aside from a number of individuals, a structured system of relationships among members and with other groups.

Thus a nation continues to exist even though all of its specific members ultimately will die. Conversely, a group may vanish or die without any of its members doing so.

This is not to say that social scientists ignore the physical, biochemical, physiological, and neurological processes involved in all behavior. Consideration of such influences, although it cannot *account* for behavior, does contribute to our understanding of the physical and biological substrate that makes behavior possible.

Interpretive Versus Cognitive Social Psychologies

Although we accept the concept of a division of the field of social psychology into psychological and sociological camps, we feel that a further differentiation is required. Two broad categories organize social psychological theories of human experience. The first, termed *interpretive,* is closely aligned with our point of view. The second, *cognitive,* applies to the majority of the theories now holding sway in the field. We discuss interpretive social psychology briefly below, and then discuss two particular such social psychologies: historical social psychology and ethnomethodology. As representative of cognitive social psychologies, we then present a discussion of artificial intelligence.

An interpretive social psychology has the following characteristics: First, it stresses the interactional, historical, emotional, and interpretive dimensions of human experience. Second, it tends not to rely on experimental, statistical, quasi-experimental, or survey research methodologies. Third, its goal is the interpretation and understanding of human behavior, not its prediction or control. Fourth, interpretive social psychology tends to be humanistic, existential, and historical; it is always concerned with personal experiences. Fifth, the seven basic propositions concerning human behavior that we have outlined above reflect the core assumptions of the interpretive perspective. Similarly, the 16 key assertions central to the interactionist point of view, also presented above, describe the broader contours of the interpretive approach (see Douglas et al., 1980; Douglas & Johnson, 1977; Kotarba, 1984).

Examples of interpretive social psychologies include Gergen's historical social psychology, Rom Harré's (1982, 1995) ethogeny, Giddens's (1984, 1990) action theory, hermeneutics, Douglas's (1970) sociology of everyday life, Scott and Lyman's (1970) sociology of the absurd, Garfinkel's ethnomethodology, the new Iowa school of social psychology (Couch et al., 1986), our version of symbolic interactionism, and diverse variants of psychoanalytic, feminist, and Marxist thought. In the following pages and chapters we will make reference to several of these approaches. At this point we call special attention to only two: historical social psychology and ethnomethodology. However, the reader is encouraged to explore the works of other interpretive social psychologists (see Harré, 1995).

Historical Social Psychology

Kenneth Gergen (1973, 1982; Gergen & Gergen, 1984) is closely identified with historical social psychology. In his view, the field of social psychology is historical because it deals with facts that are largely nonrepeatable and that fluctuate over time. Knowledge cannot transcend historical boundaries, nor can it be based on purely objective methods. Building on the position that the social sciences differ from the natural sciences, Gergen calls for a dismantling of the unified science thesis (i.e., a single method unifies all the sciences). He wants social psychology to be based on methods and theories that derive from human experience. His view calls into question theories based on the mind-body dualism, atomist, reductionist, and exterior models of human experience discussed earlier. Gergen views knowledge as being socially constructed and historically embedded. Human action, he argues, is based on voluntaristic principles. He feels that research should illustrate and bring theory alive, rather than merely verify or test propositions.

Gergen and Gergen (1984, p. 174) have made a series of proposals concerning the study of how humans give meaning to their experiences. They suggest that biographical narrative accounts, including life stories, and popular cultural texts (i.e., fiction) create for persons and social groups a coherence about social life that is connected, temporal, personal, and collective. These narratives may be tragic, romantic, or comic.

Historical social psychology is not new to the sociological tradition. *The Polish Peasant in Europe and America* (1927), written by Thomas and Znaniecki in the early 1920s, is a work that is historical, comparative, and interpretive. That Gergen and Gergen called for such a theory in the 1980s suggests that the field is returning to its roots (see Saxton & Hall, 1987). In 1959, Strauss called for a historical, biographical, interactionist social psychology. In many respects the work of Gergen and Gergen continues this line of thought.

We must note, however, that a fully historical social psychology is one that could be grounded in any historical moment, not just the present. Like the new history associated with such scholars as Michel de Certeau (1984), historical social psychology would address the manner of women, men, and children produced, for example, in the Middle Ages, during the Renaissance or the Industrial Revolution, in colonial America, in the postbellum South, and so on. It would be politically historical, examining the power structures and modes of economic organization that existed in any given historical period. It would be subjective, written from the point of view of those who lived during the period being studied. It would rely upon letters, autobiographies, diaries, novels, and the cultural myths of the time. It would connect lived history to the human group and to the human family, and it would do so from the standpoint of a political economy of interaction (see Foucault, 1980b; Lefebvre, 1971/1984; Mills, 1959; Sartre, 1960/1976).

Ethnomethodology

We should note that current formulations derived from the phenomenological perspectives of Husserl, Schutz, and Gurwitsch have been incorporated into the work of such scholars as Berger and Luckmann (1967) and into that loosely formulated school of thought known as *ethnomethodology* (Boden & Zimmerman, 1991; Cicourel, 1974; Garfinkel, 1967b; Garfinkel, Lynch, & Livingston, 1981; Garfinkel & Sacks, 1970; Heap & Roth, 1973; Heritage, 1984; Maynard & Whalen, 1995; Psathas, 1995; Sudnow, 1972, 1978, 1979).

Central to this line of thought are the following assumptions: First, human behavior is to be approached subjectively from the standpoint of the phenomenological reality of individual actors. Second, there are as many phenomenological realities, or social worlds of experience, as there are individuals producing such worlds. Third, social action and social order are seen as problematic, yet taken-for-granted, productions. Society does not just exist; it has to be produced by interacting individuals. Fourth, in the course of interacting with themselves and others, individuals suspend any commonsense assumptions and act as if they understand one another, when in fact they may be talking past each other. Fifth, these taken-for-granted assumptions embody the very essence of social interaction and social order. The ethnomethodologist's task is to uncover these assumptions and show how they are routinely acted on or deliberately suspended.

It is beyond the scope of this chapter to detail this approach fully, but we should note that recent work in psycholinguistics and sociolinguistics reflects the commitment to studying human behavior from the standpoint of native actors. Theorists such as Cicourel (1974) are trying to discover and chart the deep and superficial structural rules that native actors consciously and unconsciously employ in the organization of their behavior. Others carefully study everyday conversations for what they reveal about the underlying dynamics of broader social structures (e.g., Sudnow, 1972).

A central figure in this line of thought has been Harold Garfinkel. The word *ethnomethodology* is used to describe what the practitioners of this approach see as the unique features of their perspective. *Ethno,* borrowed from Greek, means race, culture, or people. For Garfinkel and his associates, *ethnomethodology* refers to the practices of an observer who attempts to discover the methods that people use when they formulate the definitions of particular situations. An ethnomethodological investigation involves at least three steps. First, the observers suspend the assumption that social situations are governed by sets of rules; that is, they withhold judgment on the functions that roles, norms, rules, or culture may have in any particular setting. Second, they observe how laypersons and sociologists alike describe and explain what it is that they do. The third step requires treating these explanations as appearances produced so as to project the image that rules have been followed. The ethnomethodologist assumes that individuals explain their behavior in ways that fit everyday conceptions of what that behavior was all about. Zimmerman and Wieder (1970) say that the ethnomethodologist is "concerned with how members of society go about the task of *seeing, describing, and explaining* order in the world in which they live" (p. 289).

The aim of such investigations is to discover the formal properties of everyday, commonplace actions; the method demands that the researcher look at behavior from "within" actual situations. Garfinkel, in an article titled "What Is Ethnomethodology?" (1967c), develops this view of research activity:

> Whenever a member is required to demonstrate that an account analyzes an actual situation, he invariably makes use of such practices of "et cetera," "unless," and "let it pass" to demonstrate the rationality of his achievement. . . . Much therefore of what is actually reported is not mentioned. . . . In short, recognizable sense, or fact, or methodic character, or impersonality, or objectivity of accounts are not independent of the socially organized occasions of their use. (p. 3)

For Garfinkel and other ethnomethodologists, all social interaction—whether it be husbands talking with their wives, students making purchases in stores, or interviewers talking with mothers about their birth control practices—involves individuals producing, describing, and explaining each other's accounts of their actions.

In one study, Garfinkel instructed students to engage a friend in conversation and then press the person to clarify his or her remarks. One student presented the following case:

> On Friday my husband remarked that he was tired. I asked, "How are you tired? Physically, mentally, or just bored?"
>
> (S) I don't know, I guess physically, mainly.
> (E) You mean that your muscles ache or your bones?
> (S) I guess so. Don't be so technical.
> *(after more watching)*
> (S) All of these old movies have the same kind of old iron bedstead in them.
> (E) What do you mean? Do you mean all old movies or some of them, or just the ones you have seen?
> (S) What's the matter with you? You know what I mean.
> (E) I wish you would be more specific.
> (S) You know what I mean! Drop dead!
> (quoted in Garfinkel, 1967c, p. 43)

Garfinkel argues that people refuse to let one another understand what they are really talking about. They anticipate that others will understand them, and for this reason everyday conversations have a vague, ambiguous tone. They rest on a body of background assumptions taken for granted by the participants. Thus the husband in the above example assumed that his wife knew what he meant when he said he was tired.

Artificial Intelligence

Collins (1986) has proposed that one of the payoffs from the microsociologies, ethnomethodologies, and cognitive sociologies of the last decade will be

> a practical contribution to the development of Artificial Intelligence. It is becoming increasingly clear that individualistic psychology has not cracked the code that will open the way to a computer that can think and talk like a human being, and AI leaders are already turning to cognitive sociologists, including ethnomethodological ones, for a better lead. (p. 1349)

These remarks suggest that theories of artificial intelligence (AI) are drawing from the works of interpretive and cognitive social psychologists. Indeed, some argue that human beings are like computers. Hence building a computer that thinks like a human and has humanlike intelligence has become a goal of many behavioral scientists, including Turing, von Neumann, McCarthy, Newell, Simon, and Minsky.

It is necessary, then, to discuss the concept of artificial intelligence. Computers have become part of the American way of life, especially in the fields of business and education. Many have criticized this development, including such philosophers as Taylor, Searle, Dreyfus, and Dennett. John Haugeland (1985) has presented a history and critique of artificial intelligence; it is primarily from his text that we draw the following discussion. We shall see that AI raises many problems that relate back to our earlier discussion of mind-body dualism and reductionism (see Taylor, 1982).

There are many versions of AI, and theories of AI continue to change and evolve. Nonetheless, some basic assumptions may be stated as follows: (a) It must be understood that AI, like cognitive psychology and cognitive social psychology, is an offshoot of behaviorism. It attempts to offer a logical, objective, experimental theory of the human mind, of talking, intelligence, and problem solving. (b) AI assumes that human thought is rational, orderly, and logical. (c) It is argued that if human thought is rational and orderly, then a machine that has these characteristics should be able to model and predict human thought. Because computers have these characteristics, they are like the human mind and brain; that is, computers can rationally and logically solve problems. (d) Computers have intelligence; this intelligence, however, is artificial, for it is not acquired like human intelligence. (e) It is argued that thinking and computing are the same. (f) Because thinking is rational, and like talking, AI argues that our minds operate on computational principles. Intelligence thus becomes the ability to say the right thing at the right time. (g) The computer is now seen as an interpreted, automatic, formal system that manipulates pieces of information, called tokens.

AI uses a formal language, which is not the natural language of everyday speakers. This formal language is a machine language, like FORTRAN or Pascal. It has been found that natural languages cannot be reduced to a computer language. In 1960, linguist Yehoshua Bar-Hillel discovered that it is impossible to create a machine language that can encode all the facts of a natural language. He stated:

> What such a suggestion amounts to, if taken seriously, is the requirement that a translation machine should not only be supplied with a dictionary but also with a universal encyclopedia. This is surely utterly chimerical and hardly deserves any further discussion. (p. 160)

As a result, computers work on a system of language that manipulates tokens, often organized in terms of oppositions, as in a digital system (e.g., positive/negative, present/absent). Computers are programmed to manipulate symbols or tokens so as to solve particular problems or puzzles. Tokens designate pieces of information that the system is able to interpret. As an interpreting, automatic, and formal system, the computer processes information within a meaning system that has its own rules of organization (syntax) and its own system of meaning (semantics).

AI works on the principle that there is a system of symbols/tokens/markers that operate in terms of a syntactic logic that is self-contained (i.e., programmed into the computer). Furthermore, it is argued that the meanings these symbols have exist in some relation to an external world. Haugeland (1985, p. 100) suggests that the formal tokens within an AI system have two lives: syntactic and semantic. The formalist motto of AI asserts, "If you take care of the syntax, the semantics will take care of itself . . . that is how the 'two lives' of an interpreted formal system go together" (Haugeland, 1985, p. 106).

The languages that computers use are, as indicated, based on systems of symbols or tokens whose meanings are arbitrary. That is, the meanings of the words within a machine language are designated by the programmer. The ability of a computer to use a language and to form a correct solution to a problem is based on the coherence principle: The meanings of tokens within the system must be logical, and must cohere and interrelate in a rational, orderly manner.

Some AI theorists argue that computers can be seen as having a sense of inner consciousness, or as having introspective abilities. It has been suggested that introspection amounts to having a built-in ability to "tell" what is contained in our mental memory banks. Because computers can access information that has been stored, the argument goes, they can be seen as having introspective abilities.

Some AI theorists contend that computers have artificial egos, or artificial selves (see Haugeland, 1985, p. 245). This argument rests on the assumption that computers also have a sense of consciousness, or an ability to access information that has been stored. Haugeland (1985, pp. 230-238) goes so far as to propose that computers may have feelings, emotions, and moods, if by these terms we mean the ability of machines to sense their environment. He suggests that many fancy computer systems can sense pain (i.e., internal malfunctions, internal damage). He goes on to propose that perhaps sensations do not matter when intelligent behavior is concerned (p. 235). In this sense, emotions are not a problem for a rational, cognitive system. Finally, Haugeland throws up his hands, stating, "The more I think about this question, the less I'm persuaded I even know what it means (which is not to say I think it's meaningless)" (pp. 235-236).

An Evaluation of Artificial Intelligence

Charles Taylor (1985) has argued that AI, in its attempt to deal with the concepts that behaviorism excludes (e.g., mind, consciousness, intentionality, self, thought, language) has run into "difficulty a lot faster, and this is all to its credit" (p. 127). He suggests that AI rests on a naive representational theory of language and on a simplistic stimulus-response theory of meaning. Further, it lacks a theory of emotionality; its conceptions of self, ego, introspection, and consciousness are forced and empty. Furthermore, the computer, as a thinking machine, contains no sense of interaction within a conflict-riddled, emergent social world. That is, it forces the external world, in the form of its user, to conform to its rules of syntax and semantics.

AI rests on a reductionist, dualistic conception of mind, language, consciousness, self, and the human body. Remembering that reductionism is the tendency to explain human behavior in terms of physiological, neurological, chemical, physical, and mechanical concepts, we can see that AI is reductionist. Computer programs are seen as having the same functions as human behavior. This reductionism is sophisticated, as Taylor (1982, p. 36; 1985, p. 127) observes, for it recognizes that "radically different forms of hardware [can] be programmed to represent the same process" (Secord, 1982, p. 15).

This reductionism is not just physicalistic; it rests on a distinction between the computing program that organizes the computer's "thought" and the physical realization of that program in terms of answers to questions. AI theorists contend that consciousness, or self-awareness, is always faulty and partial; yet their theories presume complex inner processes that are involved in problem-solving activities. They "marginalize" consciousness to the fringe of awareness. They explain thought in terms of mechanistic, rational processes. Their model presumes the operation of higher mental processes that fall outside their reductionist, mechanical model; mental process is reduced to mechanical transformations. They do not explain thinking or thought on its own terms (Heidegger, 1977, pp. 341-367). The being or self that calls us into thinking stands outside AI's computer. By creating the illusion that computers can think as humans do, AI theorists engage in a form of anthropomorphism that has long been recognized as unacceptable in the human disciplines. Anthropomorphism, or the attribution of human characteristics to nonhumans, pervades all of AI theorizing. By stripping away the essential features of human experience so that a model of the human mind can be built, AI theorists end up with a grotesque caricature of what a human being is.

Dualistically, AI maintains a separation between mind and body as radically different realities. The two lives of the computer (the self-contained world of syntax and the outer world of semantics, meaning, and performance) speak to this dualistic bias. But more is at issue. AI works with a representational theory of mind that sees the computer mapping an external world; thus mind and world are separated, to be joined only through the computer's ability to produce truthful answers to the questions that are posed to it. This model purges any bodily reality from mental processes, just as it excludes any meaningful interaction between mind and world. The AI dualistic assumption posits, then, a physical world and a mental world, yet it has no way of bridging the gap between the two.

Consider shame. Taylor (1982, pp. 46-47) suggests that AI is unable to handle the fact that in the case of human emotions it is impossible to push consciousness to the fringe of experience. Shame requires self-feeling, agency, purpose, and a language of emotionality (see Denzin, 1984a). Shame cannot be reduced to physiological sensations; it requires self-reflection. Because computers lack the ability to engage in reflective self-thought, they cannot feel shame.

Consciousness and its meanings are basic features of human existence. Computers and AI theorists are unable to theorize consciousness, self, or emotionality. This is a decisive flaw in AI. Consciousness cannot be severed from human experience. A theory of minded, human behavior that is built on a mechanical theory of language, and that cannot speak to embodied emotional experiences, contributes little to our understanding of human behavior.

A second decisive flaw in AI involves its theory of language. Bar-Hillel's (1960) conclusion that a machine language cannot recover all of the meanings in natural, everyday language sent AI theorists in search of a machine language that would be completely self-contained. The systems of language that have been produced cannot handle the shifting meanings that words take on in everyday conversations. In everyday life, speakers do not and cannot ignore meaning or semantics, nor can they just let syntax do the work of meaning. The AI assumption that syntax will do the work of semantics thus cannot be allowed.

Nor does the AI theory of language fit into the semiotic model of language produced by Saussure (1959). Words, as signs, have different values and meanings. Signs exist in both speech and language. AI's tokens and symbols exist in a never-never realm that is neither institutional nor interactional. Their languages have none of the features of language and speech as studied by Saussure, nor can their language deal with language games, signifying acts, and the rules of language use that Wittgenstein (1953) and Perinbanayagam (1985) have developed. Hence their position on language is ahistorical, non-social psychological, and noninteractional. It is of little or no use when the problems of understanding how humans think and use language are raised. (In the spring of 1997, an IBM computer named Deep Blue defeated world champion chess player Gary Kasparov in a six-game match. Kasparov expressed great frustration and sadness at his loss. The emotions of Big Blue were not reported.)

Still, AI theorists are to be thanked for the careful way in which they delineate the limits of their models. Unfortunately, the very features of human experience and thought that AI excludes are those that are closest to what it means to be human.

CONCLUSION

We have covered a vast amount of material in this chapter. We have presented the basic features of our point of view and have contrasted our viewpoint with those of other social psychologies. We have spent some time on a discussion of artificial intelligence in order to expose the limits of a purely cognitive, rational, and logical approach to the study of human experience. We hope that our discussion of AI—the most sophisticated of the cognitive social psychologies—has successfully conveyed the limitations of these approaches.

In summary, we note that all social psychologies (of whatever theoretical variety) are concerned with the relationship between persons and groups or larger forms of social organization. All of the theories discussed in this chapter share the following common assumptions:

1. Humans learn from experience.
2. Humans are symbol-producing and symbol-using organisms; this sets them apart, in one sense, from infrahuman organisms.
3. Human behavior is influenced by the presence of others.
4. Humans are capable of maintaining some control and consistency in their own actions.
5. Human behavior is constantly changing and adapting to new situations.
6. Some behaviors and influences are more significant than others.
7. Human behavior is meaningful; that is, it can be interpreted and understood.

In short, all social psychologies employ some version of the scientific or interpretive method.

Despite these shared assumptions, advocates of different positions tend to rely primarily on different kinds of research methods. Psychoanalysts employ in-depth interviewing, self-reports, and dream and fantasy analysis. Psychological social psychologists rely on laboratory and field experimentation as well as on psychological tests and questionnaires. Symbolic interactionists attempt to study persons in their natural locales and use primarily field observation, open-ended interviewing, life-history construction, and unobtrusive methods.

In this text we develop a view of human behavior that stresses that humans are social and symbol-using organisms. We attempt to cross the boundaries of sociology, anthropology, linguistics, psychology, political science, and history, and to utilize any and all data that elaborate our theoretical perspective. Our fundamental concern is to account for the structured regularity and irregularity of human conduct, and we assume that even deviance and deviant behavior are lawfully and predictably organized.

SUGGESTED READINGS

Hall, S. (Ed.). (1997). *Representation: Cultural representations and signifying practices.* London: Sage. A critical, interpretive approach to the media and to those cultural texts that represent and define gender, race, ethnicity, and nationality.

Smith, J. A., Harré, R., & Van Langenhove, L. (Eds.). (1995). *Rethinking psychology.* London: Sage. An excellent source for learning about many new approaches to social psychology, including phenomenology, symbolic interactionism, narratology, and analytic, cultural, discursive, and dialogical psychology.

Strauss, A. L. (1993). *Continual permutations of action.* New York: Aldine de Gruyter. Many of the assumptions outlined in this chapter are treated in more detail in this important book by the late Anselm Strauss, a coauthor of this textbook and a founding father of symbolic interactionist theory.

STUDY QUESTIONS

1. Select a commodity you have recently purchased, such as a CD, a piece of clothing, a meal, a book, or a print, or a movie you have attended. Using the circuit of culture model (representation, identification, production, consumption, regulation), analyze the experience of making this purchase.
2. What are the key features of the existential approach to social psychology?
3. What is the narrative turn in social psychology? How is this turn connected to the problem of experience and its representations?

2

Primate Visions and Human Symbolic Behavior

In this chapter we examine the behavior of lower species and indicate some of the major differences between that behavior and various kinds of human, symbolic behavior. We deal with the recently established field of sociobiology (Wilson, 1975; see also Dewsbury, 1987; Haraway, 1989, pp. 126-129, 349-367), which is the systematic study of the biological bases of all social behavior. Sociobiology involves primarily the study of animal societies, but it is also concerned with the "social behavior of early man and the . . . adaptive features of organization in the more primitive contemporary human societies" (Wilson, 1975, p. 4). Sociobiology is a branch of evolutionary biology, but it proposes a synthesis with modern sociology, for it attempts to isolate the underlying biological causes and functions of human social behavior.

After we offer an evaluation of sociobiology, we discuss the behaviors of chimpanzees who have been taught a version of language. We briefly address the history behind these studies, drawing on the work of Haraway (part of the title of this chapter is borrowed from Haraway's book *Primate Visions,* 1989). We then take up the topics of symbolic worlds and symbolic environments. Our intention is to secure firmly the importance of the "symbolic" in the study of human social behavior.

The Evolutionary Setting of Human Behavior

The behavior of all animals (including humans) is social to some degree; even among the lowest species, organisms stimulate one another and may live in some sorts of groups. Social groups as we know them require organization, psychological unity, a communication system, and a division of labor—however simple—whereby group members cooperate to work toward group goals. Another type of group, exemplified by a mass of people waiting for a train, is known as an *aggregate,* or an *assemblage.* Members of an aggregate, whether it is composed of human beings or animals, do not act concertedly toward group goals or in the manner of members of social groups; they do affect one another's behavior, however, thereby making the behavior social to a limited degree. An aggregate thus is not a genuine social group, because it involves only the most rudimentary social relations and lacks most of the features of social groups noted above.

Although in our discussion we emphasize the evolution of forms of behavior, we should note that cultural evolution presupposes and depends upon prior biological evolution. The evolution of the human brain, of course, has been of central significance. Specialists in this area generally emphasize that assuming an upright posture was of critical importance in the evolution of humans, because it freed the hands for the making and use of tools and for other fine manipulative behavior. This, in turn, changed survival conditions and helped produce the changes in cranial size and structure that distinguish *Homo sapiens* from the human-apes thought to have been our immediate predecessors. The human brain is not simply a relatively larger one than that of monkeys and other primates; it is also qualitatively and structurally different. For example, the areas associated with the thumb (and with control of the hands in general), language, speech, and higher mental functions are proportionately much more elaborate and specialized in humans than in apes. In the ape's brain there is no counterpart to the specialized left-hemisphere language center characteristic of right-handed humans.

In the chronology of human physical and cultural evolution, it is significant to note that although the former no doubt set the stage for cultural evolution by providing us with our human brain and physical form, the two forms of evolution seem to be unrelated after that point. Cultural evolution or change has, in recent times, accelerated at a geometric rate without any further significant evolutionary changes in the biological equipment of humans.

The Evolution of Social Behavior

We turn next to different "levels" of organisms and behavior. Just where to draw the line between the social and nonsocial in the interorganismic contact of the very lowest animals is an indeterminate matter. Jennings (1942), the well-known student of protozoa, has confessed that in his younger days he concluded that aggregates of infusoria exhibited no social characteristics; he was reprimanded later by a critic who noted that the reactions he had described actually were social relations of the protozoan kind. Although the one-celled animal requires no other to aid it in performing its vital functions, it does nevertheless on occasion gather together with others of its kind.

Dense aggregates may be produced by convergence toward a source of light or by movement against a current. These are aggregates in the literal sense of the term; there is no division of labor, no cooperative activity.

Two Aspects of Evolution: Continuity and Emergence

Although it is certain that various forms of group organization exist among the lower species, biologists find it hard to classify one as more complex or more social than another if the forms are not similar. Allee (1951), for example, speaks of small but real differences in group organization:

> We are confronted with a gradual development of real differences without being able to put a finger with surety on any one clearly defined break in the continuity. The slow accumulation of more and more social tendencies leads finally by small steps to something that is apparently different. If we disregard the intermediate stages, the differences may appear pronounced, but if we focus on these intermediates, it will be only for the sake of convenience that we interrupt the connecting chain of events at some comparatively conspicuous link and arbitrarily make this the dividing point, when one is needed, between the more and less social. (p. 158)

This statement brings out two aspects of evolution: the continuity of species and the notion of distinct "levels" or the emergence of new properties. The latter has been stated in this way:

> The principle of levels has come into current usage through a recognition of important differences in the complexity, the degree of development, and the interdependent organization of behavior functions through the animal series. The evidently superior properties that appear on a new level of organization are not to be explained as due to a new kind of energy or new vital properties, but as functional properties arising from a new system of organization which differs in given ways from "lower" and "higher" systems. (Schneirla, 1949, p. 245)

The "levels" concept thus assumes the existence of continuity and similarity among species but stresses also the emergence of new properties of organization. The differences in levels have to do with "*what kinds of processes and capacities are available* to an animal and its species mates in adapting to their environments" (Schneirla, 1953b, p. 57). Ants and bees live in organized colonies and operate at higher levels of capacity than do sponges or protozoa, which live as individuals or in aggregates. Different animal aggregations reach the same general ends—such as providing food and shelter—but the organization of the aggregates and the processes through which ends are attained may be very dissimilar.

Anthropomorphism and Morgan's Canon

The concept of behavioral levels leads us to guard against anthropomorphizing. Anthropomorphism (from the Greek *anthropos,* "man," and *morphe,* "form") is the projection of human traits upon things not human, and it is a fallacy we need to steer clear of in studying the lower animals. We often make the mistake of assigning human attributes to the behaviors of particular animals or species (for example, when a pet dog does something for which it is usually punished and is then viewed as acting guilty or looking ashamed).

In a sense, however, the human vocabulary must always be anthropomorphic. Suppose one makes a statement as simple as the following: "The chimpanzee placed the box so that by standing on it, he could reach the banana." Surely this sentence does not mean that the chimpanzee has verbally formulated his purpose within the framework of English or any other language, as might be assumed by a too-literal reader. We should remember that although we apply human words to the actions of animals, the animals themselves do not.

Asquith (1984) has observed, in regard to the use of ordinary language and anthropomorphism, that anthropomorphism

> arises through qualitative or ordinary language description in which terms such as "threaten," "appease," "chase," "greet," "submission," and so on are applied to animal behaviour. These terms already carry meanings associated with human action (that is, purposeful behaviour). (p. 38)

Asquith contends that in ordinary language usage "metaphor" is the mechanism that "allows and in fact necessitates the semantic link between human action and animal behaviour" (p. 39). "It occurs simply as a result of our language, or more specifically, meaning in language" (p. 43).

Reynolds (1980) has summarized Weber's (1946) distinction between *behavior* (*Verhalten*) and *action* (*Handein*) and a third term, *meaning* (*Sinn*), which links the two:

> If we describe what people or animals do, without inquiring into their subjective reasons for doing it, we are talking about their *behaviour.* If we study the subjective aspects of what they do, the reasons and ideas underlying and guiding it, then we are concerned with the world of *meaning.* If we concern ourselves both with what people are, overtly and objectively, seen to do (or not to do) and their reasons for doing (or not doing) which relate to the world of meaning and understanding, we then describe *action.* (p. xxii)

Drawing upon Harré and Secord (1972), Asquith (1984) writes:

> Action has significance and meaning; it occurs in a social, not a physiological context; it is inextricably bound up with the nature and limits of language (and the fabric of society), and importantly there is no way of reducing action to movement and so of setting it within a physiological context. (p. 57)

Anthropomorphic ordinary language terms, then, when used metaphorically, may offer a heuristically useful way to understand animal behavior. Asquith concludes:

> Because ordinary language terms for social behaviour have most often been used to express human action, they connote purposefulness in the animals to which they are applied. This occurs through metaphor and gives rise to generic anthropomorphism, or the treatment of animals as conscious agents. The usual connection we make between purposeful actions serves as a heuristic aid to interpretation of the animals' behaviour. The sophistication and applicability of quantitative description was argued not to replace our ultimate understanding of animal behaviour in terms of ordinary language. (p. 59)

It is not only in common speech that animal behavior is described and accounted for in human terms. Many years ago Lloyd Morgan (1894), a comparative psychologist, attacked the then general propensity of both laypersons and scholars to find resemblances between the mental processes of human beings and those of lower animals. He enunciated a canon that has been quoted with general approval ever since by comparative psychologists:

> In no case may we interpret an action as the outcome of the exercise of a higher psychical faculty, if it can be interpreted as the outcome of the exercise of one which stands lower in the psychological scale. (p. 53)

At the time of Morgan's writing, it was customary to prove similarities between animals and human beings by narrating anecdotes. The anecdotal method has long since disappeared from scholarly writing, but there are numerous references to animal reasoning, generalization, hypotheses, concepts, dominance, leadership, purpose, goals, neuroses, communication, and cooperation. The terms are often used within quotation marks to indicate that the reader is not supposed to take the analogy to human behavior too seriously; however, there is little doubt that many writers and readers *do* take the analogies seriously. Schneirla, who has attacked this kind of anthropomorphic writing, suggests that a distinction be drawn between the *description* of behavior and its causal *explanation.* We may speak loosely of protective behavior, food getting, and courtship in various species, but a genuine causal description of the behavior will make clear that several processes are involved. For example, whereas intent and exchange of information and sentiment are involved in human courtship, none need be imputed to various of the lower species when they engage in sexual activity.

We believe that the concept of levels of behavior is particularly fruitful because it focuses attention on both the continuity of species and the differences among them. It requires that concepts and hypotheses concerning the behavior of any species be inductively derived from the study of that particular species—rather than, as is common, by extrapolation to lower species of the principles derived from mammalian investigation, or by the explanation of human behavior in terms of principles derived from lower mammalian types (*zoomorphism*).

Sociobiology

Sociobiology is the study of the biological basis of social behavior in both animals and humans. Zoologist Edward Wilson (1975), in his extensive book on sociobiology, writes, "One of the functions of sociobiology . . . is to reformulate the foundations of the social sciences in a way that draws these subjects into the Modern Synthesis" (p. 4). According to Wilson, "Sociology, and the other social sciences, as well as the humanities, *are the last branches of biology* waiting to be included in the Modern Synthesis" (p. 4; emphasis added). The "Modern Synthesis" is a neo-Darwinist evolutionary theory that examines each phenomenon under study (including human behavior) according to its adaptive significance and relates it to the basic principles of population genetics.

Sociobiology, then, applies natural selection theory to behavior. According to this theory, human social and cultural behaviors have biological, or genetic, determinants. That is, an individual's behaviors are at least partially determined by his or her genetic makeup (Ehrmen & Parsons, 1976). Wilson (1975) notes that prominent social scientists such as Chomsky, Piaget, and Kohlberg have theories of language, cognitive development, and moral development, respectively, that are consistent with sociobiology in that they posit an innate, genetic underpinning to child development. Children, they contend, go through certain stages in their development because they are genetically predisposed to do so. We regard this as a careless misreading of Chomsky, Piaget, and Kohlberg, who make no such claims.

Assuming that behaviors have a biological basis, sociobiology maintains that genetic determinants of behaviors that are adaptive—in that they make the species fitter to survive and to reproduce—become more common in the gene pool of the population. To elaborate, individuals who behave in ways that enhance survival and reproduction will produce more offspring than will those who behave in ways that impede survival and reproduction; therefore the genetic determinants of those adaptive behaviors will increase in the gene pool of the population.

Altruistic behavior has been a challenge to evolutionary theory because it seemingly results in a decrease in the reproductive success of the individual yet continues to be prevalent in both human and animal. A person who sacrifices him- or herself for another will not produce more offspring, and the genetic determinant of altruistic behavior should decrease in the gene pool and eventually die out. This apparent contradiction has been explained through the process of *kin selection*. According to Greene, Morgan, and Barash (1979):

> Since natural selection operates through the representation of genes in succeeding generations, any one individual can pass on its own genes either by raising offspring or by helping a relative (with whom some genes are shared by common descent) to reproduce. Thus if two individuals are sufficiently related, then one individual may best further its own ultimate success by helping the other, even at some apparent immediate cost. (p. 422)

People, then, will be most likely to exhibit altruistic behavior toward those who are most genetically similar.

Altruism toward unrelated others has been explained in terms of the probability of reciprocity (Trivers, 1971). Given our lengthy lifetime and our high degree of mutual dependence, it is adaptive to be altruistic, assuming that others will reciprocate at some future time.

The theory has not been neutral on gender. Researchers who have conducted field studies of chimpanzees—for example, Jane Goodall—have argued that the mother-dependent offspring group is the primary stable grouping within chimpanzee social organization (Haraway, 1989, p. 174). On the basis of such evidence, theorists like Wilson argue that within the evolutionary hierarchy, females are inferior to males. Females do not exhibit the level and intensity of competitive behavior identified in males (Haraway, 1989, p. 178). Females have a maternal instinct that is displayed in the mother-child bond.

Haraway (1989) is understandably critical of such formulations. She argues, "The issue here is whether sociobiological theory *does* accurately and usefully reflect and predict animal behavior, or does it represent attempts to develop biological justifications of the belief, rather than the fact, that females are in some way inferior?" (p. 321). Facts are not neutral. Sociobiology narrates a paternalistic, patriarchal view of social organization, biology, nature, gender, and sexuality.

Sociobiology has also been used to help explain gender and parenting behaviors in humans. Alice S. Rossi (1984), in a presidential address to the American Sociological Association, has noted:

> This analysis of gender and parenthood begins with the judgment that none of the theories prevalent in family sociology—exchange, symbolic interaction, general systems, conflict, phenomenology, feminist, or development—are adequate to an understanding and explanation of human parenting because they do not seek an integration of biological and social constructs. (p. 1)

Rossi maintains that biology and sociology are interdependent, and an understanding of both is needed to further our knowledge and understanding of social life. To study one and neglect the other "may doom efforts at social change to failure" (p. 11).

Others are more critical of sociobiology. Vernon Reynolds is an anthropologist and ethnologist who posits a link between biological traits and social behavior. He maintains, however, that there is no reason to search for genetic factors to explain behaviors that can be explained as rational responses to recurring problems (see Wallace & Wolf, 1986, p. 298). Bleier (1984) denies the biological-social dichotomy and maintains that the two are so intertwined that they cannot be separated.

Donald T. Campbell (1975), in a presidential address to the American Psychological Association, maintains that humanity is a product of both biological and social evolution, but concludes that "*human urban social complexity has been made possible by social evolution rather than biological evolution*" (p. 1105). By *social evolution,* he means "a *selective* cumulation of skills, technologies, recipes, beliefs, customs, organizational structures, and the like, retained through purely social modes of transmission, rather than in the genes" (p. 1104). Both biology and sociology play a part in determining behavior, but the relative significance of each has yet to be determined.

Interpreting Sociobiology

What does sociobiology tell us about being human? How do sociobiological factors explain or account for language, culture, and those complex structures called societies? Wilson and others attempt to explain human, social, and cultural behaviors in terms of a general evolutionary model that stresses biological and genetic factors. Although Campbell and others have raised problems with a strict evolutionary point of view, we need to note the following problems and criticisms of sociobiology.

Sociologist Bryan Turner (1984, pp. 1, 35, 41, 227) argues that sociobiology is reductionist and a blind alley. He states that sociobiology suppresses the obvious fact that human beings have bodies, whose social presence is socially constructed and constituted through communal, cultural practices (p. 227). Sociobiology, he goes on to argue, suggests that the human body, in all important respects, has remained physiologically static over the past 2,000 years (p. 35). This approach tells us virtually nothing about the history of the human body, its diseases, its illnesses, or its sexuality (Foucault, 1980a, p. 185). It fails to see the body as a historical product whose meanings shift and change within social groups and cultures.

As a reductionist perspective, sociobiology attempts to explain social behavior in terms of processes that operate below the level of the social. In this respect it is anthropomorphic and violates the levels of analysis principle discussed earlier. However, Wilson (1975, p. 30) predicates his entire program on the rejection of these principles. He argues with Morgan and Schneirla on precisely those points that served to establish the boundaries of comparative psychology in the first place.

Wilson rejects the argument that the principles of selection and reproduction cannot be applied to group selection and higher social structures. He proceeds to build his sociobiology on the premise that evolutionary processes will explain not only altruism, but language communication, aggression, caste systems, family organization and gender differentiation, parenting behavior, group formation, role playing, bonding, divisions of labor, culture, ritual, religion, ethics, and societies of the future.

Clearly, for an interpretive social psychology these assumptions blur any distinction between human and nonhuman behavior. Furthermore, they distort (if not destroy) any understanding of the complex structural and interactional processes that together produce social organization, culture, and human symbolic behavior.

In these respects sociobiology is also atomistic; it attempts to explain the whole in terms of its parts. Furthermore, it is dualistic; it posits a basic division between mind and body, body and nature, genes and culture, and so on. It is unable to offer a dialectical, processual theory of human social structure (see Lewontin, Rose, & Kamin, 1984).

Although Wilson speaks with the authority of a biologist, his theory of society and human nature is dubious. He assumes that there are universals in all societies, including athletics, dancing, cooking, religion, entrepreneurship, territoriality, warfare, and female orgasm (see Lewontin et al., 1984, p. 243). He also assumes that these universal human characteristics are coded in the human genotype. He then contends that "these genetically based human universals have been established by natural selection during the course of human biological evolution" (see Lewontin et al., 1984, p. 244).

Each of these assumptions is open to question. First, the universals that Wilson ascribes to all societies are themselves social constructs, or labels. They are not natural objects having a concrete reality universally agreed upon by all persons. Wilson arrives at his terms arbitrarily. There is no a priori way to determine whether in fact his categories of nature exist. He reifies these terms, giving them a force in human evolutionary history that they do not and cannot have. He also gives social metaphors and social concepts (e.g., caste, warfare, love) a force in primate and insect societies that is suspect. This is the anthropomorphic fallacy again. How is it possible to speak of "slavery" in ants (Lewontin et al., 1984, p. 249)?

Wilson's assumption that human social behavior is coded in the genes is also wide open to criticism. Lewontin et al. (1984, pp. 252-253) observe that up to the present time no scientist has been able to relate any aspect of human behavior to any particular gene. Wilson's simple determinative model of gene control is thus wholly fallacious.

The argument that natural selection has determined the evolution and origin of human traits has also been criticized. Lewontin et al. (1984) state:

> The combination of direct selection, kin selection, and reciprocal altruism provides the sociobiologist with a battery of speculative possibilities that guarantees an explanation for every observation. The system is unbeatable because it is insulated from any possibility of being contradicted by fact. If one is allowed to invent genes with arbitrarily complicated effects on phenotypes and then to invent adaptive stories about the unrecoverable past of human history all phenomena, real and imaginary, can be explained. (p. 261)

More deeply, *sociobiology fails to offer an answer to the question of what it means to be human.* It reduces the essence of the human being to the genetic level. It is unable to address how human beings live their bodies into existence. Sociobiology thus becomes a strangely static, mechanical theory. It drives all of human experience down to the level of the gene and becomes, in the process, unable to speak to those lived disorders of the body that include alcoholism, drug addiction, and anorexia. At the same time it must be stressed that sociobiology exhibits a recurring structural sexism. It always begins with the assumption that "females lose in competition with males, and then reasons backwards to a plausible biological origin for female inferiority" (Haraway, 1989, p. 322).

Sociobiology is a new version of social Darwinism. It holds that the fittest survive and that populations display an adaptive capacity for reproduction that rests on the principles of natural selection (Wilson, 1975, pp. 1, 13-16). It is a conservative social philosophy that ignores the role of culture, religion, and political ideology in the production of the altruistic and conflictual forms of behavior that make up any society. We agree with Turner (1984) in his assessment of sociobiology: It is a blind alley. Lewontin et al. (1984) are more harsh; they claim that Wilson, who has identified himself with American neoconservative libertarianism, has offered in his sociobiology a "vulgar Mendelism, vulgar Darwinism, and vulgar reductionism in the service of the status quo" (p. 264). This latter point is well illustrated by the controversy surrounding Herrnstein and Murray's *The Bell Curve* (1994), in which the authors argue that low-IQ black parents are reproducing at an alarming rate. Accordingly, affirmative action, education, and federal government programs for the needy should be discontinued (see Kincheloe & Steinberg, 1994, p. 23). This is another example of the use of sociobiology for political purposes, to maintain the status quo.

However, we are not willing to rule out biological and genetic factors. We merely see them as constituting a stratum or level of behavior that must be analyzed at its own level. They cannot be lifted to the level of social and cultural phenomena and made to do the work of truly social psychological and psychological concepts and theories. Sociobiologists, like artificial intelligence theorists, clarify the assumptions and problems of social psychology.

In this respect, we find their work on animal communication and language systems important. We turn to a discussion of the "social" behavior of chimpanzees and the controversy surrounding the ability of apes to use language as humans do.

The Behavior of Chimpanzees

The great apes, who of all the animals stand closest to humans on the evolutionary ladder, offer perhaps the most interesting comparison with human beings, for they are unquestionably more intelligent than our usual house pets or farm animals. The great apes that have been most thoroughly studied are the chimpanzees. We shall attempt to show what sociable animals they are. In describing their behavior, we shall use language that will bring out their seemingly human qualities. We shall then point to their limitations, which emerge when we compare them with the more complex human being.

Group Solidarity

"It is hardly an exaggeration to say that a chimpanzee kept in solitude is not a real chimpanzee at all" (Köhler, 1926, p. 293). This statement indicates the extraordinary extent to which chimpanzees are influenced by the presence of other chimpanzees. When forcibly removed from his companions or group, the chimpanzee "cries, screams, rages, and struggles desperately to escape and return to his fellows. Such behavior may last for hours. All the bodily functions may be more or less upset. Food may be persistently refused, and depression may follow the emotional orgy" (Yerkes & Yerkes, 1945, p. 45). The chimpanzee in these circumstances will even risk his life in an effort to return to his group. When he rejoins it, there is great rejoicing, and the one who has been isolated displays the deepest excitement.

A chimpanzee locked alone in a cage will stretch his hands out through the bars toward his companions, wave and call to them, or push various objects through the bars in their direction. If the isolated animal's cries are audible and his gestures visible to the others, they may embrace him through the bars of the cage and otherwise give evidence of what seems to be human sympathy for their unhappy fellow. But if they cannot hear him or see him, they show no awareness of his absence. If one of their number is taken away because of illness or death, there is usually no evidence that the others grieve for their missing companion or even know that he is no longer in their midst.

In contrast, in a *National Geographic* article on Koko, a gorilla who has been taught American Sign Language, Patterson (1985) reports:

> Last year she [Koko] asked for and received a kitten. She attempted to suckle it and carried

> it tucked against her thigh, as gorilla mothers carry their babies. Tragically, All Ball, as Koko named the kitten, was killed by a car. When she heard the news, Koko remained silent for about 10 minutes, then began to cry—not with tears as humans do but with high-pitched soblike sounds. (p. 409)

Chimpanzees have a characteristic cry of distress. When this cry is emitted in connection with some action taken by the human investigator, other chimpanzees tend to rally to the support of their companion and threaten or actually attack the offender. Sometimes it is difficult to train the animals when they are in a group because of this danger of attack, particularly when the chimpanzees are adults.

Limitations of Chimpanzees

When we consider the collective achievements of civilized humans, we are overwhelmingly impressed by the vast gulf between humankind and the apes. Chimpanzees do not weep. Although they have various ways of indicating pleasure, they do not laugh. Nor do they seem to have the slightest appreciation of human laughter; they tend to respond to it with bewilderment or rage. One could go on almost indefinitely enumerating specific kinds of human behavior that are beyond the ape. It is not so easy, however, to determine the exact sources of the chimpanzees' limitations or to define the precise limits of their accomplishments. Here we can indicate only some of the main types of differences between human and subhuman behavior that are to a degree substantiated by the work of comparative psychologists.

Animals are limited to the here and now. All subhuman behavior is sharply, although not absolutely, limited to the immediate, concrete situation. This limitation is one of time and space. Thus Köhler (1926) states that a major difference between humans and chimpanzees is that the time in which chimpanzees live stretches back and forth only a little way. The ability of chimpanzees to solve problems appears to be determined principally, Köhler says, by their "optical apprehension of the situation." Sticks and other instruments are most readily used as tools when they are in immediate proximity to the problem situation. If they are moved away from it—for example, to the rear of the cage or into an adjoining room or corridor—the apes virtually cease to perceive them as potential tools, even though they may be perfectly familiar with these items and see them daily.

The assertion that animals are limited to the here and now requires some qualification: The limitation is not absolute, nor does it warrant overemphasis. Thus if chimpanzees in a cage see bananas buried in the sand outside and are not allowed out of the cage until the next day, when they are released they run quickly to the approximate spot to search for the buried fruit. Other experiments clearly indicate that delayed responses of this type are well within the range of the chimpanzee's abilities. Moreover, a chimpanzee separated from a human being to whom he has become accustomed will give unmistakable signs of recognition when he sees the person again after months of separation. But by and large, one may regard chimpanzees as limited to the here and now. Quiatt (1984) complicates this conclusion slightly:

> That social strategies of monkeys and apes may be premeditated is suggested by both naturalistic observation and experimental research . . . a review of deceptive behavior in monkeys and apes convinces me that those animals do manipulate displays in complex and subtle ways. (pp. 34-35)

Quiatt provides an interesting illustration about a chimp playing a trick by keeping his mouth full of water until a human is in range and then squirting the water at him (p. 31).

Whether primate behavior displays planning and intentionality, as we understand those terms, is problematic. Harré and Reynolds (1984) leave this topic open for discussion in the following statement:

> Whether primate intentionality is the same as human intentionality is another matter, but there seems no reason to deny the possibility of some degree of overlap between primate intentions and some kinds of human intentions. (p. 6)

The use of tools. Although chimpanzees can use various kinds of objects as tools and can even construct certain types of tools, they show almost no tendency to store the tools for future use or to transport them systematically from place to place. Moreover, chimpanzees show practically no disposition to store or hoard food against future contingencies. Other animals, especially certain insects, do store and transport food in complex and systematic ways. Such behavior, however, does not have to be learned; it is biologically determined.

Chimpanzees have what seems to be an "innate destructive impulse," according to Yerkes (1943), that expresses itself in their tendency to break down into its constituent elements any complex object made up of various movable or removable parts. Chimpanzees, like small children, will explore, pull, poke, and otherwise manipulate an object; they do not rest until it has been taken apart and the pieces strewn about. When chimpanzees do actually construct a tool—for example, by fitting two sticks together to make one long one—their action seems remarkable because it contrasts so sharply with their usual mode of behavior.

Moreover, unless they are continuously trained, there is a strong tendency for the animals to soon slough off most of the new behavior they have learned in the experimental training situation. As Köhler (1926) notes:

> If one is able to produce a—very temporary—type of behavior which is not congenial to the chimpanzee's instincts, it will soon be necessary to use compulsion if he is to keep it. And the slightest relaxation of that compulsion will be followed by a reversion to type. (p. 296)

Yerkes (1943) exclaimed over the remarkable manner in which the chimpanzees of his laboratory colony learned certain human activities. Thus when push-button drinking fountains were installed in their cages, only some animals were shown how to use them. The others learned from watching their fellows. Yerkes also observed that each generation became more tractable as experimental animals, certain of the activities required by the experiments being passed on from ape to ape "by imitative process" and from one generation to the next "by social tradition." These effects were the result of constant contact with human beings, and with an environment arranged by human beings. If the entire colony were returned to its native habitat, in a short time probably few, if any, traces of human influence would remain; a new generation would not profit from the older generation's contact with civilization. This is particularly so as drinking fountains, hammers, keys, and the like are not usually found in the ape's native environment. It is clear that such transmission as may occur among trained chimpanzees is not the result of language communication as humans know it. "When Jane Goodall saw chimpanzees fishing for termites and sopping up water with crushed leaves, her mentor, Louis Leakey, remarked that we're either going to have to redefine tools, or redefine man" (Brownlee, 1985, p. 93).

The Absence of Language Among Lower Animals

Apes never learn to speak like human beings. Little success has been achieved in training them to imitate the sounds of human speech, although many investigators have tried. Relevant to this point are the reports of two experiments in which young chimpanzees were reared for a time in the homes of psychologists (Hayes, 1951; Kellogg & Kellogg, 1933). Kellogg and Kellogg (1933) found that they were entirely unable to train their chimpanzee, Gua, to utter any words or to imitate human speech. The Hayeses (1951), on the other hand, reported that their animal, Vicki, acquired a vocabulary of three words: *mama, papa,* and *cup.* From a demonstration that we witnessed, it was clear that the imitation was so crude that the sounds could hardly be identified, and could be called words only by a stretch of the imagination. It was also clear that Vicki used them in a mechanical and uncomprehending manner.

Psychologists continue to be preoccupied with the attempt to teach language to apes. Beatrice Gardner and Allen Gardner (1969) have taught a chimpanzee to communicate in American Sign Language, and Ann Premack and David Premack (1972) have taught one of their chimpanzees, Sarah, a vocabulary of about 130 "words" that consist of brightly colored plastic shapes that can be readily placed in various combinations (sentences?) on a magnetized language board. These endeavors do not seem to have created a new situation or discredited the idea that humans are the only animals capable of learning a language. They have, however, once more demonstrated the remarkable capabilities of one of our closest and most captivating primate relatives.

The Premacks trained Sarah by rewarding her when she chose the right plastic "symbols" in a given context. For example, in order to obtain and eat a banana, she was required to put the plastic "word" for banana on the language board. In later phases of her learning, the plastic symbols were combined to form "sentences"—for example, "Give apple Sarah." When Sarah did this correctly, she was given a piece of apple. Sarah was also taught the names of various trainers, who wore their plastic symbol-names on string necklaces. On one occasion when she put on the board, "Give apple Gussie," the trainer promptly gave the apple to another chimp named Gussie, and Sarah never again made the same mistake. In the more advanced phases of her training, Sarah became able, according to the Premacks, to make complex assertions and judgments such as the following: "Sarah take apple, if/then Mary give chocolate Sarah," "Red color apple," and "Red no color of banana." She was able to match the plastic word for apple with a real apple, and the plastic name for Mary (a trainer) with a picture of Mary.

Premack and Premack (1972) cautiously conclude that "Sarah had managed to learn a code, a simple language that nevertheless included some of the characteristic features of natural language" (p. 99). They warn against asking of Sarah what one would require of an adult, but argue that Sarah holds her own in language ability when compared with a 2-year-old child. The Premacks are able to say that Sarah has a language because their definition of language is quite broad; they use the term *language* to refer to systems of communication in general, viewing human languages as particular "albeit remarkably refined forms of language" (p. 92). *They have thus conferred language upon chimpanzees by the very nature of their definition.*

Closer consideration of the highly interesting accomplishments of Sarah casts doubt even on the Premacks' comparison of Sarah with an ordinary 2-year-old child. For example, children even at this early age use their language to talk with each other, whereas Sarah talked only with human beings. In contrast to how children acquire vocabularies, Sarah acquired her vocabulary exclusively or mainly though a laborious learning process, motivated by material rewards. Although the Premacks say that Sarah mastered about 130 words, they also observe that her level of reliability was about 75-80%. This raises the question as to how well humans, even 2-year-olds, would be able to communicate if, in the process, they said approximately the opposite of what they intended to about 20-25% of the time. One may further wonder how much a colony of chimps in their natural habitat, all trained to Sarah's level and equipped with plastic words and language boards, would be likely to use this language.

In general, as we have indicated, it seems improbable that the work of the Premacks and the Gardners will result in any need to revise the belief that humans are the only animals capable of learning a language. The significance of this work is more likely to be felt in other areas, such as those that attempt to specify the basic points of difference that exist between human language and the lower-order system of communication. Anthropologist G. W. Hewes (1973) reviewed this material in connection with a proposal he made concerning the possible origin of human language. In the process of doing so, however, it seems clear that Hewes was not overly impressed with the idea that at least two chimpanzees in the world now have language, although they cannot talk to each other, because each uses a different one (whereas Sarah uses plastic symbols, the Gardners' chimp, Washoe, has been trained to use American Sign Language). We are more impressed by the ingenuity and creativity of the teachers than by that of their pupils.

Apes emit characteristic sounds of their own, but these do not constitute language in a genuine sense. This may be demonstrated easily through a consideration of three features of so-called ape language. First, the sounds are unlearned. This point has been proven conclusively by Boutan (1913), who raised an ape wholly isolated from other apes from birth until its fifth year. It uttered the same cries as those made by other apes. Second, the sounds emitted by apes, as various investigators have noted, are "subjective"—that is, they merely express emotions; they do not designate or describe objects. In the words of one writer, "Chimpanzees can exclaim *kha* or *nga* over their food just as humans delightedly cry yum-yum, but they cannot say *banana, today.*" Their cries of enthusiasm are responses to an immediate situation: Such cries "cannot be used between meals to talk over the merits of the feast" (Köhler, 1926, p. 85). And third, ape sounds do not constitute a system of symbols. Yerkes and Yerkes (1945) have summarized this lack of system:

> Certainly chimpanzees communicate effectively with one another by sounds, gestures, facial and bodily expression, postures, and visible attitudes which function as meaningful signs. Symbols probably are rare and play a subordinate, if significant, role in their linguistic expression. Therefore, the composite language of the chimpanzee differs greatly from our own. They, for example, have no system, or even assemblage, of sounds which may properly be termed speech, and nothing remotely like a written language. (p. 90)

The sounds emitted by apes, or by any other animal, clearly do not constitute systematized animal languages similar to human languages. Neither may one refer to animal sounds as words, for if one does, one is forced to recognize that human children also communicate their needs to one another and to their elders by means of cries—cries as natural for them as are chimpanzee cries to the chimpanzee. One would thus be led to say that children have language before they learn a language, and that they speak words immediately after birth. It is more in accord with accepted usage to restrict the term *language* to such conventionalized systems of sounds or words as those designated as English, French, German, Spanish, and so on. All such systems have to be learned, and they vary by communities rather than by species.

Biologist J. Bierens de Haan (1929) has clearly and conclusively summarized the arguments against the possible existence of unknown animal languages. He notes, first of all, that human language has six characteristics:

> The sounds used in it are *vocal, articulate,* and have some *conventional meaning,* they *indicate something,* are uttered with the *intention* of communicating something to somebody else, and are *joined* together to form new combinations, so that phrases of various and different content are formed. (p. 249)

On the relationship between primate sounds and objects, Cheney (1984) reports:

> Playback experiments of both the predator alarm calls of veret monkeys and the grunts used by verets during social interactions have indicated that nonhuman primate vocalization may effectively function to designate objects or events in the external world. . . . At present, our investigations of monkey vocalization are limited, in the sense that they can examine only the responses that calls evoke in listeners, and not the vocalizers' psychological or affective states. . . . However, whenever an organism communicates "about" objects external to itself, it effectively classifies objects in its environment, and in so doing re-

> veals some of the cognitive processes that underlie its signals. (p. 138)

In her research, Cheney has investigated "the manner in which veret monkeys perceive and classify objects and events in the external world" (p. 138). She uses data on alarm calls and other vocalizations to argue that classifications made by verets both of one another and of other objects are complex and hierarchical, in many respects resembling the multilevel taxonomies created by humans to describe their own social organizations.

Harré and Reynolds (1984) write, "The young veret gives a generalized alarm call to a variety of birds, later coming to restrict them to predatory birds only" (p. 8). Cheney suggests that the participation of the mother in cases where there really is a predator may be important in refining the call. We know that in humans, the broad categories of childhood are refined by learning and experience into the finer discriminations of adulthood. Harré and Reynolds (1984) state:

> Many theorists of psychology would hold that there is a strict relation between the capacity to use concepts for thought and the acquisition of language, the latter conceived as an abstract and arbitrary system of signs. . . . In this context the issue of whether "signing" chimpanzees "have language" assumes great importance. If they have, there is at least a necessary condition satisfied for their having conceptual (intentions) thought ways. It seems that the question of whether some non-human primates "have language" does not admit a simple or clear cut answer. It looks now as though even the smartest "signing" chimpanzee lacks syntactical capacity, but does have semantical capacity of quite a high order. (p. 8)

Primate Pseudolanguage

Bierens de Haan (1929, p. 249) reasons that animals possess at best "pseudolanguages," because human language is of a decisively different order. We may summarize the evidence he offers for this judgment and invite the reader to compare this analysis with that of linguist Charles F. Hockett (1965), presented in the next chapter:

1. *Vocal:* The great majority of animals—including most of the vertebrates—are mute.
2. *Articulate:* Syllables are joined together. This is impossible when sounds are produced by organs other than the mouth. Among the higher animals that possess voices, there is generally no joining together of syllables. Humans combine syllables into words.
3. *Conventional meaning:* With few exceptions, there is no direct relation between meaning and the nature of the sound. Even among the higher animals, sounds are innate and typical of the whole species.
4. *Indication:* With the aid of conventional meaning it becomes possible to indicate something—an object, situation, and so forth. Among the animals, sounds do not name objects or situations, but express "sentiments" and "emotions."
5. *Intention:* Animal sounds are generally uttered without reference to other beings. Although not made with intent to influence others, these sounds may be responded to by other animals.

6. *Joined together to form new combinations:* Combining words into phrases does not occur among animals; only humans do this.

We do not assert that there is no communication among the infrahuman species—quite the contrary. It is obvious even to the superficial observer that there is such communication. If communication is erroneously equated with language, then it is necessary to attribute language behavior to many lower species. But equating communication with language does violence to the usual meaning attached to these words and neglects the fact that there are many forms, or levels, of communication and that language is only one of these. If it is contended that lower animals have language like that of humans, it becomes necessary to explain the absence of behavioral effects of this fact upon them compared with the many profound effects of language on human behavior.

Just as there is no doubt of the existence of communication among the lower animals, there is no doubt that humans are the only animals capable of language. We discuss the nature of language behavior in Chapter 3, but we anticipate our discussion of it here by noting briefly that conversation is the fundamental form of linguistic intercommunication. Any intelligent person, given the proper training, can learn to converse with any other person on Earth. However, one cannot converse with lower animals.

Consider the comments of Seyfarth (1984), who with Cheney has studied primate communication systems in veret monkeys in their natural habitat in Africa. Seyfarth recorded an individual monkey's grunts, such as the "grunt to a dominant" and the "grunt to another group," and then played these back to monkeys in the wild through a concealed speaker. The monkeys' responses to these calls were filmed. Seyfarth concludes:

> Because veret monkey grunts transmit quite specific information, and because in some cases they clearly relate to external events, it is tempting to compare them with human words, where individuals often have a mental representation of some object or event they wish to communicate. Clearly, however, such a comparison is premature, since our experiments can only measure the responses evoked by grunts, and not what is going on in the mind of the vocalizer. . . . When a monkey hears a grunt, for example, he is immediately informed of many of the fine details of the social behavior going on, even though he may be out of sight of the vocalizer, and even though the vocalizer himself may not be involved. At this point, the monkey's system of communication, whatever its physiological or cognitive basis, begins to take on many of the functional properties of a system of communication based on true representation. (p. 54)

Some Consequences of the Lack of Language

The fundamental difference between human and animal behavior, basic to and in a sense determining all other differences, is that humans can talk and animals cannot. Human possession of language symbols and our ability to produce them voluntarily enables us to overcome the time and space limits in which, as we have noted, subhuman organisms are enclosed. Indeed, it may be more accurate to say that the possession of language has enabled human beings to "invent" time and space—past, present, and future.

We may summarize the differences between humans and the lower animals by saying that the lower animals do not have a culture. The term *culture* is generally used to refer to behavior patterns—including beliefs, values, and ideas—that are the shared possession of groups and that are symbolically transmitted. A culture also includes artifacts or products that are handed down in a physical sense, but whose significance resides in their relationships with human behavior. As language is both an integral part of culture and the indispensable vehicle for its transmission, the assertion that animals do not possess it is a far-reaching one for comparative psychology.

Another type of animal that has received considerable publicity in recent years is the dolphin or porpoise (Brownlee, 1985; Kellogg, 1961; Lilly, 1961). The adaptability of this creature has been amply demonstrated, but the rash suggestions that it can talk and that it has a language are obvious examples of the way in which enthusiasm about the accomplishments of a given animal leads people to endow it with human qualities. It has been remarked that although humans may have some success in communicating with dolphins in "dolphin language," dolphins will probably have difficulty communicating with us in human language.

We say this despite the apparent efforts of some scientists to "demonstrate" the ability of dolphins to learn the names of objects and to respond to commands. Brownlee (1985), reviewing the evidence on this matter, suggests that the question is not "so much whether animals think as what they have to do in order to convince scientists that what they're doing is in fact thinking" (pp. 85-86).

Some have suggested that what is really happening with the lower animals is not the learning of language, but the learning of patterns of behavior that produce rewards. In 1973 the psychologist Terrance attempted to teach his own sign language to a young male chimpanzee named Nim Chimp-sky (a play on the name of the famous linguist Noam Chomsky). Terrance hoped to disprove Chomsky's position that language is a uniquely human facility. After 4 years he gave up—Nim had learned 128 signs, but most of his sentences consisted of repetitive demands for food or play. Terrance concluded that chimps do not use signs as words; they learn, instead, behaviors that are rewarded (reported in Brownlee, 1985, p. 87). Terrance (1984) states:

> The question of what language is has yet to be answered by linguists, psychologists, psycholinguists, philosophers and other students of human language in a way that captures its many complexities in a simple definition. Agreement has been reached, however, about one basic property of all human languages. That is the ability to create new meanings, each appropriate to a particular context, through the application of grammatical rules. Noam Chomsky and George Miller, among others, have convincingly reminded us of the futility of trying to explain a child's ability to create and understand sentences unless one attributes to the child a knowledge of rules that can generate an indeterminately large number of sentences from a finite vocabulary of words. . . . a rote learning of a

> string of words presupposes no knowledge of the meanings of each element and certainly no knowledge of the relationships that exist between the elements. (pp. 139-140)

In his analysis of other chimp language studies, Terrance argues:

> Two films made by the Gardners of Washoe's signing, a doctoral dissertation by Lyn Miles . . . and a recently released film of Koko, the Talking Gorilla, all support the hypothesis that the teacher's coaxing and cueing have played much greater roles in so-called "conversations" with chimpanzees than was previously recognized. (p. 146)

The History of Primate Research, Sociobiology, and Chimp Language Studies

Haraway (1989, p. 11) argues that the origins of scientific discourse on simians (apes, monkeys, chimpanzees) can be traced to the following intertwined processes, all of which drew on evolutionary theory. The newly emerging scientific fields of comparative psychology and primatology called for laboratory and field studies comparing the intelligence of humans with the mental abilities and adaptive behaviors of simians and other nonhumans. These studies were organized by three goals: to find the principles that govern animal behavior, to apply these understandings to human behavior, and to compare animal behavior in laboratory and natural settings. This last goal lead to attempts to assess the animal's "overall evolutionary fitness" (King, 1987, p. 222).

Before World War II, the nations of France, Belgium, Russia, and the United States had established research stations and conservation areas for nonhuman primate study (Haraway, 1989, p. 19). Nonhuman primates were also the subjects of medical research on tropical diseases (yellow fever), polio, and syphilis (Haraway, 1989, p. 22). Private collections of nonhuman primates soon complemented collections housed in zoological gardens. The year 1915 marked the birth of the first chimpanzee born into human captivity.

The late 19th and early 20th centuries saw the "publication of numerous stories about amazing animal accomplishments" (King, 1987, p. 222). Clever Hans, a horse who could supposedly read, spell, and solve mathematical problems, was perhaps the most celebrated of these cases. Darwinian evolutionary theory supported the preoccupation with animal intelligence, especially the intelligence of monkeys and apes. Wealthy individuals treated chimps as pets, surrogate children, research subjects, and wild animals (Haraway, 1989, p. 23).

Before World War II, primatology was based primarily in laboratories and museums or in public or private collections (Haraway, 1989, p. 24). Dead simians "were in cabinets and dioramas in universities and museums. Expeditions into the 'wild' were made primarily to collect animals for circuses, the pet trade, medical research, zoos or museums, and only incidentally to record the lives of the animals in their own worlds" (Haraway, 1989, p. 24).

The scientific study of nonhuman primates can be divided into discernible projects and historical periods, defined in part by the pre- and post-World War II years. Between 1924 and 1942, Robert Yerkes directed the Yale Laboratories of Primate Biology, which consisted of a laboratory colony of chimpanzees. Using psychobiological and engineering effectiveness models, Yerkes and his students investigated the sexual, social, and cooperative behaviors of the captive chimpanzee. They attempted to generalize from the behaviors of chimps to human society, arguing that male dominance is correlated with leadership, whereas females exhibit "sexual allure and a chameleon-like personality" (Yerkes, 1943, p. 83; quoted in Haraway, 1989, p. 81).

Studies of nonprimates in natural settings gained popularity between the years 1930 and 1955. With support from the U.S. Army and the Macy and Rockefeller Foundations, primatologists such as C. R. Carpenter and S. A. Altman studied the sexual conduct and communication patterns of wild monkeys and gibbons in the Panama Canal Zone, Thailand, and Siam. Altman applied cybernetic communication theory to primate societies, formulating arguments about animal aggression and communication signals that would later be used by sociobiologists.

Postwar primatology can be divided into two phases. The first extends from the 1950s to the early 1970s, and includes the emergence of sociobiology as a new field of inquiry. In this phase there was an increase in federal and private support for primate studies, coupled with a growing medical demand for primates as laboratory material and renewed interest in using primates as models for answering psychobiological questions about humans (Haraway, 1989, p. 126). There was increasing international trade in monkeys as research subjects, and a corresponding concern about their cruel treatment. This led to formal U.S. assurances that monkeys would be given humane treatment and would be used for research that would benefit all of humanity (Haraway, 1989, p. 121).

Today there are six National Institutes of Health-sponsored regional Primate Research Centers, located in Atlanta, Georgia; Davis, California; near Boston, Massachusetts; New Orleans, Louisiana; Madison, Wisconsin; and Seattle, Washington. By 1980, approximately 1,100 scientists and support staff working in these six sites were studying 12,000 nonhuman primates representing 45 different species. This research was supported by the federal government and by private philanthropy, with grants from the Ford, Wilkie, Louis Leakey, and Wenner-Gren Foundations, as well as the National Geographic Society and the World Wildlife Fund (Haraway, 1989, pp. 122-123).

Such authors as Robert Ardrey, Desmond Morris, Lionel Tiger, Robin Fox, Jane Goodall, Ashley Montagu, and Allison Jolly produced popular books in this period. These works often celebrated humankind's domination over nature, male natural aggression, territoriality, biological determinism, and women as mediators of culture. This literature, according to Haraway (1989, p. 127), was ideologically conservative and patriarchal, emphasizing the female's natural, nurturing place in the home.

The second primate phase can be marked by the appearance of E. O. Wilson's *Sociobiology* in 1975. Wilson's work, as we have argued above, stressed the problems of genetic fitness, kin selection, altruism, and reproductive behavior (Dewsbury, 1987, pp. 66-67). Once again, monkeys were used as stand-ins for human beings, as models for arguments about population control, mother-infant bonding, pathological male aggression, innate intelligence, heterosexual relations, depression, child abuse, and "male-male social cooperation" (Haraway, 1989, p. 129). There was an increase in language and home-reared ape studies in this phase. There were also attempts to return chimps who had been confiscated in the illegal pet trade to their natural settings.

Television specials focusing on nonhuman primates also gained popularity in this period, including such programs as *Miss Goodall and the Wild Chimpanzees* (1965), *Monkeys, Apes, and Man* (1971), *Search for the Great Apes* (1975), *Gorilla* (1981), and *Among the Wild Chimpanzees* (1984) (see Haraway, 1989, p. 133). These films relocated the nonhuman primate back in nature (*Gorillas in the Mist,* a 1988 feature film about the work of Dian Fossey, is another example).

Another major scientific effort in this period involved putting chimps into outer space. In 1961, as part of the U.S. man-in-space program, the chimpanzee Ham was successfully shot into suborbital flight (Haraway, 1989, p. 137). Ham performed all of his duties flawlessly. However, in an effort to mobilize public opinion behind the space effort, NASA replaced chimps (chimponauts) with human pilots (astronauts). It was clear that humans were merely replicating what chimps had been trained to do (Haraway, 1989, p. 138). Thus was born a kind of human cyborg, a scientific construction—part human, part nonhuman, part machine. Chimps became replicas for humans (Haraway, 1989, p. 139).

A third major initiative during this period involved the continuation of language studies with home-reared apes. Work in the 1980s continued the Kellogg, Hayes, Gardner, and Premack projects. Perhaps the most interesting case in this series involves Koko, a gorilla who has been taught to use American Sign Language by Penny Patterson, who was inspired by the Gardners. Koko, it seems, understands spoken English. Patrick Suppes, head of Stanford's Institute for Mathematical Studies in the Social Sciences, designed a keyboard-computer system that allows Koko to talk by "pressing buttons linked to a voice synthesizer" (Haraway, 1989, p. 141). Koko, part computer, part ape, part English-speaking ape-human, has been turned into a cyborg.

Koko admired herself in a mirror's reflection, and soon learned how to use a camera, taking a picture of her reflection in the mirror. Koko decided she wanted a pet and asked Penny for a kitten. Penny presented her with a Manx kitten (a tailless breed), which she named All Ball. Koko bonded with All Ball, and served as his surrogate mother.

Haraway (1989) discusses this preoccupation with the ape's abilities to learn and use language. She quotes from a *National Geographic* cover story about a primatologist, Birute Galdikas, who had studied a chimp named Sugito. Galdikas stated, "I have often regretted that I would never be able to talk to Sugito, so that I could examine how she perceived and interpreted the world" (p. 141). Haraway comments, "This is the ethnographer's dream of knowing the world from the other's point of view" (p. 141).

There are other parts to the history of primate research, including the 1974 discovery in Africa of the fossil remains of Lucy, a 3.5-million-year-old full bipedal; attempts to rewrite the evolutionary history of modern humans based on this discovery; continuing debates about race and intelligence and the intellectual inferiority of dark-skinned persons; arguments about "Woman the Gatherer"; Harry Harlow's nuclear family apparatus and his experiments in the 1970s with rhesus monkeys who were taught to bond with cloth-and-wire surrogate mothers; post-World War II primatology projects in Japan and India; the 1980s mountain gorilla studies in central Africa; and the development of a female primatology and a feminist sociobiology as variations within feminist theory.

Haraway (1989, p. 4) suggests that it is useful to view the field of primatology as a "story-telling craft," as a field made up of different narratives about science, monkeys, apes, human beings, intelligence, culture, society, and nature. Primatology "is about the life history of a taxonomic order that includes people" (p. 5). This narrative system is organized by a triple code that manipulates the meanings of gender, science, and race. Haraway argues that in the primate narrative, woman mediates between the nature (chimps, apes) and culture. Woman is closer to nature than man, and hence it is she who teaches the chimp to speak, and it is she who goes into the wild and studies the chimp in its natural environment. Woman thus functions as man's channel to nature.

So the woman scientist is a key part of this story. Louis Leakey repeatedly selected young women as his assistants. He felt that his "ape women" were unbiased and would make "better observers than men because they would be more patient, not be threatened by the male apes in masculine rivalry, and be sensitive to the mother-young interactions" (Haraway, 1989, p. 151). The woman scientist is critical because she is not regarded as a threat to the natural order in chimp society. This gender coding in the stories and films about Goodall and Fossey help to ground ape science in patriarchy.

Race intersects with gender. The women scientists are all white. Brown, wild apes become stand-ins for the brown Africans who live in the jungles. These people are visited by white-skinned, fair-haired women scientists. Haraway (1989) is explicit on this point. Third World people of color were systematically excluded from the primate project. In a complex process, "race of people of color is displaced onto animals and the generic status of man is displaced onto white women" (p. 153). Black people were the beast, the uncivilized other who would be trained to be human by white women.

A series of oppositions thus operated in this narrative: white/black, human/animal, mind/body, light/dark. White women mediate "between 'man' and 'animal' . . . [and] colored (dark) women are . . . [connected] to the category of animal" (Haraway, 1989, p. 154). People of color are not part of the primate story. So these are not innocent stories, these tales about chimps, their sexual habits, their dominance hierarchies, and their use of language.

Summary

In this section we have sketched the chronology of human evolution, noting that after a certain point in time, biological and cultural evolution cease to be closely correlated. The enormous acceleration of cultural evolution in recent times is linked with language and especially with the invention of writing. The social and communicative behavior of a number of subhuman species, especially of chimpanzees, is considered in comparison with that of human beings.

The study of subhuman behavior has two general purposes for the social psychologist. First, it provides a picture of response mechanisms and adaptive devices that generally increase in complexity, sensitivity, and variability as one ascends the evolutionary scale to humans. The second main purpose in studying subhuman behavior is to bring into sharper focus the differences among organisms of various degrees of complexity. As the organisms develop to more complex and more specialized levels, new behavioral possibilities and properties emerge. These new behavioral possibilities and properties, if they are to be investigated as such, must be conceived of as related to the previous possibilities and properties from which they have evolved. This does not mean, however, that they are to be identified with that from which they have evolved.

With reference to understanding human social behavior, the study of subhuman organisms enables us to form tentative conceptions (Allee, 1931, 1951) of similarities (common features) of human and subhuman behavior and differences (unique elements) that distinguish human behavior from that of other living forms. We must give adequate attention to both of these aspects. Experimental and comparative psychologists frequently stress the similarities and underplay or disregard altogether the differences between humans and other animals; theologians and philosophers, on the other hand, often stress the differences to the point of failing to recognize that humans, after all, are animals themselves.

Social scientists are largely concerned with political, economic, legal, moral, religious, and other specific forms of behavior that are found almost exclusively in human beings living in groups. In other words, they are concerned with analyzing the unique phases of human behavior; therefore, it is inevitable that they should seek explanations of this behavior in terms of something that human beings have and that other organisms lack. Such expressions as culture, mores, institutions, traditions, laws, politics, economics, philosophy, religion, science, art, literature, and mathematics all point to unique attributes of human behavior. These differences between humans and apes cannot be logically explained through reference to things that human beings and animals have in common.

Social psychology as the study of the influence of groups on the behavior of individuals is merely a part of the broader comparative study of species, each of which presents its own particular problems, but all of which share certain attributes in the sense that they are all living forms. It is unnecessary to insist either that only the differences be investigated and emphasized or that exclusive attention be focused on the similarities. It is understandable that economics, political science, and sociology, which deal with behavior that is not found outside of human society, should not concern themselves directly with subhuman behavior. As social psychology is a part of comparative psychology, it must concern itself with the behavior of and narratives about lower animals in order to understand the evolutionary emergence of civilization, culture, reason, and intelligence.

Symbolic Environments and Cognitive Structures

Earlier in this chapter we broadly outlined the study of humankind's physical and early cultural evolution and indicated some of the basic differences between humans and lower animals. We extend the argument here by noting that with the acquisition of language and conceptual thought, human reactions to the external social and physical worlds have become increasingly indirect. These reactions are increasingly affected by *ideas* that represent to humans an unknown and unknowable ultimate reality. Language—by enabling humans to be observers of their own actions, objects in their own thought processes—adds new dimensions to the simple and more direct consciousness of lower animals. It also ushers into awareness a private, incommunicable aspect of experience, commonly described as "subjective."

Symbolic Environments

In Chapter 1, we noted that language has several dimensions—including the institutional, the syntactic, the semantic, the cultural, and the interactional—and we argued that signs are fundamental features of language. We now need to introduce some additional terms.

The word *symbol* refers to the ability of a sign to stand for something else—for example, the symbolic environment, or the world of symbolism in art. On occasion, we shall use the words *sign* and *symbol* interchangeably. Signs that refer to representations, such as the cross, will be called *icons*. Those signs that point to or measure something else will be called *indexes*. A barometer, for example, is an index of impending weather conditions. With these distinctions in mind, we can now discuss symbolic environments.

Humans live in a symbolic environment because (a) they are responding directly to symbols, and (b) their relationships to the external world are indirect and organized by means of symbols. As Cassirer (1944) has aptly stated:

> Man lives in a symbolic universe. . . . [He does not] confront reality immediately; he cannot see it, as it were, face to face. . . . Instead of dealing with things themselves man is in a sense constantly conversing with himself. He has so enveloped himself in linguistic forms . . . that he cannot see or know anything except by the interposition of this artificial medium. (p. 25)

The symbolic environment may be thought of as a substitute environment, but it is important to note that this environment is not a mere reproduction or reflection of the external world. Indeed, some believe that the "real" external world can never be known "for what it is"; what humans know of it, they know by virtue of their particular

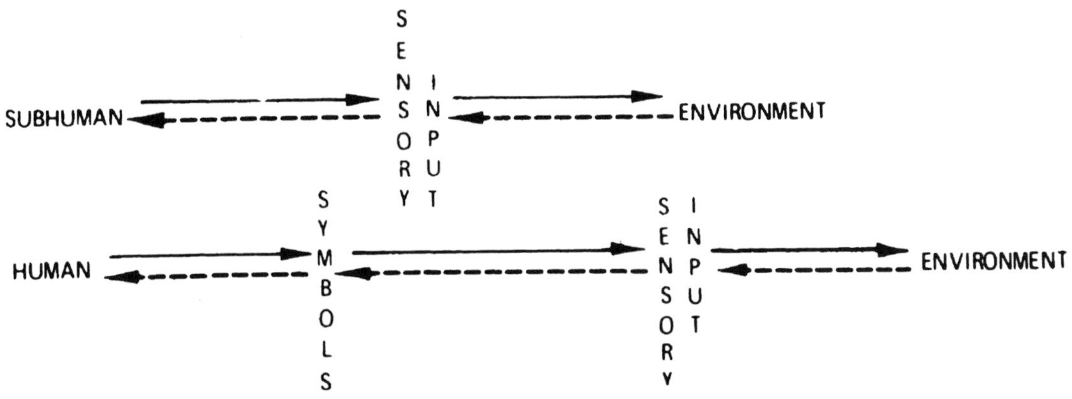

Figure 2.1. Two Types of Relationships With the Environment: Subhumans and Humans

sensory equipment and their particular socialized experience of it. The world in which human beings live and act is, in a sense, "constructed" by them in terms of the requirements of human conduct. That humans can invent symbolic structures and are affected by them introduces new dimensions and levels of interaction into the relations of humans to humans, humans to the external world, and humans to themselves.

The two types of relationships with the environment discussed here can be illustrated by contrasting the relations of primitive and civilized humans to microbes (see Figure 2.1). Primitive humans generally are unaware of the existence of microbes and thus have no symbols with which to designate, describe, and comprehend them. Nevertheless, microbes influence them and may even cause death. We therefore may say that microbes form a part of the nonsymbolic environment of primitive humans, but are not represented in their symbolic environment. They are not, as Mead (1934) would have said, "social objects."

By contrast, civilized humans are aware of the existence of microbes and are able to formulate elaborate statements about them. Microbes today are represented in our symbolic environment, and this fact is of great significance. To have symbols for microbes means to be conscious of them, to comprehend them; it also means that microbes may be controlled and subordinated to human purposes. That civilized humans are able to make statements about these forms of life, which are invisible to the naked eye, is thus of utmost intellectual and practical importance. We may add that human conceptions of the world are rarely static or unchanging; thus microbes have become linked by biologists in new and complex ways with each other, with viruses and cells, and with physiological and genetic processes.

Humans also use language to describe themselves, devising terms and concepts for the human body and its parts and finding various means of describing processes that go on within the body. Humans, in short, become objects to themselves; they become conscious of their own thought processes and of consciousness itself. They not only learn to make and be influenced by statements about their physical world, they also learn to formulate verbal propositions about themselves and to be influenced by them. Insofar as humans are aware of their own responses, those responses become part of the human environment too.

The human environment, therefore, does not consist merely of natural and external events and processes; it also includes the symbols by means of which humans name, classify, and form conceptions of things as well as of the world of ideas and values. These symbols are products of group living; they reflect the fact that the members of groups—in the process of intercommunication and adaptation—devise linguistic schemes for classifying, describing, and responding to persons, objects, and events. These schemes form part of the social heritage and are the most significant aspects of the human environment. It is not just a matter of complexity that is involved (as the astronomer's world is more complex than that of most lay stargazers); rather, quite literally, the world is differently constructed by different groups. *In a sense, most of this text illustrates not only that point, but how those different constructions affect interaction between particular groups of human beings.*

Humans as Actors and Observers

From the foregoing discussion an important point emerges: Humans engage in activity while simultaneously observing their own actions. It is as though human beings, acting out parts on the stage, are also sitting in the audience watching their own performance and evaluating it as it unfolds. Sometimes these two processes interfere with each other, and people tend to switch from one activity to the other. They may become so absorbed in what they are doing that they fail in their observer role and do what they had not intended to do. Or, as observers, they may become so preoccupied in watching their own performance—or that of the others involved in the real-life drama—that they distract themselves in their role as actors and forget their lines or miss their cues.

This aspect of human behavior arises from the fact that humans live largely within a symbolic environment of their own creation. We can describe this in general terms by saying that humans become both subjects and objects; that they become conscious of consciousness; that through their conceptualizations they establish a distance between themselves and their experiences of the real world. This distance, or detachment, enables them to deal conceptually with their own experiences and gives them a new dimension by making them objects within their own thought processes. Presumably, lower animals are incapable of this activity; they may be conscious, but they are not conscious of their own consciousness. They obviously have experiences of a direct sort, but they are unable to observe their own actions. For such reasons, a distinction is made between the one-dimensional consciousness of lower animals and the two- or more-dimensional consciousness of humans, which is often called *reflective self-consciousness* or, more simply, *self-reflectiveness* (see Chapter 1).

Subjective and Objective Reality

It has been said that human beings live simultaneously in three kinds of worlds: the real world of things and events; a subjective, private world; and a symbolic or cultural world of shared beliefs, accepted ideas, and *objective* knowledges that are distilled from experience and observation and transmitted via language.

Concerning the first of these worlds—reality as it really is—little need be said here, although philosophers have said much about it. As physical beings we are part of this reality, deny it or not, no matter how imperfectly we understand it. Presumably, this world exists independent of our intellectual grasp of it.

The second world—the private, subjective realm—is one in which we are alone. All our experiences have a unique personal reference in the sense that they are ours and no one else's, and that we alone have direct access to and awareness of them. This is true regardless of whether an experience is artistic, religious, or of any other kind.

The third realm is the cultural world of beliefs, ideas, knowledge, theories, and logic. It has the appearance of objectivity because—as we note more fully in Chapter 4—it is communicated and shared within groups, which act toward the presumed real world of objects, people, and events in terms of it. The cultural world actually is created through "a process of consensual validation of experiences" that in their origins are inherently subjective—that is, unique experiences of unique individuals. The connection between "objective knowledge" of the real world and the real world itself is always problematic, as Henri Poincaré, the famous French mathematician and scientist, has indicated by posing the question: What would happen if an omniscient being were to appear on Earth and go from one scientist to another, telling all of them the final truth about the problems they were investigating? Poincare's answer is that nothing would happen, because the scientists would be unable to comprehend what they were told. Indeed, one might wonder whether the omniscient being would be able to state the absolute truth in any existing language (or be able to stay out of jail or a mental institution long enough to complete the mission).

The term *subjective* is commonly misused to describe events that transpire in the heads or brains of humans and presumably of other animals. These events, however, can no more be called subjective than those that presumably occur in the interior of the sun. Both events occur in a real, material world; those in the human brain are material events that involve a substratum of complex interlocking neural, chemical, and electrical occurrences that use up energy. It is therefore erroneous to call mental processes subjective merely because they are internal and relatively inaccessible to observation, as are those inside the sun.

Clearly, *subjective* means something other than simple inaccessibility. What it actually refers to must be not the material occurrences themselves, but some aspect of how these occurrences are perceived by the organism. Our analysis suggests that the term refers to the communicability of experiences; there are aspects of all experience that escape the communication network and cannot be fully shared with others because they are the peculiarly private property of unique individuals. This aspect of experience can properly be called subjective.

We may, for example, tell a friend that we have a toothache, and because she has had similar experiences, she understands what we are saying. Nevertheless, the toothache remains our own personal experience. This latter aspect is the private, or subjective, part of the experience; it is difficult to describe because it is essentially incommunicable. We know that it is there—"in ourselves"—by introspection and infer that it can also be present in others, but beyond that we can do little else beyond advising other people that they will not understand all of what we are trying to say unless they have had exactly the same experience themselves. For example, how does it feel to die? We suppose there is only one obvious way to find this out for oneself. In matters like this, the languages of poetry and art come closer to communicating than does the precise, didactic language of science.

It is thus meaningless to assert that falling in love is a subjective experience, because there are no other kinds. By the same token, it is equally meaningless to claim that weighing an object is an objective experience. The difference between these two experiences is simply that the latter is more readily transmitted to others than is the former. The terms in which both are conceived, perceived, and communicated are intimately related to the symbolic coordinates of the speaker's world. We turn now to this topic.

Social Worlds, Symbolic Coordinates, and Fictions

The idea of a symbolic environment implies that all humans live in what can be termed *social worlds.* These can be thought of as groupings of individuals who are bound together through networks of communication—whether the members are geographically proximate or not—and through the sharing of important symbols. Groups also share common or similar perspectives on reality. For simple societies, as described classically by anthropologists, one might think of the society as equivalent to a single social world whose members have essentially a single organized outlook on reality. But as Shibutani notes (1962): "Modern mass societies . . . are made up of a bewildering variety of social worlds. . . . Each . . . is a cultural area, the boundaries of which are set neither by territory nor formal group memberships but by the limits of effective communication" (p. 136). In short, a nation is not the equivalent of a society—there are many societies, many social worlds, within each nation; and people may have membership in international communities (such as the community of biologists or Jehovah's Witnesses) regardless of where they live.

The members of social worlds conceive of reality in terms of certain basic *symbolic coordinates.* To grasp the notion of symbolic coordinates, consider the early Christians' ideas of reality following from their interpretations of the teachings of Jesus—ideas linked with concepts of God and His Son and the implications of those concepts—then compare this view of reality with that of the modern atheist, who accepts a strictly materialistic, "scientific" view of the universe; or compare both with the Nazis' conceptions during the 1930s. One philosopher has suggested that perspectives on reality can be represented by quite different metaphors: a prison, a battlefield, a stage, a garden, and so on. Each metaphor has different implications for how reality is conceptually organized. Each metaphor also has a perspective on what space looks like and what time feels like—indeed, what time periods (past, present, future) are most important and how they relate to each other. The basic items concerning all these are what we mean when we refer to the social coordinates of a given social world.

From the individual's standpoint, the symbolic environment that he or she thinks of as "reality" itself seems like an objective "thing." Berger and Luckmann (1967) have phrased this in similar terms:

> I apprehend the reality of everyday life as an ordered reality. Its phenomena are prearranged in patterns that seem to be independent of my apprehension of them and that impose themselves upon the latter. The reality of everyday life appears already objectified, that is, constituted by an order of objects that have been designated *as* objects before my appearance on the scene. The language used in everyday life continuously provides me with the necessary objectifications and posits the order within which these make sense and within which everyday life has meaning for me. . . . In this manner language marks the co-ordinates of my life in society and fills that life with meaningful objects. (pp. 22-23)

Berger and Luckmann add that this reality presents itself to the individual as a world that he or she shares with others. And—a very important point—this "reality" is taken for granted *as* reality. It does not require verification over and beyond its simple presence; it is simply *there.*

This reality, the symbolic coordinates and symbolizations, may be regarded by later generations as mistaken, misguided, or dreadfully immoral. Obviously, the same judgments can be made by contemporaries. Insofar as the members of one social world are concerned with the views and actions of people from other social worlds, they will take corrective action. This can be argumentative, rhetorical, persuasive, or directly coercive, giving rise to fights, imprisonment, or warfare.

Prejudices and Stereotypes

Social scientists and language students have mistakenly referred to the "incorrect" symbols of others as *fictions.* A striking contemporary example is that of commonly held ideas of *race.* Whatever scientists may say about the pitfalls attending the classification of humans by biological characteristics, certain socially important classifications of race still exist. Just as humans classify objects into categories and act toward them on the basis of class membership, they classify other humans into racial groupings and behave toward them on the basis of presumed racial membership. The ways in which one perceives other humans as black or white are as much part of social heritage as the words *Negro, black, African American,* and *white.* The same individual may be classified differently in different parts of the world or in different social groups in the same place, and behavior toward him or her will vary accordingly.

In the United States some people have held truly nonsensical attitudes about "black blood." Because among Americans it has been customary to regard a person as black if he or she has any "black blood," "mulattoes" are described as "blacks having some white blood"—never as "whites having some black blood." During World War II, "black blood" and "white blood" were sometimes kept in separate blood banks. The idea underlying this practice was that if white people received a transfusion of "black blood," then their skin color might change, or they might have been said to have "black blood" in their veins. It was sometimes supposed that this would affect the individuals or their progeny.

These conceptions are absurd. In the first place, the blood of a pregnant woman does not flow through the vessels of the unborn child; hence we are not justified in saying that we have our parents' blood in our veins. Moreover, there is no difference between the blood of blacks and that of whites; all blood types are found in both races. Neither the physical nor the mental traits of parents or their future offspring can conceivably be affected by blood transfusion. Popular thinking on these matters is based on certain misconceptions—the scientist would say—about the nature of races, blood, and heredity. These ideas have no biological foundation; indeed, scientific evidence points to the essential biological unity of all human types. Not only are all blood types common to all racial groupings, but the human organism is so uniform throughout the world that for experimental work in physiology and anatomy, the "race" to which subjects belongs does not matter. But as long as the members of some social world regard other persons as belonging to a genuine race, they will act toward them accordingly.

Another term that is similar to *fictions* (especially racial ones) is *stereotypes.* Sociologists have long and customarily used this term to refer to certain oversimplified, fixed, and usually fallacious conceptions that people hold about other people. Etymologically, the first part of the term is derived from the Greek word *steros,* meaning solid or firm. Historically, it is derived—at least in American technical usage—from a book on public opinion by Walter Lippmann (1922), who uses it to refer to "the pictures in our heads." Lippmann asserts that because people approach facts with preestablished classifications, they do not see the facts clearly or in unbiased fashion: "For the most part, we do not first see and then define, we define first and then see." There is stereotyped imagery of races, nationalities, national groups, occupational groups, social classes, and the sexes, but it is in the racial area that stereotypes have most often been studied. It has been found that although the practice is changing, our movies, radio and television programs, and popular literature have rarely portrayed blacks in any roles other than those of servant or low-class person—roles that fit the old white stereotype of blacks. Similarly, stereotypes influence the depiction of females in the mass media. Until recent years, women were most commonly cast only as wives and mothers in situation comedies and television commercials.

Once formed, a stereotype tends to persist even in the face of contradictory evidence and experience. So long as an individual classifies certain persons as belonging to a group or race and attributes certain characteristics to that group or race in general, he or she will dismiss those who do not have these characteristics as exceptions to the norm—and we are told that "the exception proves the rule." The rule, as we have already seen, is what the group is supposed to be "by nature."

The notion of stereotypes has been useful for social psychologists in the investigation of intergroup hostility, but it is not really a special and distinct concept. It provides an effective means of calling attention to erroneous and oversimplified concepts that people have about other people. By their very nature, all classifications are selective responses to a complex environment, and thus are necessarily somewhat simplified versions of reality. Stereotypes often are strongly tinged with emotion, but this is also true of many other conceptions. Likewise, as classifications are embedded in systems, many of them resist easy change even when confronted with contradictory evidence.

Some students of language phenomena advocate that such fictions—*all* fictions—should be eliminated from the language, as they refer to nothing real and are socially harmful. "No other animal produces verbal monsters in his head and projects them upon the world outside his head" (Chase, 1938, p. 14). Such a proposal, of course, demonstrates a radical misconception of the nature of language and associated forms of symbolization.

CONCLUSION

The reactions of humans to their surroundings are mediated ones. They are not based on reality, but on ideas of that reality expressed mainly by means of linguistic symbols. Hence the symbolic environment of humans, the names, words, terms, concepts, categories, fictions, stereotypes, prejudices—in short, the symbolic meanings—are social, interactional productions. They are the means by which humans make sense of the world around them. The acquisition of language habits generates in humans the motivation to name, classify, and explain the significant aspects of their environment.

In this chapter we have seen how human biological and cultural evolution have set the boundaries for the development of language. We have presented and criticized the sociobiological point of view, which attempts to reduce human experience to the level of genes and to universal evolutionary principles. We have also discussed the behavior of chimpanzees and indicated how their experiences reflect the absence of language, as we understand language at the human, group level. It should be clear from our discussion that it is impossible for chimps to have prejudices, form stereotypes, or mediate their worlds with the complex structures of meaning that language provides. In the next two chapters we discuss in greater detail language, social structure, and groups.

SUGGESTED READINGS

Bateson, G., & Bateson, M. C. (1987). *Angels fear: Towards an epistemology of the sacred.* New York: Macmillan. This very important book by Gregory Bateson in collaboration with his anthropologist daughter, Mary Catherine Bateson, explores the nature of the mental process and its connection with the biological world.

Haraway, D. J. (1989). *Primate visions: Gender, race, and nature in the world of modern science.* New York: Routledge. An influential analysis of primatology from a critical, feminist point of view.

Harré, R., & Reynolds, V. (Eds.). (1984). *The meaning of primate signals.* Cambridge: Cambridge University Press. A highly informative collection of research studies on the latest findings on primate communication systems.

Köhler, W. (1926). *The mentality of apes.* New York: Harcourt, Brace. This study might be described as one of participant observation; it remains an early classic account of the behavior of chimpanzees.

Wilson, E. O. (1975). *Sociobiology: The new synthesis.* Cambridge, MA: Belknap. The controversial source that sparked the recent debate over sociobiology.

STUDY QUESTIONS

1. Do chimps experience freedom? How?
2. What are the major limitations of sociobiology?
3. How is subjective reality experienced?
4. What factors shaped the emergence and development of the field of primatology?

PART II

SOCIAL STRUCTURE AND LANGUAGE

3

The Nature of Language

The four chapters in Part II speak to the "symbolic" aspect of symbolic interactionism. The symbolic interactionist perspective demands an immediate and direct focus on various forms of symbolizing activity. Chief among them and central to an understanding of human conduct is *language.*

In this chapter, however, we consider only one general aspect of language: its nature and the various theoretical perspectives that have been brought to its study. (In Chapter 4 we take up language's relation to group life, culture, and social structure.) We consider here recent developments in the field of semiotics as they relate to the symbolic interactionist view of language.

Semiotics and Symbolic Interactionism

Semiotics, as we noted in Chapter 1, is the science of signs within a society. It is an integral part of social psychology because social psychology is, in part, the study of the social foundations of language. This social aspect of linguistics is called *sociolinguistics,* the aim of which is the study of language in use in social contexts and of "how speech (and other language in use) simultaneously influences social interaction and has its 'meaning' constrained by its interactive context" (Grimshaw, 1981, p. 241). Semiotics and sociolinguistics constitute integral parts of the field of social psychology.

We need to define a number of terms carefully. A linguistic *sign,* as we noted in Chapter 1, is a two-sided psychological entity, represented by the terms *signifier* (sound-image) and *signified* (concept). *Signification,* as we have said, is the process of using signs in speech. Perinbanayagam (1985) has given the term *signifying acts* to this process. Language, as we have proposed, is a social institution and a system of values that give meanings to words. *Speech,* in contrast to language, is essentially an individual and interactional production of selection and actualization. Extended speech, in any context, is called *discourse.* Language and speech exist in a dialectical relation to one another; each achieves its full meaning only in relation to the other (Barthes, 1964/1967, p. 15).

Language can be seen as existing on three planes: first, as a structure, a form, a framework, or an institution; second, as a norm—that is, as an ideal; and third, as usage. Every social group has its own norm-usage-speech pattern. After Barthes (1964/1967, p. 21), we use the term *idiolect* to refer to the speech and language of a specific linguistic community or a particular speaker. Others have used the words *argot* and *special languages* to refer to idiolect.

The term *code* refers to how a message, or spoken utterance, is formulated in terms of the syntax of speech, numbers, writing, and so on. All messages are coded, wrapped in a framework that allows the speaker and hearer, or writer and reader, to comprehend and define what is being communicated. Some codes are formal and logical (e.g., computer programs), whereas others are based on commonsense frameworks (e.g., where there is smoke, there is fire) (see Manning, 1987, p. 93).

Sign Systems

Within any social group there are a number of different sign systems that extend beyond the language-speech distinction. A sign, then, need not refer just to the *words* of a language; anything that can be represented by a group can be organized into a sign system. Barthes (1964/1967, pp. 25-31) discusses such sign systems as the garment system, where clothes are (a) written about, (b) photographed, and (c) worn. Other sign systems include the food system of a society, where there are rules that (a) exclude certain foods from being eaten, (b) specify how certain foods are to be associated, and (c) dictate rituals of use. The menu in any restaurant can be interpreted as a sign system—for example, (a) appetizers, (b) main courses, (c) à la carte items, (d) desserts, and (e) beverages.

Any sign system is organized in terms of a set of rules and a set of oppositions and similarities that are somewhat arbitrarily organized. The automobile system in U.S. society is organized this way. Each American automobile manufacturer distinguishes its models from those of other manufacturers, and models are presented in terms of the status they confer on the buyer. Freedom in choosing models is severely restricted; that is, only a few different models are available for purchase. The car system turns cars into objects, and the meaning of the object is given in ownership and in the act of driving.

Barthes (1957/1972) has analyzed the worlds of wrestling, films, soap powders and detergents, children's books, ornamental cookery, and striptease performances as sign systems, which he calls *mythologies*. Myths are sign systems that are based on everyday phenomena (e.g., advertisements for new soaps). These myths convey a sense of naturalness about our world that masks reality or hides meaning. Myths tend toward proverbs; they attempt to quantify quality (e.g., "Our soap is this much better than their soap"; "Excedrin cures headaches 10 times faster than aspirin"). Myths are often presented as self-evident truths and present objects in a kind of timeless historical moment.

Myths attempt to rid viewers of prejudice. Consider the following example in which Barthes (1957/1972) describes an advertisement for margarine in a French magazine:

> The episode always begins with a cry of indignation against margarine: "A mousse? Made with margarine? Unthinkable!" "Margarine? your uncle will be furious!" And then our eyes are opened, one's conscience becomes more pliable, and margarine is a delicious food, tasty, digestible, economical, useful in all circumstances. The moral at the end is well known: "Here you are rid of a prejudice which cost you dearly!" (p. 42)

Barthes contends that myths are language systems that convey particular sets of meanings about our contemporary world. He began his analysis of these myths in order to understand how the media, books, art, and common sense present things and experiences with a "naturalness" that dresses up reality and hides the history that exists behind these representations.

The Classification of Signs

We must distinguish the term *sign* from other related terms. According to various authors, *sign* can mean the same thing as *symbol, cue, signal, index, icon,* and *allegory* (Barthes, 1964/1967, p. 35). All these terms share a common characteristic: They refer to relations between two or more things. We cannot distinguish these terms on this ground, and so must turn to other considerations. First, does the relation between the two terms (e.g., symbol and thing, sign and thing) imply the mental representation of one of the terms? Second, does the relation imply an analogy between the terms? Third, is the link immediate? Fourth, does the relation imply an existential connection with the user? (That is, does it refer directly to the user?)

Use of these terms varies by author (for a comparison of Mead, Peirce, Saussure, Barthes, Baudrillard, and White, see Harman, 1986, p. 149; for a comparison of Wallon, Peirce, Hegel, Jung, Walton, and Saussure, see Barthes, 1964/1967, p. 37). The controversy centers on the difference between *sign* and *symbol.*

Saussure (1959, p. 68), for example, rejects the term *symbol* in his semiotics. He asserts that it is restrictive, because its meanings are never arbitrary. For instance, the symbol of justice—a pair of scales—cannot be easily replaced by another symbol, such as a car. Peirce (1960) offers a semiotic that defines *sign,* the basic concept in his system, as "something which stands to somebody for something in some respect or capacity" (p. 135). Icons, indices, and symbols are different types of signs. Mead (1934) uses the

TABLE 3.1 Classification of Signs

1. *Signal:* A term that establishes an immediate, existential relation between two terms; for example, a traffic light and a moving automobile.
2. *Index:* A term that is a measure of something else; for example, a barometer.
3. *Icon:* A figure or image that represents something else (e.g., the cross in Christianity). An icon implies an analogy—the link is indirect to the thing being represented, and it must be existential.
4. *Sign:* A term that is exact; there is no analogy implied. The word *ox* and the image of an ox implies a direct relation that is not existential.
5. *Symbol:* A term that implies a relation that is analogical and indirect ("Christianity 'outruns' the cross"; Barthes, 1964/1967, p. 38).
6. *Learned cue:* A term that carries an immediate and direct relation between two things; for example, the sound of a gong that triggers a dog's salivation. Animals respond to learned cues.
7. *Natural sign:* A term and what it relates occur in the same space-time framework; for example, the sound of a siren and the passing of a fire engine on the street.
8. *Conventional sign:* A term that derives its meaning from social consensus and is arbitrary.
9. *First-order sign:* A sign that operates for lower animals, such as a natural sign or a learned cue.
10. *Second-order sign:* A sign applied to visual or auditory data; for example, the word *box* applies to our sense impressions of a box. Second-order signs are like conventional signs.

term *universe of discourse* to describe how language works in interaction; his significant symbols are gestures that call out consensual meaning in another person. Meltzer (1972, p. 8) suggests that signs are directly linked to immediate situations, whereas symbols have arbitrary meanings that transcend situations. MacCannell (1976, p. 102) proposes that a symbol is a sign that lacks a syntactic component, whereas a sign lacks a semantic component.

Following Barthes (1964/1967, p. 38), we adopt the set of meanings displayed in Table 3.1 for these terms. In this text we try to maintain the *sign/symbol* distinction as much as possible. A sign and a symbol both represent something that stands for something to somebody. Signs are relatively unmotivated representations, whereas symbols are motivated and nonarbitrary. When we speak of the "symbolic environment," we are referencing all the meanings (given in Table 3.1) that have been applied to language. Similarly, when we discuss the categorical, or language, attitude, we are assuming all of these meanings.

Components of Signs

Before turning to the language attitude and human experience, we must note the following features of signs and symbols. First, it is impossible to separate a sign or a symbol from the object it represents. We cannot, for example, think of the object *automobile* without immediately giving that object a set of meanings (new, old, American) that are contained in the sign we attach to the object. Signs invade the objects they represent (Baudrillard, 1972/1981). When we attempt to unravel how signs give meanings to objects, we must ask how signs have come to be connected within any sign system. For example, we might ask how it is that Cadillac automobiles have come to carry such prestige and status in American society. The sign "Cadillac" immediately confers status on a person who owns a car so labeled, just as the signs "BMW," "Audi," and "Jaguar" do for other individuals.

Second, the objects upon which signs and symbols are conferred are cultural in nature. Cultural objects are organized in terms of four overlapping logics, or meaning systems. Every object (car, table, TV, stereo) has (a) a use value, (b) a market value (i.e., how much it costs), (c) value as a gift, and (d) value as a status or prestige marker. Objects that are signified can thus have meanings as instruments, commodities, gifts, and prestige markers.

Third, we live in an age of simulation. Baudrillard (1983) calls this the age of the hyperreal, in which "the very definition of the real becomes: *that of which it is possible to give an equivalent reproduction*" (p. 146). Disneyland is an excellent example of this. In such a setting, one finds perfect models of simulation: the worlds of pirates, the frontier, the future, and so on. All of these worlds are presented in perfect simulations or representations of the real thing—but they are *not* the real thing. We live in an age where objects and meanings are mass-produced. We find, as symbolic interactionist Harvey Farberman (1980) has argued, that "the subject matter that now confronts us supersedes symbolic interaction; rather it is the process surrounding the autonomization of signs; signs that stand for—and refer to—nothing but themselves" (p. 18). The commodity that is now bought, sold, and signified within our language and sign systems is experience. How that experience is lived and given meaning is the subject matter of the symbolic interactionist and the semiotician.

The Categorical, or Language, Attitude

We organize or adjust our behavior toward things and persons by means of symbols, and these symbols come to embody a plan of action. "A category . . . constitutes a point of view, a schedule, a program, a heading or caption, an orientation" (Dewey, 1938, p. 237). Thus if one hunter shouts to another, "A duck!" the second hunter immediately looks into the sky and makes the appropriate preparations to shoot at a bird on the wing. If the first hunter shouts, "Rabbit!" his partner responds in a different manner. Language symbols do not merely stand for something else—they also indicate the significance of things for human behavior, and they organize behavior toward the thing symbolized.

Some writers have gone further, pointing to a general attitude toward the world that is implicit in language use and therefore common to all those who use language. They have called this general attitude the *categorical attitude.* In its simplest terms it can be described as the realization that (a) things can be named and talked about, (b) events and objects may be grouped or classified, and (c) by naming and classifying the features of our environment, we bring into existence new modes of behavior, as well as new possibilities for manipulating that environment.

Children first demonstrate this attitude when they learn that everything has a name; they soon exasperate their parents with persistent questions: "What's this?" "What's that?" At first they are satisfied with mere names, as they identify the names with the things named; they have acquired an initial appreciation of the importance of language symbols. Later, when they start to ask "Why?" children exhibit a second, more mature phase of the categorical attitude.

We can illustrate the adult categorical attitude with an analogy. Let us suppose that a boy who has lived all his life in an isolated rural section of Africa is suddenly placed in the middle of Johannesburg. He sees large numbers of people hurrying past, hears a chaotic jumble of sounds, and sees a bewildering array of buildings, billboards, neon signs, automobiles, and other objects. The people he encounters respond to him in ways that utterly confuse him. He does not know what to do or where to go. To him, the city is merely an immense buzzing confusion.

We can compare this boy's view of Johannesburg with the view of the world that a person without language would have. The longer one lives in a large city, the more one grows accustomed to it; one gradually is able to classify or categorize "things." One disregards as irrelevant most of the sounds that assail the ear; they simply form part of the roar of the city. One ignores the countless motor vehicles; they are only hazards that one must consider in crossing a street. The newcomer is astounded by the skyscrapers, but soon grows used to them and thereafter may scarcely look at them. The attitude of a city dweller compares with the attitude that humans acquire toward the world in general through their use of language symbols: We organize things into systems or categories in terms of their significance for behavior. Consider Mark Twain's comments in his essay "Two Ways of Seeing a River" (1976):

> Now when I had mastered the language of this water and had come to know every trifling feature that bordered the great river as familiarly as I knew the letters of the alphabet, I had made a valuable acquisition. But I had lost something, too. I had lost something which could never be restored to me while I lived. All the grace, the beauty, the poetry, had gone out of the majestic river! (p. 41)

We use the terms *concepts* and *categories* almost synonymously here, although they have different connotations that should be kept in mind. *Concept* has a broader meaning that includes "categories" as a special kind of concept. To have a concept of something means that one is able to picture it, to describe or represent it to oneself or another, or to grasp it intellectually. A concept is a way of thinking about something—therefore, it is also usually a way of talking about it; conceptual thought is communicable thought. Concepts of classes or types are called *categories*. Through the use of such categories of classification, we are able to group things together and to distinguish one type of thing from another and, ultimately, to see the world as orderly. Indeed, without categories one could not think in a sophisticated human sense. The expression *categories of thought* refers to basic concepts (such as space, time, substance, and motion) that are regarded as fundamental in human reasoning about the material world.

We have indicated that the categorical attitude impels human beings to group things into classes. By categorizing or conceptualizing our experiences, we are able to analyze them and respond selectively to some aspects of experience while ignoring others. By using categories and concepts, we are able to picture the world as relatively stable, predictable, and orderly, and to find unity in its limitless diversity.

An example indicates the connection between concepts and the language attitude. There is a certain animal that we call a "cow." When we use the word *cow,* we refer to all the cows in the world and also, in a sense, to all the cows that have ever existed or ever will exist. But no two cows are ever exactly alike; cows vary greatly in size, color, and disposition. Nevertheless, we lump all cows together, disregarding their differences. In this way we identify them, thus indicating to ourselves and others their significance for human beings. By means of the concept "cow," we have created unity out of diversity and multiplicity. There are millions of cows, but one single concept refers to them all.

Still another implication of the categorical attitude then follows. When we see objects, we see them not only as concrete entities, but also as representatives of the classes to which they belong. Every time we see and recognize an animal as a "cow," we bring into the picture, in an implicit or indirect way, all the other cows in the world that we cannot see and have never seen. For these reasons, language concepts are called *universals.*

One should not suppose that any given object can be classified in only one way. It can be placed in a number of different categories according to the way in which it is being viewed or used. Thus it may be classified in a series of classes on an ascending scale of abstractness, so that each is more inclusive than those preceding it and less inclusive than those following it. The more abstract the classification, the fewer and more general are the criteria of classification.

According to Alfred Schutz (1964), a famous German phenomenologist, classification is a process of typification, and the sign system of language is the "typifying medium par excellence" (p. 96). Typification is based on a generalized knowledge that categorizes objects or events into like groups. Each object, although recognized as unique, is classified as similar to other objects. This typification process provides the individual with a frame of reference from which to deal with the object. A person does not need to understand fully the unique differences surrounding each object or event; it is sufficient that he or she recognize the general type and act toward it on the basis of previous experience.

Meaning, for Schutz, can be attributed to a sign insofar as both the person using the sign and the person interpreting it can rely on similar past experiences in understanding what the sign represents. This sharing of meanings for signs leads to reciprocal perspectives between people. Language, then, allows us to classify similar objects within the same category and develop recipes for interaction that enable us to manage our social worlds (Schutz & Luckmann, 1973, p. 146; Stone, 1982, p. 101).

Conversely, the more concrete the classification, the more numerous and specific are the criteria. For example, a particular cow may be classified on an ascending scale of abstractness as follows: Farmer Jones's cow, cow, mammal, animal, living form, material object. Cows can also be classed as four-legged creatures, objects weighing more than 100 pounds, edible animals, economic assets, sources of milk, livestock, and so on. Each classification carries its own connotation of point of view and potential use. None of them is "natural," or inherent in the nature of the world, although some are obviously more effective than others for certain purposes.

To complicate matters further, a cow can also be seen as a composite—rather than unitary—object. To a butcher, it is made up of sirloin, porterhouse, T-bone, and other cuts of meat. A biochemist, a physiologist, and an anatomist would each describe and classify the cow's components in wholly different ways. Farmer Jones himself might well think of his cow as something compounded mainly of hay, corn, grass, water, and a little salt.

Dale (1954), discussing the child's growing understanding of the concept of "dog," has made much the same series of points that we have in discussing cows:

> One of the child's earliest learnings is the name for the shaggy thing that barks. It is called *Rover.* Next he learns that *Rover* is like *Sport* and *Shep,* and finally that things that look and act like them are called *dogs.* Once he has the *dog* classification, he may move in either or both of two directions in further classification. He may learn that there are terriers, St. Bernards, shepherds, and poodles; and then subdivide terriers into wirehaired, rat, Boston, and so forth. He can also go in the direction of more general classification—a dog is a quadruped, an animal, a vertebrate, or a mammal. If he continues, he may arrive at classifications used by the zoologist, involving abstractions that are extensive, precise, and increasingly complex. There are, of course, a variety of other paths that crisscross the two chief directions . . . indicated, in the course of which his concept of *dog* grows richer. (p. 31)

That humans have concepts and categories with which to classify, subclassify, and cross-classify the objects of their environments is thus greatly important. Our concepts and categories give us a flexible point of view and a multiplicity of perspectives, enabling us to see connections among things that otherwise would be impossible; they also enable us to think of things in terms of their constituent parts rather than as undifferentiated wholes. They are therefore indispensable tools in any analytic procedure. This implies that concepts alter our behavior by making it more discriminatory, selective, and flexible (that is, more intelligent).

Some students of human behavior object to the implication of the term *meaning,* which is often thought of as a metaphysical essence residing in symbols, a person's brain, or objects themselves. In this book, we use *meaning* in a behavioral sense. *The meaning of an object or a word is determined by the responses that are made to it; that is, meaning is a relationship and not an essence.*

It is easy to fall into the habit of locating a word's meaning in the word itself. But, as noted previously, meanings arise out of group activities, and they come to stand for relationships between actors and objects. Our position has been stated clearly by Lee (1954), who says that language

> is not a system of names for passively sensed objects and relations already existing in the outer world; but neither does it fit experience into predetermined molds. It is a creative process in which the individual has an agentive function; it is part of a field which contains, in addition, the world of physical reality, the sensing and thinking individual, and the experienced reality. In this way each word, each grammatical formation, is not an empty label to be applied; it has meaning, not because meaning has been arbitrarily assigned to it, but because it contains the meaning of the concrete situation in which it participates and has participated, and which it has helped create. (p. 74)

Thus a concept implies a unitary mode of action; it enables people to act the same way toward a variety of objects. There are many types of foods, for example, but once a substance has been identified as belonging to the food category, a common mode of behavior toward it is established. Thus every class concept is also a generalization, as it "generalizes" behavior toward everything included within its boundaries. The invention of generalizations never ends; as long as group activity and experiences continue, members of the group will discover and transmit new meanings to one another.

Symbols, or conventional signs carrying meanings upon which there is consensus, are by their nature open to manipulation. Signs operate upon signs as in algebra or mathematics, or as in argument. Concepts breed new concepts as they are manipulated in the handling of problem situations. In group action, differences of opinion and position that are expressed in conversation and debate produce new perspectives and meanings.

Symbols enable us to escape the narrow confines of the immediate natural world and participate in the artistic, religious, moral, and scientific worlds created by our contemporaries and ancestors:

> Without symbolism the life of man would be . . . confined within the limits of his biological needs and his practical interests; it could find no access to the "ideal" world which is opened to him from different sides by religion, art, philosophy, science. (Brown, 1958, p. 41)

The Nature of Language: Signs and Symbols

Classifying and analyzing symbols are exceedingly complex, controversial tasks. Generally acceptable concepts and a stable working vocabulary have not yet been achieved, although various attempts have been made to establish them. Recognizing the difficulty of the problem and the possibility for confusion, we present here a greatly simplified account and confine ourselves to only a few fundamental distinctions.

All living creatures learn to respond to environmental cues. Inevitably, some stimuli come to stand for other stimuli. "The sound of a gong or a whistle, itself entirely unrelated to the process of eating, causes a dog to expect food, if in past experience this sound has always preceded dinner; it is a sign . . . of his food" (Langer, 1948, p. 23). A dog also learns to respond to visual cues (a stick), movements (raising a hand), odors (that of a cat), and so on. Psychologists call such learning of cues *conditioning,* and in the laboratory they have conditioned many animals to respond to *substitute stimuli.* The world of any animal (human or subhuman) is full of such cues, and behavior is largely accounted for in terms of responses to them. Hereafter we refer to learned cues as *signs.*

Sign behavior runs the gamut from the simple to the complex; it ranges from the most elementary forms of conditioning to the most complex verbal behavior. One can produce a simple sign response in an animal by repeatedly sounding a buzzer and always feeding the animal immediately after. One can make this situation more complex in various ways: by delaying the reward, by introducing the factor of punishment, by giving the animal multiple-choice problems, by requiring the animal to respond to two simultaneous signs, and so on. Thus an animal can be taught to obtain food by pressing a lever; later the animal can be taught that pressing the lever will yield the usual reward only when a green light is on and not when a red light is on. Experimental psychologists who study the conditioning processes in animals can investigate only the nonverbal sector of the sign range, because there is no verbal sign behavior among subhuman animals.

All psychological behavior probably involves sign behavior at some level. Perhaps more correctly, psychological behavior is sign behavior. Let us consider a simple psychological act—the perception of a box. If we ask a physiological psychologist to describe what happens when a person perceives a box, he or she will begin by noting that light reflected from the box reaches the eyes. From that point on, the physiological psychologist's account will be concerned entirely with descriptions of how the light impinges on the retina of the eye, how the retina is connected with the central nervous system, and how impulses pass through the nerves. The act of seeing is described as occurring entirely inside the individual. In short, the process of seeing is a representational or sign process in which the things that occur within the individual function as signs of the real box. However, this account does not explain why the person sees the box outside of him or her, or why the person sees it as a box and not as an image of his or her retina or as something in his or her head.

Human beings display a tremendous range of sign behavior, from the simple thought processes of the developmentally delayed to the complex thinking of geniuses. Almost any object, act, occurrence, or quality can function as a sign of something else. A red glow coming from wood indicates that it is hot; a gesture may reveal anger; a cross is a symbol of religious sentiment; a falling barometer forecasts a change of weather; and so on, endlessly. Words are our most versatile signs, for by means of them we can talk of anything, whether or not it is before us, and whether it is in the past, in the future, or only in our imagination.

From such examples we can see that signs are related to the thing signified in a variety of ways. The relationship of the falling barometer to an impending weather change is different from the relationship of the cross to the sentiment to which it refers, and both of these differ from the relationship between words and their meanings. Signs of the type represented by the cross have been called *icons*; those represented by things like the barometer, *indexes*. Note that what is signified may be even more varied in nature than signs; aside from referring to all kinds of real acts, events, and objects, signs can also indicate nonexistent things that can only be imagined, and they can also indicate other signs.

The Second Signaling System

To complicate things further, signs may be classified as conventional or natural, and they may be classified in other ways as well. A *natural sign* is a movement, sound, smell, gesture, or other stimulus that is perceived to be connected with something else. The natural sign and what it indicates occur together in the same space-time framework, and both are thus parts of a concrete situation. For example, the dog that follows the rabbit's trail connects the scent with the actual rabbit because he has learned that the two go together. By contrast, the *conventional sign* derives its meaning from social consensus and is "movable," or arbitrary, in the sense that different signs (for example, in different languages) can mean the same thing and that the sign (for example, a word) may be used in situations in which the object referred to is not present. Conventional signs relate to social groups or language communities in which the same signs are interpreted in the same ways by a number of persons.

Natural signs are not "natural" in the sense that they occur only in nature; they also can be human artifacts, such as the psychologist setting up a sequence of buzzes (food in a dog's experience) or the lines in a spectrum being taken as evidence of the presence of certain elements. Similarly, the click of a Geiger counter is a natural sign of the passage of an electron. Symbolic analysis enables humans to notice and respond to much more subtle cues than the natural signs that the lower animals are able to master.

Another way of expressing the ideas developed in the preceding paragraphs is to say that signs may also represent other signs; for example, when we use the word *box* to refer to the visual data relayed to our central nervous system when confronted with a boxlike object. For lower animals, these sensory experiences are natural signs of an external but unnamed object. When we call the object a *box*, this word functions as a *second-order sign* to designate the sensory experiences that in their turn are *first-order*, or direct, signs of the actual boxlike object before our eyes. An essential difference between natural signs and conventional signs is that the latter are always at least second-order signs, which are related only indirectly to physical reality through the mediation of *lower-order* signs (that is, sensory experiences or natural signs). This idea has been expressed succinctly by Pavlov (1929, 1960), who calls the simple sensory cues the *first signaling system* and language and speech the *second signaling system*.

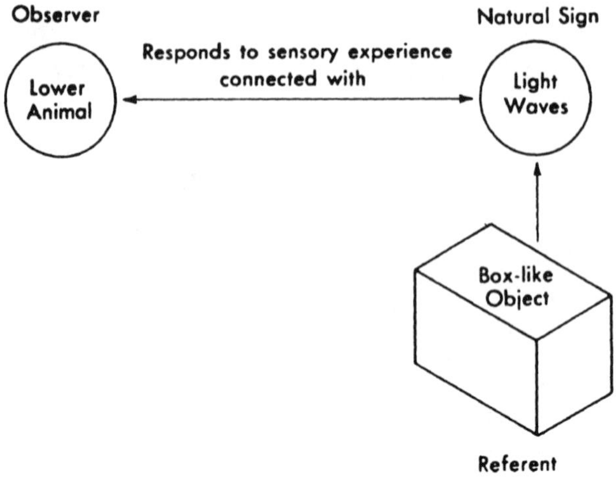

Figure 3.1. First-Order Signs (Pavlov's First Signal System)
NOTE: An animal is enabled to act with reference to the object it sees.

Although signs function in place of the objects they represent, keep in mind that the word *box* is not the box itself, and that the light reflected from the box (which enables us to see it) also is not the box itself. When we see the box, we respond to the light waves that it reflects; when we name it, we respond to the sound waves that constitute the spoken word. All organisms respond to the external world not as it really is, but in accordance with the information they have about it. They respond to signs that *represent* external objects. Although the organism's information may be adequate for its specific behavioral needs, it is always highly schematic, incomplete, and inaccurate when judged by the standards of, for example, the physicist, who does not claim to tell us what the world is actually like but only tries to indicate how it can be represented or conceived (Morris, 1946, pp. 3-5).

In Figure 3.1, the fact that there are no arrows linking the box directly with the observer indicates that, in a profound sense, the observer never can have any direct communication with a box as it really is, whatever that may mean. All the observer's contacts with it are indirect, mediated, and shaped by the nature of the sense organs and the sensory input from it, be it visual or tactile. Lower animals with different kinds of eyes, for example, may see objects without color or in simplified color schemes, whereas others attend primarily to movement and evidently perceive stationary objects only vaguely.

Determining the precise effects of symbolic behavior, and the differences between human and animal behavior, is thus the study of the interrelationships of different levels or systems of sign behavior. One basic consequence of the existence of second-order signs such as words is that they make sensory experience a subject of discourse and an object of reflective thought and analysis, thus establishing the behavioral

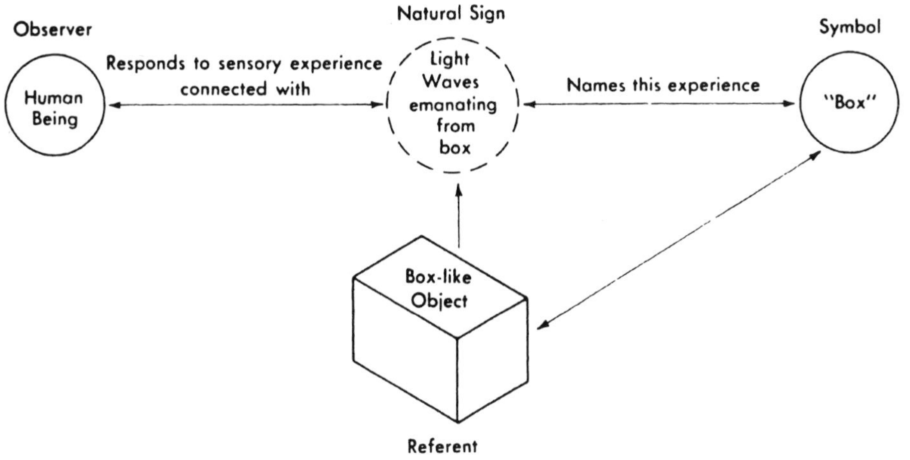

Figure 3.2. Second-Order Signs (Pavlov's Second Signal System)
NOTE: A human being is enabled to act toward, use, remember, imagine, and conceptualize boxes and to reason, talk, and plan about them with other human beings.

foundation for all the higher cortical functions in humans. Being human social inventions, they are basic to human society.

As Soviet psychologist Luria (1976) has observed:

> Language, which mediates human perception, results in extremely complex operations: the analysis and synthesis of incoming information, the perceptual ordering of the world, and the encoding of impressions into systems. Thus words—the basic linguistic units—carry not only meaning but also the fundamental units of consciousness reflecting the external world. (p. 9)

We shall return to this point about consciousness when we discuss the relationship between thought and language.

In this book we designate all conventional signs by the term *symbols*, recognizing that the characteristic forms of human symbolic activity have to do with language or are derived from it. We can briefly summarize three important characteristics that distinguish language symbols from other kinds of signs:

1. Language symbols constitute symbol systems, so that the meaning of any single symbol cannot be grasped in isolation but must always be understood within the system. For example: "Wife" is intelligible only in terms of a wider linkage of symbols—"husband," "marriage," and the like.
2. Language symbols are inherently social in character and meaning. They evoke from the person who produces or uses them the same or similar responses as those elicited from the person to whom they are directed. If communication is faulty or if the speaker talks past the listener, the words do not function as symbols.
3. Language symbols can be produced voluntarily even when the external events or objects to which they refer are absent or

> nonexistent. We can thus say that although people carry their symbolic systems around with them, the fact that an individual makes assertions about an object does not prove that the object is present or that it even exists.

However, we should not think of language merely as a system of words, a combination of phonemes, or the contents of a dictionary. Language is, first of all, a form of behavior. It is not merely a system of symbols, but the activity of using and interpreting symbols. Speech is often said to be the most primitive form of language behavior, but speech is meaningless unless it is addressed to an understanding listener. Hence conversation is the essential and original form of language; language behavior not only originates in cooperative social action, it is such action. This is why parrots are not given credit for language behavior, even when they produce words.

Viewed in this manner, language becomes at once more significant and more complicated. The act of listening and comprehending, for example, does not itself involve an act of speaking, but only appropriate response to the other's verbalizations. The response evoked by the other's utterances may be a bodily act or it may be a covert or internal response, perhaps leading to a reversal of roles, in which the listener becomes the speaker and vice versa.

Conventional signs or symbols are not necessarily linguistic, as a brief reference to such cultural items as flags, rings, pins, uniforms, monuments, and music makes clear. However, all nonlinguistic symbols of this sort—as well as all ceremony and ritual—have meanings based on group consensus and are deposits of collective experience; hence they fall into the general category of conventional signs. If we return to the triadic relationships of observer, sign, and thing signified, the added element appearing in conventional signs is this: Instead of a single observer, we have a group that interprets the sign in the same way and gives it its meaning. For this reason, conventional signs, unlike natural signs, always involve group reference and communicability.

We should not assume that humans operate exclusively on the level of linguistic symbols, although that is their most characteristic mode of behavior, or that this symbolic behavior is itself a single, unified process: It falls into many different types, which in turn represent a scale graded from most simple to most complex. The use of proper names is a simple symbolic process, as a person's name refers only to a single object and can be fairly adequately defined by pointing. Using a class name such as *human being* is more complex, because the name refers to many objects and involves differentiation between "human" and "nonhuman." The use of terms like *tautology, contradiction, truth, generalization,* and *abstraction* is even more complicated, because these symbols refer to other symbols and to the ways in which they are interrelated. The manipulations of abstract orders of symbols by mathematicians, logicians, philosophers, and other scholars are among the most complex kinds of symbolic behavior.

Analyzing language from the viewpoint of modern linguistics, Charles F. Hockett (1965, p. 574) has enumerated key properties of language as follows:

1. *Duality* is the combination of a relatively small number of basic sounds—meaningless in themselves—in a relatively large number of meaningful words (for example, *tack, cat,* and *act,* which are composed of three sounds in different combinations).
2. *Productivity* refers to the fact that words can be combined in completely new ways to say something that has never been said before and can nevertheless be understood.
3. *Arbitrariness* of linkage between symbol and what is signified is a feature that delimits what can be talked about.
4. *Interchangeability* refers to the ability of speakers of a language to reproduce any linguistic message they can understand and is closely associated with the fact that speakers hear what they themselves say.
5. *Specialization* involves the sharp functional distinctions between words even when they are poorly pronounced—in contrast, for example, to the gradations of anger expressed by raising one's voice.
6. *Displacement* is the ability to talk of things remote in time and place from where the talking occurs.
7. *Cultural transmission* is transmission by learning rather than transmission through the genes.

Nonverbal Communication

Those who dispute the importance that we attach to language behavior sometimes emphasize that a lot of communication between people occurs on the nonverbal level—without speech. For example, people may communicate by *touch.* In romantic attachments of past years, young people were expected to go through a long preliminary dating period during which they first got to know each other solely through verbal communication. At a certain point, if everything seemed to be going well and if he was encouraged to do so by the young woman, the young man was supposed to clasp the young woman's hand. If she responded positively by squeezing, there followed a predictable period of hand-holding and mutual squeezing and stroking, leading to a new gambit—the first kiss. Assuming a positive response from the young woman, the young man would put his arm around her waist, and then would follow a series of warmer and closer embraces, along with kissing and considerable body contact, leading to breast manipulation, then genital manipulation, and sometimes to the culminating act. In any case, gestures and "tactile communications" took precedence over verbal ones, or if the communications were verbal, they were expressive rather than representational.

This series of steps was quite clearly prescribed, as was the order. "There is usually a well-established code for these communications, with degree of intimacy of direct tactual contacts" (Frank, 1966, p. 208). The boy who omitted a step was regarded as "fast," whereas the one who was unable to read the signs given by his partner to signal the next step was seen as "slow." As the process proceeded, senses other than the tactile—such as taste and smell—entered into the interaction.

To be systematic about nonverbal communication, we should make the following distinctions: Words themselves can be used expressively to designate additional or contradictory meanings in addition to their "actual" meanings. Thus Pittinger and Smith (1967) remind us that words can be drawled or clipped; they can be spoken loud or soft, with raised or lowered pitch, with a spread or squeezed register, with a rasp or with openness, and with increasing tempo. There is also *body language*, which, as the term is commonly used, refers to several kinds of phenomena. It can include gestures (made in the air or against someone else's body), which can either replace words or accompany verbal language. Such gestures can be highly stylized or idiosyncratic, but they are generally readable by anyone from the same general social background. There is also a class of highly stylized gestures, such as saluting and nose thumbing. Finally, there is an iconic sign language connected with the body, consisting of the messages flashed by an individual's posture, grooming, hairstyle, facial expression, eye movements, and so on.

Most of these nonverbal gestures or body movements are not natural signs. If a person involuntarily squirms in pain or moves restlessly in hot weather, we might speak of these movements as uncontaminated by symbolism, but it is difficult to draw that conclusion with most other body movements. Birdwhistle (1970), one of the most sophisticated researchers in the area of *kinesics* (nonverbal communication), is highly instructive:

> Early in the investigation of body movement patterning, I had to deal with that deceptively transparent set of phenomena commonly called *gestures*. A considerable body of ethnographic data was extant demonstrating that these varied from culture to culture. An even larger body of philosophical and psychological literature maintained that these could be understood as "signs" as distinct from less transparent or easily translatable "symbols." Examination of these phenomena in context, however, soon revealed that this was at best a dubious interpretation of their activity or function. (pp. 182-183)

What Birdwhistle means is that gestures are no less "conventional signs" (in our terminology) than are words themselves. One must know the interactional context in which the gesture is made. "A 'salute,' for example, depending upon the integrally associated total body or facial behavior, may convey a range of messages from ridicule and rebellion to subservience or respect." This is true of a smile, wink, wave, or bow. "To call these 'signals' is to indicate a specificity such behavior lacks in actual practice" (Birdwhistle, 1970, p. 183).

One proviso needs to be added to Birdwhistle's general point: the possibility that there are a few cross-cultural facial expressions of emotion. Research by Ekman (1970, 1973) and Eibl-Eibesfeldt (1970) has found that similar facial expressions are used across cultures for expressing happiness, sadness, anger, fear, surprise, and disgust. Ekman (1970) observes, however, that "universals in facial expressions of emotion can be explained from a number of nonexclusive viewpoints as being due to innate neural programs or living experiences common to human development regardless of culture" (p. 151), and notes that future research is needed to determine this matter. Ekman severely criticizes extreme views such as LaBarre's that "there is no 'natural' language of emotional gesture" (p. 151) because they do not distinguish facial gestures from facial expressions of emotion. However, Ekman does admit that many facial gestures are independent of facial expressions of emotion and that these "may well be culturally variable" (p. 151).

In another study, Ekman (1972) investigated how emotional displays vary from culture to culture. He compared Japanese and American adults viewing a distressing film alone and in the presence of an interviewer. When they were alone, both the Japanese and the Americans showed similar reactions to the film, but when the interviewer was present, the Japanese showed less distress; they appeared to be masking their emotions behind polite smiles.

Ekman (1980) further maintains:

> Having taken some time to explain a number of different ways in which culture and various experimental factors could shape facial expression, let me say that I don't think there is complete plasticity. . . . It seems unlikely that experience will be organized and maintained directly in opposition to biological predisposition. However, there is ample room for enormous cultural differences in emotional expression. (p. 59)

This discussion deals only with facial expressions as they express rather basic emotions —compared with all other gestures that may stand for less basic matters and even for finely differentiated emotions like love of country or embarrassment over a spouse's behavior.

Let us return to Birdwhistle's point about the conventional-sign aspects of gestures, which he illustrates with an interesting description of the various types of gestures (he calls them *markers*) that accompany verbal communication. He notes that markers may be used to indicate the specific person(s) referred to when the pronouns *he, she,* and *them* are used; in this case, the markers may be slight movements of the head, finger, hand, or eyes in the direction of the person(s) referred to. When the reference is to *I, me, us,* or *we,* the gestural markers are different. The markers indicating future events are likely to be different from those used in speaking of past occurrences. Verbal communication including such words as *in, behind, on top of* ("area markers") or *quickly, lightly, roughly* ("manner markers") is also accompanied by characteristically patterned gestures; such markers sometimes replace speech rather than merely accompany it, as, for example, when one is in the dentist's chair and unable to talk but wishes to tell the dentist to "take it easy."

This information is relatively simple compared with what Birdwhistle calls the total body language used when, say, one woman tells another about the intricacies of dressmaking. The concept of gestural markers, he says, is insufficient to describe the various processes involved; he adds that he is inclined to view total body language as an example of "derived communicational systems"—derived, that is, from prior verbal communication.

The ways in which nonverbal communication as interaction occurs can be represented schematically as shown in Table 3.2, by indicating whether the messages are transmitted or received knowingly or unknowingly. Thus a speaker who arouses an audience's hostility may feel a vague discomfort without knowing why. The audi-

TABLE 3.2 **Nonverbal Communication as Interaction: Four Possibilities**

Receiving	*Sending*	
	Knowingly	Unknowingly
Unknowingly		
Knowingly		

ence members, on the other hand, without consciously doing so, may lean back in their seats with folded arms and blank faces. Here the message is transmitted unintentionally and received without clear awareness.

To illustrate another of the four possibilities: At a class reunion, one of the authors met a former classmate who told him that many years earlier, during their student days, she had tried for a year to attract his attentions—a fact of which he had been totally unaware. In this case, the messages were deliberately sent but were not grasped by the person to whom they were directed. The opposite situation (unknowing-knowing) is demonstrated when someone becomes irritated but is unaware that this irritation is apparent to bystanders, who easily read his or her gestures and facial expressions.

The last situation, in which both sender and receiver are quite aware, hardly needs illustration, but we might note that a particularly pleasant example from the theater is found in the elaborate but shared facial and body movements made by a skilled mime like Marcel Marceau. This French artist can be understood by Americans because he draws upon social situations and gestures that are cross-cultural. On the other hand, some of the cultural limitations of mime are suggested by an American student of French culture, Laurence Wylie, who attended a Parisian school of mime. In a 1973 interview, he remarked that when Americans were required to act out what happens when fire meets water, rubber meets glass, and glass meets steel, "they could not prevent themselves from getting involved in the idea of winning a contest. They become a street gang defending its territory" (quoted in *San Francisco Chronicle,* July 8, 1973, p. 2).

In sending these messages, the Americans were drawing not only on national imagery, but undoubtedly on what Ekman would call wittingly sent and culturally shared "emblems" and "illustrators." When emblems are used, the receivers usually know not only the message but also that it was deliberately sent to them. Such emblems are most often used when verbal discourse is prevented by agreement (as in miming), by external circumstances, or by distance. Thus an emblem for sleeping might be moving the head into a lateral position perpendicular to the body while bringing both hands below the head to represent a pillow. According to Ekman, many messages are emblematic in more than one culture, but often different movements are used in different cultures. For example, to represent suicide, an American places a finger at his or her temple, the hand arranged in the shape of a gun; in New Guinea, the emblem for suicide, representing hanging, is to grab the throat with an open hand and push up; in Japan, one plunges the fist into the stomach to represent hara-kiri, or draws an index finger across the neck to represent throat-slitting.

Ekman's illustrators are essentially the same as Birdwhistle's markers; they are "used with awareness and intentionality, although . . . usually in peripheral, not focal, awareness" (Ekman & Friesen, 1972, pp. 358-359). Referring to hand gestures, Ekman (1980) distinguishes the following types of illustrators:

- *Batons:* movements that accent or emphasize a particular word or phrase
- *Ideographs:* movements that sketch the path or direction of thought
- *Deictic movements:* movements that point to an object, a place, or an event
- *Spatial movements:* movements that depict spatial relationship
- *Rhythmic movements:* movements that depict the rhythm or pacing of an event
- *Kinetographs:* movements that depict bodily action or some nonhuman physical action
- *Pictographs:* movements that draw a picture in the air in the shape of the referent

These illustrators are intended to explain further what has already been said verbally. They are socially learned and culturally derived. Their interactive function—and that of emblems too—is suggested by Ekman's finding that they are hardly ever used when the person is alone or not actually communicating with someone. American Sign Language, which is taught to the deaf, represents an attempt to standardize a nonverbal gestural system; in ASL, every letter in the English alphabet is given a different gestural configuration.

Our own interactional scheme—the four cells shown in Table 3.2—does not take into account either the misreading or the failure to receive an intended message or the failure to recognize that there is anything to read, like the teacher so involved in her subject that she is oblivious to students' impatience after the bell has sounded. These interactions, too, although nonverbal, fall within the realm of the symbolic, of "communication." Without shared understandings from prior verbal communication or from participation in common culture, nonverbal communication would be primitive indeed.

Internalized Speech and Thought

From Egocentric Speech to Thought

From the ages of about 3 to 7 years, the speech that growing children redirect at themselves becomes more and more abbreviated and less and less intelligible to outsiders. (See Chapter 9 for a critique of this formulation.) Their self-directed remarks may become increasingly truncated, and they use various abbreviating devices (for example, the subject of the sentence tends to be omitted because it is implicitly understood).

What happens to the egocentric speech of children is interesting. It does not simply disappear without a trace; rather, it gradually becomes internalized, becoming transformed in the process. It ceases to be speaking and becomes thinking.

Using some ingenious experiments, Vygotsky (1939) discovered and described some features of this gradual transformation. His evidence indicates that the internal speech of adults retains many of the characteristics of childish egocentric speech. For example, it is highly abbreviated, much concerned with self, often highly fragmentary and disjointed, and filled with irrelevancies. It should be emphasized that the egocentric speech of the child is not mere verbal play; like the adult thought that grows out of it, it serves an adaptive function. Thus when children are alone or in places that are noisy, or if they think that they are not being understood, their egocentric utterances diminish. However, when children are faced with problems, both their references to self and assertions of their own egos increase in number. Speaking apparently helps them solve problems by "thinking them through" aloud.

The process that transforms external language into thought may be illustrated by how we learn to count. Children at first count aloud, touching or pointing with hands or head to the objects they are counting. If they are prevented from pointing or saying anything, they are usually unable to count at all. They begin also by counting similar objects, for their counting depends on external features and overt processes that are not essential to the adult. As children grow, these external props are discarded one by one. They learn to count dissimilar objects, it becomes unnecessary for them to point, and later it becomes unnecessary for them to count aloud. They may continue to move their lips and count inaudibly to themselves, but eventually this external activity also may disappear. For the person with mathematical ability, the very awareness of number words may vanish, so that mathematical thought often appears to proceed without any dependence upon language symbols.

A similar process of internalization is involved in learning to read. Here, as in learning to count, children first learn to read aloud, progress to reading inaudibly to themselves, and end by following a sequence of ideas with relatively little attention paid to specific words.

The Dualistic Error

Many people erroneously conceive of thinking as independent of the more overt forms of language behavior that precede it and make it possible. Laypersons are not the only ones who commit this dualistic error; as Vygotsky (1939) has written, "The fundamental error of most investigations in thinking and speech, the fault which was responsible for their futility, consisted in regarding thought and word as two independent and isolated elements" (p. 29).

Language behavior is erroneously supposed to have a material or behavioristic basis, whereas thinking is regarded as something separate, distinct, and of a purely "mental" or "spiritual" character—in short, disembodied. The "mental powers" involved in thinking are viewed as seeking external means of expressing themselves, and language becomes merely their external agent or tool. Language is said to be "a vehicle for the transmission of ideas"; it is a way of transferring the ideas occurring in one person's mind to the mind of someone else. Thus the indissoluble unity of language and characteristically human thought is destroyed and placed outside the realm of empirical research.

Although it is generally agreed that language and thought are interconnected processes and forms of human behavior, specifying the precise nature of the interrelationship is a moot point among philosophers and scholars. We cannot enter into the detailed arguments that are advanced on this question by numerous schools of thought except to indicate that they exist, and that they constitute a considerable body of literature.

As a working conception suitable to the limited purposes of this discussion, language behavior and thinking can be pictured as two intersecting circles with considerable overlap. This scheme oversimplifies and to some extent misrepresents the situation, but makes the points that lower animals and infants have some sort of thinking processes and that language behavior may sometimes be relatively mechanical in nature and have little or no communicative significance. We think that behaviorist John Watson's (1968) assertion that thinking is simply talking to oneself is a considerable overstatement, and that the opposite position (that thinking and talking are two radically separate and independent kinds of activity) is demonstrably false. For socialized human beings, we postulate that there are levels of psychological activity (similar to those in the lower animals) that do not enter into explicit awareness; Freudian psychologists place heavy emphasis on this type of subliminal thinking. On the other hand, it is also plausible that in some of its most complex manifestations, thinking may occur in some sense without language, transcending the limitations of existing language structures. Without the latter assumption, it would be difficult to understand human creativity. The creative drive of human imagination and inventiveness constantly tends to outrun the capabilities of existing formal symbolic devices; as a result, new forms of language, mathematics, and other notational or coding systems are constantly being produced.

Symbols cannot represent the real world completely and exactly, nor can they convey the full content of human experience. If thinking were completely confined within the limits imposed by language, there would be no way to account for the progressive expansion of knowledge and the emergence of new ideas.

At this point we should consider the thought processes of creative artists. Do painters or musicians have to use language as they paint or compose? Do sculptors use language as they shape stone figures with live models before them? From the subjective reports of artists and musicians, it is clear that they can manipulate musical and artistic symbols with or without verbal formulation of their means and ends to themselves. When artists are asked what a given picture "means," they often reply in what seems to be gibberish—or they refuse to talk at all, stating that the picture should speak for itself. The symbols they create and use are nondiscursive and nonlinguistic; they cannot be translated into verbal symbols. Some people naively believe that such nondiscursive thought is purely recreational when compared with the strenuous thinking of scientists or mathematicians. Dewey (1934), among others, has countered with the following:

> The idea that the artist does not think as intently and penetratingly as a scientific inquirer is absurd. A painter . . . has to see each particular connection of doing and under-

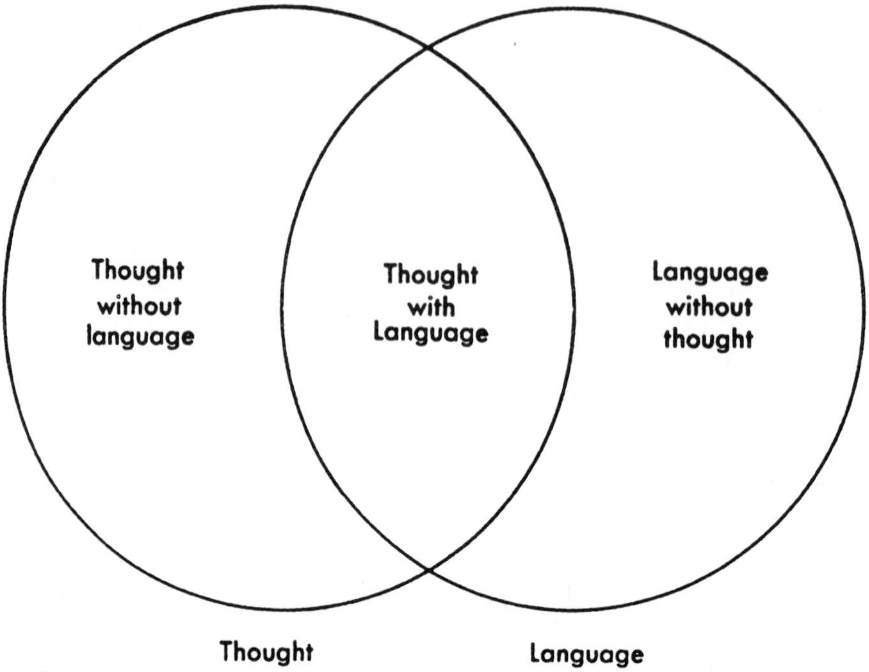

Figure 3.3. Vygotsky's Representation of the Interrelationships of Language and Thought

> going in relation to the whole that he desires to produce. To apprehend such relations is to think, and is one of the most exacting modes of thought. (pp. 45-46)

Soviet psychologist L. S. Vygotsky (1962) represents the interrelationships of language and thought with two intersecting circles (see Figure 3.3). He notes:

> Thought is not merely expressed in words; it comes into existence through them. Every thought tends to connect something else, to establish a relationship between things. Every thought moves, grows and develops, fulfills a function, solves a problem. . . .
>
> The relation between thought and word is a living process; thought is born through words. A word devoid of thought is a dead thing, and thought unembodied in words remains a shadow. (pp. 125-126)

Interestingly, Vygotsky's ideas, and the research that he and his followers (Luria and Yudovich) have conducted, take their point of departure from an aspect of Pavlov's thought that has received little attention in the United States—that is, Pavlov's description of language as the second signaling system. Soviet psychologists and physiologists, led by Vygotsky and Luria, have reported on the results of extensive observation and experimentation concerned with the relationship between complex mental and cortical processes and language behavior. The conclusions are practically identical to the theoretical perspective developed here. Luria and Yudovich (1959) discuss the significance of the point of view that links complex mental activity with language and the processes of social interaction:

> Perception and attention, memory and imagination, consciousness and action, cease to be regarded as simple, external, innate mental "properties." They begin to be understood as the product of complex social forms of the child's mental process; as complex "systems of functions" which appear as a result of the development of the child's activity in the process of intercourse; as complex reflective acts in the content of which speech is included, which, using Pavlov's terminology, are realized with the close participation of the two signal systems—the first signal system being concerned with directly perceived stimuli, the second with systems of verbal elaboration. (p. 15)

A similar position has been developed by Werner and Kaplan (1963).

When we discuss aphasia (Chapter 5), we note that aphasic patients can perform acts of direct reference but not acts of symbolic reference—in other words, they characteristically fail to organize their activities on the highest level of abstraction. Such simple dichotomies as "concrete attitude" and "abstract attitude" or "direct reference" and "symbolic reference" merely suggest the immense range of sign behavior, from the simplest to the most complex. No human thinks systematically, logically, and on the highest planes of abstraction at all times, nor do all matters require abstract thought. Some people may never learn to think consistently at the highest levels—that is, they may deal with similar matters at varying levels of abstraction. Various classifications of sign behavior and thought have been suggested as preliminary to investigation of the full range of thought. Dewey and Bentley (1949, p. 16) offer a tentative hierarchy. The idea that thinking covers a range of sign behavior is likely to be a fruitful one; study of this range is a task for the future.

Return to our opening discussion of semiotics. It is easy to confuse speech, consciousness (or self-awareness), and writing with language—to presume, as Saussure (1959) does, that language is the "norm of all other manifestations of speech" (p. 9). Although language may operate in this normative sense, it is a social institution, a collective act. Speech is an individual act. Self-reflection is an interior, mental act, inner speech that may have no direct connection to spoken utterances. Writing, which inscribes language signs, mirrors neither language nor speech. Barthes (1985) reminds us that speech is "always fresh, innocent, and theatrical" (pp. 3-5). Written or transcribed speech is dead—it destroys speech's theatricality.

Still, there is often the presumption that the voice is "consciousness itself. When I speak, not only am I conscious of being present for what I think, but I am conscious also of keeping as close as possible to my thought" (Derrida, 1981, p. 22). This view presumes that speech, via language, is a mirror of the self—this is too simplistic.

The Metaphysics of Presence

From its birth, modern social psychology has been haunted by a "metaphysics of presence" (Derrida, 1972, p. 250), which asserts that real, concrete subjects live lives with meaning and that these meanings have a concrete presence in the lives of subjects. This belief in a real subject, who is present in the world, has led sociologists to continue to search for a method that would allow them to uncover how these subjects give subjective meaning to their life experiences. This method would rely upon the subjective verbal and written expressions of meaning given by the individuals being studied, these expressions being windows into the inner lives of these persons.

Since Dilthey (1900/1976), this search has led to a perennial focus in the human sciences on a subjective, autobiographical approach and its interpretive biographical variants, including hermeneutics (see Heidegger, 1927/1962). Derrida (1972) has contributed to the understanding that there is no clear window into the inner life of a person, for any window is always filtered through the glaze of language, signs, and the process of signification. And language, in both its written and spoken forms, is always inherently unstable, in flux, and made up of the traces of other signs and symbolic statements. Hence there can never be a clear, unambiguous statement of anything, including an intention or a meaning.

One of our tasks in this book is to reconcile this concern with the metaphysics of presence, and its representations, with a commitment to the position that interpretive social psychologists study real people who have real lived experiences in the social world (see Bruner, 1984).

Speech as Discourse

Bakhtin (1986) reminds us that all discourse (everyday speech, poetry, drama, novels, music, scientific articles) is contextual, immediate, and grounded in the concrete specifics of the interactional situation. Discourse is dialogical; it joins people in tiny little worlds of concrete experience. In every situation there are three parties: the speaker, the addressee (the person who hears), and the superaddressee (a third party who is presumed to understand what is being spoken) (Bakhtin, 1986, p. 126). The dialogues that occur in these thickly peopled worlds cannot be repeated. They are always first-time occurrences; each attempt at repetition creates a new experience.

No text, or utterance, can be repeated without a change in meaning and in context. The reproduction of the text is a new, unrepeatable event in the life of the text (Bakhtin, 1986, p. 106), a new link to the historical moment that produced it. This life always exists between two subjects, the self and the other. The basic, underlying structure of the text lies in its connectedness to the boundaries that join two consciousnesses, two selves (Bakhtin, 1986, p. 106). Two speakers (or a reader confronting a text) create a context for meaning that cannot be easily transferred to another context. This life is thoroughly contextual, grounded in the moment of its existence.

Consider the following Russian parable analyzed by Bakhtin: "Two people are sitting in a room. They are both silent. Then one of them says, 'Well!' The other does not respond" (Clark & Holquist, 1984, p. 203). For an outsider, this exchange is without meaning. For Bakhtin, four crucial elements are absent in this text: the intonation of the speaker (that is, how the word "well" was pronounced); the visible, concrete, historical situation the two subjects shared; their shared knowledge of the situation; and their shared interpretation of it (Clark & Holquist, 1984, p. 203).

Bakhtin fills in this discourse. (This can be read as a violation of his framework, for he presumes an external, all-knowing position in this situation.) The two Russians were looking out the window of a railway station and saw that it had begun to snow. Both knew that it was time for spring to finally come, and "*both* were *sick* and *tired* of the protracted winter, *were looking forward* to spring, and were *bitterly disappointed* by the late snowfall" (Clark & Holquist, 1984, p. 204). All of these assumptions are unstated. The spoken word "well" contains many meanings. "The snowflakes remain outside the window; the date, on the page of the calendar; the evaluation in the psyche of the speaker; and nevertheless all this is *assumed* in the word *well*" (p. 204). One can understand the meaning of the word "well" only by "analyzing the relationship between what is said and what is unsaid" (p. 204).

A discourse is always more than what is said, or seen. It never reflects an extraverbal situation "in the way that a mirror reflects an object" (p. 204). Discourse is always productive; it brings a situation into play, enunciates evaluations of the situation, and extends action into the future. "Discourse does not reflect a situation; it is a situation" (p. 204).

This context of the utterance encompasses the visible (what is seen), the auditory (what is heard), and the sensory (what is felt). This context rests on shared knowledge and taken-for-granted assumptions that are unique to the moment. The unsaid, the assumed, the silences in any discourse provide the flesh and bone, the backdrop against which meaning is established. Intonation is the bridge that joins the speaker, the word, and the listener. The way a word or utterance is inflected and given bodily and facial expression (surprise, incomprehension, doubt, affirmation, refutation, admiration) is critical. Intonation creates the double-voicedness of talk. It mediates and connects a speaker's meanings with the text of his or her talk. Discourse is thus always both specular and productive. It is not a mirrored reflection of what is seen or heard, but an emergent, unpredictable occurrence, a specular production.

Comprehension (understanding) is made possible when two speakers enter into a dialogic relationship with one another. In this relationship each person becomes a party to the utterances of the other. Together the two speakers create a small, dialogical world of unique meaning and experience. This universe cannot be reduced to mere transcripts. It cannot be captured in logical structures, or in the relationship between linguistic units. It must be treated as a whole, as a slice of experience unique to itself. An outside observer has no place in this dialogue. Only by entering into the dialogue can one gain understanding—and even then understanding will be problematic. The best one can hope for is a version of naturalistic generalization, vicarious emotional experience, naturalistic verisimilitude.

In discourse, cultural values are enacted and social structures come alive. The self, a constantly shifting process, is always the incomplete sum of its discursive practices. In speaking, I hear myself being created. I hear myself not as the other hears me (and sees me), but as I want the other to hear me. In this cracked acoustical mirror (Silverman,

1988, p. 80), I hear the sound of my own thoughts, knowing that you will never hear me as I hear myself. I am a constant acoustical production. These sounds, and their meanings to me, anchor my inner (and outer) meanings in this specific act of speaking and hearing. My voice creates the public context for my articulated thought.

The other, always embodied, moving, and shifting, inhabits this space. They fill it with the sound of their voice, their eyes meet mine, glance off my shoulders and my head. I talk to and at them, and they talk at me. They hear my thoughts against the sound of their own voice, which reverberates in the spaces that lie between us. Inner and outer dialogues merge, interact, shape and inform one another. Punctuated by silences, dramatic pauses, and gestures, these two dialogical orders are the said and the unsaid, the heard and the unheard of everyday life. Together we create a historical situation, a social structure, a moment of experience, enlivened culture.

On occasion this enlivened culture can become problematic, especially so when the spoken word is printed. The printed text allows an inspection of what was spoken, and inspection may produce interpretations that are at odds with the speaker's intent. Disavowals are often created. Dick Armey, a member of the U.S. House of Representatives, called it a slip of the tongue, a mispronunciation, when he was quoted as having referred to his colleague Barney Frank as Barney Fag (Bauman, 1995). Similarly, when the tapes from a question-and-answer session with faculty members were published, Frank L. Lawrence, the current president of Rutgers University, denied that he meant anything racist when he was quoted as having said three words: "genetic, hereditary background." (Lawrence uttered these words in reference to scores on the Scholastic Aptitude Test.) He later claimed that these words slipped into his conversation because he had been reading reviews of *The Bell Curve* (Herrnstein & Murray, 1994), a book that "examines the links between genetics and intellectual achievement" (Carvajal, 1995).

Any account of this byzantine social world must, then, address this complex event that two or more speakers (and then readers) have shared and created. The person who wishes to understand (comprehend) the text must be given a way to enter into the parts and spaces of listener and speaker. Only in this way will it be possible for interlocutors to bring to (and take from) the text the same depth of understanding and sympathy they bring to their own experience. This is Bakhtin's moral and epistemological imperative: an ethical aesthetic that demands that texts be written and read in ways that morally move readers and viewers.

CONCLUSION

We have covered a great deal of theoretical material in this chapter. We have attempted to elaborate and develop the general relationship between language and other forms of social behavior and have indicated how semiotics, the science of signs, bears directly on the symbolic interactionist view of language. We have dealt at length with the language of categorical attitude and have shown how a word's meaning lies in its relationship to human experience and human action.

We have also discussed signs and symbols and different levels of signal systems (first and second). We have also addressed nonverbal communication, internalized speech and thought, and the dualistic error. In Chapter 4, we anchor language more firmly in the human group.

SUGGESTED READINGS

Bakhtin, M. M. (1981). *The dialogic imagination: Four essays* (M. Holquist, Ed.; M. Holquist & C. Emerson, Trans.). Austin: University of Texas Press.

Bakhtin, M. M. (1986). *Speech genres and other late essays.* Austin: University of Texas Press. These two collections of work by Bakhtin, the great Russian literary scholar, present his arguments about the dialogical nature of language, discourse, and speech.

Barthes, R. (1985). *The grain of the voice: Interviews: 1962-1980* (L. Coverdale, Trans.). New York: Hill & Wang. A valuable collection of Barthes's later writings on voice, speech, writing, and language.

Baudrillard, J. (1988). *America.* London: Verso. This controversial book offers a reading of the hyperreal sign systems that make up the mythical symbolic environment of the United States.

Saussure, F. de. (1959). *A course in general linguistics.* New York: McGraw-Hill. The classic statement on European semiotics—the science that studies the life of signs in a society.

STUDY QUESTIONS

1. Outline the key terms in Saussure's semiotic theory.
2. How does gender influence nonverbal communication?
3. What is the dualistic error?
4. How does Bakhtin's system modify Saussure's semiotic scheme for analyzing language, speech, and discourse?

4

Language, Groups, and Social Structure

In this chapter, we are concerned with the ways in which human group life structures language, its use, and its meanings. The emphasis on group life is both a necessity and a virtue—a necessity because all languages are rooted in groups, and a virtue because groups are at the core of the interests of sociological social psychologists.

Consensus and Human Groups

Coordinated group activity presupposes communication, shared goals, and shared perspectives. It is obvious that group activities are consequences of linguistic communication. Membership is essentially not a physical matter, but rather a question of how people think, how they conceptualize their social worlds and themselves, and how they relate themselves to others through the communication circuits available to them.

Communication among members of social groups and the sense of belonging to groups may vary greatly. For example, there may be little direct communication among the members of an audience. In a *primary group*—to use Charles Horton Cooley's (1902) term—such as the family, communication is on an intimate face-to-face basis. A sense of intimacy, solidarity, and "we-ness" characterizes primary groups. In more formal groups and associations, however, communication often takes the form of written correspondence, telephone calls, or highly formal notices and announcements disseminated from a central office. These may be supplemented by annual conferences ordinarily attended by a relatively small proportion of the total membership or by small seminars of exclusive groups.

The Small Social Group

The small social group is a network of one-person, two-person, and three-person social relationships. Groups exist within a symbolic structure or framework of experiences and are characterized by a sense of supraindividuality that connects one-person, dyadic, and triadic relations into a complex structure that encompasses all the members. Groups have a common interest—often a desire to combat loneliness—and they may be fused and pledged to a set of meanings that brings the members back to one another. (An Alcoholics Anonymous group, for example, is pledged to the concept of sobriety. Recovering alcoholics keep coming back to A.A. groups out of a commitment, in part, to this pledge; see Denzin, 1987b.)

In small groups, interpersonal biographies are joined. Each member brings a unique personal history that becomes part of the group's culture and emotional life. Every group has its own "emotional frame of reference." This framework may include the periodic or regular production of togetherness, horror, fear, dismay, joy, reverence, love, intimacy, and warmth. Emotions, which are self-feelings, are social processes that join group members into felt mood states.

A group's special language, or idiolect, contains words and references that give meaning to the selves, emotions, and relationships that combine to make the group unique to its members. This language is woven into the cycle of group life and serves to give each group its own special sense of history and temporality (Denzin, 1984b).

The Group Bases of Language

Anthropologists' study of primitive cultures demonstrates that all human societies have language. Although there are hundreds of different languages in the world, and often numerous dialects within languages, linguistic behavior as such is universal. Differences among languages are apparent, as any traveler to a foreign land can attest. Not so apparent, although equally true, is that the language of every human society is complex, intricate, and systematic—the carrier of a great wealth of experience and attitude. "The mechanics of significant understanding between human beings," writes linguist Edward Sapir (1942), "are as sure and complex and rich in overtones in one society as in another" (p. 78).

Every existing language contains at least 5,000 words. As examples of primitive language complexity, we might note that in the speech of the Abipones, a South American Indian tribe, a verb can take more than 400 endings to indicate mood, person, and tense; and in some Australian aboriginal tongues, dual, triple, and even quadruple forms of nouns are in use (Hiller, 1933, pp. 401-415). Sapir has perhaps overstated the case for the equal complexity of all languages, but all linguists agree that speech is highly developed throughout the world. For this reason, one writer has referred to language as humankind's "fundamental institution" (Sapir, 1942, p. 78).

The social heritage of any society consists of its traditional ways of acting, believing, and speaking. This social heritage—often referred to as *culture*—is distinct from biological heritage, which is transmitted from parents to infant by way of parental genes in the chromosomes. (The genes determine such physical characteristics as hair color and eye color.) A basic difference between biological and social heritage is that social heritage is never passed on biologically; the child must acquire social heritage through some process of learning.

Howard Becker (1986, p. 12) suggests that the word *culture* refers to the conventional understandings people share about the things they do together. Bruner (1984, p. 7) argues that we should study culture and its meanings through an examination of cultural performances. Performances represent the meanings people give to experience, and to their shared understandings. Thus culture is simultaneously a process and a text that is undergoing constant transformation through the performances of cultural members.

Traditional ways of acting, thinking, speaking, and handling language vary widely from country to country, and from place to place within the same country. The language of a given nation or segment of it is part and parcel of its social heritage; for example, Muslims, Christians, and Jews who have lived in close contiguity in Baghdad for hundreds of years nevertheless speak three quite different versions of Arabic. Like other traditions, language is passed down from generation to generation nonbiologically. Newborns are unable to speak their parents' tongue, nor do they acquire the ability to do so as a result of later bodily maturation. They must learn word order, pronunciation, and—if they learn to write—spelling and punctuation.

The language learned by children is not primarily *their* language so much as it is that of their society and of their primary group. Adults have linguistic standards to which children must conform. Although different individuals may set unique distinctions of pronunciation, enunciation, and meaning upon established ways of speaking and writing, there is nevertheless a common core to all these individual treatments. Language is a group product that, like every other part of the social heritage, must be learned:

> The child playing in the sand invents a word for the pebbles that fill its hand. The new word is "pocos." Does society adopt this word . . . ? Not at all. Society has an expression of its own for the designation of pebbles, and it does not look with favor on the exercise of further inventive genius. So the child's word "pocos" lingers for a time in the tolerant memory of the immediate family and then passes into oblivion. (Judd, 1926, p. 195)

Many children invent a baby talk of some complexity that the parents learn, participating for a while in a bizarre linguistic game. But if children are to be understood by persons outside the family, if they are to become adjusted members of society, they must eventually employ generally accepted linguistic forms (see Chapter 7).

Indeed, marked individual deviation from the accepted language meets with disapproval. To be sure, a certain amount of latitude is allowed—all Americans do not pronounce, enunciate, or construct sentences identically—but one must not stray too far from certain linguistic patterns. Generally speaking, a future tense cannot be substituted for a past tense to indicate something that has happened. In the United States, American word order must be used; German word order is scarcely permissible. In France, inflection and intonation must approach a common French standard; they must not be appreciably American or Chinese. Marked deviation from the community's linguistic norm will fall stridently upon the ears of one's friends and associates; they are likely to respond with expressions of distaste, amusement, or ridicule. Deviants may even be punished—witness how "bad" grammar may deprive a person of career opportunities or prevent college students from passing freshman English.

The meanings of correct American speech in the world of the early-20th-century Central European immigrant have been beautifully captured by Alfred Kazin (1951):

> A "refined," "correct," "nice" English was required of us at school that we did not naturally speak, and that our teachers could never be quite sure we would keep. This English was peculiarly the ladder of advancement. Every future young lawyer was known by it. . . . It was bright and clear and polished. We were expected to show it off like a new pair of shoes. When the teacher sharply called a question out, then your name, you were expected to leap up, face the class, and eject those new words fluently off the tongue. (p. 22)

Reactions to the violation of linguistic rules are no different from reactions to the transgression of other customs and rules. Linguistic ways are public property and must not be grossly violated. As with other items of social heritage, individuals can use language to private ends; language can be made to fit the patterns of unique personalities. But individuals must operate within a framework of what is deemed permissible. Language is essentially a group product, the outcome of the common experiences of members of social groups.

The social character of language is underscored by the existence of what linguists call *special languages*:

> By the term "special language" we mean a language which is employed only by groups of individuals placed in special circumstances. The language of the law is a case in point. In the exercise of their profession lawyers employ a language very far removed from that of ordinary speech; it is a special legal language. Another example can be found in ecclesiastical language. A special language is often used in addressing the Deity. . . . All forms of slang are special languages. Students, artisans, and thieves all use a language of their own. . . . They all have this in common . . . when their structure is examined they are found to be the outcome of a common tendency to adapt the language to the functions of a particular group. (Vendryes, 1925, p. 249)

Each special language is based upon and utilizes the framework of the larger society's language. Yet people who are outside a group are aware of being strangers to that group's ways when they encounter its distinctive vocabulary. All of us have probably undergone experiences in which we felt like strangers to some group in our own society because we did not possess its language.

Language and Group Experiences

It is said that the history and interests of a people are reflected, to an astonishing degree, in their language. The British have a language rich in nuances and expressions for the sea; Eskimos make minute distinctions among numerous kinds of snow and snowfall (Hiller, 1933, p. 115). Klineberg (1954) comments on the Arabs' concern with the camel:

> There are said to be about six thousand names connected in some way with "camel," including words derived from the camel and attributes associated with it. These include, for instance, names and classes of camels according to function—milk camels, riding camels, marriage camels, slaughter camels, and so forth; names of breeds of different degrees of nobility of lineage, derivation from different lands, and so forth; names of camels in groups, as several, a considerable number, innumerable, and with reference to their objectives—grazing, conveying a caravan, war expedition, and so forth; as many as fifty words for pregnant camels, states of pregnancy, stage at which movement of the foetus is first felt, mothers who suckle and those who do not, those near delivery, and so forth. (p. 50)

The special languages of any society's subgroups provide additional examples of this mirroring of interests. The idioms and vernacular of sociologists, journalists, bankers, college students, and football players all reflect their respective dominant interests and concerns.

Language is also the carrier and the embodiment of environmental features that group members feel are important. People's words designate, refer to, and select aspects of the world relevant to their lives. As de Laguna (1927) notes, "Not everything in the world has a name. . . . Language singles out for specification only those features which are, in a peculiar sense, *common* to the social group" (p. 272). According to Lewis (1948):

> Among the Solomon Islanders . . . there are nine distinct names for the cocoanut, signifying stages in its growth, but no word corresponding to our general term "cocoanut." On the other hand, they have only one word which covers all four meals of the day—breakfast, dinner, tea, supper—but no special name for each of these. It is of practical importance to them to distinguish the nine stages of the cocoanut but not to discriminate between "dinner" and "tea." (p. 224)

Many social groups develop concepts or categories that refer to major or dominant statuses and positions in the life cycle. They are likely to have words designating sex, age, and marital and economic status, and they may have complex vocabularies to indicate positions in the kinship structure of the group. The socialization of children into the group requires that children learn the group's language. Furthermore, a group's standing in the broader society is in part reflected in the degree to which its private or peculiar language is spoken by the members of that society. Thus Black English is seldom spoken by white school-age children, and central Hebrew phrases have seldom become incorporated into the American national vocabulary. Colonizing nations have long recognized that language control leads to group control; the British, for example, were quite skilled in making English *the* language for the countries they controlled. As a group or a nation gains control over its own fate, one of its first actions is to require the learning of its "native" language. Indeed, it may insist on conducting all public business in that language, and may ban the languages of its prior oppressors from its schools in the process.

Listening and Comprehending

Conversation is a complex activity, as each participant is engaged almost simultaneously in a number of distinct processes. Thus while *A* speaks to *B*, *B* listens to *A*. But *B* is also busily engaged in formulating the remarks that she intends to make as soon as *A* stops speaking. *B* also may be commenting to herself upon what *A* is saying. Some of these comments may not even be explicitly formulated, and generally they will not be uttered aloud. Thus *B* may silently remark that *A* is stupid or confused or dishonest, but when her turn to speak comes she suppresses these comments in favor of others that meet the conversational requirements of courteous social intercourse. To complicate matters further, *A* not only speaks to *B*, he also listens to what he is saying to *B*—correcting, revising, retracting, and evaluating as he goes along. Both *A* and *B* alternate between listening to their own speech and listening to the speech of the other. The remarks made by each are called forth by, and adapted to, remarks made by the other as each assesses the other's intentions and motives. Each is involved as both participant and observer.

Comprehension of someone else's speech presupposes mastery of the language and is the counterpart of speech. The other person's words act as stimuli that produce in the listener an internal symbolic process that constitutes the act of comprehending. When we listen attentively to another person, our own word schemes are not directly involved, as we temporarily cede control to the other.

Speech and comprehension of speech are not so much different processes as they are different phases of the same process. None of us can communicate linguistically with others unless we comprehend our own remarks. Conversely, we do not adequately comprehend others' ideas until we are able to formulate them for ourselves. The crucial test of comprehension of a word is the individual's ability to use the word correctly—that is, to be able to evoke on the part of the listener the same response the word evokes for the speaker.

As we note in our discussion of aphasia in Chapter 5, if we shift our attention to neurological and physiological levels and ask what goes on in the brains of two people engaged in conversation, the situation becomes infinitely more complicated. Only some of these internal processes have been roughly identified. It is impossible, for example, to provide a meaningful description, in neurological and physiological terms, of the simplest conversational episode or to distinguish one type from another. Thought, speech, and conversation unquestionably require the participation of various neurological and physiological mechanisms and processes. They are not, however, identical with these processes. They must be viewed in a broader sociohistorical perspective (Luria & Yudovich, 1959). Nevertheless, sociologists, psychologists, and other behavioral scientists share with biological scientists a profound interest in the nature of the functioning of the human brain.

Although some hold that dogs and other animals "comprehend" things said to them, the standard of comprehension for dogs is not the same as the standard for human beings. Parents, for example, do not assume from isolated correct responses that their children understand all the words directed to them. Children are subjected to another, more crucial test: They must be able to use the words correctly—not just once or twice, but in a wide variety of situations and in various combinations. If we remember that *the fundamental prototype of language behavior is conversation,* we shall not be confused by the fact that lower animals such as dogs seem able to comprehend verbal cues. As we have seen, children show a similar subverbal comprehension before they learn to speak.

Writing and the Literate Tradition

It is virtually impossible to exaggerate the importance of the invention of written symbols in the evolution of culture (Couch, 1984a, p. 302). Primitive writing systems developed early in the evolution of ancient civilizations, arising out of the practical necessities and problems that arose when human beings first began to live together in large permanent settlements and to form political units. The term *civilization* implies the existence of literacy, political organization, and city life. Cultures that lack writing are located in an oral tradition. Without writing, history gives way to myth, and organized intellectual activity is limited; there can be no mathematics, algebra, science, or any of the other numerous disciplines incorporated within the literate tradition. In preliterate societies, customs, practices, and beliefs are passed down through the generations essentially through long chains of person-to-person conversations. This method of transmission is sharply limited in the kinds of information that can be transmitted, and it also tends to distort the past because of people's tendency to reinterpret and understand the past in terms of the present (Goody & Watt, 1972).

Writing probably began as pictures or drawings representing external objects, people, and animals; marks were used to indicate numbers. From the latter, various types of number systems were invented and elaborated on; from the former, the modern alphabet was created, primarily by the Phoenicians and the Greeks during the first millennium B.C. The earliest writing systems were cumbersome, hard to master, and restricted to elite segments of the population. The emergence of a phonetic alphabet not only made it much easier to become literate, but also radically altered the function of writing. This function, at first, was to represent the world by means of pictures or simplified drawings. In contrast, the alphabet permits us to describe and record the sounds people make when they speak, regardless of what they talk about. It took several thousand years after the first appearance of primitive forms of writing for humans to develop the modern phonetic alphabet.

Writing was initially a response to the practical necessities created by the development of commerce, trade, agriculture, and organized government. The earliest writers wrote laboriously on stone or clay. The Egyptians later learned to write on papyrus;

paper was first produced about A.D. 200 in China, whence its production and use was acquired centuries later by the rest of the civilized world. The Arabs introduced papermaking into Europe in the twelfth century A.D., and in 1452 Gutenberg invented the printing press. These advances added revolutionary new dimensions and possibilities to the social and intellectual significance of writing and literacy.

The invention of writing has a more subtle intellectual implication in that writing converts language and the thoughts it expresses into material objects in the external environment. Oral speech, in contrast, consists only of sounds or events that occur and vanish except as they may be remembered by individuals. Recorded speech or writing invites sustained attention and analysis with respect to both the structure of language and the structure of thought. Writing also facilitates thinking; try to imagine what mathematics would be like without it. Because of writing, talk about talk and thinking about thought are stimulated and facilitated.

In view of this discussion, it is probably no accident that the flowering of Greek civilization during the first millennium B.C. was preceded by the adoption of the modern phonetic alphabet and accompanied by an expansion of literacy in Greek society (Couch, 1984a; Goody & Watt, 1972). It also makes sense that the Greeks invented logic, cultivated rational discourse, speculated on human nature and the nature of the world, practiced mathematical reasoning, and wrote plays and poetry.

The development of writing in a society creates a complex literate tradition that contributes to an accelerated rate of cultural evolution, the accumulation of knowledge, and the development of science and technology. Recorded history begins and a new sense of the past emerges. New modes of symbolic operation become possible, and new conceptions of the world, of humans, and of the past and the present emerge. The literate tradition does not displace the oral tradition, but rather supplements it. Writing, as we have argued in Chapter 3, differs drastically from oral communication in that (a) it is not supplemented by the wide variety of nonverbal signs that routinely accompany conversations and (b) what is written acquires an objective public character that ordinary conversation lacks. Writing is thus a purer example of linguistic communication than oral communication, and by the same token it is more exacting. Thoughts tend to evolve and change as one tries to represent them on paper, and sometimes they may simply evaporate.

The oral and literate traditions coexist in modern societies; they also interact with each other, and items pass from one to the other. The oral tradition is the carrier of what is called "practical common sense," whereas the literature is represented by what is learned from books and through advanced training and education. There is often conflict between the two traditions. No one in our society can avoid the influence of the oral, but it is quite easy to minimize the influence of the literate tradition.

Language and the Social Structure of Thought

The social environment affects the content of a person's thoughts as well as the form of his or her thinking. Sapir (1949), making a point akin to that made earlier concerning symbolic environments, suggests the importance of particular languages for the construction of thought and environments:

> Human beings do not live in an objective world alone . . . but are very much at the mercy of the particular language which has become a medium of expression for their society. It is quite an illusion to imagine that one adjusts to reality essentially without the use of language and that language is merely an incidental means of solving specific problems of communication or reflection. . . . the "real world" is to a large extent unconsciously built upon the language habits of the group. No two languages are ever sufficiently similar to be considered as representing the same social reality. The worlds in which different societies live are distinct worlds, not merely the same worlds with different labels attached. (p. 120)

The influences of language structure upon the structure of thought are illustrated by the problems of translation. The translation of other languages into English, for instance, involves more than merely finding equivalent words; the translator must try to convey meanings and nuances of meaning that may be practically impossible to express in English. The translation of non-European languages into English is even more difficult, because the modes of thought are likely to be even more divergent. Consider the differences between the Chinese and American styles of thinking. For example:

> Chinese poets seldom talk about one thing in terms of another. . . . If a metaphor is used, it is metaphor directly relating to the theme, not something borrowed from the ends of the earth. . . . For our Western taste, used as we are to the operatic in poetry, that is, the spectacular or shocking effect produced by some unusual analogy or metaphor, the substance of Chinese poems seems often mild or trivial. (Brynner, 1929, p. 27)

The following newspaper account suggests some of the problems conscientious translators encounter when they try to interpret English expressions into Chinese:

> Some of the great difficulties among the diplomats sitting around the international table [at the United Nations] arise from the differences in languages, alphabets, and, consequently, ways of thinking; and in no tongue is more ingenuity required for accurate, precise translation than Chinese.
>
> The Chinese ideograph script is one of the world's oldest written media, but the talk at Lake Success is so brimful of new ideas, new concepts and new words that, to translate even the basic Charter itself into Chinese, it was necessary to devise almost 2000 new combinations of characters.
>
> A perfect example of the troubles faced here by Chinese translators is the word "uranium," which has a persistent way of cropping up with a decision to call the atomic base "U-metal." That, however, only started their headaches.
>
> The symbol of "U" was found in the Chinese word for grapefruit, which in literal translation is the "U-tree." What was just as disturbing, from a purist point of view, was the discovery that the symbol for metal was contained in the first part of the word for "bell," which literally translated meant "metal boy."
>
> After some cudgeling of brains, however, the calligraphers came up with the proposal to shave off the "tree" part of the "U-tree"

> character, discard the "boy" part of the "bell" character, and then in the best manner of diplomatic compromise, join the severed remains to form a new symbol: "U-metal" or, as we would say, uranium. (quoted in Vinacke, 1953, p. 37)

Although new words can be added to a language with relative ease, the language's basic structure is highly stable and resists change. Most people who speak a given language are unaware of its structure as something that differs from the structures of other language systems. Consequently, the uniform modes of thought imposed upon them by their native tongue are not recognized, but are accepted as part of the "real nature of the world," or as among the elements of "common sense."

Because most Americans are acquainted with only the general family of Indo-European languages, they are likely to view skeptically the contention that thinking is not essentially the same the world over. They know that the content of thought varies from group to group; nevertheless, they are likely to believe that the form of all "correct" thinking is the same everywhere. Americans often regard the divergent modes of thought of other peoples—which actually do exist—as merely varieties of error.

It would be revealing to know what effect the English language has on our thinking processes. It is probably impossible for individuals operating within the framework of English to become aware of the influences it exerts upon them without their first being acquainted with other languages (preferably non-European ones). For this reason, we shall illustrate our point with material from the Navajo Indian language, which is quite different from our own:

> [Navajo language] delights in sharply defined categories. It likes, so to speak, to file things away in neat little packages. It favors always the concrete and particular, with little scope for abstractions. It directs attention to some features of every situation, such as the minute distinctions as to direction and type of activity. It ignores others to which English gives a place. Navaho focuses interest upon doing—upon verbs as opposed to nouns or adjectives. . . . The important point is that striking divergences in manner of thinking are crystallized in and perpetuated by the forms of Navaho grammar. Take an example of a commonplace physical event: rain. . . . To give only a few instances of the sorts of discrimination the Navaho must make before he reports his experiences; he uses one verb form if he himself is aware of the actual inception of the rain storm, another if he has reason to believe that the rain has been falling for some time in his locality before the occurrence struck his attention. . . . Similarly, the Navaho must invariably distinguish between the ceasing of rainfall (generally) and the stopping of rain in a particular vicinity because the rain clouds have been driven off by the wind. The [Navajo] people take the consistent noticing and reporting of such differences . . . as much for granted as the rising of the sun. (Kluckhohn & Leighton, 1946, p. 149)

Kluckhohn and Leighton (1946) point out that Navajo is a very literal language that gives concreteness and specificity to everything that is said. The result is that Navajo thought is more exact and particular than English thought. This is demonstrated by the way the Navajo express the meaning conveyed by the English verb *to go.* The Navajo specify precisely whether the journey was made on foot or by horseback, wagon, auto, plane, or train; they also indicate whether they are starting to go, going alone, returning from somewhere, or arriving at a point; and, if they make a trip astride a horse, different verb forms indicate whether they moved at a walk, a trot, or a gallop (pp. 197-201).

The study of non-European languages makes it evident that there are different modes of reasoning. Every child is introduced to a system or systems of language embodying certain peculiar and nonuniversal conceptual distinctions. Thus children are inducted into traditions of thinking—traditions consisting not only of certain kinds of ideas but of certain ways of thinking. This point is made particularly clear by a consideration of time divisions. If certain temporal distinctions are not made by one's language, one cannot think in terms of them. A person's behavior can scarcely be organized, systematized, arranged, defined, regulated, or coordinated in terms of temporal categories of which the person is unaware. Whereas our own language

> always expresses tense with perfect definiteness there are languages . . . which are incapable of doing so . . . in Samoyedic (Siberian) only two temporal forms of the verb are recognized . . . one of these . . . signifying present and future . . . the other indicating the past. . . . The minute temporal distinctions which we recognize as "present," "present perfect," "past," "past perfect," "past future," "future perfect," and "past perfect" are impossible in these languages.
>
> A number of languages clearly reveal the efforts which have been made to render intelligible the elusive and abstract nature of time by interpreting it in terms of space. . . . [In Sudan language, for example,] the locations in space are crudely expressed by means of body-part words, and these spatial expressions then serve as indicators of time. . . . here the fundamental institution of time is quite different from that to which we are accustomed. . . .
>
> [For] some people future and past fuse linguistically into what might be called a "not-now." . . . in Schambala (African) the same word designates the distant past as well as the distant future. For them there exists only a "today" and a "not today." (Werner & Kaplan, 1963, pp. 126-129)

Other critical categories, such as number, action, and quality, also differ in various languages.

Because the language people use is largely inherited from previous generations, the modes of thought it conveys are also derived from the past. This has disadvantages as well as advantages, for the experiences of past generations are not always comparable to those of later ones. The errors of the past are tenacious because they become embedded in the language and popular thought—so much so that they become unquestioned assumptions. Note, for example, the sayings that the sun rises in the east, and that members of a race are related to each other by blood. Scientific progress often depends upon individuals' freeing themselves from the implications of popular speech. Sapir (1949) reminds us that "language is at one and the same time helping and retarding us in our exploration of experience" (p. 11).

In setting forth the general hypothesis that profoundly influences the forms of thought, we are not saying that a given language rigidly determines the form of thought of the society in which it is spoken. But language so thoroughly penetrates the modes of experiencing that at the very least it limit the possibilities of perception and thinking.

Componential Analysis

During recent years, anthropologists who take a position close to our own have begun to develop what has been termed *componential analysis.* This is a sophisticated linguistic analysis undertaken in an effort to avoid projecting the ethnographer's modes of cognition and perception onto his or her subjects, and instead attempting to discover *their* modes. Charles Frake (1962), a leading exponent of this view, expresses the position in terminology that will sound familiar to our readers:

> A successful strategy for writing productive ethnographics must tap the cognitive world of one's informants. It must discover those features of objects and events which they regard as significant for defining concepts, formulating propositions, and making decisions. The conception of an ethnography requires that the units by which the data of observation are segmented, ordered, and interrelated be delimited and defined according to contrasts inherent in the data themselves and not according to prior notions of pertinent descriptive categories. (p. 54)

Frake points out that anthropologists customarily do what he suggests when they study kinship systems. No ethnographers describe social relations in alien societies by referring to the doings of uncles, aunts, and cousins; however, when they describe utensils, trees, shrubs, and other features of the environment, they customarily do so "solely in terms of categories projected from the investigator's culture" (p. 59). Frake suggests that if investigators were to follow the sensible strategy used in the study of kinship, "then the problem of describing a tangible object such as a plant may become rather more complex than the relatively simple task of defining contrasts between categories of kinsmen" (p. 59). Why? Because the plant world is frequently differentiated in the amazingly complex ways that we have noted. Frake gives the example of a Philippine rain forest agricultural society whose members "exhaustively partition their plant world into more than 1600 categories" (p. 59).

What Frake suggests ethnographers should do is not an easy task, but the componential analysts believe that it must be done. That task is not necessarily easier when investigators study a group within their own nation if that group's symbolic worlds are markedly different from their own. Investigators cannot simply be satisfied with penetrating the symbolic worlds of their subjects; as social scientists, they must develop their explanations *after* they grasp these other worlds.

Sociolinguistics

Sociolinguistics, as we have noted, is the study of the social organization of language behavior in social situations. Sociolinguists examine how such structural factors as age, sex, social class, race and, ethnicity mold the talk that occurs in social situations. Their research indicates that the dominant power structures in society come into play in the talk that occurs between people. Thus in a study of encounters between doctors and patients, West (1984) found (a) that male doctors interrupt patients more than do female doctors, (b) that male doctors interrupt blacks and females more than they do whites and males, (c) that doctors ask more questions than do patients, and (d) that doctors do not give preference to patients' questions.

Sociolinguistics has taken several turns. Some analysts perform what is called *discourse analysis* (see Manning, 1987, for a review); they examine the stories and texts produced in institutional settings, such as the courts, hospitals, physicians' offices, and clinics. They study linguistic units that are larger than utterances or sentences. The problem with discourse analysis is that, too frequently, analysts assume that meaning is given in the rules of procedure that organize the texts under analysis. Manning (1987) suggests that meaning and its interpretation remain unresolved issues within discourse analysis.

Conversational analysis (CA) focuses on naturally occurring units and forms of talk—including openings, closings, turn taking, next speaker selection, repairs, and question-and-answer sequences. Manning (1987) regards CA as a highly sophisticated technique of sociolinguistic analysis. Much of the work in this area draws on the original work of Harvey Sacks, Emanuel Schlegoff, and Gall Jefferson. The study by West (1984) mentioned above is an example of conversational analysis in an institutional setting.

CA involves the study of how people use talk in interaction. CA researchers examine social life "in situ, in the most ordinary settings" (Psathas, 1995, p. 1). They assume that social actions "are meaningful for those who produce them and that they have a natural organization that can be discovered and analyzed by close examination" (Psathas, 1995, p. 2). They also presume that the orderliness of action is accomplished in situations by individuals taking account of one another's actions. Much CA research has focused on conversational exchanges, greetings, questions and answers, and compliments and responses (Psathas, 1995, p. 52). Other CA scholars locate talk in specific social structures or organizations, like hospitals or the workplace, and examine how institutional talk (and work) gets done (Psathas, 1995, p. 54).

Conversational analysis involves a transcription system for converting recorded speech into written texts (Manning, 1987). CA researchers assume that speech as heard is the object of study, and such speech can be converted into printed texts. It is unclear how these analysts are able to record and transcribe speech "as it is heard" and given meaning in an interactional situation. This mode of analysis also assumes that what is heard, and then transcribed, is what is meant. An orderliness is given to spoken speech that may not actually be present in "talking situations"; indeed, Manning (1987) notes that CA researchers avoid analysis of messy conversations and group sociable talk. The context-dependent features of conversation remain to be explored in detail.

Symbolic Behavior as Shared Behavior

Let us suppose that a dozen dogs have been conditioned so that whenever a buzzer sounds, they all produce saliva and otherwise behave as though they anticipate being fed. Then suppose that all 12 dogs are together in one room and the buzzer is sounded. Presumably, all will respond in the same way to the same stimulus. Can we say that all of them are responding as a group to a sign that all understand in the same way? To answer this question, let us compare such a situation with that existing in an Eskimo settlement where the food supply is running low. A hunting party sets out to kill seals to replenish the food supply. Can we say that the Eskimos, like the 12 dogs, are making similar responses to the same stimulus, and that therefore the two types of activity are the same?

A moment's reflection will reveal that there is a fundamental difference between these two situations. Through intercommunication, the Eskimos respond as a group, acting collectively rather than individually. Their behavior is shared; that of the dogs is not. Each member of the Eskimo community grasps the common purpose. In terms of that common purpose, which each understands and knows the others understand, they respond in different ways in order to attain the common goal. Some members of the settlement stay at home and prepare to take care of the kill; others form the hunting party, within which members play different but coordinated roles. It is no accident that the Greek word *symbola,* from which the word *symbol* is derived, originally referred to "the two halves of a broken stick or coin which were kept as tokens of a contract." Thus the word came to mean an item—such as a word—employed as an instrument of communication (Lorimer, 1929, p. 83).

Gestures as Shared Symbols

We can emphasize the shared character of language by noting how conventional gestures are utilized and understood. Gestures such as shaking hands in greeting, showing affection by kissing, and waving good-bye all seem "natural" to Americans. Yet these acts do not seem natural to the people of other countries and societies. A Palaung woman in Southeast Asia said, after several Englishmen had heartily shaken her hand: "I suppose that they mean to be kind, but what a strange custom. I am very glad it is only my hand that they wish to shake and not my head!" (quoted in Hiller, 1933, p. 121).

Most human gestures are highly conventionalized and stylized, taking on their meaning through cultural definition. The same gesture may stand for very different meanings in different lands; conversely, different gestures may stand for the same meanings. Only if both people—the one who makes the gesture and the one who sees the gesture—attach the same significance to it can there be communication between them. An "outsider" will attach the wrong meaning (or no meaning) to the gesture; hence communication will be impaired.

Even gestures of assent, dissent, and beckoning—which most Americans probably assume to be among the most natural and nonconventional gestures—are conventionally defined. Hiller (1933, pp. 103-104) notes that inhabitants of the Admiralty Islands express a decided negative reaction by making a quick stroke of the nose with a finger of the right hand. If the reaction is doubtful, the finger is rubbed slowly across the nose. To beckon a person, the hand is held half erect with the palm forward, moving in the direction of the person addressed.

Pseudocommunication

Often, two people will become involved in an argument in which both use the same words, but the words have different meanings for the two individuals. When this occurs, a genuine interchange of ideas does not take place, as each person makes remarks inappropriate to the meanings the other has in mind. The two talk past each other and grow angry at what each feels to be the other's stupidity. If the two parties do not realize that they are using words in different ways, communication is seriously impeded or made impossible; this is called *pseudocommunication.* They are interacting *at,* rather than *with,* one another.

If the disputants grow aware of the different meanings common terms can carry, their discussion may develop into a consideration of proper linguistic usage. Unless there is agreement as to the meanings of terms, people who believe they are discussing the same thing may actually be talking about different things.

Up to now, we have been discussing language symbols as symbols whose sole function is to refer to objects or to designate meanings. If someone says, "We are having lovely weather," we have treated such a statement as an indication by one person to another that the sun is shining and that it is pleasant outside. Obviously, however, this statement may mean something entirely different: Speakers may be in a social situation in which they are expected to talk whether or not they feel they have anything to say. As all the people present are generally aware of the weather that day, there is really no point in saying anything about it; nevertheless, all are likely to feel more at ease if there is conversation. Here the purpose is not to tell people something they do not already know, but rather, by uttering certain sounds, to give evidence of goodwill and sociability. Hiller (1933) has called this kind of conversation "social ritual." Language so used may be termed *expressive* rather than *representational.* Another example of purely expressive speech is swearing—although swearing *at* someone usually also involves some communication. Words used expressively cannot be understood through reference to a dictionary; they can be understood only as conventionalized ways of giving vent to certain feelings. Thus the nervous woman at a tea discusses the weather; an angry man swears; two people greet each other by saying, "Hello." In these situations, the function of language is not so much communication as expression—though of course some meaning is definitely being communicated.

In Chapter 5 we discuss aphasia, the loss of the power to use language symbols. Studies of aphasia and other speech disorders offer experimental evidence that expressive speech is more primitive than representative speech. Aphasics whose powers of speech are nearly gone and who cannot name even the most familiar objects in their everyday environment nevertheless usually retain the ability to swear and to exclaim (Head, 1926; Luria, 1972; Sacks, 1985).

Humor, Interaction, and the Resources of Language

It is sometimes said that humans are the only animals who talk, weep, and laugh. We should take that assertion with some skepticism, given that animals certainly exhibit playful behavior, and chimpanzees, at least, seem to engage in practical jokes. Yet, as Wolfenstein (1954) observes, "humor is a distinctively human achievement: among living things only human beings laugh" (p. 11). Whether humans learned to laugh before they learned to talk is an open question, but there is little doubt that once they developed language they probably laughed and joked a great deal more. Even in the face of disaster, humans satirize their oppressors and make bitter jokes about their own plight. Humor—in the form of jokes, puns, and witticisms—has often been compared to dreams. Like dreams, jokes have latent meaning; they also disguise hostile emotions and may reflect underlying definitions of the sect or of social relationships. Through humor, people reflect their responses to problematic situations. A dramatic example is that of the criminal who is led to execution on Monday morning and remarks, "Well, this is a good beginning for the week" (Wolfenstein, 1954, p. 212).

There are so many forms of humor that we can hardly begin to list them: satire, irony, gallows humor, ethnic jokes, sex jokes, puns, slips of the tongue, misprints, spoonerisms, in-jokes, black humor, jibes. Whatever its form, humor usually draws directly on the resources of language—even when the humor is gestural (as in takeoffs) and does not involve actual speech.

To say that humor depends on language means much more than merely that words and sentences are used to create humor; it also presupposes a common universe of discourse and shared experiences. To take the most obvious example: Understanding the humor of a foreign culture is one of the last and most difficult accomplishments of newcomers. What they do understand quickly, of course, is humor about those matters they share with the culture's citizens. But the subtleties and styles of humor in particular countries and cultures depend on the intricacies of their social relationships and the linkages of their social groups. On the other hand, certain jokes, such as sex jokes, are relatively easily transferable from country to country—although they tend to carry a particular cultural stamp or style. This is illustrated by the contrast between British and American styles, which often leads Americans to think the British lack a sense of humor—to the amazement of the latter.

Insofar as a universe of discourse is widely shared, the audience for given bits of humor can be huge—for instance, jokes about leading politicians. Every informed English citizen during the days of Gladstone and Disraeli understood the humor in the following exchange between the two men: Gladstone said that Disraeli would either be executed on the scaffold or die of a loathsome disease, to which Disraeli replied that this depended on whether he embraced Gladstone's principles or Gladstone's mistress.

Certain types of puns and other sayings can be understood and used by citizens of very different backgrounds, again because they can share certain general perspectives. For instance, the conundrum: "What did the ram say as he fell off the cliff?" Answer: "I didn't see that damned ewe turn." The phenomenon of in-jokes exists because the universe of discourse, the shared communication, is limited in scope. In-jokes are always related to some social world, be it ethnic, sexual, occupational, or recreational. Each social world has its particular stock jokes, humorous sayings, and fabled humorous stories about personages, social types, or important concerns in that world. For example, golf: A newcomer to the game, looking for his ball, which had strayed in the midst of trees and underbrush, rises from his search with the ball in his hand and says to his partner, "Here's the ball, now where's the course?"

In reviewing the jokes related above, it is apparent that their effectiveness as humor depends not only on language as a body of words, but language as sets of meanings and the interaction that sustains these meanings. Humor's persistence and pervasiveness—as well as its many forms—suggest that in the face of taboos and threats, humor is a vital and basic form of human behavior. The few social psychologists, psychiatrists, and philosophers who have tried to analyze humor as a phenomenon have tended to restrict their foci to the so-called functions of humor, or have simply classified its forms, or have attempted to account for humor by applying remarkably overgeneralized theories. The conditions for and the consequences of telling jokes, laughing at slips of speech, creating irony, and other settings for humor are multitudinous; no simple theory could account for them all. For the social psychologist, the important task is to get humor back into the interactional picture as an essential part of human behavior.

Being Humorous

Lynch (1982), Flaherty (1984), and Fine (1984) have contributed to our understanding of how humor and playfulness in everyday life are constructed and given meaning. Following Bateson (1979), Lynch notes that playful humor involves a process of creative exploration in a relationship. Consider the following excerpt from his field notes. The occasion is a sociable gathering attended by seven people. The principal interactants are Shan, a 40-year-old professor of social psychology from Japan; Paul, a 45-year-old professor in the social sciences; and Rob, a graduate student. During an evening of sociable talk, it is proposed that Shan and his wife have a veranda sale to dispose of their furniture before they return to Japan. The following conversation was recorded:

> *Shan:* Actually, garage sale is an interesting phenomenon—we don't have such a recycling system in Japan. . . .
>
> *Paul:* That's right—garage sales have much cultural significance!
>
> *Shan:* I think that in *garage saleology,* there is also great economic significance.
>
> *Paul:* What we really need then is a department of *garage saleology* to study this important phenomenon seriously. (quoted in Lynch, 1982, p. 51)

In this playful, humorous interactional episode, the participants create a new concept—garage saleology. They produce this concept out of their earlier talk about a veranda sale (itself an instance of humorous playfulness); they then turn this concept into a department and a field of inquiry. The talkers have pushed the boundaries of their relationship into new realms of playfulness, and they have done this by turning talking and language into resources for interaction. Lynch (1982) shows how talkers construct play in social situations. He shows how play originates, gains momentum, becomes serious, breaks down, changes course, builds on itself, suffers disruption, and then fades away (p. 60). He shows how participants signal one another about the play they are engaging in. In play and humor, interactants take a step outside literal reality and enter the realm of make-believe.

Flaherty (1984, p. 49) suggests that humorous interaction is reality play; by this he means that interactants play at not taking reality seriously. Normal interactions are organized in terms of what he calls "reality work"—the attempt to organize interaction and talk in terms of taken-for-granted rules regarding proper interaction. In reality play, interactants trifle with, alter, and change the normal expectations that are themselves "constitutive of reality work. In turn, this leads to a formal definition of humor as 'every event which manifests itself as reality play' " (p. 60).

Compare an actual interview between a patient and a psychiatrist with the following account from Woody Allen's film *Annie Hall*:

> A boy goes to a psychiatrist, and he says "Doctor you must help us, my brother thinks he's a chicken." And the psychiatrist exclaims, "You must have him committed at once!" But the boy retorts, "We can't, we need the eggs." (quoted in Flaherty, 1984, p. 67)

This short strip of humor challenges normal expectations concerning a patient-psychiatrist dialogue. The joke releases us from the ordinary world of reality work and makes us laugh. This is what reality-play-as-humor is all about. Flaherty argues that reality play exists everywhere. With Lynch, he would suggest that in reality play and humor, people step back from literal reality and creatively insert playfulness into their ordinary routines.

Fine (1984) has suggested that humor in social interaction plays an important part in shaping how people define themselves and their situations. He asserts that jocular or humorous interaction has three features: First, it demands an immediate reaction from its listeners; second, it allows the person who is joking to place some distance between him- or herself and the joke he or she tells; and third, humor carries deep, often metaphoric meaning that extends beyond what is overtly intended. Fine gives an example of how people use humorous talk to justify their actions, especially when those actions might be questioned. A girl (Bev) makes the following statement after she throws some food from a car window:

> I littered, but it's biodegradable. A peanut butter and jelly sandwich. (Bev laughs.) No big threat to ecology. (Bev is giggling while she says this.) (All laugh.) (p. 74)

In this episode Bev presents a humorous denial of any deviance or harm she might have created as a result of littering the roadside and places distance between herself and her action by calling the sandwich biodegradable. This account elicits an immediate reaction from her listeners.

Daydreaming and Dreaming

How do our previous discussions of thinking, shared symbolic behavior, expressive verbal behavior, and humor contribute to our understanding of such related mental and interactional phenomena as daydreaming, fantasy, and dreaming? These processes—unlike thinking, which involves conscious and reflective attempts to enter into the activities of another individual—represent, as Singer (1975) suggests,

> a shift of attention *away* from some primary physical or mental task we have set for ourselves, or *away* from directly looking at or listening to something in the external environment, *toward* an unfolding sequence of private responses made to some internal stimulus. (p. 3)

Daydreaming

The inner processes to which the daydreamer attends involve "pictures in the mind's eye" that may anticipate future experiences in which the thinker will take part, or the pictures may recall past experiences of some significance to the person. Daydreaming is a normal mental process.

In psychological writing, it is common to make a distinction between objective, rational thought and autistic, or fantasy, thought. The former is supposed to be more or less impersonal, systematic, objective, and logical; the latter is supposed to occur because it satisfies the subjective wishes and desires of the person and so is more or less irrational, illogical, and out of touch with reality. The assumption that fantasizing is a process apart from rational or systematic thinking is associated with the belief that daydreamers substitute the satisfactions of the daydream for those denied them by the exigencies of actual life.

It is said that daydreamers derive three main types of satisfactions: compensation, escape, and release. Compensatory daydreams allow the person to attain goals imaginatively that are otherwise unattainable. The Cinderella legend has its counterpart in the fantasies of anyone who wishes for something he or she cannot get. Daydreams of escape occur under such conditions as anxiety, boredom, hardship, and fear; the fantasies temporarily transport the dreamer into more pleasant surroundings. Daydreams of release function as safety valves by allowing the individual to dissipate anger, hatred, resentment, or jealousy in a harmless imaginary form.

Although fantasy is supposed to serve the functions of escape, compensation, and release, it is not easy to prove that these are its only functions. It is hard to determine the function of a given daydream merely by examining its content; even if one knows a great deal about the personality and background of the daydreamer, the fantasy activity may still not fit into any of the three conventional categories.

The attempt to uncover the function of daydreams is based upon the assumption that fantasizing is something apart from rational thinking; it is assumed that it must yield special satisfactions or it would not occur. Hence daydreaming is supposed to occur mainly in connection with situations of stress, anxiety, boredom, and the like. This is underscored further by the vivid and elaborate fantasies of the psychotic and the excessive daydreaming of maladjusted people. However, closer scrutiny of daydreaming (without previous commitment to a dichotomization of "reality thinking" and a substitute for it) brings some other relevant matters into focus.

Normal adults know perfectly well when they are daydreaming, and they will sometimes set aside time to engage in this often pleasant activity. Young children often have difficulty distinguishing between reality and fancy; they sometimes get them mixed up, to the amusement or exasperation of their elders. The requirements of adult life eventually make it necessary for the child to draw a strict line between fact and imagination. Severe psychosis and the condition of senility cause their victims to lose the ability to make this clear separation, at least in their less normal moments. In the psychotic, various types of fantasizing seem to constitute "thinking" and "reasoning." These commonplace observations do not lead to a separation of fantasizing and reasoning, but suggest quite the opposite—namely, that fantasizing is a type of reasoning.

As fantasizing is not a single process but embraces many types of covert activity, we can say that reasoning of various kinds may occur when anyone fantasizes. The fantasy life of the young child may be one of his or her dominant lives; the child has not yet been sufficiently socialized into correcting his or her perspective by checking it against the facts or by comparing it with the views of other people. Severe psychotics, for the most part, do not operate with *consensual validation* (public verification) in mind; the various types of fantasizing in which they engage constitute their modes of handling social relationships and responding to the physical world. Maladjusted persons become absorbed in their fantasy lives; this is the way they meet the impinging world. Normal adults, although they know the difference between reality and fancy and between public knowledge and private secret, are not constrained to reason only in socially sanctioned and verifiable modes or in systematic or rational ways. It is well-known that even though scientists present their findings and check them for public appraisal in systematic ways, their guiding ideas may have occurred to them through processes that are like reveries.

A *stream of consciousness* or of *associations* is likely to be a peculiarly rich mixture of covert mental processes. Visual and auditory images, subverbal comments, daydream dramas, recollections, review of past scenes, self-judgments, internal dialogue, and many more elements jostle each other. Even a daydream with a fairly tight plot or progression may have intrusions in the form of the daydreamer's comments or judgments. Individuals may exert a certain amount of control over daydreams by repeating and reviving them. Many daydreams appear to be fragmentary and of short duration, and are preceded and followed by conscious, rational thought processes. Like the latter, the fantasizing may be absorbing enough to exclude external stimuli that might otherwise impinge upon the daydreamer's awareness (or the stimuli may break the line of reasoning or fantasizing). It is easier to daydream when other people are not around to break the reverie, but this is perhaps true for any kind of thinking (except the kind that depends upon immediate reciprocal stimulation and verification).

Some writers have contended that it is "more plausible to consider [daydreaming] as preparation for hypothetical activity than as consummation" (Faris, 1952, p. 100). This is certainly a function of all thinking, and there is little doubt that it is the function of much fantasizing. It should be noted that interaction between humans is dramatic in character, and thus dramatic imagery is required for both actual and imaginary participation in it. For example, a man prepares for such interaction when he pictures in his mind various ways of getting acquainted with a woman who attracts him. In order to imagine the play of gestures and to judge the effects of conversational lines, he plays out various dramas in his imagination. Out of these, a plan may emerge.

It is a moot point whether persons about to enter knowingly upon a new status, or about to embark upon any enterprise involving new interpersonal relationships, can initiate their lines of behavior without daydreaming themselves in their new roles. Cues for actual behavior seem to be derived from this kind of thinking, which is also intertwined with less pictorial reasoning. Anticipatory fantasizing can even occur in an overt or shared form, as when husband and wife plan an exciting trip or anticipate the birth of a child. The preparatory functions of fantasizing—rather than the merely wish-fulfilling functions—can be suggested by the experience of immigrants who imagine what the new land will look like and what will happen to them there. Visionaries, utopians, and leaders of social movements do not merely plan, organize, and execute; the label of *dreamer* can be applied to them literally. In order for the symbolism of a movement to recruit members and help retain them, it must be kept vivid and rich. Retrospective fantasizing may occur when an individual reconstructs a particular pleasurable act. Indeed, as we suggest in Chapter 12, the sexual act may be grounded in retrospective and prospective fantasy.

Like other forms of thinking, fantasizing may turn to the past. It is true that one may help eradicate shame and other unpleasant feelings by refurbishing a past conversation or incident in daydreams, but it is also characteristic of humans to seek explanations of the past and to "rethink" incidents and discover new meanings in them. Some of this reinterpretation and reconstruction presumably goes on in the form of reverie. Reveries abound in times of personal crisis, when individuals are questioning themselves about where they are going and must consequently consider where they have been.

These processes are also implicit in any thinking or imagining in which people seek to establish relationships with real or imaginary others. Some people clearly get pleasure out of imagining meeting celebrities, and they may daydream long conversations occurring in such improbable situations. This kind of fantasizing may not merely be pleasurable; it may transform the individuals in their own eyes. Such shifts of self-conception occur even though the dreamers are aware that they are fantasizing. Another kind of vision is that sought by Eastern mystics who fast in order to achieve an elaborate reverie, or series of reveries, in which sacred animals and gods appear. Here there is social sanction for both the vision and its lifelong effects upon the individuals, and perhaps upon their social group. This last example suggests the close connection between ritual and reverie. Ritual, when it is not merely routine, represents a collective acting out of hallowed dramatic sequences, and these, like reverie, may orient one for future conduct. In Langer's (1948) felicitous phrasing:

> [Rituals] are part of man's ceaseless quest for conception and orientation. They embody his dawning motives of power and will, of death and victory. They give active and impressive form to his demoniac forms and ideals. Ritual is the most primitive reflection of serious thought, a slow deposit, as it were, of people's imaginative insight into life. (p. 128)

Seen in such wider contexts, fantasy processes are multiple in kind and function, and are orienting as well as wish fulfilling.

Most of the literature on autistic thought and fantasizing behavior has been produced by psychiatrists and clinical psychologists who are impressed with the great amount and truly fantastic quality of the reveries of their patients. This latter fact, combined with certain assumptions about the nature of humans and their relationship to reality that are made by many psychiatrists and psychologists, leads to an undue stress upon the crippling or merely compensatory effects of fantasy life. Excessive fantasizing does not lead to maladjustment, but it may be a symptom of it.

Dreaming

The meaning of dreams has long intrigued and sometimes worried humans. In the Old Testament, Joseph is rewarded for correctly interpreting Pharaoh's troubling dreams; indeed, books on dreams go as far back as the second century A.D. There are "dream books" that purport to offer guidance in interpreting dreams by supplying the meanings of dream sequences and events, usually in terms of predictions for the future of the dreamer. Eating cheese in a dream, for instance, has been said to portend good fortune. The symbols interpreted in dream books are universal in the sense that, for instance, anyone eating cheese is in for happy times. The questions of what specific dreams "mean" and whether a universal symbolism exists have had lively treatment by scientists during the past century, largely in the fields of psychiatry and psychoanalysis. Social psychologists seem less interested in dreaming, presumably because they do not utilize dreams to obtain insights into the mental and emotional processes of patients; but dreaming is an interesting and important psychological phenomenon in its own right.

Many studies of dreaming deal with physiological correlates, duration, speech, and frequency of occurrence of types of imagery (visual, auditory), as well as with the dream imagery of the blind or the deaf-blind, with sex and age differences, with types of dreams, and so on. The psychiatric literature is replete with examinations of the meanings of dream symbols and with the roles of certain kinds of dreams in the lives of certain types of neurotics. Despite the considerable bulk of this literature, both empirical and theoretical, the nature and significance of dreaming are areas of dispute.

The most influential theory of dreaming is that of Sigmund Freud. Freud's dream theory is part of a much wider and elaborate theoretical system concerning the psychological nature of humans in general. For our purposes, we need stress here only a few of the chief features of Freud's views on dreams. Freud believed that various wishes threaten to disturb the sleeper's rest, and dreams perform the function of seeming to fulfill these wishes. Usually the wishes are unacceptable in the sense that the person does not care to admit that he or she has them. Hence they tend to be *repressed,* or excluded from consciousness, during waking hours. In sleep they appear as dreams, but in disguised forms, because even during sleep the person's psychic mechanisms are operating. The obvious, or *manifest,* content of the dream is an expression of its *latent,* or real, meanings. Freud (1933a) writes that "we have got to turn the manifest dream into the latent dream, and we have to show how the latter became the former, in the life of the dreamer" (p. 19). Through the technique of evoking the patient's free associations, or nonlogical linkages, the patient and analyst eventually arrive at an interpretation of latent content and a knowledge of the connections between this and the manifest content.

The transformation in the dream of latent content into manifest content is termed *dream work,* and it proceeds through a process termed *secondary elaboration*—that is, the person *attempts* to give a rational account of his or her otherwise unaccountable and unfathomable dream. Dream work is an example of primitive modes of operation, which are characteristically unconscious. These modes are not rational and objective, and furthermore, they do not involve logical connections between propositions. Their hallmark is associations, or nonlogical linkages. Freud terms this type of mental functioning *primary process,* and the sharply contrasted logical type he considers to be a *secondary process.* The primary process of mental functioning manifested in the dream is *regression.* The reason that dreams are visual is that there is censorship of undesirable wishes and of *instinctive impulses* that causes these wishes and impulses to emerge in disguised forms. "On account of the . . . process of regression, ideas are turned into visual pictures in the dream; the latent dream thoughts are . . . dramatized and illustrated" (Freud, 1933a, p. 31). Some associations that appear in the dream are not unique to the dreamer but are universal or at least common.

Indeed, Carl Jung, an associate of Freud, contended that all human beings share a collective unconscious, which is a storehouse of latent memory traces from the ancestral past (Hall & Lindzey, 1957, p. 80). The collective unconscious is made up of archetypes—primordial, mythological images connected to birth, death, magic, the hero, the child, the earth mother, the old wise man, the child, and so on (Hall & Lindzey, 1957, p. 81). Jung documented the existence of archetypes through the analysis of dreams (Hall & Lindzey, 1957, p. 104; Jung, 1953).

Freud points out that there are certain possible objections to his wish-fulfillment theory of dreams. People who have had serious traumas reexperience these in their dreams. Freud questions what possible satisfaction of impulse can be had by this painful experience. Likewise, the reappearance in dreams of exceedingly unpleasant incidents from early childhood causes pain to the dreamer. Freud (1938) tentatively accounts for this partly contradictory evidence:

> The sleeper has to dream, because the nightly relaxation of repression allows the upward thrust of the traumatic fixation to become active; but sometimes his dream-work, which endeavors to change the memory traces of the traumatic events into a wish-fulfillment, fails to operate. (p. 18)

The Freudian theory of dreams has been considerably amended by American psychoanalyst Thomas French (1952), who contends that the mode of mental functioning exemplified in the dream is neither Freud's secondary process nor his primary process:

> In fact, it is not associative thinking at all . . . but rather thinking in terms of a practical grasp of real situations: "If I act upon this wish, then I must expect such and such consequences. Shall I renounce the wish or suffer the consequences? Or is some compromise possible?" The dream's solution may not be very good from the point of view of waking life, but it is always intelligible, once we grasp the nature of the conflict. (p. 38)

French sees dreaming as much like ordinary processes of practical thought, which generally are neither overly logical nor verbally formulated. He rejects the associational psychology that was prevalent in Freud's day, suggesting that the connections between specific latent and manifest meanings are related to dreamers' attempts to reconcile their conflicting wishes. We should note particularly in French's account that although the notion of wishes is retained, the nature and functioning of dreaming are conceived of quite differently.

The psychoanalytic conception of dreaming as wish fulfillment has been attacked repeatedly. Faris (1952, pp. 101-104), for instance, contends that dreaming is an effort to solve problems, although the nocturnal effort is far less efficient than the efforts of waking life. A more systematic attack has been launched by C. S. Hall (1953), who argues that dream symbols are not disguised, but are merely representations of ideas: "Dreaming is pictorialized thinking; the conceptual is more perceptual. . . . A dream symbol is an image, usually a visual image, of an object, activity, or scene; the referent for the symbol is a conception" (p. 175). Because different people may have different conceptions of "woman," for instance, the dream symbols for woman vary accordingly. Hall, who counts 102 symbols for the male organ in psychoanalytic writing, concludes that "since the referent is not an object, person, or activity, but a conception, the 102 different phallic symbols represent 102 ways of conceiving of the male genitals" (p. 186). Of course, the dreamer may hold different conceptions, and hence may utilize different symbols referring to these conceptions. Dream symbols, consequently, are not universal, although they may be widespread in a given culture. Hall's criticism of Freud seems to stem mainly from two objections: (a) that Freud's "disguise" theory of dream symbolization makes sleep a more active period than seems likely on the basis of studies and observation and (b) that Freud's associational psychology is "passé."

H. S. Sullivan (1953), a thoughtful psychiatrist whose views we shall encounter again, criticized any account of dreaming as cognition on the grounds that dreamers cannot help distorting their reports of what happens during their dreams; there is an impassable barrier between the covert process of dreaming and the verbal formulations of waking life. Even if dreamers wish to remember the exact details of their dreams, they cannot:

> People who feel that they should analyze . . . a dream . . . into what it stands for, seem to me to be in exactly the state of mind of the person who says to a child of two-and-a-half, "You ought to show more respect for your mother because God on Mt. Sinai said to Moses, 'Honor thy father and thy mother.' " The psychiatrist is dealing with the type of referential operation which is *not* in the syntaxic (verbal) mode, and one merely stultifies himself . . . by trying to make this kind of report syntaxic. (p. 343)

For Sullivan, dreaming is like other mental processes that go on in waking life but outside of awareness, and that have to do with the avoidance of severe anxiety. During sleep, people have less need to defend themselves against anxiety-arousing events, so that dreaming functions to guard against anxiety during sleep and (symbolically) to satisfy needs unslaked during the day. Sullivan imputes no regression to dreaming, and he is wary of interpreting symbols in any but a purely personal context. In Freud's defense, we must note that he too was sensitive to the fact that dreamers could never have direct access to their own dreams, and his concept of secondary elaboration refers to this.

These alternative treatments of dreaming suggest the controversy surrounding the topic. Is dreaming like logical reasoning—that is, practical, everyday thinking—or is it vastly different? Is it problem solving or wish fulfilling? Are the symbols unique to individuals or groups, or are many of them universal? We shall not try to mediate in this free-for-all; however, because we generally reject many of the Freudian assumptions about motivation (and make this explicit in Chapter 6), we do reject the view that dreams are disguises for unsanctioned and unconscious instinctual impulses and wishes, and that there is unvarying correspondence between a given manifest content and the latent content of a dream.

In our view, the living organism is engaged in covert symbolic processes even when asleep or unconscious. The processes involved in dreaming are on "lower levels" than those involved in self-conscious rational thought, particularly when the latter is being prepared for public appraisal. It is unlikely that the modes of sign manipulation employed in dreaming should differ much, if at all, from those employed in waking hours, particularly when the person is at a low point of self-awareness.

As for reporting dreams, we agree with Sullivan as to the great difficulty or impossibility of reporting dreams accurately; no one can possibly remember a dream without converting the dream sequence into words and so distorting and probably oversimplifying it. For the social psychologist, an important aspect of dreaming is that dreams, like any other private experience, can be responded to by self-conscious persons afterward. They may be pleased or ashamed of themselves for dreaming what they did; they may accept the views of their dreams offered by their analysts or by other persons, including fortune-tellers or the authors of dream books; and, as with all other interpretations, they may change their minds about their dreams at later times.

Sociologists have recently taken the position that dreams should properly be the topic of sociological investigation (Fine & Leighton, 1993, p. 95). This position follows logically from the call for a sociology of emotions (Hochschild, 1983), a cognitive sociology (Cicourel, 1974), and a sociology of culture (Becker, 1986). Fine and Leighton (1993) contend that dreams are more than individual productions. Dreams belong to the larger society, to the media, cinema, television, and everyday culture. Dreams are anchored in the interaction process. Dreams, of course, occur during times of sleep, hence a sociology of dreams presumes a sociology of sleeping, the who, what, when, where, why, and how of sleeping practices (Schwartz, 1970).

According to Fine and Leighton (1993, p. 101), the following features define a sociology of dreaming. Dreams are social in nature. They have a social content; that is, they are experienced and presented to others in terms of social and personal meanings and narratives. Dreams are social objects; they are given meaningful interpretation within the larger frameworks of the surrounding culture and society. And of course dreams are gendered, and they are also connected to recurring meanings located in racial and ethnic groups.

Metaphor, Analogy, Flexibility of Thought, and Metonymy

Events and objects can be classified in many different ways. We can make a game of this by trying to see some common object, such as an apple, from as many different perspectives as possible. Besides thinking of an apple as an edible fruit, one may imagine it as a ball, a table decoration, a magical object, a pupil's gift to a teacher. Each idea leads us to view the apple from a different perspective and to act as if it were what we assume it to be or what we use it for. This ability to switch perspectives and regard the same event or object in many different contexts is uniquely human.

When something is treated linguistically as if it were or might possibly be something else, we employ *simile* or *metaphor.* Thus a novelist might describe a helicopter hovering over an airfield as if it were an insect. Metaphoric language is not merely poetic or simply a colorful embellishment; it is necessary to communication. If it is said that a party was "like a funeral" or that a man's speech was "like the braying of an ass," it is understood that the analogy is to be taken descriptively, not literally. Metaphors are often used in humor and satire; for example, in the occupational lingo of funeral directors the person in charge of cremation is called the "chef."

According to German linguist P. Wegener (cited in Langer, 1948, pp. 111-115), all discourse involves a context that is well-known to speaker and listener as well as a novel element. To express the latter, the speaker will utilize a metaphor or analogy—if precise descriptive terms do not already exist—and the context tells the listener that the analogy is not to be taken at face value. It is impossible to strip explicit or implicit metaphor from speech, for many novel elements cannot easily be handled with extant vocabulary; so the speaker must hint, suggest, and evoke. The same is true of speech to oneself. In other words, *analogy* is at the heart of new perspectives, new orientations, vision, and advances in thought.

However colorful and "concrete" metaphors and similes appear, they betray a process of abstraction. As Langer (1948) points out, a word like *run,* when used in connection with rumors, brooks, and competition for political office, has nothing to do with leg action. She suggests that originally all the uses of the verb were probably metaphoric, but now "we take the word itself to mean *that which all its applications have in common,* namely *describing a course*" (p. 124). Wegener has termed such a word a "faded metaphor"; he hypothesizes that "before language had any faded words to denote logical subjects, it could not render a situation by any other means than a demonstrative indication of it in present experience" (Langer, 1948, p. 125). We need not agree with Wegener's account of the development of language to see that abstraction rests in some part upon analogy. As Langer (1948) notes, "The spontaneous similes of language are our first record of *similarities* perceived" (p. 125). But *analogical thinking* is integral to abstract cogitation of even the most abstract and systematic sort. Of course, people use it constantly in developing new political and social positions and in justifying them.

We are properly advised against taking an analogy too literally, as in relying upon analogy to prove a point in an argument. "The great danger of analogy is that a *similarity* is taken as evidence of an *identity*" (Burke, 1936, p. 128). However, as economist John Maynard Keynes has argued, one must always generalize by analogy from a sample of a class to the entire class, because in many respects each instance is unique and there is no absolute identity of all instances in the class. Keynes's point, as well as our previous discussions of the nature of categories, makes clear that all abstractions and generalizations are inevitably oversimplifications of reality. Hence all analogies, however fruitful, will be questioned sooner or later.

The danger and necessity of analogy are the danger and necessity of language itself. No classification covers all qualities of the objects it embraces. Yet without classification and metaphor there would be limited flexibility of behavior, and our attention would be focused directly upon immediate situations. The danger and fruitfulness of metaphor can be epitomized by a strategy—an old and necessary technique often used by philosopher John Dewey. Dewey would take two sharply opposed philosophical positions and show that from yet another and "transcending" position, the opponents were really rivals on the banks of the same local stream. In turn, we can be sure that Dewey's position could be lumped with many that he attacked. From a historical perspective, the positions of even the bitterest opponents often appear to be much closer than the rivals would have thought possible.

Metonymy

Metonymic thinking and speech, in which the name of one thing is used denote another thing related to it—for example, the effect for the cause, the bottle for the drink—parallel metaphoric thinking. Metonymy reveals how events and objects can be classified in different ways. Whereas metaphor relates things that are similar, metonymy relates things that are closely associated with one another in a contiguous manner. Both are figures of speech that establish equivalences in that they "characteristically propose a different entity as having 'equivalent' status to the one that forms the main subject of the figure" (Hawkes, 1977, p. 77).

Generally speaking, metaphor exploits a proposed similarity or analogy between a literal object and its metaphoric substitute—for example, a car's movement compared to a beetle's movement (Hawkes, 1977, p. 77). Metonymy, on the other hand, is based on a sequential association between the literal object (e.g., the president) and its adjacent replacement (e.g., the White House, where the president lives).

Jakobson and Morris (1956) have proposed that language use reveals a tendency toward one of two polarities. Romantic poetry, surrealist paintings, Charlie Chaplin films, and Freudian dream analysis tend toward metaphor. To the metonymic order, in which associations of a linear (syntagmatic) nature predominate, belong heroic epics, narratives of the realist school, and Griffith and Hitchcock films (see Barthes, 1964/1967, p. 60).

Jakobson and Morris propose that certain types of aphasia (see Chapter 5) tend toward either metaphor or metonymy—that is, similarity disorders versus contiguity disorders. Patients suffering from similarity disorders preserve metonymy (e.g., fork for knife, table for lamp, smoke for fire). Patients with contiguity disorders organize speech in terms of metaphors (see Hawkes, 1977, p. 78).

Lacan (1977, pp. 158-159) has suggested that in the unconscious, dreams are organized in terms of metaphor and metonymy. He sees the unconscious dream processes of condensation and displacement as structured by metonymy and metaphor. Metonymy, with its word-to-word movement, is like displacement (Coward & Ellis, 1977, p. 99); metaphor, which combines things that are similar, is like condensation. Thus Lacan argues that language is organized in the unconscious, as it is at the conscious level, in terms of the two great poles of language identified by Jakobson—metaphor and metonymy.

This formulation extends Saussure's (1959) position that the mental activity that takes place within language occurs along two dimensions, which he calls the *syntagmatic* and the *associative* poles. Word and thought combinations supported by linearity are syntagmas, for example, "God is Good" (Saussure, 1959, p. 123). On the other hand, words also acquire meaning by virtue of their association in memory. The French word *enseignement* (teaching) will "unconsciously call to mind a host of other words (*enseigner* 'teach,' *renseigner* 'acquaint,' etc.)" (Saussure, 1959, p. 123).

Jakobson and Morris (1956) consolidate Saussure's two poles of language (syntagmatic and associative) into the metaphoric, metonymic polarity; these then become the "two great poles of language." Lacan (1977) then argues that the unconscious, structured like a language, is organized in terms of these two processes.

More work needs to be done on metaphor, metonymy, and the everyday thought processes that these terms organize. Clearly, Lacan has metaphorically redefined two Freudian terms (*displacement* and *condensation*) and reasoned, by analogy, that they operate in terms of metonymy and metaphor. Jakobson and Morris have made similar moves in their studies of aphasia and in their classification of modern art, literature, and film. In these efforts we can see attempts to join semiotics with literary criticism, psychoanalytic theory, film theory, and the study of disturbed thought processes. Metz (1982) has systematically applied these concepts to the semiotic, psychoanalytic analysis of film.

CONCLUSION

In this chapter, we have shown how human groups form the basis for language, thought, symbolic behavior, humor, daydreaming, and dreaming, and we have discussed the various forms of analysis that constitute sociolinguistics. Language behavior is universal among all human groups, although each separate group tends to develop a special language of its own as an expression of its particular points of view, interests, and way of life.

Concern with human groups is a central focus of social psychology. Groups vary widely in size, duration, and complexity. Individuals who are born into groups or join them must learn the appropriate behavior and beliefs of each. A basic characteristic of groups is that they exist because of and through communication, especially spoken and written language. Language is always a group product; it is both an intrinsic part of the social heritage and the mechanism by which this heritage is transmitted from one generation to the next.

SUGGESTED READINGS

Cooley, C. H. (1902). *Human nature and social order.* New York: Scribner. The essential work of a forerunner of contemporary symbolic interactionist thought.

Fine, G. A., & Leighton, L. F. (Eds.). (1993). Symbolic interaction [Special section]. *Sociology of Dreams, 16,* 95-145. A special journal section devoted to the sociological analysis of dreams.

Mead, G. H. (1934). *Mind, self, and society: From the standpoint of a social behaviorist.* Chicago: University of Chicago Press. Mead, along with Cooley, laid the foundations for much of the material in this chapter.

Strauss, A. L. 1993. *Continual permutations of action.* New York: Aldine de Gruyter. A very important extension of Mead's work that offers a grounded theory of language, meaning, embodied social action, social worlds, and negotiated orders.

STUDY QUESTIONS

1. Briefly discuss the relationship between language and culture as a performance text.
2. What are the key assumptions of conversational analysis?
3. Compare and contrast psychoanalytic (Freudian, Jungian) and sociological theories of dreams and their meanings.

5

Emotions and the Naming Process

In this chapter we take up the following topics: (a) the body and pain; (b) emotional experience; (c) madness, the uncanny, aphasia, and Alzheimer's disease; (d) body images, medicine, AIDS, and anorexia nervosa; and (e) opiate and other addictions. We intend to explore the internal environment of the human so that we can gain a deeper understanding of how language and symbols structure human experience. The topics addressed here reflect points of entry into the inner, symbolic world of the human body.

The Body and Pain

The human body, or the "lived body," as Merleau-Ponty (1968, p. 256) calls it, is a complex structure. At one level, it is a physiological body and a sounding board for bodily sensations. At another level, it is a source of experience for the person, as when one feels fatigued after a long day at work. The body is also a source of information about the person; as others gaze upon an individual, or catch him or her in a glance, they gather and make inferences based on the body's appearance (Stone, 1962).

Human beings have a threefold relationship to their bodies. They are their bodies. They live, so to speak, inside their bodies, and they can get outside their bodies, and view themselves, sometimes objectively, as when they consider their reflections in a mirror. The lived body is the point of reference for the person's social and emotional experiences in the social world; it is also the symbolic and physical extension of the person in the situation. No dualism is implied in this statement, for the body and the self are intertwined presences in the world of experience.

French physiologist Claude Bernard has said that the stability of the internal environment is an indispensable condition for a free life. This statement points up the fact that in the routine business of living we tend not to pay much attention to our bodies as long as they remain healthy and respond properly in their customary manner. Our attention is focused much more on the outside world and on external events. In certain situations, however, we receive from the body unusual types of messages to which we are not accustomed. These experiences include pain, anxiety, and other types of problematic or extraordinary sensations, such as those involved in sexual activity or those experienced by psychotics or drug users. Experiences of this kind require that we learn how to respond to them, cope with them, label them, and interpret what they signify. For example, on first using marijuana, a person must commonly learn both how to identify the effects and how to enjoy them.

The preceding points are vividly attested to by that pervasive and seemingly quite physiological phenomenon known as pain. Most of us are likely to recognize that "pain is subjective," despite its physiological sources. Pain is rooted in the body, of course, and in its internal malfunctioning or in wounds received from the outside. People with different physical constitutions appear to have different capacities to withstand pain, as well as different thresholds for feeling pain. Also, people from different ethnic backgrounds reveal varying propensities to define and act on pain and illness. Nevertheless, there is no one-to-one relation between some physiological experience and the sensation of feeling a particular pain. In short, the messages coming from within the body that we label "pain" are interpreted just as any other perceptions are. Like other perceptions, pain has a private coloration, but its meanings are deeply social in nature; and as with other meanings, we act upon them.

Among pain's properties are its (a) placement (where within or on the surface of the body), (b) frequency of appearance, (c) duration, (d) degree of intensity, and (e) quality—as described using adjectives such as *burning, searing, flooding, annoying.* These properties seem "natural" to pain, but they are also matters of definition and social experience. If a person's knowledge of internal organs is imperfect or vague, then he or she will attribute pain to "the stomach area," "in there," or "down there" (pointing). Children and adults whose vocabularies are inadequate to describe certain pains will use crude approximations, and we may wonder whether they have that intense a pain, or if they really experience it as "searing" rather than as just "burning" or as "lots of pain." Experience plays a part, too, as when a sufferer of occasional backaches comes to recognize the beginnings of a severe and lengthy "session" if she does not quickly correct her sitting position.

Pain is rarely just pain; it is set within a context of meanings. Thus a new or unexpected pain brings about an etiological search—Why this pain? An expected and socially legitimate pain—for example, the experience of childbirth—needs no such search, for its interpretation is obvious. Evaluations as well as interpretations are placed on various pains, as when a dentist angrily reproved a friend of ours, telling him he deserved his toothache because he had neglected his teeth for at least a decade. On occasion, pain can be received joyfully because it stands for something valuable, as in circumcision rites or other rites of passage wherein pain signals passage into manhood. Pain can be endured and accepted as inevitable, as when a man needs an operation that he knows will be followed by a few days of postoperative pain.

In terms of the complexities of "the naming process and the internal environment," the search for etiological meaning is among the most interesting. Ordinary pains get self-diagnosed. However, extraordinary or persistent ones bring the sufferer to some presumably knowledgeable agent—a physician, a faith healer, a pharmacist. Through the person's experience, or through diagnostic procedures, the agent will arrive at some decision about what in the body is causing the pain. If the agent cannot find a reasonable explanation, he or she has various options: to say so, to give a false answer, to refer the client to another agent, or to suggest a psychological rather than a physiological cause. Modern medicine frequently employs technology and a complex division of labor to obtain proper diagnostic answers—requiring the drawing and examination of blood, taking and reading of X rays, and examinations by specialists. Some diagnostic procedures themselves inflict pain, so that the patient must undergo further pain in order to be rid of a major pain. Of course, procedural pain is usually of short duration; but sometimes, as with bone biopsies, it is exceedingly hurtful.

Thus in discussing a phenomenon like pain, the social psychologist moves from considerations of "naming" internal bodily occurrences to quite external considerations involving interaction, social relationships, and alternations in identity and self-image.

Emotional Experience

Emotional experience provides an excellent example of a type of behavior that involves an unusually complex combination of events and processes of different natures occurring at different levels. Thus an emotional response may be triggered by an external social situation; as it occurs, it often conspicuously involves visceral and glandular changes that are accompanied by psychological processes. Emotional reactions traditionally have been regarded as distinct from other types of responses (such as the cognitive), probably because they are not readily communicable and seem, therefore, to have a distinctively private aspect. Different aspects of total emotional response have tended to form the basis for mutually incompatible theoretical formulations found in different disciplines.

The nature of emotion has been a controversial question for centuries, and there are countless theories concerning it. Students of emotion have written about it in terms ranging from the physiological to the cultural. Most of the efforts of psychologists have been concerned with the physiology of emotion; for example, attempts have been made to determine what muscular and glandular patterns of response accompany specific emotions, whether the sources of emotional awareness are in bodily movement or in attitude, and what part of the brain is involved in emotional behavior (see Kemper, 1978; Scheff, 1979).

Like many other aspects of human behavior, our emotions are profoundly affected by the fact that we live in complex societies. To the student of human behavior who seeks to take into account the types of feelings and emotions that are found in various societies, the situations that call them forth, and the many-sided conventionalized ways in which they are expressed, it appears that they are to an amazing extent regulated, prescribed, and even defined by groups (Hochschild, 1983; Lofland, 1985).

What arouses given emotions is determined by social situations rather than physiological processes. For example, embarrassment is caused by different situations in different societies. Similarly, shame is an emotion aroused in accordance with prevailing social definitions. Even an emotion like fear is not invariably kindled by specific situations; in one society fear may be aroused by the occurrence of a bad omen—such as an eclipse—and in another society by anticipation of the collapse of the stock market. As we shall see, the emotions connected with even such commonly assumed biological drives as sex and hunger are also aroused by different situations in different societies.

The expression of emotions is also socially influenced, for the physiology of any emotion does not determine how the emotion will be expressed. In our society, anger is likely to be shown by sudden, impatient, or violent movements, but it may be expressed differently in other societies. In the United States, one may express love in one way in the bedroom and in another way in public; anger is manifested differently in private and in the presence of company; expressions of hate may be avoided in the presence of children, but may be displayed when children are not present.

Much anthropological research has pointed to another, more subtle aspect of emotional patterning. Each society provides differential conditions of life for its members, so that certain emotions are aroused more frequently and intensely in one society than in another (see Ekman, 1980).

Many emotions are undoubtedly universal, but because the conditions of life vary so widely and the experiences of groups are so diverse, allowance must be made for variation from society to society. In societies where there is no elaborate organization of social classes, emotions that have to do with class mobility and the maintenance and change of status can scarcely exist. The very languages of such societies lack vocabulary for indicating the experiences and the events around which these emotions occur. Americans cannot easily imagine how it would be to experience a medieval sense of religious awe, nor can they appreciate the abasement of self that a caste system implies or feel the anticipation of the Brahmin as he looks forward to death and reincarnation (see Perinbanayagam, 1985).

The Linguistic Aspect of Human Emotions

The arousal and expression of emotion may be categorized into three phases, listed here in their order of occurrence:

1. A stimulus or situation that is defined or interpreted in certain ways

TABLE 5.1 Interpretations of an Act and Resulting Emotions

Act	*Situation*	*Definition*	*Resulting Emotion in the Victim*
Slap in the face	two quarreling people	insult	fury and resentment
Slap in the face	in a play	playacting	none or simulated
Slap in the face	father slaps child for lying	punishment	shame
Slap in the face	20-month-old child slaps father	good spirits	amusement

2. An internal response to the defined situation, involving both physiological and symbolic processes
3. An outward conventionalized expression (by means of words, gestures, facial expressions, and the like) that serves to indicate the emotion to others

A given external situation or act does not call forth an emotion until the individual has interpreted it in a certain way. The emotion is a response not to a raw stimulus as such, but to a defined, classified, and interpreted stimulus, to signs with meanings that vary according to situation, as shown in Table 5.1. The physiological aspects of emotional response (such as rising blood pressure, a changed heartbeat, and increased activity of the ductless glands) are not learned forms of behavior. On the other hand, the symbolic processes involved in emotion are learned. The third phase of emotional behavior has sometimes been called the "mimicry" of emotion because persons may voluntarily utilize the conventional means of emotional expression without actually experiencing the genuine emotion. Actors do this constantly, but people in ordinary life commonly use the same sort of mimicry as they strive to conform to the polite usages of social intercourse.

The actual learning of emotional behavior considerably reverses the chronology of the arousal and expression of emotion just discussed. The child is first encouraged to imitate the outward manifestations of adult emotions, even though he may not grasp the significance of a particular situation, such as a funeral. Only as the child acquires a better understanding of the significance of death, for example, will he be able actually to feel the expected emotions and conform inwardly as well as outwardly.

An adult who moves into a new social group may find that the modes of emotional expression of the group seem strange at first. The pressure to conform causes the person to adopt the external forms of behavior quickly, even though at first she may be merely playacting. As the person adopts the group's perspectives and begins to see the world as other people see it, her playacting becomes instead a genuine expression of experienced emotions.

We have been speaking of the first phase as if the stimulus that arouses the emotional response always comes from outside the organism. Actually, in humans the stimulus may lie within the symbolic processes. This can be seen plainly in the case of the arousal of emotion through daydreaming. A soldier may dream of going overseas and become fearful at the "thought" of it. Fantasy may also revolve around past events. While fantasizing, a person may recall a past insult and undergo emotions similar to those that were aroused by the actual insult; or the individual may reinterpret the event, and perhaps laugh once she realizes no insult had been intended. Whether in daydreaming forward or backward in time, the stimulus to emotional arousal is not externally present.

Humans are aware of their own emotional responses, and they name, evaluate, and interpret them in accordance with definitions provided by the groups to which they belong. People not only experience anger, they label their feelings as such and are able to tell other people about them. Because of this capacity, humans have the power to control and inhibit their own feelings to some degree. Thus a devoutly religious person who recognizes that she is becoming angry may check her response and seek a new interpretation of the situation that will allow her to respond, for example, by feeling compassion for the person who has insulted her. An individual may stifle an almost uncontrollable impulse to laugh in church at a minister's gesture by formulating a quick redefinition—perhaps taking the form of "This is church, laughing would be awful" or of acute fear of embarrassment or shame (see Hochschild, 1983).

Cognitive-Social Aspects of Emotion

As the preceding discussion indicates, it is difficult to conceive of an experience that is purely emotional or an emotion that is purely physiological. Apart from the difficulties inherent in the idea of a purely physiological experience, Skinner (1953, pp. 161-162) has observed that the scientific study of emotional behavior that is based on the idea that each emotion has its own characteristic pattern of emotional response offers a far less reliable basis for identifying emotion than does common sense.

A decisive consideration here is that many of the physiological accompaniments of emotion can be produced through the use of drugs. When this happens in a situation that has no emotional significance, subjects do not report that they feel "angry," "afraid," or "unhappy," but rather that they feel as though they were experiencing one of those emotions without actually doing so. This suggests that rapid heart action, increased blood pressure, and other such phenomena do not signify emotion except when they are part of an appropriate behavioral context. In short, even if all the biological aspects of feeling terror were to be artificially produced, an individual evidently would not actually *feel* terror unless there were something in the environment that might cause this feeling. In absence of the appropriate situation, the physiological accompaniments of emotional behavior produce only "mock" emotion, not the real thing.

Schachter and Singer (1962), taking their point of departure from the general idea that the interpretations of internal physiological processes that intrude on consciousness depend on how people view them or what they know about what is happening to them, have performed experiments of special significance to this argument. Subjects were given a drug in a variety of ways for control purposes. Some subjects were grossly misinformed as to what to expect from the drug. The drug given was adrenalin, which normally produces palpitations, hand tremors, and a warm, flushed face. The misinformed subjects who experienced these unexpected effects were then put into different types of emotion-producing situations. The results indicated that they were more prone to become emotionally involved, but that the same state of physical excitation led to different and contradictory types of emotion, depending on the situations in which the subjects were placed. In contrast, subjects who were correctly informed as to the drug being given and its effects tended simply to explain how they felt as a consequence of the drug. The investigators concluded that when individuals experience physical excitation they do not understand, they tend to account for it with whatever cognitive schemes are available to them.

The situation faced by the subjects in Schachter and Singer's experiments was much like that of persons who experience unusual abdominal symptoms and pains that do not fit into any pattern they know about. They are not only likely, but virtually bound to explain them with whatever cognitive terms are available or make sense to them. If they are perplexed, their friends cannot help them, and their symptoms are serious and persistent, they will normally consult a physician who will diagnose their ailment (name it, explain it, indicate its probable cause, apply a cognitive structure to it, and issue prescriptions and instructions to deal with it).

If the essentials of emotional behavior are not physiological, it is incongruous to think of them apart from the cognitive features with which they are inseparably entwined. How, for example, can people be expected to experience fear in a situation in which they are unaware of danger? How can people feel anger at insults if they do not know they have been insulted? As new knowledge accumulates, new threats and new emotion-stimulating situations are created. For example, fear and anger have been generated by reported levels of strontium 90 in the milk or water supply, and by secondhand reports of high radiation levels produced by fallout from distant atomic explosions.

Our discussion suggests that emotion should be viewed as an aspect of certain types of behavior rather than as a distinct form of behavior in itself. The specifically emotional portion of behavior is elicited by the relationship of the emotion-provoking situation to the values of the person as seen by that person.

If we accept the idea of emotion as an aspect of a behavioral sequence within a situation that is cognitively grasped, it is easy to understand that the emotional responses of any two people may be radically different in the same situation. *A*, for example, devoutly religious, believes that his immortal soul is in jeopardy; *B* is certain that she has no immortal soul and cannot, therefore, be worried about it.

It is also interesting to note that, perhaps because the involved multiple phases of emotional experience are sometimes spread out over appreciable intervals of time, the process may be interrupted, so that during a dangerous event no subjective feeling of fear may be noticed. Victims of automobile accidents often report that when their accidents began, events seemed to slow down in a curious way. They may have attended only to this and to the strange sensations created by the spinning or rolling car. The feeling of fear may not have appeared as a completed experience until after the accident. Other self-observations by individuals indicate the same points; it is often remarked that one may observe the first surges of an emotional reaction with a certain detachment and even surprise, and have time to remark to oneself about it. Another observation is that a person can experience strong reactions without knowing for certain what the emotion is—whether it is anger, fear, embarrassment, or self-consciousness.

Emotion as Symbolic Interaction

We can extend these remarks on emotional behavior by arguing that the processes of symbolic interaction organize all emotional experiences. By this we mean that the process of self-reflection, the organization of social acts, the meaning of time, and the labels we bring to our emotional experiences are themselves based on the interactional process. We suggest that emotions are *embodied self-feelings that arise from emotional social acts persons direct to self or have directed toward them by others* (Denzin, 1984a, p. 50). Emotions are social acts and self-interactions; self-feelings refer to any emotion the person may feel—including bodily sensations, intentional feeling states such as grief, and feelings of self such as shame or guilt. Every feeling a person has unfolds within a process that involves, first, a sense of feeling in terms of awareness; second, a sense of self feeling the feeling; and third, a set of self-feelings (for example, guilt, shame) in relation to the emotion.

Linguistically, we can see how every emotional word in our language contains hidden referents to self and to other people. We feel embarrassed, for example, in situations where we have acted in a way that causes others to react negatively to us. Emotional terms and labels, then, are interactional words; they locate persons in emotional situations. We can never have a completely private emotion, nor can we have an emotion or self-feeling that is not felt in the real or imagined presence of others.

Types of Emotions

We can distinguish four types of lived emotional experience. The first type is *sensible feelings,* or sensations felt in the lived body (pain, for example). Sensible feelings are not deliberately produced by the person. The second type of lived emotional experience is termed *feelings of the lived body.* These are feelings captured by such words as *sorrow, despair, happiness,* and *anger.* Lived feelings communicate an emotional definition of the person in the situation. People, for example, can see our grief or "feel" our sorrow about the loss of a loved one.

Intentional value-feelings constitute the third form of lived emotion. These are feelings that reference the ways we intend or want to feel in a situation, but they are not the actual feelings we will experience. These are feelings about feelings, so to speak. If a person is ill and vomits, and then turns back on this experience, he may experience a feeling of self-anger—"Why did I eat that last piece of rich dessert anyway?" In this example, the person intends a feeling about an emotional experience he has just felt.

Intentional value-feelings can reference feelings that will occur in the future or events that have happened in the past. These feelings are produced through self-conversations, and they may or may not be accompanied by sensible feelings or feelings of the lived body.

Feelings of the self, or the moral person, are the last form of lived emotion. Unlike intentional value-feelings, which originate in values that lie outside actual emotional experiences, feelings of the self originate from within the self and are located in the inner stream of experience of the person. These feelings may carry deep implications about how we feel about ourselves. Consider the following excerpts from Malcolm Lowry's novel *Under the Volcano* (1947/1984). A deep wrenching of the self from its inner moral meanings is illustrated by the crisis of Lowry's protagonist, Geoffrey Firmin, known as the Consul. At one point, the Consul thinks about "that bloody nightmare he was forced to carry around with him everywhere upon his back, that went by the name of Geoffrey Firmin" (p. 223). Later, the Consul prays:

> "Deliver me from this dreadful tyranny of self. I have sunk low. Let me sink lower still, that I may know the truth. Teach me to love again, to love life.... Let me truly suffer. Give me back my purity, the knowledge of the Mysteries, that I have betrayed and lost.—Let me be truly lonely, that I may honestly pray. . . . Destroy the world!" he cried in his heart. (p. 289)

Here we see a lonely, frightened individual, feeling a series of self-feelings that cut to the core of who he sees himself as being. Self-feelings are part of being human.

In studying and interpreting emotional experiences, it is important to keep in mind the following points: First, all emotions have a linguistic foundation; second, all emotions are interpreted by the self, at some level of awareness; and third, the way in which the self and the lived body enter into the experiencing of emotion varies according to whether the emotions are sensible feelings, feelings of the lived body, intentional value-feelings, or feelings of the self.

Interpreting Drug Experiences

Increasing attention to the effects of drug use has accompanied the growth in popularity of marijuana, cocaine, and other drugs among persons of the middle class. The effects of a drug are not easy to communicate to those who have not experienced them. In order to conceptualize what such an experience is like, one must either talk with and observe those who know from direct experience or try it oneself. The final authority on the question of how drug effects are experienced by a given user is the user and no one else.

Carrying the argument further, we can note, as Becker (1953, 1973) has pointed out with respect to marijuana, that users must generally learn how to "smoke pot," how to identify the effects, and how to feel "high" or "stoned." The most common report of those who try marijuana for the first time is that they feel nothing; the first experience may also be unpleasant. This may be due to faulty technique or false expectations—and if the individual's expectations are based on reports in the mass media, they will almost certainly be wrong. Because beginners look for effects that marijuana does not produce, they fail to notice those that it does produce. This error is quickly corrected by the first-time users' associates, who assist users in learning and validating in their own experience the viewpoints and shared conceptions that cause marijuana users to experience the effects as pleasurable.

A fairly elaborate ideology and mystique has grown up around the drug from its collective use and from the sharing of experiences with it. Its dangers, techniques of dealing with uncommon effects, ways of counteracting excessive doses, and the effects of drugs on various activities—all become part of an ideology that carries the authority of a considerable tradition built up by generations of users. Just as with alcohol, marijuana users are instructed in what to expect under various circumstances and therefore are not alarmed by what the drug does to them.

Similar points can be made concerning alcohol, but in this case there are many millions of people who have experienced various possible effects and have described them to others. Because knowledge of alcohol's effects is widespread in U.S. culture, the alcohol experience seems less mysterious and less subjective than do the experiences associated with LSD, cocaine, or marijuana. The person who gets a hangover for the first time and takes it too seriously is promptly reassured by the laughter and advice of associates, who instruct her about hangovers and what to do about them. If, while drunk, she has done things that would otherwise be viewed as proof of a psychotic condition, or if she blacks out and cannot remember what happened the night before, this too is explained as ordinary and unalarming. At higher levels of sophistication, such as those represented in Alcoholics Anonymous, other more advanced phenomena such as "the shakes" and delirium tremens are similarly handled by group definitions consensually validated by the experiences of other members.

Becker (1967) has applied this kind of reasoning to LSD, which is a drug of greater potency than alcohol or marijuana. As a new drug in the 1960s, LSD had not been thoroughly explored as a pleasure-producing agent. Consequently, there was uncertainty even in the minds of users as to what to expect, what the dangers were, and how they might be dealt with. It is noteworthy, however, that users at the time already emphasized that before taking a "trip" one should be briefed and coached on what to expect and what to do when the effects took hold. Techniques for dealing with bad trips were reported. We suspect that similar processes are now occurring for cocaine users, especially in light of the growing numbers of deaths associated with cocaine use.

Madness, the Uncanny, and Aphasia

French psychiatrist Charles Blondel (1928a, 1928b), speculating some years ago on the uncanny impression that the psychotic creates in the nonpsychotic, proposed an interesting and relevant interpretation of this type of mental abnormality. Some of his ideas were derived from Durkheim, who has been an influential figure in the development of American sociological thinking.

According to Blondel, the ordinary activity of an individual presupposes a smoothly functioning internal psychological and biological environment, and goes on against a background of internal stimuli arising from various parts of the body and from normal psychological reactions. Blondel calls these internal stimuli, which are largely ignored except when they signal a disturbance of bodily equilibrium, or homeostasis, the "kinesthetic mass." In the nonpsychotic person these processes are the setting within which the higher functions occur. The socialized individual responds to these internal stimuli in terms of the categories provided by the society of which he or she is a member. Thus people respond to certain types of internal stimulation by reporting, "I am hungry" or "My foot is asleep."

Blondel believed that in the psychotic, this kinesthetic mass is disturbed; the individual becomes aware of internal stimuli that he or she cannot identify with the usual labels. Psychotics develop the notion that curious and fantastic things are happening within them, and when they attempt to describe their experiences to other people, they are not understood. Others regard the remarks of psychotics as queer or crazy; their responses lead the psychotics to withdraw, and this in turn accentuates the break in communication.

Finding themselves rebuffed by others, psychotics withdraw into their own private worlds but continue to attempt to adapt themselves verbally to their strange sensations. In their struggle to assimilate their essentially unique and unassimilable experiences, they build up ideas that seem fantastic and senseless to others. The curious speech and distorted reasoning of the psychotic as conceived of by Blondel is an attempted symbolic adaptation to an organic disturbance. Blondel does not account for the origin and nature of this organic disturbance; presumably, however, the disorder would be in the central nervous system, whatever its causes might be.

Blondel's theory, whether or not it will stand the test of verification, has interesting implications because it avoids the usual mind-body fallacy. Even if all psychoses should turn out to have organic causes, the study of psychological symptoms would not be irrelevant to the study and understanding of psychotics.

H. S. Sullivan's (1953) conception of schizophrenia resembles Blondel's, for Sullivan also stresses the crucial role of the uncanny and of the inability to communicate and designate it. But he does not make physiological stimuli the cornerstone of his analysis:

> In the schizophrenia state, very early types of referential process occur within clear awareness, to the profound mystification of the person concerned. And since many of these referential processes are literally historically identical with the composition of the not-me components in personality, their presence is attended by uncanny emotions. . . . [These] schizophrenic processes which we encounter represent attempts on the sufferer's part to communicate types of processes that most of

> us created to have within awareness by the time that we are two and one-half. (p. 327)

According to Sullivan, there are three modes of experience: the prototaxic, the parataxic, and the syntaxic. These terms refer to the manner in which experience is registered and to the nature and degree of inner elaboration that it is accorded. In the prototaxic mode, there is an absolute minimum of inner elaboration, and experience consists mainly of discrete series of momentary states that cannot be recalled or discussed. The syntaxic mode, in contrast, involves a maximum of inner organization and elaboration; because it is fully encompassed by symbolic formulation and is logically ordered, it can be discussed and completely communicated to others. In the parataxic mode of experience, which lies between the two, experience is partially organized or organized in a quasi-logical manner, but there are also elements of which the individual is unaware. Parataxic experience can be discussed by the adult human subject, but Sullivan (1953) states:

> The mode which is easiest to discuss is relatively uncommon . . . experience in the syntaxic mode; the one about which something can be known, but which is somewhat harder to discuss, is experience in the parataxic mode; and the one which is ordinarily incapable of any discussion is experience in the prototaxic or primitive mode. (p. 29)

Children's earliest experiences (as we note in Chapters 7 and 8) are in the prototaxic mode, but they quickly progress to the parataxic once they start to make sense out of their environment and note certain interconnections and simple sequences. Lower animals also are capable of reaching the parataxic level, according to Sullivan. The syntaxic mode appears with the learning of language and is hence confined to human beings, although Sullivan emphasizes that it is rarely possible for us to express all aspects of an experience in words. Roughly, we can say that the three modes represent the incommunicable or ineffable (prototaxic), the partially communicable (parataxic), and the wholly communicable (syntaxic). This scheme allows a considerable place for unconscious behavior without positing an "unconscious mind" or instinctual urges as the mainsprings of behavior.

Although Sullivan stresses childhood experiences as the probable origin of some psychoses, he does not rule out organic causes in other psychoses. Blondel, on the other hand, emphasizes organic causes but leaves open the question of the nature and causes of these organic conditions. Both stress that the psychoses conventionally said to be characterized by a radical detachment from reality—or, in our terms, by a breakdown in the communication mechanisms—are linked with disturbances within the internal environment that are uncanny and incommunicable. The symptoms of psychoses are conceived by psychiatrists in terms of the individual's efforts to grapple with this situation. These conceptions are clearly related and applicable to certain types of effects produced by drugs, such as those we discuss later in this chapter.

Interestingly, strange internal experiences of the type Sullivan and Blondel address, and those produced by certain drugs, are often interpreted in religious or mystic terms. There are numerous cults and religious groups in different parts of the world that either are organized around the use of substances that change mental functioning or include the use of such substances as an integral part of their ceremonies and rituals. The psychedelic movement that focused on LSD is one case of this; the peyote religion that flourishes among American Indians is another prominent example (Aberle, 1966, p. 28). In Mexico the "sacred mushrooms" from which psilocybin is obtained have been used for centuries, and were known to the Aztecs as "God's flesh" (Solomon, 1964, p. 153). In India and the Middle East, hemp or marijuana has been linked for centuries with religious beliefs and practices (Carstairs, 1954; Ebin, 1961). Some writers have suggested that the origins of religion may be traced to experiences of the type that scientists today label "psychotic" or "drug induced."

Aphasia and Related Neurological Disorders

We have noted how various forms of madness and the uncanny illuminate the complex relationship between people's internal environments and their speech and language abilities. We shall now briefly discuss aphasia—a language disturbance produced by lesion or disease in the brain—and related neurological disturbances that alter the "normal" relationships among speech, thought, and the internal environment.

Gardiner (1987) observes that research on "cognitive incapacitates following damage to the brain . . . relies heavily on the travesties of war. As in the era of the First World War, much was learned during the Second World War about aphasia . . . agnosia (difficulty in recognition) and other forms of mental pathology consequent upon injury to the brain" (p. 220).

Aphasia is often, though not necessarily, brought about by cerebral injury. Aphasic conditions may also be produced under hypnosis or by traumatic experiences. The loss of function associated with aphasia can assume various forms, including the inability to read, write, or name familiar objects. Consider the following statement made by a young Russian soldier who during World War II sustained a severe brain injury that altered his ability to read, think, speak, and write. He is discussing his attempts to write with a pencil:

> I'd forgotten how to use a pencil. I'd twist it back and forth but I just couldn't begin to write. I was shown how to hold it and asked to write something. But when I picked up the pencil all I could do was draw some crooked lines across the paper and finally moved the pencil across the paper. But looking at the mark I'd made it was impossible to tell where I'd started. It looked something like the scribbling of a child. (quoted in Luria, 1972, pp. 71-72)

Often, in the aphasic's world, there is no memory of the past. This means that the patient has difficulty connecting internal, bodily processes with the words that represent those processes. The same Russian soldier quoted above describes trying to relieve himself:

> After dinner, when the other patients were going to sleep, I suddenly had to relieve myself. To put it plainly, I needed the bedpan. But what a complicated thing it was for me to remember the word and call the nurse. For

the life of me I couldn't think of the word *bedpan*. . . . I saw the nurse. . . . I yelled . . . calling her *sister*, a word that suddenly entered my mind: "Sister . . . I also . . . need the . . . what's it!" (quoted in Luria, 1972, pp. 87-88)

Oliver Sacks (1985), professor of neurology at the Albert Einstein College of Medicine, discusses a patient who had suffered a lesion in the visual cortex. The patient had difficulty converting sensations into recognizable objects. When shown a glove, he described it as a continuous surface unfolded on itself with five outpouchings. When by accident he put it on his hand, he exclaimed, "My God, it's a glove!" At the end of one consultation session, the man attempted to put his hat on and instead seized his wife's head, tried to lift it off, and attempted to put it on his own. He had "mistaken his wife for a hat!" (p. 11). This patient's wife made the following statement about his condition:

He does everything singing to himself. But if he is interrupted and loses the thread, he comes to a complete stop, doesn't know his clothes—or his own body. He sings all the time—eating songs, dressing songs, bathing songs. . . . He can't do anything unless he makes it a song. (quoted in Sacks, 1985, p. 45)

The patient was a doctor of music; he learned to use melody, sound, and rhythm as a guide that gave meaning to his actions, but had lost the ability to connect his thoughts with words and the actions of his body.

In the 1890s, Charles Sherrington, a British neurologist, discovered what he called our sixth sense, which he named *proprioception*. By this he referred to our normal ability to know where our bodies are, what position or posture we are in, and so on. We know this subliminally, without looking. Some aphasics appear to lose this proprioceptive sixth sense.

Sacks had a patient named Christina, who, after routine surgery, developed an acute infection in her nerves that permanently destroyed her proprioceptive nerve fibers. She became, and remains, disembodied. She lacks all instinctive sense of her body, its position, its posture, and its movements. She feels that her body is dead, not-real, not-hers, blind and deaf to itself.

There are a number of different ways to classify aphasia. In a review of the research available up to the early 1980s, Wallace (1984, p. 80) suggests that there are two basic types of aphasia. The first involves language disturbances that primarily affect the ability to speak (expressive, or Broca's, aphasia), and the second involves the ability to understand language (receptive, or Wernicke's, aphasia). Broca was the first to link types of aphasia with areas of the brain. He demonstrated an association between damage in the left hemisphere and aphasia. Patients who suffer brain damage in this area of the brain usually show disturbances in the ability to produce written and spoken language. They often speak slowly and with difficulty. They display poor articulation, improper sentence structure, and omission of small grammatical words and word endings. They may, however, understand written and spoken speech and often have the ability to sing familiar songs. Wernicke identified another type of aphasia that results in disturbances involving how language is understood, as well as in speaking (see Wallace, 1984, p. 80). Patients often have fluent and rapid speech, but their utterances are devoid of meaning. Other types of aphasia have also been identified. Word deafness, for example, refers to a patient's inability to understand spoken language, even though he or she can hear normally, read, and write.

Wernicke proposed a theory of language production that is still held to be valid (Wallace, 1984, p. 80). This theory argues that an underlying utterance originates in Wernicke's area (the temporal lobe of the brain) and then is transferred to Broca's area, where a coordinated program for the utterance is produced. This program is then passed to the motor cortex, which "activates the appropriate motor sequences required for the specific utterance" (Wallace, 1984, p. 80). Those theories that explain aphasia in terms of disturbances to specific brain areas are called *localization* theories (Schutz, 1962, p. 263).

The Nature of Aphasic Experience

In analyzing the aphasic's experiences, we must maintain a distinction between inner speech and external speech performances (Schutz, 1962, p. 264). Inner speech finds its expression in thought and in the selection of words and word categories that fit the subject's ongoing flow of experience, including how he or she interprets bodily sensations. External speech performances, or speech acts, locate the inner speech and thought of the subject in a social conversation. In aphasia, this connection between inner thought and outer speech is broken; thought and speech become problematic, and words are no longer immediately and directly linked to experience. Clearly, those theories of aphasia that explain it in terms of localized injuries to specific areas of the brain speak not to language disturbances per se, but rather to disturbance in memory. The aphasic loses the ability to deal with concrete, immediate experience. However, localization theories have problems explaining how the same word, spoken by different people in different contexts, is understood as the same word (Schutz, 1962, p. 270).

Merleau-Ponty (1962) has developed this point. The normal mind is able to organize spontaneously its perceptual field and its symbolic structure. It experiences no breaks or gaps separating sensation, perception, memory, thought, speech, and action. These accomplishments occur in the lived present. The aphasic's mind is incapable of doing this; for the aphasic, the world suddenly becomes strange and problematic. A theory of aphasia that accounts for these disturbances solely in terms of the localization of brain function becomes a mechanistic, physiological account that does not explain how the person engages the world in a continuous process of interaction. Localization theories fall into the dualistic trap of separating mind from body. We can illustrate these points by taking up the introspective reports of some aphasics.

Introspective Reports of Aphasics

Some of the most significant materials on aphasic thought are found in the work of Head (1926). The comments of some of Head's patients are interesting and allow us insight into their condition. One of them said:

> When I think of anything, everything seems to be rolling along. I can't hold it. . . . I can see what it is. I seem to see it myself, but I can't put it properly into words like you ought to. I can see what it is myself like. My mind won't stop at any one thing. They keep on rolling. Myself, I imagine when you're talking you're only thinking of what you're talking about. When I'm talking to anybody it seems a lot of things keep going by. (quoted in Head, 1926, p. 256)

Another patient attempted to explain the difficulty he had in finding his way around London:

> "You see it's like this: with me it's all in bits. I have to jump like this," marking a thick line between two points with a pencil, "like a man who jumps from one thing to the next. I can see them but I can't express. Really it is that I haven't enough names." (p. 371)

A number of comments made by Head's patients indicate that images and the flow of imagery are profoundly affected by the loss of language that occurs in aphasia. Head always asked his patients to draw pictures, both from a model and from memory. One of the patients who had drawn a jug from a model could not draw the jug from memory. He commented:

> I was trying to see the glass bottle: the picture seemed to evade me. I knew it was a bottle, and I could describe the drawing. But when it came to seeing it as a picture, I was more or less nonplussed. I often seem to have got the picture, but it seemed to evade me. (quoted in Head, 1926, p. 193)

When this patient was questioned further it became clear that he experienced images, but they appeared to be unstable, and he could not control or evoke them at will. He said, "The more I try to make them come the more difficult it is to get in touch with them, as one might say" (p. 193).

Head performed the following test with one of his patients: He rolled bits of paper into wads and had a contest with the patient to see who could toss the improvised balls more accurately into a basket placed some distance away. The aphasic proved more adept than Head. Then a screen was moved in front of the basket so that the basket was not visible, and the contest was repeated. This time Head did far better than the patient; the patient was at a loss as to what to do. He explained his difficulties:

> When I could see the basket I could follow the line of vision; when it was in the same place . . . I'd seen the basket before you put the screen there; I knew you hadn't changed the position, but in some odd way I didn't feel perfectly confident in my own mind that it was in that position. (quoted in Head, 1926, p. 208)

We noted in Chapter 3 that through the internalized use of language, humans are able to imagine objects and events that are removed in time and space. This point is corroborated in the study of aphasia, for the aphasic's flow of imagery is so disturbed that he or she is unable to visualize objects adequately when they are not in view.

The inability of some aphasics to deal with objects they cannot see or touch is brought out in a curious manner by their inability to strike an imaginary match on an imaginary matchbox, to drive an imaginary nail with a nonexistent hammer, or to demonstrate with an empty glass how one drinks water. These same patients can strike actual matches, drive actual nails, and drink water from a glass when they are thirsty. Goldstein (1940) describes these and other inabilities of the aphasic as a regression from an abstract or categorical attitude toward the world to a more concrete attitude.

Disturbances of Voluntary Activities

Clearly, aphasics appear to have lost a certain flexibility of orientation, so that they no longer seem at home in the world. Their inner life is impoverished and simplified, and freedom of thought and action is largely lost. Aphasics are more or less at the mercy of the external stimuli that play upon them.

Aphasics are often able to function normally in simple, concrete relations. But when required to act on the basis of long-range goals or abstract principles or merely of remembered events, objects, or persons, as all people constantly are, aphasics tend to fail. This limitation to the concrete present makes impossible many of the voluntary, "creative" kinds of human behavior—behavior that seems normal because human beings think about things, events, and people and adapt their behavior to these verbal formulations or interpretations. Aphasics are unable to make these verbal formulations; therefore, their responses are piecemeal and unintegrated. Aphasics respond to each concrete situation as such, and when no immediate demands are made upon them, or when excessive demands are made, they tend to lapse into inactivity or anxiety, realizing that there is something wrong with their inner life.

In a fundamental sense, normal adult social interaction rests upon a person's ability to anticipate and appreciate the actual and possible reactions of other people—in short, to assume the role of another person. The loss of this ability in aphasia (to varying degrees, depending upon the severity of the disorder) thus provides powerful experimental and clinical evidence to support the thesis that language is the basic social and socializing institution.

Language Impairment and Thought

We have said a great deal about language and thought in past chapters, emphasizing that the latter cannot exist without the former. Thought without language is reduced to the level of thinking—if we may call it such—that is characteristic of lower animals. Those who study aphasia sometimes erroneously conceive of thinking and language as two entirely distinct and separate processes. Thinking, speaking to others, and speaking to oneself are inextricably interrelated and dependent processes. Head (1926) has compared the aphasic with a man in solitary confinement whose only contact with the outside world is a defective telephone. Although this comparison is picturesque, it is incomplete; when the aphasic tries to talk to himself to formulate his own thoughts, he uses the same defective telephone.

The normal human finds it difficult to imagine how it feels to be aphasic. There is little in our experience that enables us to project ourselves, as it were, into that position, or to see and experience the impairment of thought that hinges upon the aphasic's speech difficulties. To understand better, suppose you are in a foreign land whose language you know only moderately well. Conversation with others is reduced to simple concrete levels, as you would need considerable facility in the language to exchange views on complicated, abstract, or philosophical matters. It is easier to talk—with the aid of gestures—about concrete objects that are present, such as the immediate scene and the weather. If you try to speak of events long past or far in the future, or of objects out of sight, your vocabulary is insufficient. However, if you try to carry on such a slightly involved conversation, the effort is likely to prove exhausting. As an acquaintance of ours once said:

> I went to bed exhausted every night from trying to speak German, particularly when I was with a lot of German people who were engaging in a crossfire of conversation. It was simply exhausting—after a while you felt you wanted to sit down and recuperate. And you felt absolutely frustrated and bottled up; you wonder if you're ever going to think a complex thought again in your life. You can ask for beer and coffee and potatoes, but when you have to discuss a complex feeling or reaction or analyze a political situation, you're simply stalled. You struggle to speak, but you're reduced to the level of your vocabulary.

Suppose that in addition to conversing with others in the foreign language, you also had to converse with yourself (that is, think) using only this same restricted vocabulary. How difficult it would be to carry on internalized conversation that had any semblance of complexity!

Alzheimer's Disease

It will be instructive to compare aphasia briefly with Alzheimer's disease, which has been called the disease of the century, for it is now the "single most devastating illness of old age" (Gubrium, 1986, p. 38). Alzheimer's leads to a progressive decline in mental functioning; victims experience forgetfulness, depression, disorientation, confusion, and inability to plan and organize activities, including simple daily tasks. It is often called the disease that "dims bright minds" (Gubrium, 1986, p. 39). One Alzheimer's patient's spouse describes her husband's actions:

> I just don't know what to think or feel. It's like he's not even there anymore. . . . He doesn't know me. He thinks I'm a strange woman in the house. He shouts and tries to slap me away from him. . . . he makes sounds more like an animal than a person. Do you think he has a mind left? . . . Sometimes I get so upset that I just pound on him and yell at him to come out to me. (quoted in Gubrium, 1986, p. 41)

Each occurrence of Alzheimer's disease has two victims: the person with the disease and the caregiver. In a particularly insightful interaction analysis, Gubrium (1986) has described how caregivers struggle with the meaning of mind and agency in the Alzheimer patient. Especially distressing for caregivers is the fact that these patients, often the caregivers' spouses or parents, no longer display actions that indicate they know who they are, how they feel, or how they feel toward their caregivers. This leads the caregivers to impute a "hidden mind" to the victims, and behind that hidden mind they impute a biographical theory of "agency" that assumes the victims still love and care for the caregivers. The following two accounts indicate how the caregiver struggles to maintain the belief that the victim still has a mind. A man named Jack is discussing his spouse, who he says is just like the living dead:

> That's why I'm looking for a nursing home for her. I loved her dearly but she's just not Mary anymore. No matter how hard I try, I can't get myself to believe that she's there anymore. . . . I just know that's not her speaking to me but some knee-jerk reaction.

Another caregiver, Sara, replies:

> Well, I know what you've gone through, and I admire your courage, Jack. But you can't be too sure. How do you *really* know that what Mary says at times is not one of those few times she's been able to really reach out to you? You don't really know for sure, do you? . . . I face the same thing day in day out with Richard [her husband]. Can I ever finally close him out of my life and say, "Well, it's done. It's over. He's gone"? How do I know that the poor man isn't hidden some where, behind all the confusion, trying to reach out and say, "I love you, Sara"? [she weeps]. (quoted in Gubrium, 1986, p. 42)

Gubrium's analysis reveals how the spouses and children of Alzheimer's disease victims impute a theory of minded, intentional, loving conduct to them. Such beliefs keep alive the hope that a "mind is still inside," and that that mind still cares for them. In these ways caregivers indicate how mind is a social, interactional process.

There is no known cure for Alzheimer's disease; however, victims of aphasia can be treated and in many cases there is hope of recovery. These two disorders reveal how disturbances in language ability strip from humans their basic abilities to be feeling, thinking, expressive beings.

Body Images and Medicine

As in other areas of symbolic behavior, one must distinguish carefully between the *ideas* that people have of their bodies and the *concepts* of biological scientists of anatomy and physiology. Scientific views, in their turn, should be distinguished from objective reality, which is always somewhat problematic. We are concerned here with popular images of the body and with some of the behavioral consequences that follow from them.

People have always had conceptions of what is inside their skins and how those insides might function. Inasmuch as the study of anatomy arose only recently, and then only in Western cultures, the anatomical ideas of even sophisticated early societies such as that of the ancient Greeks seem crude. Their conceptions of physiology also seem ludicrous and primitive when judged by our standards.

It follows that conceptions of the body's insides and functions vary greatly from society to society. The Chinese practice of acupuncture exemplifies this point. In recent years, some anthropologists studying underdeveloped countries have been concerned with the theoretical and practical consequences of native medical beliefs. Their research reveals the tremendous variety throughout the world in conceptions of the body, its functioning, and the manner in which it should be treated when it does not function normally. Their research also indicates that people believing particular ideas tend to form conceptual systems that are related to other conceptual systems, such as those concerning the supernatural or those having to do with people. Popular medical ideologies also specify the persons who are viewed as capable of diagnosing and dealing with disorders.

Charles Frake (1961) has reported that among the Subanun of Mindanao, there are 186 names of diseases that classify specific illnesses, symptoms, and stages of illness. The diagnostic criteria that distinguish one disease from another are conceptually distinct. Every person is his or her own herbalist, as there is no separate status of diagnostician or curer. Each person diagnoses and names his or her own illness and then turns to appropriate remedies. Elsewhere in the Philippines, another anthropologist has reported that both natural and supernatural causes of illness are recognized, and that one way of staying well is to not violate the society's mores. Five types of practitioners exist, each with his own qualifications, modes of treatment, and types of illness in which he specializes (Nurge, 1961). In still another Philippine community, where sorcery is recognized as a cause of some illnesses, the sorcerer is called upon to cure the supernaturally caused sickness, whereas other types of curers are called on to handle illnesses regarded as biological malfunctions (Lieban, 1966).

Perinbanayagam (1982), in a study of self, society, and astrology in Jaffna, the northern peninsula of the island of Sri Lanka, found that astrologers are key medical personnel in the treatment of mental and physical illnesses. For example, a young woman, aged 20, is brought to an astrologer with her horoscope:

> Once the calculations have been made, the astrologer inquires about the patient, and is told that she is a recent mother (two weeks), suffering from sleeplessness, loss of appetite, "fear," "anxiety" . . . "indifference." Now the astrologer proceeds to do a horoscope for the newly born and then gives the following discourse: "According to the child's horoscope, this period is one of danger to the mother. There is a fault in the child's horoscope—it is, however, temporary, and there is really nothing to worry about. It will pass in time. But go to the temple and do a Navagrapha pùja—pùja to the nine planets." The subject leaves, and subsequent inquiries establish that such a pùja was in fact performed and that the medicine prescribed by the Ayurvedic physician was also taken. In any case, subject recovered from her "postnatal depression." (p. 143)

Here astrology blends with a theory of self, society, and illness. The astrologer prescribes specific lines of action for the patient to take. These actions are believed to be valid treatments for the illness in question. The patient, after all, was relieved of her postnatal depression.

From the viewpoint of modern science, such systems of concepts and the therapies based on them are often erroneous. Indeed, one reason for the increase in research in medical anthropology is that in the underdeveloped countries of Asia, Africa, and South America, various governments are trying to effect some transfer of native allegiance to whatever Western medicine may exist within their countries. Even in the most technologically and scientifically advanced nations, however, ideas generally accepted by the scientific or medical community compete with many other systems of conceptualization.

Manning and Fabrega (1973) have summarized the differences between modern, technologically impersonal medicine and the personalistic medical systems that exist in the so-called underdeveloped societies. They contend that the differences between these medical systems revolve around conceptions of self, society, and the body. Impersonal, modern medical systems have the following characteristics: (a) body and self are seen as separate entities, (b) bodies and/or selves may be sick or normal, (c) the body is described within a biological framework and is seen as a biological machine, and (d) the body is partitioned into parts, systems, and functions. In contrast, personalistic medical systems (a) do not treat the body and the self as different entities, (b) see health and illness as part of the same process, (c) use few biological terms to describe the body, and (d) view the body as a unified whole that is responsive to the social environment of the person.

Western medicine tends to be atomistic, whereas non-Western medicine is holistic. Entirely different ways of perceiving and defining the body (and its illnesses) thus derive from these two conceptual schemes. Westerners have medicalized the body and the mind (O'Neill, 1985, p. 123). Health engineering has produced an industrialization of the lived body; medical technology now provides life-support systems to keep bodies alive long after many patients and their families desire.

The Morality of Medicine

Modern medicine is a decidedly moral enterprise; the consequences of its practices extend far beyond the treatment of illness, disease, and pain. Indeed, many have argued that modern medicine takes a distinctly moral position on defining normal behavior (Foucault, 1980a; O'Neill, 1985; Saukko, 1996, p. 55; Turner, 1984; Walstrom, 1996, p. 79). Furthermore, medicine has shaped the history of the human body and the meanings that have been brought to our bodies.

Take the case of AIDS. This is partly regarded as a sexually transmitted disease; some view it as the "black plague" of the 1980s and 1990s. Homosexuals have been singled out as the population most likely to get and transmit the disease. In many cases, AIDS is associated with illicit or promiscuous sexuality. Professional pronouncements on the disease have approached the level of hysteria, and the public response to AIDS has been likened to medieval attitudes toward leprosy (Turner, 1984, p. 220). Persons with AIDS have been systematically isolated and excluded by the public. Some have been fired from their jobs because they had the disease. In 1986, a political party in one state campaigned using a slogan that called for the killing of all AIDS victims.

One result of the AIDS epidemic has been an emphasis on monogamy, sexual fidelity, and celibacy. In contrast, some within the gay community—members of the group

Sex Panic, for example—equate sexual liberation with nonmonogamy. Sex Panic represents a challenge to the so-called assimilationist, "queer" politics of the larger gay community (see Green, 1998, p. 88; also Preston, 1989, p. 7). Clearly, modern medicine has been anything but morally neutral about AIDS. Indeed, some have suggested that modern medicine has contributed to the latent "homophobic" attitude that already existed in American and other Western societies.

Anorexia nervosa provides another example of how medicine moralizes. Foucault (1980a) argues that one of the consequences of modern medicine has been the "hysterization of women's bodies" (p. 104). He means that certain "disorders" of the body have been found to be peculiar to women. In many cases, the mental illnesses that women have suffered have been found to be caused by their sexuality and their relation to their sexual bodies. Thus, in the late 19th century, women became hysterical and were even hospitalized for it. Like hysteria, anorexia is a disorder almost entirely specific to women. The French psychiatrist Charcot found, in the late 1880s, that hysterical women were anorexic.

Anorexia is an illness found mainly in young women, and it has become a popular diagnosis among medical practitioners. Sociologist Turner (1984, pp. 183-184), following the lead of some feminists, suggests that anorexia is an "illness" that reflects the contradictory expectations of beauty in a consumer society where male criteria of aesthetics predominate. The clinical symptoms of anorexia include at least a 25% loss of body weight, a distorted attitude toward food and eating, and no prior medical illnesses that could account for the disorder.

There are several interpretations of anorexia (see Saukko, 1996, p. 63; also Bordo, 1988). Some argue that it is an attempt by middle-class daughters to exert greater control over their lives. By not eating and by attempting to conform to a cultural concept of thinness and beauty, such women conform to the ethic of consumer beauty. Because anorexia disrupts and often delays the menstrual cycle, extreme dieting may be "associated in puberty with a rejection of sexuality through the suppression of menstruation" (Turner, 1984, p. 185). However, anorexia can end in death. It has been described as

> a disease in which the concept of the whole person is so confused, so dialectically divided, that "I" can at the same time be choosing to live, as the self, and choosing to die, as the body, however unconscious those choices may be . . . both suicide of the schizoid type and anorexia nervosa involve a denial of reality which depends upon an acceptance of a split between self and body. (MacLeod, 1981, p. 88; quoted in Turner, 1984, p. 186)

In recent years men have also been found to have this disorder, as have African American, Latina, and white lesbians, for whom "starving and binging and purging are strategies to cope with racism, classism, poverty and heterosexism" (Saukko, 1996, p. 63). Chinese anorexics have recently been discovered. Anorexia is not an anomaly of Western culture. As Saukko (1996, p. 63) argues, the crystal called anorexia includes many contradictory perspectives, edges, and sides. The multiple discourses on the disease push and pull persons first in one direction and then in another (see also Walstrom, 1996, p. 92).

From a social psychological perspective, the labels of scientific medicine are not statements about "real" disease entities (Turner, 1984, p. 182). They are the effects of particular power-knowledge structures within our society regarding women, sexuality, beauty, health, and illness.

Opiate and Other Addictions

The phenomenon of drug addiction provides a complex example of how behavior is shaped and directed by the ways in which inner experiences are defined. The patterns of use connected with addictive drugs such as opiates, barbiturates, and alcohol contrast sharply with those connected with nonphysically addictive drugs like marijuana and cocaine.

The Fixation Process

An outstanding characteristic of addictive drugs is that withdrawal from them after regular use over a period of a few weeks or more produces an automatic painful physical reaction. Opiate drugs (those derived from the opium poppy) and their synthetic equivalents are the most important drugs of this type. However, alcohol and barbiturates also produce physical dependence and withdrawal distress. Barbiturate withdrawal is more severe and dangerous than opiate withdrawal. Barbiturates are widely prescribed by physicians for insomnia and other ailments; addiction to this type of drug, however, requires that it be used in much larger quantities than those ordinarily prescribed by doctors. The withdrawal distress connected with opiates varies with individuals, and its intensity depends upon duration of use, amount used, and other factors. Withdrawal symptoms form a characteristic pattern that in its severe form is unmistakable. These symptoms begin about 4 to 5 hours after the last injection; if no further drugs are taken, they increase in intensity for about 72 hours, and the more noticeable ones disappear only gradually over a period of about 2 weeks. An injection of drugs during the withdrawal period causes all symptoms to vanish in a matter of minutes. Withdrawal distress occurs in newborn infants whose mothers are addicts and in various animal species when drugs are regularly administered. This shows that the withdrawal reaction is biological in nature; this has led some students to declare that drug addiction is essentially an organic condition or disease.

In view of the publicity given in recent years to teenage addiction, it is not necessary for us to describe addiction or withdrawal distress in detail here. It should be noted, however, that much of the popular literature is aimed at frightening or warning young people; this has led to inaccurate and exaggerated descriptions of the alleged evil physical effects of drug abuse. The facts are that with the full establishment of addiction after several weeks of regular use, a bodily condition of tolerance or "drug balance" is acquired. When this has occurred, the main effect of the drug is to maintain this balance, to prevent withdrawal symptoms, and to cause the addict to feel normal. The user may experience a physical "kick" when he or she takes a shot, especially if it is "mainlined" (injected into the vein), but during the several hours between injections it is exceedingly difficult to determine with certainty whether or not the person is under the influence of the drug. People who take drugs by means other than hypodermic injection (for example, orally) may never have experienced physical pleasure from taking them; this is especially true when the initial use occurs during an illness.

During the initial period of use, several radical changes occur that amount almost to a reversal of the drug's effects. Thus the original depressing effect on bodily functions tends to vanish, to be replaced by a stimulating one. Also, the euphoria of beginning use vanishes and is replaced by the negative effect of relieving withdrawal distress and achieving approximate normality between the shots. Bodily functions originally disturbed by the regular injection of drugs generally return to an approximately normal level when tolerance has built up. The long-continued use of such drugs as morphine or heroin, contrary to popular belief, does not lead to major tissue destruction or to insanity; tooth decay, constipation, and sexual impotence—which are relatively frequent among drug addicts—are not necessary consequences of addiction, and some addicts, especially those who are well-to-do, do not experience them. The principal deleterious effects are psychological in nature and are connected to the taboo and secret nature of the habit, the extreme cost of obtaining a supply of drugs at black market prices, and resulting changes in self-conception, occupation, and social relationships.

In asking why people become addicted to the opiates, we might also ask about the nature of the experience in which the craving for drugs is generated. It will not suffice, as we shall see, to say that the reason is the pleasurable sensations or inner experiences that occur when the drug is used. Marijuana, cocaine, and other substances produce such pleasure without many of the unpleasant consequences associated with opiates, but they are nonaddicting (in a physical sense, that is).

A crucial element in the fixation of addiction appears to be the user's understanding of what is going on. If a person receives drugs unknowingly, he or she will not develop a craving for them. Even if an individual knows that he or she has been receiving morphine regularly, that person will still evidently not get "hooked" if he or she does not grasp the nature of the withdrawal distress that occurs with the cessation of regular use.

It is the repetition of the experience of using drugs to alleviate withdrawal distress (when the latter is recognized and properly identified) that appears to lead rapidly to the changed orientation toward the drug and to the other behavior that constitutes addiction. An addict does not get hooked on the pleasures of opium, but on the experience of relief that occurs immediately after a shot. This effect depends on cognitive elements and is absent when the person does not understand the withdrawal distress that is suffered. Psychologists who rely on reinforcement explanations might describe the process as one in which a response pattern is established by negative reinforcement (that is, the removal of an unpleasant stimulus). These psychologists would leave out the cognitive and emotional aspects of the situation, which, from our point of view, are crucial, as they probably account for a number of aspects of addiction that otherwise appear paradoxical.

To clarify, let us assume that the beginner, on the way to addiction, takes a shot every 4 hours. The theory we present here is that addiction is established in the experiences that occur approximately 10 minutes after each shot, and not by the way the user feels during the other 230 minutes. Those who think of drugs in terms of users being "high" or "stoned" are likely to emphasize the 230 minutes rather than the 10, and to think of addiction in terms of ecstatic pleasure that is often presumed to extend throughout the interval between shots and to be renewed by the next one. A major problem with this view is that addicts (who are, after all, the only real authorities on how they feel) uniformly deny that it is accurate. Between injections they feel normal, or, as one user remarked on a television program, the way one feels after a good breakfast.

The Pleasure Theory

Those who try to explain heroin addiction in terms of pleasure ordinarily emphasize that the pleasure of the "high" is the key to addiction. They may admit that between shots, during the steady state—as opposed to impact effects immediately after—the fully addicted individuals may feel normal. Nevertheless, they insist—and many addicts also contend—that the high is the key motivating factor. Addicts often describe this experience in ecstatic terms (see Lindesmith, 1975; McAuliffe & Gordon, 1974).

What is wrong with this view? It is essentially a tautology, like a person saying a disease is caused by a high fever or a man explaining that he is in love with a woman because she makes him feel wonderful—that is, the condition that is said to explain the phenomenon is simply a part of the phenomenon itself. The addict's assertion that she "loves" the high that heroin produces is only an indication that she is addicted; it does not tell us why she loves the heroin high or anything about the learning process through which she acquired this attitude.

To explore this line a bit further: The initial experience with heroin is often perceived as unpleasant or unimpressive, or may not even be noticed, almost exactly the same as with initial marijuana use. Even when the first experience is pleasurable, the attitude it then engenders scarcely compares to what it later becomes in addition. This is readily seen in the contrast between reports on heroin or morphine effects given by the same persons before and after their addiction. This means that falling in love with the effects of heroin does not occur prior to addiction, and therefore cannot be viewed as a causal factor, given that causes must precede effects, not follow them.

We can understand what happens to the heroin addict by contrasting the addict's attitude with that of a hospital patient. We may represent the total of an individual's life activities and concerns with a large circle. The hospital patient who has, let's say, received morphine for 3 weeks regularly without knowledge and been withdrawn from it

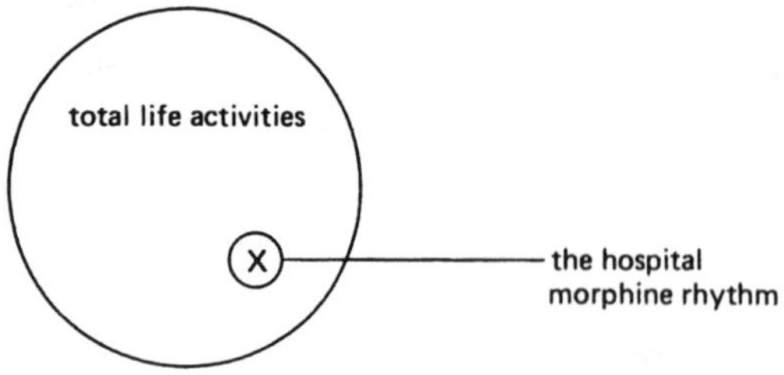

Figure 5.1. Hospital Patient's Experience With Morphine

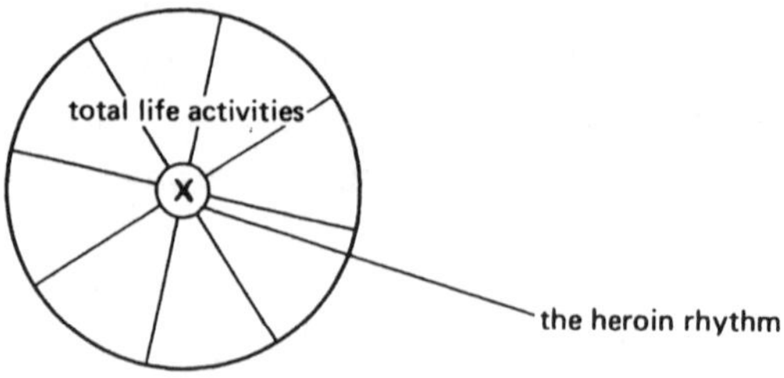

Figure 5.2. Addict's Experience With Heroin

may be represented as shown in Figure 5.1. The hospital experience for such a person remains an isolated, minute item of experience, which he or she may occasionally recall or talk about, but that has little influence on the remainder of the individual's life, despite his or her having been physically dependent on the morphine and having experienced its effects.

In contrast, the addict's situation appears as shown in Figure 5.2. The rhythm of regular "fixes" of the drug moves into the center of the person's attention, as he or she becomes addicted, or falls in love with, or learns to crave the drug. All other activities tend to be progressively drawn into the orbit of the heroin rhythm, organized around it, and subordinated to it.

At this point, those who assume that heroin must produce intense pleasure to be as powerfully addicting as it is have problems explaining the apparent absence of such pleasure in the addict between shots. Far from being a happy person, the addict is one of the most miserable and unhappy types in our society. Strategic devices used to salvage the pleasure theory are to deny the addict's claim that he or she feels normal between shots, and to argue that the addict continues to use drugs in a futile attempt to recapture the original euphoria of early use during the "honeymoon" period. This comes to an end after a number of weeks, like other honeymoons.

Relapse

If we ask why people who have been "hooked" tend to relapse after they have been apparently "cured," the answer implied by the viewpoint presented here is clear in its broad outlines. To be hooked on drugs means to be pervasively changed by experience, to acquire new conceptions and attitudes as well as new knowledge of one's own body and its capabilities and the effects of the drug. This experience in many respects is comparable to that of having one's first sexual experience or going to war. These are not experiences of which one can be readily "cured," even when they lead to unhappiness or disaster. Similarly, after people have been hooked on drugs like heroin or morphine, their changed conceptions and new knowledge remain after the drugs are taken away, and create in them an impulse to relapse. Thus they sometimes resist this impulse for varying periods of time, but it is doubtful that it can ever be wholly eradicated.

Paradoxes and Problems

Among the many paradoxical aspects of opiate addiction are the apparently contradictory reports on the subjectively experienced effects of these drugs. Nonaddicts, given single shots of heroin and placebos without their knowing which, report greater pleasure from the placebos than from the heroin. Hospital patients who are given morphine regularly over periods of time sufficient to establish physical dependence, as we have indicated, may be prevented from becoming addicted by being kept ignorant of the drug they are receiving and of its effects. When this is successfully done, and a patient who is physically dependent upon morphine without knowing it is asked about the effects of the medicine, he reports nothing out of the ordinary. He may merely observe that it reduces the pain and discomfort connected with his ailment, makes him feel reasonably comfortable, and makes it easier for him to sleep. Should this same patient later become addicted, his description of the drug's effects will change dramatically, for he will now talk of it in terms generally used by addicts. He will do so even when the quantity of drugs and the methods used are exactly the same as when he was a patient. This indicates that, like Becker's marijuana users, opiate users learn how to react to the drug; their subjective experiences are profoundly altered by the fact that they have learned to crave it. Similar processes appear to work for cocaine addicts.

Another facet of addiction that is of interest to the social psychologist and that poses interesting theoretical problems is the fact that addicts can—under certain circumstances—be deceived into believing that they are under the influence of drugs when they are not, and vice versa. During the 19th century, for example, it was customary to take addicts off drugs through a gradual withdrawal method over a period of weeks. Under this system, the user might be placed in a hospital and given the drug every 4 hours in diminishing doses, so that after a couple of weeks the drug would have been wholly withdrawn without the patient's knowledge, and he would be receiving an inert substance instead. Under this system the withdrawal distress was reduced and spread out over time, and the patients did not ordinarily realize that they were off drugs as long as the placebo doses continued to be given regularly.

Conversely, addicts who are accustomed to intravenous injections may be given heroin or morphine by other means (such as in solution or by suppositories) without their realizing it. When the administration of drugs is taken out of a user's hands and the intravenous injection method is replaced by others, the addict may become uncertain or confused about whether he is receiving drugs and, if so, in what quantity. This confusion appears to stem mainly from the fact that when the intravenous method of administration is not used, the addict cannot "feel" his shots. If from its inherent pharmacological nature the drug automatically produced great euphoria or pleasure, the addict would surely not be confused. The fact that he can be suggests that his state of mind between injections is not sufficiently extraordinary to explain the power of the habit (Lindesmith, 1947, 1965, 1975).

CONCLUSION

People react to their bodies, and the processes that occur in them, on the basis of sensory cues that are assimilated in conceptual schemes that include ideas of the nature of the body and its functions and malfunctions. Like cognitions of the external world, these ideas are socially derived and vary from one society to another. The interpretations of the bodily changes associated with emotional reactions are an example of the manner in which internal processes are brought into the social sphere by being named, explained, and talked about. Experiences induced by drugs such as marijuana, LSD, cocaine, and opiates are other examples. Subjective experiences that cannot be shared or communicated, such as those of the psychotic, are felt to be "uncanny" and are often interpreted by the individual and others as evidence of insanity or as religious or mystic experiences. The measures that people resort to in order to cure their illnesses depend upon their ideas of the nature and sources of their ailments, and vary widely from group to group even within Western societies.

In this chapter we have examined such related phenomena as the body and pain, emotional experiences, madness, the uncanny, aphasia, Alzheimer's disease, body images, medicine, and opiate and other addictions. Our extended discussion of aphasia reveals how disturbances in language processes can alter and change an individual's relationship to the internal environment of the body and the external world of social experience. We have seen how relatives of Alzheimer's disease victims impute a sense of mind and emotion to victims. We have contrasted modern medicine with the treatment of health and illness in "underdeveloped" countries and have discussed the morality of medicine, as seen in the treatment of AIDS. We have also briefly addressed the phenomenon of anorexia nervosa. Finally, we have taken up the topic of opiate addiction and discussed how behavioral theories of addiction are unable to explain the addict's relationship to opiates and other drugs.

Our purpose has been to show how language structures and shapes our interpretations of what goes on inside our bodies. The naming process is absent in the lower animals. In the next chapter we continue this line of thought by showing how humans learn and construct explanations for their actions in problematic situations.

SUGGESTED READINGS

Biernacki, P. (1986). *Pathways from heroin addiction: Recovery without treatment.* Philadelphia: Temple University Press. A powerful extension and elaboration of Lindesmith's theory of addiction.

Denzin, N. K. (1984). *On understanding emotion.* San Francisco: Jossey-Bass. An interpretation of emotion as symbolic interaction.

Ehrenreich, B., & English, D. (1978). *For her own good: 150 years of the experts' advice to women.* New York: Columbia University Press. A history of medical practices as related to the treatment of women.

Lindesmith, A. R. (1968). *Addiction and opiates.* Chicago: Aldine. A detailed presentation of the views of opiate addiction briefly presented in this chapter.

Preston, J. (Ed.). (1989). *Personal dispatches: Writers confront AIDS.* New York: St. Martin's. A powerful set of essays and stories by writers narrating their experiences with AIDS.

Rosenbaum, M. (1981). *Women on heroin.* New Brunswick, NJ: Rutgers University Press. A moving analysis of the female addict's experiences, which are rooted in emotional social relationships.

Turner, B. (1984). *The body and society: Explorations in social theory.* London: Basil Blackwell. A sociological theory of the body and its relation to society, medicine, religion, and modern cultural practices.

STUDY QUESTIONS

1. What are the three phases in the arousal and expression of emotion? Apply these phases to your own experience of being hungry.
2. What is emotion? What are the various types of emotion?
3. Why would a symbolic interactionist study aphasic experience?

6

Perception, Memory, Motives, and Accounts

In this chapter we explore the language and group foundations of human perception, memory, and motivation. We examine the temporal foundations of human experience, as seen in those behaviors directed to the past, present, and future. In other parts of this book, we deal with the other consequences that follow from the internalization of language. Here, perception, memory, planning, and motivation are grouped together because they are interpretive adjustments to the past, present, and future. When we consider how these four fundamental processes differ in human (and nonhuman) subjects, the importance of language internalization becomes evident.

We take up, in order, the following topics: (a) the social and cultural patterning of perception, (b) the social and historical bases of memory and remembering, (c) the planning of human behavior, and (d) motives, accounts, and human activity.

Preliminary Considerations

It is pertinent to remind the reader of Pavlov's distinction between the first and second signal systems, which we touched upon in Chapter 3. We noted that sensory input or stimulation is transmitted to the brain in the form of "messages" that are coded in terms of impulse frequency. These messages serve a representational function when they are processed in the central nervous system so as to orient the organism within its environment. In other words, sensory input from seeing, touching, hearing, tasting, and smelling provides both human and nonhuman organisms with *signs,* or *cues,* representing the environments of these organisms. This is what Pavlov has called the first signal system.

At the neurological level, what Pavlov refers to as the second signal system consists of the new or additional neural circuits established in the central nervous system when humans acquire language. These new neural patterns are established largely within the left, or dominant, hemisphere of the brain in those areas in which the most complex and least understood regulatory and integrative processes linked with voluntary behavior and consciousness are believed to take place. The processes involved are viewed as second-order signs or symbols, because they represent the lower-order sign processes involved in simple sensory experience. Because these language-derived sign processes of the second signal system merge with, absorb, or dominate many of the lower-order neural patterns, and because the second signal system is social in nature and origin, the existence of the latter has the effect of making many of the psychological activities of human beings subject to social influences transmitted symbolically in a communication or interactional process.

Perception and memory, considered here as symbolic activities, have often been viewed as though they were mechanical, whereas planning is usually not thought of as a separate activity. Thus visual perception has been treated as though it were a process of photographing, and the human visual apparatus has been treated as though it were a camera. Ignored by this view is that the past experiences of the organism influence its perceptions, and that cameras do not have experiences, desires, aspirations, or attitudes. The same mechanical approach has been used to reduce human emotions to purely physiological functions located in the viscera or in some part of the brain. Memory has been treated in a similar manner; it has been conceived of as a mechanical record akin to the "memory" attributed by some to electronic calculating machines. Although this conceptualization has shed light on some aspects of remembering, it has not clarified other important aspects.

Obviously, we reject these mechanistic approaches. Perception, memory, planning, and motivation are human, material practices, actions, and interactions. They are symbolic activities lodged in the ongoing flow of human experience (see Coulter, 1989, p. 6). We will develop the views of activity theorists on these topics (see Holland & Reeves, 1994; Keller & Keller, 1996; Vygotsky, 1978).

Activity Theory

Activity theory is based, in part, on the work of Vygotsky (1978). Its main features are compatible with many of the assumptions of symbolic interactionism (see Clarke & Fujimura, 1992; Star, 1991). Activity theory assumes that the knowledge and information humans have about the world is based on concrete practical actions, including the use of tools. These material practices transform experience. Perception, memory, planning, and motivation are forms of activity that are shaped by these practices. Human intelligence is framed in the context of this kind of activity (Keller & Keller, 1996, p. 20).

For example, persons preparing an elaborate meal engage in complicated material practices, including organizing trips to the grocery store, buying food items, assembling pots and pans and other cooking utensils, cutting up food items, cooking various foods, setting the table, stirring sauces, locating serving bowls, and planning when the meal will be served. This example speaks to a basic feature of activity theory; that is, the structure and meaning of an activity are understood to be mutually constitutive (Keller & Keller, 1996, p. 27). Persons recognize what they are doing by defining it as an instance of what they are doing, in this case cooking a meal.

Activity theory assumes that knowledge is purposeful. A dialectic exists between knowledge and forms of practice. Imagery plays a central part in this process. Cooks imagine how a meal should look when it is served, but they may be forced to alter that imagery if, say, the meat is overcooked. Much of daily activity is repetitive and routine. That is, persons carry stocks of knowledge from one situation to another, yet they are able to adjust these understandings, images, and perceptions to fit new situations (Keller & Keller, 1996, p. 15).

According to some activity theorists, understandings are organized in terms of schemata, which involve plans, procedures, and specific practical actions. These actions are shaped by larger plans, or constellations of understandings (for example, preparing a complex meal). These skilled performances are embedded in ongoing activities; their production shows how cultural meanings are made public through situated performances. Meaning always occurs in the context of naturally occurring events (Keller & Keller, 1996, p. 173).

Motives and Activity

One especially perplexing aspect of the study of humans arises from the fact that they, unlike any other objects of scientific study, have ideas of their own about why they act as they do. Consideration of what people say in explanation of their behavior inevitably leads to consideration of motives and motivation. The concept of motivation is especially applicable to human behavior. It is less applicable to the lower animals, and when applied to them is usually translated into biological terms. In this chapter we are concerned with the concept of motivation as it is applied to human behavior; as we will show, it poses some of the most difficult and controversial problems in the social sciences.

The issues of motives and motivation are often confused in the social and psychological sciences. It is useful at the outset to state our position in this matter. We assume that the human organism is active from birth to death. Accordingly, activity per se is a constant factor across all human situations. The explanations for the directions, shapes, and forms that activity takes, however, are varied and variable. The explanations that persons give for their behavior we shall call *motives* or *accounts*; these are often subsumed under what Mills terms *vocabularies of motive.* As humans act, they may alter their reasons for acting. In this sense, accounts and motives are embedded in ongoing activity. This suggests that "What motivates human behavior?" or "What are the motivations for a particular action?" are erroneous and misleading questions. *Motives,* not *motivations,* are what concern us here. We turn first to common conceptions and misconceptions concerning these points.

When specific acts are explained in ordinary discourse, the explanations rest upon assumptions about behavior in general. Systems of philosophy also require that assumptions be made concerning the nature of behavior and its motives. In this connection, the problem of motivation is an old one, and it has been handled in many different ways. The various hedonistic philosophies have tended to conceive of pleasure seeking and the avoidance of pain as the bases of most action. Another approach has been to think of humans as motivated by certain powerful drives or combinations of drives, such as sex, hunger, love, self-interest, and self-preservation. The sources of the purposes that move human beings have been found also in supernatural beings or superordinate structures such as God, the state, the community, the economic system, and the class system.

Because humans have curiosity about and deep interest in the "why" and "how" of behavior, every generation makes a fresh attack on the problem of motivation. Nevertheless, we are struck by the tenacity with which certain classical conceptions reappear in new guises. The terminology may be new, but the themes are not.

Three Views of Motivation and Action

At the outset, it is useful to distinguish three different approaches to the problem of motivation and action. *Internal models* explain conduct in terms of deterministic psychological or physical processes located in the individual, such as needs, drives, desires, and sexual orientation. Such positions may rest on essentializing arguments. They seek invariant, or essential, differences between individuals. These differences are often seen to be rooted in biology or genetics. They are then fitted to a theory that attempts to explain, for example, differences between men and women, between blacks and whites, or between straights and gays and lesbians (see Kitzinger, 1987, p. 8).

External, structural models, in contrast, locate the causes of human behavior outside the individual in the social structure, in the economy, in the categories, codes, and meanings embedded in the culture and reproduced by the media, embodied in the very terms of language itself. This approach contends that "human consciousness and human experience cannot be the ground for explaining anything" (Hall, 1980, p. 66). Humans can live experience only "*in and through* the categories, classifications and frameworks of culture" (Hall, 1980, p. 60).

Interactional models rest on nonessentializing arguments. They take a position, not unlike the one we take here, that recognizes how structure shapes meaning and experience. However, interactionists seek always to examine how humans represent their experiences through the categories and meanings the culture makes available them. This model seeks always to interrogate those mainstream cultural discourses that operate behind people's backs, showing how these texts structure and shape human experience in predetermined ways. This is the view we are developing in this book.

The imputation of motives to others is an integral aspect of human interaction. It is inconceivable that social life could exist if people did not make guesses or assumptions about the purposes of others. The mark of human behavior, as opposed to animal behavior, is that it is organized around anticipation of others' responses to one's own actions. Anticipation involves assumptions as to how and why others will react. It also involves judgments about previous acts of others, as they have bearing upon their possible future acts. A knowledge of the purposes of others is the most effective basis for understanding what they are doing now and knowing what to expect from them in the future.

Incorrect assessment of such purposes has important consequences, as it may lead to embarrassment, misunderstanding, loss of money and time, or other even more unfortunate effects. When acts are familiar, traditional, and routinized, the assessment of motivation is easy and taken for granted. No one questions why people walk erect, build houses, or wear clothes, although the question of motivation is brought into sharp focus when they do *not* do these things. If the reasons for customary behavior are inquired after, usually by an outsider, the person who is questioned may be at a loss for an answer. In relatively homogeneous societies, the questioning of motives may be relatively infrequent, because the bases of customary behavior are infrequently challenged.

In heterogeneous societies, actions more frequently raise questions, because certain behaviors are unfamiliar to some or because they are performed in contexts that make them unclear. Then some guesswork, and sometimes some sleuthing, is called for on the part of the investigator. The difficulties of correct assessment are further increased by the fact that people very often do not clearly formulate to themselves the purposes of their actions and so can give little help to others who wish to understand them. There may also be several purposes, or levels of purposes, involved in a given act. The importance of clues to future behavior is further underlined by the existence of duplicity in interaction. The concealment of motives and the deliberate misleading of other people is sometimes cultivated as an art, and it appears to be necessary for the smooth functioning of social relationships, even relationships among friends, lovers, and kin. "Nothing but the truth" would thoroughly disrupt human relations.

Social Patterning of Perception

Selectivity in Perception

Perception refers to the ways in which organisms respond to the stimuli picked up by their sense organs. It refers to processes of immediate experience. Perception has often been distinguished from *cognition* and *interpretation*, which refer to how perceptual experiences are ordered and given meaning, often in terms of symbolic, individual, group, and cultural meanings and categories (see Dougherty, 1985, p. 4; Tajfel, 1969, p. 317). The disciplines of cognitive psychology and cognitive anthropology study the relationships among perception, cognition, meaning, culture, and language.

The subject of visual perception has traditionally included such topics as the perception of space and form and the "close mapping of stimulus and experience" (Kolers, 1983, p. 130). Over the past 20 years, research has shifted from these traditional interests to such phenomena as iconic memory, backward masking, apparent motion, and imagery (Kolers, 1983, p. 130). We shall briefly discuss two of these phenomena. *Iconic memory* refers to the ability of people to describe various features of letters and digits that were briefly presented but are no longer in view. It is seen as a first stage in the process of information extraction in perception. *Backward masking* refers to how an event perceived later in time interferes with the perception of an earlier event. Kolers (1983) describes this process:

> When the time interval separating two flashes is appropriately brief, the two stimuli tend to be seen as a single object. As the interval increases T (the original flash) is seen less distinctly; later still, during the recovery stage, they are often seen as two temporally distinct objects. Not only was the "backward" aspect of masking counterintuitive, the fact that visibility of T first decreased and then recovered as time between T and M (second flash) increased violated many assumptions about visual perception; particularly it violated the assumption that perceptions were coded immediately and were realistically faithful to stimulus events. (p. 136)

It was once thought that perception was something analogous to such mechanical processes as photographing an object or recording sound on a record. That analogy to a mechanical sequence is inadequate, however, because it ignores the fact that perception is influenced by interests, needs, and past experiences. The analogy also does not take into account the fact that the total volume of physical stimuli reaching us from sources both within our bodies and in the environment is so great, most of them must be ignored and therefore can neither function as cues nor enter significantly into the determination of behavior. Physical illness sometimes reminds us painfully of some of the multitudinous processes that normally go on inside of us without our being aware of them. The hypochondriac illustrates par excellence preoccupation with stimuli originating in bodily processes. Ordinary healthful living requires that we be highly selective of the stimuli to which we pay attention and, at the same time, that we consign whole ranges of stimuli to the background and ignore them.

Response to environmental cues constitutes the reality orientation of the organism. The data that are supplied by the sense organs and the receptor nerves are interpreted and acted upon as signs of the nature, location, size, movement, and quality of objects and occurrences. The degree and nature of inner elaboration or "interpretation" of experience vary among species and among individuals. The degree of interpretation reaches its peak in humans, in whom the elaboration may be very great, and in whom it assumes a symbolic form. Individuals' reports of what they perceive, and their ideas of what they see or hear, include matters of inference, interpretation, and judgment—in short, people do not discriminate between what may be called direct perception, or physical stimulus, and the meaningful elaboration of the perception that occurs when it is classified, named, analyzed, and judged:

> On the face of it, to perceive anything is one of the simplest and most immediate, as it is one of the most fundamental, of all human cognitive reactions. Yet . . . it is exceedingly complex. . . . Inextricably mingled with it are imagining, valuing, and the beginnings of judgment. (Bartlett, 1932, p. 31)

This point is illustrated graphically in Keller and Keller's (1996, p. 65) and Dougherty and Keller's (1985, pp. 162-163) discussions of how blacksmiths organize their tools in their shops. A person unfamiliar with how a blacksmith works might organize the tools by size or by common labels—such as hammers, including ball-peen, claw, sledge, mallet; or saws, including hacksaws, coping saws, Japanese carpenter's saw, ripsaws. Tongs, clamps, and chisels might be categorized as well. As one blacksmith stated, "We could sort them into tools with wooden handles, single pieces of metal, pivoted metal tools, and multicomponent tools, too" (quoted in Dougherty & Keller, 1985, p. 163). The question this smith asked was, "What do you want to make?" Thus one linguistic sorting of the perceptual objects in the blacksmith's shop—that done on the basis of common labels—was found to be unsuited to how working smiths organize their work. In this case, perception and cognition are based on the task at hand and what the perceiver is doing. Perceiving, naming, categorizing, and labeling are individual and cultural matters. The meaning of the perception of an object is not just given, as in a camera's image of the object perceived.

Stimuli viewed as purely physical events are presented to us by our environment and are not changed in any way by being named, classified, or interpreted. Stimuli become cues, however, when attention is paid to them or when they are responded to. Individuals learn to select and interpret the stimuli relevant to their actions and interests, and to ignore others or take them for granted.

It is easy, but fallacious, to conceive of perception as a single passive act, as if an organism looks out upon an environment and receives impressions of it through the sense organs. This *copy conception* has been attacked by Dewey (1922, 1925) and others who stress that perceiving is part of a larger organization of activity. Some persons do sit idly and allow stimuli to flow in upon them, but usually they are engaged in some sort of activity. What is noted and how it is interpreted affect the course of action. As the action enters new phases, new kinds of cues are sought and evaluated. Lines of activity are typically intermittent and extend over periods of time—as, for example, when an individual is buying a house, planning a vacation, or making a garden. When a given line of behavior is temporarily suspended, individuals have time to ruminate over the past and anticipate the future. Both past and future may influence their perceptions when they resume the earlier activity.

Perceiving as part of the larger pattern of activity is necessarily focused on the future, even though it occurs in the present. As Ittelson and Cantril (1954), following Dewey's general position, note:

> Perception certainly seems to be of the world as it is right now, or, perhaps, as it was a few minutes ago. Indeed, the definition of perception frequently appears in psychology

> texts as "the awareness of immediately present objects." . . . [But w]hile present and past are involved in the perceptual process, the chief time-orientation in perceiving is toward the future. The primary function of perception . . . is prediction of the future. (p. 27)

The facts are that perception is selective, that motivation and needs sensitize us to specific stimuli or sometimes lead to distorted perception, that stimuli are often misinterpreted, and that perceptions of the same situation may vary from individual to individual. But these facts should not cause us to ignore the further fact that reality sets limits to perception. People who persistently see nonexistent objects such as pink elephants or who hear voices when no one is speaking are out of touch with reality; they are hallucinating. Perception, therefore, is not arbitrary, but is limited by what is actually present in the environment. None of us can live in the real world if we see only what suits us.

Learning to perceive causes behavior to become more discriminating and flexible with respect to environmental reality. It does not, however, free behavior from reality. Admittedly, the complications introduced into the perceptual processes when they become linked with higher-order conceptualizations and symbolic systems (such as the individual's conceptions of self) increase the probabilities of distortion and error. The perceptions of the lower animal or the child are probably less subject to error than are those of the sophisticated adult.

Selectivity of perception is especially marked in social interaction in which the person's self-esteem is at stake. Psychiatrists and clinical psychologists have long noted the tendency of humans to ignore or misperceive things that would be damaging to their egos if correctly noted. Psychiatrist H. S. Sullivan (1953) coined the expression *selective inattention* for this process, in which "we fail to recognize the actual import of a good many things which we see, hear, think, do, and say, not because there is anything the matter with our zones of interaction with others, but because the process of inferential analysis is opposed by the self system" (p. 374).

Social Factors in Perception

Social or cultural influences affect perception in marked ways. Laypersons, of course, have noticed this phenomenon. A real estate broker looking at a house is not likely to observe the same details as would an artist, an insurance agent, or an architect. When viewing a landscape, an artist will perceive details and relationships of line, space, light, and color that escape ordinary "seeing." What is selected and emphasized in perceiving is connected with the observer's perspective, with his or her value system, interests, needs, and the like. Perception is clearly dependent upon previous experiences, interests, and concerns. These in turn are related to such factors as the perceiver's occupation, class, and age—in short, to the perceiver's social background.

Perception, Language, and Groups

We have noted that humans act toward objects in light of their classifications of them. The term *schemata* has been employed by cognitive psychologists and anthropologists to describe the conceptual abstractions that mediate between stimuli received by the sense organs and behavioral responses (e.g., Agar & Hobbs, 1985; Bartlett, 1932; Casson, 1983). Schemata "are abstractions that serve as the basis of all human information processing, e.g., perception and comprehension, categorization and planning, recognition and recall, and problem-solving and decision-making" (Casson, 1983, p. 430).

Schemata are based on group languages and group perspectives. Group influences on perception have been well illustrated in a study by Boster (1985) of the Aguaruna Jivaro, a forest-dwelling tribe in the northern Peruvian *montaña*. Boster studied how the Aguarunas classify and name manioc, a starchy root that contributes about 60% of the calories in the Aguaranas' daily diet. The root is also used for making beer, and it is the main ingredient in tapioca pudding.

In Boster's investigation of Aguaruna manioc identification, two experimental gardens were planted; the first had 61 different varieties of manioc, the second had 15 common varieties. One group of 58 women participated in the identification of the manioc in the garden that had 61 varieties; this was designated the hard task. A group of 43 women and 21 men participated in the easy task—identifying the manioc in the garden with 15 varieties of the plant. The findings of this study may be summarized as follows: (a) All women in both tasks (hard and easy), with only two exceptions, had higher overall agreement on the classification of manioc than did men; (b) younger women who had gone to school were more likely than those who had not to disagree with others in their classifications; and (c) women from the same kin groups were more likely to agree with one another when compared with women from different kin groups.

How do we interpret these findings? First, we must note that in this cultural group men do not garden, hence the fact that women were better able to classify manioc is explained by this sexual division of labor. Second, a woman who leaves the group to go to school is deprived of her "education as a horticulturalist with her mother in the garden" (Boster, 1985, p. 189). Third, women within the same kin groups share intimate knowledge about manioc that is not shared in other kin groups (Boster, 1985, p. 193). Fourth, "different layers of agreement corresponded to different layers of social identity and also to different modes and intensities of communication about manioc" (Boster, 1985, p. 183). Fifth, the variations among individuals can be explained by these layers and forms of social identity.

We can see that different cultural schemata are associated with the sexual division of labor and the organization of women within kin groups in this culture. These schemata lead to differences in the perception of the object manioc. Boster's study points out the implications of different learning situations for the ways in which objects and concepts are organized (Dougherty, 1985, p. 175).

As the above example suggests, objects are perceived characteristically not as isolated items, but as members of classes. The class to which a perceiver fits a given object is in turn related to the perceiver's task at hand. We do not perceive bare, unnamed, isolated objects. Glance around the room, making note of what you "see." Do you not see class representatives such as walls, books, pencils, chairs, and flowers? Linguistic classification is not external or incidental to such perceiving but an integral part of it. What we term *perceiving* involves linguistic distinctions, for an observer cannot perceive objects as class members unless his or her language has already designated these classes or enabled the observer to invent new categories.

F. C. Bartlett's (1932) careful work, which is still a point of reference for current research in this area (Casson, 1983, p. 430), indicates also how linguistic elements influence perception. Subjects in Bartlett's studies who were briefly shown the figure  sometimes thought the rectangle was completely drawn in. In a figure such as 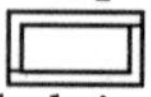, naming was of great importance in helping to shape perception. Subjects looking at this figure who saw "picture frames" perceived an object that looked like 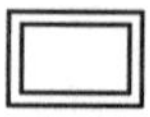 or 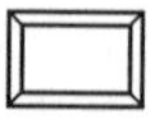. The figure  was called a "pick-ax" by one observer and reproduced with pointed prongs; another person called it a "turf cutter" and drew it with a rounded blade. Several persons called it an "anchor" and exaggerated the size of the ring on the top. Only one person correctly perceived the pointed blade; he had seen it as a prehistoric battle-ax. Bartlett found that if a figure seemed odd, disconnected, or unfamiliar it was usually seen in terms of an analogy—that is, in terms of the identity of a known object. He concludes that "a great amount of what is said to be perceived is in fact inferred" (p. 31).

A commonsense maxim holds that, in general, "people see what they are looking for." This is not always true, but as the saying indicates, verbal frames of reference organize perceptual responses. A person's perceiving is likely to follow along the lines of familiarity and expectations. The illustrations taken from Bartlett's (1932) work demonstrate this well, as does the existence of some types of "suggestion." Thus when Binet showed subjects "a series of lines of gradually increasing length, but with occasional 'catches' where the lines did not lengthen as expected . . . not one of his forty-five pupils completely escaped the suggestion of increase in length in all lines" (Murphy, Murphy, & Newcomb, 1937, p. 173). We can account for this kind of suggestion very simply by supposing that Binet's subjects were *set* to see successively longer lines.

If simple perception such as that studied by Bartlett involves naming, analogy, and inference, it can be assumed that more complex acts of perceiving will involve more complex uses of language.

Complex Perceptions and Codability

The Solomon Islanders have a complex and detailed perception of coconuts, Eskimos make fine discriminatory classifications of snow, and Arabs have many words for camel (including 50 that describe various stages of camel pregnancy). These fine discriminations make it possible for those who make them also to draw associated perceptual distinctions. It can be said that without the linguistic distinctions, people can still make the same perceptual distinctions; for instance, Brown and Lenneberg (1954, p. 455) argue that Americans distinguish as many kinds of snow as do Eskimos. But the Eskimos' categories have what has been termed *high codability.* This means that the classes of things to be talked about have established single names that permit the members of the language community to respond quickly and consistently from one situation to another, to both the names and the things. Such terms are especially useful in communicating perceptual distinctions, and probably in making them. Possibly, there may sometimes even be links connecting social structure, norms, and specific categorical distinctions.

The Social Basis of Memory

Perceiving involves the response to or interpretation of signs in the form of sensory stimulation resulting from the organism's contacts with the external environment or arising within the organism. *Remembering* is a response to signs of past experiences, which in some form or other are preserved within the organism. In the one case the sign bridges a spatial gap; in the other, a temporal gap. Thus remembering, like perceiving, is a complex form of sign behavior. Like perception, memory is profoundly influenced by the communicating we do in the groups to which we belong.

Human Remembering as a Symbolic Process

Remembering's Dependence Upon Categorization

Without language, humans, like animals, would be tied down to concrete situations. They would have no conceptions either of history or of a personal past. On reflection, it becomes clear that much of our remembering revolves around memorable events, holidays, and dates. We cast back "in our memories" to last Friday, last summer, the weekend before last, the day we entered college, our 16th birthday. We often recollect by means of such notational devices. If we are asked where we spent last Thanksgiving and what we did, the task of recalling is relatively easy. If, on the other hand, we are asked what we did last November 6, recollection is likely to be either weak or totally absent (unless that is some memorable date, such as a birthday).

To hear a melody and recognize vaguely that you have heard it somewhere does not perhaps clearly depend upon language. However, to say to yourself, "How does the first movement of Beethoven's Fifth Symphony go?" and then by an act of "concentration" to call up themes from that movement, is clearly dependent upon a linguistic framework. Music is so closely linked with language that you could not keep your attention focused on that symphony and that movement if the linguistic framework were missing. Similarly, if you ask, "What is the color of my house back home?" it is by virtue of language that you can call up that house and name its color. Without language categories, such acts of remembering would be impossible. Again, suppose you are asked to meet a friend for lunch at 12:00 in such-and-such a restaurant, and at a quarter of 12:00 you remember your engagement. Could you have remembered without the aid of the appropriate names—time categories—that you verbalize to yourself, perhaps repeatedly, or that you actually write down on a memo pad? Moreover, how would you remember the past or keep appointments in the future without systems of time notation?

The psychology of legal testimony supplies an interesting instance of the organization of memory around verbal plans or labels. People may erroneously remember details as having happened, provided that the details fit into a frame of reference. An instance of this is provided by early litigation concerning patents on the telephone:

> Certain people in a little town . . . gave at a second court hearing testimony totally different from that which they had given several years earlier at the first hearing. The first testimony was vague and uncertain. In the interval between the two hearings the major subject of discussion in the town had been the apparatus in question. At the second court hearing the people recounted as fully established facts incidents which had apparently been generated by their discussions. (Judd, 1939, p. 354)

Studies of distortion in the transmission of rumors show the same sort of inaccurate remembering. As it is passed from one person to another, the content of a rumor undergoes alteration according to how the transmitting person hears and remembers the rumor—both activities dependent upon the person's frame of reference (Allport & Postman, 1947; Shibutani, 1966).

Not only does society provide the linguistic and other devices that individuals use in registering events, in recalling, identifying, and placing them, but human memory has other important social dimensions as well. French psychologists and sociologists particularly have elaborated the idea that the things people remember form interlaced and mutually reinforcing systems organized around group situations. Thus Halbwachs (1925, 1950) notes that students' memories of given professors, and the courses they took with those professors, are different from the professors' recollections of the students and the courses. The students' memories are generally much more precise, Halbwachs deduces, because their experiences are part of a unique group situation shared with others. Professors, on the other hand, experience each class and the individuals in it primarily as one of a series of similar situations occurring in their professional activities. They have met successive classes in the same room or in similar rooms; class follows class, and, as the professors have no special group framework for each, they retain only the haziest ideas of what they did, what happened, who was present in any of the classes, and in which buildings and rooms they were held.

Most of our memories, Halbwachs observes, are organized in this way within a framework provided by the group to which we now belong and by those groups to which we have belonged. When we are within a given group (for example, our families) over a period of time, the members talk about past experiences and keep them fresh in our minds. Familiar faces and old haunts become linked with memories of past events. When we leave the group for a long time or permanently, the memories fade, along with the faces, places, and names, until a skeleton or almost nothing remains. If we return after many years to the old group and the old environment the memories are revived, although they are not the same. As we remember and reconstruct the past, according to Halbwachs, we project ourselves into a group framework and use it to revive and organize past experiences. This argument is used to explain the tendency for memories of experiences in temporary groups—for example, the kind formed aboard an ocean liner—to shrink and disappear quickly. This is especially true if no lasting relationships are established and if one does not again meet any of the persons involved. Human memory, Halbwachs contends, is therefore *collective,* or social, in nature. We are able to think of memory as individual only because we overlook or take for granted its group connections.

Amnesia for Childhood Memories

Why is it that there is such a dearth of recollections of childhood experiences, and virtually total amnesia for the period of infancy? Some writers have hypothesized that repression of memories takes place. This is an unsatisfactory explanation, because it does not account for the forgetting of pleasant happenings or for the complete absence of memory of the earliest experiences of a fully sentient infant.

Schachtel (1947) has argued that infants and young children live in a world of feeling and fantasy in which their experiences are such that they quite literally cannot be formulated in words. Hence they cannot be recollected, for infants lack symbolic means to retain them and adults do not have the proper mentality to recapture them later. Schachtel lays great stress upon the stereotyped, abstract, and schematic character of adult language, which transforms growing children in socializing them and renders them in a sense unfit to be children even in memory. We need not adopt Schachtel's nostalgic attitude toward the richness and vitality of childhood imagery, but his emphasis on the crucial import of symbolic structures for remembrance is important. Infants, lacking these symbolic structures, have nothing to record them with so that they can recapture them later.

A subsidiary but also important point is that the transformations of children during the course of their socialization make recollection difficult or impossible. The Luria (1928) experiment suggests this same conclusion. In a study of the development of children's concepts of money, Strauss (1952) found that it was unusual for the children to recollect any of the concepts held at earlier ages. In fact, they rejected notions once firmly believed with no awareness that they had once accepted them—rejected them with ridicule, laughter, and incredulity. This is precisely what one would expect if it is assumed that development implies genuine transformation of behavioral organization. In his studies of children, Piaget also observed that when children are asked where they learned their most recent conceptions, they often remark, "I have always known that."

Halbwachs (1925) has suggested that although certain childhood memories can be recaptured, at least in a gross sense, certain others cannot, because the individual's perspective changes. For example, one can often remember the name of a book one read as a child, conjuring up the look of the print and some of the imagery of the pictures and possibly even recapturing some of the overtones of the feeling experienced while reading the book. (However, it takes a rare person, like novelist Marcel Proust, to recapture feeling.) But, as Halbwachs shrewdly notes, it is literally impossible to divest oneself of the experiences of the intervening years so as to feel exactly as one did when reading the book as a child. He remarks that the effort to recapture feelings poses the same problem as the effort to recapture the spirit of preceding periods in history. We may add that even Proust, dredging up minute and poignant details of his childhood, gives only the illusion of an accurate recollection. Recollection is active, not passive. Proust's *Remembrance of Things Past* is an artistic and artful reconstruction, a creative act, not the record set down by a passive watcher as his memories file by like a parade. Adults, moving through the life cycle to new perspectives and abandoning old ones, can be expected to find it difficult to recapture any but the grossest or most static, or most poignant, moments of their pasts.

The Child's History

Taking our lead from Proust, we can argue that the resources for producing a childhood history are present in most children by the age of 3 years. By this age, children have mastered language (see Chapter 8) and are capable of self-reflective thought and action. They are able, that is, to produce events that can and could be remembered at a later date (Denzin, 1982). However, as our remarks on childhood amnesia suggest, children lack the complex symbolic equipment necessary for grasping or recapturing any but the most vivid events of their pasts.

Nonetheless, families keep histories of their shared and significant experiences. Family photo albums, mementos from vacations, souvenirs, and gifts all mark significant moments in historical time. They serve to locate the child's self in the memories of this past. We may ask, what things from childhood are remembered? Alice James (1964), sister of William and Henry James, considers the question in the following passage:

> I wonder what determines the *selection* of memory, why does one childish experience or impression stand out so luminous and solid against the, for the most part, vague and misty background. The things we remember have a *firsttimeness* about them which suggests that may be the reason of their survival. . . . I remember so distinctly the first time I was conscious of a purely intellectual process. (pp. 127-128)

One's remembered childhood may hinge, then, on the experiencing and the cataloging of first-time, significant events. In between these first-time events are chains of repetitions—habitualized routines and daily doings. One establishes the credibility of one's childhood by remembering it well and in vivid detail.

Henry James (1913) offers the following remembrance of one of his early childhood perceptions. It involves his temporal standing in the James family, behind his older brother William:

> One of these, and probably the promptest in order, was that of my brother's occupying a place in the world to which I couldn't at all aspire . . . as if he had gained such an advance of me in his sixteen months' experience of the world before mine began that I never for all the time of childhood and youth in the least caught up with him or overtook him. He was always round the corner and out of sight,

> coming back into view but at his hours of extremest ease. We were never in the same schoolroom, in the same game, scarce even in step together or in the same phase at the same time; when our phases overlapped, that is, it was only for a moment—he was clean out before I had got well in. How far he had really at any moment dashed forward it is not for me now to attempt to say; what comes to me is that I at least hung inveterately and woefully back, and that this relation alike to our interests and to each other seemed proper and preappointed. (pp. 9-10)

Now consider the following statement from another member of the James family. Robertson James, the youngest of the James sons, says of himself in a fragment of an autobiography:

> I was born in the year 1846, in Albany, N.Y. I never remember being told anything extraordinary about my babyhood but I often like to contemplate myself as a baby and wonder if I was really as little appreciated as I fully remember feeling at that time. I never see infants now without discerning in their usually solemn countenance a conviction that they are on their guard and in more or less hostile surroundings. However that may be, in my own case, at a very early age the problems of life began to press upon me in such an unnatural way and I developed such an ability for feeling hurt and wounded that I became quite convinced by the time I was twelve years old that I was a foundling. (quoted in Burr, 1934, p. 25)

We have, in these statements, painful remembrances of childhood. Henry James felt that he was always behind his brother William, no matter where they went or what they did. Robertson remembers himself as feeling hurt and wounded, and not fully appreciated. He generalizes this childhood memory to all infants and young children. These accounts from the James family suggest that memories of childhood can take on an influence that is still felt in adulthood.

The Symbolic Nature of the Past

Maines, Sugrue, and Katovich (1983), commenting on Mead's (1929, 1932, 1934, 1936, 1938) theory of the past, suggest that the past has four identifiable dimensions: (a) the symbolically reconstructed past, (b) the social structural past, (c) the implied objective past, and (d) the mythical past.

In the symbolically reconstructed past, individuals redefine "the meaning of past events in such a way that they have meaning in and utility for the present" (Maines et al., 1983, p. 163). We have seen how members of a family symbolically reconstruct past events so as to give them meaning in the present.

In the social structural past, events in the past *structure* and *shape* experiences found in the present. In the preceding account, Robertson James explains how his experiences in early childhood led him to see infants in the present with the conviction that "they are on their guard." His past experiences structure and shape his present perceptions and actions.

The implied objective past is the third dimension in Maines et al.'s theory. Mead (1929) states, "The past is that which must have been before it is present in experience as a past" (p. 28). He refers here to the existence of previous events, to the fact that they must have existed in order for them to exist in the present as a past. Mead is suggesting that past events have an implied, objective existence in that "they exist in the present through memory" (Maines et al., 1983, p. 164). The present structures what is remembered from this implied past. Henry James gives an implied objective past to his relationship with his brother William. He states that William "was always round the corner and out of sight"; this is how he objectively remembers William.

Mythical pasts are "creations, rather than re-creations, because they are not empirically grounded." They are fictitious, but they are "empirical in their consequences because they materially affect relationships" (Maines et al., 1983, p. 164). Returning to Henry James's biography once again, he creates a mythical past that includes his brother and their relationship. Mead suggests that we create myths (stories whose origins are forgotten, ostensibly historical, that usually serve to explain some practice or belief) because they have practical value in solving problems.

Each of these dimensions of the past flow through the "specious," or immediate, present. The existence of these events that occur in the past is never doubted, because they are given meaning in the present. What is problematic is their meaning in the present (Maines et al., 1983, p. 165). We develop these points in the next section.

Historical Communication, Perception, and Memory

We have shown how perceiving and remembering are selective processes. Selectivity is socially influenced. Schemata are social constructions. Because groups, organizations, and institutions exist for long periods of time, memories of past events and dead personages are passed along from generation to generation. Each generation, however, symbolically reconstructs, structures, and creates its own version of the implied objective past and weaves this past through its myths. Let us consider several instances of collective heritage, historical communication, and collective memory.

A relatively simple instance is the garden-variety remembrance that most of us have about the relations between Native Americans and white Americans during the 19th century. Unless we have heard or read specifically to the contrary, we tend to believe the mass media's version of "how the West was won." We even tend to equate Indians with the West! A more complete version would include the idea that rarely has a group of natives been so completely swept clean off their land and with such cruelty. Our individual memories of these events are nonexistent, so our views of this past, and to a large extent our views of Native Americans today, are rooted in our induction into channels of communication represented mainly by the mass media. Because European children may also read the same stories and see the same movies, they too may be inducted into the standard set of legends. Recently, some Native Americans have been trying—with difficulty, for collective memories are tenacious—to refashion Americans' conceptions of the past relations between whites and Native Americans.

With more passion and perhaps more face-to-face interaction, most American southerners have images of both what the "War Between the States" was like and what followed directly thereafter, during the Reconstruction period. The present generation has heard about these events from their parents through folk tradition. Southerners who were not born in the South have been inducted into intense communication about these events through friends and acquaintances, perhaps through teachers, as well as through the various mass media that circulate in the South. Indeed, some of the nonnatives may have sharper and more passionately held images than do southerners whose forefathers fought in the Civil War. These collective memories have helped to shape the subsequent course of events in the South and in the North also. Attempting to answer this legendary tradition, both black and white historians have done firsthand research that has shown that both popular and scholarly historians (mostly southern whites) have often made errors in fact and in interpretation regarding the Civil War era (Beringer, Hattaway, Jones, & Still, 1985; Franklin, 1956; Jordan, 1968). More recent emphasis on black pride and other attempts to counter the destructive effects of being black in a white-dominated society have also sought to rectify the remarkably inaccurate history of race relations in the United States.

We need not attribute deliberate distortion to historians, the press, or ordinary conversationalists as they reshape the past through their interpretations of it. Quite enough distortion occurs through the selective processes of perceiving, remembering, and retelling without the necessity of our assuming deliberate manipulation, although assuredly falsification of history often does occur. The selective processes can be seen at work in "house organ histories," whether these are histories of corporations, voluntary organizations, religious denominations, cities, or professions. These accounts are almost certain to be slanted in the direction of self-aggrandizement, if only because those who write them are biased in the direction of "progress" or have seen events from particular positions, or both.

Continuity of the legendary tradition of any group is broken when the communication channels either disintegrate or are captured by people who wish to change the information transmitted by those channels. The latter strategy is shown by what happens when authoritarian governments begin to beam different interpretations of national history over the mass media, blocking out as completely as possible all competing versions of the past. The disintegration of communication channels generally means the disappearance of either the communication-bearing group itself or the persons who acted as key transmitting agents for the old days. Another possibility is the transformation of the group itself so that in some sense the original group has disappeared, as happens with minority groups that become assimilated into the mainstream of a nation's life. Its members are likely to forget much of their ethnic heritage—such as foods, religious beliefs, and customs—whereas an embattled minority group, as in the Balkan countries, may persist for centuries with collective memories of its distant past as vivid as those of yesterday.

A new group, organization, or social structure may also appropriate as part of its functioning heritage various events and objects that either were forgotten and have been rediscovered or genuinely had little connection with its actual past. History is full of such events. The rediscovery by Renaissance scholars of the Greek past, and how this past was interpreted in contemporary terms, is one of the great stories of Western civilization. In turn, this story becomes part of *our past*—if we know about it.

The Planning of Behavior

As we have stressed repeatedly, the human is a planning animal, making continual references to the past, present, and future. As individuals move through the present into the future, the past is recast and reformulated to fit the images of the future. This merger of the past and future in the present constitutes what G. H. Mead terms the *specious present.* That is, as we act in the present, we bring our previous actions to bear upon our anticipated actions in the next moment. These anticipations, in turn, shape our actions in the present. In the specious present, past, present, and future flow into a single temporal phase of experience. William James describes this as the *stream of consciousness* of the person.

In their plans, however ill defined and vague, humans reveal an ability to take control over their own behavior so as to give it a semblance of organization and predictability. Plans, then, take many forms. They can be well thought out, written down, and made public, as when a president or other head of state lays out a 10-year economic plan. They can refer to private affairs or public affairs, and they can refer to individual actions, to the actions of large collectivities, to the actions of families, or to the actions of two lovers.

People vary in their ability to formulate plans. Young children, for instance, seldom have any control over when they will enter school, be taken on vacations, or be permitted to open savings accounts. Furthermore, people vary in their power—legitimate or illegitimate, institutionalized or informal—to formulate plans. This ability and authority to make plans varies according to individuals' locations in the power networks that make up social groups and complex bureaucracies. We can also see that individuals' plans vary by where they see themselves in their overall moral careers. The plans of the elderly, which reflect some attempt to control their last years of life during retirement, are quite different from those of persons just beginning their work careers.

Plans are always about the future, even when formulated in the present, for they refer to how individuals will organize their actions in the next moment, day, year, or decade. Finally, we can note that some plans are hidden from others (embezzlers, for example, seldom make their plans known), whereas other plans are matters of public information (e.g., a phase of an anti-inflationary economic plan).

By virtue of their higher mental processes, then, humans can, on a symbolic level, engage in true deliberation—which is, as John Dewey (1922) notes with his usual emphasis on behavior, "a search for a *way* to act, not for a final terminus" (p. 193). Dewey also emphasizes, as we have, the unified character of past, present, and future, reminding us that we judge present "desires and habits" in terms of their probable consequences, with which knowledge is linked. "We know . . . by recollecting what we have observed, by using that recollection in constructive imaginative forecasts of the future, by using the thought of future consequences to tell the quality of the act now proposed" (p. 207).

Planning, Feedback, and Probabilities

The process of deliberation to which Dewey refers is actually much more complex and delicate than it seems at first glance, especially when plans involve the presumed reactions of other people. One way of illustrating this point is by referring to what are called *self-fulfilling* and *self-negating* predictions. The former are exemplified by the person who seeks to make money in the stock market by following some of the well-known formulae disseminated in financial circles. If there are many investors who believe that stocks should be sold when stock averages behave in certain ways that are believed to constitute sell "signals," then stock prices will fall when the signal occurs, simply because there are enough people who heed the signal to force prices down.

The self-negating prophecy, or prediction, is one that induces the person whose behavior has been predicted to prove that the prediction is wrong. Some years ago, before going barefoot was as common as it is now, a professor arguing before a class said that it was easy to predict human behavior and made his point by predicting that everyone would be wearing shoes and stockings at the next meeting of his class. At the next class, a number of students arrived with bare feet to prove him wrong.

These examples indicate some problems of planning and predicting that are introduced by the fact that people tend to seek information about the plans others make concerning them and then alter their own plans accordingly. As activity proceeds, information concerning its effects and the reactions of others tends to flow back to the persons involved in what is called a *feedback* process. Feedback data are then interpreted and utilized to confirm, negate, or alter the ongoing course of action.

Kristin Luker (1975) conducted a study in which she interviewed more than 600 women who had had abortions. Her findings illustrate our points on planning and probability. She found that for all the women she interviewed, the decision to "seek an abortion has been serious, thoughtful, and carefully considered" (Luker, 1984, p. 285). She found that many of the women had unwanted pregnancies (unwanted because of the women's ages, the health status of their spouses, the numbers of children they already had, their job situations, their personal health and goals, and other reasons) because the predictions they had made about getting pregnant were incorrect. Her respondents made subjective probability predictions about not getting pregnant, and these predictions underscored their decisions not to contracept. Their decisions, and the consequences of those decisions, then led them to form accounts (explanations) of their conduct in which they justified their actions to themselves and to others, including abortion counselors. They were required in many cases (a) to have reasons for not contracepting and (b) to have reasons for seeking abortion.

Motives, Activities, and Accounts

At the start of this chapter we suggested that human beings have a deep interest in the "how" and "why" of behavior. In this section we examine three theories that address these issues. The first is the Freudian conception of human behavior, the second is the Marxist position, and the third is the social psychological point of view we hold in this text.

Freudian Conceptions

Probably the most influential motivational scheme of this century is the Freudian, which was most popular in sociology between the years 1930 and 1939. Some variant of it is still utilized by most clinical psychologists and psychiatrists. Social workers, child psychologists, and anthropologists have often found it useful or acceptable, although sociologists have found it far less so. Fragments of Freudian terminology and Freud's conceptual scheme have also found their way into popular thought.

It is difficult to set forth current Freudian ideas in a form that would be subscribed to by all Freudians, because there are considerable differences in viewpoint, formulation, and emphasis among them. Whatever these differences may be, there is a fair amount of agreement on a number of basic points and assumptions (see also Chapter 8). The psychoanalytic view has also gained a great deal of interest in literary criticism in recent years. The work of Lacan (1977) has been especially influential in this regard (see Coward & Ellis, 1977; Ragland-Sullivan, 1986).

Some basic points. Among the basic assumptions underlying the Freudian view of motivation are the ideas that all human behavior is motivated, that the explanation of any behavior requires that its motives be analyzed, that the energy sources of motives are biological in nature, that motives range from those that are entirely conscious to those that are altogether unconscious, that most important ones are either unconscious or partly so, and that the conflict of motivational forces plays a dominant role in personality development. Thus, according to the Freudian position, human behavior is activated either by innate biological needs or by elaborations of them. Human culture is conceived of as an agency that both frustrates and disciplines primitive urges, and, as a consequence of such frustration, the basic sources of energy are undirected and goalless and are channeled through cultural forms. According to Freud (1933):

> Our civilization is built up at the cost of our sexual impulses which are inhibited by society, being partly repressed but partly, on the other hand, made use of for new aims. However proud we may be of our cultural achievements . . . it is by no means easy to satisfy the requirements of this civilization and to feel comfortable in its midst, because the restriction of the instincts which it involves lays a heavy psychological burden on our shoulders. (p. 151)

However complex the social proliferation of instinctual demands may be, these demands are nonetheless a "facade behind which the function of the underlying innate drives are hidden" (Miller & Dollard, 1941, p. 19).

Freudian emphasis on unconscious drives and motives involves a corollary skepticism concerning the purposes that people consciously assign to their acts. Psychoanalysts believe that not only is there much duplicity and concealment about motives, but most people actually know very little about their own motivations.

The Freudian scheme of motivation applies to human behavior the *conservation of energy principle,* which holds that energy can be neither created nor destroyed. Repressed wishes carry energy charges, and this energy must be discharged in some way. Hence the occurrence of such processes as *sublimation,* in which forbidden sexual impulses obtain indirect gratification through acceptable modes of behavior such as artistic creation, intellectual pursuits, simple labor, and other outlets that are not obviously sexual.

Evaluation. The Freudian system is complex and, as we have stated, has many variants. We therefore content ourselves here with commenting critically upon those aspects that have to do most explicitly with motivation.

We have already examined the idea that all human behavior and all cultural forms stem directly or indirectly from primal biological sources. We may add that Freudian theory is an especially elaborate form of modified biological determinism. Despite the ample allowance that contemporary analysts often make for social or cultural factors, the theoretical scheme still presents an extremely oversimplified view of the relationship of humans to groups. This is perhaps to be expected, given that this body of theory arose from therapeutic practice with individual patients and that its main focus is still on therapy.

Because orthodox Freudian psychoanalysts view society and its functions as growing out of individual biological urges, they are compelled to view the urges that derive from group life as entirely secondary. The sociologist's position is usually that groups, by their very interaction, generate new "needs"—that is, wishes, aspirations, ambitions, ideals, values, and goals—and that these needs constantly change and proliferate. This is a pervasive feature of group life that need not and cannot be explained in terms of primal urges. Individuals are born into or join groups that are already going concerns, often with long histories, and learn the appropriate motives for action in them. As groups change and develop new interests, individuals change with them, dropping old motives and acquiring new ones. The Freudian idea that culture is a dependent variable, that it merely reflects the psychology of the individual, does not square with history and has led to strained and improbable interpretations of many institutions and historic events—war, social movements, marriage, drug addiction, the Nazi revolution, and international affairs, for example. Freud (1933) himself set this pattern, and his statement about the origin of religion gives an idea of the flavor of some of these interpretive efforts: "Psychoanalysis . . . has traced the origin of religion to the helplessness of childhood, and its content to the persistence of the wishes and needs of childhood into maturity" (p. 229).

One feature of Freudian psychology that is still relatively popular, despite its stress upon instinctive drives, is that it does assign an important role to learning. The instincts that are recognized are only two in number—Life and Death (Eros and Thanatos)—and these are seen mainly as energy sources having no implicit direction or goals. The direction, form, and content of the resultant pattern of behavior, as well as the objects toward which it is directed, are regarded as a matter of learning. In the actual acquisition of specific behavior, primary stress is placed upon the interaction between a child and his or her parents and siblings. Although behavioristic psychologists and social scientists usually do not accept the whole Freudian scheme, some are receptive to the idea that organic drives become harnessed to social motives through a conditioning or learning process.

At the heart of Freudian psychology lies the *energy postulate*, which asserts that individuals have fixed quantities of energy at their disposal. What this means is that all socially learned motives are merely transformations of basic urges and do not have autonomous status of their own. The energy postulate leads Freudians to assume further that motives acquired in adult life are merely complex permutations of old ones. As Piaget (1951), criticizing Freud, says, "When there is transfer of feeling from one object to another, we must recognize that in addition to continuity there is construction of a new feeling through the integration schema" (p. 186). Allport (1937, pp. 190-212) makes much the same point when he insists upon what he calls the *functional autonomy of motives*. By this he means that a form of behavior first performed as a means to a given end may become an end in itself when the original purpose has long since disappeared. The error involved in the Freudian view of motivation is that of confusing historical continuity with functional continuity. The motives of acts being performed now obviously must be operative in the present. The fact that these motives have histories does not mean that they are determined by early childhood antecedents.

One major objection to the Freudian system hinges on the conception of "the unconscious" and unconscious motives. There is no question that people are often unable—or unwilling—to give adequate grounds for their acts or that there is much irrationality in human behavior. Considering the complexity of human interaction and personal life histories, individuals can hardly be expected to account fully and accurately for their behavior and all its antecedents. This fact was recognized for generations before Freud.

However, the Freudian view of unconscious functioning is open to question on a number of points. First, it exaggerates the extent of unconscious motivation. A great deal of human behavior certainly appears to be routine, standardized, planned, or otherwise rational. The Freudians have been accused—and we think rightly—of taking a dim view of the rational processes and tending to look for motivational complexities where they do not exist. In the hands of a novice, this can be a form of "motive-mongering." At best, such an analytic approach tends either to reduce complex phenomena to terms of individualistic motives or to shy away from these phenomena, many of which, like the establishment of the United Nations, are of a conscious and planned character.

Another criticism often made of the Freudian conception of the unconscious is that the term *unconscious* is used so loosely that it confuses issues. It can be used to indicate an experience that an individual has forgotten or to designate an innate drive. It can be used to describe an experience that an individual has never had, in the sense that he or she failed to notice that certain things were happening. It can also designate individuals' simple ignorance about themselves and their acts, or it may refer to their failure to analyze their own behavior.

An examination of any one portion of Freudian theory tends to lead to a consideration of the whole system. However, we shall confine ourselves to a few comments on the Freudian theories of repression, memory, and unconscious purposes.

One does not have to deny the existence of repression, or something like it, to quarrel with the Freudian interpretation of it. People sometimes do bury memories so deeply that they are entirely unconscious of their existence, and they are often unaware of impulses and desires that influence them. In much of Freudian theory, however, the concept of repression is overextended, as when it is used to explain why people do not recall experiences during infancy. The total volume of anyone's experience is so great, and behavior is so complex, that it seems inevitable that everyone should forget much and that none of us should be fully aware of all the reasons for our actions. Sullivan (1953) refers to *selective inattention*, which enables us to maintain our self-esteem by not noticing things that may threaten it. The concept of repression calls attention to an important psychological process, but a satisfactory description of the process remains to be formulated.

The Freudian conception of repression rests on a particular view of memory. "For Freud, the whole of the past is preserved in the unconscious. . . . another conception of memory has been opposed to it, that of reconstruction-memory" (Piaget, 1951, p. 187). The latter concept, as we have stated, interprets memory as a reconstructive act, dependent upon the nature and organization of the material and the linguistic categories available to the person. Forgetting is regarded as a complex and not necessarily repressive process. It is clear that repression is often associated with anxiety and threats to self-esteem, but the precise nature of the connection is not clear.

A final point concerning unconscious motivations: By definition, they are inaccessible to the individual. This means that evidence concerning their existence cannot be obtained through direct testimony, but their existence must be inferred from what the person says and does. Evidence of this sort is subject to interpretations that differ according to the school of thought followed by the interpreter. The acceptance or rejection by the patient of a specific interpretation in itself proves nothing concerning the correctness of the interpretation. Taken with other evidence, the patient's rejection of an imputed motive is often viewed as proof of its existence, as is the patient's agreement with the analyst in other circumstances. We can even ask if a wholly unconscious motive can exist at all. Take oxygen deprivation as an example: A person may desperately need oxygen and be entirely unaware of it; as long as this is the case, no appropriate behavior to satisfy the need occurs, and thus the biological need can scarcely be called a motivational force. So-called unconscious motives should probably be called by some name other than *motives* to indicate that they are not like the ordinary conscious motives for which the term might well be reserved.

We have offered this long, detailed analysis and criticism of the basic Freudian position on motivation because of its continuing influence upon contemporary thought. (For example, a revised version of Freudian thought has resurfaced in recent years in the statements of feminist scholars who have reassessed Freud's and Lacan's theories concerning sexuality, gender, and the family.) There is no doubt that it has provided a needed corrective of rationalistic and static psychologies and has suggested new depths and dimensions of behavior. It has fostered a well-warranted skepticism about easy explanations of behavior in terms of its face value. As Langer (1948) notes, "The great contribution of Freud to the philosophy of mind has been the realization that human behavior is a language; that every *move* is, at the same time, a *gesture*" (p. 18).

The Marxist View

Another very influential motivational terminology in the contemporary world is that provided by Marxism. Most American social psychologists pay scant attention to it, although in other social sciences—anthropology and political science, for example—it is more influential, and it constitutes an essential feature of the cultural studies position (see Chapter 1). Also, among some younger sociologists there has been considerable reliance on, or stimulation from, Marxism. European social scientists give considerable attention to it (see Ibanez-Gracia & Rueda, 1997). A brief general consideration of the Marxist view offers an interesting contrast to the Freudian scheme.

The Marxist social scientist conceives of the individual as the product of institutions, whereas adherents of the Freudian scheme consider institutions to be the products of individuals. The Marxist locates sources of motives in the social structure in the apparatuses of culture, in the media, and in the communications industries of the society, rather than in the individual. Like the Freudians, Marxists do not take seriously the expressed purposes of people, regarding them as mere surface manifestations or rationalizations of fundamental economic and class interests that may go unrecognized. In Marxist theory, these interests have nothing to do with primal biological urges, but are seen as arising from the social structure and its particular historic past.

The details of Marxist theory are complicated; however, the major theme is that the economic system, as it is mediated by the ideological apparatuses of culture, is the source from which the important motivations flow. An individual's position within the material structure has a pervasive effect upon his or her thought and action. Because individuals share or have similar positions, they form different social classes and other somewhat less massive and important interest groups. The course of history is seen as the struggle for power among these groups.

According to this view, all thoughts, beliefs, philosophies, writings, art, and the like are determined by the basic economic facts of the society and reflect the position in the class structure of those who have formulated or created them. In Marxist terminology, mental products are *superstructure.* Marxists have used the term *ideology* to suggest that ideas are reflections of class interests. The Marxist use of the term *ideology* is not identical to the Freudians' use of the term *rationalization,* because the former refers to a collective, or group, rationale. Because Marxists hold that ideas are derived from class position, they theoretically disparage as "idealistic" any psychology that attaches much importance to the motivational aspect of ideas, although they make practical use of this aspect in the political sphere.

The Marxist position is radically environmentalistic and hence comes into conflict with views stressing hereditary or biological factors in the determination of behavior.

The Marxist recognizes a difference between the real interests and the perceived interests of a person or class. Thus in the Marxist view, the real interests of white-collar clerks may be identical to those of factory workers, because both stand in opposition to an oppressing elite. However, white-collar workers usually ally themselves with their employers and thus, according to the Marxist, betray their own class interests. They do this because their eyes have not been opened to the way in which society really functions; in this sense they have a *false consciousness.* Marxists explain white-collar attitudes by referring to the special occupational position of this group of workers. They contend that only through Marxist analysis—that is, analysis in terms of class structure—can white-collar workers see their true position and recognize their affiliation with the working class. This distinction between real and perceived interests is paralleled by the Freudian dichotomy of unconscious and conscious motives. Like the Freudians, Marxists try to help their adherents to bring the real sources of their behavior into the open (Laclau & Mouffe, 1985).

Marxist theory involves some ambiguity, as many critics have pointed out. However, the theory of historical epochs, which predicts alterations in symbolic, cognitive skills, has guided the research of Luria and, earlier, of Vygotsky. Paradoxically, however, "Marxist materialism" as reflected in the work of some Soviet psychologists turns out to be the approximate equivalent of American "behaviorism."

As suggested in Chapter 1, in the cultural studies version of Marxism, the "circuit of culture" shapes the meanings things have for human beings, including the meanings humans have of themselves. These meanings are shaped by the mass media. They flow through a political economy that regulates and articulates the production, distribution, and consumption of cultural objects. This political economy structures the production, distribution, and consumption of wealth in a society. It provides the motivational apparatus for the consumption of cultural objects. It makes connections among such cultural objects as cars, clothing, and the personal identities consumers form of themselves as gendered human beings.

There is some significance and truth in the idea that occupation and class position are important sources of motivation. The Marxist theory is much too one-sided, but it has played an important historical role in social science by counteracting individualistic assumptions concerning the motives of humans. It has placed a needed emphasis upon institutionally derived loyalties and has called attention to economic interests, the media, group allegiances, and intergroup conflicts as determinants of individual action (Althusser, 1969; Anderson, 1984; Giddens, 1981).

A Sociological Conception

Rationalization and interpretation. As we have seen, both Freudians and Marxists regard as suspect the verbal accounts that individuals give of their own purposes. Marxists often regard such accounts as cover-ups of real economic motives or as evidence of ignorance. Freudians call them "rationalizations" and heavily discount them. Although they admit that some statements of purpose of a rational and conscious sort are in accord with reality, they are mainly concerned with irrational and unconscious motivations.

A technical definition of *rationalization* is that it is "a common technique by which the ego keeps certain tendencies repressed. . . . Emphasis upon the acceptable motivation allows the ego to keep the unacceptable repressed, since the selected motives can sufficiently explain the act in question" (Alexander, 1952, p. 13). The psychoanalytic concept of rationalization implies that when acceptable motives are substituted for unacceptable ones, individuals are actually unable to think of the latter; when they deny their existence, they are not being dishonest or "kidding" themselves. In popular discourse, the term *rationalization* is usually taken to mean giving socially acceptable but "phony" reasons instead of the socially unacceptable but "real" reasons for one's acts. Thus a woman quarrels with her husband in the morning and throughout the day deals harshly with her coworkers on the grounds that they need discipline. This conception implies that individuals usually know the real reasons for their acts, and hence tends to equate rationalization with dishonest or deluded thinking. It is a common belief that honest people do not rationalize, or that they do so infrequently.

Strictly speaking, dishonesty has nothing to do with rationalization, for a person who deliberately makes false statements is not rationalizing at all, but merely lying. A genuine rationalization is a formulation that the individual believes to be true even though it may be labeled self-deception by outside observers. The concept is probably used so widely by laypersons because it allows them to disregard or discredit the opinions of other people. As Burke (1935) has said:

> Much deep sympathy is required to distinguish our reasoning from another's rationalizing. . . . As people tend to round out their orientations verbally, we sometimes show our approval of their verbalizations by the term reasoning and disapproval by the term rationalizing. Thus these words also serve as question begging words. (pp. 19-20)

The central sociological conception of rationalization is that people interpret their behavior and the entire situation in which it occurs either before or after the act—or both. Such interpretations sometimes represent distortions of the facts, however subtle, so that the individual's face or self-esteem is preserved. Concerning the interpretations that are made after the act, they may have to do mainly either with "purpose"—that is, motive—or with "the objective situation" in which the act occurred. For example, suppose that a man shows cowardice when he is attacked or threatened at a party by another man. He may avoid the implications of cowardice, in his own eyes or in the eyes of others, by a rationalization in terms of motives ("I didn't fight because I wanted to wait until a better moment to answer him"), or he may rationalize by interpreting and perhaps distorting the objective situation ("He had a number of friends there and they would have helped him"). Whether the interpretation after the act is chiefly concerned with purpose (of the self or of others) or with the objective situation, distortion or inaccuracy may creep in because of the person's self-involvement.

In order to obtain a true or correct interpretation of an event or situation, one thus attempts to rule out all bias stemming from personal involvement and to base interpretation upon genuine evidence, so that if possible all disinterested observers may agree on "the facts." Procedure in courts of law is the classic example of a formalized, if not always successful, attempt to accomplish this. No sharp line can be drawn between a rationalization about a situation and a description of it, for it is difficult to rule out the influence of all personal interest and bias.

Accounts. Scott and Lyman (1968) have pointed out that rationalizations, which they term *accounts,* are called forth when the social actor needs to explain unanticipated or untoward behavior—that is, problematic rather than accepted routine behavior, whether past, present, or future. They note that in general there are two types of accounts: excuses and justifications.

Excuses are the accounts used in situations in which individuals admit their acts were bad, or that they made mistakes, but they deny responsibility for what they did, stating that the causes of their acts were accidents, mistakes, or misunderstandings, or that what occurred took place because of fatigue, emotional problems, or perhaps drug or alcohol abuse. Persons who use excuses separate themselves from their behavior and its consequences. For example, in a study of convicted rapists, Diane Scully (1991) found many men who used excuses. They admitted having committed rape, but claimed that they were drunk at the time, had emotional problems, or were really nice men who had made mistakes.

Persons who use *justifications* accept responsibility for their problematic acts, but deny that what they did was wrong. In Scully's study, men who used justifications denied that they had committed rape. These men argued that their victims enjoyed it, that they did nothing wrong, that the women asked for it.

Scott and Lyman also distinguish five linguistic styles that "frame the manner in which the account will be given" and that often indicate "the social circle in which it will be most appropriately employed." First is the *intimate style,* used among those who share deep, intense, personal relationships. There is a tendency to use single sounds or words and jargon for the communication of ideas. Scott and Lyman give the following example: A husband caresses his wife in bed but gets no endearing response; the wife just says, "Pooped." Second is the *casual style,* used among peers, in-group members, and insiders. In this style, typically, words are omitted and slang is used. Thus among regular users of cocaine, the question "Why did you sell your stereo?" might be answered simply, "Coke." Third is the *consultative style,* which ordinarily is used when the amount of knowledge available to one interactant is unknown or problematic to the others. In response to the question "Why are you using cocaine? Don't you know it's addictive?" the individual might reply, "You don't know anything about addiction; cocaine's not addictive because there are no physical withdrawal effects, like there are for alcohol." Fourth is the *formal style,* used in groups perhaps larger than six persons, where listeners must wait their turn to speak. The formal style is typically used in bureaucratic organizations, courtrooms, and organized meetings. Fifth is the *frozen style,* an extreme version employed by people who are required to interact while yet remaining strangers—for example, telephone operators speaking to customers and airplane pilots talking to air traffic controllers.

Scott and Lyman also emphasize that accounts may or may not be honored, so each person must learn a repertoire of proper accounts for appropriate audiences as well as proper styles of wording the accounts. When an account is not honored, it will most frequently be viewed as illegitimate or unreasonable.

In common experience, many acts are interpreted more than once. Indeed, if an act is important, it may receive several interpretations, sometimes distributed over a number of years. Individuals usually are not aware of these reinterpretations. This kind of reseeing of the past we have already discussed as *reconstructive memory.* It should be apparent that a large proportion of the later interpretation is not concerned with the preservation of self-esteem—that is, it is not rationalization in the narrower, Freudian sense of the word.

Interpretations of an act may also be made before the act takes place. Such a *preinterpretation* includes an estimate of the situation in which behavior is called for—including the possible actions, intentions, and expectations held by others—and some judgment of how and why the individual proposes to act with regard to the situation. The how and why of the coming act have to do with the individual's purposes, and if the person should happen to phrase the matter aloud to someone else and explicitly to him- or herself, he or she will generally use the word *because* when referring to these purposes. For example, someone is asked what he is going to do next summer and answers, "Go to Europe." When asked "Why?" or "Why next year?" he offers a statement that includes purpose: "Because I am getting to the age where I feel I can spend my savings and because I have never been there." The initial statement of purpose is likely to be somewhat condensed; if he is encouraged, the person may present his reason in more detail. "I have never been there" may be expanded to an explanation that he wants to go to Europe so that he, too, can talk about Paris when others speak of their experiences there.

Purpose, as we use the term, is synonymous with *motive.* Mills (1940) has called statements about purpose *motivational statements,* whether offered to others or to self, because they are formulated, at least partially, in verbal terms. When others ask us to account for our acts, either forthcoming or past, we usually give them motivational statements so that they may understand the reasons for our acts. The statements that we offer them may be—but certainly need not be—quite false. We may couch them in terms that appear reasonable to our questioners so as to "get by," or we may conceal our real motives for various other reasons. As Schwartz and Merten (1971) have remarked, "The ease with which people shift from what [Alfred] Schutz calls 'in order to' to the 'because of' motivational explanations gives the actor considerable latitude in the way he can construe his actions" (p. 294).

Disclaimers. Hewitt and Stokes (1975; see also Hewitt, 1984, pp. 167-168) discuss a second form of motive talk, the disclaimer. A disclaimer is "a verbal device people employ when they want to ward off negative implications of something they are about to do or say" (Hewitt, 1984, p. 167). A person might say, "I'm not prejudiced, because some of my best friends are Jews, but . . ." or "This may seem strange to you, but . . ." or "I'm no social psychologist, but . . ." (Hewitt, 1984, p. 167). In these statements, the individual introduces an act or statement that contradicts the premise of the disclaimer. A person claiming not to be prejudiced makes a racist statement; a self-proclaimed nonexpert makes a pronouncement that one would trust only if it comes from an expert (Hewitt, 1984, p. 167). Disclaimers are *prospective social acts*; they reveal how people attempt to protect their identities in the eyes of others. In some cases, disclaimers support prejudices and stereotypes.

Motive, disclaimer, purpose, and cause. Motive, disclaimer, and purpose should not be confused with cause. Cause and causation have backward references, whereas motive, disclaimer, and purpose have forward references in time. Motive, disclaimer, and purpose are concerned with the anticipated consequences of acts; *cause* refers to antecedent processes that precede an event and that influence it decisively or determine it. (Motives are in a sense personal and private, whereas causes are general and public.) *Causation* applies to classes of events, and causal explanations are subject to public verification. The causation of human behavior is poorly understood, but it is known that much more than motives is involved.

Motives appear or are mobilized at the beginning of an act and indeed are a part of the act, because they persist throughout its course. They may, of course, change during the act by becoming more complicated or more simple; they may be joined by other motives, or they may even be replaced, particularly if the act has considerable duration. Hence, in describing any complicated event in a person's life, reference must be made to the purposes the individual had in mind. But in addition, a whole range of other conditions must be taken into account—namely, the motives of others and the material or objective situation. Individuals themselves are in a sense the final authorities on their own purposes, because they know better than anyone else what they had in mind, even though the mechanisms of repression or rationalization may have operated to distort their knowledge of their actions. With respect to the objective situation, on the other hand, individuals usually cannot be well informed, because it is impossible for them to possess all the information concerning their own nervous systems, physiological states, and past experiences that might be relevant to any explanation of why they performed specific acts exactly as they did at exactly the times they did.

Before an action is completed, the purposes of the behavior are likely to loom large to the person engaged in it. After the action is completed, the person may often have second thoughts, and may then wonder whether his or her reasons were as simple as they seemed. When asked to account for past actions, people often give commonsense, causal explanations rather than motivational ones. For example, a husband may scold his wife at the breakfast table, believing that he is scolding her because she has spoiled his coffee. He may later explain the quarrel by saying that neither he nor his wife had gotten enough sleep the previous night.

Because motives appear at the beginnings of acts or in preparation for action, and because each individual feels his or her own motives in a direct way, it is easy to understand how motives have come to be viewed as causes of the behavior of which they are a part, and indeed as "forces" that "make" the behavior occur. It was common earlier in the 20th century for sociologists to explain institutional and other cultural behavior in terms of the operation of wishes, interests, needs, and other "social forces." However, the idea of causation no longer includes the conception of force in this sense. There are many different ideas of causation in the philosophy of science, but on this particular point there is general agreement.

Scientific cause. The scientific concept of causation, of course, is a general feature of many scientific fields in which no problem of motivation exists. Indeed, in view of the instability and variability of human purposes and of the fact that purposes are really part of behavior rather than mysterious forces lying behind it, motives are not so much explanations of behavior as they are behavioral problems, themselves requiring analysis and explanation. From this viewpoint, explaining such behavior as stealing, for example, includes the problem of accounting for the fact that people steal because of so many different motives.

We have seen how Freudian psychoanalytic and Marxist "scientific" theories attempt to offer causal analyses of complex forms of human behavior. We have also seen how individuals construct their own "causal" interpretations of their conduct. It is therefore useful to distinguish, as Alfred Schutz (1962, pp. 3-5) does, between commonsense and scientific thinking on causal matters. Commonsense causal explanations are based on matters that lie outside, but may draw upon, scientific formulations. They tend not to be strictly logical; they are often based on unclear meanings or vague definitions given to words, and they are not predicated on scientific knowledge (Garfinkel, 1967b, p. 271). Scientific explanations are derived from scientific theories. They are based on knowledge that has been scientifically verified, and they are typically logical and semantically clear. Accounts and disclaimers are examples of commonsense causal interpretations. The Freudian and Marxist schemes are examples of scientific causal interpretations.

These examples point up the truism that people and groups may do the same things for different reasons and different things for the same reason. Because causal generalizations are based upon elements that are common to various instances of a given form of behavior, in problems like the above these generalizations cannot be stated in terms of motive. Psychoanalysts have attempted to meet this difficulty by looking for uniformity and common motivations on the unconscious level. What is suggested here is that the matter may be dealt with in another way, provided that one conceives of motive as something other than a specific determinant of behavior. It may be conceded that most significant human behavior is and must be motivated, but this is a far cry from contending that any given form of behavior must always be motivated in the same way.

Social Sources of Individual Motivation

Mills (1940) asserts that "motives are of no value apart from delimited societal situations for which they are appropriate vocabularies. They must be situated. . . . Motives vary in content and character with historical epochs and societal structures" (p. 906). One implication of this statement is that although our motives generally appear to us as peculiarly personal and private, many of them are learned from others and are furnished to us tailor-made by the society or the groups in which we live.

When an individual joins a group of long standing, he or she finds that the proper codes of conduct, including the ends and means of group activity, are spelled out in considerable detail. They may even be formalized and embodied in written documents such as the Hippocratic oath or an oath of allegiance, or in constitutions, contracts, or codes. When persons leave groups and join new ones, they must learn new motivations. As Weber has pointed out in connection with work, for instance: "The motives which induce people to work vary with different social classes. . . . When a man changes rank, he switches from one set of motives to another" (paraphrased in Mannheim, 1936, pp. 316-317). Even when people live rather stable lives, changing their group memberships very little, some of their motives nevertheless change with advancing age according to prevailing social definitions. Although the physical processes of aging are much alike in all cultures, the motivational adaptations to them are endlessly varied.

The above statements of Weber and Mills point to a phenomenon that is immensely important to the social psychologist. How individuals see their own behavior and how they may explain that behavior to others, as well as how they may interpret it to others—including themselves—is crucially important. It is important for understanding their interaction, as well as for understanding their thoughts about themselves. But social psychologists cannot comprehend the full significance of this accounting, interacting, and thinking unless they link them with both the personal biographies of the individuals and the social biographies of the groups to which the individuals belong. This point closely relates to our earlier discussions of the group contexts of language and thought as well as to the group and historical contexts for remembrance. Said another way (although this quote pertains to identity rather than to motives), "Personal identity is meshed with group identity which itself rests upon an historical past" (Strauss, 1959, p. 173).

The fallacious commonsense imputation of motives has its academic counterpart. For example, psychoanalysts have reinterpreted the private lives of famous people such as St. Augustine and Leonardo da Vinci in terms of 20th-century sexual symbols, thus ignoring the fact that these historical characters viewed the conduct of others and themselves in very different terms than do people of our own era. Such scholarly interpretation is equivalent to translating other rationalizations into our own. Because humans are interested in the lives of past generations, such translating is inevitable. The only corrective to a superficial handling of the past is an adequate understanding of the period under consideration through exhaustive examination of historical sources. The accuracy of the account should rest upon an understanding of the actual symbols available to the historical personages; it should not rest upon the degree to which their motives appear plausible to us in the light of our own motives at the present time.

It follows that individuals cannot express purposes or rationalize behavior in terms they have not learned. We cannot motivate people to act by using terms outside their comprehension; we must appeal to purposes that they understand and that make sense to them. Conversely, it is incorrect to impute rationalizations to individuals when these involve motivational terms they do not possess. Nevertheless, such imputation is a common recourse of individuals who find it impossible to assess behavior in their own terms. There is almost always a tendency to explain other people's behavior in terms of one's own vocabulary of motives. This form of incorrect assessment is called *projection* and is seen in a crude form in most romantic historical novels. The characters, supposedly living a century or two ago, are made to rationalize their activities according to the symbols of the 20th century. Likewise, in American movies, heroes and heroines dress in the clothes of other eras but act as if their incentives are those of 20th-century Americans. But the projection of motives may take more subtle forms.

Apropos of motives and explanations, Alan Blum and Peter McHugh (1971), influenced by critical positivistic tendencies in ethnomethodology, have also severely criticized symbolic interactionist conceptualizations of motivation. They reject, as we do, the idea of motivation as simple "cause," but contend that symbolic interactionists accept the actor as "a research informant, whose report acquires analytic status because the actor is thought to be a privileged and exclusive source on questions of his motives" (p. 101). They argue that the researcher ought to try to learn systematically how a motivational statement is generated to begin with—how, for example, the actor is constrained to cite a reason at all; how it takes the form it does (giving a reason for, say, telling a joke); how it comes to be acceptable to the hearer as an answer. We believe that Blum and McHugh have badly misread the conceptualizations of motive and motivation by symbolic interactionists. However, they make an excellent point, provided one mutes their criticism, when they say that there is often an inadequate formulation of the "conditions" under which specific types of motivational statements are given, chosen from alternatives, offered or given to others, or accepted or rejected by those who give them as well as by others. This leads us to considerations touched on in the next section.

Motives, Morale, and Social Structure

The stability and endurance of social groups or structures depend upon the members' carrying out necessary lines of action. This means that group members must be motivated to perform these actions.

When a structure recruits "from the inside," as when persons are born into it, the problem of motivation is handled early through the socialization of the young. But when members are recruited, as in an army or a vocation, the new members must be taught to act in accordance with the essential purposes of the body or group. Because many recruits join voluntarily, some learning of appropriate motivations starts beforehand; for example, future doctors learn something about the aims and aspirations of the medical profession long before they go to medical school. Involuntary membership may present the group with the problem of apathy or lack of enthusiasm, because new members may find the purposes of the organization to be irrelevant, or they may even be antagonistic. These attitudes are exemplified by political apathy among citizens and the act of "going AWOL" among soldiers. Insofar as good citizens and good soldiers decry unmotivated or badly motivated colleagues, they exemplify their own attachment to the long-range functions of the state and the army. Considerable variation in personal motivation may exist among the membership of any group, but in general, motivations must be geared to, or at least not antagonistic to, the group's purposes.

Social structures vary tremendously in the amount of latitude permitted to their memberships in this regard, and the degree of latitude is related intimately to the nature of the structure. For instance, if an embattled religious sect is to survive, it must arrange matters so that group and individual motivations are virtually identical. The very existence of a revolutionary or radical political elite, such as the Communist Party leadership in a capitalist country (at least in earlier years, when the party was revolutionary), also requires that individual and institutional motivations be closely intermeshed. The concept of "party discipline" requires that individuals make the party's decisions and policies their own, regardless of how they may vary from week to week or how they may appear to the individuals personally. They are required to sacrifice personal comforts and immediate personal desires to the long-run interests of the party, and they are willing to do so because they identify their own essential interests with those of the party. A group characterized by this attitude is said to have a *high morale* or *high solidarity*. This is equivalent to saying that even in the face of setbacks, the membership persists in pursuit of group aims and, indeed, may thrive upon a certain amount of opposition or suppression, because this adversity supplies additional justification for revolutionary ardor. Self-interest and group interest coalesce so completely in groups of this kind, whether political or otherwise, that individuals may sacrifice their own lives for the good of the cause and may do so not only willingly but with elation.

Most organizations, of course, allow more latitude between individual and group purposes, and demand lesser degrees of allegiance and sacrifice. For these groups to function effectively, they must have a certain amount of consensus concerning matters relevant to group survival. Individuals may retain membership for a variety of reasons, some of them quite peripheral. For example, people belong to churches for business and social reasons as well as for religious ones.

In any society, some parts of the total structure are generally recognized as more vital than others. There is a corresponding difference in the pressure upon individuals to conform to the controlling norms. People who "buck the system" because they do not value it or because they will not support the group's endeavors are liable to be punished severely. Court martial, imprisonment, and so on are deterrents to deviance, but positive allegiances operate more efficiently.

When a social structure fails to elicit the minimal allegiance necessary for its proper functioning, then we speak of *poor morale* or *low solidarity.* Presumably, there are different types of poor morale, depending on the kind of group structure, but essentially it comes down to a lack of effective coordination because of discrepant individual aims. To take the simplest case first, there may be so little consensus about group values and such diversity of individual purposes that the group cannot act in concert. A more complicated form of poor morale stems from discrepant definitions of group ends on different social levels represented in the group. Whenever the structure is complex, there is a problem of obtaining a working consensus shared by the various echelons. This condition can exist in a political party, industrial corporation, religious organization, or university. Of course, some segments of the organization may have excellent morale and others poor morale, because they evaluate differently the way matters are progressing.

CONCLUSION

The distinctive qualities of human mental activity are the consequences of humans' incorporation and use of language symbols. *Goal behavior* involves response to signs representing the future, *memory* is response to signs representing the past, and *perception* is response to signs representing the present environment. Skill in interpretation of and response to signs on any level is *intelligence.* Reason involves the interpretation and use of symbols and is the equivalent of conceptual thought. It is a peculiarly human activity.

Such complex mental functions as perceiving and remembering are examples of complex human sign behavior. Individual human beings take over language symbols as part of their repertoire of behavior. Activity theory is geared to the study of these kinds of practices. Human beings are able to assimilate socially developed symbolic systems that transform their psychic life, add new dimensions to their behavior, and make it possible for them to profit from the experience of past generations and to anticipate and plan for the future in ways unparalleled in the rest of the animal world.

Motivation presents an old and thorny problem for the student of human behavior. The ways in which social theorists handle the concept of motivation are likely to determine how they will deal with a great many other problems. Through the course of group interaction, individuals develop motives and accounts, or linguistic explanations, of their behavior. These accounts are lodged in ongoing interaction. A common conception of motives, which we reject, gives them a biological base, as when hunger is identified with the contractions of the walls of the stomach and other bodily conditions. A biological condition by itself has little motivational significance, except as it is perceived or interpreted by the individual in whom it exists. The influential Freudian conception of motivation, which emphasizes unconscious wishes and desires, has serious weaknesses arising mainly from the fact that no theory about the content of the "unconscious" can be proved because the unconscious is, by definition, virtually unknowable. Marxist theory presents an interesting comparison with Freudian theory, for in the former the emphasis is placed upon unconscious economic, rather than sexual, motivations. A conception of motives held by symbolic interactionists treats them as essentially verbal in nature, as part of behavior, but as something other than causes of behavior. Knowledge of motives, in this conception, is used primarily to enable a person to project him- or herself into the outlook of another person—that is, for "understanding," rather than for "explaining," behavior.

Motives are learned in social experience, vary from group to group, and are relative to social context. A consideration of group morale, or solidarity, gives some indications of the ways in which persons are motivated by their identifications. The research implication of this discussion is that the accounts people offer for their own behavior, far from explaining it, themselves require analysis and explanation. Motives are social and interpersonal products. They emerge and may be observed in the interaction process. They are often after-the-fact explanations of human conduct.

SUGGESTED READINGS

Bentz, V. M. (1989). *Becoming mature: Childhood ghosts and spirits in adult life.* New York: Aldine de Gruyter. A powerful account of how the memories of childhood haunt us in adulthood.

Burke, K. (1945). *A grammar of motives.* Englewood Cliffs, NJ: Prentice Hall. A sensitive and sophisticated discussion by a literary critic of the linguistic nature of motives and the functions of motivational accounts.

Clarke, A. E., & Fujimura, J. H. (Eds.). (1992). *The right tools for the job: At work in the twentieth-century life sciences.* Princeton, NJ: Princeton University Press. An important collection of essays that extends interpretive activity theory to the work of scientists.

Perinbanayagam, R. S. (1985). *Signifying acts.* Carbondale: Southern Illinois University Press. A seminal presentation of the symbolic interactionist theory of motives.

STUDY QUESTIONS

1. What are the differences among causes, motives, and accounts?
2. Compare and contrast Marxist and Freudian theories of motive (and motivation).
3. Why is there a dearth of recollections of childhood experiences?

PART III

CHILDHOOD SOCIALIZATION

7

Learning Language in Early Childhood

The three chapters that make up Part III discuss how the social object called *child* is produced by social groups in and through the process of language acquisition. In this chapter we turn to the issue of childhood socialization, taking up the topic of the acquisition of language and concepts in early childhood. We hope this analysis will provide a framework through which the reader may better grasp our earlier discussion of language. As social psychologists, we are obliged to devote a considerable amount of time to childhood socialization; the nexus between self and society lies in the socialization process. Any theory of how society is possible must be able to account for the social and socializing experiences of the young child. The term *childhood socialization* refers to those experiences and interactive relationships that build human nature into the child (Denzin, 1977, p. 3; see also Miller, 1996, p. 183). Central to this process is the acquisition and use of language (Markey, 1928/1978).

The learning of language is not merely a matter of mastering the mechanics of speech. The symbols that make up a language are concepts that represent ways of acting and thinking. Infants must learn to classify objects and to act appropriately toward them. They also must learn that some words refer to things that do not exist as material objects, but only as ideas, abstractions, or relationships. To teach anyone the conventional meaning of a word is to teach him or her how to act or think with reference to the object or the concept to which the word refers. The meanings of words are not locked up in dictionaries, but are found in people's acts. In this chapter we review the growing literature on language acquisition, paying particular attention to the speech patterns of young children (see Hulit & Howard, 1997, pp. 108-152; O'Grady, Dobrovolsky, & Aronoff, 1997, pp. 437-471). As children acquire language, they develop the ability to be consciously self-aware, as we shall discuss in Chapter 8. Language acquisition is basic to the genesis of self in early childhood. We also examine the research and theories of Piaget, Vygotsky, and Chomsky in this chapter. We argue that the "universal" features of language usage may reflect "universal" characteristics of the primary group and may not, as Chomsky argues, be based on grammatical knowledge that is inborn. This view is known as nativism (O'Grady et al., 1997, p. 466).

The child's learning of language is not merely an intellectual process. Language puts children in touch with their parents and peers in new and significant ways and initiates their acquisition of broader and more socialized perspectives. It introduces them to new pleasures and satisfactions and also creates a great many new needs and problems. Through learning a language, children learn the rules and standards that regulate social relations, and they develop ideas of mortality and religion. Language is also the means whereby children are gradually prepared for and later inducted into the roles they are destined to play, and through language they learn to grasp the viewpoints and understand the feelings and sentiments of others. Through language, children become aware of their own identities as persons and as members of groups in which they seek status, security, and self-expression and that in turn make demands upon them.

Because newborn babies cannot be aware of their caretakers' symbols, they remain relatively unsocialized for some time. Socialization begins even before infants begin to learn language, because they are responding to all kinds of stimuli. On the other hand, until they begin to comprehend and use conventional speech, their humanness is only partial. Children become socialized when they have acquired the ability to communicate with others and to influence and be influenced by them through the use of speech. This implies socially acceptable behavior toward named objects.

However, learning concepts one by one in piecemeal fashion is not enough, for concepts are interrelated. A word such as *spoon* refers to more than a piece of shaped metal, although "metal" and "shaped" are themselves complex concepts. The meanings of *spoon* (that is, modes of response toward it) are linked with and contingent upon a whole system of related meanings (for example, what foods are eaten with spoons, how spoons are handled, what they are made of, and where they are placed as part of a table setting).

Just how the child comes to a consistent and conventional use of words is a crucial problem for social psychology. We do not really know the full details of this transformation from babbling and initial imitation to adult verbal behavior, or the use of spoken words with conventional meaning. In the following discussion, we consider the materials that are available (see Hulit & Howard, 1997, pp. 109-159).

Instrumental Use of Gestures

Children make meaningful as well as sheerly expressive bodily movements long before they speak conventionally. Such gestures may be accompanied by vocalizations. At first these may not be understood by even extremely solicitous parents, but gradually, their meanings are discovered so that approximate interpretations are readily made. As late as 18 months, babies communicate needs largely through gestures and expressive utterances rather than through actual words. *Neologisms,* or made-up words, may also be used (Brown, 1970; Cook-Gumperz, 1975; Denzin, 1977; DeVilliers & DeVilliers, 1979; Taine, 1877).

The infant's gestural communication gradually recedes and becomes secondary to his or her other gradually evolving vocal language. Some children are retarded linguistically because they develop elaborate gestural "languages" that are so well understood by their parents there is neither incentive nor urgent necessity for them to learn genuine speech. Parental refusal to respond to gestures, however, usually results in the abandonment of such systems.

The most important point about infants' use of gestures is that it is instrumental. They use gestures—although they are not aware that they are using them—to reach for objects, to avoid certain things, or to call for certain things. Infants' expressive bodily movements occur within a context of social relations; that is, people react to their gestures and the infants respond both to people and to their actions with still further gestures. Although at first children make expressive movements toward a brute physical environment, the responses of their parents soon transform the environment into a thoroughly social one in which their early expressive movements become endowed with social significance.

The foregoing considerations suggest that language might best be viewed as a *conversation of gestures.* Language and speech behavior are processes that vary by context, speakers, listeners, and their intentions. Any language contains a set of rules, however implicitly organized and recognized, that governs the expression and interpretations given to both spoken utterances and nonverbal gestures. This view of language is crucial for understanding early childhood speech, for infants speak in a highly personal, often nonverbal language. Indeed, the family must be viewed as a complex language community. The child must master the language of all family members before he or she can successfully take their perspectives in any speech encounter.

Children learn to speak before they learn to think (in a verbal sense), for their first utterances bear no meaning for them and are unlikely to have clear, conventionalized meaning for their caretakers (Vygotsky, 1962). Their verbal sounds begin to get attached to concrete objects and concrete movements. Initially, the young child may develop a complex "crying" vocabulary, as Roger Brown (1958) has noted, with as many as seven different cries designating such diverse states as happiness, pain, anger, discomfort, hunger, and frustration. Often a verbal utterance is combined with a particular nonverbal gesture. The sound "jeewsh" (which the parent translates as "juice") may be accompanied by pointing to the refrigerator or to a container filled with juice. The child has elaborated the contextual meaning of his or her nonconsensual utterance with an unspoken gesture. Whereas many have argued that the family is basically a monolithic speech community, our remarks suggest that each speaker in the family has a unique mode of speaking and gesturing. Each has a unique style of pronunciation, accent, and gesture as well as a particular pattern of intonation and resonance.

Learning to Use and Comprehend Symbols

Bilingual Children

Berk (1997) observes that although most American children speak only one language, current estimates indicate that "6 million American school children speak a language other than English at home, a figure expected to increase steadily into the twenty-first century" (p. 1). Nearly 40 years ago, Bossard and Boll (1960, p. 265) contended that at least one in every five white Americans had grown up in a home where a language other than English was dominant.

Bilingual children may adopt a set of *protective devices* that aid them in the production of their speech acts. They may speak in restrained fashion and attempt to be inconspicuous speakers, seldom talking in "mixed linguistic" company. On the other hand, they may overcompensate and adopt a meticulous mode of talking. As bilingual children, they may develop a stigmatized view of self based on their linguistic status. This is especially so if they come from a disadvantaged ethnic or racial group that is stigmatized by the broader society. Labov (1968) has gone so far as to argue that many American blacks speak a form of "nonstandard" English that gives them a distinct linguistic disadvantage in public schools.

If one of every five Americans comes from a bilingual family, the above remarks suggest that indeed all Americans are socialized into multilingual speech communities—if nonverbal features of language are incorporated into the definition of "language." The problems of the bilingual child are simply more complex than those of the child who comes from a family where only Standard English is spoken. Both kinds of child speakers, however, must learn complex sets of verbal and nonverbal languages.

Learning the Speech Act

The *speech act,* to paraphrase Searle (1970, p. 16), can be defined as the production of a set of sounds that are understandable to at least one other person. Searle, taking a pragmatic approach to the use of language, argues that when people use words they do more than follow a set of conventional language rules—they use words "to get things done" (Hulit & Howard, 1997, p. 37). They perform activities with their speech acts, and every speech act can be said to have three components. The *locutionary act* is what is heard, the expression of words, the sentence that is spoken. The *illocutionary* or *indirect act* is the motive behind the act, what the speaker means or wants to listener to do. For example, a woman says to her husband, "It is cold in the bedroom." Behind this statement is a motive, an intention, perhaps a request for the husband to close the window. The *perlocutionary act* explicitly takes the listener into account and is directed to the effect of the utterance on the listener. For example, a speaker assumes that his or her listener will respond favorably to a compliment.

Such acts are the basic units of linguistic communication and may be verbal or nonverbal. The infant, of course, enters the world with no conception of the speech act and must be taught how to speak. Initially its utterances—the cry, the whimper, the giggle—are not attached or linked to an internal second signal system that would give referents to the sounds. The child must learn how to produce speech acts that are meaningful for others. In this context, it is useful to recollect Vygotsky's (1962, p. 17) distinction between vocal speech (verbal utterances) and inner speech (silent thought). Thought is "soundless" inner speech. The child's first speech acts are global, social utterances that are understood by the recipients of the sounds but not by the child; they are undifferentiated sounds that are not attached to internal symbolic or categorical referents. As children acquire speech act repertoires, their talk becomes increasingly egocentric, or self-centered, in nature. *Egocentric* utterances progressively merge with *sociocentric* formulations such that children are increasingly able to place themselves in the perspectives of others and to view their actions from those standpoints. *Sociocentric speech* is possible because of the emergence of inner speech, or thought. Vygotsky's remarks (1962, p. 19) summarize our position on this point.

Vygotsky's model can be contrasted to the proposals of Piaget. Vygotsky views speech as having a social origin that stands outside the infant. The infant's speech is first social in nature and then becomes egocentric in nature. Egocentric speech progressively translates into inner thought and speech. Piaget, on the other hand, views the origins of speech and thought as first arising within the infant. His model works from the individual to society, whereas Vygotsky's model works from the social environment to the individual. Thus Vygotsky reverses the more traditional psychological views of speech and thought development. Piaget's choice of the term *egocentric* to describe the child's thought is perhaps unfortunate (see Chapter 9).

For children to become credible and understood members of the family speech community, they must relinquish their private, autistic speech for the differentiated symbol system consensually understood by all members of the family.

The Characteristics of Baby Talk

The emergence of speech, or articulatory skills, begins around 6 months of age with babbling, which by 12 months evolves into understandable words (O'Grady et al., 1997, pp. 440-441). A predictable developmental order of word and sound use emerges. The relative order in which a child acquires words and sounds seems to be related directly to the frequency of the use of words and sounds in the child's world: Those used most often appear first and so on (O'Grady et al., 1997, p, 441). As the child's skills improve, his or her verbal activity begins to follow more closely the syntactic rules regulating speech. The child moves from one- to two-word sentences to more complex grammatical structures. This is called telegraphic speech—for example, "Daddy like book," "Chair broken," "Me wana show Mommy" (O'Grady, 1997, p. 450).

The child's speech acts tend to move from undifferentiated utterances to progressively refined categorical statements. In an intriguing study of baby talk in six languages, Charles A. Ferguson (1964) found that the words in baby talk are modifications of normal adult words. The child, for example, says "choo-choo" for "train" or "itty bitty" for "little." Ferguson's research reveals the following features of this form of speech. First, baby talk items consist of simple consonants, stops, and nasals, and only a few vowels. Second, there is a predominance of reduplication (repetition) of particular sounds in baby talk. Third, in each of the six languages Ferguson studied (Arabic, Marathi, Comanche, Gilyak, English, and Spanish) there was a typical morpheme form of talk. The most typical was a sound that began with a monosyllable and ended with a consonant. Given those cross-cultural commonalities, Ferguson (1964) notes:

> In view of this similarity one is tempted to make the hypothesis that every language community provides a stock of baby-talk items which can serve as appropriate material for babies to imitate in creating their phonemes but which do not interfere with the normal words of the language and can gradually be discarded as real words emerge in the children's speech. . . . The baby-talk lexicon of a language community may thus play a special role in the linguistic development of its children. (p. 110)

Thus, by differentially rewarding or showing indifference, adults contribute to the child's progressive speech skills. They may encourage excessive baby talk or talk to the child in more adult language. If the latter, then the child's use of baby talk will be at a minimum. However, it must be noted that the human's ability to make certain vocal sounds is a function of the speech apparatus itself, and certain sounds are easier to make than others. Furthermore, cultures vary in the kinds of sounds they emphasize. As a consequence, the character of the child's speech acts is to a certain degree conditioned or influenced by the child's physiological development—for example, the size of the tongue and the ability to move the lips or to bring the tongue to bear against the teeth, as when the *f* sound is made. The ease with which some sounds are produced may account for the remarkable similarity in baby talk across cultures that Ferguson observed. All of the cultures in Ferguson's study, for example, had a word for mother, and it assumed the "ma-ma" form. The *m* sound is an easily produced sound. Thus, although mothers may delight in their infants' first utterance of "ma-ma," this sound is really one of the most simple phonological sounds the infant can make.

Indeed, the first word spoken by infants the world over is usually a syllable or repeated syllable, such as *mama, dada, bebe, nana, wawa,* or *papa.* The word is expressive of either pleasurable or unpleasurable states. These syllabic phonetic forms become stabilized in the infant's speech with the help of delighted elders, who pick out certain ones and repeat them to the baby until he or she uses them correctly. The use of other words soon follows, especially when the infant somehow makes the momentous discovery that things have names. When children have managed to discover that every object has a name, they have taken a conspicuous step toward learning parental speech.

Aside from discovering that things have names, children may also be said to discover that names have things—that the words they learn correspond to aspects of the real world. In complex types of learning, especially, the progression may be from words to things rather than the reverse. The fact that racial prejudice can be learned before contact with the racial group in question is an illustration of this point. The acquisition of vocabulary sensitizes individuals to certain aspects of the environment that they may encounter later, and predisposes them to notice those that correspond with or confirm what they have previously learned through verbal communication alone. It is in this sense that we may say that the world is not made up of ready-made, discrete objects, events, and qualities waiting to be perceived and named, but rather is built up through collective experience and crystallized in linguistic forms. As learning proceeds, this type of movement from words to things tends to become more and more important.

Usually, as noted above, the infant's first words are employed as sentences rather than as single words; they do duty as one-word sentences. Analyzed merely as parts of speech, they are characteristically nouns or interjections. The infant, however, uses these words as complete—although, by adult standards, crude—sentences. Thus *mama* will have to be interpreted by parents in a variety of ways, depending upon the situation in which the word is spoken as well as the intonation and gesturing that accompany it. *Mama* may mean that the infant "wishes" the mother to come, or that the infant is hungry, or content, or that he or she sees the mother enter the room. *Ball* may mean "There is a ball," "Where is the ball?" "I want the ball," and so forth. These earliest word sentences cannot be understood out of context or without observation of the associated inflection and gesture.

At this stage of language development, children possess words that have only partly socialized meanings (that is, they have learned to employ words conventionally) with approximately the same meanings that their parents attribute to them. Their use of words is close enough to conventional adult usage that from the contexts in which they speak the words their parents are able to understand them.

Children are able to use words in an amazing variety of ways because they have not caught on to their full public meanings. As de Laguna (1927) has written:

> It is precisely because the words of the child are so indefinite in meaning, that they can serve such a variety of uses. . . . A child's word does not . . . designate an object *or* a property *or* an act; rather it signifies loosely and vaguely the object together with its interesting properties and the acts with which it is commonly associated in the life of the child. The emphasis may be now on one, now on another, of these aspects, according to the exigencies of the occasion on which it is used. (p. 270)

Adults, who are much more conscious of the "real" (conventional) meanings of words, cannot employ words so irresponsibly or variously.

Children use these early words as a way of responding to situations. A child does not merely name an object with a word (such as naming his or her mother by using the word *mama*). *Mama* means "Mama come here" or "I'm glad to see you," and so forth. As Lewis (1959) has noted, "When he speaks the sounds it is his way of dealing with the situation" (p. 91). The child's words are instruments; they are means of handling the environment. We shall see how children progress rapidly to the point where words become very effective means for managing the environment and manipulating certain key environmental objects.

Declarative and Manipulative Functions of Language

We previously noted the instrumental use of gestures and word sentences; it's implications now call for further analysis. We closely follow the work of M. M. Lewis here, because in our judgment his is the most careful inquiry into this aspect of our problem.

Children use their early "conventional" words instrumentally in ways that are either *declarative* or *manipulative*. Declarative use involves drawing adult attention to some object. By uttering a word such as *chair* or *doll*, the child directs adult attention to the named item. Manipulative use of words by the child involves, in addition to drawing attention to a particular object, a demand that his or her needs with regard to that object be satisfied by the adult. For example, the word *cookie*, when used in manipulative fashion, is equivalent to a demand for aid in reaching the cookie jar and getting a cookie. The word *tick-tock*, used manipulatively, might mean, "Papa, show me your wristwatch."

The child's instrumental use of language, whether declarative or manipulative, results in drawing other people into his or her circle of activity:

> In the declarative use he attracts another's attention and so assures himself of company. If he is delighted, the presence of another person enhances his delight; if he is afraid the presence of another person alleviates his fear. . . . In the manipulative use the child is again using the word as a social instrument; this time as a means of securing the help of others in satisfying his practical wants. (Lewis, 1936, pp. 147-149)

Even before infants learn any real words, they use their own vocalizations for declarative and manipulative purposes. But when they learn real words, those two instrumental functions become more effective, because they enable children to point more precisely to the objects that attract their attention.

A series of significant points is involved here. First, children's instrumental use of sounds is rooted in the children's pasts, and their instrumental use of sounds merges imperceptibly into their acquisition of conventional speech. Second, children's learning of conventional speech rests upon their using it as an instrument—that is, upon their calling adult attention to more specific objects and aspects of their environment than was possible with their ambiguous baby vocalizations. Finally, children's gradual approach to conventional speech presupposes the cooperation of adults. If adults paid no attention to them, or if children could not use words as social instruments, it is difficult to imagine how they could ever learn conventional usage.

Inaccurate Initial Use of Words

When children discover adult words, they do not employ them to specify precisely the same objects that are referred to by adults. To put this into commonsense terms, children do not at first use adult words with their correct adult meanings. To the adult, the child's application of words often seems haphazard and frequently amusing.

Infants, in fact, apply sounds and homemade words to objects long before they master adult words. It is out of these initial vocal references that their ability to use adult words correctly eventually develops. Taine (1877) gives us an instructive example of how children begin to apply vocalizations to the objects of their infantile world in this description of his daughter:

> She was in the habit of seeing a little black dog belonging to the house, which often barks, and it was to it that she first learnt to apply the word *oua-oua*. Very quickly and with very little help she applied it to dogs of all shapes and kinds that she saw in the streets and then . . . to the bronze dog near the staircase. Better still, the day before yesterday when she saw a goat a month old that bleated, she said *oua-oua*. . . .
>
> *Cola* (chocolate) is one of the first sweetmeats that was given her and it is the one she likes the best. . . . Of herself and without or rather in spite of us she has extended the meaning of the word and applies it now to anything sweet; she says *cola* when sugar, tart, a grape, a peach, or a fig is given her. (pp. 254-256)

From this description it is clear that when children first apply learned words to objects, they do so with different meanings than do adults. Although Taine thought he had taught his daughter the essential meanings of the word *baby*, he had not. Similarly, although the child applied the word *cola* to the correct object, she also applied it to other, incorrect objects. Children sometimes use adult words to designate objects outside the adult definitions, and sometimes they do not use words to designate enough objects.

Inaccurate Usage Reflects the Child's Point of View

Why is the child at first unable to grasp the correct adult meanings of given words? For an answer, we may refer to our discussion of language in Chapter 3, where we note that the vocabulary utilized by any given society or social group necessarily reflects its interests and preoccupations. To state this another way, the distinctions implicit in a society's words are distinctions that members of the society consider important and relevant.

It may be assumed that infants, before becoming overly influenced by human association, will make distinctions of importance to themselves. They choose features of their world that appear similar and group them together under identical words. Whereas adults make a distinction between, say, prunes and carrots as fruits and vegetables, infants at first may use the same sound (say, *teterre*) to pick out similar features of a solid—something that tastes good.

Children cannot very well group objects that are the same together as adults do, for the latter see the world from points of view derived from participation in certain social groups. Children have yet to acquire these standardized categories. Features of their environments that strike them as similar are features that grow out of their own experiences. Thus, because chocolate tasted sweet, peaches tasted sweet, and grapes tasted sweet, Taine's daughter called them all by the same name, *cola.* A young acquaintance of ours came to call a small doll *putzibabe*; he then extended the name to other small objects, including small dogs, and later to his baby sister. Similarly, when an infant touches a rose, the infant's mother may carefully call it *rose,* whereupon the child is likely to apply *rose* to all flowers. The child's need to deal declaratively or manipulatively with an object—calling our attention to it, or to his or her needs with reference to it—often leads the child to make naive and unique use of words.

The child's adoption of adult words is encouraged by the adult's readier response to conventional sounds than to the child's private vocalizations. The conventional sound proves to be a more efficient instrument for calling attention to an interesting object or to one's desires with regard to the object; hence the child has an incentive for appropriating the conventional sound.

Perhaps this is an instance of social pressure. But children do not automatically conform to social pressure; their choices and use of words are selective. The child's experience determines the range and extension of his or her words; the decision does not lie with the adult. For a time, a child may stubbornly resist the adult's word, so that even after he or she is aware of the conventional word and has imitated it correctly, the child may continue to use his or her own unique word form. Or the child may alternate, sometimes using the adult word and sometimes his or her own. The child has to accept the conventional term as the more efficient instrument of the two before he or she will finally adopt it.

Contemporaneously with and, undoubtedly, as a partial result of adult intervention, children learn to make increasingly adequate distinctions among classes of objects. For instance, they begin to discriminate between a solid-something eaten with a spoon (potato) and a solid-something eaten by hand (bread). The adult encourages the child to make such distinctions and helps to crystallize and fix them by supplying the necessary conventional words. Growing discrimination and adult intervention/cooperation go hand in hand; it is fruitless to inquire which contributes more. Both contributions are crucial to the gradual convergence of child and adult symbols. Children thus stand on the threshold of mastering their native language; they are becoming capable of employing voluntarily the symbols of the society to which they belong.

Theories of Language Acquisition

Currently, three basic theories provide differing accounts of how language is acquired (Berk, 1997, p. 377). According to the *behaviorist* position, language, like other behaviors, is learned through a complex process of operant conditioning. The *nativist* position, associated with Noam Chomsky (see below), is that humans are born with a "language acquisition device" that permits children "to speak in a grammatically correct fashion" (Berk, 1997, p. 377). In contrast, a middle position, termed *cognitive* and *social interactionist* or *pragmatist*, contends that biological and contextual factors interact to produce language development (Hulit & Howard, 1997, p. 38).

Language Acquisition According to Chomsky

Linguist McNeill (1966) has commented on the character of early childhood speech:

> At the age of about one, a normal child, not impaired by hearing loss or speech impediment, will begin to say words. By one-and-a-half or two years, he will begin to form simple two and three word sentences. By four years, he will have mastered very nearly the entire complex and abstract structure of the English language. In slightly more than two years, therefore, children acquire full knowledge of the grammatical system of their native tongue. This stunning intellectual achievement is routinely performed by every preschool child, but what is known about the process underlying it? (p. 34)

Thus by the age of 4 children have acquired the major linguistic categories and meanings of their social groups. They quickly become masters of their own behavior. That this linguistic ability appears so early in the developmental cycle is the subject of considerable controversy. Chomsky (1965), a linguist whose writings have had great impact on other linguists and on psychologists, argues that language may be, in some sense, an innate ability. He makes this point quite explicit in the following passage:

> On the basis of the best information now available, it seems reasonable to suppose that a child cannot help constructing a particular kind of transformational grammar to account for the data presented to him, any more than he can control his perception of solid objects or his attention to line and angle. Thus it may well be that the general features of language structure reflect, not so much the course of one's experience, but rather the general character of one's capacity to acquire language—in the traditional sense one's innate ideas and innate principles. (p. 59)

The suggestion that innate ideas and principles, as part of a general capacity to acquire language, may be inherited, poses formidable difficulties if one tries to imagine how these might be translated into specific genetic mechanisms, as Piaget (1970) has pointed out. However the problem is conceived, it should be formulated so as to bring it, theoretically at least, into the realm of empirical inquiry. The human brain and nervous system are without doubt amazingly complex structures that unquestionably play a central role in the easy acquisition of language in early childhood, but it is extraordinarily difficult to conceive of their being programmed with innate ideas and principles, or with what some call an underlying *language acquisition device* (LAD). It is possible that better understanding of the brain and its functions, coupled with further study of the nature of language and how it is learned, may take the mystery out of this problem.

Another point that might be made concerning those who, like Chomsky and McNeill, are greatly impressed by the child's ability to acquire language is that *small and seemingly insignificant causes fairly com-*

monly produce large and even revolutionary effects. The invention of writing may be taken as an example. Spoken language had been in existence for tens of thousands of years before the absurdly simple idea of a primitive form of writing came into practice. Those who participated in and contributed to the early evolution of writing would surely have been incredulous if they could have been told of the revolutionary consequences that were to follow from their invention (see Brown, 1958; Couch, 1984a).

We ourselves adopt a *constructionist* view of language acquisition. From birth, the infant is exposed to linguistic experiences, and these experiences are progressively adopted by the developing child. The regularity of speech behavior is contingent on the symbolic environment to which the child is exposed. In this respect we side with Sullivan (1953), who suggests that

> the learning of gestures, by which I include the learning of facial expressions, is manifested by the infant, certainly well before the twelfth month, in the learning of the rudiments, one might say, of verbal pantomime. And this learning is, in good measure, learning by trial-and-error approximation to human example. (pp. 178-179)

As the foregoing suggests, we need not resort to an innate, "deep-structure" interpretation of how language appears in the child's behavior. Sullivan's observations suggest that the infant is constantly involved in the process of mimicking the languages and sounds of the adult world. Sullivan's remarks can be framed in terms of two propositions: First, *the more complex the linguistic community of the primary group, the more elaborate and complex will be the speech patterns of the young child*; and second, *the greater the complexity of this community, the more rapid will be the child's acquisition of speech.* These propositions are consistent with our earlier discussion of social isolation. If social behavior is not directed toward the child, his or her rate of social development will be correspondingly retarded or impeded. The basic similarities between languages (similarities that impress Chomsky), rather than being the result of inheritance, may simply be a reflection of the basic similarities of primary groups throughout the world. In the primary group, speech is acquired by infants, just as Charles Horton Cooley suggests that "human nature" is derived from this source.

The Syntax of Thought and Speech

Sounds, gestures, and thoughts are organized and made intelligible through the use of a set of syntactic rules that are specific to language communities. Written speech is governed by a set of rules that are quite precise and rigorously governed and studied by grammarians. Thought, on the other hand, has its own set of rules that may bear little relationship to the specifications governing the printed word. Finally, spoken vocal utterances are governed by another set of rules. Speakers, for example, develop their own styles of punctuation, exclamation, and interrogation.

Of concern in this context are the peculiarities of inner speech. Many students of early childhood thought and speech have erroneously judged the child's speech behavior from the standpoint of the syntax of formal, written utterances. Furthermore, when they claim that the child thinks "egocentrically," they are making that judgment on the basis of adults' thought and speech rules. There is no "thought rule" governing the organization of a thought, nor is there a rule concerning the prominence of the thinker's self in his or her own thoughts. We turn then to a further elaboration of *thought,* following Vygotsky's (1962, pp. 146-147) formulation. We note that (a) thought is truncated, abbreviated, and often abstracted from concrete experience; (b) its meaning is embedded in a larger context of perhaps unformulated thoughts; and (c) it is grounded in words that flow together. The word *love,* for instance, merges into a number of other images and experiences that are involved in the love relationship. Unlike vocal speech, thought does not fall into separate categories or units. We quote Vygotsky's (1962) remarks on this point:

> When I wish to communicate the thought that today I saw a barefoot boy in a blue shirt running down the street, I do not see every item separately: the boy, the shirt, its blue color, his running, the absence of shoes. I conceive of all this in one thought, but I put it into separate words. A speaker often takes several minutes to disclose one thought. In his mind the whole thought is present at once, but in speech it has to be developed successively. A thought may be compared to a cloud shedding a shower of words. (p. 150)

Thus, as Vygotsky notes, there is no direct transition from thought to speech. The same relationship holds for the various transitions that move thoughts into printed or written sentences, sentences into paragraphs, and paragraphs into books. To understand another speaker's speech, "it is not sufficient to understand his words—we must understand his thought" (Vygotsky, 1962, p. 151; see also Hulit & Howard, 1997, p. 91). In other words, listeners or readers must penetrate the subjective side of speech if they are to comprehend and place themselves in the perspective of the utterer or the writer. One author has noted that the message that is sent is seldom, if ever, the message that is received (Hulett, 1964).

Rather early in the process of acquiring language symbols, children begin to use them to influence their own behavior. Lorimer (1929) describes an amusing instance of this:

> A child of about eighteen months was warned not to put her hand into a certain open chest and not to take out things in the chest. The inhibition was clearly established, but the original impulse was strong. For ten enormous minutes I watched with fascination the battle between the impulse and inhibition, as the little hand reached forward toward the things in the chest and withdrew to the verbal accompaniment "no, no, no!" uttered by the child herself. Then the battle subsided, called to a close by the distraction of other interests. (p134-135)

Such self-command (the beginnings of what is commonly called willpower) derives from previous adult commands and prohibitions.

Children will eventually internalize their self-directed words so that they will say no to themselves silently, or will merely think the command. But at an early age, self-directed language is not completely internalized. Let us take another example: Ask a young child to say how many pencils are lying on a table. The child is likely to touch each pencil, counting aloud, "One, two, three," while doing so. If you hold the child's hands, thereby preventing her from touching the pencils, she either will be unable to tell you the total number or will nod her head in the direction of the pencils and count, "One, two, three," and so on. Youngsters at play are often overheard giving themselves commands like "Put this block there." As children grow older, language becomes internalized, so that counting, commanding, and expressing desires can be carried out silently. The external conversation of gestures and vocal speech merges into inner thought, or into "the internal conversation of gestures."

The Learning of Concepts

Learning language, as we have stressed, requires the child to master systems of interrelated concepts. A number of investigators have studied how children's conceptions of gender, time, space, movement, shape, weight, and numbers become progressively more sophisticated and differentiated. Studies of children's notions of social relationships, such as those bearing upon social class and race, also show in a general way how knowledge of these matters gradually becomes more discriminative and systematic.

Most studies of children's learning of concepts have been of the very general kind described above. Emphasis has been placed upon revealing what children of varying ages know about certain topics, rather than upon the exact tracing of stages and mechanics involved in the development of that knowledge. Our discussion of the nature of symbols and of concepts indicates that change in a given concept is clearly linked with the development of related concepts. As the child finds or learns new classifications, he or she revises or qualifies the old concepts, or they are assimilated by the new ones. The refinement of concepts waits upon the development of related concepts. Later meanings are built upon and absorb earlier and simpler ones, although children themselves do not usually recollect most of their earlier conceptions. Children at the same stages of conceptual development tend to commit similar types of errors.

The Categorical Self

With increased language skills comes a sense of self-awareness. In early childhood, by age 2 or earlier, this sense of self-awareness is based on what some have called the categorical self (Berk, 1997, p. 426). This is a set of self-differentiations that enacts the salient ways the surrounding culture uses to classify people. These categories are, of course, embedded in language. Depending on the family, the social group, and the culture, this will include such circumstantial identities as those based on age ("baby," "boy," "woman"), sex ("boy" versus "girl," "man" versus "woman"), and race and ethnicity. It will also include situational identities (things the person can change), including moral categories (goodness and badness), competencies, and personal preferences (see Berk, 1997, p. 426).

By age 3 or 4, race and ethnicity become operative categorical terms for the child. Young children quickly connect race and class with power, wealth, and poverty, and assume that white people have more power than persons of color (Berk, 1997, p. 449). Young children also form negative attitudes toward out-groups to which they do not belong, although some of this prejudice may decline with age (Berk, 1997, p. 449).

Concepts of Gender and Gender Stereotypes

Even before the age of 2, children label themselves as male or female. With this classification comes a set of interrelated understandings concerning differences in the attitudes, behaviors, and performances of males and females, boys and girls. As Berk (1997) notes, young children associate toys, styles of dress, clothing, color preferences (pink and blue), household items and duties, games, even occupations "with one sex as opposed to the other" (p. 503).

Gender differences are reflected in language. Even though males and females learn the same language, little boys and girls learn to select different words when they talk; these words are gender coded (Hulit & Howard, 1997, p. 324). Little girls learn to use feminine, polite words, such as *please, thank you, lovely, adorable,* and *pretty.* Little boys learn to use profane and crude words. Boys are more likely than girls to interrupt during conversations, and they are more likely to interrupt girls than they are to interrupt other boys (Hulit & Howard, 1997, p. 324).

These gender differences are not firm; they are performative, established in and through the interaction process. That is, young children enact gendered selves, drawing in the process on mediated cultural understandings concerning proper male and female conduct (see below). This process of performing gender produces a gendered social order. In these performances there are no originals against which a particular gendered performance can be judged. On this Butler (1993b) is clear: "Compulsive heterosexuality sets itself up as the original, the true, the authentic; the norm that determines the real implies that 'being' lesbian is always a kind of miming, a vain effort to participate in the phantasmatic plenitude of naturalized heterosexuality" (pp. 642-643).

There is no true, naturalized sexuality; rather, Butler (1990) argues, "in the place of an original identification which serves as a determining cause, gender identity must be reconceived as a personal/cultural history of received meanings subject to a set of imitative practices which refer laterally to other initiations and which, jointly, construct the illusion of a primary and interior gendered self" (p. 138; see also Butler, 1993a, 1993b, 1997). That is, each person constitutes, through his or her interactional performances, a situated version of a heterosexual or nonheterosexual identity. Every performance is a masquerade, a copy of the real thing, an imitation of an imitation.

Butler (1993b) elaborates: "If heterosexuality is an impossible imitation of itself, an imitation that performatively constitutes itself as the original, then the imitative parody of 'heterosexuality' . . . is always and only an imitation of an imitation, a copy of a copy, for which there is no original" (p. 644). The following discussion of gender develops these points.

Lacan (1977, pp. 151-152) suggests that young children enter or learn language as "sexed" or "gendered" beings; that is, they learn language from the standpoint of being boys or girls. Many authors have suggested that children learn gender concepts early—in the primary socializing agencies of the family, day care, and preschool (see, e.g., Joffe, 1971). We review some of these findings in Chapter 9. At this point we wish merely to note that of all the concepts young children learn, perhaps gender is the most important. This is the case because the gender stratification system in any society rests on the gender concepts a group passes on through the socializing process. We understand *gender* to refer to the cultural and social patterning of maleness and femaleness; gender encompasses such concepts as sex role. In later chapters, we use the term *sexuality* to refer to the actual sexual experiences associated with gender identities in this or any other society.

Boys and Dolls

In a series of ingenious studies, William Damon (1977, pp. 240-281; see also Damon, 1988) asked children of different ages to respond to the following scenario: A little boy, named George, likes to play with dolls. His friends think he is silly to play with dolls. His parents tell him that little boys don't play with dolls; only little girls play with dolls. His mother has purchased all kinds of other toys for him, including model airplanes, trucks, and baseballs. Damon then phrased the following questions:

1. Why do people tell George not to play with dolls? Are they right?
2. Is there a rule that boys should not play with dolls?
3. What will happen if George keeps playing with dolls?
4. Should George's parents punish him?
5. What if George wore a dress to school? (p. 242)

He asked these questions of 56 boys and girls between the ages of 4 and 9. Following are some representative responses from children of different ages; their answers reveal different conceptions of correct gender behavior for young boys:

- Jack (4 years old) said that it was okay for George to do these things because there are no rules against it. Jack did not think that George should wear a girl's dress "because boys don't wear them" (p. 240).
- Jane (4 years, 6 months) stated that she didn't think George should play with dolls "because he's a boy . . . and he'll get in trouble" (p. 254). She said that "dresses can only be for girls" (p. 254).
- Eugene (7 years, 4 months) was firmer on these understandings. He stated that George can't play with dolls "because it's not right for boys to play with dolls because boys play with other toys like cars and girls play with dolls" (p. 256).
- Laura (7 years, 9 months) argued that "boys play with boys' stuff and girls with girls' . . . because girls don't like boys' stuff" (p. 262). Laura went on to say that boys should be allowed to play with dolls if they want to because it's not fair to say they can't.

Damon (1977, pp. 246-247) proposes that there are four levels, or stages, of children's reasoning about social regulations like gender:

- *Level 0:* All types of social regulations are seen as situationally specific and to be followed only if the child wants to.
- *Level 1:* Social regulations are seen as constraining and as conflicting with personal preferences.
- *Level 2:* Social conventions are seen as being arbitrary and may be rejected because of this.
- *Level 3:* Social conventions are respected and followed.

At Level 0, the child respects only those conventions that conform to his or her desire. At Level 1 there is an appreciation of the importance of conventions that extend beyond personal desire. At Level 2 the conventions are seen as being arbitrary, and at Level 3 they are seen as being necessary.

The children quoted above span Levels 0 to 2. Here is the response of a child at what Damon, following Turiel (1975), calls Level 3: Todd (9 years, 6 months) stated that George "should tell his mother that he likes to play with them (dolls), and then if his mother says he can't play with them, then he can't play with them" (Damon, 1977, p. 270). Here the convention is followed because it is respected.

We can extract several points from this discussion. First, children ages 4 through 9 do have firm understandings regarding "correct" male and female behavior. Second, these understandings are gender specific; that is, they are connected to boys or girls. Third, the fact that there *appears* to be a general movement from personal-situational views of gender conventions to a more abstract, less personal position suggests that as society gets inside children, the arbitrary nature of rules becomes more and more acceptable. Fourth, there is some suggestion that girls grasp these understandings more quickly than boys do. Fifth, it is clear that there are two gender codes operating in early childhood, and these codes are tied to the acquisition of language and the group's point of view. Nonetheless, return to Butler's arguments. The rules that regulate gender work back and forth between acceptable and unacceptable gender-specific conduct. That is, heterosexual norms are, to paraphrase Butler (1993b, p. 644), running commentaries on these performances that appear to deviate from what is acceptably normal. Children learn these norms very quickly.

Reasoning and Child Development

Sensorimotor Intelligence

It is incorrect to maintain that babies and very young children do not give evidence of intelligent behavior, for even prior to the acquisition of language they are capable of primitive kinds of "mental" activity. Following Piaget (1950), we may term this activity *sensorimotor,* because through touch, sight, and movement the infant locates and relates objects in space and time (see also Berk, 1997, p. 214; Crain, 1992, pp. 103-108). Sensorimotor intelligence has nothing to do with language; it develops partly as a result of biological maturation and partly as a result of the child's experiences with objects. At a crude cognitive level, the infant begins to make distinctions between his or her own body and objects that are external to it.

At first, infants do not even realize that objects that have disappeared from their field of vision still exist. The objects do not have any temporal permanence. Thus if one covers an object with a cloth while a 5-month-old infant is reaching for it, he will cease reaching and lose interest. "The primitive world is not made up of permanent objects . . . but of moving perceptive pictures which return periodically into non-existence and come back again as a functional result of the proper action" (Piaget, 1950, p. 27). Nor do young infants have any clear idea of objects in space. Through exploration of objects—rotating and touching them, seeing their various sides—they soon arrive at some elementary notions of space and of the permanence of objects.

Through sensorimotor "reasoning," the infant eventually becomes vaguely aware of his or her body as one among many stable objects. This represents a considerable advance over the infant's initial picture of the world as made up wholly of impermanent objects.

Logic in Children

Many child psychologists believe that "the child's reasoning processes at the age of six are [not] essentially different from his reasoning processes at the age of twelve or eighteen" (Jersild, 1947, p. 380). This belief involves several assumptions: First, children's logic is essentially the same as that of adults; second, the more frequent errors committed by the child are a consequence of false premises rather than inferior logic or inability to reason abstractly; third, these false premises exist because the child has had inadequate experience with the given subject matter; and fourth, adults, when confronted with unfamiliar subject matter, also are likely to commit errors in logic and judgment. This belief in the general equivalence of child and adult reasoning can easily lead to a subtle form of anthropomorphism concerning the child. Our earlier discussion of the evolution of sign behavior implies that children should be expected to acquire mastery of the higher orders of symbolic activity only gradually. This is obvious if we consider some of the difficulties with logic that children encounter. Casual observation of the child's speech reveals some of these, but others are not apparent unless the child is trapped into revealing his or her thought processes through clever questioning and verbal testing. Some of these deficiencies in logic are shown in Table 7.1, in which we paraphrase Piaget (1950).

The ability to reason abstractly has a lengthy developmental history. We once observed an episode in which a child could not describe correctly the kinship relations between his mother and his two maternal aunts, nor could he indicate how many sisters each had. When questioned about this in the women's absence, he fell into the confusions and contradictions typical of a 5-year-old. However, when all the women were seated with him at a table and he was asked how many sisters each had, he was able to answer correctly. The effort that this task cost him was unmistakable: He looked fixedly at his mother, then turned and looked at her two sisters one by one, naming

TABLE 7.1 Children's Difficulties in Logic

Difficulties in	*Illustration*
Classifying abstractly (generalizing)	Four trays, each holding a small wooden dog and one other object, are shown to the child. The child is asked to name the common element (the dog). Few children under 4 or 5 years of age could name it by saying, "All the trays have dogs."
Realizing that the class name is only a convenience	The young child believes the name is "in" the object—is inseparable from it. For example, the sun's name is "in" the sun.
Understanding the relativity of relationships	The child maintains that a pebble is light and that a boat is heavy. The child does not realize that a pebble is light for him or her and heavy for the water in which it sinks, or that the boat is light for the water, but heavy for him or her. Another example—the child cannot grasp the following set of abstract relations: "Edith is lighter than Suzanne. Edith is darker than Lily. Who is darkest—Edith, Suzanne, or Lily?"
Imagining the merely possible	Asked to suppose that the sun is really called the moon and vice versa, the child is likely to argue that that is impossible. Asked, "If your brother is a year older than you, how old is he?" a child with no brother will protest that he or she has no brother.
Avoiding logical contradictions and inconsistencies	The child will maintain that big bodies are heavier than small ones, but that a small pebble is heavier than a large cork. He or she will state that rivers have strength because they flow, and a moment later maintain that rivers have no strength because they can't carry anything.
Understanding logical necessity	If asked why water goes down and smoke goes up, the child answers that heavy bodies fall and light ones rise. This answer is based not on logical necessity, but on moral obligation: The object must rise or fall because it is morally obliged to, rather than because it is lighter or heavier than air.
Dealing simultaneously with several logically related matters	The child is asked the following question: "If the animal has long ears, it is a mule or a donkey; if it has a thick tail, it is a mule or a horse. Well, this animal has long ears and a thick tail. What is the animal?" The child cannot answer correctly. Example: "The animal can be a donkey because you say that if it has long ears it is either a donkey or a mule. But it can be a mule, for you say that if the animal has a thick tail it is either a mule or a horse."

each as he did so. Then he repeated the same process for each of his two aunts. This child's behavior clearly represents a phase in learning to understand relationships. At 5 years of age, a child's comprehension of abstractions tends to be on a relatively low level—the comprehension is concrete rather than abstract, as Goldstein (1940) would say. The persons or objects in question must be physically before the child if he or she is to solve even the simplest kinds of questions concerning their interrelations.

Here is an illustration of how children may apply what they have learned in a relatively concrete situation to one in which a higher degree of abstraction is required. The child has learned, by making purchases in stores, that the more pieces of gum are bought, the more pennies are needed. He or she is then shown one stick of gum and asked what it costs. "One penny" is the reply. Then the stick of gum is broken in halves, in full view of the child, and the question is repeated. "Two cents" is the answer. One of the halves is divided in half again, in front of the child, and the answer is "Three cents."

Piaget (1950) has analyzed the failures of children on certain tests dealing with concepts of space, number, movement, and the like. His technique is suggested by the following:

> To study the formation of classes we place about twenty beads in a box, the subject acknowledging that they are "all made of wood," so that they constitute a whole, B. Most of these beads are brown and constitute part A, and some are white, forming the complementary part A′. In order to determine whether the child is capable of understanding the operation A plus A′ equals B, i.e., the uniting of parts in a whole, we may put the following simple question: In this box (all the beads still being visible) which are there more of—wooden beads or brown beads, that is, A < B? (p. 133)

Piaget has suggested that there are four fairly clear stages in the learning of logical operations. We do not need to describe these stages here, but the import of his theory is that as children move from stage to stage, the organization of their behavior changes accordingly.

Vygotsky's (1962) very interesting experimentation has influenced American research and theory about child development. One of Vygotsky's most general findings is that children reason according to *chain complexes.* This term means that in putting together objects that "belong" together, children do not use a consistent classificatory system; rather, they use a succession of similarities (they look yellow, then they look blue), but the successive similarities have no constancy. Bruner and Oliver (1963), influenced by both Piaget and Vygotsky, also conclude that children form chain complexes. They offered children pairs of words (for example, *peach* and *banana*) and then asked them in what ways those two objects were alike. Next, they presented additional words (*meat* and *potato*) and asked the children how all the words were alike. The children gave answers such as that the banana and peach are yellow, the peach and potato are round, and the potato and meat are eaten together.

Roger Brown (1965, pp. 385-388) has questioned these kinds of experiments. He agrees that children in such experiments tend to sort objects on a part-whole basis and form chain complexes; he also agrees that they seldom are able to formulate rules that accurately describe the classes they form, and they do not fully understand the relation of class nclusion. He argues, however, that even adults cannot always give the rules describing their use of words, and although it is probably true that adults understand class-inclusion relations and children do not, knowledge of these relations is not required for referential use of words, or for most propositional purposes. He asserts, therefore, that the "intellectual characteristic of children that seems most likely to be reliably characteristic and to have general implications for their understanding of words is their use of chain complexes" (p. 388). Brown cautions against supposing that because adults seldom reason with chain complexes in experiments, they also seldom do so in real-life solving of problems.

CONCLUSION

In children's acquisition of language—from their earliest babblings and simplest vocalizations to the final convergence with adult speech—the progression is from the instrumental use of words, word sentences, and gestures to the more complicated forms of speech. Ways of speaking are intimately connected with ways of thinking, and we have emphasized the ways in which children's assimilation of language is related to self-control and to the development of logical thought. The rules governing speech are much different from those that control thought. One's patterns of speaking and thinking reflect one's location in the social structure. Further study is needed of the relationship between language behavior and socialization. On the whole, this has been a neglected research area, but it is a field that deserves serious social psychological attention.

SUGGESTED READINGS

Berk, L. E. (1997). *Child development* (4th ed.). Boston: Allyn & Bacon. A valuable analysis of current research and theory in the field of child development.

Chomsky, N. (1975). *Reflections on language.* New York: Pantheon. Further reflections on the controversial theory of language acquisition and language competence by this important linguist.

Jessor, R. J., Colby, A., & Shweder, R. (Eds.). (1996). *Ethnography and human development: Context and meaning in social inquiry.* Chicago: University of Chicago Press. An important collection of essays that locate child development and early childhood within an interpretive, ethnographic framework.

O'Grady, W., Dobrovolsky, M., & Aronoff, M. (1997). *Contemporary linguistics* (3rd ed.). New York: St. Martin's. A very accessible treatment of the complex theoretical and empirical issues surrounding psycholinguistics and language acquisition.

Vygotsky, L. (1962). *Thought and language* (E. Haufmann & G. Vakar, Eds. and Trans.). Cambridge: MIT Press. A classic statement of this author's important position on language and thought in early childhood.

STUDY QUESTIONS

1. What is a speech act? What forms do speech acts take? What is the sequence of speech acts young children go through?
2. What are the three major theories of language acquisition?
3. What is the constructionist view of language acquisition?
4. How is language use connected to the development of gender and the gendered self?

8

The Development of Self

Consistent with our symbolic interactionist orientation, we hold that any theory of socialization and interaction must ultimately consider the question of how the newborn infant becomes a self-conscious participant in the interaction process. As Miller (1996) observes, "All children grow up to be cultural beings. . . . Child development is thus inextricably bound to the process of orienting oneself within systems of meaning, a process known variously as 'socialization' " (p. 183).

In this chapter we review the social conditions that give rise to the development of self in early childhood. We locate the origins of self in early childhood experiences with adult caretakers. We conclude the chapter with a discussion of various developmental theories, including those of interpersonal psychiatrist Harry Stack Sullivan. We extend Sullivan's arguments to those of Norbert Wiley (1994), who has recently offered a theory of the semiotic self. In our judgment Wiley and Sullivan offer the best and most coherent interactional treatment of the rise of self-consciousness in the human organism. We extend our analysis in Chapter 9, which focuses on the social worlds of early childhood. We begin with a general discussion of socialization and interaction.

Language, Performance, and Human Nature

In recent years, as Miller (1996, p. 183) notes, several powerful currents of thought have revitalized socialization theory and research, from Vygotsky's theory of mediated action to recent theories of language as a set of narrative, interpretive practices. Language is a form of situated action. Language is more than just a rule-governed, representational scheme; the speech act is a performance.

The self, as a linguistic process, is always a performance. Persons tell stories about themselves, and little children acquire selves through the storytelling process. These stories are shaped by the mass media, by children's television, by cinema, and by children's literature. This narrative, performance approach to the development of the self has the advantage of locating the processes of socialization in the "forms and functions of everyday discourse" (Miller, 1996, p. 184).

From this perspective, the child is viewed as an active participant in the process of self-development. The self is viewed as a *dialogical process*, a process constantly grounded in interpersonal, interactional dialogues with itself and with others. This dialogical process is temporally reflexive—it works back and forth among the present (I), the past (me), and the future (you).

We will continue our argument that there is a universal human nature rooted in language and in the structures of the primary social group. The self arises from and embodies these features of human nature. Following Wiley (1994, p. 1), we argue that human nature has the distinguishing feature of being symbolic and linguistic. We can call this the reflexive, or semiotic, self. This is what we mean by *generic human nature* (Wiley, 1994, p. 1). All humans are part of this semiotic apparatus. This is where dignity, self-sacredness, and emotional, moral power are located. The self is a sacred, emotional structure of meaning (Wiley, 1994, p. 15).

Self and Identity

We use the term *self,* rather than *ego, actor,* or *subject,* to refer to the adult human and the young child as reflexive, language-using beings. The self, as we argue in Chapter 1, references, on one level, all the person calls his or her own at a particular moment. We use the word *identity* to describe differences between humans and to refer to the interpretive meanings brought to these differences. "Identities individuate and allow us to recognize individuals, categories, and types of individuals" (Wiley, 1994, p. 1). Identities can be imposed from without by social processes, for example, race, class, and ethnicity. Identities can come from within the social interaction process and can refer to situational identifications, or *situational identities.* The term *social identity* is used to describe identification based on first appearances, including manner of dress and speech (Goffman, 1963b, p. 2). *Personal identity,* in contrast, references the specific biographical details of a given, named individual (Goffman 1963b, p. 56)—for example, the personal identity of the sociologist named Erving Goffman. *Ego identity* or *self-* or *felt identity* describes the self-feelings of the individual, the subjective sense of meaning the person gives to his or her personal situation, the "continuity and character that an individual comes to obtain as a result of his social experiences" (Goffman, 1963b, p. 105). Social identities draw on markers of the self that the person has little control over, the markers of race, ethnicity, age, and gender. These are what Gregory P. Stone (1981b, p. 33) calls the *circumstantial facts* of the self, circumstantial identities. In contrast, the *situational facts* of the self reference those markers of identification that the person can control and manipulate (Stone, 1981b, p. 33). Thus it can been seen that social identities are build on the circumstantial facts of the self. Personal identities build on the situational facts of the self. These facts become part of the individual's self-identity.

As we argued in Chapter 7, young children develop particular personal and ego identities and generic selves. The child's self is born out of a politics of identity. There are constant struggles over the qualities and social meanings attributed to the child, and to his or her self. These struggles center on those meanings attached to race, ethnicity, and class, as well as to gender and—later in the development process—sexual orientation (Wiley, 1994, p. 2).

Socialization and Interaction

Humans have to develop self-control and a sense of self; the infant is born with no sense of self, other, or social situation. The cardinal task of the child's caretaker is to transform this socially neutral infant into a symbolically functioning human being. The child enters an ongoing world of social interaction that is presented through the symbolic and behavioral actions of his or her most immediate caretakers, typically those persons who make up the primary group of the family. Assuming there are no organic or neurological deficiencies, the object called *child* possesses at birth the necessary equipment to become social and self-conscious (Bullock, 1987; Damon, 1977; Richardson, 1969; Zigler & Harter, 1969).

We assume that the child immediately after birth is exposed to the necessary interactional experiences that will eventually become incorporated into his or her behavioral repertoires. In short, before socialization can occur, the child must be exposed to face-to-face interaction. Once interaction begins, every succeeding exchange between the child and the mother can be viewed as an instance of socialization. Should interaction cease, or be deflected for a period of time, the child will symbolically regress to an earlier level of development.

Attachment, Bonding, and Deprivation

The research on maternal deprivation pioneered by John Bowlby (1953) and his associates in the mid-1950s clearly revealed that infants in orphanages who were not exposed to face-to-face interaction rapidly began to lose weight, and many were so understimulated, interactionally, that they began dying at the ages of 3 and 4.

Attachment is an affectional bond that ties one person to another over an extended period of time. Following Bowlby's pioneering work, attachment—as it is used in developmental theories—typically refers to the bond between mother and child. Children can, and do, form attachments to persons other than their mothers, but the mother-child attachment is usually primary. Through behaviors such as smiling, gazing, touching, talking, crying, and physical proximity, people promote and maintain interaction with those to whom they are attached. Distress often occurs in attached infants when they are separated from their mothers.

It is widely believed that healthy mother-infant attachment is essential to normal child development. One reason for this is that children learn about their worlds through exploration and play. It appears that children who have developed healthy attachment use their mothers as secure bases from which to venture forth and explore their physical and social worlds. As these children's sense of security strengthens, they feel more comfortable leaving their mothers for longer periods of time. Healthy attachment, then, can foster later independence.

Research by Klaus and Kennell (1982) indicates that there may be a sensitive period shortly after the birth of a child that is important for mother-infant attachment. These authors contend that when mothers are separated from their babies during the first hours and days after delivery, they may have difficulty forming an attachment. They recommend that, whenever possible, mother, father, and infant should be left alone for about 30 minutes after birth to facilitate bonding. The duration of this sensitive period has not been determined, and it seems that under appropriate conditions attachment can occur after this phase.

According to Ainsworth (1973), the amount of mother-infant interaction determines whether the infant becomes attached, whereas the kind of interaction shapes the quality of the attachment. Pediatricians, psychologists, and social workers see scores of children who are strongly attached to abusive parents. The quality of attachment is largely determined by maternal responsiveness. The mother, however, is not solely responsible for her ability to respond to her infant; some infants are easier to respond to than others. Premature and handicapped infants, for instance, do not make as much eye contact with their mothers and are slower to respond to maternal cues; this makes it more difficult for mothers to be appropriately responsive to these babies.

Bowlby (1980) contends that the process of attachment to the parent or other immediate caregiver takes place in four phases: preattachment (birth to 6 weeks), attachment-in-the-making (6 weeks to 6 months), clear-cut attachment (6 months to 18 months), and, finally, a reciprocal relationship (starting at 18 months; see Berk, 1997, pp. 406-407). According to Bowlby, this close relationship forms for the child the base out of which other relationships are developed.

Maternal deprivation implies inadequate or insufficient maternal care, and under such circumstances attachment often does not occur. It has been found that infants who are maternally deprived often develop abnormally; these infants have lower IQ scores, exhibit social deficits, and have poorer health than do infants with normal attachment to their mothers. One of the most profound long-term effects of extensive deprivation in infancy and early childhood has been found to be inability to establish and maintain deep and significant interpersonal relations—that is, inability to become attached.

Childhood as Status Passage: Children as Optional Objects

We must make clear, however, that there is nothing intrinsic to the object called *child* that makes it more or less human. Accordingly, depending on the actions taken toward the child, different types of selves will be produced. When a society does not have a status called *childhood*, "children," in a sociological sense, will actually not be produced; consequently, childlike behavior as it is known in current scientific theory will not be found in societies and social groups that have no conception of childhood (Goodman, 1970). It would be expected that children in such groups would be permitted to engage in the behaviors normally reserved for adults only. They would own property, exercise political power, make sexual contracts, and engage in the vices of their groups (Linton, 1942; Van Gennep, 1960).

A group's stance toward the desirability and inevitability of childhood will determine whether or not that group produces children. Six categories have been suggested. Childhood may be viewed as desirable or undesirable, as Wolfenstein (1955) claims is the case for the Parisian French. Next, childhood may be regarded as inevitable, or as optional, or it may not exist. Middle-income Americans regard childhood as desirable and inevitable. The French view (according to Wolfenstein) is that it is undesirable and inevitable; the French think that individuals should move through childhood as rapidly as possible. The Amish view childhood as optional and desirable, although for those studied by Kuhn (1954a) it ceased to exist after age 2. The Balinese have no period called *childhood*; children in that society are immediately transformed into adults (Mead, 1955).

The Changing Value of Children

Some authors have asked in recent years if children are becoming emotionally dispensable (Degler, 1980; Elkind, 1981; Leavitt, 1994; Packard, 1983; Postman, 1982; Skolnick & Skolnick, 1977; Suransky, 1982; Winn, 1983; Zelizer, 1985). They point out that increasing numbers of women are delaying childbirth and that increasing numbers of children are cared for by persons other than their parents. In 1998, approximately 70% of American children under the age of 3 with mothers who work outside the home were in some form of family- or center-based day care (see Berk, 1997, p. 568; Leavitt, 1994, p. 2).

Zelizer (1985, pp. 223-228) sees a shift in U.S. society back toward the view of children as useful participants in family life. She envisions a changing world of childhood emerging within the new egalitarian ideologies of male-female relations of the late 20th century. Still, to the degree that day-care centers become institutionalized in our society, children will be treated as commodities whose time, emotions, and experiences are managed by others (Leavitt, 1994; Power, 1985, p. 221). Clearly, the meanings of the social object called *child* are changing. Whether a new place will be found for children within the family unit remains to be seen (Zelizer, 1985, p. 228).

Groups that view childhood as undesirable produce adults at a much faster rate than do those who define it as desirable. This suggests that distinct cultures of childhood and adulthood will exist in those groups that prolong entry into the adult world. Thus, although we would argue that "childlike" behavior as it is known in current scientific theory will not be found in those societies and social groups that have no conception of childhood, nonetheless we contend that the steps or phases by which the self develops are universal in nature. The specific contents will vary from group to group, but the forms are universal. With the foregoing reservations and points in mind, we can turn to a discussion of the self and its emergence in early childhood. We must first treat the general place of the concept called *self* in the literature of social science (see Calhoun, 1994; Wiley, 1994; see also the discussion of self in Chapter 1, including the phenomenological, linguistic, material, ideological, gendered, and racialized selves). This will require a discussion of several interrelated issues, including current theoretical approaches to the self as well as issues surrounding social constructionism, essentialism, identity politics, and theories of agency and action.

The Concept of Self

A concept such as person, self, ego, or identity appears to be essential to any account of human social nature or the socialization process (see Calhoun, 1994, p. 9; Wiley, 1994, p. 1). Humans characteristically act with self-awareness, exercise self-control, and exhibit conscience and guilt, and in the great crises of life they make decisions with reference to some imagery of what they are, what they have been, and what they hope to be. The wider social community enters the person through its language, which in turns furnishes the foundations for the self.

Proponents of the "self" idea have gained the advantage in the past few decades. The concept was never entirely rejected in all fields of psychology; it was granted some validity, particularly in child and social psychology. Then, with the increase in influence of psychoanalytic theory, there came a revival of interest in problems of self and identity. Since the 1960s, a considerable amount of research has been conducted that has involved or focused on the idea of self. One reason for this has been a growing discontent with theorizing about self, which is done without some empirical base in research; another reason has been a growing awareness that the concept has implications that can guide significant research provided those implications are followed through. Our view is that some of the most significant research is research that focuses on implications of the self-concept. We concur with Newcomb, Turner, and Converse (1965) that the original emphasis on the self as a product of social interaction has been reinforced rather than altered by more recent investigations. As they say, now we "know much more about the psychological processes by which children learn to perceive themselves, but the earlier conclusion that the self is a social product has scarcely changed at all" (p. 142).

Two Views of the Self

Charles Lemert (1994, pp. 100-101) has observed that current writings about the self can be divided into two categories. The first is represented by a group of writers who believe in the self, and who write from the position of a universal human nature, of a generic self and its identities. Theorists in this group include William James, Freud, Lacan, Anthony Giddens, Norbert Wiley, and Charles Taylor. The second group is made up of individuals who write about an aspect of experience "that appears to be closely related to the self. . . . Yet, when using the term

'Self,' if at all, those in this second group . . . frequently write in verse. . . . often they tell personal stories" (Lemert, 1994, p. 101). Gloria Anzaldúa, Patricia Hill Collins, Donna Haraway, Trinh T. Minh-ha, and Judith Butler are representative of this second group.

Lemert (1994) observes that writers in the first group, which he calls the "strong-we" group, tend to be white, heterosexual, middle-class males. Lesbians and women of color tend to be in the second group, which he calls the "weak-we" group. For the first group, self-experiences are referred back to an essentialist position; humanity itself constitutes the final and sufficient identifying group for all human beings. For those in the second group, experiences are connected to immediate, "concrete historical relations with local groups" (p. 104).

Theorists in the first group present elaborate conceptual models of the self, offering stage theories, theories of language and the unconscious, and so on. For theorists in the second group there is "either no explicit theory of the Self, or a theory is stated in terms that retain but the thinnest rhetorical association with the strong-we Self" (Lemert, 1994, p. 105). To illustrate this point, Lemert quotes Patricia Hill Collins (1990): "By insisting on self-definition, Black women question not only what has been said about African-American women but the credibility and the intentions of those possessing the power to define" (pp. 106-107; quoted in Lemert, 1994, pp. 105-106).

Writers in the strong-we group theorize invariant, universal conditions that shape the self experiences of all individuals. Lemert (1994) notes that the likelihood that "such conditions could pertain in *fact* are slim" (p. 106). In contrast, writers in the weak-we group offer first-person accounts of meaningful social experiences. Here is an example from bell hooks (1990):

> When I was young the journey across town to my grandmother's house was one of the most intriguing experiences. . . .
>
> . . . In our young minds houses belonged to women. . . . There we learned integrity . . . of being; there we learned to have faith. . . .
>
> . . . I would not be writing this essay if my mother, Rosa Bell, daughter to Sarah Oldham, granddaughter to Bell Hooks, had not created homeplace in just this liberatory way. (pp. 41, 45-46)

Clearly, these two groups take entirely different approaches to the self and how it should by written about. Symbolic interactionists can learn from both perspectives and the controversies surrounding each. In the past two decades considerable discussion has focused on the topics of social constructionism, essentialism, and identity politics.

Social Constructionism, Essentialism, and Identity Politics

Social constructionism challenges the idea that the self, or its identities, is given naturally by virtue of biological or social or cultural factors such as race, ethnicity, or class (Calhoun, 1994, p. 13). Constructionists challenge essentialist notions that "individuals can have singular, integral, altogether harmonious and unproblematic identities . . . constructionist arguments challenge accounts of collective identities as based on some 'essence' or set of core features shared by all members of the collectivity and no others" (Calhoun, 1994, p. 13).

Advocates of essentialism invoke invariant, or essential, identities based on race, nationality, gender, sexual orientation, or social class. Some gay men, for example, are drawn to research "suggesting a genetic foundation for homosexuality and to claims that gays should be accepted not because they are free to choose their own identities [constructionism] but because they have no choice in the matter" (Calhoun, 1994, p. 25).

As discussed above, recent narrative, performance approaches to the study of interaction and the socialization process stress the fragile, incomplete, fragmented, and contradictory nature of the self and its social, personal, and felt identities. These arguments attack essentialist positions. However, it is inappropriate to create a simple opposition between essentialism and constructionism. This kind of thinking creates a false nature-culture dichotomy, a dichotomy that should be deconstructed rather than dismissed. Keeping the two terms alive creates a space for conversations about the body, the embodied self, and the social and cultural discourses that create male and female bodies, genders, and sexualities (see Calhoun, 1994, p. 17; Haraway, 1991). On occasion it may be useful to invoke a provisional quasi-essentialism. This would especially be the case in those situations where a particular category of social identity has been repressed, or deligitimated, or "devalued by dominant discourses" (Calhoun, 1994, p. 17).

The politics of identity can never be avoided or easily dismissed. Calhoun (1994) observes that the "various versions of identity politics have shaped and have been shaped by a range of specific liberation and lifestyle movements that have flourished in the relatively rich countries since the 1960s" (p. 22). These new social movements include those connected to gays and lesbians, African Americans, Chicanos, Asians, Native Americans, the elderly, deep ecology, and the environment. But these movements are not new, and identity politics in the United States extends back at least 200 years (Calhoun, 1994, p. 23).

Gilroy (1996, pp. 228-229) suggests that the politics surrounding identity has clustered around three poles connected to gender (feminism), race and ethnicity, and social class and nation. *Identity-as-subjectivity* describes what we earlier called felt identities. Gilroy argues that feminist and critical race theorists have focused on this dimension of identity, studying how " 'subjects' bearing gender and racial characteristics are constituted in social processes" (p. 227). *Identity-as-sameness* is given in those identifications connected to collective, communal identities: "nations, genders, classes . . . 'races,' and ethnic groups" (p. 229). At this level, persons may be given a collective identity—for example, African or Native American. However, arguments about sameness are tenuous. Differences always exist within personal and felt identities, "as well as between them" (p. 228). No two individuals have the same self-feelings. *Identity-as-solidarity* looks at those historical, economic, cultural, and discourse structures that "both regulate and express the coming together of individuals in patterned social processes" (p. 230). At this level, groups of individuals share common social and personal identities, thereby forging a sense of group solidarity.

These three forms of identity anchor discussions of the self and its identities in a multicultural, political, and historical context. They refer back to our discussion of the circumstantial and situational facts surrounding the self and its meanings. A multicultural society is one based on multiple, conflicting, and overlapping social, personal, and felt identities—identities of sameness grounded in competing and shared feelings of moral solidarity.

The dialogical, performance view of the self sketched above further suggests that these multiple meanings are always in motion, provisionally anchored in the situational performances of the self and the other. Just as there is no true, naturalized sexuality, there is no true, fixed original self or set of identities to which the person can refer. Rather (elaborating Butler, 1990, p. 138), every individual creates through his or her interactional performances a situated version of who he or she is. This version works against and within racial, ethnic, and gendered identities. To repeat, every performance is a masquerade. As Hall (1996b) observes, "The fully unified, completed, secure, and coherent identity is a fantasy" (p. 598).

Theories of Agency and Action

It is necessary to take up briefly the problems surrounding two additional concepts: action and agency. These bear directly on theories of the self and the socialization process. *Action* references subjectively meaningful conduct, experiences that are reflexively meaningful to the person. *Agency* describes the locus of action, whether in the person, in language, or in some other structure or process. Theories of action and agency are common to the many theoretical branches of interpretive sociology, including phenomenology, linguistic philosophy, ethnomethodology, and symbolic interactionism. These theories are connected to the linguistic turn in 20th-century social theory. They have been shaped by Wittgenstein's linguistic philosophy, C. Wright Mills's arguments concerning vocabularies of motive, Schutz's reworking of Weber's concept of meaningful action, Peter Winch's application of Wittgenstein to the idea of a social science, Blumer's extension of Mead to symbolic interactionism, Goffman's dramaturgical sociology, Garfinkel's ethnomethodological project, Giddens's structuration theory, Habermas's theory of communicative action, and various feminist theories that locate action and agency in the unconscious or in the field of performance (Benhabib, 1992, p. 215; Butler, 1990, p. 143; Clough, 1994, p. 153).

At issue in these formulations is the place of an autonomous, reflexive individual in the construction of meaningful action. That is, do persons, as agents, create their own experience? Is agency, or meaning and intention in the actor, in the experience or in the social structure (see Clough, 1994, p. 153)? Do persons, as Karl Marx argues, make history, but not under conditions of their own making (Hall, 1996b, p. 606)? If history goes on behind people's backs, then structures, not persons as agents, make history. If this is the case, then the real subject of social psychology is not the person or a single individual. Rather, external systems and discursive practices create particular subjectivities and particular subjective experiences for the individual. Of course, we do not accept this position, for experience, structure, and subjectivity are dialogical processes.

Giddens (1976, 1981, 1984, 1991) uses the term *duality of structure*, which is central to his theory of structuration, to describe this process.

> According to the theory of structuration, all social actions consists of social practices, situated in time-space, and organized in a skilled and knowledgeable fashion by human agents. . . . A crucial move in this theory is an attempt to transcend the opposition between "action" theories and "institutional" theories. . . . By the duality of structure I mean that the structured properties of social systems are simultaneously the *medium and outcome of social acts.* (Giddens, 1981, p. 19)

Thus it can be seen that every individual is a practical social agent, creating meaning and structure through personal action; social life is "the skilled accomplishment of knowledgeable social actors" (Livesay, 1989, p. 266). Human agency is bounded and constrained by the very conditions that shape the duality of structure. Knowledgeable agents, human actors, are constrained by structural rules, material resources, and the structural processes connected to class, gender, race, ethnicity, nation, and community. The processes of childhood socialization create little children who act as practical agents who create their own meanings and situated experiences. However, the duality of structure suggests that these experiences are constrained by larger cultural and discursive practices located in the adult world.

With Giddens's theory of action and agency in hand, we can now turn to the development of self-awareness in childhood.

Development of Self-Awareness

Observers of child behavior have long noted that the child develops a kind of crude self-awareness within 2 or 3 years and that it takes many more years before full adult self-awareness comes into being. The abilities to think of oneself as an object and to have feelings about oneself evolve throughout the childhood years. The observation that self-awareness has a gradual development has misled many philosophers as well as laypersons into thinking of this development as a biological process. It was once assumed that infants lacked self-awareness because they were physically incapable of experiencing it; bodily maturation was supposed to provide the capacity to conceive the self. Self-consciousness, in other words, was seen essentially as a natural outgrowth of innate physical endowments. Although this hypothesis was completely disproved by studies made in the 19th century (see Sherif & Cantril, 1947, pp. 156-178), it is easy to see how it could have been formulated (Baldwin, 1897). Now, however, there is general agreement that socialization, over and beyond mere biological maturation, is essential to the development of self-consciousness. Deprived of human association, the biologically developing infant could scarcely develop a sense of self (Bowlby, 1953; Schaffer, 1971).

Body Awareness and Body Display

The infant at first has no conception of what belongs to his or her body and what does not, but seems to develop several patterns rapidly:

> At six or eight months he has certainly formed no notion of himself. He does not even know the boundaries of his own body. Each hand wandering over the bedspread for things which can be brought into the mouth discovers the other hand and each triumphantly lifts the other into his mouth; he draws his thumb from his mouth to wave it at a stranger, then cries because the thumb has gone away. He pulls at his toes until they hurt and does not know what is wrong. (Murphy, Murphy, & Newcomb, 1937, p. 207)

This is not to say that others in the immediate environment of the newborn do not make social judgments about the child's body and its relative degrees of perceived attractiveness. The newborn enters the world with a physical body that, given the presence of others, is constantly on display and under evaluation. At the outset, the infant passively enters into the display rituals that surround the presentation and inspection of his or her body. At this age, the child lacks any ability to adorn, dress, or systematically manipulate his or her own body. As the child grasps a sense of self, he or she more actively controls these ritual elements of self-presentation.

Slowly infants learn the boundaries of their own beings and learn to make distinctions between what is part of their bodies and what is part of other things. M. W. Shinn (1891) has described two incidents in this process:

> The 181st day her hand came into contact with her ear; she became at once very serious, and felt it and pulled it hard; losing it, she felt around her cheek for it, but when her mother put her hand back, she became interested in the cheek and wished to keep on feeling that. . . . To the end of the year, she would . . . feel over her head, neck, hair, and ears, the hair she discovered in the eighth month, 222nd day, while feeling for her ear, and felt it over and pulled it with great curiosity. (p. 143)

This lack of differentiation between body and surrounding environment is merely a specific illustration of the infant's generally blurred perceiving (Piaget, 1929/1967, pp. 236-237). Piaget has used the term *indissociation* to describe this undifferentiated perception.

In considering the case of the blind child, the following findings have emerged:

> While the environment of the blind child may fade in and out of his awareness, his own body remains constant. The child may be unable to experience the impact which his manipulations have on the toy which he holds, but he can experience the impact which he has upon his own body . . . his own body becomes the vehicle for feedback. (Scott & Stanford, 1969, p. 1032)

Compared with the sighted child, "the blind child explores his own body whereas his sighted counterpart" can more directly explore his environment as well as his body (Scott & Stanford, 1969, p. 1032).

This lack of differentiation, as we have discussed in Chapter 7, exists because the child has yet to acquire the necessary linguistic skills that will permit him or her to differentiate self from others. To have a sense of self—to be able to objectify his or her own activity and separate it from that of others—the child must be able to see him- or herself as a distinct object and realize that the self is not the same as the material-body self. Further, as Mead (1934) argues, the child must be able to see him- or herself from the perspectives of others. The genesis of self involves an awareness that other perspectives outside the child's direct control exist and must be taken account of. The child's knowledge of self is contingent on a separation of self from others.

Naming the Object Called *Child*

Central to the creation of the self as a social object is an identification of the object that will be termed *self.* Identification, as Stone (1962), Strauss (1959), and Allport (1961) have argued, involves naming. Once an object has been named and identified, it can be acted toward. This is true for children as it is for any other object—whether a chair, a cigarette, or a scientific theory. For children to acquire a sense of self, they must be named and singled out from other objects; they must be labeled as distinct objects. Such identification permits their differentiation from other persons or selves. As Allport (1961, p. 115) has argued, the most important linguistic aid becomes the personal name. Elaborate rituals surround the selection of first and middle names for American children. Rossi (1965) has shown that kinship, generational, and religious processes enter into the selection of names for newborns. Similar processes have been observed in other countries. Thus Young and Willmott (1957) have shown that lower-class London families also employ rather complicated rules in the selection of names for their children.

Allport (1961) has commented on names and the emergence of a separation of the material-body self from the social self:

> By hearing his name repeatedly the child gradually sees himself as a distinct and recurrent point of reference. The name acquires significance for him in the second year of life. With it comes awareness of independent status in the social group. (p. 115)

Confusion of "Self" with "Nonself"

Even after infants learn to distinguish between their bodies and the world, they do not have full self-awareness. They continue for several years to have difficulty in properly locating processes that go on "within their own minds" and in keeping them separate from external processes. Thus Piaget (1967) notes that if a child were asked, "Where is the dream when you dream?" he or she would say that it is "in the room" or "beside the bed." Asked by Piaget where the name of the sun is located, children usually answered that it was very high in the sky. Conversely, they attributed to words qualities signified by the objects or events. Thus they declared the word *elephant* to be a very "strong" word in comparison to *mouse.* Children, of course, also project human attributes onto various animate and inanimate objects. They may believe, for example, that fish eat three meals a day; that if a pin is poked into a tree, the tree feels it; or that it hurts a rock to be broken by a hammer. They assume that all people are like themselves, that animals are like humans, and that inanimate objects are alive. They may even identify themselves with material things.

Young children have a particularly difficult time learning to use personal pronouns correctly. Their initial use of *I, me, mine,* and *you* may be confused and inaccurate. They hear their mothers use the word *you* toward them, and so will address themselves as *you* instead of *I*. They may speak of themselves in the third person instead of the first person; for example, "Donnie wants that." As Allport (1937) says, "The two-year-old often confuses quite sadly the first, second and third persons. He may be overheard to say to himself, 'You be careful, William get hurt. NO! I won't get hurt.' He is first, second and third person all at the same time" (p. 161).

Cooley (1930, p. 200) has suggested that young children misuse pronouns because they cannot directly imitate them. Ordinary words such as *apple* or *doll* can be easily imitated, whereas words like *you* and *I* have to be reinterpreted by the child rather than copied directly. Actually, as we have seen, children at first do not imitate such words as *apple* or *doll* very directly. However, they have their chief difficulties with relationship terms, such as *brother, father, I,* and *you*, because during their early years they are unaware of perspectives other than their own.

Increasing accuracy in the use of pronouns shows children's maturing conceptions of their own existence and individuality. This is reflected also in the acquisition of new pronouns. Before age 5, first-person pronouns in the plural (*we, us, ours*) appear infrequently in children's vocabularies; they increase as children grow older and become more conscious of their own participation in groups.

Bain (1936), following Cooley's lead, studied his young daughter's acquisition of pronouns. The first pronoun appeared at the age of 15 months, but she did not systematically employ it until the age of 20 months. By the age of 2 years and 9 months, she was using 71 proper nouns (persons) and 13 pronouns (*I, me, my, mine, myself, we, us, your, something, it, both, any, none*). By the age of 10 months and 20 days, she was answering the question, "Where's Sheila?" with "She-e! She-e!" Although she also had a term for mother and father, she did not make these designations until she was a year old.

The Looking-Glass Self

There is a close connection between self-awareness and imagining how one looks to other people. To illustrate, we can consider what is properly termed *self-consciousness.* Almost every one of us has been placed in situations in which we have felt an acutely heightened sense of self; that is, in which we were extremely conscious of our existence and appearance. Consider, for example, a student making her first speech in a public speaking class. She perspires, fidgets, feels tense, and may even have "butterflies in her stomach." Although she may be on good terms with everyone in her audience, she concentrates on thoughts such as "What are they thinking of me?" "How do I look?"

"What kind of impression am I making?" Nor does our imaginary fright-stricken student have to face an audience to feel acutely self-conscious; she need only think of facing the audience to experience some of the same symptoms. "Mike-fright" has been known to happen to radio speakers before a "dead" microphone. *Self-consciousness* is an extreme example of being self-conscious; it illustrates well the connection between self-awareness and imagining what one looks like to others.

Cooley (1902) had this connection in mind when he coined the phrase *the looking-glass self.* His analysis is worth quoting:

> As we see . . . our face, figure, and dress in the glass, and are interested in them because they are ours, and pleased or otherwise with them according to as they do or do not answer to what we should like them to be; so in imagination we perceive in another's mind some thought of our appearance, manners, aims, deeds, character, friends, and so on, and are variously affected by it.
>
> A self-idea of this sort seems to have three principal elements: the imagination of our appearance to the other person; the imagination of his judgment of that appearance; and some sort of self-feeling such as pride or mortification. The comparison with a looking-glass hardly suggests the second element, the imagined judgment, which is quite essential. (p. 184)

This emotional-affective response of self-feeling, which appears when people present themselves in front of others, is not present in the early stages of self-awareness.

As we have noted, newborn infants lack the ability to visualize themselves through the eyes of others. They must acquire this ability through learning; essential to this is language acquisition, which permits children to take the roles of other individuals.

Learning to Take the Attitude of the Other

Language is necessary to the development of self-awareness. Many writers have recognized this relationship and have expressed it in various ways. Some have suggested the importance of linguistic anchorages like address, salutations, and property. Others have regarded parental use of the child's name as an important factor. Still others have assumed that the use of pronouns by both the child and the child's elders helps to fix the child's idea of self-reference. But none of these views is as concrete or convincing as that of G. H. Mead (1934).

Mead notes that from the standpoint of children, among the most significant adult vocalizations are those that have to do with themselves. Children pick up, imitate, and gradually incorporate these in the evolving systems of signals, or cues, that they use to stimulate themselves. They hear their names repeated over and over by others who accompany the names with appropriate gestures and activities to indicate what they mean. The remarks that they are able to remember and repeat to themselves gradually increase in complexity. At first they can use only simple words, then groups of words, and later simple sentences. Finally, they become capable of rehearsing in their imaginations entire conversations in which they have been involved. They learn to ascribe motives to their actions and to become concerned over others' reactions to their behavior. As a person converses with him- or herself, an inner dialogue can be observed: The person takes the attitude of another person and judges that attitude in terms of his or her own response to the situation at hand. Mead describes this as an exchange between the "I" (the person) and the "me" (the reflected attitudes of the other).

Through this process of self-stimulation, children learn to think of themselves as persons with personal points of view, feelings, ambitions, and goals. Such recognition necessarily means that they recognize or conceive of themselves along lines similar to the conceptions that others have of them. In this inner forum, this personal rehearsal and dramatization of roles, young individuals learn to apply symbols to themselves and to their behavior. As Mead has pointed out, young children are characteristically less adept on the "me" side. They respond directly to stimuli, but do not have the means—or have inadequate means—of taking the other's attitude.

In the course of responding to themselves, children (a) develop an awareness of their own responses, (b) learn something of their consequences, and (c) achieve a certain objectivity about them. Fundamental in the process is the medium of language. Individuals become aware of objects when they are able to name and classify them; similarly, they become aware of themselves when they learn to apply symbols to themselves and to their acts.

Concerning the necessity of symbolization for the realization of selfhood, we should emphasize the turmoil that may accompany this development of self-symbolizing. Baldwin (1987) notes this succinctly, pointing to the fact that self-conceptions depend upon assessments of others' perspectives toward one; because wrong assessments as well as correct ones are made, children learn about themselves not without some turmoil. In the writings of Freud and other psychoanalysts, this point is raised to a central theme. Children identify closely with one of their parents, take over some of the parent's moral perspectives, and apply these to their own behavior. But the identification is fraught with peril, and the internalization of parental views may result in harsh control over basic attitudes.

Individuality and the Social Character of the Self

The preceding discussion indicates that the self is a social product; it is a consequence of the individual's incorporation within his or her own emerging sense of self of a social process, which involves ongoing conversations between the "I" and the "me." Indeed, the self is just this process of intraindividual communication. Selves do not exist except in symbolic or social environments from which they cannot be separated. Intraindividual communication is only a part of the total communication network, which extends also to relations between individuals and between individuals and groups. The very idea of an isolated self as an atomistic unit is an error. Symbolic behavior is shared behavior; "self" therefore implies "others" and is inseparable from them. The meanings of the symbols by which selves are organized are based on the responses of others. The fact that a self always seems to belong to an autonomous biological organism should not cause us to neglect the fact that it is built upon a social foundation and that it continues to draw its sustenance from its roots in social relations. As Mead (1934) notes, "No hard-and-fast line can be drawn between our own selves and the selves of others, since our own selves exist only insofar as the selves of others exist" (p. 164).

However, a commonsense idea of individuality runs counter to this. It is thought that because persons have unique bodies and somewhat unique experiences, they are quite autonomous products. There is no need to deny individuality in affirming the basic social nature of self. As Cooley (1930) has said, the use of the word *I*—which expresses individuality—would be inconceivable in the absence of an audience to address or exert power over. But in an even more subtle sense, the social nature of the self necessarily implies, rather than denies, individuality. The *generalized other,* the organized community of attitudes to which the person responds—the "me"—is not a mere importation into the person; it is an assimilation attended with anguish, anxiety, concern, and care. In a report of a series of observations of his young daughter, Cooley contends that a sense of appropriation is crucial to the development of a sense of self. He points to the early and passionate use of pronouns such as *mine* and *my.* In a limited way, Cooley is getting at a much larger point—namely, that people are not compliant automatons.

The Nature of Self

The use of such expressions in common speech as "self-consciousness," "I hate myself," "I hurt myself," "I am a problem to myself," and "I will be here myself" is an indication of the self in action. However, popular usage of self-words is often inconsistent and confusing, particularly because the self is sometimes identified with the body and sometimes not. *Self* has both an objective and a subjective reference. Using *self* as a noun seems to imply the existence of a corresponding entity or object. This, however, is an erroneous conception—as erroneous as it would be to think of *speed* in the same manner. Both terms refer to events and relationships rather than to entities having definite locations in space. For these reasons the self has been described as a "grammatical illusion."

If the self is thought of as a thing, it is reified; that is, it is either conceived of as the body or thought of as an entity somewhere within the body. It is universal to refer—at least poetically—to some part of the body that is especially favored because it is the seat of selfhood (perhaps particularly the heart, the eyes, the breath, and the brain). Horowitz (1936) has reported some amusing answers by subjects to the request that they locate their selves: They named such varied zones as head, face, brain, eyes, heart, chest, lungs, teeth, hands, and genitals. Kluckhohn and Murray's (1948) definition of the personality as "the organization of all the integrative (regnant) processes in the brain" (p. 9) is a sophisticated example in the technical literature of the tendency to locate the self in a part of the body.

In order to have a self, one must first have a body. Hence some psychologists have spoken of the "physical self " as apart from the "social self." Little is gained by this, as we already have a word to designate the body, namely, *body.* The self is not in the body as a physical part, neither is it a spiritual or mystical entity located somewhere or everywhere in the organism; yet the body is implicated in the very notion of self.

The Self as Organization

A definition. We will note in Chapter 11 how persons' conceptions of themselves serve to evoke and organize appropriate responses and, as part of the same process, inhibit other responses. Such conceptions have a much greater effect on the control of behavior than do simple verbal commands or a single inhibiting response. In the same way, at a higher level of integration, one may think of self as (a) *a set of more or less consistent and stable responses on a conceptual level* that (b) *exercises a regulatory function over other responses of the same organism at lower levels.*

This definition of self does not imply that the self is a "motivating force." It is not the ultimate vital source of behavior and energy; neither is it a suprabehavioral court to which all behavior is somehow mysteriously referred. Dualistic notions of this kind often pervade popular thinking about human behavior and are also found in the scientific literature.

The self is an organization or integration of behavior imposed upon the individual by him- or herself and by societal expectations and demands. Social requirements and pressures impose limitations upon the degree of inconsistency tolerated in the behavior of individuals and impel the person to eliminate or reconcile such inconsistencies. The organization and integration of lines of activity that appear contradictory or inconsistent to the outsider are essential parts of what is referred to as the self. For the person, they merge together in the conversations between the "I" and the "me." Clearly, each person has multiple "I"s and multiple "me"s.

The self, as we have defined it, does not enter significantly into all behavior but is differentially involved in various acts; at one extreme, involvement is slight. Psychological experiments dealing with "level of aspiration" have shown that when involvement in a task is increased (that is, when the individual is appropriately motivated), performance is improved or otherwise changed. In many involuntary and automatic activities, little of the self is implicated, although even in these the action may have significance of which individuals are not aware. Moreover, an automatic action, like tapping the table with your fingers, may acquire significance if it is singled out for attention or criticism by other persons so that it takes on meaning for yourself.

Self and self-control. Self-control is usually thought of in connection with self-awareness; for example, we speak of people controlling their appetites or curbing their passions. However, regulatory functioning is not necessarily accompanied by acute self-consciousness. For example, a driver may pilot a car quite skillfully for many minutes while engaged in conversation or sunk deep in thought. Any physical skill tends to assume an automatic character, although when first acquired it is at the forefront of attention. Some skills may become the basis of self-esteem, as in persons who use them professionally or competitively, so that they continue to be at the center of attention in a somewhat different way.

The mechanism of control. Self-regulation is inseparable from social control. The language mechanisms by which self-control is exerted are derived from social sources, and the regulatory process itself occurs largely in the form of internalized conversation. As we have noted, Mead has distinguished two phases of internalized conversation, the "I" and the "me." These can be made clear by means of a simple illustration. Let us suppose that a man walks into a bank and finds himself in a position where he can make off, without fear of detection, with a large sum of money. We shall suppose that our hypothetical man is not above temptation in this particular situation. Something like the following inaudible and greatly abbreviated conversation might take place:

Phase 1: "I"	*Phase 2: "Me"*
I could use that money.	But it's stealing.
So what! Everyone steals if they have a chance to.	You know it isn't so.
I could get a new car.	No. Better be honest.
No chance of getting caught.	Dishonest.
Banks make lots of money; they won't feel it.	Isn't right to take it. Isn't theirs either.

If the man is above temptation, Phase 1 does not exist, and this conversation does not occur.

Internal conversation does not go on in terms of complete sentences or words alone, but rather as a kind of mental tug-of-war between conflicting impulses interspersed with visual and auditory images and daydreams, and accompanied by corresponding feelings. Such conversations are not necessarily short, nor do they always take place in single episodes. The battle against a particular temptation may be a sporadic and long one that is brought alive periodically by external circumstances.

Much of our thinking, particularly when we are dealing with difficult or problematic situations of a moral or volitional kind, involves these two general phases of conversation. Mead calls Phase 1 the "I" and Phase 2 the "me." The "me" in his scheme represents internalized group standards; that is, the "me" is the community in the individual. To Mead, the "I" represents impulses that are supervised by the "me," either being squashed as they get under way or afterward or being diverted into acceptable channels.

The widespread popular conception that the impulses of the "I" always require supervision and are of a negative and unsocialized character requires considerable qualification. Impulses may be perfectly socialized, but nevertheless judged inappropriate to the situation after brief consideration. We are continually making such judgments, given that life is anything but routine. Control is not necessarily a matter of stemming ignoble temptation or putting the lid on passions; it may be quite the reverse, as when one checks overly generous impulses in favor of other considerations. Furthermore, control may be positive in the sense that we have to urge ourselves to do things, the urging representing the regulatory side of our action. We shall draw a sharp line between negative and positive self-control, because lines of action necessarily involve both the eliciting of certain responses and the negation of others. Puritanical traditions emphasize the repressive aspects of control and disregard the fact that the "I" may become socialized and need not be an expression of the brutish side of human nature.

Social control is not based exclusively—and certainly not primarily—upon coercion. Nor can effective group action be based upon the continuous direct surveillance of individuals. If this were false, humans would revert to sheer brutality and opportunism whenever they were out of sight or earshot of others, or whenever the chances of detection were slight. Orderly social controls are based on contract, obligation, trust, and responsibility. Even limited alliances involve these.

Theories of human nature that postulate opposition between individual and society picture society as a kind of police officer watching over the individual. Self-interest is seen either as being in opposition to collective interest or as utilizing the latter to gain its primary ends. This is a misconception of the nature and function of ethical codes and of the requirements of group life. Compliance with community norms and with contractual obligations is not only a requirement of effective collective action, but a necessity for the creation and fulfillment of individual aspirations. There is no natural opposition of humans and society.

Conscience, guilt, and shame. Internal control in moral matters is referred to as *conscience.* What is regarded as right and wrong varies widely among societies, among groups, and even from situation to situation within homogeneous populations. Also, as Cameron and Magaret (1951) point out, "The behavior which one man views within an ethical context of 'right' and wrong may be for his neighbor a matter of expediency, taste, or arbitrary cultural control" (p. 285). We sometimes make naive judgments about the acts of others because we do not take into account the varied content of consciences. Sometimes conscience is identified with religious precepts; religion and morality are frequently so closely intertwined that a coalescence of ethical and religious teaching seems part of the natural order of things. However, in some societies large areas of morality lie outside the religious sphere.

In Western theological writing and in commonsense thinking, transgressions of the dictates of conscience are associated with guilt. One stands alone before one's God—or conscience—and suffers remorse for what one has done or left undone. We hardly need dwell upon the subtleties of guilt and self-judgment and the means of expiation.

The Self in Early Childhood

The child is not born with a sense of self. The self develops out of the matrix of experiences to which the child is exposed. In the foregoing sections we have implicitly presented a number of notions central to a social psychological theory of self-development. Below, we review the work of Cooley and Mead, contrast it with the psychosexual formulations of Freud, Lacan, and Erikson, and conclude with an appreciative statement about Sullivan's *The Interpersonal Theory of Psychiatry* (1953).

Cooley and Mead

Mead and Cooley present views of early childhood that could be termed interactional and developmental. They argue that the self emerges in three sequential phases. In Mead's work, these phases are termed *play, the game,* and *the generalized other.* In each phase, the child is progressively better able to differentiate self from other. In the play phase of self-development, the child is seen as unable to take more than one role at a time. In the game stage, the child can segregate multiple roles, but he or she cannot, as in the generalized other phase, combine them into a consistent symbolic perspective. *The generalized other* describes persons' interpretations of their experiences with others who make up their world. They need not be an actual group per se. In the generalized other stage of self-development, individuals are capable of standing over and against the outside community and capable of seeing themselves clearly in terms of the moral and symbolic expressions of others. This is what Mead means by the "I" and the "me." The "I" component of the self describes the individual's distinctly personal views of self, whereas the "me" refers—in Sullivan's terms—to the "considered and reflected appraisals" of others. The self, for Mead and Cooley, reflects constant interaction between (a) the individual's definitions of situations and (b) the definitions reflected to the individual by others. Cooley locates the emergence of the self in the primary group of the family. *Self-feeling* is basic to his theory. Mead, on the other hand, argues that the genesis of self is based not on self-feeling per se, but on the child's ability to respond *reflexively* to the attitudes of others.

Stages of Selfhood

We may call the three phases of selfhood the *preparatory stage,* the *interactional stage,* and the *participatory stage.* In the preparatory stage, the child imitates and mimics the words, actions, and feelings of others. In the interactional stage, he or she is able to take the attitudes of specific others, and a process of anticipatory socialization begins to occur. The child is learning the languages, feelings, emotions, and ways of acting that are shared by other family members. In the participatory stage, the child learns to take the attitudes of the family and play group, and can grasp the generalized outlook of the group. Socialized speech of a nonegocentric nature is produced (see Mead, 1934; Meltzer, 1972, pp. 9-10; Stone, 1981a, pp. 200-201).

Gender and Selfhood

In Chapter 7, we discussed gender codes and conventions and noted how young children quickly acquire understandings of gender-specific behaviors. We can now note that selfhood is directly connected to gender. The self that emerges in childhood is not gender-free. An axis of value and mood (Stone, 1981a), or instrumental and emotional attachment (Gilligan, 1982, pp. 8-9), differentiates males and females in U.S. society. These may be termed *gender codes*; one is masculine, the other feminine (Erikson, 1950; Kohlberg, 1981). The masculine code in our society represses emotionality; the feminine code releases emotion. To the degree that males and females are socialized into these two codes, the emotional experiences for the two gender classes will differ. At the same time, the ability of each gender to take the attitude of the other will vary and be differentially difficult or easy. Thus it is easier for boys to understand boys than it is for them to understand girls. The same holds for adult males in their relations with other males and with females. Kohut (1977), a psychoanalyst, has suggested that the goal of socialization is to produce a human being who is cohesive and responsive to the needs of others, irrespective of gender. This may be a utopian goal, given the current arrangement between the sexes in our society.

Lever (1978) has noted sex differences in children's play and games. She observes that whereas boys tend to participate in more formal games, girls are more often involved in small group play that mimics primary group relationships. She writes, "In Meadian terms, it may be that boys develop the ability to take the role of the *generalized other* while girls develop empathy skills to take the role of the *particular other*" (p. 481). When children live in a shared environment and are part of the same community, they tend to take the attitude of the same generalized or particular other, and thus respond to the same set of rules—including feeling rules.

Thorne and Luria (1986) have observed that 11-year-olds form separate gender play groups, and these groups foster ritualized and asymmetric relations between boys and girls. Hence sexual scripts for adolescence are learned in these play groups. This finding is consistent with Sullivan's theory, which we discuss later.

We must, however, return to Butler's (1990) arguments about gender. Recall her point that "gender ought not to be construed as a stable identity or locus of agency from which various acts follow" (p. 140). Gender is a socially constructed identity. Its meanings are given in performances, through the body, its stylization, bodily gestures, movements, hairstyles, and so on.

Early Selfhood

Wiley (1979) has outlined a theory of infant selfhood. He indicates three stages in the genesis of self in the first year of life. The infant's first sense of self-awareness emerges in the "me" stage, when the infant defines him- or herself through the mother. This stage flows into the second, the "we experience," in which mother and child merge in a field of shared social experience. The third stage is the "I" stage, which develops when the infant can turn back on his or her behavior from the standpoint of the "me" and the "we experience" and see him- or herself as a "psychological I," or self. In the "I" phase of self, the infant is able to reflect temporally and interactionally upon his or her own conduct from the double standpoint of the infant's and the mother's points of view in the social situation. Wiley's formulations locate selfhood earlier in the life cycle than do many other theories. His emphasis on the "me," "we," and "I" phases strengthens Mead's theory, which does not locate a social relationship in the center of the self-experience. That is, Mead's "me" is not closely joined to the self in a "we" relationship.

Other Developmental Views: Freud, Lacan, Erikson, Sullivan

Whereas Mead and Cooley see self-reflexivity as a problematic element in every interactional episode, other theorists take a more deterministic view. We term them the *psychosexual* or *psychosocial developmentalists.* The two most prominent theorists in this tradition are Freud and Erikson. Each, in a somewhat different fashion, stresses age, sex, and family experiences as crucially determining variables in the emergence of the self and personality. Each adopts a relatively fixed sequence of stages through which the infant must pass on the way to adulthood. Each assumes that processes internal to the organism enter significantly into the developmental process. We turn first to Freud, whose work is still highly influential in the fields of psychiatry and clinical psychology. (See also our discussion in Chapter 6, and see Table 8.2 for a summary view of the theories to be discussed in this section.)

Freudian Developmental Theory

The general Freudian thesis of personality development has been concisely stated by Benedek (1952):

> The integration of the *sexual drive* from its pregenital sources to the *genital primacy* and to functional maturity is the axis around which the organization of the personality takes place. From the point of view of personality development, the process of interaction is the same in both sexes. Men and women alike reach their psychosexual maturity through the reconciliation of the sexual drive with the superego and through the adjustment of sexuality to all other functions of the personality. . . . *The sexual drive is organized differently in men and women, in order to serve specific functions in procreation.* (p. 100)

In our presentation of Freudian developmental theory, we rely mainly on Benedek's summarization. The reader should bear in mind that there is some divergence of opinion among Freudian psychoanalysts and others who subscribe to the general outline as Benedek gives it. She herself indicates some of the points of divergence (see also Benjamin, 1981; Coward & Ellis, 1977; Mitchell, 1983; Rose, 1983).

The Stages. The early developmental history of the child is described in terms of the dominance of certain sensitive—or *erotogenic*—zones, such as the oral, anal, and genital regions. Infants' earliest libidinal pleasures are connected mainly with their mouths. They suck at their mother's breasts and their own fingers, and they also use their mouths to explore and test the objects they encounter in the external world. The oral phase of development occupies approximately the first year. The psychoanalyst Abraham distinguishes two phases of this stage: the *passive-receptive,* in which children merely have things done for them, and the *active-incorporative,* in which children are able to reach actively for objects. During the oral period, if the infant's instinctual needs are not adequately met, insecurity, anxiety, and conflict develop. Throughout this period, children are "narcissistic," deriving most of their gratification from themselves and their own bodies, with little reference to external objects. However, they are learning what causes them pain and which of their actions bring disapproval and withdrawal of love. The differentiation of id and ego has begun, as children begin to establish relationships with their mothers and with objects.

In the second phase, the anus becomes the dominant erotogenic zone. "Its double function—retention and elimination—becomes the center of interest and the source of pleasure" (Benedek, 1952, p. 71). Toilet training then becomes critical. Parents, in a fashion that depends on their cultural and

TABLE 8.1 Erikson's Eight Stages of Psychosocial Development

Stage	*Psychosocial Crises*	*Significant Social Relations*	*Favorable Outcome*
1. First year of life	trust versus mistrust	mother or mother substitute	trust and optimism
2. Second year	autonomy versus doubt	parents	sense of self-control and adequacy
3. Third through fifth years	initiative versus guilt	basic family	purpose and direction; ability to initiate own activities
4. Sixth year to puberty	industry versus inferiority	neighborhood; school	competence in intellectual, social, and physical skills
5. Adolescence	identity versus confusion	peer groups and out-groups; models of leadership	an integrated image of self as a unique person
6. Early adulthood	intimacy versus isolation	partners in friendship; sex, competition, cooperation	ability to form close and lasting relationships; to make career commitments
7. Middle adulthood	generativity versus self-absorption	divided labor and shared household	concern for family, society, and future generations
8. The aging years	integrity versus despair	"mankind"; "my kind"	sense of fulfillment and satisfaction with life; willingness to face death

personal backgrounds, attempt to teach the child sphincter control. By this time, the child understands adults well enough so that he or she can cooperate with or resist them, depending upon the kinds of relationships that have been established. "Toilet training," Benedek (1952) says, "is the ego's first conscious struggle for mastery over an id impulse" (p. 72). The mother's approval is balanced against the instinctual pleasure of soiling. When mastery of the impulse becomes a goal in itself, a new phase begins. The ego, even in the absence of the mother, resists the id impulse. This represents a big forward step in building personality structure. One of its immediate results is that the child is now vulnerable to threats from id impulses that may break through against the controlling ego. This conflict also represents a clash between the *pleasure principle* and the *reality principle.* The former, in the service of the id, strives for immediate gratification; the latter postpones immediate gratification for later gratification through a mastery of the reality situation.

The particular method of toilet training employed is important, as it causes the child to react in certain ways. Thus severe training seems punitive to the child and may lead him or her to rebel and become hostile toward the mother. This creates a vicious circle as the mother reacts to this rebellion. When sphincter control is secure, the conflict situation diminishes and the child is ready for the next step. During the anal period, differences in learning between the sexes begin to appear. Benedek remarks that mothers generally recognize that girls are more easily trained than boys. This is because the girl identifies with the mother more readily, whereas in boys a good relationship with the mother is merely preliminary to self-assertion and eventual identification with the father. The roots of competitive behavior are said to lie in the achievement of sphincter control. A British analyst, Jones, has even stated that the model for competitive behavior among men derives from boyish competition in urinating.

The third general stage is called *oedipal*, or *phallic*, because the child's sexual urges, originally directed toward his or her own body, now become intensified and directed toward the parent of the opposite sex. For obvious reasons, boys become aware of genital gratifications earlier than do girls. The mother is the object of the boy's first heterosexual interest. The girl's development is slower and more complex; her sexuality remains more diffusely located in sensations of the skin and in motor coordination rather than focusing on the genitals. Freud postulates that the sight of the male genitals arouses "penis envy" in the girl, and that this is instrumental in breaking the girl's attachment to her mother and directing her erotic impulses toward her father and eventually to other males. Freud believed penis envy to be the key to feminine psychology. (This is one point on which some analysts disagree with Freud.) In any case, the girl is said to turn toward the father, thus arousing an instinctual conflict between attraction to the father and the potential loss of gratification of needs by the mother. However, sometimes after lengthy conflict and vacillation, the girl develops her own kind of Oedipus complex—the *Electra complex*. The boy's oedipal development is more direct, yet there is a crucial conflict associated with it. The boy is in competition with his father for the mother, but cannot win. Although he cannot actually consummate his urges, he feels guilty and "expects retaliation to be directed toward the organ from which he receives pleasure. The fear of castration—mutilation—develops in varying intensity, even if a threat of physical punishment was never uttered" (Benedek, 1952, p. 82). Fear of castration brings about ambivalence toward the father. The boy tries to please him by identification with him in nonsexual areas of behavior and tends also to idealize him. Identification with the father leads to internalization of the father's moral code, although the working out of the Oedipus complex, and the associated development of a mature super ego, takes many years. In the meantime, genital urges may find expression in masturbation or other substitute activities and attachments. Benedek also lists various ego defenses against sexual tendencies that help to repress and resolve the Oedipus complex. These include the intellectualizing of curiosity about sex, development of infantile sexual theories, denial of sexuality in the parents, and identification with the opposite sex. The latter is a defense against the dangerous heterosexual urge. This is known as a "negative Oedipus complex" and is usually temporary, because it is not a feasible solution of the sexual problem. The various phases of the resolution of the Oedipus complex do not occur in a fixed time sequence, but may occur more or less simultaneously.

During the oedipal period, the structure of the personality becomes much more complex and differentiated. The superego is developing and is in conflict with the id. The ego now undertakes the function of mediating between (a) the id and the superego and (b) the id and reality. At this stage, the ego represses the sexual tendencies, thus initiating the latency period.

The beginning of the latency period coincides, in our society, with the beginning of school. "The desexualization of the child's interest enables him to comply with environmental requirements and thus to expand in mental and social growth" (Benedek, 1952, p. 88). The basic biological tendencies of giving and taking, retaining and eliminating, and other tendencies from the anal and oral stages continue to develop into more complex forms. Oral receptive pleasure continues in the form of pleasure in the reception of material and spiritual gifts. During latency, children learn how to share. Aggressive incorporation appears in the form of envy, jealousy, and maliciousness. Passion for collecting betrays the retentive tendency. Boys characteristically collect masculine objects (stones, strings, keys) and girls accumulate feminine objects (beads, dolls). If either sex evinces much interest in the wrong kinds of objects, this is an index of bisexuality. The existence of the latency period as a biologically determined stage is another point upon which all Freudians do not agree.

The next phase is brought about by the onset of puberty and is coterminous with adolescence. The physical maturation that occurs in this period reawakens latent conflicts, and the ego must again master them. Girls, for example, become sensitive to the changes in their bodies and may become ashamed or shy. In both sexes, attempts are made to master sexuality through repression, a technique that was successful in the earlier oedipal stage. As the sexual drive becomes more urgent, "all the available resources of sublimation are mobilized, and expansion of interests and achievements is generated" (Benedek, 1952, p. 97). Safe ego gratification is afforded by these interests. Yet "the ego . . . cannot withstand for long the pressure of the instinctual impulses; the defenses yield and the instinctual tension is released" (Benedek, 1952, p. 97). During adolescence the child discovers new values and ideals and appraises those of the parents, thus reactivating the old conflict with them: The boy quarrels more with his father, the girl with her mother. As the child becomes more independent of the parents, the superego becomes less rigid, and a more complex level of personality integration is reached. Sexual maturity requires a personality that accepts both the sexual drives and the social regulation of them.

The systematic account of development offered by Freudians ends at this point. Later events tend to be interpreted as a working out, in relation to an adult environment and advancing age, of earlier genetic occurrences. This account of development must be viewed as an ideal, or average normal, picture. Children, it is said, vary in the rates at which they pass through some or all of the phases; some experience one or more phases only in dreams or fantasies. Sometimes part of a phase may be repeated as a consequence of regression, which is in turn a consequence of disappointments. Adolescence is such an especially tortuous process that some analysts refer to the "normal psychopathology" of the period. It is also noted that some individuals do not go through adolescence to the final stage but remain fixated at earlier points, and that if the process goes awry, libidinal urges may find expression in a wide variety of curious or abnormal ways.

Criticism and appreciation. In criticizing this account, we can quote Benedek herself to show what is left out of it. In discussing the anal stage, she comments briefly on the development of speech during the second and third years:

> It is in another area of maturation that the child learns to speak. . . . This complex process is considered to be the result of the progressing maturation of the speech apparatus and of intellectual accomplishments and is, therefore, not usually discussed in connection with the psychodynamic aspects of personality development. (Benedek, 1952, p. 74)

She touches briefly upon initial learning of words and sentences, noting that the child "has stored in his mind symbols related to . . . experiences" that occur before the development of language, and that these experiences and symbols may never reach the level of verbalization, but may form the content of the unconscious (p. 76). This is virtually all Benedek says of language behavior. The separation of "emotional experience" from cognition, which is implied in Benedek's quotation, is characteristic of psychoanalytic thinking. It stems from the classical tripartite distinctions among cognition, conation, and affect (intelligence, will, and emotion). Those who make these distinctions neglect the fact that emotional experiences do not exist as pure states, but are shot through with cognitive elements. The fiction of the separation of intellectual development and personality development can be maintained only if one disregards or underrates the role of language in the organization of behavior, including emotional behavior.

A second major criticism is that a *genetic fallacy* is persistently maintained when the last event in a chronological series is identified with the first, as illustrated by Benedek's frequent use of the term *model* (as in the suggestion that urinary competition provides the model for all later male competition). The attribution of sexuality to both newborn infants and adults is another example. Some analysts have made note of the resulting confusion, and have differed with Freud on this point. The same type of fallacious genetic reasoning is evident in the conception of the biologically rooted drive as the theme that unites all processes throughout the developmental sequence. Although learning is given important place, its primary function is seen as the harnessing of the id drives in socially acceptable ways. The genetic approach of Freudian analysts gives their explanations a narrative character. If they are asked why two persons whose childhood experiences appear to be substantially the same turn out very differently as adults, the analysts' answers will frequently consist of two biographical narratives.

A third problem arises from the general character of analytic theory itself, which makes it difficult or impossible to subject it to empirical tests at crucial points. In a review of psychological studies of children, Koch (1954, p. 22) has pointed out that there is virtually no evidence of a nonclinical sort on which to base an evaluation of psychosexual stages. With respect to some minor points, it has been possible to check the implications of the analytic account. The existence of the latency period, the validity of the concepts of sublimation and repression, and the Oedipus complex itself, as described by Freud, have been found to be questionable. Anthropologists, by using comparative data, have raised serious doubts about the alleged universality of some of the central factors in the developmental process, such as Freud's concepts of the superego and oedipal attachments. The assumption that development is virtually over—except for minor variations—when adulthood is reached is questionable from the viewpoint of sociologists (see Chapter 11).

Despite the many objections that have been raised concerning it, Freudian developmental theory also has some clear-cut virtues. The fact that it is a general theory concerning areas of human behavior that are vital to self-esteem makes it significant and challenging. It at least proposes explanations for many forms of behavior that are ordinarily passed over by other psychological systems. Analytic theory has also performed the function of calling attention to the subtlety of human interaction and the existence of concealed factors that subjects themselves are unable to report. It has sought to isolate and analyze crucial experiences in the life of the child and has described, with much clinical detail, various significant processes, such as identification with parents and other mechanisms of interaction and ego defense. Close contact with patients provides the analyst with a continuous flow of clinical data of great value to anyone interested in childhood development, regardless of how it may be interpreted. Some suggest that Freud's theory should be read as a myth, and others regard it as supporting male dominance over women.

Lacan

Jacques Lacan (1977), a French psychoanalyst, has undertaken a complete rereading of Freud's works. In the process, he has modified and changed a number of the key Freudian concepts. Positing that language is central to an understanding of the unconscious, Lacan has produced a semiotic-psychoanalytic framework that has become quite controversial. Lacan's works are difficult and are subject to many different readings (see Coward & Ellis, 1977; Metz, 1982; Ragland-Sullivan, 1986). We will now discuss Lacan's theory of the "mirror stage" and the phases of development the young child moves through on the way to resolving the crisis of identity that Freud locates in the oedipal phase.

Sensorimotor phase. To borrow Piaget's (1954) term, the sensorimotor phase sees the infant like a "hommolette," or a little man, spreading without hindrance in all directions (Coward & Ellis, 1977, p. 101). The infant moves around its environment, crawling here and there. In this phase, the child experiences a sense of "oneness" with the other. This is like Wiley's "we" phase.

Splitting phase. In the splitting phase, the infant begins to detach from the mother. The mother receives all the infant's demands and is the object of its desires. In this phase, the infant divides the world into two categories: self and world. An emerging sense of prelinguistic self-awareness develops in this phase; this may begin as early as the age of 3 months, although some say it appears at birth (Feld, 1979; Martin & Clark, 1982).

Mirror phase. In the mirror phase, the infant sees his or her image in the mirror and forms an ideal, unified picture of him- or herself. This image splits the child from the mother because it provides a picture of self that is no longer dependent on the mother's attention. Simultaneously, it unifies the child's sense of self and creates an ideal, imaginary self. Soon the mother becomes another "mirror" for the child, for the infant sees him- or herself mirrored back in the mother's actions.

Lacan argues that the mirror stage creates an ideal yet fictional self-image for the child. It gives the child a false sense of unity. The mirror stage is critical to all later experiences of self because it establishes the infant's first reflective relationship with the external world on an error, or on what Lacan terms *méconnaissance.* Because the "I" of the infant is ushered in under imaginary, false circumstances, the underlying social foundations of the self are unstable and fragmented. This genesis of the self in the mirror stage prefigures later personality disorders that appear in adulthood, including narcissism, aggression, neurosis, and madness (Lacan, 1977, p. 7). For Lacan, the mirror stage means that there is no firm, steady center to the self.

Language and subjectivity. Lacan (1977, p. 2) argues that the child emerges as a subject when he or she acquires the pronoun *I.* However, he argues that the *I* of language is a false ego ideal, for the *I* has no real permanence in the child's world. Arguing that children enter language as gendered beings, Lacan proposes that the mother is the first ego ideal of the child. The child attempts to become like the mother, but always fails. Finding his or her place in language, the child confuses him- or herself with the mother. This means the child has an imaginary ego that is located in the mother; he or she has another imaginary ego that is located in the mirror phase. These two ego ideals create confusion and ambiguity. Ultimately the child's subjectivity is located in language, but language separates the infant from him- or herself. Hence language gives a false sense of self-unity. The infant's self exists in a vacuum; it is neither in language nor in the mirror and the mother. In no sense is self connected to validating self-experiences that would promote security and self-assurance.

Identity crisis. As the infant is detached from the mother and acquires language, another crisis occurs. The infant is unable to identify with the ideal type of his or her sex. The infant is not the mother and is not the father, but is a gendered individual—that is, the infant is called a girl or a boy. In the triadic family drama with the mother and the father, the child experiences what Lacan, after Freud, terms the "castration complex." The male child cannot use his penis to express his desire for his mother because of the incest taboo. The female child is deprived of a penis, as is her mother. She experiences herself as a lack or an absence. Her sexual desire is repressed, and she is forced to sub-

TABLE 8.2 **Theories of Psychosexual Development**

Theorist	*Stages*	*Drives*	*Language*
Mead	play, game, generalized other; me/I/we	no	yes
Freud	oral/anal/pre-oedipal/oedipal	yes (sex)	yes/no
Lacan	sensorimotor/splitting/mirror	yes (sex)	yes
Erikson	first year through old age	yes (anxiety)	yes/no
Sullivan	infancy through adulthood	yes (anxiety)	yes (three modes)

mit to language and to the symbolic order of the family, where her subjectivity and sexuality are regulated. A similar process occurs for males.

Lacan's image of the infant and young child suggests that this period is filled with anxiety and fear. His emphasis on gender and sexuality suggests that the self-genesis experiences will be considerably different for males and females, although the broad outlines of the identity crisis surrounding the castration complex will be the same for males and females. His suggestion that language mediates and structures self-awareness fills out a part of Mead's theory that was only hinted at by Cooley's study of pronoun use in early childhood. The discussion of the splitting phase and the mirror phase is also useful, for it points to experiences that are missing in Mead's play, game, and generalized other phases. Whether the mirror stage lays the foundation for unstable self-other relations later in life is problematic. Clearly, however, Lacan's mirror is not like Cooley's looking-glass. Important here is that both authors see the child's identity being reflected back not only through mirrors, but also through the actions of other people—most especially the mother.

It is important to note, however, that for this version of psychoanalysis, there is no direct knowledge of the world of experience (Clough, 1994, p. 77). No subject can escape the realms of discourse and the unconscious.

Erikson's Model of Developmental Stages

Another Freudian approach to developmental stages that has gained a wide audience in recent years is that proposed by Erik Erikson (1950, 1959, 1962, 1965, 1969). Although a psychoanalyst trained in the Freudian tradition, Erikson had experiences while doing research among Native American and while treating patients in the United States that led him to still another approach to developmental stages. His scheme has gained great popularity, principally among child and adolescent psychiatrists and among clinical psychologists. Many enthusiasts take it as a rather definitive picture of developmental reality, although Erikson himself apparently meant it only as a suggestive guide. We shall not outline this scheme in any detail, for it is not very different in some important assumptions from the Freudian one.

Erikson rethought Freud's theory of infantile sexuality, developed a diagram that emphasizes the step-by-step (progressive) nature of the mind's development, and stressed the ways (modes) that the body's sensitive zones (openings, organs) work (Coles, 1972, p. 75). He linked this with a sequence of social experiences, emphasizing critical periods that the child must manage, either doing well or failing in some degree (Coles, 1972, p. 137). Later he added additional stages and developmental tasks, eight in all (see Table 8.1). Erikson does not regard these stages and tasks as rigidly sequential; rather, he remarks:

> If the chart . . . lists a series of conflicts or crises, we do not consider all development a series of crises. Development proceeds "by critical steps—critical being a characteristic of turning points, of moments of decision between progress and regression, integration and retardation." (quoted in Coles, 1972, p. 138)

In a sense, the developmental tasks run all through the adult years, perhaps in any individual never being accomplished once and for all.

An interactionist must view such a scheme as not remarkably different from the Freudian, to which Erikson was reacting. Thus there still is a great emphasis on psychosexual linkages, and despite the disclaimers, it attempts to give a "stage" picture of development. The earlier stages, in which the family is implicated, receive much more emphasis and are discussed in greater detail than the later, or adult, years. And Erikson focuses considerably—and understandably, given that he is a psychoanalyst—on psychic health; hence the abilities to become trustful, autonomous, industrious, and truly able to exhibit initiative and share intimate relations are crucial. There is nothing "wrong" with emphasizing these things, but this focus on psychic health tends to restrict the scheme unduly for more wide-sweeping social psychological purposes. Certainly it tends to restrict the focus—despite Erikson's own interest in history and in famous figures such as Gandhi and Luther—to individuals rather than to interlocking social biographies.

The point is underscored by the largely clinical use to which Erikson's chart and writings have been put. A painful example is given by Schwartz and Kahne (1973), who document how college psychiatrists have picked up Erikson's scheme and applied it faithfully to college students as a "real" explanation of adolescence. Consequently, when the campuses felt the effects of the events of the 1960s, beginning with the civil rights movement, college psychiatrists simply translated students' memberships in all the emergent social movements into Eriksonian language. The scheme allowed them to discount the students' complex memberships and commitments to political movements, and allowed them to misread almost totally the students' participation in a variety of other social worlds. Indeed, Parsons and Platt (1970), in their efforts to elaborate the Freudian and Eriksonian schemes, have suggested that between adolescence and early maturity is a clearly discernible developmental stage that they term "studentry." In this sense, Erikson's scheme may be restricted to only certain classes of individuals. Finally, with his emphasis on sequential *identity crises* in adolescence, Erikson often gives less attention to the transformations in self that occur in middle and late adulthood. The foundations of these identity crises are also not fully clear. They, too, may be relevant only to certain groups of individuals.

Sullivan's Developmental Theories

We turn now to the developmental scheme of Harry Stack Sullivan. His approach, in our judgment, overcomes many of the flaws in the theories of Freud and Erikson.

Theorists who do not subscribe to the central tenets of the Freudian position are disposed to locate the critical junctures in development at other points and ascribe somewhat different significances to them. This is true even of formulations that focus exclusively on children. One of the most systematic and thoughtful accounts of personality development—and one that differs in important ways from the Freudian position—is that of Sullivan. Like Freud, Sullivan developed his position mainly out of his experience with psychiatric patients. Through his close association with anthropologists and other social scientists, he placed more emphasis on the social environment than Freud had. He repudiated much of the Freudian vocabulary and developed one of his own. The *interpersonal theory* of psychiatry he formulated has found expression in an influential journal and has also been disseminated through the work of his students. Perhaps because of the great difficulty of communicating with schizophrenes, he became concerned early on with the nature of communication. Sapir, who markedly influenced Sullivan's thinking on communication, was a pioneer anthropological linguist. The roles in development that Sullivan ascribes to communicative processes and the cultural milieu give his work special significance for the social scientist. Our discussion of his position is based primarily on Sullivan's (1953) posthumously published lectures.

Some central concepts. For Sullivan, the avoidance of severe anxiety is central to human behavior. He argues that a *self-system* starts to develop in infancy as a protection against overanxiety. The process of *selective inattention* is mentioned in this connection. Sullivan formulated several other concepts that require elaboration before an account of his developmental stages will make much sense to the reader.

From the first moments of life, infants interact with adults—mainly with their mothers, who are concerned particularly with satisfying the infants' initial bodily needs. The mothers also have needs, which in turn are met by their general activity in caring for their infants. Sullivan thus says that the situation is *integrated* insofar as it is meaningful for both organisms. In adults, a mutually satisfying friendly conversation would exemplify an integrated situation. Situations may be *resolved* when the needs are met. There is then no longer any reason for continuing the immediate interaction unless new bases immediately arise. Situations *disintegrate* when they are terminated before they are resolved. Anxiety may play a large role here; it arises, for example, when one makes friendly overtures to a desirable person and is rebuffed.

According to Sullivan, there are three types of experience: the prototaxic, the parataxic, and the syntaxic. These terms refer to the manner in which experience is registered and to the nature and degree of inner elaboration that it is accorded. In the *prototaxic* mode there is an absolute minimum of inner elaboration, and experience consists mainly of discrete series of momentary states that can be neither recalled nor discussed. The *syntaxic* mode, in contrast, involves a maximum of inner organization and elaboration, and, because it is fully encompassed by symbolic formulation and is logically ordered, it can be discussed and completely communicated to others. The *parataxic* mode of experience lies between the other two; in it, experience is partially organized or organized in a quasi-logical manner, but there are also elements of which the individual is unaware (Sullivan, 1953, p. 29).

Children's earliest experiences are in the prototaxic mode, but they quickly progress to the parataxic as soon as they begin to understand the environment and note certain interconnections and simple sequences. Lower animals also are capable of reaching the parataxic level, according to Sullivan. The syntaxic mode begins to appear with the learning of language and is hence confined to human beings, although Sullivan takes pains to emphasize that it is rarely possible for us to express all aspects of an experience in words. Roughly, the three modes represent the incommunicable or ineffable (prototaxic), the partially communicable (parataxic), and the wholly communicable (syntaxic). This scheme allows a considerable place for unconscious behavior without positing an "unconscious mind" or instinctual urges as the mainsprings of behavior.

Sullivan's treatment of needs is fluid. The infant quickly develops new needs in addition to the initial bodily ones, through both experience and maturation. Needs appear chronologically, some not until several years have passed. Thus the sexual drive—or, as Sullivan terms it, the *lust dynamism*—does not arise until puberty. (Here Sullivan explicitly departs front Freud, who views the sexual drives as present from birth.) In Sullivan's theory, the various needs are given sophisticated treatment and are not regarded as inner forces. Apart from elementary biological needs of the infant, most of the needs with which Sullivan is concerned arise in interpersonal interaction and have nothing to do with biology. Needs are satisfied in highly complex ways through interaction. Much satisfaction, Sullivan holds, must take place through *sublimation*—that is, by indirect means. This is because the initial means adopted are met with reactions by significant others that arouse anxiety in the person.

Stages. Sullivan's (1953, pp. 33-34) designation of stages is a clue to important differences between his position and that of orthodox Freudian psychoanalysts. Sullivan distinguishes seven stages of personality development: infancy, childhood, the juvenile era, preadolescence, adolescence, late adolescence, and adulthood. *Infancy* extends from birth to the appearance of speech. *Childhood* covers the period from the onset of articulate speech to the appearance of a need to have playmates. The *juvenile era* covers the period of grammar school through, as a result of maturation, the desire for an intimate relationship with a companion of the same sex. *Preadolescence* ends with the display of sexual awareness and the desire for an intimate of the opposite sex.

Adolescence, which varies from culture to culture, ends when the individual has developed some social relationship and pattern of activity that fulfills his or her lust, or desire, for sexual activity. *Late adolescence* extends the individual's attempts to form a socially acceptable pattern of intimacy and sexual behavior. At *adulthood* the person enters into a love relationship (which may or may not satisfy the person's sexual desires). During this era the person establishes a relationship with another person who is regarded as a significant other. That person becomes highly important to the individual, and his or her concerns may take precedence over the individual's own view of his or her life situation.

Sullivan's account of *infancy* and *childhood* covers much of the same ground that has been covered in chapters of this text dealing with the development of language, thought, and self. Sullivan emphasizes the role of anxiety in the origin of the self-system. The Freudian concepts of the ego, id, and superego are not included, and there is no discussion of instinctual drives or the Oedipus complex. In childhood, along with the gradual learning of the syntaxic use of language, children may also use language as an anxiety-reducing instrument, as when they verbally disown certain of their actions—"I didn't do that, it was my hand," or "I did it. I am sorry." Parents' demands for apologies and explanations further this use. During childhood the need for tenderness, which appeared during infancy, is manifested and elaborated in the desire for play and physical contact with others, particularly the mother. If the mother is consistently unable to respond with tenderness, the child may be compelled to sublimate the need or may give it up. Like other observers, Sullivan remarks upon the fact that children learn to deceive adults and so escape rebuff and anxiety. Sullivan is constantly concerned with inadequate means of handling issues that may be taken by the child and notes a number of appropriate modes of concealment that may lead to trouble later. One of them is the use of *verbalism,* or *rationalizations,* to ward off punishment.

Vicious cycles of malevolent development may start through interaction of the sort that occurs when the mother continually disparages the father and explains the child's behavior by saying the child is like the father. This may establish the conviction in the child that he or she is detestable and unworthy and must expect always to be treated badly. This unfortunate turn of events may "very easily prevent a great deal of profit from subsequent developmental experiences. . . . There is literally a slowing down of healthy socialization" (Sullivan, 1953, p. 217). Important to Sullivan is the idea that any developmental mishap may prevent or slow the learning process. The arrest of development is not a static thing, for the person continues to change and develop; however, "the freedom and velocity of the constructive change are very markedly reduced" (p. 218).

In *late childhood,* children become more aware of their identity as males or females and begin to adopt appropriate behavior. Their knowledge of other cultural perspectives also broadens. Like Piaget, Sullivan emphasizes the necessity—imposed by the requirements of others—for the child to begin to distinguish between reality and fantasy (autism, or autistic thought). Toward the end of this period, children have learned to sort out what they must conceal from what they can talk about because it will make sense to adults.

Even when malevolent or other inappropriate personality organization has developed, the transition to the next stage introduces a real possibility for correction. Sullivan (1953) is impressed by the amount of change that can occur "as one passes over one of these more-or-less determinable thresholds of a developmental era" (p. 227). This means that children, to some extent, are given the choice of a fresh start, although the older they grow, the more they become the heirs of their own pasts.

The *juvenile era* starts approximately the time the child begins school. School plays a key role in various ways. Many more "authority figures" appear on the child's horizon—teachers, playground bullies, traffic police, other parents—and the child has to learn to live with all of them. By the end of this era, the child is comparing authority figures—including the parents—with one another as persons. The child no longer regards the parents as the most perfect people on earth, nor does he or she endow them with omniscience any longer. At the beginning of this era, the child typically begins to desire contact and play with other children; this sociability contrasts with the greater egocentricity of younger children. Hence schoolchildren are open to tremendous influence from their peers. They learn that their peers have points of view, and they discover how many perspectives there are. Through interaction with their peers, some of it brutal and antagonistic, they learn a great deal about how to handle themselves without suffering unduly from anxiety. They must face the possibility of ostracism. Toward the end of this period, especially, they begin to be sensitive to their reputations—that is, their general self-conceptions deriving from juvenile groups. Sullivan notes that mobility of the parents may be disastrous, as it causes children to continue to be strangers as they go from one school to another.

Sullivan (1953) gives the juvenile era tremendous weight as a determinant of future development. It is "the time when the world begins to be really complicated by the presence of other people" (p. 232). Through rough-and-ready interaction with these new people, children correct their misconceptions of self and acquire a wider grasp of selfhood and their place in the community. If they are fortunate in their development, they emerge with an "orientation in living"—that is, an idea of how to satisfy their needs without arousing too much anxiety (p. 244). This represents their first and most important socialization experience; if they have not learned this, they are in for trouble. They may, for example, use the technique of disparaging others as a protective device; this is equivalent to saying, "I am not as bad as the other swine." This does not provide a secure base for a sense of personal worth.

Preadolescence is ushered in by an interest in a new type of personal relationship: friendship with a person of the same sex. This is quite different from previous relationships, for it turns upon intimacy and collaboration in satisfying each other's expressed needs: "Because one draws so close to another, because one is newly capable of seeing oneself through the other's eyes, the preadolescent phase . . . is especially significant in correcting autistic, fantastic ideas about oneself or others" (Sullivan, 1953, p. 248). Participation in preadolescent gangs has a similar desirable effect. The need for chums arises as a result of both interpersonal development and maturation. Sullivan emphasizes the great therapeutic effects of these preadolescent intimacies in saving persons from previous unfortunate courses.

However, the preadolescent period is also one of danger because of differences in rates of development among friends. Children reach puberty at different ages; variation within the same sex may be as much as 3 or 4 years. Hence some preadolescents lag behind others. Some still require intimate friendship when others no longer do, or one child may not yet need such an intimate relationship when most of his or her peers do, and so later may have to establish relations with a much younger or much older person.

Sullivan (1953) defines the early stage of adolescence as "extending from the eruption of true genital interest, felt as lust, to the patterning of sexual behavior which is the beginning of the last phase of adolescence" (p. 263). Sullivan considers lust as the last of the maturation needs, drawing a sharp line between it and the need for intimacy. *The need for intimacy* starts much earlier and has an independent development. At the onset of adolescence, there is a significant change in the object of intimacy. *If there has been no very serious warp in development, the child begins to seek increasing intimacy with a member of the other sex,* the pattern of intimacy being much like that of preadolescence. In the United States, the fulfillment of this need faces serious obstacles, because it runs into sex taboos. The obstacle that prevents access to intimacy leads to *reverie* and *fantasy*, and in "the gang," children may engage in discussion pertaining to it. The discussion of "who's who and what's what" in the heterosexual world is of great profit for those of the gang who are already in the adolescent stage.

In adolescence, life becomes tremendously complicated by the elaboration of potentially conflicting needs. The appearance of lust—a powerful need—adds greatly to the problems of the period. There may be collision between the requirements of lust and the maintenance of self-esteem. Genital urges may create acute self-doubt, puzzlement, embarrassment, and other unpleasant reactions. Because of the way sex is viewed in Western society, the desire for sexual activity often clashes with a sense of security in interpersonal relations. This is true in adolescence and in later life as well. Intimacy and lust requirements may also conflict with each other. A common manifestation of this conflict is the separation of persons into two mutually exclusive classes: those who can only satisfy one's lust, and those who can only satisfy the need for intimacy and friendship. The distinction between "good women" and "bad women," "sexy girls" and "good girls," conveys this idea:

> Thus satisfying one's lust must be at considerable expense to one's self-esteem, since the bad girls are unworthy and not really people in the sense that good girls are. . . . The trouble . . . is that lust is a part of personality, and no one can get very far at completing his personality development in this way. (Sullivan, 1953, pp. 269-270)

The shift in the sex of the desired object of intimacy may also clash with security needs. For instance, the parents may disparage and ridicule the adolescent's interest in the opposite sex; the parents may be jealous, may not wish the child to grow up too fast, or may fear sexual accidents. The various collisions of needs may lead in this stage to homosexual play, but more usually produce autosexual behavior (masturbation).

Sullivan (1953) points out that the "number of wretched experiences connected with adolescents' first heterosexual attempts is legion, and the experiences are sometimes very expensive to further maturation of personality" (pp. 271-272). They may be destructive to self-esteem and may erect permanent barriers to satisfactory heterosexual consummations.

Several unhappy long-term outcomes include the following: Some people feel pursued by members of the opposite sex and expend a great deal of energy trying to avoid them. Lust may be dissociated from consciousness and may be expressed only in fantasies. Lack of potency may be connected with failure to resolve the lust-intimacy problem. In some persons, the appearance of lust may be accompanied by the continuation of intimacy needs on the preadolescent level, leading to transient or persisting homosexual tendencies, with the genital drive handled in a variety of ways—homosexual reverie, homosexual relations, autoeroticism. In some persons, lust may mature although the individuals remain chronically juvenile. The ladies' man and the persistent "tease" are often chronic juveniles, according to Sullivan. These people need to be envied by others of their sex, and hence often boast of their conquests.

Sullivan indicates the extreme diversity of alternatives that face the adolescent. The adolescent has to discover "what he likes in the way of genital behavior and how to fit it into the rest of life. That is an achievement of no mean magnitude" (p. 297). Sullivan demonstrates the range of alternatives by showing that there are about 45 patterns of behavior that are "reasonably probable." He reaches this figure by setting up classifications of intimacy, kinds of objects of lust, and types of sexual activity.

Late adolescence, for Sullivan, is the period when the mode of sexual activity is decided upon. In addition, he stresses the great growth of experience in the syntaxic mode of communication. Through formal education and work experience, persons acquire greater insight into their own and others' behavior and may develop enormously in knowledge and maturity. Many adults, because of their developmental heritage, are greatly restricted in what they can learn from a potentially enlightening environment: "Large aspects of living are, as it were, taboo—one avoids them" (Sullivan, 1953, (p. 306). As for truly mature persons, Sullivan confesses that psychiatrists have very little to say, because they do not meet them in their offices as patients. With the progress of patients toward maturity, psychiatrists lose sight of them (p. 310).

Evaluation. Sullivan's view has much in common with the Freudian conception. Both give considerable attention to unconscious features of behavior, and both focus attention on the dynamic interplay of personal relations. Both have a place for bodily maturation and posit a close relationship between this maturation and the development of personality. They are also alike in that they are mainly derived from clinical experience with adults rather than from firsthand intensive study of children. One further point of similarity is that both Sullivan and Freud more or less terminate their systematic accounts of development at the threshold of adult life. The differences between the two conceptions will become apparent as we review some of the main features of Sullivan's scheme.

Sullivan's account provides an important place for needs that arise sequentially. Sex appears late—rather than early, as in Freud's account—and is not given supreme priority. Many of the important needs arise from interpersonal relations rather than biological bases.

Those needs that are of biological origin, such as the infant's need for "tenderness," quickly become transformed as they are felt and interpreted and as they enter into progressively more complex interpersonal patterns. Even what Sullivan calls "lust," with its obvious biological concomitants, is of this nature. The needs that arise in interpersonal relations, although associated with biological maturation, are essentially consequences of the developmental complexity of the communicative processes and the self system. Instinct is not inevitably in conflict with society—indeed, Sullivan explicitly rejects the instinct theory and the id concept, which makes humans essentially evil beings held in check by social proscriptions. The "unconscious mind" in which Freud locates the instinctual impulses does not appear as such in Sullivan's theory, although he makes ample provision for the unwitting aspects of behavior.

Sullivan clearly specifies the crucial experiences of each period, and in such a form that empirical testing of his views is possible. He presents his position as a tentative one, recognizing the need for empirical validation. He acknowledges that many of these critical experiences, and even the stages themselves, might vary from culture to culture. He always recognizes and specifies the role of various adults as representatives of culture, rather than as unique personalities. Like other writers, Sullivan emphasizes the important fact that the differential rates of biological and experiential development of children may crucially affect personality development. His treatment of some of these consequences, as in his discussion of the transition to adolescence, shows great insight. Following a line of thought that has generally taken hold in recent years, he also emphasizes the uselessness and possible danger of training children before they can assimilate the training experience.

Sullivan's scheme is genuinely developmental in the sense that he introduces no genetic fallacy. No stage is a repetition of a preceding one, and in each stage genuinely new behavior emerges. Sullivan acknowledges a tremendous possibility for change, particularly during transitions into new stages.

Sullivan does not view so-called arrests of development as "fixations" or "regressions." The capacity to learn from experience is greatly reduced by such arrests, but change and development go on. In Sullivan's scheme this change is not conceived of as merely a new form of an old personality organization, but as a genuine, if unfortunate, innovation.

A central concept in Sullivan's system is *consensual validation,* by which he means the manner in which the meanings of symbols and the validity of ideas, including ideas of self, are confirmed in the process of the individual's communicating with others. (We discuss this idea in numerous places in this text.) Sullivan notes that symbols do not carry meaning, but evoke it in user and listener, and that consensual validation makes symbols precise and powerful instruments for handling both people and ideas. Through his emphasis on the effects of the communication process upon the developing personality, Sullivan introduces a social dimension to the center of individuality. This is in line with his explicitly stated idea that the scientific analysis of interpersonal relations requires a *field theory* rather an elementaristic or atomistic approach. Sullivan's main contribution has not been in the analysis of what he calls the syntaxic mode, or public communication, but in his discriminating treatment of the "unconscious."

Sullivan reinterprets the unconscious as a distortion of the communication process through such mechanisms as (a) selective inattention, (b) dissociation, (c) misinterpretation, and (d) masking processes. Cottrell and Gallagher (1941) note:

> Sullivan attempts to show the influences within a given culture which channelize awareness. . . . If we accept [G. H.] Mead's analysis of the way in which meaning emerges from an incorporated verbal structure of rights and duties, Sullivan's work suggests an important amendment. The meaning that is borne by verbal interchange in interpersonal relations can be completely distorted by the dissociated elements which are at work to set the tone and color of the situation. (pp. 23-24)

Our criticism of Sullivan's developmental scheme is based mainly on what it leaves out. The omissions can be attributed partly to Sullivan's explicit psychiatric interests and partly to the scantiness of his actual writings. The gravest omission is the lack of consideration of personality change after the initiation of adulthood. By implication, the importance of such change is suggested, but it is not discussed. The consequence of this is that such influences as the following are left out: occupational status and other adult statuses; the shifting of age memberships, including the effect of children on parents; adaptations to the approach of death; and the handling of slow or abrupt changes of statuses of many kinds.

The developmental account itself, insofar as it deals with children, must be amplified, as Sullivan himself recognizes. It can be extended, of course, by actual investigation of children. Cultural variation as well as variation by sex and the general influence of social structures must be taken into account more extensively. A wider range of psychological processes also needs to be included.

One major reservation about the account itself is justified. Sullivan makes anxiety virtually central to—actually, the basic motive of—human behavior. No one, of course, should deny anxiety's great importance. Despite Sullivan's sophistication about the ramifications of anxiety and the associated needs for security and intimacy, however, his treatment of this central concept is like that of the older motivational theories. In his defense, it should be said that he is tentative about the centrality of anxiety: "In discussing the concept of anxiety, I am not attempting to give you the last word; it may, within ten years, be demonstrated that this concept is quite inadequate, and a better one will take its place" (Sullivan, 1953, p. 8).

The research on children that has been done by anthropologists and sociologists since the 1950s considerably amplifies our knowledge of cultural variations in child rearing and child development. However, this research does not—except as it accepts and details the psychoanalytic developmental account—provide an overall systematic developmental theory; Sullivan's does.

Limitations of Stage Theories

It is useful to review Lemert's comments on the stage theories of the self. These theories, written by males, presume a universal human nature. They use a singular view of humanity as the reference point for all experience. They seek to locate a single cause, or set of drives, that motivates action and experience. They presume a normative model of the family—the heterosexual, two-parent nuclear family unit. They do not take up race, ethnicity, and social class as processes and structures that shape the politics of childhood. They do not take the child's point of view. In these ways the stage theories differ from the work of those authors who narrate childhood from the site of personal memory and autobiography.

CONCLUSION

In this chapter we have surveyed several interrelated topics, including process and performance views of the self; "strong-we" and "weak-we" group models of self-development; theories of identity, agency, and action; the politics of identity; and recent research and theory, including psychoanalytic stage models bearing on the process of self-development. The human infant enters the world with no self-conception. Exposure to interaction produces the socialization experiences that progressively mold and build the child's emerging self-conception.

The self is not a part of the physical body. The self is not a thing. The self is a set of symbolic indications that the individual makes to him- or herself on the basis of interpersonal experiences with others. We have reviewed the formulations of Cooley, Mead, and Wiley and contrasted them with the developmental schemes of Freud, Lacan, Erikson, and Sullivan. Of the Freudian models, we find Sullivan's to be the most satisfactory. Freud's original scheme lacks any systematic view of the self, and Erikson's formulations stress individual crises that must be overcome if a "healthy" personality is to form. Both Freud and Erikson stress sexual experiences heavily, and Freud posits that the sexual drive is the major motivating force for the human organism. Sullivan, on the other hand, locates the origins of the self in interpersonal relationships, thus his views extend the statements of Cooley and Mead.

These classic formulations do not anchor the child's self in the televisual and cinematic apparatuses that mediate daily experience. In their emphasis on the family as the site of critical interaction, the male theorists discussed in this chapter fail to address how the mass media enter into and shape the self and the internal conversations children have with themselves. Nor do their theories systematically interrogate the narrative, storytelling side of selfhood in early childhood. These are promising areas for future research.

SUGGESTED READINGS

Chodorow, N. (1978). *The reproduction of mothering: Psychoanalysis and the sociology of gender.* Berkeley: University of California Press. A controversial and highly criticized treatment of gender from an object-relations psychoanalytic perspective. Lacan scholars, in particular, have criticized this work, but it should be examined for its alternative psychoanalytic treatment of the problems raised in this chapter.

Erikson, E. H. (1950). *Childhood and society.* New York: W. W. Norton. Contains a treatment of the author's well-known child developmental stages and presents the research on children that led to his theoretical modification of Freud.

Freud, S. (1938). *The basic writings of Sigmund Freud* (A. A. Brill, Ed. and Trans.). New York: Random House. Contains all the basic elements of Freud's theory and includes such writings as *Psychopathology of Everyday Life, Totem and Taboo,* and *The Interpretation of Dreams.*

hooks, b. (1990). *Yearning: Race, gender, and cultural politics.* Boston: South End. A wonderful collection of personal narratives about childhood, youth, and early adulthood by a major African American feminist scholar.

Lacan, J. A. (1977). *Écrits: A selection.* New York: W. W. Norton. Contains a number of important essays detailing Lacan's departure from Freud as well as Lacan's essay on the "mirror stage."

Mead, G. H. (1934). *Mind, self, and society: From the standpoint of a social behaviorist.* Chicago: University of Chicago Press. Contains Mead's most important essays on the emergence of self out of interaction.

Sullivan, H. S. (1953). *The interpersonal theory of psychiatry.* New York: W. W. Norton. Presents the most comprehensive picture of Sullivan's developmental theory. Students are encouraged to explore the works of Erikson, Mead, and Sullivan and to draw their own conclusions concerning which theory is most viable for an understanding of the emergence of self in childhood and adolescence.

STUDY QUESTIONS

1. What are the major differences between the "strong-we" group and "weak-we" group of theorists of the self?
2. Distinguish the various meanings and types of identities that are discussed in this chapter. Connect this discussion to the concept of identity politics.
3. What is the place of the unconscious in psychoanalysis?

9

The Social Worlds of Childhood

A major consequence of children's linguistic socialization is that they become involved in increasingly larger systems of social relationships. The acquisition of the verbal and nonverbal languages that make up the family speech community permits children to become more adept participants in complex social situations. As they become increasingly more self-reflexive, they are able to stand outside their own behavior and view it from the stances of others; they begin to move from the *play* stage of social awareness to the *game* and *generalized other* modes of social interaction.

In this chapter we examine the complex social worlds that make up childhood. Social worlds consist of groupings of persons bound together by networks of communication and common understandings. Often widely distributed in geographic space, members of the same social world share similar views of reality. The social worlds of childhood embed children in common interactive experiences with significant others. Like members of other social worlds, children come to develop their own patterned ways of thinking and acting. In examining these patterns, we employ a developmental, or sequential, model of analysis to lay bare the underlying processes that make the child a more competent interactant. One of the more popular theories that has gained increasing interest in recent years is that of the Swiss psychologist Jean Piaget. Although we have drawn upon his work in earlier chapters, in this chapter we depart from his specific developmental scheme and offer a set of criticisms of his perspective. In the last section we take up the topic of gender and gender performances.

As Corsaro (1996) observes, recent work in the field of child development has moved away from "theories that view development as the solo child's mastery of the world on her terms" (p. 419). Socialization is now seen as a collective process that occurs in "a public rather than a private realm" (p. 419). From this interpretive, interactionist perspective, children are seen as active participants in the negotiations and experiences that connect them with others, including adults, other children, and the taken-for-granted culture that is mediated by language, television, cinema, and children's literature.

This interpretive approach differs from "traditional theories of development and socialization" (Corsaro, 1996, p. 419) in several important ways. First, there is a greater emphasis placed on language and on an examination of how children participate in the cultural routines that make up their world. Second, traditional models of socialization (see below) are linear; they assume that children pass through "a transition from purely biological beings through a period of childhood into socially competent membership in a social group" (Corsaro, 1996, pp. 419-420). This approach focuses on the end point of development, the movement from immaturity to adult competence.

The interpretive approach views development dialogically, within a narrative, performance framework. From this perspective development is seen as constantly emergent, dialectical, and nonlinear. Building on activity theory and the theory of structuration, proponents of the interpretive model examine how children construct meaningful cultures with their peers. These peer cultures consist of "a stable set of activities, or routines, artifacts, values, and concerns that children produce and share" (Corsaro, 1996, p. 432). This culture creatively enacts, reproduces, and becomes a part of the so-called surrounding adult culture (Corsaro, 1996, p. 420).

The Child's Egocentrism

In a series of books, Piaget (1937, 1948, 1951, 1952a, 1952b, 1952c, 1959, 1960, 1929/1967) has documented what he calls the *egocentric* character of childish thought. Piaget describes the entire intellectual development of children—from the time when they begin to speak with relative adequacy to the point at which they acquire approximately adult views of themselves and the world—as a gradual process of overcoming this initial egocentric tendency. It is unfortunate that Piaget selects the term *egocentric* to describe the child's early thought patterns, for it implies that such thought is not social in nature and origin—although it decidedly is. James F. Markey, in his long-ignored work *The Symbolic Process and Its Integration in Children* (1928), suggests that Piaget's "encumbrance with the psychoanalyst's conception of . . . autistic . . . thought . . . permits him to ignore its essential aspects" (p. 152).

Children are at first enclosed in their own point of view and see all things from within it. They are, as Markey notes, the centers of that universe. Their perceptions and judgments tend to be absolute or egocentric, because they are unaware of any other points of view and perceptions. Thus Piaget points out that most young children of 5 years old or so believe quite firmly that the sun and moon follow them as they walk about. At this age, children are not troubled by the logical difficulties that confront adults. They do not attempt to account for the many sudden changes in direction of the movement of moon and sun, or to account for the ways in which these bodies may appear to other people who are moving in various other directions. Their conviction arises from their own perception of movement. Because children do not take perspectives other than their own into account, their own perceptions appear absolute—the only possible ones.

Another example is furnished by young children's difficulty in properly using such terms as *brother* and *sister.* John and Paul are brothers, aged 4 and 5, respectively. If we ask Paul how many brothers he has, he may say "One," or "Two, counting me." If he has decided that he is not his own brother and is asked how many brothers his brother John has, he usually will deny that John has any. By questioning Paul, we may sometimes induce him to say that there are one, two, or three brothers in his family.

Paul's confusion over the significance of the term *brother* arises because the word refers to different persons when he and John use it. Paul is fairly clear about the fact that John is his brother. But because he views the situation absolutely rather than relatively, he becomes confused when required to take any point of view other than his own. He cannot view the family of which he is a part from John's standpoint.

The following is another illustration of child's egocentricity:

> What will happen when it is a question of imagining distant objects, and of coordinating the perspectives of different observers? . . . The child is placed opposite a small model of three mountains, and given a certain number of colored pictures of these mountains; he is then asked which of the pictures show the mountains from the position occupied successively by a doll on the mountains in the model. The function of age in this development of these reactions is very clear. The little ones do not understand that the observer sees the same mountains quite differently from different points of view, and hence they consider their own perspective absolute. But the older ones discover the relativity necessary to objectivity after a number of systematic errors due to the difficulty of coordinating the relationships in question. (Piaget, 1937, p. 32)

The egocentrism of young children is also reflected in their play activities. Parten (1932) has asserted that "since the young children lack the power of expressing themselves with language, they have difficulty in playing in cooperative groups" (p. 263). Children playing in the sandpile usually do not play *together,* although they are fond of playing in company; older children, however, are likely to play together cooperatively. Another investigator, Bridges (1931), notes that "two-year-olds usually play or work by themselves with little reference to others except to claim their toys or otherwise interfere with them. . . . Older children engage more often in group play than younger ones and seldom play alone" (p. 72). These and other researchers have asserted that as children grow older, they learn to play cooperatively, and that in the earlier years, although children may like to play in the presence of others, they do not in a genuine sense play *with* them. Because children do not at first grasp the roles of others, and because they lack an adequate time perspective, they tend to act in terms of short-range egocentric goals. Their ideas of fair play and of the "rules" are inadequate or absolute (see Corsaro, 1981; Selman, 1981).

A Critique of the Egocentric Perspective

Vygotsky (1962) has remarked that psychology owes Piaget a great debt, for he revolutionized the study of children. He observes:

> Like many other great discoveries, Piaget's idea is simple to the point of seeming self-evident. It had already been expressed in the words of Rousseau, which Piaget himself quoted, that the child is not a miniature adult and his mind not the mind of an adult on a small scale. (p. 9)

Piaget assumes that the child is unlike the adult, and this difference sets the tone for early egocentric thought. It is on this point (and others to be elaborated below) that we part company with Piaget. As we have argued earlier, there is ordinarily little—if anything—intrinsic to the human organism that upon birth will make it more or less responsive to the symbolic environment to which it is exposed. In short, we argue for a model of social development that begins from ongoing social worlds of experience, not from traits and attributes that the infant brings into the world at birth.

This point warrants elaboration. Piaget isolates three modes of thought: autistic, egocentric, and rational. As Vygotsky (1962, p. 13) notes, Piaget's conception of development is psychoanalytic in origin, for it assumes the child is initially autistic and will change to rational thought only after a long and arduous process of socialization. Furthermore, Piaget repeatedly implies or asserts that autism and egocentrism are tied to the child's psychic nature and are impervious to social experience. He asserts that until age 7 or 8, real social life does not exist among children. Children engage in open monologue conversations; they are incapable of placing themselves in the perspective of others; they are essentially self-centered and egocentric in nature.

We reject the two assumptions underlying this formulation. First, there is nothing intrinsic to age that makes a 7- or 8-year-old child more or less egocentric. Second, the degree of egocentric thought present in a child's behavior repertoire will be a direct function of the complexity of that child's social environment. Consequently, thought and its complexity are *not* functions of organic and psychic factors but are inextricably bound up in the world of social experience. In short, thought is a product of social interaction. To argue otherwise, as Piaget does, is to construct a psychologistic, not a sociological, model of thought and development. Piaget assumes, then, that thought moves from inner, autistic experiences to outer, sociocentric utterances that are mediated by a lengthy period of egocentric thought. As we have outlined in Chapter 7, in our discussion of Chomsky's formulations, our model of linguistic development assumes that thought follows vocal utterances, that initial utterances are global and nonspecific in nature, and that thought and speech progressively merge into one.

We wish to make two more points concerning egocentric speech. First, we concur with Vygotsky that egocentric speech quickly joins with inner thought. Furthermore, egocentric, or self-centered, speech and thought always involve the utilization of a social perspective. The dialogue between the "I" and the "me" is a social process. Egocentrism, or the primacy of the "I" over the "me," is always a matter of degree and is not as clear-cut as Piaget's work would imply. But more important, the presence of egocentric speech in the young child can be taken as evidence that the self as a distinct object is starting to emerge in the child's thought patterns; this is Markey's (1928) point also. The presence of pronouns in the 3-year-old child's vocabulary is unequivocal proof that a linguistic conception of self as actor is forming. In this sense we wish to reverse the usual meanings of *egocentric* and argue (a) that all individuals are egocentric from the perspectives of others and (b) that young children who think and talk egocentrically are in essence separating themselves from others, however unsuccessfully, and in that process are making distinct objects of themselves.

The following excerpts from a study conducted by one of the authors in a preschool underscore this position, Two girls are standing below the large dollhouse inside the preschool:

> *First girl:* They're people up there. [Points to three girls playing upstairs.]
>
> *Second girl:* Shall we go up there?
>
> *First girl:* No, they'll say "you can't come up here."

A 3-year-old girl has just finished working at the painting table. She gets up and goes across the room to get a book. An instructor confronts her:

> *Instructor:* Are you through painting? Don't you want to hang up your painting?
>
> *Girl:* No, I don't want to!
>
> *Instructor:* Don't you really?
>
> *Girl:* No. [Shakes her head and walks off.]
>
> *Instructor:* I'll do it for you. [Grimaces.] (Denzin, 1972, pp. 299-300)

These examples reveal that young children, at least in preschools, use personal and impersonal pronouns with ease, and in direct reference to ongoing activity systems. There are few elements of egocentric thought in either episode. The examples also suggest that the children were capable of placing themselves in one another's perspectives and formulating lines of action on the basis of that role-taking process.

It would be expected that the more familiar the situation to the children, the more reflexive and accurate the children would be in separating themselves from the selves of other individuals. In those worlds that children control—sectors of preschools, their own bedrooms and playrooms—greater levels of reflexivity will be observed.

The argument to this point can be quickly summarized: *The child actor is a sophisticated interactant. Many child development researchers gloss over children's interactional skills either by studying children in unfamiliar test-taking situations or by focusing on solitary individuals without attempting to catch them in moments of serious play.* Too many students of early child development, as Markey observed in 1928, have failed to check their findings out in nonlaboratory settings; this situation has not changed significantly since 1928. Piaget's view of the egocentric child may hold for those children he observed in his institute, but our position is that if left to their own devices, and if exposed to a sufficiently rich and complex interactional environment, 3- and 4-year-old children will act in ways that are essentially adultlike.

Perhaps the point can be underlined with one more example taken from the field observations of one of the authors. A very alert 4½-year-old child was observed making quite adultlike remarks in which she made clear distinctions between "mine" and "mummy's." A few minutes later, watching her mother turn the pages of a book of art reproductions, she "dropped" to the level of pointing at objects and naming them ("tiger," "mother," "baby"). Later in the afternoon, she tried to explain to the author that she and her mother had looked for the author's parked car—where they thought he would be but was not—and did it not have something blue in it (a coat)? And several minutes later, when the author said, "Let's go get your parents," she objected that they were not her parents, but her "mummy and daddy"—denying that she knew what *parents* meant! Interviewed à la Piaget about what were a "mummy" and a "daddy," and how did they get to be that (and was the author without children a daddy?), the child displayed thought processes that perfectly fit Piaget's descriptions of children of that age. She said that her parents had gained their status by passing the age of 7—which she counted up to—and becoming grown-up, then became "daddy" or "mummy" (see also Berk, 1997, pp. 255-256; Crain, 1992, pp. 131-132).

The Child's Network of Significant Others

Infants, as Mead and Cooley have observed, are born into an ongoing network of interconnected social worlds that are filled with individuals who will later become their *significant others.* That is, these people will stand in some position of influence and authority over the children, and they will come to view those people as influential in organizing their own behavior.

Six categories of significant others can be identified. The child is likely to confront and interact with his or her various significant others at predictable times and in predictable places. The first class of significant others is made up of those termed *sociolegal;* they are the child's parents or guardians, siblings, and other members of the kinship system. The second class of significant others are *socio-others,* drawn from the sociability network that surrounds the primary group of the family. These individuals assume "fictional kinship" in the family and may be called "aunts" and "uncles"; baby-sitters also fall into this category. Third are the *co-equal,* or *compeer,* significant others. These may include siblings, but more important, this group is made up of playmates and children in the neighborhood and at school who come to assume a high degree of socializing influence over the child. By age 3 or 4, compeers may rival parents and other sociolegal significant others in their influence over the child. Certainly by the first grade, and by age

7 or 8, the child may have moved nearly entirely into a peer-oriented world of social control.

The fourth class of significant others are *child-care experts.* These persons have attained some legitimate authority over child care and child evaluation. Pediatricians, child psychologists, child-care workers, psychiatrists, teachers, lawyers, politicians, and social workers dictate and shape the broader process by which a society produces its children. A fifth class of child caretakers and significant others is drawn from the mass media: *Media others* enter the child's world through television, radio, CD and audiotape players, movies, storybooks, and nursery rhymes. These others may view themselves as experts on childhood, but more important, they staff and populate the child's world of fantasy and entertainment. Captain Kangaroo, Mr. Rogers, and Big Bird and Cookie Monster on *Sesame Street* represent such fictive and real others who regularly enter the child's world of interaction. Media others may have more contact with the child than people in any of the aforementioned classes of individuals. Those with access to cable television now have entire networks dedicated to children's television, from the Disney Channel to networks devoted entirely to cartoons (e.g., the Cartoon Network) and to reruns of family sitcoms (e.g., Nickelodeon). Recent research indicates that 4- to 6-year-olds may watch up to 4 hours of television a day. This exceeds the interactive experiences they may have with adults.

The last major class of significant others comes from the world of public places. *Public place others* include police officers, firefighters, mail carriers, clerks and strangers in stores, and individuals whom children and their caretakers normally meet when in the public arena. These others fall into a residual category, and their influence on the child is likely to be specific to particular situations or services.

The six categories of significant others described above constitute what may be termed the child's interactive world. The most important significant others in a child's social world are drawn from the sociolegal and compeer groups. These persons make up the child's primary group, and they provide the sources of self-worth and self-awareness that the child first experiences. They are, in Kuhn's terms, *orientational significant others.* They shape conceptions of self, provide vocabularies of motive, furnish symbolic environments, and promote a sense of "we-ness" and solidarity. Depending on the stances that these others take toward the child, the child's rate of social development and lingerings within the egocentric mode of thought will be hastened or retarded. We turn now to a discussion of the decline in egocentrism in early childhood.

The Decline of Egocentrism

As a consequence of entering into more extensive and complex social relations, children become increasingly and more systematically aware of the points of view of other persons. They learn that these are often at variance with their own viewpoints and that they must be taken into account. The young boy learns that though he has a brother, his brother also has a brother (himself); that a pebble is light in weight from one point of view but heavy from another point of view; that an object may be to the left of one object but at the same time be to the right of another. Children's thinking becomes increasingly relativistic. They come to realize that the sun follows neither them nor anyone else; they learn to conceive of it as the center of a solar system and think of the earth as one of several spherical bodies revolving about the sun. When they have achieved this mature point of view, they have, in a sense, synthesized virtually all conceivable views of the sun as a physical object and can assume the perspective of anyone in any location with respect to it.

Piaget places the age of transition, learning to grasp other points of view—learning to become nonegocentric—at approximately age 7, but some English and American investigators have challenged this. In accordance with our own position, as stated earlier, we suggest that the age of transition—aside from being different in different individuals—varies from society to society, from social world to social world. Presumably a young child might remain relatively egocentric in some respects and achieve somewhat greater social awareness in others. The important point is not the exact age at which egocentricity disappears, but that the disappearance is gradual. Of equal importance is the child's *interactional age,* or the amount of time he or she has spent in exposure to a given social experience. *Chronological age,* as such, is often superseded by interactional age. Hence rates of cognitive development cannot be predicted simply on the basis of how old a child is.

Mead (1934) has described graphically how children playfully imitate the roles of elders or associates, thus gradually developing an ability to see objects, other persons, and themselves from a nonegocentric standpoint. He emphasizes what Piaget merely notes in passing—that language is basic in the development of the ability to play roles:

> [There are] countless forms of play in which the child assumes the roles of the adults about him.... In the play of young children, even when they play together, there is abundant evidence of the child's taking different roles in the process; and a solitary child will keep up the process of stimulating himself by his vocal gestures [spoken words] to act in different roles almost indefinitely. (pp. 150-151)

Further, Mead notes:

> A child plays at being a mother, at being a teacher, at being a policeman; that is, it is taking different roles.... He has a set of stimuli which call out in himself the sort of responses they call out in others. He takes this group of responses and organizes them into a certain whole. (pp. 364-365)

Children's playing at being people other than themselves is paralleled in their actual lives in their interactions with parents and playmates. One theory of play is that it is a preparation for later adult activity wherein individuals apply the skills they have acquired (Denzin, 1977). Thus the standards of fair play and the proper attitude toward defeat in competition are often said to be learned on the gridiron or on the "playing fields of Eton." No doubt it is from considerations of this kind that the widespread absorption of children (and adults) in comic strips and comic books concerns and alarms some who feel that constant identification with comic-strip characters of doubtful virtue may lead children to emulate these fictional "heroes." Without accepting this position, one may recognize that this kind of play activity and fantasizing gives children a repertoire of roles and practice in switching from one to the other.

The initial role taking of young children (placing themselves in the perspectives of other persons) is simple and limited, involving only limited and brief fragments of behavior and the imitation of a few specific persons. As children's circles of acquaintanceship are enlarged, as their mastery of communication develops, and as their real roles multiply in number and become more complex, the role-taking processes become more complicated (Cahill, 1994; Corsaro, 1996; Opie & Opie, 1969; Musolf, 1996, p. 305; Selman, 1981).

Perspectives and the Generalized Other

When a child has developed the ability to grasp the role or attitude of one other person at a time, he or she is on the road to becoming a social being. However, before the child can participate in organized adult activity, he or she must be able to conceive his or her own social identity systematically from the standpoint of all other participants.

An illustration will clarify this: Suppose that a group of Air Force men are on a bombing mission. Each man has a definite, assigned general identity that involves certain duties and obligations. Each man has a clear conception of his general identity as he imagines it from the points of view of all the others. He also has a clear picture of how his own identity fits in with the identity of each of the other men.

Mead asserts, by contrast, that the very young child is able to take the point of view of only one other person at a time. From this simple kind of role taking, the child eventually develops the abilities (a) to take the standpoints of others in the situation, (b) to organize these perspectives into an integrated whole, and (c) to view his or her own behavior from this standpoint. Mead's (1934) suggestion of how this learning takes place is as follows:

> If we contrast play with . . . an organized game, we note the essential difference that the child who plays in a game must be ready to take the attitude of everyone else involved in that game, and that these different roles must have a definite relationship to each other. . . .
>
> In a game where a number of individuals are involved . . . they do not all have to be present in [his] consciousness at the same time, but at some moments he has to have three or four individuals present in his own attitude. (pp. 151-152, 154)

Through their participation in organized games, play, and other activities, children learn to take the points of view of the other participants and to grasp the fact that the identities of others are intertwined. At the same time, they begin to see how their own activities within given situations look from the standpoints of the others. They see their own actions as part of a whole pattern of group activity.

Mead coined a term for this organization of the roles of others; he calls it the *generalized other.* He uses this expression because it means that one is taking the related roles of all the other participants rather than the role of just one other person. This concept of the generalized other applies to the organized roles of participants within any defined situation.

The term *generalized other* does not refer to an actual group of people, but rather to a conception or an interpretation that persons derive from their experiences. They then regulate their behavior in terms of these supposed opinions and attitudes of others. They stand outside their own behavior and view it from the perspective of these others. They imagine what people would say "if they knew" or what they will say "when they know." The term *people* may not have any specific reference to actual persons, but may merely represent the child's conception of abstract moral standards. These standards widen as role playing becomes more generalized. Internal "I"-"me" conversations become increasingly more complex.

We disagree with Mead's view on one important point. If one observes them closely, one can see young children taking the roles of multiple others (mother and father, for example) quite nicely in some situations but regressing in other situations to Mead's "able to take only one person at a time." Some children take the roles of multiple others very easily. Mead's points about their increasing ability to do that, along with the general direction of their development, seem accurate enough.

As children's conceptualizing ability approaches the adult standard, their concepts become more numerous and the interrelationships of those concepts become more complex. Children's abilities to play parts and to be different persons and to understand the actions and motives of others develop in a parallel course.

The earlier identity conceptions of children are, from an adult viewpoint, rather curious and often amusing, although in their own way they represent a primitive if incorrect systematization of how identities (behavioral expectations) vary for different individuals. Thus very young children know there are storekeepers and customers, but they think that the customer buys and both customer and storekeeper pay each other. Only the customer buys goods; the storekeeper never does. Monetary activity is confined to buying and selling. Although one storekeeper may help another sell, the distinction between owner and employer is unclear and is not involved in the buying-selling transactions. There are no other parts, such as that of manufacturer (Strauss, 1952, p. 278).

At one step of concept development, children will deny that two identities are compatible; later, having grasped their relationship, they will agree that they go together. Thus a child at a young age will deny that a teacher can be a storekeeper or vice versa, because the two belong to different worlds. Later the child agrees that a teacher could be a storekeeper "after school," but still denies that a storekeeper can be a customer. Still later the child sees that a storekeeper can buy in a store and still in a general sense be a storekeeper. The child does not yet perceive that the storekeeper must be a customer of manufacturers.

Much of children's early learning about identity relationships occurs in concrete

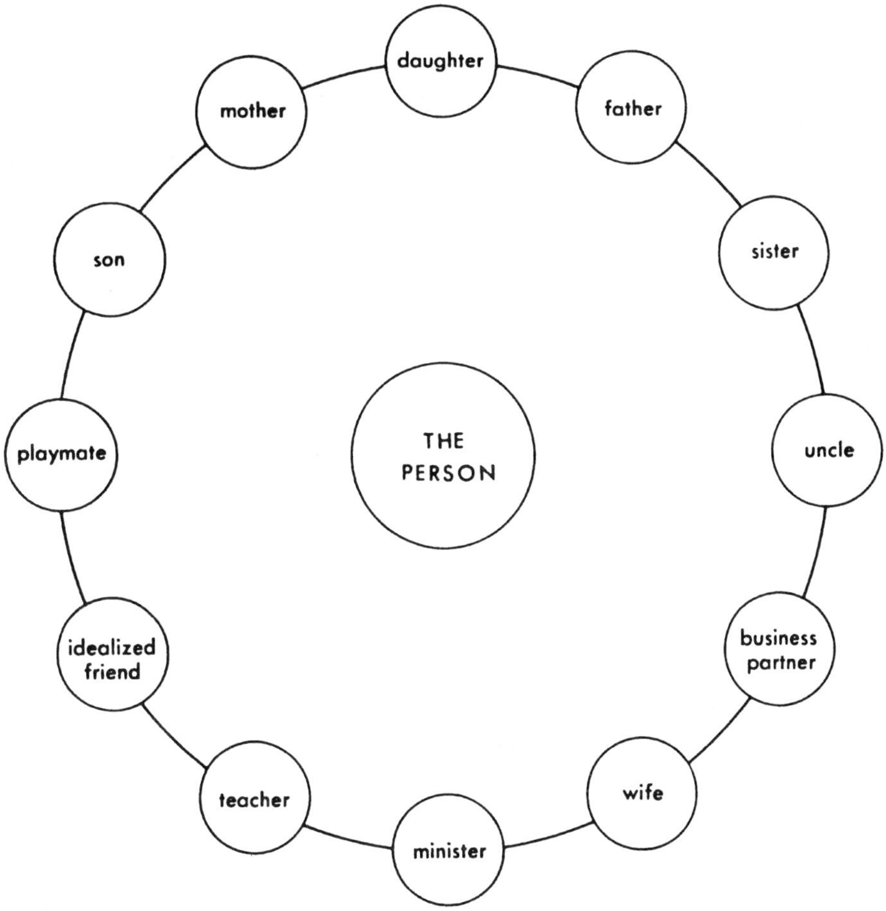

Figure 9.1. The Person and the Points of View of Others
NOTE: Persons learn to look upon their own behavior from the points of view of all these people. They learn the various points of view at different periods of their lives, and these points of view have varying importance for the organization of their behavior.

situations in which the identities are played out before their eyes. However, most relationships are rather abstract. Even those relationships that seem most concrete and visible—for example, those between a teacher and a pupil—involve much more than is visible on the surface. Greater maturity and breadth of experience are necessary before the child can be expected to understand the subtler aspects of such relationships.

The Generalized Other and Moral Behavior

That generalized others are learned conceptions has two important implications: (a) Children do not acquire moral views automatically or mechanically, and (b) even persons belonging to the same groups cannot have identical generalized others. Children are rewarded, punished, and exhorted so that they will conform to adult expectations. However, every parent knows that learning is not a rubber-stamp process and that one cannot mechanically or forcibly inculcate adult ideas into a child.

The concept of the generalized other has been mildly criticized by Mills (1939, p. 672) on the grounds that it implies too great homogeneity and does not account for the multiplicity and heterogeneity of modern societies. It has been argued that the generalized others of given persons are always relative to particular groups and persons, and that not all participants in given social acts have equal influence. A person is said to build up his or her moral and intellectual standards in terms only of significant other persons rather than all others in the situation. There is obvious truth in this. The standards of the criminal, for example, do not enter into the generalized other of the law-abiding citizen except to reinforce them by negative example. Even significant others are significant in different ways and to different degrees. One may describe a student's intellectual orientation in a gross way by relating it to a specific university, specific subject, and specific department. Closer scrutiny may reveal, however, that really decisive influence has been exercised by certain professors, or perhaps by one professor. The same can be said of moral standards, which are perhaps most usually acquired from parents. The mother's and father's influences upon the child may be very different, and in some cases, neither parent may exercise the dominant influence—that is, the child may acquire moral conceptions from peers, a well-liked teacher, or someone else. (See the discussion of child development as conceived by Freud and Sullivan in Chapter 8.)

Athens (1994, 1998) has both criticized and extended Mead's model of the self and his concept of the generalized other. Athens (1994) contends that persons are constantly conversing with themselves, and the self is a soliloquy. He introduces the concept of the *phantom other* to describe others who are not physically present in a situation but "whose impact upon us is no less than the people who are present during our social experiences" (p. 525). The phantom other is both a single and a multiple entity. People are constantly conversing with their phantom others, and the conversations are always operating at multiple levels. In these conversations, raw sensations are transformed into emotions, self-images are developed, moral positions are adopted, and forms of radical self-change are contemplated (Athens, 1994, pp. 525, 529-531). It is easy to fit this model to the socialization process. Children are constantly expanding the universe of others with whom they converse, constantly engaging in soliloquies and in conversations with real and imagined phantom others.

Social Structure, Membership, and Self-Conception

As children become adults, their self-conceptions undergo a variety of patterned types of changes and become increasingly anchored in the groups and broader societal structures in which they participate. Kuhn (1960, p. 40) has developed this point in a study in which people of various ages were asked to make 20 statements in answer to the question, "Who am I?" Kuhn found that children's answers to the question tended to scatter over a wide range of topics focused on particular, individualistic, or idiosyncratic aspects of their lives. With increasing age, the conceptions of personal identity funneled into the kinds of broad social categories that also are employed to describe the social structure. Adults identified themselves more often by occupation, class, marital status, sex, age, race, religion, and other similar criteria. Thus when a very young child who has lost his parents in a crowd is asked who he is, he may be able to supply his first name and a variety of irrelevant information that does not give much help to those who are trying to return him to his parents.

Two examples from Kuhn's study underline this point. A fourth-grade girl replying to the question "Who am I?" wrote a series of negative statements about her behavior, obviously reflecting parental discipline and admonition: "I boss too much. I get mad at my sisters. I am a show off. I interrupt too much. I waste time. Sometimes I am a bad sport. I fiddle around. I am careless at times. I forget." In contrast, the response of a university senior included the following items: "I am of the female sex. My age is 20. I am from [city and state]. I have two parents. My home is happy. I am happy. I am of the middle class. I am a [sorority name]. I am in the Waves Officer School. I am an adjusted person. I am a [department major]. I attend church." It is apparent that the latter series tells us much about the person's position in society, whereas the former tells us about almost nothing except the parental discipline imposed upon a fourth-grade child.

As children are processed through the educational system and drop out of it at various stages to assume adult responsibilities, they are distributed in a variety of jobs, places, and positions. This process of distribution is complex but not haphazard; it is regulated in a general way with respect to occupation by gender, race, the number of job opportunities existing in each field, and price mechanisms that offer differential economic rewards for different occupations in rough proportion to the balance of supply and demand.

In order for a job, rank, office, or any other status to exert a pervasive and decisive influence upon a person, it must become linked with that individual's self-conception and with the networks of social relationships that make up his or her social worlds. At the heart of this linking of self-regard and social position is a fateful commitment to doing well as "that kind of person." A civilian soldier is not insulted by being told that he is not a soldier, but a professional military man is. The latter's behavior is largely oriented toward his being a soldier. It is therefore a matter of some importance to him to believe that he is a good one, in a good army, preferably one of the "best soldiers in the best damned army in the world."

We say that a person's commitment to central statuses—those identities that are important to him or her as a person—is fateful because the individual will read the failure to uphold the standards as failure, and this will cause him or her to feel guilty or ashamed, to lose self-respect, and to make efforts at redemption. When conception of self is based on a simple central status, all other statuses tend to become subordinate to that one and to be judged by reference to it. To continue the example of the professional military man: He will tend to judge many nonmilitary phases of his life in terms of the bearing they have or are likely to have upon his military career. The higher his status, the greater will be the demands of his profession on him for more total commitment, and the greater will be the probability that this commitment will eclipse or take precedence over any others. In discussing morale, we have already seen that certain social organizations demand almost total devotion and allegiance of members, even to the exclusion of familial and other roles that may run counter to the group purposes. Even family roles may become impossible to maintain, or may become subordinate to and subtly colored by more essential loyalties.

Morality and Objectivity

Studies of the development of children's moral ideas and judgments demonstrate that the child moves from predominantly egocentric to increasingly relativistic moral standards. Piaget (1948) has analyzed this aspect of childhood (see also Berk, 1997, p. 469). In his study of lower-class children of Geneva, Switzerland, he discerned a series of transformations in their moral conceptions. He found the young Genevan up to 4 or 5 years of age to be characterized by "moral realism." That is, right is right and wrong is wrong: if a person does wrong, he or she should be punished regardless of motives. Later the child realizes that moral rules are not objectively real but reflect group values—a realization based upon the recognition of multiple perspectives. The children Piaget studied remained at this stage until age 9 or 10, when they reached a third level at which the rules are allowed to be altered by considerations of equity; for example, a lame boy may be given a head start in a race. According to Piaget, these findings demonstrate that the child's conception of moral rules changes from the belief that rules are absolute to the knowledge that they are agreed upon. Other studies of children have supported Piaget's conclusions (Lerner, 1937; Strauss, 1954).

Piaget's specific explanation for the direction of moral development is dubious. He hypothesizes that the early conceptions of moral rules are absolutist because of the authoritarian relations that exist between parent and child, and that conception grows more relativistic, general, and systematic as cooperative relationships grow between the child and others, particularly peers. Nor does it seem adequate to explain the growth of morals merely as a consequence of reward and punishment or of learning from specific direct experiences "to recognize a common element in a variety of situations" (Erikson, 1950, p. 438). Conceptions of roles and of rules grow side by side. Built into identity conceptions are the justifications and canons appropriate to the positions. When children are young, their moral standards lack relativity and generality because they cannot grasp the fuller meanings of acts as seen from wider perspectives. It is therefore worthwhile to distinguish between the full and general comprehension of moral values and the learning of specific rules.

These remarks are supported by some imaginative research reported by Lawrence Kohlberg (1966, 1963a, 1963b, 1969, 1971, 1976), a psychologist who has been stimulated by both Piaget and Mead. To children varying in age from 7 to 17, Kohlberg (see also Brown, 1965) posed stories that embodied moral dilemmas. For instance:

> In Europe, a woman was near death from a special kind of cancer. There was one drug that the doctors thought might save her. It was a form of radium that a druggist in the same town had recently discovered. The drug was expensive to make, but the druggist was charging ten times what the drug cost him to make. He paid $200 for the radium and charged $2000 for a small dose of the drug. The sick woman's husband, Heinz, went to everyone he knew to borrow the money, but he could only get together about $1000, which is half of what it cost. He told the druggist that his wife was dying, and asked him to sell it cheaper or let him pay later. But the druggist said, "No, I discovered the drug and I'm going to make money from it." So Heinz got desperate and broke into the man's store to steal the drug for his wife. Should the husband have done that? Why? (Kohlberg, 1963a, pp. 18-19)

One can resolve such dilemmas by subordinating a rule of law or authority to a higher principle. Kohlberg's results concerning moral judgment are much more complex than Piaget's; he enumerates 6 stages of development and distinguishes 30 aspects of morality. His evidence does not support Piaget's conclusions about the origins of absolutism (authoritarian relations) or the sources of relativism (peer group cooperation). Kohlberg studied children as old as 17, and found that developmental stages continue throughout the entire age range. In the sixth stage, children judge their conduct in accordance with their own internal standards, doing right to satisfy their own consciences. Although an operating conscience exists earlier, only considerably later do children explain conduct to themselves in terms of their consciences.

Roger Brown (1965) offers some comments on Kohlberg's findings with which we agree. He notes that to speak a language, the speaker must have a system of general rules, and so also a person must have a set of general rules in order to act morally. But parents "do not provide lessons in what to do if your wife needs a medicine you cannot afford or in how to resolve the conflicts that may arise in a bombing raid. We have no rote answers to Kohlberg's dilemmas" (p. 407). Such dilemmas can be resolved only by reference to general rules. Brown's comments are in accord with our previous contention that it is worthwhile to distinguish between learning specific rules and comprehending general moral values.

Criticisms of Kohlberg: The Case of Gender

A number of authors have criticized Kohlberg's formulations of moral judgment. Lever (1978), whom we cited in Chapter 8, found that gender differences operate in the games that boys and girls play. Boys are fascinated with the legal aspects of the rules that apply to their games, whereas girls are more pragmatic and tolerant of exceptions to rules. Although Lever does not elaborate the implications of her work for all of Kohlberg's theory, she does suggest that the interactional contexts for the learning of morality differ for males and females.

Gilligan (1982) suggests that Kohlberg's work is colored by a bias that judges moral development in terms of a male model. She quotes Virginia Woolf (1929), who states, "It is obvious that the values of women differ very often from the values which have been made by the other sex . . . yet it is the masculine values that prevail" (p. 76; quoted in Gilligan, 1982, p. 10). Gilligan contends that the traits contained in Kohlberg's moral development scale mark women deficient because they reflect a male view of morality, judgment, and responsibility: "The very traits that traditionally have defined the 'goodness' of women, their care for and sensitivity to the needs of others, are those that marked them as deficient in moral development" (p. 18). Kohlberg's conception of moral development is derived from the study of men's lives, not women's. Women, Gilligan argues, define and judge themselves in terms of such moral values as care, responsibility, helping, and nurturing. Men, on the other hand, emphasize individuality, achievement, legal rights, instrumentality, and control. These two moral domains are often in conflict in male-female relationships, and they continue the gender stratification system in our society. Clearly, any model of moral development that stresses the male model over the female model is deficient. It is apparent, however, that these two models clash in the social worlds of childhood (Cahill, 1994; Damon, 1977; Thorne & Luria, 1986).

The Socializing of Emotionality[1]

Emotions play a central role in childhood socialization, for it is through their emotions that children come to understand themselves, others, and situations. The *socializing of emotionality* refers to the process by which socially constructed meanings for emotions vis-à-vis situations are passed on to the members of a social group (in this case children) and the ways these persons interpret and construct meanings into self-feeling such that they can share their emotions with each other interactionally. Children are born into a social and emotional world and quickly learn to order, interpret, and understand their experiences, including their emotional experiences. In learning about emotions, they must learn when and where they "should" experience and how they "should" express various emotions. They must learn to manage their emotions in the interactional arena (Hochschild, 1979, 1983).

Central to emotion management is a knowledge of feeling rules and the ability to do emotion work. According to Hochschild (1979), feeling rules are "guidelines for the assessment of fits and misfits between feelings and situation" (p. 566), and emotion work is "the act of trying to change in degree or quality an emotion or feeling" (p. 561). Feeling rules tell us how we should feel in a particular situation, and emotion work enables us to change our emotions so that they will fit the situation's social expectations. Hochschild (1983) also maintains that "feeling rules are what guide emotion work by establishing the sense of entitlement or obligation that governs emotional exchanges" (p. 74).

The socializing of emotionality occurs through interactions with *emotional associates*, using *emotional talk*, in *emotional situations*. These three components, which provide the basic structure of emotionality in early childhood, are discussed below.

Emotional Associates

Emotional associates are those persons who, both directly and indirectly, share in emotional experience (Denzin, 1984a, pp. 92-93). In the socializing of emotionality in early childhood, caregivers facilitate a child's understanding of emotions in several ways. Lewis and Michalson (1983) contend that parents overestimate their children's emotional development. They note, "To teach children . . . the socializing agent must 'preview' such capacities to infants in order to promote the children's acquisition of them. Previewing may involve attributing skills and capacities to infants before they actually exist" (p. 221). In support of previewing, Lewis and Michalson cite a study conducted by Pannabecker, Emde, Johnson, Stenberg, and Davis (1980) in which mothers were asked to report on the emotions of their children from birth to 18 months: 66% of the mothers reported that interest, joy, surprise, anger, disgust, and fear appeared in the first 3 months. Important here is not how the mothers made their assessments, or even if these emotions actually existed in their babies, but that the mothers saw these emotions and acted "as if" they existed.

Another way that adults might facilitate a child's learning about emotions is through the way they respond—or don't respond—when the child is expressing an emotion. Brooks-Gunn and Lewis (1982) found that, as their children get older, mothers respond less to their crying, but they increase their responsiveness to positive expressions of emotion. Seemingly, mothers facilitate their children's emotional socialization by teaching them that it is more appropriate to express positive emotions than it is to express negative ones.

Caregivers can also influence children's emotional experiences by trying to manage when children will be exposed to various experiences. Hartup (1979) writes: "Parents manage the social lives of their children directly. Mothers and fathers consciously determine the timing and circumstances under which their offspring will have contact with individuals outside the nuclear family" (p. 949). Parents often attempt to manage their children's emotional lives as well; typically, they try to prevent their children's exposure to experiences that will have negative emotional impacts (e.g., experiences that will upset or frighten them). This can include restricting their television viewing to nonviolent shows or restricting their contact with certain other children, such as neighborhood bullies or children with mental or physical handicaps.

Emotional Talk

Language, in the form of emotional talk, is the means by which the socializing of emotions typically occurs. Adults, both intentionally and unintentionally, use emotional talk to express and explain emotions to children. It is through emotional talk that children come to develop emotional intersubjectivity. They come to identify and confer meaning on their recurring self-feelings and concurrently come to interpret and understand emotions in others. This gives people a way of sharing their emotional meanings. Using emotional talk, children gradually come to recognize and use the commonly held linguistic labels for emotions. By acquiring this socially shared knowledge, they are able to join their subjective meanings for their self-feelings with others. Through intersubjectivity, based on language, children are able to take the perspectives (including the emotional perspectives) of others. Through interactions with others, they come to recognize expressions of emotions in themselves and others; come to assume these expressions are indicative of recurrent, identifiable self-feelings; and learn the commonly held linguistic labels that often are attached to these self-feelings.

Consider the following example of a young boy learning to label and share his feelings. A mother and father are talking with their 5-year-old son about his day in kindergarten:

Mother: Did you play with Sam today?

Son: No. I'm not playing with him anymore.

Mother: Why not?

Son: Because he said he didn't want to be my friend anymore.

Mother: How did that make you feel?

The son looks puzzled by the question, so the mother elaborates.

Mother: Did it make you feel happy or sad or something like that?

Son: [pausing, apparently groping for a word] It made me feel truant.

Mother: [looking confused] Truant? What do you mean?

Son: You know. That's between sad and mad. First there's happy, then there's sad, then there's truant, then there's mad.

Mother: I think I know how you felt, but that's not the right word. A truant is someone who doesn't go to school when they're supposed to be in school. I don't know of a word that means between mad and sad.

Father: Maybe bitter's the right word.

Mother: Yeah. Bitter sounds like it might be between sad and mad. (field notes, September 7, 1984)

This boy is trying to share his self-feelings with his parents, but before this can be accomplished, they must agree upon a commonly held linguistic label for his emotions. This problem is compounded by the fact that our vocabulary of sharable emotional terms does not have a definitive, unambiguous label for his emotional experience. This is always the case, but as we become emotionally socialized we learn to typify our emotions; we attach to them labels that approximate what we feel. In so doing, we tend to group potentially different self-feelings under the same rubric.

Emotional Situations

Emotional situations are those socially structured, constructed, and emergent interactional episodes in which emotions are recognized, interpreted, managed, hidden, shared, or defined. Emotional situations are structured by rules and rituals. Through emotional talk with emotional associates, children come to recognize smiles, frowns, and grimaces; come to assume these expressions are indicative of recurrent identifiable feeling states; and gradually learn the commonly held linguistic labels that can be attached to these feeling states and their expression. We teach our children both the linguistic labels for their self-feelings and various linguistic rituals that may accompany emotions in self and others. *Linguistic emotional rituals* are those gestures, words, and phrases that children (and adults) use to acknowledge regard toward or to confer respect on others. We teach children the social niceties, the rules of "polite" interaction, such as saying "please" and "thank you." The significance of this ritual can be seen in the deference (Goffman, 1967, p. 56) that saying "please" and "thank you" affords another. If a child (particularly an older child) does not show deference to an adult, the adult may feel upset by the child's "lack of manners." Further, parents frequently become distressed by their children's lack of interactional skills and are pleased when they "behave appropriately."

Another linguistic ritual that we teach our children is the *apology ritual.* This includes saying such things as "excuse me" and "I'm sorry." The "I'm sorry" ritual can take several forms. The most common form, especially for very young children, is adult initiated, in which the adult prompts the child to make the apology. Another form is the misdirected apology, where the wrong child initiates the action. A variation of this form is when both children respond simultaneously. Regardless of the direction of the apology, it provides a satisfactory close to the episode.

Temporal rituals involve teaching children when they should experience or express different emotions. They can be seen as attempts to control children's behavior through the use of time, thereby influencing children's emotional interactions with others.

We tell children when to get up, when to go to sleep, when to get dressed, when to eat, when to go outside and come inside, even when to go to the bathroom. Day-care centers further rigidify their time; in that setting, children's activities and interests are typically subordinated to the teacher's agenda of scheduled activities. Often a child's day is scheduled according to what activity it is time for—snack time, story time, potty time, nap time, play time. Efforts are made to control children's disruptive behaviors by telling them it's not "time" for that—"It's not time to be running around—we do that during gym time—now it's time to sit still and listen to the story."

We need more research on the socialization of emotion in childhood. We need to connect children's games with emotional experiences and with the rituals that structure emotional expression. Gender should be located centrally in our studies of childhood emotion.

Gender Differentiation

As we have argued in Chapter 1, no society fails to embody in its practices and language the fundamental biological distinction between the sexes. Every human being belongs to a specific sex class. Femininity and masculinity are socially defined terms added to these sex classes. *Gender* (like *sexuality*) is a discursive term; its meanings are established through discourse and performance. Gender "is a performance that *produces* the illusion of an inner sex or . . . psychic gender core" (Butler, 1993b, p. 631). Many societies recognize still further categories, which include men who act like women and women who act like men. These in-between persons are sometimes taken for granted, sometimes looked upon as biological abnormalities. Scientists and sophisticated laypersons recognize another intermediate hermaphroditic class of persons who at birth have some of the genital apparatus, and perhaps physical traits, of both sexes (Edgerton, 1964).

Regardless of these intermediate classes, we can take for granted that humans universally recognize the existence of polar biological types—that is, men and women. It is easy to understand why the incorrect assumption is frequently made that infants "naturally" know to which sex they belong. Every child must learn not only the meanings of *male* and *female,* but how to classify him- or herself with both or neither.

This poses a problem. How do children learn to identify themselves as members of one or the other sex? The reader who seeks a detailed, exact answer to this question will be disappointed, for pertinent scientific data are meager. However, the larger outlines of the process of sex identification are clear enough.

Recognition of Sex Differences

When young children start to learn sex distinctions, they employ criteria that betray rudimentary conceptions of the differences between men and women. These criteria vary according to the opportunities available to children for observing and conversing about sex behavior. In the United States, such experiences vary widely among differing social classes, social worlds, and conditions of housing and is also influenced by the number of siblings in the family, sibling position, moral philosophies of the parents, and other relevant factors.

The institutions that any society assembles for the production and rearing of children differentially stress sex role attributes as they structure the socialization process (Aries, 1962). This is particularly evident in the education arena, where males and females are segregated in the bathroom and in physical education activities. Perhaps more critical are the lessons in sex role socialization young children receive in preschool and day-care centers. Bathroom interactions in nursery schools may provide occasions for conversations about anatomical differences between the sexes; the bathroom becomes a "social place." Observers such as Joffe (1971) and Henry (1963) have noted that many preschools are explicitly organized so as to set males and females against one another. Teachers expressly value and reward appropriate "male" and "female" behavior and often discourage "female" behavior on the part of boys and aggressive "male" behavior on the part of girls. One of the authors observed a preschool teacher in a racially mixed middle-class preschool who repeatedly embarrassed a 4-year-old boy who insisted on dressing each day in the garments of a bride. Joffe (1971) reports the following episode drawn from a parent-cooperative nursery in Berkeley, California, in 1970:

> L. and N. have been arguing over the use of a spade. N. pushes L. and L. responds by delivering a solid punch to N.'s chest. A mother who has witnessed the scene says to the observer (within hearing of L.), "Did you see the punch L. gave N.? He really can take care of himself like a man." (p. 470)

Young children find that they are rewarded when they act on preferred sex role stereotypes and often bring "sexual rhetoric" into their games. Joffe (1971) observed the following exchange between two girls and a boy: "C. and two other girls are playing on top of a large structure in the yard. A. (male) comes over and C. screams, 'Girls only!' to which A. screams back, 'No, boys only!' " (p. 472).

Phrases like "Your hair looks nice today" and "What a pretty dress you have on" inform girls that they will be positively addressed and identified if they look nice—that is, if they are dressed nicely and have their hair and other physical features properly in order. Thus, by the early age of 3, young children begin to assign to themselves and others quite specific self-identities with sexual dimensions.

Gender Performances

Recall Butler's argument that heterosexual norms are running commentaries on these gender performances that appear to deviate from what is acceptably normal. It is not surprising that children learn these norms very quickly.

Cahill (1986) suggests that at a very early age young children are using the words *boy, girl, baby, mommy,* and *daddy.* Use of these terms indicates recognition of gender difference. More important, through gender performances, including cross-dressing and games like "mommy and daddy," little boys and girls acquire interactional understandings of how gender is socially constructed.

Cahill (1986) suggests that the acquisition of gender identity involves several interrelated performance and participation-based processes. Through self- and other-labeling, children try on gender identities, modeling same-sex behavior from a variety of referents, including TV, movies, stories, peers, and parents (Musolf, 1996, p. 311). Participation rituals involving game playing—for example, mommy, daddy, and baby—anchor gendered identities in the family context. Gender masquerades involving cross-dressing allow children to try on the identities of the opposite gender. Nonetheless, as Butler (1993b, p. 646) observes, there are no hard-and-fast lines separating sex, gender, and gender presentation. Still it is clear that at least for heterosexual families, a compulsive heterosexuality governs the gendered performances that are staged by little children. Butler (1993b) notes, "If a regime of sexuality mandates a compulsory performance of sex, then it may be only through that performance that the binary system of gender and binary system of sex come to have intelligibility at all" (p. 648).

Learning the Meanings of Sexual Behavior

Children must learn the meanings associated with sexual activities. They do not in any significant degree invent them, nor do they acquire them through biological endowment or maturation. They may not understand the full adult significance of many sexual words and acts until they are well into adolescence, or later.

Although humans everywhere recognize the existence of sexual excitement, coitus, masturbation, sex organs, and the like, they nevertheless take dissimilar attitudes toward these objects, acts, and events. Words convey or mirror attitudes—that is, they have meanings. When the child—whether American, Japanese, or Marquesan; upper or lower class; boy or girl; rural or urban—learns words, he or she learns also the conventional points of view that they express.

Misconceptions of Child Behavior

Laypersons and even students of child behavior frequently make the mistake of anthropomorphism; they project adult attitudes and conceptions onto children or regard children's ideas and modes of thought and behavior as curious forms of error. This tendency to interpret the behavior of children from the perspective of concepts derived from and appropriate to adults is also noticeable in the study of children's sex behavior.

The fallacy is aggravated by the use of the same terms to describe child and adult behavior, or by the use of such hazily defined terms as *libido* and *sexual.* Although the popularization of psychoanalytic theories and concepts has undoubtedly swept away many puritanical and mid-Victorian misconceptions about children, it has opened the way to errors of another kind. Thus when one states that the infant masturbates, it is usually assumed that infant and adult masturbation are equivalent acts—a dubious assumption indeed. The rebellion against the reluctance of past generations to face sexual facts has led to excessive zeal in discovering sexuality in the behavior of children. It must be emphasized that *children live in a world of their own; they have their own concepts, their own ways of acting, and their own perspectives.* It is just as erroneous to judge children's behavior by adult standards or to read adult motives into it as it is to measure African Bantu behavior by American standards.

Illustrating an extreme example of this type of error, Isaacs (1933) writes: "Penelope and Tommy were playing 'mummy and daddy' and Tommy insisted upon being the mummy" (p. 160). Isaacs interprets the boy's act as an attempt to quiet his fear of castration, yet he presents no data regarding the actual state of the child's sexual knowledge or how he may have obtained it. The child analyst Klein (1932, pp. 42-46) provides an even more flagrant example: Her patient was a 3-year-old boy who between the ages of 18 and 20 months slept in his parents' room and had occasional opportunities to witness coitus (if one can stretch the meaning of the word *witness*). The child, writes Klein, is therefore fearfully jealous of his father, feels inferior because of his own lack of physical potency, fears that his mother was hurt by coitus, wishes to smash his father's genitals, wishes to kill his father, and so forth. How can such complex ideas be attributed to young children?

Other child psychologists and psychoanalysts have been much more circumspect in their interpretations. Cognizant of the social origins and learned nature of sexual behavior, many psychoanalysts have pointed out weaknesses in Freud's theory that feminine character may be largely explained in terms of "penis envy" and reactions to it. According to this theory, when the young girl discovers that every boy has a penis, she is disappointed and shocked at her own lack of the same organ (see Chapter 8). Hence she develops a sense of inferiority, or penis envy. The traits of character she develops in her childhood and adult years are, according to Freud, the consequences of her attempt to adjust to her sense of inferiority. But the sociologist is inclined to note that reactions of this type are associated with the patriarchal organization of Western European society—that is, a society in which men and masculine values are relatively dominant. This patriarchal situation, however, is by no means universal, even in Western society.

Disinterested investigation of girls' reactions to the discovery of genital differences, such as that by Conn and Kanner (1947, pp. 44-48), shows without question that girls do not always respond with penis envy; some girls exhibit envious feelings, but most do not. Instead, they accept these differences matter-of-factly or react with amusement. In the light of the learned character of such behavior, one would not expect all girls to react identically. Freud's overstatement of the case should make us wary of equating children's sexual responses with those of their elders.

By word or act, by punishment or reward, and through the various media of communication, the young boy and girl learn the sex behavior associated with their roles; they learn to avoid those acts that will evoke reactions of ridicule, disgust, or anger. Children internalize the taboos to such an extent that they become angry and ashamed if they break them.

CONCLUSION

Children's early years involve complex sets of significant others who take part in the process of socializing children into the complicated area of causal understanding about the physical world as well as into the more intricate topics of morality and sex role behavior. Children quickly relinquish an egocentric conception of their surrounding world, replacing that biased view with a more relativistic perspective that is grounded in the multiple perspectives of their generalized others. Children enter the world with no knowledge of sex or gender differences. Through their interactive experiences with peers, parents, and other adults, they soon develop sophisticated images of proper "male" and "female" behavior. A society's educational institutions take on the major assignment of teaching children what these differences between the "sexes" are.

In this chapter we have considered the importance of gender and moral judgments, noting that different moral codes appear to hold for males and females in our society. These codes are located in Western religion, culture, and philosophy; they are also deeply intertwined in the economic and stratification systems of our society. A crucial phase of childhood socialization involves emotion. We have shown how children's caretakers teach various emotional meanings, rituals, and understandings. The topics of gender, morality, and emotionality remain important areas of social psychological study.

SUGGESTED READINGS

Leavitt, R. L. (1994). *Power and emotion in infant-toddler day care.* Albany: State University of New York Press. A very important ethnographic study of the lived experiences of infants and toddlers in day-care centers.

Musolf, G. R. (1996). Interactionism and the child: Cahill, Corsaro, and Denzin on childhood socialization. *Symbolic Interaction, 19,* 303-322. Significantly extends the Mead-Cooley model of self and interaction in early childhood.

Steinberg, S. R., & Kincheloe, J. L. (Eds.). (1997). *Kinderculture: The corporate construction of childhood.* Boulder, CO: Westview. A seminal collection of original essays that examine the corporate construction of childhood, from Disney movies to video games, day-care centers, children's magazines, McDonald's, and children's television.

STUDY QUESTIONS

1. Compare and contrast performance- and stage-based models of child development.
2. How are emotionality and gender learned in early childhood?
3. How does the concept of the phantom other fit with Mead's concept of the generalized other?

NOTE

1. This section was written by Martha Bauman Power.

PART IV

SELVES AND SOCIETIES

10

Reading the Interaction Order

The five chapters in Part IV return to our opening themes of freedom, constraint, and existential crises in human societies. The everyday world of social interaction is this chapter's topic. The issues we discuss include the interaction order; race, gender, and public, civil society; rules and roles; social situations; social relationships and identities; status passage and interaction; and awareness contexts. We begin by situating the interaction order within the cinematic society, that social formation that knows itself through the reflected gaze of the television and movie camera. We then locate this society in its contemporary, historical moment.

The Cinematic Society

In the space of 30 years (1900-1930), cinema became an integral part of American society.[1] Going to the movies became a weekly pastime for a majority of Americans. American films were regularly exported to Europe. Motion pictures became a national institution. Hollywood stars became personal idols, fan clubs were formed, and a movie theater with its marquee was a permanent part of virtually every American community. A new visual literacy was being produced; Americans were learning to look and see things they hadn't seen before.

The sociological impact of cinema on the newly industrializing societies and its import for social theory was virtually ignored or at least slighted by the great classical social theorists. Hollywood's cinematic apparatus ushered into American civil society a new way of looking that initially privileged the visual over the aural (see Jay, 1988, p. 3), but quickly this loss of voice was overturned, merging the panoptic with the panauditory. The cinematic, surveillance society soon became a disciplinary structure filled with subjects (voyeurs) who obsessively looked and gazed at one another, as they became, at the same time, obsessive listeners, eavesdroppers, persons whose voices and telephone lines could be tapped, voices that could be dubbed, and new versions of the spoken and seen self.

American cinema created a space for a certain kind of public, communal urban life. Inside the new movie palaces, Americans entered the public realm. But this was a self-contained realm, the public made private by the darkness of the theater. In these darkened spaces, utopian stories, political fantasies, and mythic narratives were told. These stories effectively erased the corrosive consequences and features of an oppressive racial and gender stratification system in the United States. The kernels of utopian fantasy contained in these stories "constituted the fulfillment of what was desired [yet] absent within the status quo" (Stam, 1989, p. 224)—that is, an emotionally harmonious gender and racial system that had successfully integrated racial and ethnic differences into the core emotional elements of the American self.

Cinema made voyeurs out of spectators (Metz, 1982, p. 94). In the shadows of the theater was reproduced the concept of a private, sacred space that the spectator enters. The spectator could simultaneously (and vicariously) experience the thrills, desires, dangers, and invasions of being both voyeur and the subject gazed upon. At the same time, the cinematic apparatus operated as a technology of gender (and race) that reproduced the structures of patriarchy (and racism) by implementing a concept of looking and spectatorship that often made women (and nonwhites) the objects of the male (white) gaze. Thus did the movies create the gender- and race-biased cinematic eye and an attendant cinematic imagination fitted to the values of the larger American culture.

Cinema elaborated the epistemologies of scientific realism already deeply rooted in American culture. This epistemology held that faithful, direct, and truthful knowledge of the actual world could be produced. This belief system was firmly established in 19th-century American religion, philosophy, science, and technology, and it had quickly taken hold in journalism and photojournalism (Persons, 1958, p. 332). It found its expression in literary works—especially the novels of Stephen Crane, Frank Norris, Jack London, and Theodore Dreiser—that were both naturalistic and realistic (see Persons, 1958, pp. 332-337). Cinema helped create a realistic and naturalistic discourse about the universe of experience and appearance.

The movies became a technology and apparatus of power that would organize and bring meaning to everyday lives. They would function as adjuncts to the 20th-century surveillance society, deploying the cinematic gaze and its narratives in the service of the state. Cinema would create a new social type, the voyeur, or Peeping Tom, who would, in various guises (detective, psychoanalyst, crime reporter, investigative journalist, innocent bystander, sexual pervert), elevate the concept of looking to new levels. This voyeur would gaze into the sacred, hidden places of society. By invading private spaces, the voyeur defined the sanctity of such spaces, even as their presence was being erased by the surveillance structures of the democratic societies.

The Birth of the Cinematic Society

Thus was born, in three swift decades, American cinema and its counterpart, the cinematic society. Fittingly defined in its early modern form by D. W. Griffith's racist film *The Birth of a Nation,* the movies entered American culture under an immediate cloud of suspicion. Introduced as a new form of entertainment for the masses, an art form for some, a source of profit for a few, a challenge to Christian morality for others, a threat to the human eye for some, an educational vehicle for others, this new apparatus fundamentally transformed American society. With this birth the United States became a cinematic culture, a culture that came to know itself, collectively and individually, through the images and stories that Hollywood produced.

Like a mirror, the camera's cinematic gaze answered a double reflective desire to see and be seen (see Metz, 1982, p. 45). This reflection was visual and narrative. At the visual level it articulated the 20th century's version of the reflected self, "each to each a looking-glass reflects the other that doth pass" (Cooley, 1909/1956, p. 184). This reflected self saw itself reflected back in the face, gaze, figure, and dress of the cinematic self, that larger-than-life self that gazed back from the theater's screen. From this reflection arose self-ideals and self-appraisals, self-feelings and feelings toward others. The reflected, everyday self, and its gendered presentations, attached itself to the cinematic self. Blumer (1933) provides an example by quoting the words of a white female college freshman, age 19:

> When I discovered I should have this coquettish and coy look which all girls may have, I tried to do it in my room. And surprises! I could imitate Pola Negri's cool or fierce look. Vilma Banky's sweet and coquettish attitude. I learned the very way of taking my gentlemen friends to and from the door with that wistful smile, until it has become a part of me. (p. 34)

Blumer also quotes a white male college sophomore, age 20:

> The appearance of such handsome men as John Gilbert, Ben Lyon, Gilbert Roland, and the host of others, dressed in sport clothes, evening attire, formals, etc., has encouraged me to dress as best possible in order to make a similar appearance. One acquires positions such as standing, sitting, tipping one's hat, holding one's hat, offering one's arm to a lady, etc., from watching these men who do so upon the screen, and especially if they do it in a manner pleasing to your tastes. (pp. 33-34)

These selves, reflected back from the screen, were interiorized in the imaginations and fantasies of the moviegoer. They became part of individuals' imagined self-feelings and were incorporated into their interactions with others.

The Everyday Gaze and Narrative Reflexivity

The spectatorial gaze of cinema would elaborate and build upon the structure of the gaze as it already operated in everyday life. It would, that is, bring more precision and more voyeurism to visual interaction. It would increase the sensual pleasures derived from gazing at the other and introduce an increased emotionality to the forms of "civil inattention" persons would accord one another. Goffman (1963a) suggests, in this regard, that "what seems to be involved is that one gives to another enough visual notice to demonstrate that one appreciates that the other is present (and that one admits openly to having seen him), while at the next moment withdrawing one's attention from him so as to express that he does not constitute a target of special curiosity or design" (p. 84). Cinema taught people how to both respect and violate the norms of civil inattention. At the same time, the movies established a reflexive interaction between cinematic representations and the real-life experiences that occur offscreen.

This visual structuring of the spectator's gaze had to be embedded in a narrative, a story, a system of discourse. As Metz (1982) observes, "The cinema was born . . . in a period when social life was deeply marked by the notion of the *individual*" (p. 95). Cinema was made for private individuals (p. 96) and their fellows. Like the classical novel, it told realistic, gothic, and melodramatic stories about the lives of men, women, and children in contemporary society (see below). In narrativizing cinema's gaze, filmmakers introduced a new form of visual and oral storytelling into the new industrial societies. Hollywood's stories were myths, public dreams, secular folktales. Ritualized and emotional, these stories allowed people to make sense of their everyday lives. They used the logic of the hero and the heroine to tell stories about individuals and their families. They unified audiences by reinforcing key cultural values (e.g., the horrors of violent crime).

They produced a reflective illusion that the "world out there" is controllable and under control. That is, the modern individual, like a screen character, could take control of his or her life. Two further examples from Blumer (1933) illustrate this. The following quote is from a Jewish white male college junior, age 20:

> When I was sixteen years old, I saw the picture . . . *The Ten Commandments* . . . and from that time on I have never doubted the value of religion. The many hardships which my people went through for the sake of preserving our race was portrayed so vividly and realistically that the feeling of reverence and respect for my religion was instilled in me. (p. 177)

These remarks were made by a white female high school junior, age 16:

> I can remember very distinctly that when I was thirteen years old, I saw a moving picture in which the heroine was a very young, pretty girl. In school she had taken a business course and after working hard she had been promoted to the position of private secretary. To this very day I would like to be a private secretary. I used to sit and dream about what my life would be like after I had that position. (p. 169)

In these dreams and fantasies the movies created emotional representations of self, sexuality, desire, intimacy, friendship, marriage, work, and family. These reflective representations drew upon the ideological structures of everyday life. They created an everyday politics of emotionality and feeling that shaped real, lived emotional experiences.

The cinematic gaze left no corner of society untouched. It entered the worlds of home, work, leisure, sexuality, sports, medicine, science, prison, school, church, the courts, and war. The movies and the cinematic eye introduced into the social world forms of feeling and thinking that mediated the harsh realities of the everyday with the fantasy world of Hollywood dreamland. These stories were gender and racially specific and were molded by the ideological structures of domination that existed in the larger social structure. This visual hegemony opened up the cinematic society to itself and destroyed forever the boundaries that separated the private lives of individuals from the public life of the larger society. All personal, political, sociological, cultural, and economic dilemmas were converted into personal melodramas. By making public stories out of personal troubles, the movies "trivialize[d] issues into personal squabbles, rather than humanize[d] them by asserting their meanings for you and for me" (Mills, 1956, p. 335).

This new gaze was owned by the state, perfected by its agents, the scientists, and the Hollywood filmmakers. There soon developed the belief that a form of democratic surveillance was needed if an informed public opinion was to be produced in the industrialist and capitalist societies (Foucault, 1980b, p. 162). In particular, there was a need for an impartial, objective source of information about society and its workings (Davis, 1976, p. 77)—the filmmakers and the news makers who would create accurate newsreels of the events of the day (see Foucault, 1980b, p. 162).

The impartial renderings of reality that the camera could produce through photography and cinema were beneficial for democracy. They made the American citizen an informed participant in history (Davis, 1976, p. 72). These pictures and stories awakened public interest in democracy. They aided the war effort (p. 95), promoted national solidarity and patriotism, and, by being available to all people, made all citizens equal, thereby reinforcing basic democratic principles (p. 61).

Cinematic Reality and the Cinematic Imagination

Several implications followed from the cinematization of American society. Reality, as it was visually experienced, became a staged, social production. Real, everyday experiences soon came to be judged against their staged, cinematic, video counterparts. The fans of movie stars dressed like the stars, made love like the stars, and dreamed the dreams of the stars. Blumer (1933) provides another example in this quote from a white female college senior, age 24:

> During my high-school period I particularly liked pictures in which the setting was a millionaire's estate or some such elaborate place. After seeing a picture of this type, I would imagine myself living such a life of ease as the society girl I had seen. My daydreams would be concerned with lavish wardrobes, beautiful homes, servants, imported automobiles, yachts, and countless suitors. (p. 64)

Blumer quotes another person: "I used to look in the mirror somewhat admiringly and try to imagine Wallace Reid or John Barrymore kissing that face" (p. 66).

The metaphor of the dramaturgical society (Goffman, 1959, pp. 254-255) ceased to be just a metaphor. It became interactional reality. Life and art became mirror images of one another. Another of Blumer's (1933) respondents said:

> I have fallen in love with movie heroes. . . . I imagined myself caressing the heroes with great passion and kissing them so they would stay osculated forever. . . . *I practiced love scenes either with myself or the girl friends. We sometimes think we could beat Greta Garbo, but I doubt it.* (p. 71; emphasis added)

The main carriers of the popular in the cinematic society soon became the very media that were defining the content and meaning of the popular; that is, popular culture quickly became a matter of cinema and related media, including television, the press, and popular literature.

Cinema entered a metropolitan American culture that would soon be filled with segregated public spaces, including baseball fields, amusement parks, boardwalks, libraries, museums, picture palaces, theme and national parks, and world's fairs. These carnivalesque sites erased while they maintained racial, gender, and ethnic differences.

Hollywood manipulated its mass audiences, creating texts that located spectators within these multiple visual and auditory cultures. By the early 1930s, marketing specialists had learned how to carve up this mass audience into innumerable segments based on gender, age, income, and race. This segmentation of the audience destroyed the republic of pleasure seekers. A unified public of moviegoers no longer existed. The integration of public spaces destroyed the "race-based privilege that had [previously] held the white audience together" (Lears, 1994, p. 29). The spread of television and the increased privatization of suburban entertainment further contributed to the destruction of this common visual culture.

This instantiation of the gaze, in its multiple forms, led to the production of a *cinematic imagination*, an imagination that circulated through the private and popular cultures of American life. This imagination was visual, narrative, and aesthetic. It defined central personal experiences, especially those anchored in the cultural identities of race, class, and gender, within a master narrative derived from classic theater and Victorian melodramatic literature. This imagination suggested that lives had beginnings, middles, and ends. It argued that the preferred cultural self found its fullest expression in the love and marriage relationship (Clough, 1992, p. 13).

This imagination argued for stories with happy endings and valorized the central American values of individualism, freedom, the frontier, love, hard work, family, wealth, and companionship (Ray, 1985, pp. 56-59). Such stories became ingrained in the cinematic imagination; they became master tales, myths that structured how lives were evaluated and judged. Aesthetically, this imagination mediated the individual's relationship to the popular and the everyday world. It judged stories and images in terms of their human elements. It valued a realist aesthetic grounded in a realist epistemology.

The cinematic imagination mediates these complex, intersecting visual cultures, constantly attempting to make sense of two versions of reality: the cinematic and the everyday. But a paradox is created, for the everyday is now defined by the cinematic. The two can no longer be separated. A single epistemological regime governs both visual fields. Cinema not only created the spectator in its own eye, it created what the eye of the spectator would see. It then subjected that eye and its vision to the unrelenting criteria of realism and the realistic image of reality given in the camera's image.

Today, as we have argued in Chapter 1, people live in CNN, televisual, satellite TV—a postcolonial world. Boundaries between nation-states have collapsed. We must now think beyond the nation or the local group as the focus of study. The electronic media amplify the changes in meanings that now surround the performances of gender, sexuality, family, nation, and personhood.

The circuits of culture, woven through the apparatuses of the mass media, turn ordinary people into consumers. In the United States, a conservative political regime has defined the historical period extending from the 1980s to the present. This regime is connected to the rise to power of conservatives and the radical right in the United States and Europe. This reflects a new worldwide "antistatism" coupled with a vigorous rhetoric of law and order and human right. It may be seen, in part, as a backlash against the 1960s. It also reflects a conservative, late-capitalist response to the worldwide economic crises of the 1970s and the emergence of contradictions in social democracy, communism, and the international labor movement.

Throughout the 1980s and the 1990s, the New Right has constructed conceptions of who its ideal subjects are and how they personify the sacred values of religion, hard work, health, and self-reliance. This new ideology has redefined the "ordinary, normal, commonplace" individual as it has put in place a politics of health and morality. This morality involves debates about abortion, child abuse, sex education, gay rights, AIDS, health care, aging, family violence, drug and alcohol abuse (including the "war on drugs"), homelessness, and the general social health and moral hygiene of U.S. (and British) society. A new, repressive politics of the body, sexuality, desire, the family, and individuality has emerged in the decades of the 1980s and 1990s.

The Logic of the Present

The postmodern, the logic of the present, is everywhere and nowhere. It has no zero point, no fixed essence. It contains traces of everything that has come before. Its dominating logic is that of a hybrid, never pure, always compromising, not "either/or," but "both/and." The postmodern impulse is playful and paradoxical. It mocks and absorbs historical forms, always having it both ways, always modern and postmodern. Nothing escapes its attention. Its logic of use and utility can turn anything from the past into a commodity that is sold or used to sell a commodity in the present. On the surface benignly playful, this "both/and" posture disguises ideology as entertainment (e.g.,

The Cosby Show). It makes the spectacle and the newsworthy event the emblematic sign of an age in which lifestyle advertising has become the accepted popular psychology. At the same time, the electronic image is the only sign of reality that counts.

Late capitalism's "both/and" logic expands constantly, like a rubber band, to fit all that has come before, turning everything, including lived experience, into a commodity that is bought and sold on the contemporary marketplace. This logic requires a positive nostalgia that infuses the past with high value, for if the past were worthless, it could not be sold in the present. Old is good. New is good. Old and new together are best. This popular ideology scripts a politics that keeps ancient narratives alive. These myths are many; they include the nuclear family, heroes with white hats on horses riding into frontiers that remain to be conquered or into cities (and nation-states) that need to be saved, and rugged individualists who overcome enormous handicaps (e.g., the stigma of the age) on the way to finding wealth, happiness, and personal fulfillment. In short, capitalism needs and uses anything and everything to perpetuate its hegemonic control over popular culture. These are the spaces that surround and define the interactional order.

Interaction Rituals and the Interactional Order

Goffman (1983) has suggested that a neglected area of sociological study is the interactional order, which is the world of interaction that occurs whenever persons come into one another's presence. This is the world of face-to-face interaction, encounters, and behavior in public places. We briefly discuss here Goffman's analysis of interaction rituals and the interactional order; throughout his work, he has directly confronted how etiquette rules, or ceremonial prescriptives, enter into interaction (see Goffman, 1956, 1959, 1961a, 1967, 1971, 1974, 1981, 1983).

The core of Goffman's position is that social regulations subtly govern interaction. This conception of regulated interactions is clearly illustrated in his essay "On Face-Work: An Analysis of Ritual Elements in Social Interaction" (1955). Goffman begins by noting that everybody "lives in a world of social encounters" that involve face-to-face contacts with others. During these encounters, people tend to act out "lines"—whether deliberately or not. Lines are patterns of verbal and nonverbal acts by which individuals express their views of both given situations and the participants in them, including themselves. The term *face* is "the positive social value a person effectively claims for himself by the line others assume he has taken during a particular contact" (Goffman, 1967, p. 5). The person "may be said to *have* or *be in* or *maintain* face when the line he effectively takes presents an image of him that is internally consistent," supported by others' gestures and confirmed through "evidence conveyed through impersonal agencies in the situation" (p. 6).

Goffman (1967) emphasizes that the line "maintained by and for a person . . . tends to be of a legitimate institutionalized kind" (p. 7). During certain socially defined situations, "an interactant of known or visible attributes can expect to be sustained in a particular face" (p. 7). A person is "out of face" when he or she is not ready with the kind of line that participants in given defined situations "are expected to take." When a person is out of face, the ordinary regulated interaction is out of balance: "Expressive events are being contributed to the encounter which cannot be readily woven into the expressive fabric of the occasions" (p. 8). Thus the person may be embarrassed, shamed, or confused, and may show these reactions. If the person can control or conceal these reactions, he or she has "poise."

All participants in these encounters share the responsibility of maintaining face. Concerning the individual's own face,

> each person takes on the responsibility of standing guard over the flow of expressive events. . . . He must ensure that a particular *expressive order* is maintained—an order which regulates the flow of events, large or small, so that anything that appears to be expressed by them will be consistent with his face. (Goffman, 1967, p. 9)

Rules of considerateness and self-respect help the person to conduct him- or herself so as to maintain not only his or her own face but that of the other participants. Consequently, these encounters embody much "face-work," which "serves to counteract 'incidents'—that is, events whose symbolic implications threaten face" (p. 10).

Goffman has focused on one class of rules: "rules of etiquette" or "ceremonial directives." Other rule-based categories, such as those that protect the civil-legal order, or those that are specific to intimate relationships, have gone basically unnoticed in his studies. Thus he offers a restricted account of interactional rules. Furthermore, Goffman's model of interaction assumes a "threat-based" view of human interaction. His individuals genuinely are actors, always on a stage, rarely if ever able to relax and "drop their guard." In this sense an uneasy dramaturgical analogy underlies a good deal of Goffman's work. He offers insights into the drama of action in public places, but seldom takes the student into the "safe" regions of comfortable, at-ease interactants; nor does his perspective suggest leads for studying a common everyday situation—the case of two interactants, experienced in working together, who are now working on a common task.

Goffman's analysis is primarily concerned with *stabilities* in interaction. He makes this quite clear with his closing points, which touch on the relation of face saving to social relationships. When a person enters an encounter, "he already stands in some kind of social relationship to the others concerned, and expects to stand in a given relationship to them after the particular encounter ends" (Goffman, 1967, p. 9). That is how social contacts among people are linked with wider society. Much of the activity during an encounter is understandable as an effort by everyone to get through the encounter "without disrupting the relationships of the participants" (p. 12). What about relationships that happen to be changing? "And if relationships are in a process of change, the object will be to bring the encounter to a satisfactory close without altering the expected course of development" (p. 13). Understandably, this kind of accommodative behavior requires the socialization of all the participants. This view of interaction perceives it as governed or guided not only by explicit rules but by implicit rules. The informal control that society exerts on individuals is not rigid or mechanical, but subtle, resulting in a corresponding subtlety of interaction.

Public Places and Civil Society

The interaction order is located in those spaces of civil society marked as public places, "*those sites and contexts that our society understands to be open to all*" (Gardner, 1995, p. 3). As Gardner (1995) notes, persons are assumed to dress and act differently in public as opposed to private settings. Civility is a norm in public places. The norm of civil inattention holds that persons should not stare at or verbally harass others. Dress in public is expected to be less casual than in the home. Personal, biographical, and social attributes and identities of the person are not to be called attention to. It is presumed that everyone in a public place should be treated with civility—politely, with respect. However, public harassment is normative. Gardner (1995, p. 228) observes that any category of persons can be assaulted in public places, including gays, lesbians, African Americans, Asian Americans, Native Americans, the physically handicapped, children, the elderly, even male members of the white middle class.

In public places, persons are rightfully fearful of public harassment in the form of shouted remarks, vulgarities, insults, and innuendo; ogling; stalking; and sometimes physical assaults, including pinching and slapping (Gardner, 1995, p. 4). A lesbian African American marketing executive in her 40s described her experiences of being harassed:

> Sometimes all this that happens in the streets makes me think: Is it worse to be black, or a *dyke,* or just to be a woman? And I've got to tell you that being a woman doesn't bother me much.
>
> Having the white people rag on me because I'm black doesn't scare me so bad either. . . . worst is being a dyke. . . . lesbians *do* get attacked, sometimes killed, by strangers. *That* makes a wolf-whistle because you got a short skirt on look pretty harmless. (quoted in Gardner, 1995, p. 229)

Anderson (1990) provides background to Gardner's observations: "Around the nation, urban residents feel intimidated by their streets, parks, and other public places, particularly after dark or when too many strangers are present. The national problem of safe streets has become especially acute in . . . underclass ghetto communities" (p. 1). Streetwise people learn how to recognize and respond to danger in these situations.

The Cinematic Racial Order

Consider the following dialogue from Spike Lee's 1989 film *Do the Right Thing.* In a pivotal moment near the film's climax, as the heat rises on the street, Lee has members of each racial group in the neighborhood hurl vicious racial slurs at one another:

> *Mookie to Sal and his sons Vito and Pino* (Italians): Dago, Wop, guinea, garlic breath, pizza slingin' spaghetti bender, Vic Damone, Perry Como, Pavarotti.

Pino to Mookie (and the other blacks): Gold chain wearin' fried chicken and biscuit eatin' monkey, ape, baboon, fast runnin', high jumpin', spear chuckin', basketball dunkin' ditso spade, take you fuckin' pizza and go back to Africa.

A Puerto Rican man to the Korean grocer: Little slanty eyed, me-no speakie American, own every fruit and vegetable stand in New York, bull shit, Reverend Sun Young Moon, Summer '88 Olympic kick-ass boxer, sonofabitch.

White policeman: You goya bean eatin' 15 in the car, 30 in the apartment, pointy red shoes wearin' Puerto Ricans, cocksuckers.

Korean grocer: I got good price for you, how am I doing? Chocolate, egg cream drinking, bagel, lox, Jew asshole.

Sweet Dick Willie to the Korean grocer: Korean motherfucker . . . you didn't do a goddamn thing except sit on your monkey ass here on this corner and do nothin'. (see Denzin, 1991, pp. 129-130)

Lee's speakers are trapped within the walls and streets of a multiracial ghetto (the Bedford-Stuyvesant neighborhood of Brooklyn). Their voices reproduce current (and traditional) cultural, racial, and sexual stereotypes about blacks, Koreans, Puerto Ricans, Jews, and Italians. The effects of these "in-your-face" insults are exaggerated through wide-angle, close-up shots. The speakers' faces literally fill the screen as the racial slurs are heard. These black and white, Korean, and Puerto Rican men, women, and children exist in a racially divided urban world, a violent melting pot. Here there is little evidence of assimilation to the norms of white society. (There is no evidence of the black middle class in this film.) Complex racial and political ideologies (violence versus nonviolence) are displayed in subtle levels and layers of sexuality, intimacy, friendship, hate, love, and a lingering nostalgia for the way things were in days past.

Prejudice crosses color lines, but racial intolerance is connected to the psychology of the speaker (e.g., in *Do the Right Thing*, the character of Vito). It is "rendered as the *how* of personal bigotry" (Guerrero, 1993, p. 154). The economic and political features of institutional racism are not taken up—that is, in Lee's film, "the *why* of racism is left unexplored" (Guerrero, 1993, p. 154).

Even as racial insults are exchanged, Lee's text undoes the notion of an essential black, white, Korean, or Hispanic subject. Each speaker's self is deeply marked by the traces of religion, nationality, race, gender, and class. Blacks and Koreans uneasily inhabit a shared space where, in the moment of the riot, the Korean grocer can claim to be black, not Korean. Lee's world is a microcosm of the racial underclass in American today. This is a world where persons of color are all thrown together, a world where words like *assimilation, acculturation, pluralism,* and *integration* have little if any deep meaning. Lee's people have been excluded from the social, economic, and political structures of the outside white society.

In this little neighborhood, differences are ridiculed and mocked. Separatism is not valued, although intergroup differences are preserved through speech, music, dress, and public demeanor. Indeed, like ethnic voyeurs or middle-class tourists, the members of the different ethnic groups stare at one another and comment on how the racially and ethnically different other goes about doing business and daily life. These separate racial and ethnic groups are not merging into a single ethnic entity.

Only in his later film *Clockers* (1995) does Lee take up the "insidious, socially fragmented violence" (Guerrero, 1993, p. 159) of the "hood films" of Singleton, Van Peebles, and the Hughes brothers. Cheap guns, crack cocaine, and gang and drug warfare are not present here. But a seething racial rage is, a rage that is deeper than skin color. This is a rage that, even when muted, attacks white racism and urges new forms of black, Korean, and Latino nationalism.

Thus is evidenced a reverse form of ethnic nativism: disadvantaged racial group members stereotyping and asserting their superiority over the ethnically different other. Victims of racial hatred, they reproduce that hatred in their interactions with members of other racial and ethnic groups. The benefits of the backlash politics of the Reagan and Bush years are now evident (Guerrero, 1993, p. 161): 15 years of playing the race card, 15 years of neoconservative racial nativist national politics come home to roost. The nation's racist, crumbling, violent, inner-city ethnic enclaves have become "violent *apartheid* environments" (Guerrero, 1993, p. 159).

And so *Do the Right Thing*, as realist ethnographic text, marks one ending for one history of the race relations story in the United States today—the ending that has race riots and racial minorities attacking one another. This ending demonstrates the paucity and tragedy of nativist, and liberal assimilationist (and pluralist), desegregation models of race and ethnic relations (McKee, 1993, pp. 360-367). It is as if the clock had been turned back to 1914 and everyone was watching D. W. Griffith's *The Birth of a Nation*; white men in Klan hoods attacking "coons" who are sexually threatening the sexuality and lives of white women. The birth of a new racist nation. But how to start over?

Reading the Cinematic Racial Order

Films like *Do The Right Thing* can be read as realistic ethnographic texts, stories, and narrative histories that privilege whiteness and an assimilation-acculturation approach to the race relations problem in the United States. Such films present situated versions of the racial order. Many of them have created and perpetuated historically specific racist images of dark-skinned ethnics. This racist imagery extends, like a continuous thread, from *The Birth of a Nation* through *Boyz N the Hood.*

This century's history of cinematic race relations has been shaped by what Myrdal (1944) has called the American dilemma. This dilemma reflects a deep-seated conflict between a national creed that endorses the fundamental equality of all persons and the segregationist and discriminatory realities surrounding the actual treatment of racial and ethnic minorities in the United States (McKee, 1993, p. 227; Myrdal, 1944, p. 24). Historically, this conflict has produced a two-sided race relations agenda, one played out both in real life and on the screen. The white man's burden obliges whites to lead nonwhites into full assimilation. This will produce integration, "Americanization," and a version of the melting pot that dissolves racial and ethnic differences (McKee, 1993, p. 131). Only individual prejudice and the absence of self-will and diligence will prevent this ideal racial order from coming into existence.

The social science history of U.S. race relations has attempted to explain why full integration and assimilation have not occurred. This same history has tried to explain why multiculturalism, or the mutual respect of ethnic groups for one another, has been so infrequent (McKee, 1993, p. 264) and pluralism and segregative separatism have been normative. And few predicted the race riots of the 1960s, 1970s, 1980s, and 1990s. Current social science theory, along with Hollywood cinema, now struggles to define the meanings of such terms as *separatism, diversity, pluralism,* and *multiculturalism* (see Chapter 1; see also Friedman, 1991, p. 20; McKee, 1993, pp. 360-367). Hollywood, like the rest of society, has not been immune to this social science utopian discourse (see below) and the politics of representation that shapes it. Recall Du Bois's (1903) observations, noted in Chapter 1, concerning how white America had yet to learn how to accord respect and dignity to the black self.

The "hood movies" of the 1990s, which include *Do the Right Thing* (1989), *New Jack City* (1991), *Boyz N the Hood* (1991), *Straight Out of Brooklyn* (1991), *Juice* (1992), *Deep Cover* (1992), *Menace II Society* (1993), *Just Another Girl on the I.R.T.* (1993), *Clockers* (1995), *American Me* (1992), *Bound by Honor* (*Blood In, Blood Out,* 1993), *My Family/Mi Familia* (1995), and *Mi Vida Loca* (*My Crazy Life,* 1994), are stitched into a contemporary version of the American dilemma. These films enact a post-civil rights racial politics. This politics shapes a cinema of racial violence. It contributes to the production of a new racial discourse that connects race to a culture of violence (see also Park, 1996, p. 497).

A majority of Americans know and understand the American racial order through the mass media. Accordingly, those who control the media, including cinema and television, shape and define a society's discourses about race and race relations. As Hall (1996d) argues, there is "no escaping the politics of [racial] representation" (p. 473). Gray (1995) elaborates, contending that in the 1980s the New Right, under the leadership of Presidents Reagan and Bush, constructed notions "of whiteness that . . . [made] appeals to . . . black male gang members, black male criminality, crumbling black families, black welfare cheats, black female crack users, and black teen pregnancy" (p. 14).

The New Right "had to take away from blacks (and other persons of color) the moral authority and claims to political entitlements won in the civil rights movements of the 1960s" (Gray, 1995, pp. 17-18). Negative images of "blackness" and "brownness" (dark skin) were constructed and cinematically arrayed "along a continuum ranging from menace on the one end to immorality on the other, with irresponsibility located somewhere in the middle" (p. 17).

Persons of color commingled in this complex, multidimensional space. But in white popular middle-class culture this was not a rainbow coalition; it represented instead a menacing blur of dark-skinned, non-English-speaking others that included African Americans, Asian Americans, Mexican Americans, Cuban Americans, Puerto Ricans, and other Spanish- or non-English-speaking subaltern persons (e.g., Indians). Of course, as we have argued in Chapter 9, no racial identity is pure—solely white, black, Hispanic, or Asian. Instead, hybrid cultural forms interact in the gendered, racial, and ethnic spaces of popular culture: Chicano and black rap, the violent gang and gangsta rap, Chicano and black gangs, all-woman gangs (on this process, see Hall, 1996d, p. 471).[2] These cinematic and televisual representations of race, ethnicity, and gender constitute, at the national popular level, America's system of race relations. A seemingly out-of-control classroom is nonetheless managed by a white woman who is a former Marine (*Dangerous Minds,* 1995), and by the skin of his teeth, and with the help of a good black man, a white man escapes from the violent racial ghetto streets of Los Angeles, a frightening place presented as if it were a bombed-out foreign city (*Grand Canyon,* 1991).

This cinematic version of the racial order situates race in the hood, in the barrio, in Chinatown. In these foreign sites the viewer confronts dark-skinned youth, baseball hats on backward, driving low-riding cars. Threatening, cacophonous sounds of Chicano and black rap music reverberate from boom boxes. Complex mixes of black and brown faces confront the white viewer: blacks, Asians, and Latinos, the subaltern threatening, youthful other is in the viewer's face.

The hood, barrio, and gang films of the 1980s and the 1990s answered to and attempted to salvage this political situation. Through the complex act of cinematic representation these films defined this new (but old) racial order. African American, Chicano, Asian American, and white filmmakers produced a conservative cinema of racial violence, a cinema focused on the violent, destructive features of ghetto life, the very features stressed by the New Right: drugs, the cocaine wars, gangs, gangsta rap, drive-bys, and gang warfare (Reeves & Campbell, 1994; Sanders, 1994). And thus did these situated versions of race and gender simultaneously disrupt and make problematic one version of the interactional order in civil society. For many, the televisual and cinematic racial order perfectly mirrored life in the real world, wherever that was.

Two Approaches to Interaction: Rules and Roles

Two approaches have dominated the study of social interaction: In one, the emphasis has been on regulated and patterned interaction; in the other, the emphasis has been on relatively open-ended, albeit patterned, interaction between self-reflexive interactants. Here we attempt to achieve some balance between these two views.

Very little (if any) interaction occurs, even between total strangers, without some element of code, norm, or rule entering in. This is true even when conflict exists between individuals or when interaction actually takes place around a conflict—as in warfare or an athletic contest. Rules, as prescriptions for conduct, come closest to determining interaction when the interaction is ritualistic—as, for example, in the case of religious ceremonies. Anthropologists and sociologists some years ago employed a loose terminology of *rights* and *obligations* when analyzing such repetitive and standardized forms of interaction; they also used terms like *roles* and *statuses* and applied them to situations in which interactions were either relatively narrow or quite wide in scope (as in the institution of slavery, master and slave having reciprocal rights and obligations associated with their respective statuses). These concepts were often combined with others, such as contract, custom, codes, and mores. A newer generation of social psychologists and sociologists has sustained the interest in socially regulated and patterned behavior, but has abandoned most of the older terms—except for *role* and *status*—and substituted ones like *negative sanctions, positive sanctions, norms, reciprocity, distributive justice, the exchange process,* and *rules of conduct.*

The second traditional approach to interaction emphasizes that it is often "fluid" and that, even when standardized, it can break out of bounds into the unexpected, the surprising, and the novel. As we shall see, social psychologists in this tradition talk about "the self in interaction" and about role taking. They are wary of confusing patterned regularity in interaction with rules, norms, and roles—which supposedly determine that regularity. They tend to think of interaction as Blumer (1962) does—in terms of interactants working out their relationships: "Interpretations have to be developed and effective accommodation of the participants to one another has to be worked out" (p. 190). Or, as Blumer also takes the position: "In modern society, with its increasing crisscross of lines of action, it is common for situations to arise in which the actions of participants are not previously regularized and standardized" (p. 188). Social psychologists who take this position tend to think that those who represent the other viewpoint remove the self from the interactional process while assuming that "their" structural or psychological variables cause humans to act in relatively fixed and predictable ways.

Our own position is that (a) rule-guided or -influenced behavior is extremely important, but not all-important; (b) a simple vocabulary, such as that offered by sociologists who are functionalists and by many social anthropologists, is not useful for examining or researching how interaction actually might be affected by rules that the interactants are "following"; and (c) an analysis of rules and interaction is empty if it ignores the place of the self in the negotiation process.

Interactional Repertoires

In light of these considerations, it can be argued that in most, if not all, interactional episodes persons orient their behaviors toward the emerging standpoints, or lines of action, of those whom they confront. These standpoints represent unique configurations of meaning and interpretation and may be termed *interactional repertoires.* Such repertoires are characteristic lines of action associated with particular selves or persons. When all members of a class of individuals share the same repertoire or similar repertoires across situations, then it is appropriate to speak of a common interactional role. However, all interactants are obliged to assess the special line of action taken by any individual whom they confront, and in such assessments they must turn some amount of attention to the special features of the other's definition of the situation. All interaction, and all interactants, display some complex mix of self and role taking. Individuals take one another's perspectives, and to term that *role taking* has meaning only if it is remembered that it is selves interacting with one another—not roles, not role sets, but networks of interactional repertoires. To divorce the self from the interaction process is to produce an empty, mechanistic view of human behavior.

The Social Situation

All interaction occurs in social situations, and all such situations have three components. First are the objective features—the physical aspects of the room, hallway, playing field, street corner, or other location of the social situation. The second component is the subjective side of the situation—the definitions people bring to the situation and work out inside it. The third component is the people who interact in the situation. We can see how a given objective situation can take on different meanings depending on who is interacting in it. Compare, for example, the meanings brought to a house by a real estate agent versus the meanings of that house to the people who are selling it. For the realtor, the house is a piece of property to be sold; for the people who live in it, the house is "home," and it has the meanings of a personal space where important transactions and experiences have occurred. Sociologists Thomas and Thomas (1928) suggest that "if people define situations as real they are real in their consequences" (pp. 571-572). This often-repeated sociological dictum speaks to the subjective side of social situations.

Situations exist, then, only insofar as people define them and make them real. All human experience is situated, and every situation is unique. However, situations have historical meanings as well; these meanings are passed on from one generation to the next, and they shape the interactions that occur within them.

In addition to the objective, subjective, interactional, and historical features of situations, we may note that some situations may exist only in a person's imagination—for example, the dream world of a child. Other situations are completely objective and push themselves into the person's world of experience. When two cars collide at an intersection, there is no way to avoid the fact that an automobile accident has occurred.

In social situations, individuals enact and play out interactional repertoires. Situations provide the points of contact for the person and the social structure. This brings us to our next concept: the two streams of experience (see Figure 10.1).

In any situation, there are two streams of experience flowing alongside one another. The first is the interactional stream, which references the face-to-face interaction that occurs between two parties in a concrete or imagined social situation. The second stream, the phenomenological stream, describes the inner side of interaction, which occurs when the person interacts with him- or herself and with another in a social situation. In the phenomenological stream, the person (A) takes his or her own attitude toward self (A-A) and toward the other (A-B) and turns the imagined attitude of the other toward him- or herself (B-A).

Interaction in any situation will involve person A initiating a line of action toward B that calls out in B a significant emotional and cognitive gesture that is present in A's action and thought. Person A turns this

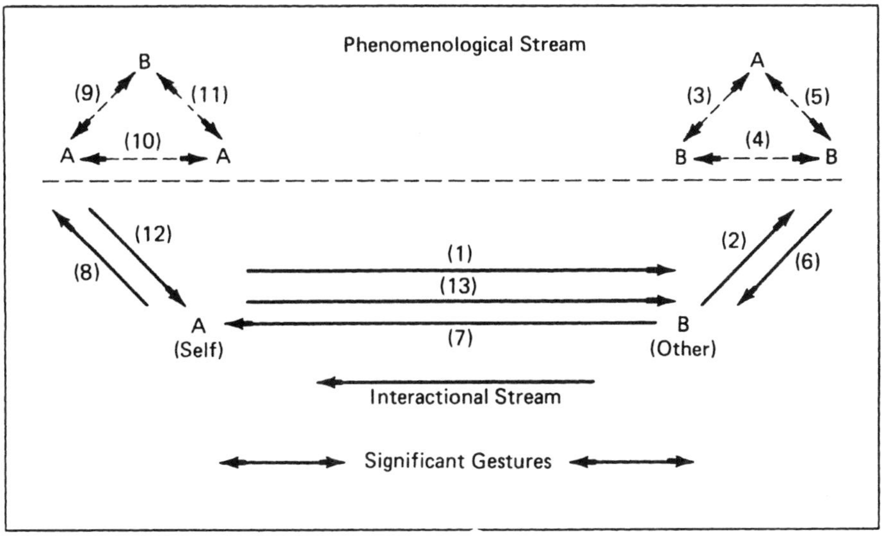

Figure 10.1. Interaction in the Social Situation
SOURCE: Adapted from Denzin (1984a, p. 55). Used with permission.

emotional and cognitive gesture inward, judging and interpreting the meaning of B's actions in light of A's own incipient emotional and cognitive attitudes (A-A, A-B, B-A). This interpretation becomes part of A's emotional and cognitive self-feelings and is then incorporated into A's next gesture or statement to B. Thus A's self-feeling and self-definition become part of an emotional, cognitive, social act that enters B's inner phenomenological stream and becomes part of B's emotional social act (toward both B and A).

A "circuit of selfness" (Sartre, 1943/1956, pp. 155-158) attaches each person to the social situation and to the other person(s) in the situation. In this circuit emotion, meaning, and self are joined. This field of experience anchors the self and the interactional repertoire in the other's phenomenological and interactional streams.

Defining the situation. Implicit in our discussion is the fundamental idea that interaction occurs in episodes, scenes, or situations. Individuals must recognize, name, and catalog these so that they may take appropriate action. No two situations are exactly alike, but there is often enough resemblance between new situations and those individuals have formerly encountered to permit them to recognize what is called for and thus behave in an orderly and regular manner. Many situations can be immediately "tabbed" because they are routine, traditional, or familiar. When individuals are able to "sense" particular situations, they can immediately gear themselves to respond to them. At the other pole, many situations are problematic and subject to different interpretations. Defining situations, both familiar and new, involves the interpretation of a multitude of clues.

In problematic situations, individuals may have to delay action while they search for relevant clues; or they may act tentatively, without committing themselves, in order to elicit further information. In any case, people can never see the totality of the situations in which they are involved, as an omniscient being or a playwright might see them. Individuals can perceive only what their abilities, categories, and interests lead or enable them to see. As MacIver (1942) indicates, the situation is not a mere physical inventory of external data:

> The situation he assesses is one that he has selectively defined, in terms of his experience, his habit of response, his intellectual grasp, and his emotional engrossment in it. The dynamic assessment limits the situation by excluding all the numerous aspects that are not apprehended as relevant to the choice between alternatives. At the same time it includes in the situation various aspects that are not objectively given, that would not be listed in any merely physical inventory. . . . it envisages the situation as impregnated with values and susceptible of new potential values. (p. 296)

The situation includes, besides the individual's own values and motives, those he or she imputes to others. No hard-and-fast lines can be drawn between the definition of a situation and the behavior thought to be appropriate to it. Any definition necessarily implies and carries with it a plan of action. A person does not usually name the situation and then sequentially decide what to do; defining the situation and exploring alternative courses of action usually occur simultaneously. These processes are often tied up with a review of preceding events and a reinterpretation of them and of past lines of action.

To illuminate these points, we offer the following excerpts from the opening and closing paragraphs of Raymond Carver's short story "The Calm" (1981):

> I was getting a haircut. I was in the chair and three men were sitting along the wall across from me. Two of the men waiting I'd never seen before. But one of them I recognized, though I couldn't exactly place him. I kept looking at him as the barber worked on my hair. (p. 115)

> The barber turned me in the chair to face the mirror. He put a hand to either side of my head. . . .
>
> We looked into the mirror together, his hands still framing my head. . . .
>
> He ran his fingers through my hair. He did it slowly, as if thinking about something else. He ran his fingers through my hair. He did it tenderly, as a lover would.
>
> That was in Crescent City, California, up near the Oregon border. I left soon after. But today I was thinking of that place, of Crescent City, and of how I was trying out a new life there with my wife, and how, in the barber's chair that morning, I had made up my mind to go. (p. 121)

Several processes are at work in this story. Carver is interactionally and phenomenologically connected to the barber, to himself, to the barber's movement of his hands through Carver's hair, to his own emotions, and to his recent past. The circuit of selfness joins Carver to the barber and to the emotions he feels and remembers in the situation.

Now reflect on the description of Preedy, a fictional Englishman on vacation, in this excerpt from a short story by William Sansom (1955). Here we see an interactional repertoire fitting itself to a social situation:

> But it was time to institute a little parade, the parade of the Ideal Preedy. By devious handlings he gave any who wanted to look a chance to see the title of his book—a Spanish translation of Homer, classic thus, but not daring, cosmopolitan too—and then gathered together his beach-wrap and bag into a neat sand-resistant pile (Methodical and Sensible Preedy), rose slowly to stretch his huge frame (Big-Cat Preedy), and tossed aside his sandals (Carefree Preedy, after all). (pp. 230-231)

Preedy is interacting with the situation. He is presenting himself to any who will look. He has an interactional repertoire—the way he walks, the book he is reading, his beach wrap, his sandals, and so on. He is set on making an impression on others (Goffman, 1959, p. 6). He has turned the beach into a personal situation, thereby making it a public place for the presentation of himself. Preedy is preparing himself for a *social relationship*—our next topic.

Social Relationships

Gregory P. Stone (1984, p. 5) divides social relationships into interpersonal and structural relationships. The difference between them consists of the fact that the structural relationship exists for the lifetime and participation of the individual member. An example reveals the difference between these two types of relationships: University students assemble for courses and are taught by members of the faculty, who have been appointed by members of the administration. In the case of the university, we are dealing with a real social structure that outlives any given member.

Now look at a small group of friends who live in the same rooming house. They have come together through the exchange of personal names. No external social structure brought them into the rooming house. When they leave, or when one moves out and another person takes his or her place, new names will be exchanged and a new informal, small social group will be formed.

Stone (1981a, p. 189; 1984, p. 7) argues that the key difference between structural and interpersonal relations lies in how one enters them. In structural relations, the person exchanges a name for a title that refers to a position in a social structure (e.g., student, physician, nurse). In interpersonal relations, the individual exchanges only a name or nickname.

Stone (1981a, p. 189) distinguishes two other types of social relations. *Human relations* are those based on such universal identities as age, gender, race, ethnicity, and community membership. Social relations that occur for members of the *larger public* (i.e., the masses) are entered anonymously. Social relationships can now be viewed as ongoing social interactions between two or more persons that are classified according to the "identities which must be placed and announced to permit entry into the transaction" (Stone, 1981a, p. 189).

Human and mass relations can form the basis for interpersonal relations—as when strangers meet at a political rally, exchange names, and form a friendship. Similarly, structural relations can lay the basis for workers' interpersonal relations; office co-workers can become friends. Furthermore, interpersonal relations can introduce persons into structural relations; friends, for example, can sponsor friends into exclusive clubs or fraternities (Stone, 1984, p. 7).

Identities

Building on the discussion in Chapter 9, and following Stone (1981a), Strauss (1959), and Maines (1978), we can define identities as "social categories through which people may be located and given meaning" in some situational or interactional context (Maines, 1978, p. 242). When "one has identity, he is situated—that is, cast in the shape of a social object by the acknowledgment of his participation or membership in social relations" (Stone, 1981a, p. 188).

Social, personal, and interactional identities are established as a result of two processes. The first situates the person with other persons in a situation, and the second separates the person from others.

We can see that identities are created in social situations. Furthermore, identities involve social relations. Larger interactional forms (groups, organizations) give persons identities and locate them in social relationships. Self, identity, names, titles, interactional repertoires, social situations, and social relationships are all closely related.

To return to our earlier example from the work of Sansom (1955), Preedy appears quite willing to be situated in the identity of a handsome man looking for interactions with members of the opposite sex. He will exchange his name for an interpersonal relationship. He is prepared, in a sense, for a status passage.

Status Passage and Interaction

Social structure is often conceived of as a system of interrelated "offices," "statuses," roles, or other designations that stand for social positions. People are said to act in accordance with the requirements of those social positions insofar as they play those roles, fill those offices, or occupy those statuses. In short, social positions carry with them guidelines for those who are "in" them. The guidelines can be in the nature of general expectations by others (and often internalized, so that the actor has those expectations too), but sometimes they are rather rigorously prescribed, being more in the nature of rules and regulations and even of laws. Offices, statuses, and roles can therefore be conceived of as somewhat independent of the specific individuals who happen to fill them. This also implies that people must be induced to fill those positions, as well as to leave them at some appropriate time.

> Insofar as every social structure requires manpower, men are recruited . . . to move along through social positions or statuses. Status is a resting place for individuals. But while the status itself may persist for many years, no matter how long an individual remains in, say, an office, there is an implicit or even explicit date when he must leave it. (Glaser & Strauss, 1971, pp. 2-3)

The movement of individuals in and out of statuses has long been referred to as *status passage.* A great many such passages (into and out of the presidency of the United States; into and out of the statuses of "accused" and "witness" in a court trial) are governed by fairly clear rules concerning when and how the passages are made, who is involved in them, the prescribed sequences of steps that must be gone through, and the like. If all passages were so neatly governed, then there might not be much change in the social structure of any group, organization, or nation. However, a large share of passages in modern societies are much less regulated, prescribed, and organized. American passage into marriage, for example, although guided by implicit rules of dating and more explicit ones pertaining to the wedding itself (e.g., the woman's family pays), may have many ill-defined features: the length of the engagement, whether there is an engagement, whether the couple lives together before, even what the details of the wedding will be. Similar unstandardized features mark the passage into the divorced status. Probably most status passages leave those who pass, and the agents who help in the passage, with a fair degree of latitude about a great many details, including major ones that relate to sequences of steps and timing.

We can see also that interactions during a passage will vary considerably in accordance with other properties of the passage. Sometimes the passage is undesirable to the person passing or to others involved in the passage. Sometimes the passage is not very important to the individual, but sometimes it may be central in his or her life. Some passages are reversible (e.g., studenthood), whereas some may be irreversible (e.g., parenthood). Other conditions of passages include whether they are inevitable (e.g., childhood to adulthood), voluntary or involuntary, and whether the person goes through the passage alone or with others (e.g., classmates). Also, some passages are left to the person passing to initiate or consummate; others are actually initiated and controlled by agents, rather than by the person passing. All these properties affect how the participants will act toward each other. In turn, their actions will have consequences for self- and other evaluations, which then will affect some of the next steps of the passage.

This general manner of looking at the relations among statuses, offices, and positions brings out two important points. First, one can see the processual or more dynamic side of social structures. Even if given statuses do not change in character, there is a good deal of movement going on as people pass into, through, and out of them. Second, it is clear that social interaction has two sides: the structural side and the self-other side. We cannot understand interaction without taking both into account.

Twin Processes: Presenting and Assessing

We noted previously that in interaction, each actor necessarily is assessing—not necessarily with full consciousness—the other. The assessor has various cues to go on: verbal, expressive verbal accompaniments, nonverbal (including posture, gesture, management of body in space, eye gaze), and also stylistic cues related to how the other dresses, arranges his or her hair, or surrounds him- or herself with household or decorative objects. The type of people with whom the other surrounds him- or herself is also a cue (Argyle, 1969; Goffman, 1959).

The counterpart of this interactional assessment process is what Goffman has called *impression management*—that is, the organization of the presenting person's cues so as to elicit desired responses in the assessing other. This management of the other's assessment may be completely sincere or coldly manipulative; it may be done deliberately and consciously, or virtually without awareness. Impressions are created by a large variety of communicative devices and interactional tactics and through the use of external props. Many of these involve teamwork, as when husband and wife collaborate to give a party for the boss, or when several members of a confidence mob separate a mark from her money.

Stone (1962) has further developed the analysis of self-display strategies by looking closely at clothing. He notes that people select the clothes they will wear, and how they will wear them, in an effort to get others to form the desired impressions. He notes, "Identifications of another are facilitated by appearance and are often accomplished silently or unverbally" (p. 90). Stone's analysis indicates that the use of clothing to create an appearance is quite complex: "By appearance, a person announces his identity, *shows* his value, *expresses* his mood, or *proposes* his attitude" (p. 101).

Of course, people not only display aspects of themselves but also attempt to suppress or hide those aspects they do not wish to reveal. They do this, for instance, by arranging clothes to hide potentially stigmatizing disease systems or by using perfumes or deodorizers to disguise or suppress smells (Largey & Watson, 1972).

The phenomenon of "passing"—of blacks for whites, Jews for gentiles, spies for ordinary citizens—necessarily relies on both the suppression of giveaway signs and an emphasis on signs that represent the desired appearance. Thus John Griffin (1962), a white journalist, for some weeks passed as a black in the South, having first taken the precaution of having his skin color changed temporarily with chemicals. We need not think of such suppression of signs of "true self" as being so esoteric; we all engage in such suppression from time to time. Indeed, to use Stone's terminology, depending on how we feel today, we may wish to "appear" that way, choosing clothes appropriate for that appearance, simultaneously suppressing those signs, including clothing styles, that are inappropriate to today's desired appearance.

Analyses such as Stone's and Goffman's are valuable extensions of the idea of self-presentation. These examples bring us to the assessor's tasks. The assessor in an interaction has to read the other's signs accurately or face the consequences of misreading them. Thus if the other is seeking to present a false appearance, the assessor has to be able to "see through" that fiction or have developed countertactics to elicit important giveaway signs. Some countertactics for recognizing persons who are suppressing their identities depend on passing as a member of their group—an FBI agent posing as a Communist—or on getting information from others within the group. Persons of similar status may use conventional signs, both to avoid mistaken recognition of the assessing person and to further recognition if their own assessment of the assessor is accurate. Thus homosexuals flash signs readable only by those who are either homosexual or "wise" (sympathetic insiders). Usually there are places where gathered insiders can forgo efforts to disguise or suppress identifying signs, but like drug addicts, they may need countertactics to avoid betrayal even in such secluded places (Goffman, 1969).

The assessing person is aided not only by astuteness, experience, and slips of control by the presenting other, but by the latter's flashing of cues of which he or she is not even aware. Only practiced actors, like spies, are intensely aware of all those features of their nonverbal behavior that act as potential revelations of selves, or aspects of selves, that they would rather not be seen. Freudians would term these "unconscious" slips—that is, they represent loss of control of which the presenting person is not even aware. Examples would be slips of the tongue, too rapid breathing, and blushing. It is notable, however, that most persons are flashing cues all the time—most of which they cannot notice because their attention is somewhere else. The assessing person may happen to notice them or may make it his or her business to notice them. Those are the same nonverbal cues that we mentioned before: posture, gesture, eye gaze, verbal expressivity, movement in space, and the like. One must also recognize that skilled actors who are intent on presenting a desired appearance may flash cues in such a way that the assessor falsely interprets what he or she assumes are unwitting signs. The entire question of "accurate" interpretation turns out to be very complex (Icheiser, 1949; Weinstein & Deutschberger, 1963).

Awareness Contexts

In considering the strategies and problems of self-presentation and of the assessment of others, it is relevant to introduce the concept of awareness context, as developed by Glaser and Strauss (1964, 1968). *Awareness context* refers to "the total combination of what each interactant in a situation knows about the identity of the other and his own identity in the eyes of the other. The total awareness is the context within which are guided successive interaction . . . over periods of time—long or short" (Glaser & Strauss, 1964, p. 670). Four principal types of awareness context are relevant to the presentation and assessment that goes on in interaction. An *open* awareness context prevails when each interactant is aware of the other's true identity in the eyes of others. A *closed* awareness context prevails when one interactant does not know either the other's identity or the other's view of his or her identity. Examples of such a context would include a spy whom the other believes to be an ordinary person, a virgin who either is deliberately passing as or is mistakenly assumed to be a sexually experienced person, and, more simply, a Japanese American visiting Japan who is mistaken for a native. A *suspicion* prevails when one interactant suspects the true identity of the other, the other's view of his or her own identity, or both. A *pretense* context prevails when both are fully aware, but pretend not to be.

The concept of awareness context is applicable in a great many interactive situations, for such situations have the potential for deliberate misrepresentation of self as well as honest presentations of self; likewise, mistakes are inherent in both presentation and assessment despite each actor's attempts at honest presentation. Moreover, the need for fictional acting, through what everybody can see through but feels the need not to state bluntly, is inherent in many situations. Some social philosophers, as well as laypersons, have been so impressed by the fictional and misrepresentation as to believe that most human relations are governed by hypocrisy. Others have merely emphasized the Machiavellian character of interaction.

McCall and Simmons (1966) have expressed a similarly pessimistic view, although they mitigate its full implication with a last qualifying phrase: "Owing to the very peculiar nature of knowledge about other persons, relationships necessarily turn on somewhat misguided and misleading premises about the other parties, social order rests partly on error, lies, deception, and secrets, as well as upon accurate knowledge" (pp. 195-196). A more balanced characterization of interaction, and the social order that it both expresses and makes possible, is that *all* types of awareness contexts are potentially operative in interaction.

Furthermore, the types are not mutually exclusive but tend to move from one to another, depending on the stage of development to which relationships have evolved (Icheiser, 1970). Thus in the early stages of friendship formation it is likely that pretense and suspicion awareness contexts predominate; but as the individuals acquire more information about one another, they can more easily and more fully reveal their perceived ambiguities about each other and about themselves as well. Indeed, friendship formation may be contingent on breaking out of the pretense and suspicion awareness contexts.

Small Groups and Problematic Interaction

There is a voluminous literature concerned with "small groups." Although this literature reports research that is far from homogeneous in character and intent, the investigations on which the literature is based share three features. First, the groups are newly formed—the members have little or no previous relationship to each other. Second, the groups are formed under the aegis of researchers, who bring them together for their own purposes. Third, the research almost always takes the form of an "experiment."

We offer a brief account below of how interaction occurs in natural social groups. We take our example from the interactions of the groups that form the basis of how Alcoholics Anonymous works (Denzin, 1987b). In so doing, we attempt to draw together the preceding discussions of identities, situations, social relationships, awareness contexts, and selves.

The Alcoholics Anonymous Group

There are more than 50,000 Alcoholics Anonymous groups in the United States, ranging in size from 5 persons to 30 or more. A.A. groups meet at least once a week. Every group has a chairperson who calls the meeting to order, announces him- or herself as an alcoholic, asks for a moment of silence, and then asks the members present to say the "Serenity Prayer." The chairperson then asks a member to read aloud "How It Works," which is a statement from the text *Alcoholics Anonymous* that contains A.A.'s Twelve Steps (Alcoholics Anonymous,

1976). After this text is read, another member reads A.A.'s Twelve Traditions (Alcoholics Anonymous, 1953). After this reading, some A.A. groups ask a member to read from a thought-for-the-day book that contains a prayer, a meditation, and a thought for the day.

After these three texts are read, the chair asks (a) if there are any visitors to the group, (b) if anyone has an A.A. birthday (i.e., has been sober for 1 year or more), (c) if there are any announcements, and (d) if anyone has a step, problem, or topic to be discussed. At this point in the meeting, a member may raise his hand and make a statement such as, "My name is Bill and I'm an alcoholic. I'd like to talk about not drinking today." The chairperson will typically say something like, "Okay, let's talk about the First Step. Who would like to go first?" A member will raise his or her hand and begin speaking, always with the announcement, "My name is _____ and I am an alcoholic." After each group member has talked, the chairperson will ask, "Does anyone have seconds?" At this point a member may speak again. Having given everyone this option, the chairperson then closes the meeting by asking everyone to join in saying the Lord's Prayer. All members of the group rise, join hands, and say the prayer in unison. This ends the meeting.

A.A. meetings last an average of 1 hour. Each member typically speaks for no longer than 2 to 5 minutes. When members speak, they speak only for themselves as individuals, not for A.A. or for the A.A. group.

Group ritual and interaction. We can extract several social psychological processes concerning how small groups operate from this description of the A.A. group meeting. First, we can see the operation of ritual. Reciting the Serenity Prayer, the Lord's Prayer, and the readings from A.A. texts ritually organize the group; they draw it together and create moments of ritual solidarity at the beginning and end of the meeting. Thus ritual, as a social act that confers special status on one or more persons, is central to the organization of the group. Second, the group exists in and through talk. Communication in the form of talk represents the central activity of the A.A. group. Third, the group is organized in terms of a "pledge," or a larger purpose that encompasses every member. This purpose is twofold. First, it tells the members that their primary purpose is to carry the message of A.A. to the alcoholic who still suffers. Second, it subordinates individual purposes to a larger group goal.

Fourth, the A.A. meeting is organized in terms of a shared personal and social identity, which is contained in the word *alcoholic.* Every member of the group identifies him- or herself in terms of the label *alcoholic.* This shared identity locates every member within the ritual structure of A.A. This identity is passed on the merger of quasi-formal title (I'm an alcoholic) and the personal name; thus the A.A. meeting merges structural and interpersonal relationships. This is underscored by the fact that A.A. members seldom exchange last names—hence the word *anonymous* in the name of the organization.

Fifth, all members share an open awareness context involving the identity of alcoholics, although some members may suspect that they are not alcoholics. They may pretend to be alcoholics by announcing themselves as alcoholics, but they may not believe this about themselves. They may also suspect others of not really being alcoholics.

Sixth, the A.A. group, through its meeting, is a temporal production. That is, action and talk within the meeting are based on shared pasts, a shared present, and a common projected future (Couch, 1984a, p. 1). Members share their past experiences with alcoholism. They locate themselves in the now of the present as they take part in the A.A. rituals. When the meeting closes with the phrase "Keep coming back," the members project a future that will be shared at the next A.A. meeting. The A.A. meeting is a coordinated production resting on shared identities, interpersonal relationships, and a shared perspective on the past, the present, and the future.

Emotional understanding. There is an additional feature of the A.A. experience (Maxwell, 1984), the phenomenon of *emotional understanding.* By this term we refer to knowing and comprehending through emotional means, including sympathy and imagination, the intentions, feelings, and thoughts expressed by another (Denzin, 1984a, p. 282). Alcoholics understand one another emotionally because they have had similar experiences with alcohol, including being drunk, hung over, depressed, remorseful, guilty, fearful, and dependent upon alcohol for courage. By sharing these experiences with one another in A.A. meetings, alcoholics build up a form of emotional understanding that is unique to the A.A. experience. This form of understanding brings them back to meetings.

We are suggesting that every social group, at a basic level, rests on a form and type of emotional understanding that is unique to the group. Because every social group organizes itself around this phenomenon, we can argue that this is a universal feature of ongoing human groups. In and through emotional understanding, groups and their members form attachments of a longstanding and often intimate nature.

CONCLUSION

The everyday interactional order is anchored in public and private life, in the public spaces of civil society. This civil order has historically been tangled up in its cinematic representations. The establishment of Hollywood's cinematic apparatus ushered in new ways of looking, being, and acting in civil society. Cinematic society, in turn, articulated particular ideological versions of race, gender, and ethnicity in American culture. The cinematic society helped establish the importance of narrative storytelling in everyday life. Hollywood movies created socially shared representations of love, intimacy, and sexual desire.

Face-to-face interaction is a rule-governed but emergent social process. All interaction occurs in social situations. In social situations, social relationships and situated identities are established. Many small group interactions are based on shared emotionality and on shifting contexts of awareness.

SUGGESTED READINGS

Anderson, E. (1990). *Streetwise: Race, class, and change in an urban community.* Chicago: University of Chicago Press. A very powerful analysis of inner-city life and of black-white relations in a mixed neighborhood.

Blumer, H. (1969). *Symbolic interactionism.* Englewood Cliffs, NJ: Prentice Hall. The classic symbolic interactionist statement on self and interaction.

de Certeau, M. (1984). *The practice of everyday life.* Berkeley: University of California Press. Should be read in conjunction with Lefebvre's *Everyday Life in the Modern World.*

Gardner, C. B. (1995). *Passing by: Gender and public harassment.* Berkeley: University of California Press. An uncomfortable documentation of the decline of civility in America's public places.

Goffman, E. (1974). *Frame analysis.* New York: Harper & Row. Goffman's most difficult book on the problematic and ritual nature of interactional experience.

Lefebvre, H. (1984) Everyday life in the modern world. New Brunswick, NJ: Transaction. This and de Certeau's The Practice of Everyday Life, both by French sociologists-philosophers, analyze the forms of domination and resistance that exist in the contemporary world of experience. They provide an alarming contrast to Goffman's perspective.

STUDY QUESTIONS

1. What is the cinematic society, and what are its key features?
2. What assumptions seem to organize the cinematic racial order?
3. How do interaction rituals shape face-to-face interaction?

NOTES

1. The material in this section draws on Denzin (1995, chap. 2).

2. Precedents for contemporary Latin and black hybrid musical forms can be found in the Latin (Afro-Cuban) and bossa nova jazz traditions. The first bossa nova recordings appeared in 1954 (Laurindo Almeida). Afro-Cuban jazz can be traced to the early 1920s and extends into the present, with the performances of Tito Puente, Dizzy Gillespie, Mario Bauza, and the current Afro-Latin world musical scene (e.g., Rubén González).

11

Selves and Identity Transformations

We have continually emphasized that the individual's self-conception and sense of self-identity are mediated by the communication process, lodged in the circuits of culture, and grounded in the person's interpersonal relationships. The contemporary self is bombarded with social and media experiences, saturated with information from such sources as electronic and voice mail, faxes, around-the-clock cable-television and broadcast news, and stories and narratives in special-interest magazines and newspapers (see Gergen, 1991, p. 16). Fractured and split identities are now taken for granted. Persons develop multiple images of who they are and shape these images around shifting hyphenated meanings attached to racial, religious, ethnic, sexual, national, and family identities. These identities are lodged in the circuits of culture, filtered, constantly defined, and represented in the mass media.

In this chapter we discuss the individual's self-identities and moral careers in relation to membership in social worlds. The self is not fixed at the conclusion of childhood, as Freud might have implied. We examine here some of the transformations and radical changes of self that occur in later phases of the life cycle. Some have divided the life cycle, without great success, into the phases of *infancy, childhood, adulthood, middle age, old age,* and *death.* We intend to demonstrate that the self changes as its social relationships and social worlds undergo transformation.

At least three generic views of self now circulate in the social science and popular literature. The 19th century gave us a "*romanticist* view of the self, one that attributes to each person characteristics of personal depth: passion, soul, creativity, and moral fiber" (Gergen, 1991, p. 6). With the rise of the modern world, Gergen (1991) suggests the romantic self was challenged by a rational view of the person. Depth for the *modern self* no longer resided in the soul, or in emotion; rather, persons were judged by their ability to reason, to be predictable and rational. Gergen suggests that the forces of late modernism have produced the conditions of *social saturation.* These conditions are eroding the foundations of the romantic and modern self, thus emerges the *postmodern self.* This self throws into doubt the very notion of personal essence, of selves as possessors of rationality, reason, emotion, or will (Gergen, 1991, p. 7).

Of course the self has been gendered, connected to those ongoing performances that establish sexual and gender identity. Trinh (1991, p. 157) suggests that the feminine standpoint is always fragile, illusive, plural. The figure of postcolonial woman, for example, always writes from a position of triple jeopardy: "as a writer, as a woman, and as a woman of color" (Trinh, 1989, p. 28). This woman is constantly crossing ff a hyphen, a hybrid, Asian American woman, African American feminist (Trinh, 1991, p. 157), constantly negotiating "the difference not merely between cultures, between First and Third World, but more importantly within culture . . . a plural singularity . . . [that problematizes] the insider-outsider position" (Trinh, 1992, p. 144). This space is fluid, infinite, unnameable, the space of becoming (Trinh, 1991, p. 157), the site of feminist consciousness (p. 112).

But this is not a state of consciousness arrived at after a new body of knowledge has been acquired. It is not a personal or group consciousness. It is a process, "a dialectical understanding and practice of identity and difference . . . [where] the ethnic me and the female me [become] political" (Trinh, 1991, p. 113). From this space, culture is rewritten from within, on the borders and silences of the body (p. 129), where women bring their stories to bear on the stories they tell (p. 131).

However, it would be an error to think of the modern self of the person as if it had no grounding in the world of experience, as if it had no sense of inner agency, purpose, or direction. Perhaps in reaction to Gergen's arguments about the saturated self, Gubrium and Holstein (1995) assert the utility of "a more modernist perspective . . . centered on the local, everyday practices of self-construction" (p. 556). In formulating their arguments, Gubrium and Holstein draw on narrative and ethnographic materials from a variety of different settings, including parent self-help groups, community support programs, and other self-help programs, such as Alcoholics Anonymous (p. 559).

They show how interacting individuals use locally shared meanings, biographical particulars, and material objects to give a sense of unity and stability to their senses of self. Here is an example. A wife of an aging, frail, and perhaps demented man uses the metaphor of a ticking clock to describe her decision to place her husband in a nursing home: "That there clock's me. It'll keep ticking away until it's time to decide and won't stop for a minute until it winds down I guess" (quoted in Gubrium & Holstein, 1995, p. 563).

Gubrium and Holstein (1995) suggest that the postmodern picture of the self as a thing with fleeting agency "seems far less ephemeral when viewed in relation to ordinary social moorings" (p. 566). The contemporary self, or contemporary agency, is "as concrete and varied as the everyday practices and sites that call forth and supply its meanings" (p. 566). We do not quarrel with this position; we only note, with Gergen, that the postmodern scene makes these practices more variable and more ephemeral. Giddens (1991) is helpful here; he notes that "against the backdrop of new forms of mediated experience, self-identity becomes a reflexively organized endeavor" (p. 5).

We begin with a treatment of the concept of *career,* focusing on the varieties of careers (work, friendship, leisure, political, religious, intimate) that any given person has; we then move to the related concept of the *social world* and show how individuals move in and out of small-scale careers into more complex worlds of discourse.

Careers

To say that an individual has a career involves three interrelated notions (Becker, 1973; Goffman, 1961b; Stebbins, 1970). The concept designates objective movements that the person may make through a social structure. Here we refer to status passages: movements in and out of the labor market, educational settings, marriages, friendships, or groups. *Objective careers*—these movements through statuses and positions—produce counterparts termed *subjective careers.* In this category are the subtle and sometimes manifest changes in self-conception that accompany positional relocations. As Hughes (1937, 1958) has noted, alterations in the objective career lead to changes in self-identity. The objective and subjective components of the career are especially important because they set the stage for the larger redefinitions of self.

Goffman (1961b) has conveniently summarized the threefold nature (objective, subjective, self) of career:

> Traditionally the term *career* has been reserved for those who expect to enjoy the rises laid out within a respectable profession. The term is coming to be used, however, in a broadened sense to refer to any social strand of any person's course through life. . . . One value of the concept of career is its two-sidedness. One side is linked to internal matters held dearly and closely . . . the other side concerns public position, jural relations, and style of life. . . . The concept of career, then, allows one to move back and forth between the personal and the public, between the self and its significant society. . . . The main concern will be with the moral aspects of career—that is, the regular sequence of changes that career entails in the person's self and in his framework of imagery for judging himself and others. (pp. 128-129)

The sacredness of the self-conception, as noted by Goffman (1956), must be emphasized. He has written that it is important to see that "the self is in part a ceremonial thing, a sacred object which must be treated with proper ritual care and in turn must be presented in a proper light to others . . . practices must be institutionalized so that the individual will be able to project a viable, sacred self" (p. 497). Any alteration in an individual's moral worth, then, alters that person's standing in a network of others. Goffman's remarks suggest that individuals go out of their way to protect one another's self-conceptions; in this sense each individual is the guardian of others' *moral careers* as well as of his or her own.

Aspects of Moral Careers

Any moral career is a temporal process that flows through the strands of the individual's life. Individuals have multiple careers, each linked into distinct universes of discourse—that is, into unique social worlds. In this sense individuals have careers with all of their interactive fellows. Some of these careers are short-term, as in a fleeting friendship. Some are long-term—marriage, for example, or the work career of the individual who retires from the same university that hired her 40 years earlier. Some careers have zigzag contours; a heroin user may, for instance, periodically "kick" the habit or move off hard drugs to soft drugs, and an alcoholic may move in and out of the drinking world. Careers have peak points of involvement, during which times the individual fully embraces the moral and subjective consequences of that involvement; at other times the involvement recedes into the background and may carry little, if any, implications for the individual's other career commitments.

Careers are situated productions as well—that is, they are located in specific social situations. Careers are also "peopled productions": They involve interactions with other individuals. These other persons, in turn, influence the directions the individual's career will take in the future. Thus careers are joint productions that are temporarily and situationally specific to each person. David L. Westby's (1960) study of the career experiences of symphony musicians illustrates this point. Westby notes that images of conductors can significantly influence the career decisions of musicians. One violin player stated: "As far as symphonies are concerned I'm better off here. I could have gone to [name of a somewhat more prestigious orchestra] last year on viola. The salary is better there, but I couldn't stomach the conductor" (quoted in Westby, 1960, p. 224).

Other people, then, positively and negatively influence the person's moral career. This is especially so for those careers that have an organizational locus (Blankenship, 1973; Faulkner, 1973). To have a career is to be involved in a set of commitments with other persons. Accordingly, it can be seen that trust and its imputation are central to the stability and shape of any career. An individual may overestimate or misrepresent, through selective inattention, the trustworthiness of another person. Or that person may misrepresent him- or herself to others. Such misreadings, deliberate or accidental, often result in betrayals and blocked or negative careers. Thus many persons find themselves in mental hospitals or jails and only later learn that their spouses were responsible for their commitment. A career is accomplished in the company of a set of *career others*—those individuals whose presence, commitment, and trust the individual comes to depend on.

As the individual moves through any specific career—say, in the academic or work world—his or her set of career others will change with the individual's changes from one position to another. That is, as the individual's career takes on new forms or leads him or her into new areas, the individual comes into the presence of others who at earlier times would not have been available. An individual has as many career others as he or she has ongoing careers; it should be clear, however, that these others may no longer be living, or they may have moved out of the person's immediate interactional world. Still, they continue to exert symbolic influence, and the individual may assess their imagined reactions as he or she makes new decisions.

The multiple careers of any individual may be in harmony or in conflict with one another. Involvement in one social world—work, leisure, politics—may intrude into others—family, friends. As Simmel (1953) has noted, the person is led to develop a set of strategies to keep these competing career demands in some kind of balance. In the company of one set of others, the individual simply does not talk about or act on the perspectives of other competing worlds. Spouses may leave their work at their offices, and children may not talk about their school experiences.

Career visibility. Although at any moment in time any individual is involved in multiple careers, some are more visible than others. The work career, for example, is highly prominent and visible and may go on display 5 or more days a week. Some careers are less visible—for example, a person's interest in stamp collecting, or in a particular musician or artist, may never be known or may be made public only to a small set of others. A related characteristic is that some careers are over and done once traversed. Thus when a medical student completes residency, his or her formal relationship with the medical establishment may be terminated. Similarly, many persons terminate careers (divorce) or have them terminated (death, demotion). Terminated careers are less visible than those that are ongoing, unless of course the previous career left the person with a set of markings that reveal his or her past. Abominations of the body—stigmata, such as concentration camp markings, that are still visible—give away past involvements. Some careers, however, are simply buried; failures, broken love affairs, past criminal offenses may be kept secret or may be known only to a few people. All of us, then, give off clues to our career involvements through our verbal or nonverbal gestures. Our clothing and other personal possessions may be the basic conveyors of information about what these commitments are.

Career entrance and access. Careers may be entered voluntarily (the dating market), involuntarily (the military), or by recruitment (medical school). Depending on the mode of entry and on how the individual defines other career involvements, a person may show great attachment, detachment, or simple neutrality. Thus people just beginning to date may enthusiastically throw themselves into the pursuit of a partner. In general, if their entry into given careers has been voluntary, individuals may be more likely to commit and attach themselves to the identifications that follow from their location in those social worlds.

The topic of career entrance raises the related matter of career access. Some careers are closed off to many groups of individuals, whereas others are open for the taking. Factors connected to race, ethnicity, religion, gender, and sexual orientation can block entry into many careers. Becker and Strauss (1956) observe:

> There are problems attending the systematic restriction of recruiting. Some kinds of persons, for occupationally irrelevant reasons (formally, anyway), may not be considered for some positions at all. Medical schools restrict recruiting in this way: openly, on grounds of "personality assessments," and covertly on ethnicity. Italians, Jews, and Negroes who do become doctors face differential recruitment into the formal and informal hierarchies of influence, power, and prestige in the medical world. Similar mechanisms operate at the top and the bottom of industrial organizations. (pp. 255-256)

Career control. Career access suggests that people can have differing degrees of control over their own and others' careers. Although ostensibly a person should have the greatest control over his or her own life chances, that may not be the case—as small children, the elderly, the stigmatized, and the impoverished know. Power and its influence, whether legitimate or illegitimate, are central to the shaping and molding of all careers. However, any assessment of power and its application must do more than assert that organizations or societies make certain classes of individuals act in certain ways. Power and influence are always filtered through interpersonal relationships, and in the final analysis involve one individual exerting authority (however legitimate) over another. Thus negative power—the threat to kill or to punish, for example—often leads persons to act in ways they find repulsive and repugnant. But the main point is that because careers involve others, power, influence, and controlling strategies are intrinsic to careers.

Encounters, sometimes called *turning points* (Strauss, 1959) or *epiphanies,* are those moments when individuals have a new and often drastically different set of self-identities thrust upon them. Mental patients who undergo mortification rites (in which their identities may be challenged), military inductees who have their identity signs (such as their clothing) removed, and brides who walk down the aisle find that after the encounter they cannot return to the past in an unaltered form. In this sense, we can see that the career is continually being affected by matters not entirely under the control of the person.

Career phases. In general, careers can be plotted in terms of a set of phases or substages. Thus the medical career may have at least four stages: (a) wishing to become a doctor, (b) gaining admission into medical school, (c) acquiring a clientele after graduation, and (d) developing a set of informal relationships with medical colleagues. Each of these stages could be broken into subphases: making it through the first, second, third, and fourth years; securing a place to practice; and so on. Many careers have institutional markers that go with them. Thus Goffman (1961b) observes that the mental patient's career falls into three phases: prepatient, inpatient, and postpatient. Location in or out of the institution that controls the activities associated with the control will place the person in or out of that career. In this way, all persons who have not yet been—but will be—hospitalized for mental illness are prepatients. It would be wrong to assume that all careers are neatly patterned or phased, however; it is difficult, for example, to plot the marriage career accurately. In this sense many careers are open-ended.

Career flow. As our remarks on career phases suggest, careers are temporal processes that flow through ongoing elements of social organization (Glaser & Strauss, 1967, 1971). Some carry the individual into unwanted interactions (the mental patient). Others are more directly controlled by the person (marriage). The temporal elements of the career can be charted—each has a unique trajectory. Some trajectories are lingering; they speed up at certain points and then bog down, so to speak. Many deaths are like this (Strauss & Glaser, 1970). Some trajectories are rapid—a person dies soon after an automobile accident. And then, some careers move along at an even, predictable rate; a college student, for example, may move smoothly through freshman year to graduation 3 years later (Becker, Geer, & Hughes, 1968). In general, the flow—temporal shape—of a career will reflect its organizational embeddedness, which in turn is influenced by the person's ability to control time's passage—that is, a person may find that other persons or organizations structure how he or she utilizes time; persons vary in the degrees of control they can exercise over their own timetables. Organizational careers are more fixed and closed than are careers through marriages or friendships. Thus the more open-ended the career, the more likely it is that its temporal trajectory will be uneven, lingering, and emergent.

Moral Careers and Biographies

Whether or not they want to, all individuals have personal moral careers that encompass all of their experiences, actions, and commitments up to and including the present moment. Thus although many careers are optional, the personal moral career is not. Every individual, accordingly, has a set of accounts or stories that explain and justify the current status of his or her personal moral career. Sad tales are told by those who feel that their careers have gone astray; happy tales are told by those who are relatively pleased with the progress of their lives (Goffman, 1961b, pp. 150-154). In practice, most accounts fall somewhere between sad and happy; this is because a person's multiple identities are never at the same stage of completion, fulfillment, or accomplishment. So an individual will most likely develop a story that is specific to each ongoing career as well as a master story that accounts for all of them.

The presumed existence of personal careers leads people to make biographical assumptions about others. If they have only a minimum amount of information about a person's age, status, education, or family, they will almost necessarily impute a set of biographical details to that person. They will assume that he or she has a work history or a mental history. Thus the possession of a personal moral career makes everyone vulnerable to attack; we are accountable for our own careers, and occasionally may be called upon to elaborate just who we are and why we are as we are (Denzin, 1971). We turn now to the ways in which careers are linked with membership in social worlds.

The Moral Career of the Ex-Nun

Ebaugh (1984) has analyzed the career and self-experiences of women who leave the Catholic Church. Drawing on her own experiences as a former nun and on interviews with 60 women who left different Catholic orders, she analyzed the exit process and found that it could be broken down into six stages. In each stage, various different career others, different self-conceptions, and different interactional and organizational forces influenced and shaped the women's experiences.

In Stage 1, the nun began to doubt the Catholic Church and her place in it. A series of historical events created doubt for many nuns; after Vatican II, many Catholic orders were radically transformed. The three vows of poverty, chastity, and obedience remained fixed, but nuns began to doubt whether the Church was still serving their needs and whether they could meet the Church's needs. Group discussions were formed within the Church as nuns thrashed out what it meant to be a nun during this historic moment. For the first time in years, nuns began to interact with laypersons, coming into contact with changing social conceptions of men, women, marriage, God, and the Church in American society.

In Stage 2, the nun realized that she had the freedom to decide to stay or leave. Rome was granting dispensations from final vows on a regular basis, and it became well-known that one could leave the Church if one so desired. Ebaugh (1984) calls Stage 3 "trying out options." Nuns who were thinking of leaving engaged in imaginary role and self playing. They tried out new social identities they might enact if they were to leave the Church. They talked to nuns who had left the Church and visited friends who lived in apartments. They learned how to dress as laypersons, how to date, and how to establish family lives (Ebaugh, 1984, p. 166).

Ebaugh calls Stage 4 "the vacuum." In this stage the nun learned that if she left the Church her decision could not be retracted, because the orders were reluctant to readmit former members, and this caused anxiety and fear. The nuns compared the security of the order to the fear of leaving. For those nuns who wished to marry and have children, leaving had to be now or never. The fear of leaving kept many nuns in a state of nonbeing; they felt that they were both nuns and ex-nuns at the same time.

Stage 5, "the turning point," came when the nun actually crystallized the decision to leave. Many different events created this turning point: If a nun had been assigned a job she did not like, this helped her make the decision; if a nun felt that her order was not making the changes she desired, this also made the decision to leave easier. Many nuns saw the time of their final vows (the end of 6 years) as the time to leave.

Stage 6 is "creating the ex-role," or the ex-nun self. Ebaugh (1984) sees this as involving three problem areas: (a) intimacies, friendship, and sexuality; (b) presentation of self—including dress, makeup, and style; and (c) adjusting to and negotiating other people's reactions to the new identity as ex-nun (p. 171). All of the women Ebaugh interviewed resolved these problems differently. What all shared, however, was the fact they had to create a new moral career for themselves. They had to do this in the company of new career others, and they no longer had the institutional force of the Church behind them. In a basic sense, each ex-nun created a new social self with new identities and did this under uncertain social conditions (Kotarba, 1984, p. 230).

Identity Transformations

Travisano (1981) has offered an analysis of *alternation* and *conversion* as two different kinds of personal transformation. Alternations in identity are changes, transformations, and transitions to identities that are "prescribed or at least permitted within the person's established universes of discourse" (p. 244). Conversions are transitions to identities that are proscribed within the person's social world; they negate prior identities. In conversion, the person experiences intense inner struggle, great trauma, anxiety, and often fear. Travisano suggests that a typical conversion would be a case in which a person embraces a completely negative identity—for example, a Jew becoming a fundamental Christian. On the other hand, a person who shifts from being a Methodist to a Lutheran, or from being engaged to being married, experiences an alternation in identity.

Conversions in identity often involve radical changes in self-attitude, in career others, in interpersonal relationships, and in the basic languages individuals apply to themselves. Alternations in identity are less radical and sweeping in influence; changing from being a father to a grandfather, for example, is much less drastic than changing from being married to being widowed or divorced.

Identity changes, whether of the conversion or alternation kind, inform and change the individual's other identities; they also change the person's interactional world. Converts, such as ex-nuns, make their new identities central to almost all interactions (Travisano, 1981, p. 247). When identities change, social worlds change. Travisano suggests that ours is an age of alternation, but not of conversion: We pursue leisure, leave work at the office, and insist on personal fulfillment. This may be changing, however; as we noted in Chapter 1, for example, more and more people in our society are experiencing problems with drugs and alcohol. To the degree that the social worlds of recovery from alcohol and drug addiction continue to expand and grow, the identities of recovering alcoholic and recovering drug addict may become more and more common. Such identities are accomplished only through radical self-changes of the type Travisano calls conversion.

Dramatic Self-Change

Athens (1995) has recently outlined a theory of dramatic self-change that extends Travisano's insights into the process of conversion. Athens says that dramatic self-change, like conversion, is a long, arduous process involving five stages, which he labels fragmentation, provisionality, praxis, consolidation, and social segregation. In dramatic self-change a radical reorganization, or transformation, of the person's identities and personal meanings occurs: An active alcoholic becomes a recovering alcoholic, a young woman becomes an officer in the Marine Corps, a nun becomes an ex-nun. Such changes are often coerced, as in brainwashing (see below). Often this process is institutionalized, and persons are supervised or guided by mentors. But much dramatic self-change can occur outside the structures of formal organizations (Athens, 1995, p. 572). A brief discussion of Athens's five stages will help clarify these points.

Stage 1, *fragmentation,* is often started by a traumatic experience. The person confronts a loss, a death, a sudden shock. This traumatic event produces fragmentation, shattering the individual's previously taken-for-granted assumptions about him- or herself and the world. This emotional shock divides the self against itself, creating an upheaval. For example, the person is told that his or her mother or best friend has just been killed. The person is thrown into a state of shock at this news and experiences self-fragmentation.

In Stage 2, self-fragmentation is slowly replaced by a new set of *provisional* self-identities. The person tries out these identities in interaction with real and phantom others. These others are new people, different from those "of the former phantom community" (Athens, 1995, p. 575). In the third stage, *praxis,* the person subjects the new self to the test of experience. Athens suggests that if the self is validated by others, then success is experienced and the self becomes unified around this new identity (p. 578). If the self is not validated, the person can experience another crisis of confidence, another period of fragmentation.

Athens calls the fourth stage *consolidation.* In this phase the person integrates these new identities and phantom others into his or her self-system. The person begins to feel comfortable with the new self he or she has created. If this self, or set of selves, is embraced, then a dramatic transformation of self can be said to have occurred; Travisano's conversion has taken place. All that is now left is to leave the old world, where the shattered self once lived. This happens in Stage 5, *social segregation.* In this process the person moves to a new world where people who have shared experiences and identities live. The movement to the new world ends, for the time being, this particular experience of dramatic self-change.

But of course we never stop changing. We are forever entertaining new possibilities of identity alternation, conversion, and transformation.

Membership in Social Worlds

In discussing symbolic environments in Chapter 2, we touched on the concept of *social worlds*—groupings of individuals bound together by networks of communication or universes of discourse. Whether the members are geographically proximate or not, they share important symbolizations and hence also share perspectives on "reality." It is significant that the term *social world* is commonly used to refer to such abstract collectivities as the worlds of theater, skiing, stamp collecting, and bird-watching, and to occupational groupings like those of medicine and science. The concept, however, is equally applicable to almost any collectivity—including families, perhaps—if we emphasize communication and membership, for membership is not merely a matter of physical or official belonging but also of shared symbolization, experiences, and interests.

The idea of the social world implies that members may be scattered in space. A family does not disintegrate merely because the members no longer live together (Hess & Handel, 1959). People who play chess and follow chess competitions live all over the world; these players can talk about and play chess with anyone, no matter where they may travel. Stamp collectors also belong to an immensely scattered world; they can visit virtually any sizable city in the world and find a store that deals in stamps, where they can find other collectors with whom they can swap stamps and stories. Some social worlds, of course, are less than international in scope, and some may even be quite localized, but the symbolic character of their membership is no less true.

These examples imply that members of a social world can come from diverse backgrounds. Baseball fans discourse enthusiastically and heatedly across the boundaries of social class, region, and age. A cousin of one of the authors is the president of a large corporation and also an avid collector of Australian two-pence stamps. Once, when traveling on business, he arranged to meet another collector; after 2 hours of conversation about stamps, he discovered that the other collector was also a corporation official. Some social worlds, however, do not draw members from such a diversity of backgrounds; they are more closely linked with class, sex, occupation, and economic level. The world of labor union officials is closely linked with socioeconomic background; conversely, polo fans and collectors of antique Chinese porcelain generally are not "working-class." Until recent years, fishing enthusiasts have seemed to be mostly men, and mostly women have been involved with the world of fashion.

Self-Control and Self-Change

In earlier chapters we considered how the internal environment of the individual is categorized, perceived, and brought into systematic relation with the outside world. Central to this process are the development of self-awareness, the acquisition of language, and the ability to put the self in the perspective of another individual. Society, as Cooley (1902) argues, exists inside the individual in the form of language and thought. Society and the individual, to use his phrase, are "two sides of the same coin." We wish to develop this point one step further by examining in greater detail the links that join self-control, social control, and the transformations of self that emerge during the interaction process.

In Chapter 8 we noted that individuals act in particular ways to salvage and enhance their self-conceptions. Here we examine those situations in which individuals often find themselves denied the rights of esteem. Few individuals submit voluntarily to derogation, embarrassment, or self-mortification. Such activities do occur, however, and with a patterned regularity that crosscuts small groups, total institutions, and intimate friendship circles. We will examine the circumstances that give rise to these interactional experiences.

We propose the following model of analysis. Individuals can *cede self-control*—that is, give up a degree of autonomy over their thoughts and actions—voluntarily (as in hypnosis) or involuntarily (as in a mental hospital or a prison camp), or they can find, quite unexpectedly, that in the course of an emergent interactional episode their fellow individuals have suddenly turned against them. Or they may find that compounds they have ingested suddenly leave them with no immediate control over their own thoughts and actions.

If we examine the sources to which self-control can be ceded, the following distinctions are relevant. First, individuals may voluntarily give over control to another individual, perhaps a psychiatrist or a physician. Second, they can place themselves in the hands of a small group. Third, they may find that they are under the control of a complex organization, perhaps the military or a mental hospital. Fourth, they may commit themselves to, or find that they are under the control of, an ideology or an abstract cause, such as communism or a deviant cult. In a strict sense, commitment to a cause leads the individual into direct interactions with other individuals who may be caught up in organizations or small groups. This set of distinctions produces 12 possible relationships between the source of ceding control and the mode of ceding control. It is beyond the scope of this chapter to discuss these 12 ideal-type cases; we only note in passing that the relationship between who controls the individual and how that control has been gained is quite complex. Further, we must indicate that in some situations single individuals gain control over broad segments of the population, as politicians do. It must also be noted that labeling behavior as *voluntary* or *involuntary* is a fundamentally contestable judgment, Much law and psychiatry revolve around where to draw this line. Finally, throughout this discussion the question of what is given up must be raised continually. Few individuals find themselves in situations where all aspects of their lives have fallen under the complete control of other individuals or groups. Some slices of the self inevitably remain free from the control of others, even the decision to die. That is, coercion is seldom complete; only parts of the individuals' activities and self-conceptions come under the control of others. Even during instances of potentially total coercion (prison camps, solitary confinement), individuals attempt to keep control over the "deepest" and most sacred parts of their selves. They will fight to the bitter end to maintain segments of self-respect, preserve control over their own thoughts, and protect the sanctity, privacy, and inviolability of their physical bodies.

Our discussion is guided by two central questions: How is an individual's control of his or her own actions related to societal control of those actions? And how can an individual's actions be controlled by others? To answer these questions, we shall discuss several topics that may seem quite unrelated; however, each bears on the issues of self-control and social control. We discuss below the nature of voluntary behavior, the loss of self-control, and the institutionally induced changes in individuals that cause them either to cede a measure of their own control to others or to change radically the social bases of their own self-control. We also will examine the circumstances of group commitment, embarrassment, degradation, and paranoia.

Voluntary Behavior

The popular conception of voluntary behavior is that it involves control of behavior by an internal psychological force called *will* or *willpower.* This force is seen as independent of any specific biological or neurological structure and is usually believed to be "free" and, therefore, essentially unpredictable. Its most typical manifestation is in choosing among alternatives.

The discerning student will recognize in this common but naive view the same dualistic distinction that is generally made between thinking and language. Just as language supposedly expresses thinking and is its vehicle, so voluntary behavior is supposed to be merely an expression of the person's will.

A sounder, more scientific view is the conception of voluntary behavior as an activity that depends upon the internalization of language. We have noted that as one ascends the evolutionary scale from the simplest forms of life to humans, the central nervous system assumes greater and greater dominance. Internal cortical processes are not determined solely by stimuli from outside the nervous system, but depend also upon stimuli that originate within the system. Voluntary behavior, from this point of view, depends upon the ability of people to initiate responses within themselves that in turn inhibit or facilitate other responses. These controlling responses are verbal in nature or are derived from verbal behavior.

Luria (1960) notes that people do not control their behavior directly by the exertion of "willpower," but can do so only indirectly, through the mediation of verbal self-stimulation. For example, if a despondent woman is urged to "buck up and be cheerful," she cannot do so merely by wishing it. However, if one can direct her attention to more cheerful subjects by talking with her or by inducing her to engage in some recreational activity, such as a game of tennis, the desired result may be accomplished.

From this point of view, willpower ceases to be conceived as a psychological force and becomes a number of complexly interrelated central processes deriving from the internalization of language and speech. Just as one may jog one's memory by tying a string around one's finger, so the culturally derived language mechanisms function as mediating and structuring devices through which self-regulation is achieved. *Self-control and voluntary behavior are thus conceived as products of external influences emanating from the cultural environment, rather than as the unfolding of vague, disembodied innate propensities of the organism.* Some sort of conception of this general nature seems to be required to make sense of the kinds of phenomena considered in this section.

Like the notion of will itself, the idea of "free will" is based upon a false view of symbolic behavior. As a corrective, we may note several points. To begin with, "free will" is not entirely free, for it is bounded, restricted, and limited by the culture of the actor. Thus it does not occur to the readers of this book to make choices involving the values of the Bantu or Balinese, or to act like these people. This may appear to be a trite observation, but its truth is often ignored; for example, it is commonplace to blame persons who, from an objective point of view, ought not be blamed. Thus children are often held responsible for stealing before they know what it means to steal. Our blaming rests upon the assumption—often false—that persons know better and have genuine choices of attitudes and acts. Whatever "will" may be, it cannot operate outside the confining limits of the actor's system of symbols.

Human social behavior is organized symbolically. Human freedom is thus a relative matter. Humans are not entirely bound by the physical conditions of space and time, but they are enclosed within symbolic systems. The thoughts of a prisoner in solitary confinement cannot be controlled by his jailers, but they are controlled and limited by the social groups that have imposed their standards, moral codes, and symbols upon the prisoner.

Blondel (1939) modifies this position, arguing that it is not necessary to deny genuine individual autonomy merely because a person must always make choices within a framework provided by society. Freedom of the individual, he contends, is itself a social product. Human beings, in contrast to lower animals, are free precisely because they are social animals living primarily in a symbolic world. To this should be added a point that we have already made in another context—namely, that no two situations are ever completely identical. Hence all behavior possesses some degree of novelty, and some of it requires genuine decisions. The discovery of values and the consequent organization of behavior along new lines free humans from slavish obedience to tradition; at the same time, tradition enters into the organization of new as well as customary behavior.

Social Control and Commitment to Groups

Social control is often erroneously seen as something that is achieved by formal governmental agencies and officially promulgated rules and regulations. Actually, most people do what they ought to or have to do simply because they want to. It is only against this background of willing conformity that the formal agencies of control can be effective.

We can summarize this argument by saying that social control and self-control are interlocked and interdependent processes. This interrelationship is brought about because people find self-fulfillment, self-expression, and a sense of identity and personal worth primarily through commitment to various kinds of groups and the standards of those groups. This point is well stated by Kanter (1972), who, on the basis of her study of communes, remarks:

> For communal relations to be maintained, what a person is willing to give to the group, behaviorally and emotionally, and what it in turn expects from him, must be coordinated and mutually reinforcing. This reciprocal relationship, in which both what is given to the group and what is received from it are seen by the person as expressing his true nature and as supporting his concept of self, is the core commitment to a community. (pp. 65-66)

In terms of this statement, we can say that social control can be effective only when persons identify with the group and internalize its values so that it becomes essential to their own sense of self-esteem and personal worth to act so as to support the social order. They hold a sense of involvement and belonging; they think of the group as an extension or part of themselves and make its values and rules their own personal values and rules. The group has become a part of them; it exerts its influence over them in symbolic as well as direct behavioral ways. Again, we quote Kanter (1972):

> Commitment links self-interest to social requirements. . . . When a person is committed, what he wants to do is the same as what he has to do, and this gives to the group what it needs to maintain itself at the same time that he gets what he needs to nourish his own sense of self. (pp. 66-67)

As Kanter says, "A committed person is loyal and involved; he has a sense of be longing, a feeling that the group is an extension of himself and he is an extension of the group" (p. 66). That is, in social control there is always self-control, and in self-control there is always social control. By the same token, lack of self-control is often a reflection of an absence of social control. But without individuals committed to their maintenance, social groups would collapse. In this sense, persons create and contribute to the very situations that control their own lives, fates, and careers.

Embracement and Distance

When individuals have committed themselves instrumentally, emotionally, and morally to a social group, they may be said to have *embraced* that group's universe of discourse. Embracement produces both moral solidarity and a solidified group perspective. It is a mistake, however, to assume that all members of any group mutually and with equal enthusiasm commit themselves to the group's demands. In a different context, Goffman (1961a) has introduced the concept of *role distance* to describe those moments when individuals place a wedge between themselves and the role they are playing. Adults riding merry-go-rounds, for example, typically act as if they wish they were not seated on those wooden horses, whereas young children vigorously throw themselves into the activity of horse rider. In the present context, we can propose that on occasion members of all groups place a wedge between themselves and the demands that their groups place on them. These "self-distancing" activities may include refusals to meet the requests of other group members or may be displayed in progressive withdrawal from the group entirely. There is, then, a constant tension between the demands of the group and the demands individuals place on themselves. Total, complete, and continuous commitment to and embracement of social groups is an infrequent occurrence. More typical are moments of heightened involvement, followed by periods of disinvolvement, disengagement, and self-distancing.

Propaganda

The problem we are concerned with now is the relationship between self-control and propaganda. For example, consider the man who implicitly believes what he reads in his favorite newspaper, what the latest government handout says, or what a particular television commentator announces. Is this person really a free agent? Or is the dupe of propaganda comparable to the hypnotized man who says, does, and apparently believes whatever he is told to say, do, or believe? If the latter answer is accepted, then it is probably necessary for us to admit that we are almost continuously, to varying degrees, being manipulated by outside persons, agencies, and forces that shape our symbolic environments, our conceptions of the world. They do this in ways that often have little relationship to the real objective world—whatever that may be. Granting this situation, the important point really may be whether we are permitted to cherish the delusions of intellectual mastery of our environments and of being free and autonomous individuals. These, by the way, are delusions that the subject who acts out posthypnotic suggestions also ordinarily entertains.

Persons who are relatively unaware of the pervasiveness of propaganda—having committed themselves to a general political or social philosophy—tend to select media sources that present them with views that they are predisposed to accept. They also tend to have friends and belong to groups that reinforce their opinions and that rely on the same sources for support of their opinions. In this process of mutual reinforcement, there is selective inattention to information and interpretations not in harmony with the person's basic social and political assumptions, which may be anywhere on the political spectrum from the extreme left to the extreme right (Altheide, 1985; Blumer, 1978; Smelser, 1963). Some persons commonly have the comfortable illusion that they have valid and reliable information about, and are responding rationally to, their environment and have it under control in an intellectual sense.

On the other hand, there are people who feel that they are being manipulated by external forces that control events, social policy, and the flow of information. They tend to emphasize the unreliability of mass-media reports and interpretations. They commonly assume the existence of extensive behind-the-scene news conspiracies by rich and powerful persons, corporations, and other organizations to manipulate people, events, and information in their own interests for the sake of wealth, power, or other material advantage. People with such views tend to feel a sense of futility and helplessness with respect to broad social and political issues and often simply ignore them and commit themselves only to small, restricted groups like the family. Others who believe that things can be changed may commit themselves to reform groups or "revolutionary" movements.

Interactional Loss of Self-Control

In the preceding section we discussed the situations in which individuals cede self-control to a group or cause. Often voluntary and positive in consequence, these exercises in self-exchange involve planning and reciprocal commitments by the persons ceding control and by those who receive their goods, resources, and self-identities. They gain something positive for what they give. The tenuous yet complex relationship between selves and others can be further elaborated through an examination of the situation of *interactional loss.* Such moments, which may be planned or unplanned, collusively based or emergent in tone, self-initiated or other initiated, are those occasions when individuals find their fellow interactants either have unexpectedly turned against them or now define them as less-than-competent selves. Although on occasion planned—as when a person is a defendant in a divorce case—most typically these moments arise unexpectedly and catch people off guard. Incidents of this kind range from deliberate embarrassment or harassment to degradation ceremonies, self-mortification rituals, and collusively based conspiracies to drive someone from an organization. In such situations, people find that their abilities to control and protect their valued self-identities have been denied, if not suddenly taken away.

In this section we examine the conditions that give rise to this interactional loss of self-control. For purposes of simplicity we focus on three forms of interactional loss: emergent loss, as seen in embarrassment; preplanned exclusion and self-loss, as witnessed in the degradation ceremony; and emergent exclusion, which is common in instances of imputed paranoia or mental illness.

Embarrassment: The Case of Emergent Self-Loss

Any instance of emergent or planned self-loss requires time. Some moments are preceded by events that unfold in a serial fashion. That is, an individual is not just mortified, embarrassed, or degraded; a set of mutually held definitions of the situation must be brought into play if an instance of self-loss is to occur. In a sense, individuals cooperate in their own mortification, and they act so as to sustain or justify definitions in which they have been judged as less than competent. It is a mistake to assume that when self-control is ceded to others, this ceding involves only one set of actors—those taking from the individual in question. It involves at least two parties: one to offer a definition and another to accept or fight off that definition. Such moments are interactional productions.

Consequently, we can see that it takes two parties to produce an instance of embarrassment—one party who acts in a less than propitious manner and another who acts on those untoward actions. In this sense we agree with Gross and Stone (1964), who argue:

> Embarrassment exaggerates the core dimensions of social transaction, bringing them to the eye of the observer in an almost naked state. Embarrassment occurs whenever some *central* assumption in a transaction has been *unexpectedly* and unqualifiedly discredited for at least one participant. . . . Moreover embarrassment is infectious. It may spread, incapacitating others not previously incapacitated. It is a destructive disease. In the wreckage left by embarrassment lie the broken foundations of social transactions. (p. 1)

According to Goffman's (1961a) formulations, embarrassment produces moments of "flooding out." Individuals lose control over themselves, their occasions, and their respective involvements. Action stops, and attempts to smooth over the flawed episode only acknowledge that something untoward has occurred. In short, to act on an instance of embarrassment can be as embarrassing as the original episode itself. Hence individuals employ elaborate avoidance or defensive techniques to act as if an instance of embarrassment has not occurred. But these strategies need not concern us now. More to the point are those actions that produce the interactional discomfort of embarrassment. Following Goffman (1961a) and Gross and Stone (1964), we can note that any of the following acts or activities can cause an embarrassing incident in the flow of interaction. First, an individual can display a lack of poise. He or she may stumble, spill a drink, unaccountably touch another person, or perhaps give off an odor that discredits any claim of respectability. A person may also lose poise by intruding into the private settings of others, dressing improperly for a particular social occasion, or hosting a party at which there is an inadequate supply of food and drink.

By failing to measure up to the demands of the occasion, the individual calls into question the actions of all those who have conformed to social expectations. To be in the company of an embarrassing actor not only challenges one's own credibility, but raises the question of why that individual's actions should be regarded as embarrassing. And if that person is judged embarrassing, why are his or her actions so judged and not those of another person? In these instances, embarrassing actions provoke both sympathy and discomfort. All individuals can recall moments when they acted, or could have acted, in similar fashion. For this reason, actors typically cooperate to pull one another through embarrassing transactions. But for the individual in question, shame, guilt, and a lack of self-respect are produced. Credible individuals should not embarrass others.

If loss of poise produces embarrassment, then we can see that presenting an inappropriate identity or incorrect identification can also disrupt the flow of interaction. Instances of misnaming, forgotten names, forgotten titles, and mistaken kinship affiliations are in this category. A divorced woman may be asked, innocently, how her former husband is doing. A college president may be misidentified by a member of the police. A faculty member may be mistaken for a janitor, perhaps because he is dressed like a janitor. Misidentifications intermingle with actions that disturb the sequential flow of sociable gatherings. Individuals may attend a party thinking they have been invited because they are friends of the host or hostess; however, they find they have been invited not as guests, but as actors who might contribute to the status of the party givers. Having misread the character of the occasion, they may then act so as to quickly bring their role to a conclusion. They may refuse to talk, talk to excess, exaggerate the effects of alcohol, or demand to be placed center stage, thus juggling the career and development of the party. They actively intrude into the gathering so as to gain some control over their place in it. Feeling that they have been embarrassed because of their own misidentifications, they make no attempt to turn the tables.

Deliberate Embarrassment

The foregoing examples of embarrassment are focused on unanticipated acts and actions that challenge the credibility of someone in a concrete situation. These accidental acts are less consequential than those that are deliberately produced, for if the individual does not anticipate such an activity, he or she is less accountable for its consequences. Deliberate embarrassment (Gross

& Stone, 1964) is more severe. Here members of a group plan in advance to discredit one of the group's members. They may do so to facilitate socialization into a role or a preferred activity or identity—for example, hazing in the military or the college fraternity discourages one set of actions and rewards another—or to halt the performance of an individual who is challenging the social group. Scapegoating, identity slurs, misrepresentations of integrity, and charges of malfeasance set the offended party off from other members of the group. Thus embarrassment serves as a social control device for social groups. This suggests the third function of embarrassment: It reasserts and reaffirms power alignments, because only certain categories of individuals can legitimately embarrass others. Thus embarrassment typically flows from the top down. It is bad form for a low-status actor to embarrass a superior, and those with low status have less interactional power to command.

Degradation Ceremonies: Preplanned Loss

With the exception of planned embarrassment, most embarrassing incidents emerge unpredictably; neither their definers nor their actors anticipate their occurrence. These incidents are haphazardly, rather awkwardly accepted instances of status forcing. The problematic individual is forced to accept an otherwise unacceptable definition of self. Degradation ceremonies describe planned and anticipated instances of status forcing in which derelict individuals know in advance that they will lose credibility. Indeed, they may be shamed and openly required to plead guilty.

Garfinkel (1956) has described the conditions that give rise to successful degradation ceremonies. Persons who are being degraded must be placed outside the everyday moral order and defined as a threat to that order. They may be defined as political criminals, "sex fiends," child molesters, or murderers. Their actions must be cast in moral terms that threaten the existence of the social group, and their accusers must be defined as persons who are morally superior. The accusers will evoke higher moral values that witnesses accept and will be defined as legitimate upholders of those values. If the accusers are successful in their attempts, the accused individuals have no options open; they must accept their new status. Degradation ceremonies force them to yield to the wishes of others. They give up control over their own moral careers—that control now lies in the hands of others.

Paranoia: Emergent Exclusion and Self-Loss

Planned exclusionary rituals are set up in advance and give charged actors little control over their fate. Such rituals can be contrasted with emergent exclusion. Often individuals begin to sense a wedge between themselves and others. They become uneasy, hypertensive; they overreact to the thoughts and actions of others. Such persons are often termed *paranoid*—their behavior is out of line with the realities of social interaction. Lemert (1962), in a series of case studies of paranoid individuals, has come to different conclusions. He suggests that paranoid individuals indeed may be reacting accurately to the specifics of their social situations. His analysis is instructive and may be utilized as an instance of a situation in which neither the individual in doubt nor that person's fellow interactants wish to alter their social relationships. The individual has no desire to be excluded, and the other interactants have no desire to exclude. However, through a course of events, both parties come to reject one another. The person who loses the most is the actor defined as paranoid. He or she may have nowhere to turn and may be unable to pinpoint the causes of the exclusion; furthermore, the individual's fellows may not be able to recount accurately exactly why it was they came to feel uncomfortable in that person's presence.

The emergence of exclusion rituals follows a relatively predictable career. First, there is an alteration in ongoing relationships. Persistent interpersonal difficulties between the individual and interactive others lead to a collapse in trust and common understanding. The death of a relative, a threatened status loss, or a failure to be promoted can produce a sense of uneasiness on the part of the "preparanoid" individual. This uneasiness, in turn, produces a series of overreactive behaviors toward superiors and close intimates. Arrogance, insults, and exploitations of the weaknesses of others may occur. Third, the individual begins to act in ways that others judge to be unreliable and dangerous. At this point the person undergoes a set of redefinitions of both himself and others; he feels they are belittling him. A set of *spurious interactions* emerges. The individual avoids others and is avoided by them in turn; conversation drops to a minimum, and the individual begins to exclude himself deliberately from their company. At the same time, they are gossiping behind his back and excluding him from their sociable interactions. Conspiratorial actions now develop. Others openly plot to remove the deviant from their presence; correspondingly, the individual may plot to have them removed or seek relocation elsewhere. Delusion sets in. The individual is denied interactional feedback and so has no reliable "reality checks" for his inferences and hunches. No one will talk to him. Soon the individual moves into his own social world, and he may, as Goffman (1971) notes, produce an insanity of place both for himself and for others:

> The manic declines to restrict himself to the social game that brings order and sense to our lives. Through his antics he gives up "his" self-respect, this being the reward we would allow him to have for himself as a reward for keeping a social place that may contain no other satisfaction for him. The manic gives up everything a person can be, and gives up, too, the everything we make out of jointly guarded dealings. His doing so, and doing so for any of a multitude of independent reasons, reminds us what our everything is, and then reminds us that this everything is not very much. A somewhat similar lesson is taught by other categories of troublemakers who do not keep their place. (p. 390)

In the end, what began as a minor disturbance in interpersonal relationships produces a massive realignment of self and others. A new deviant appears. He loses, as does everyone else. Emergent self-loss of the exclusionary variety vividly highlights the point made earlier—namely, the social order is a symbolic order that must, however tacitly, be jointly maintained by the actions of cooperating individuals.

Recapitulation: Losses and Gains

Embarrassment, degradation, and the dynamics of organizational exclusion are descriptions of three situations in which individuals lose more than they gain in their contracts with their outside social worlds. Whether fleeting (as with embarrassment), preplanned (as in degradation), or emergent and long-term (as with paranoia), agents of social control—who after all are fellow interactants—deliberately and unwittingly deny one another's claims of self-worth and self-esteem.

This is not to imply that all instances of self- and social control result in losses for one or more parties. Indeed, our earlier discussion of communes suggests that on many occasions individuals gain a great deal by giving themselves over to a social group, a cause, or an organization.

Institutionally Induced Changes in Self-Control

Ceding Control

People may also deliberately cede a measure of their self-control under quite regulated institutional conditions. This is what happens when students allow psychologists to convert them into experimental hypnotic subjects. However, there are less equivocal and more ordinary instances of this very complicated social process. We present one from a great many possible instances to clarify this point.

Under certain conditions, people allow physicians and nurses to do things to their bodies that otherwise they would not permit. The physician says to a woman, "I must operate on you." The patient then allows the physician to use drugs that render her temporarily insensible. She allows the physician to remove a bodily part. She also allows the hospital staff to control some other sectors of her life and behavior. They regulate her movements by confining her to bed or to her room. They regulate her waking hours by taking away her control over when she will sleep (giving her drugs to induce sleep), when she will eat (feeding her in accordance with a given schedule), or how she will eat (feeding her intravenously). All these events are fairly institutionalized, regularized, or routinized, because the hospital is organized for this purpose. If the patient's condition warrants different kinds of control, she may be sent from one medical service to another within the same hospital.

If we observe closely, we also note that the ceding of control from patient to hospital staff is not a static phenomenon. As the patient's condition worsens, she may agree, explicitly or implicitly, to further loss of control over her own activities. As she gets better she is given back some of that control, or she requests or demands that some control be ceded back to her. Disagreements occur daily between staff and patients in hospitals over just this matter, and a considerable amount of negotiation that takes place within hospitals pertains to setting these matters straight. A study of cardiac patients with infarctions has shown that after patients have been hospitalized, they tend to judge their condition by the amount of pain they still experience. If there is considerable pain, they will not wish to recover as much control as the staff wishes them to regain, and the staff may be annoyed at their overanxiety. More frequently the annoyance runs in the opposite direction, because the staff will not allow patients to act as they feel they have the right to act. Because most illnesses run a course (upward or downward), negotiation over control between patient and staff is potentially, if not always actually, an explosive process.

"Brainwashing" or "Thought Reform"

In the preceding subsection we dealt with institutionalized forms of ceding control. We turn now to a related phenomenon wherein a person retains self-control but changes both behavior and the bases of controlling behavior under the guidance of others. Commonly, we recognize that any person who enters a new organization and begins to believe in what it stands for may then begin to "conform" to its standards. Even skeptics may thus be converted after they have entered a group just to scoff at it. Naturally, there are many obstacles to these kinds of conversions, especially to well-nigh total conversion, as when an Episcopalian joins a radically different religious group, such as Jehovah's Witnesses.

Radical changes require that adult persons undergo turmoil. If some group or organization wishes them to change the bases of their self-control and thought in some given direction, they must be thrown into turmoil or self-doubt while simultaneously being led to new ways of seeing themselves and the world. Thus, if their loyalties to colleagues, friends, and parents are to be loosened, these people must be impugned, attacked, shaken from pedestals, and questioned. A certain amount of self-doubt and doubt of others can be induced by verbal means, but it is also essential that crucial situations be established wherein the persons see themselves and the others, if possible, acting in ways that run counter to their cherished conceptions.

After the Communist revolution in China, and intermittently since, so-called thought-reform techniques were used all over China as part of a mass conversion of the citizenry. The explicit or implicit aims, according to Schein, Schneier, and Barker (1961), were to create a new type of Chinese citizen, change attitudes, produce an obedient and energetic Party worker, initiate into Communist society those individuals who were not yet committed ideologically, and develop ideological unanimity throughout the land. *Thought reform* was essentially an attempt to break old loyalties, principally to family and social class, and to develop new loyalties to country and Party. The tactics used on citizens varied considerably, depending both on those in charge of reform and on the status of those to be reformed. Some of the same tactics were also used on foreigners in China, and later on captured prisoners during the Korean War (Lifton, 1961, p. 25).

Hunter (1951, p. 25) has described the tactics used on students in the years immediately after the Chinese revolution. To begin with, propaganda and lectures unveiled a new terminology—that of the Communists—that ran counter to familiar concepts in a great many ways. The meanings of the new terms could not be fully grasped at first, but they provided an initial vocabulary for the reinterpretation of events, persons, and groups. Students were sent to work in the fields so that they would feel like the common people. They were sent to see village justice wreaked upon former landlords—

often a harrowing experience for the onlookers, whose parents might also be landlords. Any who could not bear to watch were accused of sentimentality—a characteristic of the ruling class. Students had to write detailed biographical essays ("thought seduction essays") and turn them in to their teachers, who criticized the essays as revealing "deep-set contradictions" in their lives. The point of this criticism was to force the students to reveal publicly their former beliefs and actions, especially when they themselves wanted to forget them because they were not in harmony with Party teachings. Students were then induced or compelled to confess their sins in class, such as admitting that they had helped the Japanese and so on. Criticism of each student by every other was encouraged, and those who held back were prodded with name-calling ("lagging-behind particle") and other punishments.

Presumably, some people were relieved by making their avowals and were supported by others' commentaries; in general, however, such public avowal and criticism are very destructive. Ordinarily, one is protected from certain kinds of adverse comments by the conspiracy of silence that governs polite intercourse. Selective inattention does not get much chance to operate effectively in procedures such as those we have described, because in such circumstances the individual's illusions about him- or herself are challenged directly. This challenge was increased by the mutual hostility engendered during these sessions. The right to privacy was invaded; not only did current acts and thoughts come under scrutiny, but the intimate details of past history were examined. Students were asked to explain the "why" of their acts, and then alternative motivations were pressed upon them.

The turning point in this brainwashing process appears to have been the genuine public concession, when students got down to rock bottom and accused themselves of having been wastrels, exploiters, cowards, and so forth. This amounted to a genuine public relinquishing of past identity. The anguish attending this process is suggested by the cutting off of contacts with parents, the renaming of one's family as "exploiters," and the sundering of relations with spouses. It was at this point that the more serious consequences of the new perspective began to come home to the converts; there was no turning back.

One of the final steps for the Chinese students was the writing of "thought conclusion essays," autobiographies written to show how far they had come in the desired direction and in what ways; these essays included ruthless renunciation of the past. Students had to read their essays aloud to the class and then submit to public criticism. When they had finished with this ordeal, they were compelled to rewrite their essays along more acceptable lines.

There can be no doubt that thought reform is a technique of what one might call *forced conversion* or *coercive persuasion,* and that it sometimes brings about fundamental and permanent changes in outlook. Lifton's extensive interviews with foreigners who had lived in China and who had been subjected to thought reform also suggest some of the operative mechanisms and personal strategies that allowed some people to escape full conversion. Lifton notes that the "first form of resistance is the acquisition of a sense of understanding, a theory about what is going on, an awareness of being manipulated." This awareness and these theories give a partial sense of control over the situation and help "to dispel the fear of the unknown and the sense of complete helplessness." A second important tactic is the avoidance of emotional participation, the prisoner remaining "as much as possible outside the communication system of thought reform." Some of the individuals Lifton studied did this by refusing to learn Chinese if they did not know it and by keeping contacts with Chinese prison-mates to a minimum. The agents of thought reform were kept somewhat off balance also by a show of stoicism and displays of humor. A final and most important "resistance technique" was that of "identity reinforcement." Thus a Catholic bishop kept reminding himself that the Communist remolding was really a test of his Catholic steadfastness. "He sought always to maintain himself as a priest struggling against his selfishness, rather than a stubborn imperialist spy. To do this, he needed a continuous awareness of his own world of prayer, Catholic ritual, missionary experience, and Western cultural heritage." Because nothing in the prison reminded him of these anchors, he had to find them within himself. One prisoner reminded himself by secretly drawing pictures of scenes from his boyhood. But Lifton notes that none of these tactics was entirely successful, for thought reform had some impact on all of the foreign prisoners he studied.

In short, brainwashing, conversion, and other socially or institutionally induced changes illustrate how the bases of an individual's self-control may shift without any genuine loss of self-control except what the person may wish to cede to some group or organization. It would be erroneous to assume that in these induced processes individuals simply are coerced to change their beliefs and behaviors. If coerced, they may leave the organization or commit suicide; they may act conformingly as if they believed, but in fact control their behavior so as to pass muster in what might otherwise be situations dangerous to life itself. In such situations, even coerced behavior may have privately derisive meanings. This is a phenomenon we all recognize, even when we cannot produce particular evidence of it—for instance, army privates who mock their officers with salutes that are executed just properly enough so that the implied disrespect is not recognized.

Demoralization

Brainwashing and thought reform are examples of situations in which persons retain self-control but change because of institutional forces. We will now consider a closely related form of institutionally induced changes in self-control: demoralization. Demoralization may occur within a military organization, in a school system, or in an urban neighborhood. After Shibutani (1978, pp. 5-6), we define demoralization as a condition that exists within an organized group when there is a breakdown of collective effort and an unwillingness on the part of persons to continue to perform tasks; it is often characterized by bickering, factionalism, fights, arguments, and a general loss of morale. A demoralized group performs its functions in a desultory and sluggish manner. Absenteeism may be high, members develop low self-esteem, and there is no group pride. Members may pursue hedonistic activities or lose themselves in drugs and alcohol (Shibutani, 1978, p. 5). When confronted by adversity, members may disintegrate and become preoccupied with self-preservation.

Consider the following example offered by Shibutani (1978). The situation described occurred at Fort Snelling, Minnesota, on October 17, 1945. The participants were Nisei (i.e., second-generation Japanese American) military trainees:

> The brawl started on a small streetcar—called the "dummy line." . . . it was crowded with soldiers. . . . in the pushing . . . one soldier, whose foot had been trampled, objected loudly and shoved the offender. . . . as the protagonists faced one another, the irate man screamed, "You white! You t'eenk you better dan me! Look at me! Yallow! . . . The outnumbered men declined to fight . . . they were set upon by the gang. One man was beaten to the ground. . . . he had been stabbed in the back. (p. 1)

This incident occurred with Company K, a Nisei unit characterized by high demoralization.

What causes demoralization? Shibutani enumerates a number of factors, including the following: First, if authority figures are disrespectful of a group, its goals, and its members, then the members may turn against the leader and act in a way that will undermine the leader's authority. In this way, the group begins to work against any conditions that could create high morale or group satisfaction. Second, if authority figures become demoralized, a state of near anarchy may be created in a group (Shibutani, 1978, p. 425). Members may then begin to fend only for themselves. Third, if violence breaks out, this contributes to more violence, which may undermine group goals. Members may then turn against one another. Fourth, as demoralization becomes established it sets in motion behaviors, emotions, and attitudes that assume a force of their own. That is, in a self-fulfilling fashion, members create conditions that promote greater demoralization. The members cede self-control to a self-destructive process that is interactional in nature. In the case of demoralization, then, individuals' control goes over to a process that is both self-destructive and destructive of a social group.

The discussion in this section suggests that the commitments that individuals make to others can carry significant biographical implications for their future career choices. For these and other reasons, people take some care over the choices they make. Furthermore, they are often led to develop and adopt sets of "self-protective" strategies that enhance their abilities to mold and direct their own lives. These strategies are often referred to as *coping devices.*

Coping Mechanisms

It is commonly remarked how extraordinarily obtuse we are in situations in which our self-esteem is involved. People often embark upon and continue in relationships with other people without much insight into the character of those relationships. Such blindness, it is generally understood, is explicable in terms of individuals' self-conceptions. Psychiatrists who deal with gross and persistent errors of this kind speak of them as *defense mechanisms, security operations,* and the like, the central idea being that the person meets supposed threats to self-regard with characteristic modes of defense. Defense modes include selective inattention, anxiety reduction, evasion of responsibility, rationalization, pretense, and the disowning of undesirable qualities in oneself.

The techniques of self-defense, or coping, that psychiatrists have characteristically stressed and that have often been picked up uncritically by sociologists are those that emphasize self-deception, avoidance, and reduction of information. Such classic forms of ego defense as repression, denial, reaction formation, isolation, and rationalization lean heavily upon minimizing the recognition of potentially traumatic aspects of experience, techniques characteristically used by those who go to psychiatrists. These coping devices are frequently pathological in nature in the sense that they may themselves create other problems for the person. There are, however, many other techniques of adjustment that are perhaps more successful and that are used by people who do not seek professional help. We refer to these more normal techniques as *coping mechanisms* rather than *defense mechanisms,* and we include a discussion of some of them along with others of the better-known classical variety.

Common Defense Mechanisms

In his theoretical treatment of anxiety, Sullivan (1953) points up some common defense mechanisms. Even in the earliest months, according to Sullivan, children encounter situations that arouse their anxiety, and they learn to grade them in terms of the anxiety they provoke and to stay away from those that are most severe. Young children handle unavoidable anxiety situations by a variety of means designed to minimize anxiety and maximize satisfaction. Sullivan states that "the self-system comes into being, because of, and can be said to have as its goal, the securing of necessary satisfaction without incurring much anxiety."

A fundamental conceptual device that children utilize, according to Sullivan, involves classifying their experiences as pertaining to the *good me,* the *bad me,* and the *not me.* The first category is for acts that are approved; the second is for acts that are disapproved, and hence induce some anxiety; and the third is for acts that are so anxiety-provoking that they are more or less disavowed or "dissociated." Sullivan notes that the *not me* is tied up with emotions of dread, horror, and loathing, and is expressed obliquely with a lack of awareness (for example, in nightmares).

The *self-system* arises from the child's attempt to avoid anxieties arising in interpersonal relations with significant others, especially with the mother. This system is not equivalent to an incorporation of the mother's perspective, but is based on the child's attempts to form a system of reaction that minimizes the anxiety that arises out of interactions with significant others (Sullivan, 1953, pp. 159-161). Sullivan maintains that protection against the paralyzing effects of severe anxiety is a necessity, and that learning to protect oneself is part of the individual's educational experience.

The self-system tends to become stabilized in a generalized defense against anxiety. According to Sullivan, the person then becomes "selectively inattentive" to happenings that could change him or her, because change itself leads to anxiety. Hence awareness of one's own acts is greatly restricted, as is the understanding of the acts of others. One need not assume with Sullivan that anxiety avoidance is the central feature of behavioral organization, but certainly ideas of self do interfere with what individuals notice and learn. People do strive to maintain self-esteem, and they raise defenses against threats to it.

A person with the insight into his own deficiencies and weaknesses and the situations in which they become manifest to others may consciously maneuver to avoid competitive games, for example, and may choose as companions persons who will not shame him by their superior skills or attainments. Thus the need to maintain self-regard often produces a vicious cycle: Those very situations wherein a weakness could be overcome are avoided. A good part of social relations is unconsciously devoted to the search for companions and activities that allow one's weaknesses to remain hidden or relatively unnoticed while one's stronger points are exploited.

Characteristic defenses of self may occur without the individual's realization of their nature. Some of these have been given names. For instance, a person who has failed to reach certain goals may substitute less ambitious ones in a general lowering of his or her level of aspiration. Another well-known device is *rationalizing,* which we use in this context to mean explaining away or excusing one's failure. Another method characteristically used by some people is the shifting of their own fault to another—this is known as *scapegoating* or *displacement.* Persons aware of undesirable qualities in themselves may bolster their self-esteem by *projecting* the same qualities onto others, as when a selfish person says that it is a selfish world (that is, that everyone else is selfish too). In the handling of personal relations, it is common for attack to be met by counterattack, whether verbal or physical. Among the more complex forms of defense is *identification* with an aggressor, which permits a vicarious sharing of some of the aggressor's strength.

The cultural patterning of defense and coping mechanisms is reflected in the existence of the conventions of politeness, which function—at least in part—to shield sensitive egos and to allow delicate relationships to exist. As with other forms of behavior, different mechanisms are stressed in different groups, and the standards of politeness and rudeness vary accordingly.

There are also conventionally sanctioned tactics for defending the self that are constantly used in a conscious manner. These include such ordinary devices as physical withdrawal, changing the subject, doing favors for one's opponent, using flattery, creating diversions, sparring for time, and exploiting the vulnerable points of the attacker. Human interaction is such that individuals' statuses are often challenged, feelings hurt, and reputations impugned by the acts—intentional or not—of others. Anyone who does not learn to cope with these occurrences is in a peculiarly helpless and vulnerable position.

Coping by Detachment

Transcendence of self is made possible by the fact that through using symbols and taking the roles of others, one may take the view of an outsider (observer) with regard to oneself and one's own actions. This may lead either to concern over self and reputation or to *detachment.* Probably relatively few people achieve any large measure of disinterestedness in their views of themselves, but those who do are recognized and appreciated for it. It is one of the most effective ways of maintaining self-esteem.

One of the outstanding signs of the achievement of such detachment is a sense of humor—especially about one's own foibles, mistakes, and weaknesses. The person who can joke in the face of failure, danger, or death exhibits detachment.

Privacy and the Self

Privacy is also related to defense of self, as the expression *invasion of privacy* makes clear. All societies have unwritten rules that allow persons to withdraw from interaction in certain situations. The retreat to privacy may be used to escape from interaction that is troubling, embarrassing, or deflating; some people who cannot successfully cope with certain kinds of social relations make a virtual fetish of privacy.

Privacy has positive values as well. It is perhaps an absolute necessity to withdraw to repair one's energies, ruminate over the significance of past events, and plan. It is only in moments in which one is not reacting to other people that communication with self can be at its best. Periods of privacy designed for this very purpose are institutionalized in all societies; an obvious example is the prescription by various religions of periods of meditation, fasting, and prayer.

When others try to get at the secret thoughts and intimate biographical details that a person wishes to reveal to no one or only to very special others, the person erects barriers. Inopportune revelation of self leaves the individual at the mercy of others. Privacy may be conceptualized as a series of concentric circles: The inner circle is forbidden to all trespassers, trusted intimates may enter into the second circle, and so on; the outer circles are accessible to all. This spatial symbolism is actually embodied in the architecture of dwellings, houses of worship, and public buildings as well as in the rules permitting or forbidding entry into various rooms.

Allowing another person to enter into the ego's central core of privacy is a delicate process fraught with peril to both parties. It is attended by misgivings and release, and by hesitations and abrupt moments of confiding. Betrayal of this degree of confidence is destructive and corrosive; its effect is like being turned over to the enemy after having sought refuge in the house of a blood relation. The recipients of confidences are also in a delicate position, because they may unwittingly betray the confidences or what they learn may put them in a moral dilemma. Impersonal, institutionalized places of confession (such as the church and the doctor's office) are designed to protect both parties.

Territoriality and the Self

Individuals maintain the integrity of their self-conceptions through the use of elaborate conceptions of *territoriality* and privacy. Lyman and Scott (1967) and Goffman (1971, pp. 28-61) offer typologies that link individuals' conceptions of self and social space. There are *public territories* where people can come and go at will, and they are open to wide classes of the population. The sacred, private features of the self are likely to remain concealed in these settings. *Home territories* are those most sacred to the self; these are backstage regions for private, unobserved interaction. *Body territories* include the area immediately surrounding the physical body, often conceived as personal space. The individual is unlikely to permit other actors into that space.

Individuals develop territorial defenses that maintain the sanctity of the places most central to their self-conceptions. Through the use of markers, names, tags, labels, and addresses, they communicate to outsiders what their spaces are, where those spaces end, and where the spaces of others take over. Spaces and their attached selves may be violated or challenged. Bodies may unexpectedly touch, glances may last too long, odors may be given off and communicate an untoward body state.

Individuals can challenge the credibility of their own self-conceptions by openly debasing themselves. Furthermore, they may befoul their own bodies or, in more drastic fashion, expose the private parts of their bodies. In each of these self-acts they cease to make the self a private and hence sacred object, thereby letting down their defenses and permitting others openly to defy or denigrate them. Hence they place others in the uncomfortable position of having to process the behaviors of a derelict self. Failures to maintain self-privacy and to keep up territorial defenses challenge the routine features of smooth, everyday interaction (Goffman, 1971, pp. 52-55).

Revelations and Self-Other Relations

It is interactionally useful to keep portions of oneself from others. In this sense, an element of secrecy, as Simmel (1950, pp. 330-333) notes, surrounds each individual: A person's most private self-conceptions and fantasies may never be known by another individual. A *pretense awareness context* exists in many relationships, even those of the most intimate nature. The members agree not to challenge each other's moods and declarations, and they act as if they fully understand one another when, in fact, they are only "pretending." Thus, although they may suspect that others are thinking something other than what they declare, they are tactful enough not to ask. But if the relationship is to take the turn toward deeper involvement, at some juncture they will be led to reveal the more private and hidden features of themselves. They move from the pretense and suspicion awareness context into the open context. This is not to say that their interactions will necessarily remain at the open level; a quasi-open context is more typical, and in time the relationship may slip back into more elaborate modes of secrecy and self-concealment.

CONCLUSION

The self is simultaneously a tenacious and a fragile thing. The postmodern self is saturated with social experiences yet constantly seeks an anchoring in the concrete practices of the everyday world. Moral careers take persons in and through complex social worlds. Often these worlds produce identity transformations, at times dramatic self-change. In this chapter we have discussed the dimensions of this process in detail.

Persons can voluntarily, involuntarily, or unexpectedly cede self-control to other individuals, groups, organizations, or causes. Self-control, free will, and voluntary behavior are all connected to the extensive place language plays in human experience. Humans are creatures of and in the symbolic worlds they belong to. The processes of brainwashing and coercive persuasion are instances of the partial loss of personal autonomy to outside forces or groups. We have discussed the coping devices persons use to maintain self-esteem and privacy. Privacy of the self is central to the maintenance of self-control.

SELECTED READINGS

Clough, P. T. (1994). *Feminist thought: Desire, power and academic discourse.* Cambridge, MA: Blackwell. A very important treatment of the major feminist theories and their implications for understanding gender, self, identity, and desire.

Gergen, K. J. (1991). *The saturated self: Dilemmas of identity in contemporary life.* New York: Basic Books. A valuable analysis, by a psychologist, of the contemporary self and dilemmas of identity.

Giddens, A. (1991). *Modernity and self-identity: Self and society in the late modern age.* Stanford, CA: Stanford University Press. An interesting analysis, by one of the world's preeminent sociologists, of the places of trust, doubt, anxiety, and intimacy in the so-called late-modern age.

Hall, S., & du Gay, P. (Eds.). (1996). *Questions of cultural identity.* London: Sage: A useful collection of essays that take the cultural studies approach to identity.

STUDY QUESTIONS

1. Compare and contrast the romantic, modern, and postmodern views of the self.
2. How does dramatic self-change occur?
3. Is there a private self?

12

Sexuality and Identity

In Chapters 1 and 7, we have argued that every human being, upon birth, in American culture at least, is placed within a specific, biologically determined sex class: male or female. Gender expectations are then fitted to this classification scheme—expectations involving sexual desire and sexual pleasure. A personal sexual identity is formed out of these interpretations. The gendered identity is an interactional production. Butler (1993a) reminds us, however, that there are no firm differences between male and female, between femininity and masculinity. Although we live in a gendered social order that enforces heterosexuality, there is no true, naturalized sexuality. In this chapter, working outward from Butler's arguments, we examine the topics of sexual identity, sexual activity, and sexual expression. We discuss the social, symbolic, and interactional foundations of sexual conduct. In doing so, we draw on recent work in "queer theory" (Foucault, 1985; Plummer, 1997; Seidman, 1994; Stein & Plummer, 1994; Warner, 1993) and other recent theoretical developments in the sociology and social psychology of sexuality and sexual identity.

We begin with the assumption that sexual motivations are not biological in origin. Sexual activity, like virtually all other complex human behavior, is primarily of symbolic and interactional, rather than biological, significance (Kuhn, 1954b). The symbolic entanglements surrounding human sexual behavior make it extremely hazardous to apply the findings obtained from the study of lower animals to human beings.

Recent Histories and Theories of Sexuality

Seidman (1994) reminds us that sexuality is a social fact: "What is imagined as sexuality, its personal and social meaning and form, varies historically and between social groups" (p. 166). We commonly assume that sexuality is something with specific traits, desires, acts, developmental patterns, and gendered sexual and psychological types. However, Foucault (1985) has clearly established that this is a recent notion. The ancient Greeks imagined a sphere of pleasures that "included eating, athletics, man/boy love, and marriage, not a realm of sexuality" (Seidman, 1994, p. 166). For the ancient Greeks, according to Foucault, sexuality was an act. *Homosexuality* described a category of acts. Only in the 19th century did the "homosexual become a personage . . . a case history . . . nothing that went into the total composition was unaffected by his sexuality. It was everywhere present in him . . . it was the secret that always gave itself away" (Foucault, 1980a, p. 430; see also Seidman, 1994, p. 171).

Thus, for Foucault, sexuality is constructed through institutional discourses that constitute specific regimes of truth. When sexuality became a mainstay of personal identity in the Victorian era, "heterosexual monogamy came to function as a norm, and sexual deviants began to see themselves as distinct persons, possessing particular 'natures' " (Stein & Plummer, 1994, p. 183). Foucault's arguments challenge the idea of a continuous history of homosexuality, the notion of an essential homosexual identity. Modern sexuality, as Stein and Plummer (1994) observe, is a "product of modern discourses of sexuality" (p. 183). These discourses assume a natural order linking sex, gender, sexuality, and the nuclear family. This produces normative beliefs about the sanctity of patriarchal heterosexuality and the traditional gender stratification system.

Clearly, then, sex and sexuality are thoroughly social. The mass media, medicine, sociology, anthropology, psychiatry, psychology, and other practices of discourse bring sexual meanings to bodies, parts of the body, embodied sensations, specific pleasures, emotions, acts, desires, images, and experiences. Which sensations are sexual and which are not involve moral and hence political matters. As Seidman (1994) notes, "Moral boundaries demarcate legitimate and illegitimate sex" (p. 166).

Seidman (1994, p. 168) argues that until the 1960s and early 1970s American sociology ignored the topic of sexuality. The counterculture of the 1960s—the antiwar, civil rights, women's, gay liberation, lesbian feminism, and black power movements—placed sexual rebellion in the national public arena. A sociology of sexuality that treated sex as a property of the individual emerged in this period. Patterns of conventional heterosexuality were studied, including premarital, marital, and extramarital sex. This literature, Seidman observes, was largely preoccupied with "deviant" sexual subcultures and "deviant" sexualities, including homosexuality, prostitution, and pornography.

A sociology of homosexuality emerged as a part of the sociology of sex (see Gagnon & Simon, 1970; Humphreys, 1970, 1972; Warren, 1974). This scientific literature, coupled with research in medicine and psychiatry, including psychoanalysis, helped define and solidify a public (and private) homosexual identity, an identity that has undergone several transformations from midcentury to the present.

Seidman (1994, p. 169) and Blasius and Phelan (1997, pp. 217-218, 239-240) have outlined this history in the United States and have found that it is connected, at nearly every point, to shifting "scientific" views of homosexuality. Blasius and Phelan (1997, pp. 840-841) divide the history into these sometimes overlapping moments:

- *1900-1950:* the period of censorship, underground subcultures, and psychiatric illness models of homosexuality
- *1950-1969:* the homophile movement, culminating in the Stonewall riots in New York City in 1969
- *1970-1986:* gay liberation and lesbian feminism, queer nation, ACT Up; essentialist and constructionist views of homosexuality
- *1982-present:* the gay and lesbian politics of AIDS; bisexual, gay, lesbian, and transgender studies
- *The present:* Stonewall 25 years later, which affirms the universal human rights of lesbian, gay, and bisexual people

From the turn of the century through the 1970s, gays and lesbians were isolated by the larger society, treated as deviants without civil rights. The American Psychiatric Association defined homosexuality as a mental illness. Gays and lesbians were defined as exhibiting abnormal, deviant sexualities. Gays and lesbians had to choose between being criminals and sinners or being sick and undergoing psychiatric treatment for their deviant sexual desires (Blasius & Phelan, 1997, p. 239). Clandestine homophile organizations provided safe harbors for gay men and lesbians in this period.

The midcentury sex surveys of the American population conducted by Kinsey and his colleagues placed sexuality on a continuum (see Kinsey, Pomeroy, & Martin, 1948; Kinsey, Pomeroy, Martin, & Gebhard, 1953). Kinsey et al. suggested that many persons are bisexual, and that many heterosexual men and women have had gay or lesbian sexual experiences. This challenged the psychiatric model. At the same time, as if in anticipation of the civil rights movements of the 1960s, new political models came into view, suggesting that homosexuals are an oppressed minority (Seidman, 1994, p. 169). In the 1950s the first sustained homophile organizations in the United States emerged: the Mattachine Society, the Daughters of Bilitis, One, and the North American Organization of Homophile Organizations (NAOHO). Gay and lesbian publications followed, including the *Mattachine Review*, the *Ladder*, and *One Magazine* (Blasius & Phelan, 1997, p. 239).

By the early 1970s, the women's and gay liberation movements were criticizing the concept of compulsive heterosexuality. At the same, these groups were presenting arguments that normalized the concept of same-sex desire. During this period sociologists approached homosexuality as a social stigma and located male homosexuals in a kind of deviant sexual underworld of hustlers, prostitutes, prisons, tearooms, and bathhouses. Becker's (1964, 1973) labeling theory of deviance and Gagnon and Simon's (1967, 1970) sexual script theory offered constructionist views of nonheterosexual sexuality and identity. However, these theories did not critically examine the basic master binary category of heterosexual/homosexual.

Some gay and lesbian discourse during this period attempted to naturalize, or normalize, nonheterosexual sexuality, thereby reversing the dominant heterosexual hierarchy. This naturalizing stance had the effect of making gayness or being lesbian a universal, or normal, category of gender and self-identification. According to Seidman (1994), the notion of "homosexuality as a universal category of the self and sexual identity was hardly questioned, if at all, in the homophile, lesbian feminist, and gay liberationist discourses during this time period" (p. 170).

However, many read the universalizing argument as an assimilationist political stance. Lesbians and gays could simply fit into the larger mainstream heterosexual culture, only now without stigma. Kitzinger (1987) calls this the liberal humanistic position. She contends that it depoliticizes a radical feminist and separatist lesbian agenda—that is, it takes the politics out by making lesbian (or gay) an individual act and choice. It labels lesbians as persons "making private sexual choices and enjoying particular kinds of personal relationships" (p. vii). This construction was regarded as incompatible with the goals of the radical feminist and lesbian separatist movements. For these groups, "lesbianism is fundamentally a political statement representing the bonding of women against male supremacy" (p. vii). The radical feminist argument rejects the institution of compulsive heterosexuality, seeing it as basic to the oppression of women. In this vein, Kitzinger asserts that lesbianism "represents women's refusal to collaborate in our own betrayal" (p. viii).

Thus as Kitzinger (1987) notes, within the above framework, there are at least two positions on women and lesbianism. The liberal humanist model declares that lesbianism helps women achieve "liberal humanistic goals (happiness, sexual fulfillment, better personal relationships)" (p. viii). In contrast, the radical feminist view believes that lesbianism "helps to achieve radical feminist goals (the overthrow of male supremacy)" (p. viii).

Bisexuality

There is still a third position, that of bisexuality. Ault (1996, p. 452) observes that bisexuality emerged as a sexual category and sexual identity in the medical and psychiatric discourses of the 19th and 20th centuries. Freud and Jung used the term, as did early sexologists, who suggested that all persons have feminine and masculine needs, desires, and identities. During the AIDS crisis of the 1980s, the bisexual body was pathologized and seen to be primarily male. In contrast, "the politicized bisexual body of the 1990s appears almost universally to be female" (Ault, 1996, p. 452); examples include the bisexual character in the 1997 Hollywood film *Chasing Amy.*

Bisexuals are stigmatized by heterosexuals, lesbians, and gays (Ault, 1996, pp. 452-453). The argument is straightforward: Bisexuals simply do not exist. Depending on the point of view, bisexuals are persons who are not yet aware of their true sexual identity—that is, as heterosexual, lesbian, or gay

(Ault, 1996, p. 453). Still, bisexuals trouble the notion of a stable, straight, lesbian, or gay sexual identity.

In this vein, Ault (1996) found in one study that bisexual women used the terms *bi, lesbian, dyke,* and *gay* as ways of aligning themselves within and against the dominant categories of sexual identification. In recent years the term *queer* has functioned as a bisexual label, signaling the person's membership in a complex social and political world that challenges the "dominant sex/gender/sexual identity system" (Ault, 1996, p. 456). Women in Ault's study adopted the *queer* label for several reasons, including its "appeal to polymorphous perversity [and] its signification of solidarity with lesbians and gay men" (p. 456). For many women, *queer* marked their criticisms of heterosexuality and created a safe space for them within nonheterosexual culture (see below).

Many of the bisexual women in Ault's study rejected a queer assimilationist strategy that would have defined them "as more like gay and lesbian people than like heterosexuals" (p. 458). These women essentialized and universalized their bisexuality. They argued that all "normal" people are bisexual. This move shifts bisexuals to center stage in the sexual drama. No longer marginal or deviant, the bisexual woman now stands in opposition to the gay, lesbian, or straight monosexual person who denies his or her bisexuality. This model makes bisexuality the dominant sexual category and pathologizes those persons who limit their sexual intimacies to "members of only one sex" (p. 458).

This position reasserts, in a somewhat different way, the liberal humanist arguments discussed above. It denies differences between men and women and makes " 'everyone' a potential object of sexual or personal interest" (Ault, 1996, p. 458). At the same time, this discourse locates the bisexual in several different places at the same time, including within the centers and edges of the gay, lesbian, bisexual, queer, and nonqueer heterosexual communities. Paradoxically, many of the bisexual women Ault studied used a sexual code taken from the larger lesbian and heterosexual culture. This code stressed "honesty, fidelity, sexual responsibility and commitments . . . [and] castigated bisexuals who are 'promiscuous,' unpoliticized, or too weak to 'take the heat' society directs at lesbians and gays" (p. 459). This code thus distinguished among true (real), trendy, and deviant bisexuals.

Lesbian, heterosexual, and right-wing opposition to bisexuality is a way of reinscribing the binary sex/gender system. This discourse stabilizes the gay/lesbian/heterosexual classification scheme and renaturalizes the oppositions between and among these categories (Ault, 1996, p. 460). Right-wing criticism of bisexuality as the ultimate perversion simultaneously advocates and ridicules the social constructionist position on an essential sexuality—that is there is no essential sexual identity (Ault, 1996, pp. 452, 460-461). This criticism is revealed in the kinds of statements that have been put forward by members of the New Right, such as "You can't make the case that on Wednesdays and Fridays you like to be with men and on Tuesdays and Thursdays you like to be with women"; "You cannot be born both lesbian and straight"; and "You either choose or do not choose your sexuality" (Ault, 1996, pp. 452, 460-461). Ironically, these criticisms work to legitimate the claims of the proponents of an essential gay and lesbian identity (Ault, 1996, p. 460). Gays and lesbians are perceived to be less depraved then bisexuals.

By the mid- to late 1970s, gay and lesbian subcultures had developed into a period of shared community building and personal and group empowerment. This was the period of new theory, especially social constructionism, which drew on labeling theory, Marxism, and feminism. It argued, after Foucault and others, that the categories of sex and sexuality are fundamentally social and cultural in nature (Seidman, 1994, p. 171). Social constructionist research challenged medical, psychiatric, essentialist, and biological models of sexuality. This research refused the "natural fact" arguments of the medical regime. Scholars examined the historical and social factors that produced various situated versions of the homosexual or lesbian identity, conducting studies on such topics as gayness in the Victorian era. Researchers argued that same-sex experiences are not uniform and that homosexual and lesbian are not transhistorical identities. According to Seidman (1994, p. 171), this research dominated studies of homosexuality through the 1980s (see Connell, 1987). It became institutionalized in lesbian, gay, and bisexual studies programs in the 1990s.

A Queer Nation

The concept of "queer nation," the organization ACT Up, and queer theory all emerged in the late 1980s as a result of collaborations between radical lesbians and gay activists. Queer theory represented a move away from the strict social constructionism of the earlier period (Stein & Plummer, 1994, p. 181); it became a rallying cry "for new ways of thinking and theorizing. For many the term *lesbian and gay studies* did not seem inclusive enough" (Stein & Plummer, 1994, p. 181). The term *queer* signifies "not only those who mark themselves as gay or lesbian, but . . . anyone whose proclivities, practices, or sympathies defy the strictures of the dominant sex/gender/sexual identity system. . . . [Queer] is a discursive strategy designed to disrupt heterosexist systems of sexual marking" (Ault, 1996, p. 456).

Epstein (1994) summarizes the meanings of *queer* and *queer nation.* By invoking and appropriating the pejorative word *queer,* a "stigmatized group . . . negates the term's power to wound" (p. 195). The term is often used in an antiassimilationist sense, standing in opposition to the civil rights and civil liberties discourses of "the inclusionary project of mainstream lesbian and gay politics" (p. 195). The term describes a politics of confrontation and provocation; the standards of liberal tolerance are constantly pushed (e.g., kiss-ins). Queer theory resists constraining sexual categories, and it can be both constructionist and essentializing in its meanings (p. 195). The term also marks generational differences and potential conflicts between younger and older members of the gay/lesbian/queer community. *Queer* also references an ideal cosexual politics in which men and women "participate on an equal footing." Some prefer the term *queer* to *gay* "(which includes women in much the same way as 'man' used to include women), or to 'gay and lesbian' (which emphasizes gender difference)" (p. 195). *Queer* functions in a shorthand way to describe all sexual minorities.

Thus bisexuals, as noted above, often use the word *queer* as an identity marker, as do transgendered persons. The transgendered category includes "people who live as the opposite sex, whether or not they have had sex-change surgery" (Wilson, 1998, p. A10). This is a large category; in it are cross-dressers, transvestites, and transsexuals—that is, persons who change from female to male and those who change from male to female. Clearly, persons in this group disrupt traditional systems of sexual classification.

Membership in this broad-based queer community, in queer nation, has been likened to membership in a racial or ethnic minority. As Warner (1991) observes, "Identity as a lesbian or a gay man is ambiguously given and chosen, in some ways ascribed and in other ways the product of the performative act of coming out. . . . In many respects, queer people are a kind of social group fundamentally unlike others, a status group only insofar as they are not a class" (p. 15; also quoted in Stein & Plummer, 1994, p. 181). Of course race and ethnicity intersect with class in the queer world. Prominent African American and Latina writers, from James Baldwin to Audre Lorde and Gloria Anzaldúa, have expanded the boundaries of queer discourse. Race is also central in such organizations as the National Coalition of Black Lesbians and Gays, Dykes Against Racism Everywhere, Men of All Colors Together (Lorde, 1997, p. 475), the Caucus of Asian and Pacific Islander AIDS Activists, and Chicana Lesbians.

Stein and Plummer (1994) suggest that queer theory has four defining features: (a) an emphasis on how sexuality is conceptualized, regulated, expressed discursively, and "enforced through boundaries and binary divides" (p. 182); (b) a problematization of sexual and gender categories; (c) revisionist readings, a rejection of civil rights strategies in favor of an antiassimilationist politics, and "a politics of carnival, transgression, and parody" (p. 182); and (d) "a willingness to interrogate areas which would not normally be seen as the terrain of sexuality" (p. 182), including doing "queer" readings of traditional heterosexual and nonsexualized texts (p. 182).

Queer theorists argue that it is never possible to be located outside the dominant discourses of sexuality. To be "out" as a gay, lesbian, bisexual, or transgendered person is to presume the existence of gays, lesbians, bisexuals, and transgendered persons still in the closet (Namaste, 1994; Sedgwick, 1990). Furthermore, it is impossible ever to be "entirely outside heterosexuality, nor entirely inside" (Namaste, 1994, p. 224). Nonetheless, the dominant sexual discourses of the 19th and 20th centuries have presumed a world in which every person is mapped into a homosexual or heterosexual space (Clough, 1994, p. 144). Queer theorists challenge this map. In so doing, they study the practices and disciplines that produce knowledge about sexuality. This is a shift from the study of experience to the study of discourse (Clough, 1994, p. 145).

The AIDS Crisis

In the late 1970s, it was possible for some to speak of the "homosexualization" of American culture (Seidman, 1994, p. 172). A kind of nonthreatening gay and lesbian presence had become normalized within the culture, especially in the fashion and art worlds and in certain branches of the music and entertainment industries. Sadly, the AIDS crisis of the 1980s would "conspire to put lesbian and gay life into crisis" (Seidman, 1994, p. 172). A conservative Republican backlash against homosexuality, spearheaded by the New Right, challenged any illusions about the culture's acceptance of the gay way of life. The AIDS crisis did several things at the same time: It energized this backlash, put the gay community on the defensive, and legitimated religious and medical models that "discredited homosexuality" as a sin and a sickness (Seidman, 1994, p. 172). It also served to destabilize the gay and lesbian community, as matters of race and ethnicity surfaced with some power and force.

Howley (1998) recently completed a study of gay male fictional and autobiographical narratives written in the age of AIDS. His research covered the years 1985 (the year of Rock Hudson's death) to 1994. He studied the works of three gay authors who wrote during this period: Armistead Maupin (*Tales of the City*), Paul Monette (*Borrowed Time, Last Watch of the Night*), and David Feinberg (*Queer and Loathing*). Howley found that these texts reflect and articulate the major moments in gay society over the past 20 years. Maupin's works pathologize and stigmatize gay men with AIDS. Monette's novels attempt to normalize gay life and AIDS. In contrast, Feinberg radicalizes AIDS and gay male society, refusing the assimilationist approach of Monette and the stigmatizing stance of Maupin.

Seidman (1994, p. 172) suggests that by the early 1980s gay and lesbian people of color were challenging mainstream gay culture because it devalued and marginalized their experiences and their modes of oppression. Gay and lesbian African Americans and Latinos/as charged that the gay movement embodied a white middle-class bias. At the same time, conflicts within lesbian feminism surfaced, including clashes surrounding lesbian feminist sexual identities, assimilationist strategies, the meaning of patriarchal oppression, and the feminist "sex wars" (Ault, 1996, p. 460; Seidman, 1994, p. 172).

One reaction in the 1980s to the AIDS crisis and the right-wing backlash was the reassertion of the "natural foundation of homosexuality (e.g., the gay brain)" (Seidman, 1994, p. 173). This move was an attempt to unify homosexuals in the face of the political backlash. The gay brain argument seeks a neurological foundation for homosexuality. This move revisits earlier essentialist-constructionist debates about a universal homosexual identity. Plummer (1991) notes that for a while this debate "threatened to tear the gay and lesbian academic community apart" (p. 175). For a period, there was tension between the terms *sexual preference* and *sexual orientation*, the former connecting to a constructionist position, the latter to an essentializing, gay brain model.

Although the gay brain concept unified many in the gay community against this political backlash, others affirmed a stronger social constructionist position. This stance, based on the politics of social difference, is seen in Butler's (1993a) performance model of gender and sexuality. As we have noted in earlier chapters, for Butler, heterosexuality is always in danger of being undone.

This more contemporary view returns to the concept of sexual identity, a concept that can be seen as affirming certain forms of selfhood while policing and disciplining others. Identities are always multiple, shifting, and unstable (Perinbanayagam, 1991, p. 196). Queer theory rejects the older binary terms of the heterosexual/homosexual regulatory system. Queer theory wishes, as Seidman (1994, p. 174) observes, to challenge the regime of sexuality itself, the regime that makes *sexuality* the dominant term for the self and its meanings. Queer theorists examine those institutional practices and systems of discourse that produce sexual knowledge, critically studying how these practices organize everyday social life. It is to some of these practices, terms, and discourses that we now turn.

The Evolutionary Picture

The general picture of subhuman sex behavior is described in terms appropriate to our purposes by Beach (1947, 1965), a psychologist who has surveyed the available literature and carried out extensive investigations of the sex behavior of the lower animals. We can summarize Beach's conclusions as follows: (a) Mating behavior in lower animal forms is controlled primarily by inherited mechanisms, specifically by hormonal secretions and by the strength and aggressiveness of the animal; (b) the central nervous system plays a relatively minor part in the control of sex behavior in the simpler animal forms, its regulatory significance increasing as one ascends the evolutionary scale; and (c) past experience, as opposed to hereditary mechanisms, increases in importance as one proceeds from the simpler forms, such as the rat and guinea pig, to the more complex apes and humans. A significant part of the sex behavior of male chimpanzees, for example, is learned.

In support of these general statements, we briefly note certain facts. In most lower forms, receptivity of the female to sexual advances is determined by hormone balance and other accompanying physiological changes occurring during the period of heat or estrus. With some exceptions, the female animal is receptive only when in heat, This, of course, is not true of the human female, who may actively desire or entirely reject sexual relations at any time during the menstrual cycle.

Removal or atrophy of the primary sex glands—the testes and the ovaries—produces relatively uniform results in the lower animals and highly variable, uncertain ones in human beings. Adult men who have been castrated, women who have had ovaries and uterus removed by surgery, and older people whose sex glands have ceased to function may all continue to desire and enjoy coitus, and many do. Men who find themselves impotent sometimes have their potency restored through injection of an actual hormone, injection of any substance that they believe to be a hormone, or psychiatric treatment.

The characteristic and differentiating features of human sex behavior can be traced to the fact that humans talk about sex and other animals do not. The possibility of engaging in any sex behavior is, of course, contained in the biological structure of the individual. The intensity of the "sex drive" and certain other general characteristics may be conditioned by biological factors.

Isolated elements of the total pattern of sex activity are not learned; they are derived directly from the human being's biological structure. The orgasm, ejaculation, and nocturnal emission of the male are examples. These relatively mechanical, nonvoluntary parts of sex behavior are natural biological acts.

Although we can designate various individual aspects of sex behavior as natural, unlearned, or inherited, we cannot say the same about the total organization and overall functioning of these aspects in given social situations. The general patterns that individuals adopt cannot be explained biologically; they must be accounted for in terms of the standards or attitudes that individuals internalize toward themselves and their sexual activities. Social influences and expressions often shape sex behavior along lines that are contrary to what would be called "natural," or conventional, in the biological and social senses. Furthermore, social influences may lead to the complete elimination of some kinds of natural biological behavior.

Hormones, Homosexuality, and Inversion

A chief obstacle to proper understanding of the nature of human sex behavior is the assumption that hormones account for the vagaries of sexual behavior. According to this view, heterosexuality is the consequence of a hormone balance, which in the male is weighted on the side of androgens and in the female on the side of estrogens. (The *androgens* are the male hormones and the *estrogens* are the female hormones; however, both are found to some extent in both sexes.) The close connection between these hormones and secondary sexual body characteristics has been scientifically demonstrated. Hence many people think that when female hormones are relatively prevalent in a male or male hormones are relatively prevalent in a female, the result is an effeminate male or a masculine female—that is, a homosexual. As we shall indicate in the succeeding paragraphs, this conception is incorrect in almost every detail (Boswell, 1980; Corey, 1951; Freud, 1933; Garfinkel, 1967a; Stoller, 1979).

It is necessary to distinguish among various aspects of sexual behavior and sexual characteristics, and to note the difference between homosexuality and inversion. *Inversion* refers to the assumption of a female role or identity by a male and, conversely, of a male role or identity by a female. *Inversion* is a term that is used to describe people, not a sex act. Indeed, it is quite possible—though improbable—for an inverted male and an inverted female to engage in heterosexual relations. *Homosexuality,* on the other hand, refers to sexual or love relationships between members of the same sex. Because male and female counterroles are usually involved in the sex act, even homosexual partners often play opposite sex roles. Hence in homosexual intercourse one partner can be characterized as inverted and the other cannot.

We must also bear in mind the distinctions between male and female secondary sexual characteristics: voice differences, distribution of body hair, and so on. Moreover, the presence in a male of relatively female secondary physical characteristics does not imply either inversion or homosexuality.

The distinction between homosexual behavior and heterosexual behavior is based on the sex of the preferred partner. In short, the terms *homosexual, heterosexual,* and *inversion* refer to behavior, whereas secondary sex traits are structural, biological features of the organism, not forms of behavior.

In the light of these distinctions, we can make several observations:

1. *Inversion* and *homosexuality* are not synonymous terms.
2. In experiments on animals, through the injection of hormones of the opposite sex, secondary physical traits of the opposite sex and partial inversion have both been produced, but homosexuality in the human sense of the term has not been brought about.
3. The injection of hormones in humans neither produces nor cures homosexuality, its main effect being to stimulate sex activity without influencing the choice of partners.
4. Homosexuality usually occurs along with heterosexuality in a mixed form; many persons are bisexual.
5. Many male homosexuals are not effeminate, and many female homosexuals are not masculine.
6. Probably most effeminate men and masculine women engage in exclusively heterosexual relations.
7. Many forms of human sexual behavior, including homosexuality, have no parallels among the lower animals.

If we account for sexuality in terms of hormones, then we must ask what possible hormonal basis is involved when humans derive their sexual gratification from intercourse with lower animals or in many other ways, some of which we allude to in the next section.

The crucial point in connection with the inversion of gender identities in humans is that a male or female identifies with the opposite sex. Thus a female invert may assert that she is a man, wear masculine clothes, act like a man, assume much of the masculine role in sexual relations, adopt a masculine name, and perhaps even apply the male terminology to her sexual organs, calling the clitoris a "penis" and the ovaries the "testes." This type of inversion is no doubt brought about by the fact that adult sexual patterns are conceptually organized and to a pervasive degree regulated by social definitions of the individual's behavior and sexual identity as well as shaped by personal experiences.

These factors point to the learned and socially defined nature of gender identities. At birth, children do not identify themselves with either sex, for they do not know that the sexes exist. They gradually learn this identification and acquire the behavior deemed appropriate in their society (Isaacs, 1933; Klein, 1932). For example, the types of partners the male child will learn to prefer—blondes or brunettes; women or men; white, black, or brown—are not determined by human biological structure any more than religious, political, and ethical preferences are so determined (Broderick, 1965; Hill & Aldous, 1969). Moreover, there may be various deflections in this learning process. Later we give examples of how this might come about—through parental desire that a child be of a given gender, through anatomical peculiarities, or through mistakes in identifying the child's gender at birth.

Newborn children respond positively to pleasant stimuli, regardless of the source; they do not classify or discriminate among sources. The male child is as likely to have an erection when handled by his father as when handled by his mother. As the child matures and learns ways of classifying stimuli and responding to them, his patterns of sexual expression gradually crystallize and become channeled. As Sullivan (1953) has observed, the patterning of sexual activity into a fixed set of identities occurs over a period of several years in the life cycle (see Chapter 8). The detailed description of this learning process as it occurs for bisexuals, gays, and lesbians is still a problem for the combined efforts of social scientists.

The Meanings of Homosexuality

We must remember that the word *homosexual* carries at least two levels of meaning. Objectively, "homosexuality refers to wanting or having sexual relations with members of the same sex" (Messinger & Warren, 1984, p. 197). Subjectively, "homosexuality refers to a belief that one is the sort of person who has those wants and experiences" (Messinger & Warren, 1984, p. 197). Too frequently, scientists try to explain homosexuality by theorizing about the sources of homosexual wants and desires. They often assume that homosexuality is a sexual deviance (Foucault, 1980a) and that it is characteristic of underlying personality disorders; hence they bring a normative stigma to the phenomenon. Seldom do such theorists inquire into the subjective meanings homosexuality holds for the person. They seldom "carefully explore whether someone labeled 'homosexual' (or gay or lesbian) by others or by the self wants sexual contact with the same-sex others, has it, or believes that it is wanted" (Messinger & Warren, 1984, p. 197). They seldom examine how the label *homosexual* works and functions for the person who uses it (see Humphreys, 1972; Krieger, 1983; Messinger & Warren, 1984; Ponse, 1978; Warren, 1974).

Following Messinger and Warren (1984, p. 205), we should see that the "label" *homosexual* is vague and, like the label of *alcoholism* or *mental illness,* does not refer to specific experiences "but to frameworks for interpreting experiences" (Messinger & Warren, 1984, p. 205). *Homosexual* is a normative label; it provides a general frame of reference that must be learned and fitted to actual personal and interactional experiences. The label serves to explain conduct and feelings and distributes responsibility for the person. For example, individuals might apply the Freudian theory of homosexuality to their personal experiences, in which case they might blame their fathers or mothers for their homosexuality. When using terms like *homosexual*—or *gay, lesbian,* or *bisexual*—we must grasp the meanings these words have for the person and connect these words and their meanings to the self-conceptions and interactional experiences of the people who use them, understanding that, in all too many cases, degradation follows their use. That is, societies impose sexual identities on members. Many, like the United States, impose a compulsive "heterosexuality," and in so doing leave little space for the "social construction" of *gay* and *lesbian* labels beyond a connotation of deviance.

The Polymorphous Perverse and Patterns of Sexuality

Research findings concerning the biology of sexual differentiation and early sexual behavior suggest that the human organism at birth probably should be viewed as essentially indeterminate sexually, with the potential of adopting one or several of a large number of modes of expression. In the early stages the fetus is not sexually differentiated, but it becomes so before birth. The mechanisms that determine whether the child is to be a boy or a girl are not completely understood. What the path of sexual development will be, presumably, is determined by early learning processes that are difficult to assess and have not been isolated. Freud's expression *the polymorphous perverse* designates the child's potentiality for moving in any of a number of directions. The term implies that knowledge of biological structures does not enable us to predict reliably how the individual will make use of these structures when he or she becomes an adult.

The modes of sexual expression engaged in by adults seem to present a picture of almost unlimited variability. In addition to the wide variety of relatively common heterosexual and homosexual patterns, there are many others. Thus some persons obtain gratification not from engaging in the sex act, but from watching it performed by others (voyeurs), or from peeping activities, looking at pictures, or reading pornographic material. Masochists obtain gratification from being whipped or otherwise being made to suffer pain, whereas sadists enjoy inflicting pain or injury on others. Pyromaniacs find sexual pleasure in setting and watching fires. Another form of sexual expression is fetishism, in which sexual interests are focused on objects that are endowed with erotic significance, such as shoes or undergarments. Sexual interests may be directed toward almost any part or function of the body. Gratification may be achieved via different sense modalities—vision, sound, touch, smell, and taste.

Transvestism, or dressing up as a member of the opposite sex, is commonly misunderstood to be an aspect of homosexuality (Newton, 1972); however, most transvestites are heterosexuals. An interesting example of transvestism is provided by the Institute for Sexual Research, which was established by Alfred C. Kinsey: A middle-aged man, happily married for many years, makes it a practice to serve his wife breakfast in bed. Before doing so, he slips on a feminine wig and carefully attires himself in a feminine costume from a special wardrobe reserved for the purpose. His wife usually compliments him on his appearance, and does not reproach or harass him. One fear does trouble him—that some outsider may appear at an inopportune time and thus create gossip or a scandal. To the outside world, he appears simply as an older married man.

The brief list of unusual patterns of erotic expression we have provided above does not constitute an exhaustive description of the full range of human sexual possibilities. There are many other forms of sexual expression, including sexual acts with lower animals, some of which are forbidden in criminal codes. Considering the immense variety of human sexual patterns—patterns that probably have no counterparts among lower animals—it is difficult to imagine that any purely biological or hormonal explanation could possibly account for them. The common assumption that heterosexuality is simply "natural" or "instinctive" is naive and grossly inadequate. Actually, there are a multiplicity of competing theories that try to explain one or more of these nonheterosexual patterns.

Apart from the unresolved etiological battle, social psychologists need to be concerned with the social contexts within which sexual patterns occur and the social consequences of sexual behaviors. Much useless theorizing goes on about why men frequent prostitutes, why they have mistresses while "happily" married, why they engage in "wife-swapping," why men and women engage in group intercourse or allow themselves to be observed while "loving" their boyfriends or girlfriends. Some have even theorized about how it is possible that married couples in their late 80s can still be lustily engaging in sex (Stoller, 1979; Turner, 1984). In his consummately funny novel *Lolita,* Nabokov wisely eschews any explanation as to why his hero is so enduringly attracted to young girls; he merely tells us what happens because of that compulsion. The book further suggests that whatever the ingenious social psychologist can possibly imagine in the way of sexual relations—heterosexual or otherwise—in terms of object, place, time, or manner, one can be certain that it has been tried and found satisfying and is practiced somewhere by some persons.

Some individuals who are viewed as sexual deviants have organized themselves to protest public and legal discrimination. Gay men and lesbians have had such organizations for some time, and in recent years an aggressive gay rights movement has attracted considerable public attention through attempts to reform criminal codes as they affects homosexuals and through efforts to educate or inform the public and to bring the issue of homosexuality into the open (Humphreys, 1972). ACT Up and the International Lesbian and Gay Association are just two of the important organizations within this movement. These organizations have been especially important in light of the recent AIDS crisis, which is worldwide. Transvestites also have established organizations, and extremely interesting accounts have been published of transvestite conferences and gatherings. There are also various informal types of "swinger" groups, which engage in unconventional sexual activity, including group sex among outwardly conventional couples. A variety of publications serve these groups (Walshok, 1971).

Transvestism suggests a number of points of special interest to social psychologists. For example, a male transvestite might appear sexually attractive to a heterosexual male who mistakes the transvestite for a woman; one may ask whether such an attraction should be characterized as homosexual or heterosexual. Or suppose that two transvestites of opposite sex mistake each other's sexual identities and become erotically interested in each other: Would this be a heterosexual or a homosexual relationship? In view of these considerations, should not the usual definitions be revised to take account of the fact that a sexual attraction between two persons might be essentially homosexual for one of the pair and heterosexual for the other? The crucial elements appear to be the beliefs that the two hold concerning each other's sexual identities and whether one or both members of the pair hold erroneous beliefs—especially when assisted by attire and cosmetics.

An extraordinary example of the complexity introduced by such considerations is the case of one male homosexual invert who had his male genitalia removed by surgery and an artificial vagina installed. Subsequently, this person married a male member of the armed forces and lived with him as his wife. When the soldier was transferred to Europe and separated from his "wife," they exchanged love letters of the standard type that any newly married couple might write. We might add that the army authorities and the church got involved in this marriage, debating whether or not it could be legal or otherwise recognized as an actual union. In such matters, the judgment of the "outside world" may or may not be crucial; thus a British male, after a similar transforming operation, married an American male. This transsexual's acquaintances back home in England simply could not believe this person was no longer what he had been (an unmarried male), but his American acquaintances knew him only as he now was (a married woman). Many transsexuals who have undergone sex-change operations keep their biographies secret from everyone except their spouses and very close friends (Garfinkel, 1967a).

The sexual identities of practically all people in any society are made obvious by a variety of external signs, such as hairstyle, dress, and demeanor. It is of theoretical interest to a social psychologist to imagine how sexual patterns and interrelationships might be altered if, instead of advertising sexual identity, people made every effort and used every artifice to make the sexes look exactly alike. Under such circumstances, budding romances might often end with the discovery that the potential sweetheart is of the wrong sex. Even in such societies as postrevolutionary Russia and China, and in certain social circles where signs of sexual identity are muted in favor of other characteristics and are unclear, men and women ordinarily do not make mistakes in their identification of each other.

Agnes: An Intersexed Person

Garfinkel (1967a) and Stoller (1967) both provide illustrative analyses of the management of sexuality that occurs in an intersexed person. At the time of these authors' research, Agnes presented herself as a 19-year-old girl raised as a boy. Her female measurements were 38-25-38 and were accompanied by a fully developed penis and scrotum. Garfinkel studied how Agnes achieved her right to live the gender identity of female; he used the term *passing* to refer to how she accomplished this feat.

Agnes was born a boy, with normal-appearing male genitals, and was raised as a boy. Yet when she presented herself to medical officials at the University of California, Los Angeles, in 1958, her appearance was convincingly female. Not considered a transsexual because (a) she denied taking estrogens and (b) there was no evidence that she had in fact taken estrogens, she was given a surgical operation to remove her penis and testes and to construct an artificial vagina from the skin of the penis (Stoller, 1967, p. 286). She subsequently married and lived a full life as a woman. Five years later, she returned, expressing doubts about the size and normality of her vagina. After being assured by a urologist that her genitalia were beyond suspicion, Agnes revealed to Stoller that she actually had never had a biological defect that had feminized her—that she had been taking estrogen since age 12.

How did Agnes manage to pass (a) as a girl who had been born a boy and (b) as a person who had not taken estrogen? The answer to the second question is easily settled: Stoller had discounted her taking the drug because he felt she did not have the knowledge necessary to do so. Yet Agnes, at age 12, discovered that her voice was getting lower and she was growing pubic hair. She immediately started taking stilbestrol—a drug her mother had been given following a pan-hysterectomy—and stole money from her mother to have the prescription refilled. She continued to take this drug until she was 15, by which time she had became "a lovely looking young 'woman,' though with a normal-sized penis" (Stoller, 1967, p. 288).

Garfinkel (1967a) answers the first question, How did Agnes pass as a girl? in the following fashion. She created a "feminine" self. She fashioned a female history for herself; she learned how to cook, how to be a "lady," how to talk and cry like a woman. In short, she talked and acted herself into the identity of a woman. Lester (1984) terms this "doing gender" (p. 51).

Agnes learned how to dress for the local Santa Monica beach (she wore tight-fitting underpants and a bathing suit with a skirt), and she avoided public bathrooms. When required to take a urine test, she persuaded her roommate to give her a sample of urine. She explained the scar on her stomach by saying there had been complications during an appendicitis operation. She refused intercourse with her boyfriend by saying that she required an operation.

Persons make gender happen by learning the cultural practices associated with the gender identities their culture subscribes to. In short, gender identities are socially produced. They are not biologically determined, as Agnes's case convincingly demonstrates. However, in a "homophobic" society such as the United States, gays and lesbians experience considerable repression, to the point of being excluded from certain kinds of workplaces because of their "sexual" preferences (e.g., the military).

The Gender Stratification System

The discussion of "doing gender" brings us to the topic of the gender stratification system in American society. Gender inequality, grounded in the social institution of gender, exists in the United States. By *the social institution of gender,* we mean the interactions and identities that exist in our society between males and females, females and females, and males and males. There are two distinct gender cultures in the United States: male and female. Distinctly different modes of interaction exist within these two cultures and are based not on biological factors but on the gender belief system.

The Gender Belief System

Lengermann and Wallace (1985, pp. 19-58) have examined the gender belief system in the United States in terms of six components: (a) the belief that there are natural differences between the sexes based on biology; (b) the belief in male authority or male patriarchy; (c) the belief that the home is the woman's place and the world of work is the man's place; (d) the belief that men and women do *different* kinds of work; (e) the belief that "love," sensual pleasure, and erotic experiences occur only within the heterosexual marriage; and (f) the belief that women should make themselves sexually and erotically attractive to males (Lengermann & Wallace, 1985, p. 51).

These six belief components are changing as radical, conservative, liberal, and traditional men and women in our society confront one another's beliefs about gender, sexuality, work, family, children, and marriage. The politics of gender shape and constrain how gender identities are formed and experienced in our society.

Sexual Identity and Self-Esteem

Adolescence

Although childhood experiences may be greatly significant in later sexual development (as we indicated in Chapter 9), establishing adult-type relationships—sexual and otherwise—with the same, or opposite, sex ordinarily begins after puberty (Schwartz & Merten, 1967; Sullivan, 1953). There is considerable anxiety and uncertainty in the minds of young people as to how they appear to the opposite sex and as to whether they will be able to function as "real" men and women. In initial intersexual relationships, there is often a period of testing and self-exploration in which the primary focus may be on self-assertion and validation. The young man venturing into the sexual world for the first time may be less interested intrinsically in his partner than in asserting and establishing his own identity and masculinity. The young woman during this period is similarly concerned with proving to herself and her peers that she is attractive to the opposite sex. Sullivan (1953) indicates that this is a phase of early adolescence.

In late adolescence, once this period of concern with self is presumably resolved and maturing adolescents have acquired greater confidence in their own essential masculinity or femininity, they are ready for more serious and enduring sexual relations than the "puppy love" of early adolescence. They are now on the verge of maturity, which Sullivan describes as the capability of becoming as concerned (or more concerned) over the well-being of another as over one's own. In Freudian terms, they have passed from the phallic to the genital stage of development (Freud, 1933). However, there are many points at which this developmental schedule on the way to heterosexual maturity can be deflected. When it is, the consequences, for obvious reasons, are often serious, both for the person's self-esteem and for his or her subsequent sexual career. We turn to a more detailed statement about the development of sexual self-conceptions.

The Sexual Self-Conception

Through the socialization process, each person comes to acquire a distinct set of self-conceptions, or identities, specific to sexual conduct and activity. These *personifi-*

cations, or images of self as a male or female, cluster into three categories: the "good" sexual me, the "bad" sexual me, and the "not" sexual me. The "good" sexual me involves those identifications and actions that bring the individual pleasure, pride, and positive self-identification. The "bad" sexual me involves those misidentifications that challenge the individual's credibility and moral worth. Furthermore, the "bad" sexual me touches on those actions in the sexual arena that arouse guilt and anxiety on the part of the individual. The "not" sexual me concerns a small number of sexual acts and identifications the individual would never see him- or herself engaging in, or that—like erotic dreams and nocturnal emissions—are automatic. These often relate to sexual taboos, and taking part in them produces shame and self-mortification. Women who have been raped, for example, disclaim any part in the sexual act and often view themselves afterward in tainted, morally repugnant terms.

Dimensions of the Sexual Self-Conception

Like the individual's other identities, or personifications, the sexual self-conception involves a number of interrelated dimensions. In addition to the components of the "good," the "bad," and the "not" me, we draw attention to the individual's (a) sexual appetite, (b) sexual prowess, (c) knowledge about sexual activity, and (d) conception of self as an experienced or inexperienced sexual actor. These latter aspects suggest that people view themselves as having particular levels of sexual desire—high, low, nonexistent. Furthermore, depending on their knowledge of sexual behaviors and the amount of their actual or fantasized sexual experience, they will see themselves as adept or not adept, powerful or impotent, interested or disinterested in sexual acts. The defined effects and outcomes of first sexual experiences (whether autophilic, isophilic, or heterophilic) will shape individuals' conceptions of themselves as sexual beings. *Autophilic,* or masturbation, experiences may become the dominant focus of the individual's sexual behavior. *Isophilic,* or homosexual, experiences may predominate, and in this case the individual does not transfer his or her sexual appetite and self-conceptions to behaviors that lead to intercourse with members of the opposite sex, as in the case for *heterophilic* actors (Sullivan, 1953, p. 292).

Individuals may move through all three sexual cycles, alternate between autophilic and heterophilic acts, or focus solely on one of these three modes of sexual expression. Sometimes without observing an individual's actual behavior, it is not easy to know which mode is dominant. In any case, the identity is potentially modified in each sexual encounter. Like their other identities, individuals' sexual self-conceptions are open to change.

Sexual self-conceptions are also differently salient or prominent in individuals' behavior repertoires. Whereas Freud and the neo-Freudians see the sexual drive as the predominant force in human behavior, the view we present in this chapter suggests that an individual may (a) never act out or act on his or her sexual identity (for example, priests who have taken a vow of celibacy), (b) engage in sexual behaviors only occasionally and then only on a fixed schedule (e.g., some Victorians), or (c) frequently act in a sexual fashion (e.g., married partners in the honeymoon phase of the marriage). Thus individuals can be studied in terms of the frequency with which they engage in sexual expression. The failure to act overtly does not suggest that the individual may not be privately and covertly daydreaming about sexual matters.

In general, it can be argued—following Sullivan (1953)—that sexual identity is most important within the confines of intimate relationships. It is there that intimacy and sexuality blend together in the tight-knit worlds of love and emotional attachment. Sexual identity finds its peak expression in those relationships. Accordingly, sexuality more or less lies dormant, or at best is less prominent, in the person's other interactive relationships. This is not to say that traces of flirtation and coquetry are not ubiquitous features of many other face-to-face encounters between the sexes; we simply suggest that sexual identity arises in predictable situations and circumstances within which it also finds its fullest expression. Sexual identity is molded and built up out of experiences with a relatively small number of individuals. Indeed, many people may have sexual experiences with only one other individual aside from themselves.

Sources of the Sexual Identity

The identity of male or female, and the sexual connotations that surround "maleness" or "femaleness," arise out of the individual's network of interpersonal relationships. Grounded in the intimate circles of the primary group, these identifications involve such matters as adornment and dress and the development of a set of covert, nonverbal gestures of a coquettish nature. Children learn to attach meanings to their sexual organs and learn "rules of privacy" concerning how these regions are clothed and shielded from the eyes of others (Conn & Kanner, 1947). Children's caretakers also instruct them in the ritual sacredness of certain behavior settings. Bathrooms and parental bedrooms take on moral significance in the daily domestic rhythms, and children are taught to respect the rights of others when they occupy these settings. Body maintenance activities such as bathing, washing, and dressing also expand children's awareness of their own bodies and those of others. Sexuality is based on the body, and the body is displayed in concrete situations. In moments of body display, children communicate (often unwittingly) a sexual sense of self.

The most direct source of sexual identity lies in the conversations and experiences that individuals have with themselves and others. Indirect sources, however, play a large role in the elaboration of individuals' sexual self-conceptions. Fantasies, reveries, and daydreams, often sparked by erotic or semierotic novels, paintings, movies, or magazines, also contribute to people's view of themselves as sexual actors. Thus with some certainty we can assume that by the middle years of childhood and early adulthood, all individuals will have developed—however unelaborated—a set of conceptions surrounding the sexual self. Research indicates that by age 17, most males and females have had at least one sexual experience leading to coitus. Luckey and Nass's (1969, p. 375) data from 2,230 college students in the United States, Canada, England,

Germany, and Norway reveal that the mean ages of first coitus at the time of their research were as follows: United States, 17.9 and 18.7 for males and females, respectively; Canada, 18.5 and 19.4; England, 17.5 and 17.5; Germany, 19.0 and 19.5; Norway, 18.4 and 18.8.

The Sexual Drama

Gagnon and Simon (1970) have remarked:

> In general, the sexual dimension in our society comprises a limited biological capacity that is harnessed and amplified by varied social uses. . . . We have emphasized that the expression of the sexual component is the celebration of a social and psychological drama rather than a natural response. We have suggested that there may be substantial change in the social drama. In the past the drama has been a silent charade. Now we appear to be giving the drama a sound track and inviting the audience to participate. (p. 20)

As our society loosens the taboos surrounding the sexual act and as sexual identity becomes a more discussed topic, we may witness a greater openness concerning its various components. In the past—and we suspect the pattern will largely hold for the future—individuals have seldom talked "openly" about their sexual appetites or their conceptions of sexual prowess, nor have they taken their partners fully into their confidence concerning their sexual fantasies. As a consequence, the sexual identity—one of the individual's most ubiquitous elements of self-identification—has remained one of the least-discussed features of the self. Discussions either are confined to same-sex friendship and gossip circles or are played out in the private imaginations of individuals. Thus, like other taboos surrounding discourse concerning the biological functions of the physical organism, the sexual self is seldom brought into the open; it represents a private set of acts and activities.

One final topic, the locus of the sexual act, remains to be treated. More specifically, what sexual identities do individuals bring into the sexual arena when they engage in sexual intercourse? The foregoing suggests that sexual identity is a complex mixture of positively and negatively defined elements. Accordingly, it can be seen that one person's "good" sexual me may be another person's "bad" or "not" sexual me. Thus any sexual encounter is likely to be a mixed and compromised expression of each individual's preferred and nonpreferred sexual desires. If a person finds that a stable sexual partner fails to conform with or support and reward a preferred "good" me, she may take her sexual behavior elsewhere, thereby separating the intimate behavior from the sexual behavior. Sexual partners are continually socializing one another, teaching one another new techniques and new modes of expression. The sexual identity is a dynamic, shifting set of self-indications that are grounded, as Gagnon and Simon (1970) argue, in the most intimate, yet biological circumstances—the human body and its meetings with the bodies of others.

Falling In and Out of Love

Failing in love has been likened to getting hooked on drugs (see Chapter 5). The process commonly begins as a "weekend habit." As it continues, it imperceptibly becomes continuous, more serious—often without the realization of the participants, who become progressively more psychologically dependent on each other as they learn more about each other and the relationship becomes more intimate and permeated by mutual trust. The lovers discover there is nobody else who gives them the same "high" that they have learned to enjoy and crave. Ultimately, they experience withdrawal distress when they are separated from each other. Despite difficulties and contrary arguments from parents and friends who urge them to break their compulsion, they tend to relapse repeatedly. Finally, there is nothing to be done but to accept the fact of their addiction to each other, and they either legalize it by marriage (methadone maintenance) or live together "in sin" (the illicit market).

Like heroin addicts explaining their habit, lovers who are asked why they love each other give varied, contradictory, and generally unilluminating answers. Like heroin users who praise the drug in exaggerated fashion, lovers often extol the virtues of their partners in extremely unrealistic terms. Both love and drug addiction have their honeymoon periods when the habits are new, before reality intrudes and brings the individual back to earth. Disillusionment sets in when the joy of the habit loses its novelty and the persons discover that they have been trapped by delusions about themselves and the objects of their craving. Like addicts who end up with "monkeys on their backs," lovers end up as "hostages to fortune" and with legal and financial obligations. When divorce occurs, the partners commonly remarry (relapse), a tendency that has been described as "the triumph of hope over experience." When people have been hooked on either love or drugs, they learn something new about the body and its potential, and it is inappropriate and futile to believe that they will ever forget it or be "cured" of it.

The worlds of both sex and drugs have their illicit markets and pushers, and in both worlds there are ways of obtaining highs without getting hooked or committed. Some individuals may avoid sexual commitment and marriage by going to prostitutes or by having episodic, temporary affairs with others who also are seeking to avoid commitment. (Men and women who are recently divorced and wary of hasty remarriage are prime examples of people who engage in friendly sex without emotional commitment; see Murstein, 1971; Waller, 1930.) In the same way, it is possible for the drug user to consume a variety of substances, switching from one to another to avoid becoming hooked on any of them.

As with drugs, young people learn about sex primarily from their peer groups, which exert pressure upon them to experiment—or, in conservative groups, not to experiment because to do so is wrong, dangerous, or sinful. Young Americans have learned "not to trust anyone over 30" on either drug or sexual questions. Parental influence is often blocked, either by inhibitions that prevent free communication between parents and children or by the dominance of peer group perspectives over those of an older generation. Today's parents, like those of past ages, are consequently confronted by new sexual realities that they often have difficulty accepting. A whimsical example is provided by a loving mother of our acquaintance who was concerned that her daughter was living with a man to whom she was not married. In response to the daughter's praise of her partner, the mother timidly suggested marriage. The daughter replied, "Oh, but mother, I don't know him nearly well enough for *that!*"

Failing in love may occur suddenly or gradually. Very little is known about why people fall in love with certain kinds of persons rather than others. It has been suggested that the falling-in-love process is something like the "imprinting" that has been observed in lower animals. It has also been suggested that it may actually be an instance of imprinting of early childhood experiences with members of the opposite sex, perhaps even with one's parents. One author has suggested that after puberty, boys and girls tend to fall in love with the first potential love object who happens to come along at the critical period when the situation is right (Murstein, 1971). It has also been asserted that the one who becomes the first love object to the budding adolescent is usually a new person in town, someone not too familiar. However naive, these speculations point to the relatively impoverished state of knowledge concerning the formation of close, intimate relationships.

Love as Process

The above discussion suggests that the act of falling in love, or forming an intimate and close relationship, must be viewed processually and in dynamic terms. To love another individual, as Sullivan (1953) remarks, "involves a situation where the person cares as deeply about another individual's fate and circumstances as they care about their own" (p. 26). A number of theories have been set forth to account for the formation of the love relationship. Goode (1959) presents a structural theory of love that argues that societies control the origins and distribution of the love emotion. Arranged marriages, child marriages, chaperoned dates, sorority and fraternity dating systems, and long engagements all represent attempts to regulate entry into the marriage market. Goode's argument rests on a simple assumption: "If societies did not control the marriage arrangement, their economic and prestige systems would collapse. Furthermore, their systems of social stratification would be thrown off balance" (p. 38).

Goode's formulations are taken to a higher level by Reiss (1971), who argues for a "wheel theory" of love. He proposes that persons with like interests are thrown together by the stratification systems of societies. These interests, in turn, are reflective of common needs. Mating follows a process whereby persons with common interests and needs meet, reveal themselves to each other, and in that process learn that they are capable of meeting each other's basic needs. Reiss's theory elaborates the earlier work of Robert Winch (1967), who formulated the complementary theory of needs.

We applaud Reiss's work on a processual model of relational formation. However, we reject the notion that societies somehow structure the lovemaking process so as to maintain their systems of wealth and prestige. People—not societies—fall in love and structure the formation of intimate relationships. Furthermore, we reject any theory that rests on some notion of needs, basic impulses, or drives. And many persons fall in love more than once. Indeed, families are held together, in part, because of the "love rhetoric." Of course, remarriages assume a repetition of the falling-in-love process (Neubeck, 1969). And members of the upper class often marry "down."

Very few studies or theories have adequately structured the process whereby intimate relationships are formed. We suggest that persons symbolically and behaviorally commit themselves to other individuals in intimate and deeply emotional ways. These commitments lead to the embracement of the totality of each other's selves and identities. This embracement, in turn, leads to interactions that reaffirm the other's uniqueness and sacred qualities. The other person comes to live an independent life in the fantasies and daydreams of the committed individual (Berger & Kellner, 1964). The selves of the two become *lodged* in one another.

Falling out of love involves a breaking-away process (Waller, 1930) that is often deeply emotional and agonizing. When lovers and intimates part, they leave portions of themselves behind. In this sense they are publicly exposed, and they may severely damage their self-conceptions in the process. This falling-out process sometimes involves name changes and entire changes in lifestyle. New social worlds are entered, and old worlds are left behind. Just as falling in love involves the construction of new social worlds (Waller, 1930), failing out of love involves the destruction of existing worlds, along with the attendant building, or attempted rebuilding, of new or modified worlds.

Sexual Activities and Erotic Imagery

We now turn to a discussion of sexual activities per se. Sexual intercourse requires that the overt behavior of the human male be accompanied and facilitated by an internal symbolic process or flow of thought, which is often called *erotic imagery.* Such a flow of erotic mental images and ideas is ordinarily, although not always, necessary before a man can achieve and maintain an erection, and it is certainly a requisite element in the desire to engage in sexual relations. The same is generally true of the human female. To be sure, a woman may engage in sexual relations without having any genuine erotic interest in such relations; however, if we conceive of the sex act as a relationship that is pleasurable and desirable to both parties, or that culminates in simultaneous or nearly simultaneous orgasms, then we may say that erotic imagery is equally necessary for both sexes. Erotic imagery may provide a common symbolic basis for the sexual act, and partners may come to share the same imagery. Social worlds differ in their vocabularies, or repertoires, of erotic imagery. Depending upon where persons are in their own sexual careers, their imagery of sexual activity will vary.

The term *erotic imagery* refers to a general process that we have already discussed in other connections as internalized language behavior, though it is not language in the narrow sense of the word. Through this process, social influences and past experiences exercise their regulatory effects on human behavior in general, including sex behavior. Because they apply some voluntary control over this internal symbolic process, individuals are able, in varying degrees, to hasten, retard, or entirely inhibit their own sexual responses.

Sexual Excitement

Stoller (1979, pp. 27-30) enumerates 15 different perspectives on sexual excitement (and erotic imagery) that might be investigated:

1. *Pornography:* Materials that represent sexual objects and erotic situations, including writings, drawings, paintings, sculptures, ceramics, private performances (recorded or spoken), plays, dance, films, religious rites, and music.
2. *Adornments:* Cosmetics, clothing, jewelry, tattoos.
3. *Taboos to heighten excitement:* The use of danger in an erotic situation to increase excitement; violence, whips, chains, and so on.
4. *Body styles:* Ways of walking, running, dancing, sitting, standing, and lying.
5. *Physical attributes:* Aesthetic-erotic ideals, lust-provoking physical characteristics, secondary sex (gender) characteristics including breast size, height, weight, bulk, penis size, muscle, fat, hair distribution, skin color, bisexual, and unisex body styles.
6. *Language:* Erotic spoken and written language, language that stimulates sexual excitement in foreplay and during and after intercourse; use of profanity.
7. *Daydreams:* Pornography as formalized sexual fantasy, the content of sexual daydreams, when they occur, with whom, how they are begun and ended.
8. *Masturbation:* The mechanism that puts daydreams to work (Stoller, 1979, p. 28); techniques of masturbation that are allowed and forbidden.
9. *Subliminal communications:* Subtle, nonverbal erotic passage of information (Stoller, 1979, p. 29), including the expressing of emotions with the eyes and face, as well as the voice.
10. *Looking at and being looked at:* What body parts excite, and what techniques there are for exposing and hiding the body and its parts; voyeurism, exhibitionism.
11. *Eroticism of body parts:* "Which body parts can be stimulated to excitement? Which techniques of stimulating are most likely to excite?" (Stoller, 1979, p. 29).
12. *Boredom:* The opposite of sexual excitement; what creates sexual boredom?
13. *Other sexually related areas:* Disgust, rage, fear, pain, cruelty, pleasure in pain, anxiety, false pleasures, or faked orgasms in erotic situations.
14. *Expectations regarding excitement:* Gender, age, class, education, and religious differences in expectations concerning excitement, including styles and frequency of foreplay, different intercourse positions, afterplay, repeated performances, sleeping after intercourse or getting up and leaving, different expectations with lovers, spouses, same- and opposite-sex partners, extragenital intercourse.
15. *Aberrations:* Violent sexuality, sex with animals, sex with young children; differences by race, class, gender, culture, age, and so on.

Stoller (1979, p. 30) suggests that we know very little about any of these dimensions. It is clear that these processes, and others like them, enter into the organization, production, and consummation of the sexual act. They are part of "doing gendered sexuality" in our culture.

Sexual Thought

The individual, as Sullivan (1953) argues, may have experiences at the prototaxic, parataxic, and syntaxic levels. A good deal of experience, he suggests, is not syntaxic. Such is the case with sexual thought and behavior; individuals seldom dissect their sexual feelings, reactions, or fantasies in a fully rational and logical fashion. Rather, they experience these thoughts and behaviors at the more primitive prototaxic and parataxic levels. This is not to say that syntaxic thought cannot be employed, for it often is—as the research of Masters and Johnson (1966, 1968) reveals.

Most modern American books on sex techniques emphasize the failure of many middle- and upper-class women to achieve climax with a sufficient degree of regularity. A great deal of advice is proffered as to techniques the man may use to delay his own orgasm while at the same time attempting to hasten his partner's. These procedures represent attempts to teach self-control and have to do with a question that apparently never arises in the rest of the animal world.

Masters and Johnson's (1966, 1968) work clearly demonstrates that this attitude toward male control is very much a middle-class one. Their conclusion is worth quoting, for it brings out nicely the class-linked differences in meaning of sexual activity; it also suggests the class-linked relationships in generalized social relationships between the sexes:

> Problems of premature ejaculation . . . disturbed the younger members of the study-subject population. These fears . . . were directed toward the culturally imposed fear of inability to control the ejaculatory process to a degree sufficient to satisfy the female partner. These expressed fears of performance were confined primarily to those . . . who had attained college or postgraduate levels of formal education. Only 7 of the total of 51 men whose formal education did not include college matriculation expressed the slightest concern with responsibility for coital-partner satisfaction. These men felt that it was the female's privilege to achieve satisfaction during active coition if she could, but certainly it was not the responsibility and really not the concern of the male partner to concentrate on satisfying the woman's sexual demands. Out of a total of 261 study-subjects with college matriculation, 214 men expressed concern with coital-partner satisfaction. With these men ejaculatory control sufficient to accomplish partner satisfaction was considered a coital technique that must be acquired before the personal security of coital effectiveness could be established. (Masters & Johnson, 1966, p. 202)

Masturbation

A number of interesting human problems about human sexual behavior arise in connection with the practice of masturbation. In their 1966 report, Masters and Johnson note that Kinsey et al. (1948) calculated that 92% of males had "positive masturbatory" histories, and that this figure had since been supported in the United States and abroad by more recent reports. In the Masters and Johnson study, all the subjects of both sexes described a positive history of "masturbatory facility" (pp. 197-198).

There are those, like Kinsey and his colleagues, who seek to discuss sexual behavior largely in terms of overt behavior, excluding the accompanying internal symbolic processes. This approach leads to some curious contradictions. If we were to define homosexual behavior in purely overt terms as a positive sexual response to stimuli proceeding from the same sex, masturbation could be subsumed as a special case of homosexuality. Kinsey et al., of course, did not do this; they classified masturbation as heterosexual, homosexual, or mixed—distinguishing among these in terms of the types of fantasies involved. That is, they distinguished in terms of criteria that they initially ruled out.

In line with our previous discussion, internal symbolic processes serve as integrative and organizing phenomena in human behavior. That they are cortical in nature and difficult to study in no way justifies our disregarding or dismissing them. As we have shown, it is through the mediation of such cortical or internal symbolic processes that the mores or ethical codes of a society exert their regulatory influences on human behavior.

The internal symbolic processes, or the erotic imagery, usually accompanying the act of masturbation do not differ in any essential detail from those attending the ordinary heterosexual act. Kinsey et al. (1948) note that before and during masturbation, Americans of the better-educated classes occasionally use erotic literature and pictures; they add that "nearly, but not quite, all males experience sexual fantasies during masturbation. . . . The fantasies are heterosexual when the primary interests of the individual are heterosexual, homosexual when the individual's overt experience or psychic reactions are homosexual." A person's experiences in a social milieu determine which specific excitatory ideas are likely to occur to that person in the course of the heterosexual act.

It is significant to note the changes in attitudes toward masturbation in the United States over the years. This practice used to be regarded as the cause of all sorts of harmful physical effects, including feeblemindedness and insanity, but research by competent investigators failed to substantiate such consequences. Today it is generally conceded that (a) masturbation is not known to have any necessarily deleterious physical consequences and (b) the negative effects it does have are chiefly psychological in nature and arise from such feelings as guilt, fear, and shame, which are frequently associated with the practice. The effects of masturbation, in other words, are bound up with the way in which the act is defined within a given group or society.

Inhibiting and Facilitating Stimuli

People sometimes speak of human sexuality in animalistic terms, implying that human sex urges are aroused, repressed, and even expressed in ways essentially identical to those of other mammals. This view is incorrect, for human sexual responses are channeled in ways that have no parallel in the animal world.

Individuals may rule out whole segments of a population as sexual or marital partners for social rather than biological reasons.

This is true of the mutual exclusion practiced by many in the white and black segments of the American population, the various castes of India, and the exogamous clans found among many preliterate peoples. Thus if a native tribe is divided into four clans or subgroups, an unmarried male in one of them may be required to seek his sexual partners only among the women of one of the three other clans. In such cases, eligible and healthy persons of the opposite sex may not even be perceived as desirable sexual objects if they fall into forbidden categories. In our own society, such barriers as social class, age, religion, race, and marital status limit individuals' choices of sexual partners.

Someone else's mother may become an exciting object, particularly if she is a widow and not too elderly; but sexual responses toward one's own mother are not permissible. Although a woman may be sexually attractive to her own male children, she is generally a sexual nonentity to them. This is but one instance of the operation of incest taboos. Human standards of incest vary considerably from society to society, applying sometimes only to the intimate family group and sometimes to a wide circle of persons, many of whom are biologically unrelated (Thomas & Thomas, 1928). Incest taboos are found only among humans; they are social, not biological, phenomena.

We may cite other instances of classificatory elimination of sexual partners. Many white Americans find it difficult to be aroused by dark-skinned blacks because of strong race prejudice against black people. Indeed, some who are attracted by white-appearing persons feel repelled when these turn out to be mulatto. Black men and women are sometimes repelled by the "washed-out" appearance of whites. Similar barriers may be created by religion, nationality, age differences, and a host of other matters connected with individuals' standards of beauty, cleanliness, and the like.

The arousal of inappropriate imagery may prevent or interrupt sexual activity. For example, laughter, anger, irritation, disgust, and shock are deterrents to sexual excitation. Conditions preventing or interrupting sexual activity may have nothing to do with relationships between the partners; such external factors as noise, light, lack of privacy, and fear of possible interruption can interfere with intercourse. Internal factors having no direct connection with the overall relationship between the partners can also prove a hindrance—fear of pregnancy or disease, or guilt feelings of any kind, for example. One newly married couple was physically incapable of carrying out the sex act as long as they lived with the bridegroom's parents. Potency was restored when the couple moved to their own living quarters.

Impotence and Frigidity

The terms *impotence* and *frigidity* are used in a number of ways that are not altogether consistent or logical. *Impotence* generally refers to the inability of a man to achieve and maintain an erection sufficient to engage in intercourse, whereas *frigidity* refers to a general lack of interest or enjoyment of the sex act on the part of a woman. Both terms are highly relative; every man would be impotent and every woman frigid in some conceivable type of situation. A woman who is exclusively lesbian would probably be frigid with respect to men, and an exclusively gay man might be incapable of performing the sexual act with a woman. This statement needs qualification to allow for the fact that in many sexual relations, one of the partners may be activated to positive response primarily by fantasies concerning someone other than the actual sexual partner. It is perhaps through the control of the fantasy process that certain individuals are able to be happily married to and have children with their opposite-sex partners although they are homosexual (Boswell, 1980, pp. 26-28; Ross, 1971).

Given that the anatomical and physiological bases of sex behavior constitute necessary, but not determining, conditions for the development of sexuality, it follows that impotence and frigidity may be consequences of either organic or psychological conditions—the latter being the more common. In terms of the usual conception of frigidity, for example, it appears that American women of the urban middle class are more likely to be sexually unresponsive than are those of the lower classes. No biological explanation of these class differences is available, whereas divergent social backgrounds may sufficiently account for them (Blumstein & Schwartz, 1983).

Although a decline in sexual interest and activity during old age is related to organic changes (de Beauvoir, 1952; Hamilton, 1939; Hite, 1976), the connection is not sufficiently close to be called a causal one. Hamilton (1939), for example, notes that many men who came to his office complaining of impotence were between the ages of 37 and 40. Their ages, in short, were much less than the age at which the cessation of sex activity could be expected on purely biological grounds. Hamilton points out that, as one might anticipate, cases of this type often respond favorably to the suggestion that there is nothing wrong with them. Seward (1946), after surveying the research literature, concludes that "impotence in the aging, to a surprising extent, is the product of psychological attitude."

Masters and Johnson's (1968) intensive study of a sample of aging men and women gives strong evidence that despite organic changes, frequent sexual activity can be enjoyed well into old age. Decline of interest and gratification is related—unless there are organic reasons, including illness—to what Masters and Johnson term *psycho- and sociophysiological problems* attendant on the aging process (pp. 238-270). These include widespread cultural attitudes toward aging as nonsexual or asexual, the monotony of monogamous relations, mental or physical fatigue, overindulgence in food and drink, and fear of performance failure in the male.

Thus impotence and frigidity occur in individuals who are biologically sound. Conversely, sexual activity is engaged in by persons who lack what are often regarded as indispensable biological prerequisites. Many women continue to enjoy intercourse after they have passed through the menopause, up to and beyond the ages of 60 and 70 years, and Kinsey et al. (1948) cite the case of an 88-year-old man who enjoyed regular sex relations with his 90-year-old wife. Males who are castrated when mature—as a consequence of war injuries, for example—often continue to desire and enjoy sexual relations. Seward (1946) cites the case of a 53-year-old man, castrated at the age of 24, whose sexual activities increased markedly after the operation. Prior to it, he had practiced coitus about once a month. Afterward, he had intercourse several times a week with his wife and sometimes with other women as well. His increased potency lasted for 30 years.

Impotence and frigidity, when not organic in origin, can be regarded as the consequences of the ways in which individuals think about themselves and about sexual matters. In other words, they are learned ways of behaving. The central aspects of this problem have to do with the nature of the internal symbolic processes evoked by sexual stimulation. Thus if a woman is so affected by her early training that sexual excitation sets up an internal symbolic response in terms of such concepts as "evil," "danger," "fear," "dirty," "pain," and "immorality," then these ideas will prevent or inhibit the flow of facilitating and stimulating erotic imagery. Moreover, if the individual has been consistently brought up in the manner implied by these concepts, she is not likely to possess an adequate repertory of sexually stimulating ideas. This means that even if she overcomes the ideas of evil, immorality, nastiness, and the like, she still may not be able to respond fully during sexual intercourse.

Masters and Johnson (1968) make a similar point concerning the problems of the impotent man. They remark that when an impotent husband goes to bed with his wife, there may be more than one spectator who watches the episode: The wife who is attempting to stimulate and arouse him also is observing her own and her husband's behavior, perhaps thinking, "If he obviously isn't responding, what could I be doing wrong?" In her role as spectator, she may so distract herself that when a sexual opportunity really presents itself, she may be, as the authors say, "psychologically caught in the corner observing the physical proceeding rather than physiologically tied to the bed totally involved with her own mating" (p. 96). Both partners thus may be so involved as observers and so worried about their own performances that sexual stimuli become relatively ineffective for both of them. Neither may realize that the other is detached from and not wholly involved in what is going on. These observations by Masters and Johnson point up a general aspect of human behavior we noted earlier—namely, that human beings are simultaneously subjects and objects; they listen to themselves talk and observe their own actions, continuously monitoring both as interaction proceeds. We use this old and cynical proverb to make a related point: "When two divorced people marry, four people get into bed."

Impotence in the male also is closely bound up with the individual's conception of self and is often associated with increasing age. The middle-aged man becomes aware of his advancing age and sexual decline. Because American society places a high value on potency as a test and proof of masculinity, many middle-aged and elderly American men conceive of diminished potency as a reflection on themselves. Often they seek to restore their self-esteem by consulting physicians or taking hormone pills. Some try to reassure themselves by seeking sexual adventures with women other than their wives. A substantial percentage of the sexual offenses committed against young girls are the acts of older men seeking to bolster their masculine self-esteem.

CONCLUSION

Sexual activity is primarily symbolic and interactional. Sexuality and gender are social facts; their meanings are constructed in and through institutional discourses, including medicine, sociology, psychiatry, anthropology, popular literature and music, and the mass media, especially cinema and television. These meanings vary historically and among social groups. There is no universal, essential sexual identity, although constructionist and essentialist theorists debate this point. There is an absence of evidence indicating that human sexual preferences are determined by sex hormones, and there is positive evidence that masculine and feminine gender identities are learned systems of behavior.

A sociology of homosexuality emerged as a part of the sociology of sex in the 1970s. Gay, lesbian, and bisexual discourse has repeatedly challenged the concept of a compulsive heterosexuality. Over the past 30 years, three different moral and political discourses have shaped public attitudes about same-sex experiences. Historically, homosexuals have been stigmatized, and homosexuality has been regarded as either a sin or an illness. Liberal humanistic discourses in the 1980s refused these negative labels and attempted to normalize lesbian and gay lifestyles. More recently, this assimilationist position has been challenged by the members of queer nation, including bisexuals and transgendered persons, who endorse a politics of transgression and parody. The AIDS crisis of the 1980s energized a conservative backlash against these efforts that undermined gay and lesbian efforts to normalize same-sex experiences and relationships.

The influence of symbolic processes on human sexual behavior is evident in masturbation, erotic imagery, the control or inhibition of the orgasm, and different ways of defining or interpreting the significance of sexual activities. Sexual identities are conferred upon persons through the socialization process; sexual self-conceptions arise out of intimate relationships. Falling in and out of love must be viewed processually. A person's standing in the sexual arena often reflects his or her location in a society's or a group's stratification system. The profound symbolism that surrounds the sexual act and its consequences can be seen in the controversy surrounding the abortion issue.

SUGGESTED READINGS

Blasius, M., & Phelan, S. (Eds.). (1997). *We are everywhere: A historical sourcebook of gay and lesbian politics.* New York: Routledge. A valuable historical guide, especially the sections on AIDS and gay and lesbian politics.

Seidman, S. (1994). Symposium: Queer theory/sociology: A dialogue. *Sociological Theory, 12,* 166-177. One of the first attempts to bring queer theory into sociology.

Warner, M. (Ed.). (1993). *Fear of a queer planet.* Minneapolis: University of Minnesota Press. An important set of statements on queer theory and gay and lesbian politics in the contemporary period.

STUDY QUESTIONS

1. What is queer theory, and how are its assumptions reflected in the concept of queer nation?
2. How have Foucault's arguments shaped recent histories and theories of sexuality?
3. Discuss the sexual politics surrounding bisexuality.
4. How has the AIDS crisis shaped gay politics?
5. What is the sexual drama, and what are the sources of sexual identity and imagery?

13

Deviance, Deviant Bodies, and Deviant Worlds

In this chapter we attempt to place the study of illness, sickness, and deviance within an expanded symbolic interactionist, cultural studies conception of social relationships, social worlds, and the circuits of culture. Individuals occupy shifting positions in interlocking and interconnecting social worlds. These worlds commit them to certain lines of action and lead to the development of special self-conceptions and moral, gendered identities. Each of these worlds is a special universe of discourse, meaning, and experience. Each world, from some perspective, is deviant, unusual, or different. We discuss a variety of these worlds in this chapter.

In addressing deviance, we draw on Michel Foucault's arguments concerning discourse and regimes of truth. Some degree of caution must be exercised when using a term like *discourse.* Foucault's critics contend that "he tends to absorb too much into 'discourse,' and this has the effect of encouraging his followers to neglect the influence of the material, economic, and structural factors in the operation of power/ knowledge" (Hall, 1997, p. 51). Still others feel that Foucault's rejection of any abso- lute criterion of truth in the human disciplines opens him to the charge of relativism (Hall, 1997, p. 51). We attempt to navigate around these charges, for there is little doubt that Foucault's work has had a major impact on "contemporary theories of representation and meaning" (Hall, 1997, p. 51).

Discourse and the Work of Representation

We have argued repeatedly that understandings about the social world are established through systems of discourse. Things have no meanings in and of themselves; their meanings emerge out of the process of interpretive interaction. This process is embedded in an ongoing world of cultural meanings and representations—what we have called the circuits of culture. We know a thing only through this process of representation. The meanings of mental illness, of AIDS, of alcoholism, of gayness, and of bisexuality are constituted in and through the process of mediated, interactional representation. In their discussion of two versions of labeling theory (mundane and constitutive, or ethnomethodological), Miller and Holstein (1993) put the issue this way: "The labeling process *constitutes* the phenomenon" (p. 14). Nothing can stand outside the field of representation. Any given object, person, or abstract idea becomes the sum of its representations.

Furthermore, these meanings are grounded in specific historical moments. The same phenomenon, as we argued in our discussion of homosexuality, will not be found across different historical periods (see Hall, 1997, p. 46). Following Foucault (1985) and Hall (1997, p. 46), we can argue that mental illness, or alcoholism, or homosexuality, is not an objective fact whose meanings remain stable across time and space. Hall (1997) discusses madness and mental illness, noting that "it is only within a definite discursive formation that the object, 'madness,' could appear as a meaningful or intelligible construct" (p. 46). Foucault (1972) elaborates, suggesting that madness was "constituted by all that was said, in all the statements that named it, divided it up, described it, explained it, traced its development, indicated its various correlations, judged it, and possibly gave it speech by articulating, in its name, discourses that were to be taken as its own" (p. 32; also quoted in Hall, 1997, p. 46).

It is only after a phenomenon such as madness is put into place that an appropriate subject—the madman, the hysterical woman, the alcoholic, the schizophrenic—can appear, and this appearance is shaped "by current medical and psychiatric knowledge" (Hall, 1997, p. 46). These practices, knowledges, and discourses include medicine, psychoanalysis, clinical psychiatry, and psychology. Based on these knowledges, experts from these disciplines define and name individuals, labeling them to fit their conditions—perhaps as mad, hysterical, clinically depressed, or alcoholic. Of course it makes no sense to talk about the "hysterical woman outside the nineteenth-century view of hysteria as a very widespread female malady" (Hall, 1997, p. 46). And the bisexual, as we discussed in Chapter 12, is a recent and very complicated discursive construction.

These systems of knowledge and representation shape experience and regulate conduct. They operate within institutional settings and existing technologies of power, including laws, regulations, and systems of surveillance. Knowledge and representation are thus closely connected to the apparatuses of power that operate in a culture and its social worlds. These apparatuses shape specific regimes of truth that are fitted to particular classes of individuals, such as the mentally ill, the sexually abused, or the alcoholic. For Foucault, every society has its regimes of truth, its general systems of power, control, and knowledge that define what is truth and what is not truth. These regimes, in turn, structure the knowledge that creates specific subjects, including those types referred to above. For example, in the United States in the 1980s a new social type was created: the violent young African American male addicted to crack cocaine (Reeves & Campbell, 1994). This social type emerged out of a conservative racial discourse that focused on the inner city, violent gangs, and drug-dealing African American males. This type of individual was not present in earlier systems of racial discourse in the United States.

Systems of power circulate throughout a society. These systems help regulate the production of deviant bodies and selves. But as Hall (1997) observes, power does not just move downward, from one source to another. Power relations permeate "all levels of social existence and are therefore to be found operating at every site of social life—in the private spheres of the family and sexuality, as much as in the public spheres of politics, the economy and the law" (p. 50). Power is not only repressive, punishing, and negative. Power as a process is productive; it produces things, from knowledge to pleasures and desires. For example, the penal system produces, as Hall (1997) observes, books and treatises, regulations, debates in Congress, and police training institutes. Attempts to regulate sexuality produce "talk about sex, television and radio programmes, sermons and legislation, novels, stories, magazine features, medical and counselling advice, essays and articles . . . as well as new sexual practices (e.g. 'safe' sex) and the pornography industry" (p. 50).

We turn now to a brief discussion of social constructionism and the medicalization of deviance (Conrad & Schneider, 1992; Gusfield, 1992).

Social Constructionism and the Medicalization of Deviance

Foucault's emphasis on discourse and representation is compatible with the social psychologist's concern for how particular social problems, from alcoholism to homosexuality, become public problems (Gusfield, 1992, p. v). Of course, before these phenomena can be "explored, their status as problems must be understood" (Gusfield, 1992, p. v). This involves a consideration of the process by which members of groups come to define particular situations as problems (see Kitsuse & Spector, 1973; Spector & Kitsuse, 1987). Social problems are "not objective situations to be studied and corrected; rather they are interpretive processes that constitute what come to be seen as oppressive, intolerable, or unjust situations like crime, poverty, or homelessness" (Miller & Holstein, 1993, p. 6). Social problems are constructed through a rhetorical process, a process that involves discourse and its meanings. Public rhetoric and claims making by particular groups bring problems into existence.

Of course, real material, bedrock conditions of poverty and injustice exist in the world, and they exist independent of their representation in some system of discourse. The concern is with how these conditions get defined and represented in media discourse and in the claims-making process.

This constructionist approach emphasizes the history of particular problems—the development of AIDS, for example, or of child abuse and child hyperactivity. Problems develop, as we have argued, within interpretive frameworks that connect to public issues, public opinion, and the media. The history of a problem does not necessarily involve a solution. The "public definitions of public problems are the outcomes and continual objects of claims that interested groups put forth in public arenas" (Gusfield, 1992, p. vi). Conflicts over these claims arise, and they involve arguments about facts and moral judgments—about who has their facts straight and what moral meanings the facts have (Conrad & Schneider, 1992, p. 277).

With Foucault, Conrad and Schneider (1992, p. 36) argue that medicine and the medical model play a central part in the social construction of many social problems today. We have moved from a society of sinners to a society of sick people. The medical model suggests that strange behavior is not a matter of choice. The homosexual is sick, ill, not a deviant doing immoral, sinful things. Ill persons are "neither criminal, nor morally responsible for their 'disease.' However, as sick people, they are both obligated and entitled to be helped" (Gusfield, 1992, p. vii).

There are negative consequences to the transformation of badness, or deviance, into illness. The medical model implies that persons defined as ill have experienced loss of control over their own lives (Gusfield, 1992, p. vii). In accepting the label, persons admit to being different, helpless, or deviant (Gusfield, 1992, p. vii). As we have noted in Chapter 12, members of queer nation no longer accept the idea that homosexuals are sick, or the idea that they are sinful.

The medical model delivers people to the medical establishment, to psychiatrists, child guidance counselors, social workers, alcohol treatment personnel, and so on (see Davis, 1997, p. 5). This places them in the hands of a new set of social control agents (Gusfield, 1992, p. viii). At the same time, the process of medicalization depoliticizes a problem. Homosexuality is one example of this.

Conceptions of Deviance

Deviance and its definitions arise out of the interactions of individuals who hold different degrees of power and authority over one another. In an ultimate sense, the state, its government, and its laws possess the final power to define what is and is not deviant or criminal behavior. The application of a deviant or criminal label to one individual or a group of individuals involves the political application of power (Becker, 1973; Cockerham, 1978; Foucault, 1980b; Gove, 1980; Gusfield, 1967; Horowitz & Liebowitz, 1968; Kitsuse, 1975; Kitsuse & Spector, 1973).

The study of deviance leads the sociologist directly into a consideration of power and its distribution within social groups and societies generally. In any society there are experts on conventional behavior, normal behavior, deviant behavior, and criminal behavior. In a complex society, some things are considered deviant in some circles but not in others. Further, there are certain behaviors that simply go unnoticed—or, if noticed, are passed off as uninteresting or irrelevant. Whether a person eats breakfast, has blue eyes, or has long hair is basically irrelevant for his or her biography and relationships with others. Other behaviors, however, traditionally become so publicly real that professional interpreters of them emerge. Psychiatrists, sociologists, lawyers, educators, and physicians all account for deviant behaviors with differing theories, some of which attain the status of scientific theories. Psychoanalysis, structural functionalism, and symbolic interactionism are some theories that purport to account for such phenomena as murder, rape, drug addiction, divorce, homosexuality, and insanity. Over time, as new issues become controversial—for example, in the last part of the 20th century, civil rights, feminism, gay liberation, and urban riots—new theories emerge and old theories are revised to explain them, and inevitably clashes in perspective occur. Militant feminists reject Freudian explanations of their behavior; politicians find irrelevant the scientific utterances of social scientists, including political scientists. Deviance and its discovery involve inherently social processes, which at root rest on political debates over what will be termed conventional, acceptable behavior (Kitsuse & Spector, 1973).

The Nature of Deviance

A basic preliminary point concerning the nature of deviance is that actions in themselves are not moral or immoral, deviant or nondeviant. It is the judgment that is passed on the behavior by others, and not the behavior itself, that determines and defines deviance. As Kai Erikson (1965) remarks:

> Deviance is not a property *inherent* in any particular kind of behavior; it is a property *conferred* upon that behavior by the people who come into direct or indirect contact with it. The only way an observer can tell whether a given style of behavior is deviant . . . is to learn something about the standards of the audience which responds to it. (p. 6)

It is difficult—perhaps impossible—to think of any type of behavior outlawed in the United States today that has not been acceptable somewhere at some time.

There is nothing about many specific kinds of activities that automatically causes them to be regarded in the wider community as dangerous, odd, or perverted. Certain acts are sanctioned in some communities and negatively evaluated in others; over time, definitions inevitably change as public orientation shifts. Addiction to opiates, for example, is regarded as a medical problem in most Western countries, and was so regarded in the United States until recent decades. Homosexuals are discriminated against in Western countries, but this particular bias is not universally shared. Indeed, when heterosexuals meet homosexuals under predominantly normal conditions, as in some occupations, the fact of their homosexuality is not much of an issue, and they are assumed to be like any other human beings.

Historical changes in definitions of deviance are striking, and we could cite many illustrations. For instance, the treatment of religious sects is a highly variable matter; acceptance of a sect in a given period depends upon whether it espouses practices that seem shocking or dangerous to its neighbors. During one period of its history a sect may be viewed as a menace to public morals, whereas at another it may be viewed as merely odd or peculiar. When politics get mixed into sectarianism, the sect may be regarded, at least for a time, as unpatriotic or even subversive. Of course, a sect or any other group may engage in practices that run counter to general moral standards and yet escape widespread attention; but if the glare of publicity falls upon the group, influential groups of "good citizens" may demand that something be done about its degenerate or dangerous practices. When public furor dies down, the group may continue its traditional practices more or less unmolested, but it remains vulnerable as long as the practices themselves fall within the current definition of deviance.

Deviance, which takes a number of forms, may be viewed at two levels. At the *group* level, it involves the public violation of group norms and the application of specialized procedures and sanctions to handle the deviant and control the volume of deviance. When the formal agencies of control lack jurisdiction over the behavior, it is dealt with through informal control mechanisms, such as gossip or avoidance. At the *personal* level, deviance may be seen as behavior that violates the person's internalized norms and is believed to be controlled by internal psychic mechanisms, such as conscience.

Deviance may have its sources in the social structure or may be generated by causes within the individual. These causes may be consciously recognized and reported upon by the persons involved, or they may exist below the level of awareness as unnamed, unconscious, or subliminal influences. As we have already touched on deviance in terms of self, generalized other, and conscience, we shall be concerned here with deviance at the group and interactional level. Any attempt to explain deviance must focus not on the act as such, but on the social evaluation of the act that causes it to be regarded as deviant (Gibbs & Erickson, 1975; Kitsuse, 1962).

Sources of Definitions of Deviance

We can summarize the foregoing discussion by noting that individuals may become tainted or "spoiled" interactants for any of the following four reasons. First, they may commit illegal acts and be apprehended, arrested, charged, and convicted; then they find that their biographies have been significantly altered, and they may be unable to return to their "normal" worlds of social interaction.

Second, as Goffman (1963b) argues, they may belong to work, ethnic, religious, or racial groups that are viewed as less than desirable by the broader social order. Jews have suffered and died simply for being members of such a group, as have members of nearly all other major religious and ethnic groups in the world's history. Blacks, Italians, Irish, Japanese, Chinese, Germans, and Russians have, at different points in their collective world histories, been defined as political, economic, and moral threats to other sectors of humanity (Kronus, 1971). Whether or not group, economic, or political membership is viewed in undesirable terms depends largely on a group's standing in the broader society. Those groups with power can legislate their own conceptions of moral desirability and acceptability; those groups that are viewed as moral or economic threats, or those individuals who perform a country's "dirty work," often find themselves outside the mainstream of political processes. As a consequence, they suffer economic and moral abuse from other citizens. This phenomenon often leads such individuals to band together by living in common residential areas, where they at least find some social support for their worldviews. Of course, processes of discrimination and segregation often make it impossible for these individuals to live their lives in morally, economically, and politically acceptable circumstances.

Third, individuals may be stigmatized because of physical deformity, because they have acquired some disease or illness, or because they have deteriorated mentally or are developmentally disabled (Bullock, 1987; Davis, 1997; Jacobs, 1969; Mercer, 1973). Fellow interactants assume that those they confront on a daily basis will "appear to be normal"; they will walk normally, speak intelligently, not be sight or hearing impaired, have the usual level of physical stamina, and be able to follow the train of a normal conversation with relative ease. Any alteration in these attributes leads others to define such individuals in less than positive terms. They have not committed deviant or illegal acts; rather, they are spoiled, stigmatized actors by virtue of how they publicly present and display their bodies.

Fourth, persons can have character flaws, or stigmas, that are not publicly visible, but that would, if made known, brand those individuals as deviant. Those who have been hospitalized for mental illness, homosexuals, the recently divorced, unmarried parents, and former embezzlers all share one common characteristic: Their deviance is not publicly visible. For these kinds of deviance to have interactional effects, the individuals must make public the hidden facts in their biographies. Often it is to their advantage to do so, for a tainted past can hover over a person's life; if they refuse to reveal their deviance, they may find that someone else will.

The Asymmetry of Social Reactions

Individuals—especially those who belong to undesirable groups or who have undesirable physical attributes—may be stigmatized without ever having committed any deviant or criminal acts (Cahman, 1968). On the other hand, it is impossible for persons not to be stigmatized, if only for short periods of time, after they have broken laws or engaged in deviant acts that evoke public outrage. There is an asymmetrical relationship between stigma and deviance, and this asymmetry shifts over time as individuals move into new and different phases of their moral careers. What was deviant at one point in time may later be viewed as an attribute of excellence, bravery, or forward thinking.

The Benefits of Deviance and Stigma

The theoretical and research literature often exhibits a rather grim, humorless view of the deviant (Mizruchi & Perrucci, 1962). It is assumed that those individuals who gain what are called "immoral" sexual pleasures, engage in illicit drug practices, or make money illegally do so without reward, benefit, personal fulfillment, or professional advancement. The fact is, a good deal of what is stigmatized as deviant and illegal is pleasurable, profitable, and rewarding. This simple fact offers one explanation for why many individuals are drawn into those pursuits that "good" people find morally repugnant, deviant, and criminal.

Fads and Fashions in Deviance

What is deviant at one point in time may become normal, acceptable behavior at other times. Thus it was once considered deviant and immoral to drink alcoholic beverages, but this view eventually gave way to the view that drinking behavior is fashionable (Beauchamp, 1980; Gusfield, 1967). This definition, however, is in the process of changing once again, as we find ourselves in an era in which alcoholism and other drug addictions have become the subject of great public concern. Similarly, the recent trend toward harsher punishments in the laws concerning cocaine reflects the fact that cocaine addiction is now regarded as a major social problem; indeed, some have spoken of a "cocaine epidemic" (Gold, 1984). In the 1980s, the cocaine "craze" was compared with an earlier epidemic of cocaine use that ended well before the 1920s. At that time, it was not illegal to possess cocaine, but it was illegal for sellers not to be registered as distributors of the drug, and it was illegal to use the drug without a physician's prescription. The fact that cocaine is no longer regarded as a fashionable recreational drug but as an addictive substance (owing to the prevalence of crack cocaine) is evidence of how social, medical, and political definitions change and shift over time.

In the late 1800s and early 1900s, cocaine was endorsed by physicians, heads of state, Pope Leo XII, Jules Verne, Auguste Rodin, Thomas Edison, and Sigmund Freud. The drug was used to prevent malaria and influenza and as a local anesthetic, and some physicians used cocaine in the treatment of morphine addiction. The popular drink Coca-Cola contained cocaine until 1905. In 1984, virtually every state had laws that prohibited trafficking in cocaine, with penalties for a first offense ranging up to 15 years.

As new issues come to the public's attention, public moral conscience is aroused and people become outraged over new forms of illegal or deviant behavior. In this sense, a nation's social control agencies continually produce new side-effects of marijuana, heroin, birth control pills, cocaine, alcohol, and so on. Nations are continually experiencing new epidemics of deviance. This keeps the social control agencies in business; it also clarifies ambiguous conceptions of what is deviant and what is acceptable (Coser, 1975; K. Erikson, 1965). Furthermore, each new form of deviance lays the groundwork for new behaviors that may eventually become fashionable and morally acceptable.

A critical question concerning fads and fashions in deviance involves the original source or locus of the deviance. That is, from what sectors of society does it emanate, and who is defining it as deviant? It appears that unacceptable fashions that flow from those lacking political power will not become acceptable until more powerful and influential citizens take up the new activity. Thus marijuana laws were not modified until middle- and upper-class youths were apprehended for using the drug and their parents began experimenting with it. So today's deviance may become tomorrow's fashion. Similarly, what is fashionable today may become outmoded and deviant in the future.

Techniques of Neutralization

On the other hand, persons who violate norms that they themselves accept as valid and legitimate ordinarily feel guilty about their behavior. *Techniques of neutralization* is a recently coined expression that refers to the symbolic devices individuals use in such situations to permit themselves to continue the behavior and to assuage their pangs of conscience. Its meaning is closely akin to that of *rationalization.* We should note that deviants do not necessarily feel guilty; this is especially true when they deny the validity of the public definition of deviance, as is the case with many marijuana smokers, political dissenters, homosexuals, and others. Sykes and Matza (1959) enumerate four techniques of neutralization:

1. *Denial of harm:* Little or no real harm has been done.
2. *Denial of the victim:* The victim provoked the action and got what was coming to him or her.
3. *Attacking the accusers:* The police are corrupt, brutal, and unfair, and the laws are unjust.
4. *Invoking other and higher loyalties:* Loyalty to particular others—one's fellow gang members, for example—takes precedence.

The sense of guilt and the ideology used to neutralize it are indications that deviants are committed to the values they violate. They explain and excuse their behavior by means of concepts and ideas that are made available by the broader society. Thus drug addicts and alcoholics account for and sometimes excuse their addiction in terms of neutralizing "motives" or excuses. The user of illicit drugs, for example, may utilize any or all of the techniques of neutralization by arguing that (a) no harm was done, (b) the laws are unjust, and (c) his or her friends also use the drug.

Deviant Careers and Social Worlds

Much of the literature in criminology and the sociology of deviance assumes a relatively static view of the labeling, or defining, process. To be termed a drug addict, a juvenile delinquent, a divorcée, a homosexual, or a radical means different things for the individual at different points in his or her moral career. One is not just delinquent (Finestone, 1957), or addicted to a certain class of drugs, or mentally ill. Rather, one becomes delinquent, addicted, or mentally ill over a period of time. In each phase of their deviant careers, individuals see themselves differently (Becker, 1973). The meanings that labels have for them and their significant others and for the public at large will vary in terms of how they act. If they exacerbate their deviance—parade it, so to speak—then it may eventually become a permanent part of their identity kit, for they will now be viewed as homosexuals or drug addicts or whatever by their interactive fellows. On the other hand, they may choose to hide or conceal their deviance; then its relevance for their day-to-day interactions is minimal (Kando, 1972). Some individuals assume dramatic and emotional responses in the first phases of their deviant careers, and then with the passage of time normalize their deviant identification (Birenbaum, 1970).

As we will show, an actor's response to an ascription of deviance depends largely on the public's receptivity to his or her altered condition. Some forms of deviance have strong and massive institutional support—for example, organized crime (King & Chambliss, 1972). Others emerge in the form of social movements. Women's liberation and gay liberation are two examples of how individuals have banded together in an attempt to have themselves collectively redefined by the broader social order. Many deviants fall heir to incipient, less well-defined social worlds. Some deviants keep their deviant identities hidden altogether, or share them with only small numbers of other individuals. What can be called *relational deviance* falls into this category. Marital partners may have their own private versions of the sexual act that, if made public, would brand them deviant; those who carry on affairs, embezzle, shoot drugs on weekends, or keep hidden stocks of pornographic magazines also usually keep their deviances to themselves. Finally, there are those deviants, or "outsiders," who belong to no organized social worlds or social relationships and who furtively and secretly practice their deviant acts; transvestites, "closeted" homosexuals, and eccentrics fall into this category.

Depending on individuals' locations in any of the social worlds mentioned above, their responses to the label of *deviant* or *criminal* will vary. Consequently, any analysis of the deviant career must simultaneously assume a temporal and interactional, or organizational, stance (Davis & Stivers, 1975). Many students of deviance have ignored these temporal, moral, and interactional features of deviants and their careers. We turn now to a consideration of a variety of deviant worlds.

Deviant Worlds and Individuals

In presenting a general framework for understanding deviant behavior, we noted that some forms of deviance are highly organized. Some shade off gradually and merge imperceptibly with conduct that is disapproved of or viewed as peculiar, yet is permitted and even protected when necessary by agents of the law. We shall examine several instances of the more organized types of deviance as well as some of the less organized or unorganized types. All persons who label others as deviant or are themselves so labeled are members of social worlds that differentially endorse those designations. All forms of deviant behavior find their locus in some social world, no matter how loosely organized (Traub & Little, 1980).

Deviant Groups and the Wider Society

All deviant groups are related to and arise from the structure of the wider society. Some quite clearly perform functions for accepted groups. Respectable men of all social worlds take advantage of the availability of prostitutes, and quasi-criminal or quasi-underworld organizations capitalize on this patronage. It is not these organizations but the persistent market for prostitution that makes it difficult to suppress. The market for the prostitute's services presumably reflects the inadequacies of those legitimate institutions that regulate sexual and affectional behavior (Davis, 1937; Heyl, 1979; Roby, 1969). Occasionally, zealous advocates of vice suppression may succeed in outlawing a particular form of activity, such as gambling, that happens to be an integral part of the way of life of some people. Illegal organization then flourishes around the otherwise unfulfilled demand for the banished activity or commodity (Polsky, 1966).

Some deviant groups may be said to constitute *deviant worlds* or *deviant communities* because, although they are located in space, they also tend to transcend particular locales. They are not tightly organized; rather, they consist of loosely connected groups or circles of deviants, not all of which know or have direct communication with other circles.

Criminal Worlds

As we have remarked, the American emphasis on success, money, and competition, as well as the great proliferation of occupations and divisions of labor, has resulted in the development of illegal occupations that are integral parts of our commercial and occupational world. Students of criminology have classified crime and criminals in a great variety of ways. The criminal underworld is a complicated social structure with occupational diversity and status systems. For our purposes, we may classify criminals into three categories: conventional criminals, white-collar criminals, and racketeers (Sutherland & Cressey, 1966).

The Criminal Occupations

Conventional criminals may be either *professionals* or *amateurs*; equivalent terms would be *occupational* and *nonoccupational*. Most instances of murder, rape, and arson, for example, are not committed as occupational activities, and a great many persons from respectable society commit occasional thefts, murders, and other offenses. The *conventional criminal occupations* probably number in the hundreds. An immense number of specific devices and skills may be employed, and new ones are constantly being invented and old ones improved. These skills may be roughly classified as (a) those involving violence or threats, (b) those involving manual or mechanical dexterity and skill (such as pocket picking, shoplifting, safecracking, and automobile stealing and stripping), and (c) those involving verbal dexterity and histrionic ability (frequently called swindling, fraud, and confidence games). In the last type, some mechanical or manual skill may be called for, as in the "shell game" or "three-card monte." The specific types of fraud are legion.

Each of the various criminal occupations has its own specific rules and norms to guide and control the behavior of its practitioners. Each has a hierarchy of status positions and possesses prestige relative to others, this prestige reflecting underworld public opinion. There are codes regulating standard performances: A "fingering job" ordinarily yields a regular 10%; "the nut" (expenses) is always subtracted from the money gained "at the top" (before dividing).

White-collar crime consists of offenses committed in legitimate occupations or business—for example, by corporations in the course of their regular business operations (Sutherland, 1949). It is perhaps unnecessary to note that considerable crime is committed by politicians and public officials on behalf of the public interest. A businessman may break the law knowingly either for mercenary reasons or because he feels that he must because his competitors do likewise; sometimes he may break a law because the law itself is vague and the boundaries of legality are not clear. Sometimes corporations challenge the legality of statutes by deliberately flouting them to see if the courts will uphold their action. There is no "world" of white-collar crime as such.

The third general type of criminal is the racketeer, a person involved in underworld business activities (i.e., the provision of contraband goods or services for a market that usually includes clientele from the respectable world; gambling, prostitution, and the bootlegging of liquor and drugs are examples). Underworld businesses are organized much like any others, with certain special features, however, such as the prominence of bribery—involving collusion of public officials—and the inability of underworld businessmen to enforce contracts and settle disputes in the courts. As a substitute for court decisions, racketeers have their own methods of settling disputes and enforcing the fulfillment of contractual obligations. Racketeers, like conventional criminals, are part of the general criminal milieu.

Criminals in the first and third categories (conventional criminals and racketeers) have identifications with a somewhat vague but nonetheless real criminal world, a world that is somewhat wider than particular occupations or rackets. This world, much like the world of the artist or the professional athlete, is not sharply set off from other worlds, but does command a certain loyalty and allegiance from its members. Criminal argot reflects something of the unity of this world when it designates all outsiders as "squares" and all insiders as "right." Marginal persons—such as lawyers who engage in dubious or dishonest practices—are called "kinky" to designate their separate status:

> The professional thief . . . has semilegitimate acquaintances among lawyers, fences, fixers, bondsmen, and politicians. These . . . are making money from the thief but are supposed to be members of legitimate society. He may call upon them, also, for assistance for the less legitimate purposes. . . .
>
> The thief is somewhat suspicious of all individuals in legitimate society other than those mentioned. He believes that whoever is not with him is against him. Any noncriminal individual not personally known . . . is a possible danger and, as an individual, is somewhat disliked on that account. This feeling is reinforced by occasional trouble which results from perfectly proper acquaintances. . . .
>
> [There is considerable] danger that the thief may run into if he tries to make legitimate contacts with strangers. Because of this, the professional thief lives largely in a world of his own and is rather completely isolated from general society. The majority of them do not care to contact society except professionally. (Sutherland, 1949, pp. 164-166)

The fact that all insiders are on the shady side of the law lends symbolic cohesion. The intense hatred felt for informers is an index of this cohesion and of the need for secrecy in the face of the outside world. Of course, all groups—occupational or otherwise—require for their very functioning that certain secrets be withheld from nonmembers. This is of special importance for criminal groups for obvious reasons. An important ingredient in the ideologies of the underworld is the preservation of trade secrets and the maintenance of a closed mouth before outsiders. Even the ex-criminal who writes a book about his experiences may feel uneasy about revealing current techniques, and may therefore write mainly of past history and well-known crimes. The lines drawn between underworld and general society necessarily involve a certain suspicion and wariness:

> One of the personal characteristics is extreme suspicion. This may be accounted for by the fact that he exists in a suspicious world. . . . The first thing in his mind in every touch is whether he is under suspicion. . . . He must decide whether there is an ulterior motive in any word or act of a prospect. He must often be courteous, kindly, and solicitous, and, because he has to play this role, he is naturally sensitive to these characteristics in anyone else. Therefore, if someone would do or offer to do something for him which is unusually kindly, he immediately becomes suspicious. (Sutherland, 1949, pp. 168-169)

Lifestyles of criminals. Although the criminals in any country resemble the citizens of that country in many ways, cherishing and striving for many of the same ends, they also develop their own lifestyle. A professional thief cheerfully says that "the professional thief rejoices in the welfare of the public. He would like to see society enjoy continuous prosperity, for then his own touches will naturally be greater" (Sutherland, 1949, p. 172).

Somewhat different styles within the criminal world arise from the different occupations, but existence within the criminal milieu lends certain general features to the criminal lifestyle. Professional criminals usually operate in terms of short-range goals; they are liberal and unconcerned spenders of money and worry only about the immediate future. Probably this is true even for members of racketeer groups whose conspicuous consumption is a matter of public comment. In recent years, racketeers have tended to move into middle-class suburban areas and to take on some middle-class manners and standards. High living, with an emphasis on drinking, horse racing, and other gambling is a feature of most criminal circles. In fact, in an economic sense, many criminals live partly off other criminals; the holdup man may spend his gains with a bookie or lose his money at gambling. There is a famous apocryphal story about a criminal who found himself in a strange town and asked an associate there where they could gamble. He was told that there was only one "joint" but that it was "crooked." This information only led him to exclaim, as he prepared to be fleeced, "What are we going to do, there isn't any other."

Criminals often do not marry (although male criminals may use the term *wife* to refer to the women with whom they are currently living). Men in this world associate with women of easy virtue who are part of, or marginal to, the criminal milieu. Professional criminals are aware of their somewhat different lifestyle and of the attitudes that respectable citizens have toward them; they often partly accept the values of respectable society toward crime, and hence show symptoms of uneasy conscience. They protect themselves against their consciences with rationalizations that are extremely varied and often ingenious. For example, if they steal from someone rich, they argue that the rich are themselves usually dishonest; if they steal from the poor, they argue that their victims would have spent the money on drink anyway. The confidence man likes to point out that victims have to be willing to cheat someone else before they themselves can be fleeced. (Incidentally, criminals invariably object to calling the victim a victim; they much prefer to call him or her "mark" or "sucker." As one thief said, "That makes it sound bad to call them 'victims.' ") Criminals also like to point out that many persons, such as the police, lawyers, prison staff members, and others from respectable society, make money from them or have jobs that depend upon the existence of crime; they point to the stimulating influence they have on the insurance business and the manufacture of safes, locks, keys, and burglar alarms.

Professional criminals often think of their activities as an occupation or a business, and they may not consider themselves enemies of society. They do not usually hate the police, lawyers, judges, and others who play roles in sending them to prison, unless those individuals violate what seem to the criminals to be the rules of the game and the standards of sportsmanship. As a famous "madam" complained:

> I didn't resent the honest cop and I was able to stay in business because of the dishonest variety. But the members of the gendarmerie who really started my adrenalin flowing like wine were the boys who believed in playing it both ways, and who wouldn't have turned a hair if their own mother happened to be the one caught in the middle. (quoted in Adler, 1953, p. 144)

Recruitment. Many criminals talk about going "legit." That they consider leaving the criminal life indicates the tensions and hazards it entails. Criminals often feel a certain envy for those of their number who have managed to go straight; there is indeed a kind of folklore among them concerning instances of this kind. Nevertheless, it is not easy for people to leave the underworld once they have become rooted in it and have an investment and involvement in it. Their friends are in the underworld; they are accustomed to its routines, satisfactions, and excitements; and their loyalties tie them to it. When they try to abandon it they are not only drawn back, they are pushed back, because they are tagged by respectable society and cannot escape their pasts. When they try the straight life, they often find it dull and frustrating, and may discover that they do not have the requisite skills and knowledge to keep up the standard of living to which they are accustomed. Not much is known about the drift out of the criminal world, but there is some evidence of a shift with increasing age to marginal, semilegitimate occupations. Individuals who make this change do not altogether renounce underworld associations, but they do manage to avoid the worst risks.

There is an extensive literature on the causation of criminal behavior, and all sorts of theories—from biological determinism to the strictly environmental—have been proposed and defended. Two broad problems exist in this area. One is how to account for the origin of criminal groups; this is a historical and sociological problem and does not deal with the behavior of individuals. The other is how to explain how a given individual comes to join a criminal group and accept its way of life; this is of interest to the social psychologist.

The criminal underworld does not maintain itself biologically, for reproduction rates are low and criminals who do have children often try to keep them from following a life of crime. (This statement does not necessarily apply to other countries; in India, for example, criminal occupations, as well as prostitution and begging, have long been matters of caste heritage and have been passed on from parents to children.) As a consequence, the criminal population is maintained through a process of recruitment about which relatively little is known. It is commonly assumed that adult criminals are recruited from juvenile delinquents, but this is only partly true and varies by types of crime. A substantial portion of adult offenders have no records of juvenile delinquency, and evidently embark on criminal careers relatively late in life. An autobiographical account by a convict doing a life term in the Iowa State Penitentiary indicates that this man's first venture into crime was as a bank robber during the Depression, when he was in his early 20s (Runyon, 1953). Statistical evidence indicates that close to one-half of the criminals apprehended each year are officially first offenders.

Most juvenile delinquents come from the slums of large cities and have been brought up in homes characterized by poverty and ignorance. Such juvenile criminals, tough as they may sometimes be, are automatically disqualified from certain types of criminal occupations (such as the confidence game) that require the manners, dress, and speech of the better-educated classes. Tough urban juvenile delinquents, if they become adult criminals, are thus likely to become thugs or to enter some part of the occupational hierarchy of crime that makes demands that their slum training enables them to meet. In the higher branches of villainy and the more refined types of fraud, superior intelligence, command of language, histrionic ability, stable nerves, and other such qualities are required. Neuroticism, psychosis, and other abnormalities of character and personality are just as much obstacles to success in crime as elsewhere. This is why criminologists are, or ought to be, exceedingly cautious about drawing conclusions about criminals from the study of persons in prison. The more capable and successful criminals are probably not sent to prison as often as are the defective, the abnormal, and the unintelligent.

Virtually all criminal occupations offering reasonable returns without unreasonable risks require a certain amount of training or tutelage. Safecrackers, it is said, are recruited from the mechanical trades. Receivers of stolen goods often come from the business world. For some years, the top American racketeers have had "heist" (holdup) backgrounds and have usually been of

Italian origin. Confidence men, according to one criminal, usually come from small towns or the country.

Perhaps no other institution contributes as much to criminal recruitment as does the prison. In prisons, persons of all degrees of sophistication are thrown together for long periods of time. The stigma of the prison sentence prevents the ex-convict from getting into noncriminal occupations, and imprisonment provides him with information concerning a wide variety of illegal ways of making a living. Prison associates become contacts the amateur may use if he wishes to turn professional.

The Aging Criminal

Horowitz (1982) and Shover (1985) have studied the adult delinquent gang member and the aging criminal, respectively. Horowitz analyzed delinquent gangs in an inner-city Chicano community and found that among the men in her sample, gang membership continued well into early adulthood. She explains this perpetuation of youth gangs in terms of the marginal economic position of the young men and in terms of their continued commitment to an honor-based subculture in which dependence and lack of domination are experienced as dishonor (Horowitz, 1982, p. 3). By remaining gang members, these young adults maintained respect in the eyes of others; they were seen as independent men of honor.

In a study of 50 men over age 40 who had been involved in ordinary property crimes earlier in their lives and who had served prison sentences, Shover found three patterns of feelings among the men concerning their past criminal lives. Shover describes the men in one group as despairing; they expressed severe regrets about their past exploits and present lives. They felt that the life of crime had not paid off for them and saw little hope of reversing these effects. One man stated:

> What I regret is that I didn't get some kind of occupation, where I could have had some security when I got this old. Like, I have such a little work record, that I couldn't even collect Social Security. So what am I going to do? I don't have nothing to fall back on. (quoted in Shover, 1985, pp. 133-134)

Shover describes a second group of men as expressing satisfaction about their past lives, about the time they spent in prison, and about their present situations. As one noted:

> Well see, the idea sticks out in my mind that it took what happened, it was necessary for what happened to me to get to where I am at now, you know. With the outlook I have. And so, if I regret that—what happened—you understand, then I regret being where I'm at. And that might be an academic thought, but I don't feel that it was a great loss, you know. (quoted in Shover, 1985, p. 138)

A third group of men expressed ambivalence about their past and present lives. As one self-employed man with a steady income said:

> I wonder at times what [my life] would have been like if I had never been in jail. And got a job and worked from the time I was younger—what my life would be like today. Where I would be. What position in life I'd

> have. Would I be better off than I am now or would I be worse off than I am now? (quoted in Shover, 1985, p. 139)

Aging criminals look back on their criminal careers with mixed emotions. The status passage into prison, the loss of self-control, and the subjective career effects on self and relations with others are felt for life. Yet these individuals also express a certain amount of irony toward and affection for the past. One ex-convict reflected on his relations with close friends from his criminal past:

> We talk to each other on the telephone from time to time, and really talk about, you know, we say "what the heck was wrong with us back then?" We just talk about it, you know. I don't understand. I never will be able to understand what was wrong with us. We sure lost a lot of time getting our act together. (quoted in Shover, 1985, p. 149)

Studies like those conducted by Horowitz and Shover indicate the importance of examining the social psychological dimensions of criminal and deviant conduct. Honor, pride, group membership, self-esteem, friendship, and subjective, objective, and moral careers all lie at the center of those experiences we term deviant.

Becoming an Alcoholic

We continue our discussion of deviance in this section with an examination of the phases a person goes through in entering a particular deviant world—that of the addict. Specifically, we focus here on the alcoholic. We confine our meaning of the word *alcoholic* here to the drinker who either (a) calls him- or herself an alcoholic or (b) displays an inability to abstain from drinking for any continuous period of time and who, when he or she starts drinking, is unable to control the amount consumed.

Jellinek (1962) outlines four phases in the alcoholic career. The first is the *prealcoholic symptomatic* phase, in which the drinker learns to experience rewarding relief from stress and anxiety in drinking situations, ascribing relief to the situation and not to the alcohol. Such a person often seeks out drinking situations so that he or she may engage in "happy hour" cocktails and so on. Over the course of 6 months to 2 years, this person becomes an almost daily drinker, although he or she may seldom be overtly intoxicated. This phase has two stages: occasional and constant relief drinking.

The second phase is the *prodomal* phase. The drinker begins to drink secretly and becomes preoccupied with alcohol. He or she may begin to feel guilty about drinking, which by now is heavy. Blackouts begin to occur. As the drinker tries to cover up the amount of alcohol consumed, he or she begins to use rationalizations and excuses (accounts). In the third, or *crucial,* phase, any drinking of alcohol starts a chain reaction that is felt as a physical demand for alcohol. This felt need for alcohol often produces a drinking bout that continues for hours until the person is intoxicated. The bout of drinking that sets off this chain reaction need not be caused by physical discomfort; any social situation can trigger the drinking chain that leads to intoxication. Critical in this phase is loss of control. Like the cocaine addict, the alcoholic seems unable to control the amount of alcohol consumed once he or she takes the first drink. It appears that the drinker has crossed a line and no longer has any control over his or her drinking. However, the drinker's pride leads him or her to deny any loss of control—and this leads back to drinking (Bateson, 1972).

With the loss of control comes denial and even stronger rationalization schemes that justify continued drinking. Heavy drinking continues; the person experiences a loss of self-esteem and at the same time begins to indulge in grandiose behaviors (e.g., extravagant expenditures). Marked aggressive behavior may appear, along with changes in drinking patterns and drinking friends, changes in job, upheaval in the family, marked self-pity, and extraordinary efforts on the drinker's part to protect his or her alcohol supply. A neglect of nutrition may also occur, as well as sexual jealousy and morning drinking. At this point in his or her drinking career the person may be drinking on a continual—rather than a continuous—basis. He or she may take a first drink upon rising in the morning, then at 10:00 or 11:00 a.m., then around 1:00 p.m., and then continuous drinking starts around 5:00 p.m. (Jellinek, 1962, p. 365).

In the fourth phase of alcoholism, the *chronic* phase, there are prolonged periods of intoxication, even in the daytime. The person may resort to drinking anything that has alcohol in it. A loss of alcohol tolerance occurs; the person gets drunk on half the amount it used to take. Thinking is impaired, and fears and tremors appear as well. Vague religious desires may be experienced. At the end of this phase the person, now truly alcoholic, may express a desire for treatment (see Denzin, 1987a, 1987b, 1987c).

In order for a person to become alcoholic, he or she must (a) learn how to drink, (b) learn to define the effects of alcohol in a positive fashion, and (c) come to see that these effects bring desired personal and social ends—that is, relief of anxiety and tension, creation of friendship and fellowship, and so on. Once these three processes are met, the person must increase his or her alcohol intake to the point where increased tolerance is created and a physical addiction for alcohol is produced. At this point, the person must experience withdrawal effects and must connect them to the absence of alcohol in his or her body. Finally, the person must see that by drinking he or she removes those effects that are defined in a negative manner. Once this has occurred, the person has established the conditions for becoming an alcoholic. Like the opiate, heroin, or cocaine addict, the individual has learned that the drug will alleviate withdrawal distress. The repetition of this experience constitutes addiction to alcohol.

Family Violence

We have noted that in the crucial phase of alcoholism, marked aggressive behavior may appear. This aggression is often associated with the violent mood swings that alcoholics experience. Others have observed that opiate, heroin, and cocaine addicts also become aggressive in the later phases of their careers. There is a subtle and complex relationship between violence and the use of drugs like alcohol. We cannot go into the complexities of this literature except to note the following: Drinking and drug use often occur in the presence of close friends and family members. Violence, including homicide, occurs with high frequency (50%) in family settings. Hence the two phenomena—drug use and violence—occur in the same settings. Which causes which is not known; that is, we do not know if persons are violent and then drink or use drugs, or if they drink and use drugs and then become violent (see Denzin, 1987a).

We do know, however, that family violence occurs in perhaps one out of every three households in the United States at least once a year (Gelles & Cornell, 1985). Below, we briefly discuss the stages of family violence. We focus primarily on spousal violence; we do not attempt to deal with child abuse, sexual abuse, abuse of the elderly, or sibling violence.

The Stages of Family Violence

We begin with the assumption that family violence is an interactional process that gets out of control. To use Kadushin and Martin's (1981) terminology, it is an interactional event that takes on negative, destructive features. The family of violence becomes a small social group that threatens to tear itself apart through violent actions and emotions.

The root meanings of the term *violence* include to treat with force, to abuse, and to attempt to regain something that has been lost. We define violence here as the attempt to regain, through the use of emotional and physical force, something that has been lost (Denzin, 1984c, p. 488). What has been lost can be traced back to the self of the violent person, who has lost or never had valued self-feelings. Through the use of force, the violent person attempts to regain a sense of self that is located in the family group. The violent person becomes locked in negative emotions that spill over into everyday family life, creating negative, hostile, fearful emotional experiences for every family member. Family members lose their statuses as just spouses, daughters, or sons; they become victims of family violence. The father, if he is the abuser, becomes a violent man who is feared by those who want to love him.

The structure of social relations in the family group is altered and transformed by violence. Cliques and factions emerge; members turn against one another; secret communications appear; family members become afraid to be in the same room with one another. When the violent family member comes home, other members make excuses to leave, and the violent person begins to feel like a family isolate. What the violent person desires most—love and care—is denied because of his or her violence. The violent home becomes an empty emotional shell, and the violence that goes on behind the closed doors of the home stigmatizes every family member. Everyone loses self-esteem; false hopes and promises fuel family life, and members attempt to deny the fact that they live in a violent household.

The negative symbolic interaction that attaches to family violence moves through several stages. The first of these is the denial of violence. Second is the pleasure derived from violence. The third stage is the building of mutual hostility between spouses and between the violent member and other family members. In the fourth stage, misunderstandings develop. The fifth stage is the appearance of sexual jealousy between the spouses. The sixth stage is increased violence, which either destroys the family or stabilizes it into a state of recurring violence.

Before violence can be denied, it must first make its appearance. Dobash and Dobash (1979) show that when violence first appears in a marriage it is isolated, attached to an oversight on the wife's part and defined as insignificant. After the violence makes its appearance, the husband may take some pleasure from being violent. He feels that by being violent he not only gets his own way, but also achieves a measure of self-esteem by keeping his wife and children in their place. Hostilities increase, however, as do misunderstandings. The husband continues to blame the wife, and she comes to see that it is not all her fault. Family members are placed in a double-bind situation (Bateson, 1972): If the husband and father loves them, why is he violent? If he is violent, it must mean he doesn't love them; yet he says he loves them. Both messages can't be true. With double binds come misunderstandings and empty communications. One wife in a violent relationship, a graduate student in psychology, reported:

> I stopped talking with my husband. . . . anything I said made him mad. We barely said hi or goodbye to each other. He just seemed to get mad when he saw me. Then he would lash out, cut me down any way he could. Then he'd say, "I was happy before I met you. Look what you've done to me." He'd slam the door and walk out, and then come back in, grab the paper out of my hand and maybe twist my wrist till it got red, or swear at me and say he'd be home when he felt like it. Once he let the air out of the tires on my car. Another time he hit me so hard I had a cracked rib. (quoted in Denzin, 1984c, p. 492)

Sexual jealousy appears in the next stage. Each spouse begins to suspect the other of sexual infidelities. The husband may be violent toward the wife when they have sexual intercourse. With sexual jealousies comes increased violence of an emotional and physical nature; not only does the violent offender become more violent, but other family members begin fighting with one another as well. Violence permeates the family. Pizzey (1974) provides an example: A woman describes how her husband, a successful businessman,

> would arrive home in a very drunken state and complain bitterly about everything I did or said to him. He was frightening when in this sort of aggressive mood . . . on my son's fourth birthday he arrived home . . . and insisted that I get James out of bed. . . . After refusing . . . he picked him up and brought him into the kitchen, where he was very insulting to me and called me a slut and a whore. . . . my husband grabbed James and punched me behind the right ear. . . . He picked up the bread-knife and threatened to put it through my throat. (pp. 26-27)

Such violent outbursts either take the family to the brink of self-destruction or drive the members to seek help. A wife may call the police, leave home with her children, go to a shelter for battered women, file for divorce, or push her husband to seek help for himself. Families appear to go in one of two directions: They self-destruct or they get better. Whichever direction they take, the legacy of violence will be felt by all members, perhaps to be carried into the family lives of the next generation.

Patterns of Violence and Abuse: Franz Kafka

Noy and Sharron (1985) have analyzed the family history of the novelist Franz Kafka, who was a victim of child abuse. Kafka's life history is instructive.

Franz Kafka was born in Prague on July 3, 1883. His father, Herrmann, was a self-made businessman, and he and his wife were from families of Jewish scholars. Besides Franz, they had three daughters as well as two younger sons who died in infancy. Herrmann was disappointed in Franz, and his mother expressed a preference for her dead second son. Franz felt humiliated by his father (who despised his artistic tendencies), neglected by his mother, and betrayed by his favorite sister. In later life Kafka had few friends and was engaged to be married three times, twice to the same woman. Like Gregor Samsa in his famous story "The Metamorphosis," Kafka spent virtually all his life depending on his parents and living in their home (Noy & Sharron, 1985, p. 263).

In November 1919, Kafka wrote a letter to his father that gave a detailed account of his feelings toward his father, whose hostility had haunted him his entire life. He gave the letter to his mother, who read it and returned it to her son; his father never received it. In 1912 Kafka had written to his closest friend, Max Brod: "I hate them all, every one of them. . . . But hatred . . . again gets directed against me" (quoted in Noy & Sharron, 1985, p. 263).

Noy and Sharron (1985) suggest—and there is considerable evidence to support their position—that Kafka's stories, especially "The Metamorphosis," can be read as autobiographical accounts of the violence and abuse Kafka experienced in his family. They suggest that his father was the "active" abuser in the family, his mother the "passive" abuser, and his sister a "first-row bystander" who sided with his parents against him.

Noy and Sharron's analysis of active and passive abuse is instructive. Active abuse includes battering; neglect; the use of threats, ridicule, and scorn; isolation; and sexual abuse and exploitation. Kafka's father used all of these forms except for sexual abuse. Passive abuse includes overfondling, overpampering, the use of double binds, interfering with decisions and choices, discouraging independence, and insulating the person from the outside world. This appears to be how Kafka's mother treated him; all the while she undermined his standing in the family and took her husband's side against him.

The victim's world. Three emotions dominate the victim's world: shame, fear, and guilt. Kafka felt shame in the eyes of his father and himself; he felt that he had not lived up to his father's expectations. The active and passive abuse he experienced created more shame, for he felt that he deserved what he received, and this created the feeling that he was unworthy of love or care. He felt fear—partly because of the active abuse he received, but also because of the isolation he experienced. He feared himself, the outside world, and his family. He felt that he had lost the capacity to speak and experienced a desperate guilt. He felt that he deserved the punishment and beatings that his father directed toward him (Noy & Sharron, 1985, p. 281).

Kafka divided this emotionally torn world into three parts. There was the world of his family, which had laws that he could never conform to. There was a second world, more remote, governed by others, where orders were issued and one worked. And there was a third world, where everybody but Kafka lived happily and free (Kafka, 1952, p. 148; Noy & Sharron, 1985, p. 284). The fact that Kafka created these three worlds suggests how destructive family violence can be. Kafka found no ideal world for himself; the violence he experienced made him an outsider to himself. Oddly enough, Noy and Sharron (1985, p. 285) note, Kafka's presence in the family as a scapegoat unified the other family members into a cohesive unity. They appeared to live "relatively" well-adjusted lives.

The study and analysis of family violence is of great interest to the social psychologist because childhood socialization occurs in families. If the home is violent, then the course of self-development will be drastically altered, as the case of Franz Kafka suggests. If family significant others, including parents, are alcoholics or drug addicts, then their ability to function as socializing agents will be dramatically altered. They may well become active and passive abusers in the senses that Kafka's parents were. We must note, however, that active and passive abuse may occur in the absence of any drug. It does not appear, for example, that Kafka's parents abused drugs or alcohol.

CONCLUSION

Neither behaviors nor people are inherently deviant or nondeviant; rather, they come to be defined or labeled one way or another in large part by virtue of the actions and reactions of others. These reactions range from strong approval to violent disapproval. Negative reactions to disliked persons may result in the application of formal control measures, such as prosecution and imprisonment or hospitalization, or may be expressed informally through gossip, rebukes, or simple avoidance. These deviance-defining actions exist within larger systems of cultural meaning and representation, including the recent tendency in the United States to medicalize deviance and deviant conduct. These systems of knowledge and representation regulate conduct. Regimes of truth connected to specific productive systems of power circulate through society. These formations serve to shape and define what is regarded as deviant, sinful, immoral, or sick behavior.

Deviance and its meanings are historical constructions; they vary from one historical moment to the next. Persons in any time period may be defined as deviant because of what they do, or they may be pushed (and pulled) into deviant social activities because of their appearance. Some drift into deviance and others actively choose it or become trapped in it through accident, ignorance, or unfortunate circumstance.

Social psychologists study the ways in which bodies and forms of conduct come to be labeled as deviant or sick, the effects this labeling has on individuals and their groups, and the symbolic devices used to counteract or neutralize such labeling. Measures designed to control deviance sometimes have the opposite effect. Deviance is a pervasive phenomenon and occurs throughout the whole range of human relationships. It is even found in the various social control agencies that are supposed to enforce the rules, as well as in deviant groups in which members violate deviant norms.

Some forms of deviant conduct are governed by norms and values of subgroups within the larger society—for example, political deviance. Other forms do not have direct group support, but are engaged in by persons as individuals rather than as group members. Criminals, recovering alcoholics and drug addicts, gays, lesbians, and bisexuals form subsocieties within our culture. But not all criminals, addicts, or queer persons join these worlds.

SUGGESTED READINGS

Conrad, P., & Schneider, J. H. (1992). *Deviance and medicalization: From badness to sickness.* Philadelphia: Temple University Press. The single best source on how American society has used the medical model to explain deviance.

Hall, S. (1997). The work of representation. In S. Hall (Ed.), *Representation: Cultural representations and signifying practices* (pp. 13-64). London: Sage. An excellent presentation of Foucault's arguments concerning deviance and social control.

Holstein, J. A., & Miller, G. (Eds.). (1993). *Reconsidering social constructionism.* New York: Aldine de Gruyter. A valuable collection of important essays on the social constructionist approach to deviance and labeling.

Reeves, J. L., & Campbell, R. (1994). *Cracked coverage: Television news, the anti-cocaine crusade, and the Reagan legacy.* Durham, NC: Duke University Press. A concrete example of how media representations create moral panics and new deviant subjects.

STUDY QUESTIONS

1. How does the term *discourse* operate in Michel Foucault's theory of social control?
2. What is a regime of truth? Give three examples of different regimes of truth in the current historical period.
3. What is the social constructionist view of deviance?
4. What are the techniques of neutralization?

14

Illness, Aging, Dying, and Medical Bodies

Illness, aging, and death, with the rituals that surround their social organization, constitute social and biological facts that affect every human society. Illness, whether painful, chronic, transitory, or terminal, dislodges persons from their ordinary rounds of activity. Aging, often associated with entry into the social worlds of the elderly, the retired, and the chronically ill, signals the movement into the final stages of the life cycle. Death disrupts and alters ongoing social relationships. All social groups and societies develop routines, rituals, institutions, and classes of experts to manage the disruptive and disorganizing effects of these three interrelated phenomena. They are of interest to social psychologists for a number of reasons.

First, illness is painful, and pain is rooted in the body. Like dying, illness and pain are not merely biological events; they involve the subjective interpretation of physiologically based events. Groups and social worlds develop their own vocabularies for interpreting pain, illness, and illness-related processes. These vocabularies transform purely physiological and biological events into socially defined events that can be consensually understood and hence acted on. They connect the internal environment of the person with the socially based "naming process" (see Chapter 5).

Second, the definitions that surround the aging experience and the social worlds of the elderly constitute realities that bring new transformations to the self and its social relationships. These transformations deserve study in their own right, for they mark significant developmental changes in the life cycle.

Third, dying is not a biological process that stands independent of social interpretation or social interaction. A death must be socially produced. The person must be defined as "dead," and this definition is becoming increasingly problematic. Social arrangements must be made for disposing of the dead; these involve rituals that signify the "passing on" of the dead (Sudnow, 1967) and may include the scheduling of funeral and interment services (Salomone, 1973). Periods of mourning and grief may be observed. Ties to the dead must be severed at least partially, and the commitment of the living to their ongoing social life among the living must be reestablished.

Fourth, the reality of death must somehow be conceptualized, within any society, such that its existence does not overly disrupt ongoing social interactions. Death must be assigned some "meaning" that minimizes its effects upon the living. Societies and groups vary in the definitions they bring to this experience; indeed, it can be said that in many societies persons die socially before they die biologically. It may take such rituals as the funeral to affirm the finality of a physiological death (Riley, 1983).

Finally, these processes involve technologies of power and the exercise of medical authority. These are topics about which Foucault has a great deal to say, as we have indicated in Chapter 13.

Technologies of Power and the Body

Foucault argues that specific technologies of power and regulation operate on and through the body, dividing, classifying, and inscribing the body in different ways (see Hall, 1997, pp. 50-51). We have, for example, the military body, the criminal body, the body of the violent African American male, the body of the erotically attractive woman, the bisexual body, the gay body, the body with AIDS, the body of the bodybuilder, the body of the professional athlete, and so on. These different types of body are produced in and through different systems of discourse, different technologies of power, truth, and knowledge (Hall, 1997, p. 51).

On this point, Balsamo (1996, p. 3) reminds us that the body is a social construction. Frank (1990, p. 134) suggests that there is no single version of the body; rather, the body and its meanings vary from one discourse to another. So we can speak of the medicalized body (see below), the sexual body, the body that is disciplined, and the talking body. The body is a social, cultural, and historical production (Balsamo, 1996, p. 3). As a product and a process, the body is a site and a vehicle for the staging of performances. These performances are the "material embodiment of ethnic, racial, and gender identities . . . of personal identity, of beauty, of health" (Balsamo, 1996, p. 3), of sexuality and power.

It is also possible to speak of the "technobody"—the body created by the new body technologies. The fetal body, for example, is a product of laparoscopy (Balsamo, 1996, p. 9). Other versions of the technobody include the cyberbody, or the cyborg. This is a hybrid body, part human and part machine, or artificial parts. A cyberbody might have an artificial heart, a voice box, or penile or cheek implants (Balsamo, 1996, pp. 7, 11).

In the medical context, specific technologies of power create specific types of bodies and selves. The disciplinary power that operates in the medical encounter "provides guidelines about how patients should understand, regulate and experience their bodies" (Lupton, 1997, p. 99). Medicine requires docile bodies, bodies that will submit to the physician's gaze. This gaze has the power to observe, examine, feel, touch, and measure the patient's body. It compares individuals and their bodies to so-called established norms in order to make judgments about the degree to which given patients are sick, diseased, well, or recovering (Lupton, 1997, p. 99).

Thus the medicalized body experiences itself through the discourses and the disciplining "practices of medicine and its allied professions" (Lupton, 1997, p. 94). There is not a single medicine; rather, modern medicine is best seen as a set of loosely linked assemblages and practices extending across diverse sites and settings, from hospitals to clinics, to the workplace, schools, homes, and the media, including TV shows (e.g., *E.R.*) about doctors and hospitals (Lupton, 1997, p. 100).

The Medicalization Critique

Lupton (1997, p. 94) has written of the medicalization critique. This critique, an evaluation of the practices of medicine, involves the following arguments. The process of medicalization, as we argued in Chapter 13, has shifted considerable power to the medical establishment (Turner, 1997, p. xiii). As this has occurred, more of daily life has fallen under the control of medicine. Rather than improving people's lives and health, this has too frequently created dependency on the medical regime, including the use of drugs. The medical knowledge of laypersons is often disparaged. Patriarchal and class biases within the medical establishment produce the systematic disenfranchisement and disempowerment of women, persons of color, and members of the lower classes (Lupton, 1997, p. 96). Feminists have argued that medicine is primarily a patriarchal institution. As Lupton (1997) notes, medicine has used masculine definitions of illness and disease to maintain power over women, in part by drawing attention to "their weakness and susceptibility to illness" (p. 97). At the same time, medicine has taken control over areas of "women's lives such as pregnancy and childbirth . . . that were previously the domain of female lay practitioners and midwives" (p. 97).

The Medical Body

The medical regime subjects the self and its body to a complex set of discourses, including those associated with health, wellness, and sickness. Embodied identities connected to these states are then created, for example, the healthy, aging, dying, or chronically ill self. A moral code is attached to these identities. Persons are expected to engage in dietary and exercise practices that produce good health—they should have healthy lifestyles.

The medicalized body—diseased, sick, in chronic pain, with broken limbs—is conditioned and shaped by the institution of medicine. The practices of organized medicine create this version of the body. So, for example, the AIDS body does not exist apart from these biomedical discourses. Of course medicine does not create the material body, but it does re-create this body through its technologies of power and knowledge, such as X rays and lab tests (see Frank, 1990, p. 135). The body with AIDS is an example. However, as Treichler (1987) observes, "the social constructions of AIDS are not based upon objective, scientifically determined 'reality' but upon what we are told about this reality: that is, upon prior social constructions routinely produced within the discourses of biomedical science" (p. 270; also quoted in Balsamo, 1996, p. 37).

Gender operates as a submerged set of meanings within the medical (and popular) discourse on AIDS. Women have historically been defined as having diseased bodies, including bodies that transmit sexual diseases. Paradoxically, as Balsamo (1996, p. 38), notes, citing Treichler (1987), the early biomedical warnings about AIDS and at-risk groups focused on homosexuals, heroin addicts, hemophiliacs, and Haitians. Through this focus on "AIDS as something you get because of who you are, not what you do, women were excluded from the list of populations believed to be at risk" (Balsamo, 1996, p. 38). As more and more women were diagnosed with AIDS, prostitutes, intravenous drug users, and Third World women were added to the list of at-risk persons. Sexually promiscuous females were thus contrasted to sexually active males (Balsamo, 1996, p. 38). Women got AIDS because of the men they were connected to. AIDS was a gay or male disease, a disease caught by sexually active men.

By studying women with AIDS, medical researchers had an index of how far the disease was spreading into the heterosexual population (Treichler, 1987, p. 265). Heterosexual women with AIDS who became pregnant placed infants at risk. Thus the "female body of this AIDS discourse is identified by its reproductive responsibilities and sexual connections to men" (Balsamo, 1996, p. 38). Sadly, as Balsamo (1996) notes, "Now that it is established that women can be infected, women's legacy as an inherently pathological, unruly, uncontainable, but essentially passive vessel returns to haunt her and render her again invisible within medical discourse" (p. 38).

It is clear that medical bodies and their illnesses are created within "a culture of social practices" (Frank, 1990, p. 138). These practices, over time, privilege different combinations of race, ethnicity, age, and gender.

We turn next to a discussion of pain and the medical practices surrounding pain and its meanings.

Chronic Illness, Pain, and Medical Technology

In Chapter 5, we discussed pain in terms of location in the body, its frequency of appearance, duration, and intensity. We exam-

TABLE 14.1 Interpretations of Pain and Resulting Emotions

Pain	*Situation*	*Definition*	*Resulting Emotion*
Contraction of abdominal muscles	during childbirth	allowable pain	pleasure that labor is starting; frustration
Contraction of abdominal muscles	onset of menstruation	normal, to be expected	irritation
Contraction of abdominal muscles	a boxing match	"He got me!"	anger, chagrin
Contraction of abdominal muscles	suffering from the flu	"Why me?"	"When will it end?" show of pain and discomfort

ined how pain is defined in terms of personal and medical labels. Here, we wish to go a bit deeper into issues related to pain, including chronic illness and medical technology. We first discuss pain-centered emotions.

The Linguistic Foundations of Pain-Centered Emotions

What arouses the emotional expression of pain is determined by social situations rather than by physiological processes. The physiology of a painful experience does not determine how it will be emotionally expressed. The arousal and expression of a pain-centered emotion may be analyzed in terms of three phases:

1. A stimulus or situation that is defined or interpreted in certain ways; for instance, a contraction during childbirth.
2. An internal response to the defined situation, involving both physiological and symbolic processes. Here, the source of the pain must be located; its frequency of occurrence, duration, and intensity may also be noted.
3. An outward, conventionalized expression (by means of words, gestures, and facial expressions) that serves to indicate and hence convey the emotion and pain to others.

A given external situation or act does not call forth a pain-centered emotion until it has been interpreted in a certain way. The emotion is a response not to a raw stimulus as such, but to a defined, classified, and interpreted stimulus, to signs with meanings that vary according to the situation, as shown in Table 14.1. The physiological aspects of emotional response (such as a rise in blood pressure, a changed heartbeat, increased activity of the ductless glands) are not learned forms of behavior. On the other hand, the symbolic processes involved in emotion are learned. The third phase of emotional behavior has sometimes been called the *mimicry* of emotion because persons may voluntarily utilize the conventional means of emotional expression without actually experiencing the genuine emotion. Actors do this constantly, but mimicry is also commonly used in ordinary life as people strive to conform to the polite usages of social intercourse and to evoke on the part of others their own felt sense of pain and discomfort.

People may pretend to be in pain when they are not, and others may suspect that they are pretending. In certain circumstances, it is clear to all parties that excruciating pain is being experienced; no pretense is necessary when a young child suffers a broken finger as the result of a slammed car door.

The Taboo of Pain

In Western societies, there is a social taboo against the excessive *experiencing* of pain, just as there are taboos against the excessive or overly dramatic *expression* of pain. Although ill persons are expected to experience and express pain, the experiencing of pain is regarded as evidence of medical neglect, just as people's repeated assertions that they are suffering unbearable pain are taken as evidence that they are not being properly treated. Properly ill persons do feel pain, but their pain and their expressions of pain should fall within socially prescribed dimensions. Modern health care systems, for example, are organized to minimize the importance of pain during the hospital stay. Those who challenge social understandings about pain and its expression make medical nuisances of themselves.

People who claim intense and worsening pain often find that medical staff members begin to ignore them. Strauss and Glaser (1970) report one such instance:

> Since Mrs. Abel . . . complained loudly for all to hear, the nursing staff found her an increasingly difficult cross to bear. . . . They reacted not only by spending less and less time within beckoning distance of the patient but by disengaging each other from her room when stuck there. They carefully arranged staff rotation, so that nobody would have to spend much time with her. (p. 109)

If it is illegitimate or deviant to express excessive pain, it is also inappropriate to acknowledge the fact that certain persons, especially those who have just died, may have actually died in pain. In contemporary Western cultures death is expected to be a peaceful event into which one slides without pain or discomfort (Aries, 1974). Sudnow (1967) observes:

> The concern over whether or not the deceased experienced any pain before his death is typically voiced by the relative, who asks, . . . "Did he have much pain before he died, Doctor?" . . . Universally, it seems, the doctor answers, "No," when asked if pain was experienced and in most instances provides a form of "elaboration" which the following recorded comment typified: "He was under heavy sedation right until the end and I can assure you that he experienced no discomfort at all." (p. 146)

Chronic Illness and Pain

Chronic illness, in contrast to acute illness and disease—such as an appendicitis attack or a sudden heart attack—is characterized by recurring, chronic pain. It has been estimated that more than 20 million Americans constantly seek medical care for chronic pain (Kotarba, 1977, p. 257; 1984). The chronic pain experience often leads to dependency on painkilling drugs and to their abuse; indeed, persons suffering from chronic pain may become drug addicts. Such persons also seek out medical doctors and acupuncturists for treatment.

According to Kotarba (1977, p. 260), sufferers of chronic pain develop a certain level of secrecy about their feelings and suffering. We quote one of Kotarba's respondents, a 60-year-old widow who injured her arm in a fall:

> I don't complain to anyone about my arm. In the first place it's nobody's business. People call you a hypochondriac if you complain all the time. . . . It's better just to keep it to yourself and your doctor. . . . My sister complains all the time and everybody makes fun of her. (p. 261)

People who suffer from chronic pain learn how to manage it. They may treat themselves with heating pads and aspirin. Not previously accustomed to being in pain, the person who begins to suffer chronic pain soon comes to believe that the pain cannot be relieved. Being in pain becomes part of how the person defines him- or herself. Some patients undergo operations in the hopes that their pain can be removed. As the pain lingers, and if operations are not successful, chronic pain sufferers learn to alter their daily routines so as to lessen the pain they experience. They may alter their patterns of lovemaking; they may change jobs and drop certain hobbies. They may "spend all leisure time on sedentary activities such as watching television" (Kotarba, 1977, p. 269).

Age significantly influences how individuals define and experience chronic pain. Middle-aged persons may accept chronic pain as part of growing old, whereas younger persons may face a crisis of self because of such pain (Kotarba, 1977, p. 270).

Self-pity and the chronically ill. Self-pity is a common emotion among those who suffer chronic illness and chronic pain. Charmaz (1980, 1991) has studied the social construction of self-pity in the chronically ill. She uses the term *self-pity* to refer to a label that includes the tendency to "overindulge" in self, to have grief and regret about one's situation, and to feel sadness, a sense of loss, a feeling of victimization, misfortune, helplessness, and injustice about one's plight. Persons feeling self-pity often ask, "Why me?" and develop resentment toward others who do not suffer from the chronic illnesses they are inflicted with.

Three factors seem to shape how self-pity is defined: the self-concept of the ill person, the ill person's lifelong pattern of self-concern, and the nature of the ill person's relationships with others. Individuals may not express self-pity to close family members because they want to maintain a self-image of not being sufferers or complainers. Such individuals may express their self-pity to others, including nurses, social workers, and physicians. The development of self-pity, according to Charmaz (1980, pp. 129-135), occurs under three socially structured conditions: (a) when the illness is discovered or defined as being progressive, (b) when the ill person has been defined as socially discredited because of the illness and because of his or her past responses to it, and (c) when the ill person comes to see him- or herself as a burden to others. Charmaz (1980) quotes one woman:

> All I can do is dissolve in tears—there's nothing I can do. I just get *immobilized*—you sort of reach a point, you can't improve, can't remedy the situation, and you're told you aren't in the right category for getting the services you need and can't get for yourself. It makes me madder and madder at myself for being in the situation in the first place. (p. 133)

Self-pity may be transitory, or it may totally engulf a person's life. Charmaz (1980) quotes a woman who went through both phases of feeling self-pity:

> I was sick of their pitying looks and concerned voices. I didn't want their pity—I would just stay away if they felt like that. So I withdrew. But after a time I realized I pitied myself more than anyone else pitied me. So then and there I decided, I wouldn't let this keep me down; I was going to do something with the rest of my life. (p. 142)

Chronic illness trajectories. People have careers with chronic illness and pain. Charmaz (1991) suggests that people experience serious chronic illness in three ways: "as an interruption of their lives, as an intrusive illness, and as an immersion in illness" (p. 9). Different relationships to time follow from each of these illness trajectories, different forms of good days and bad days. We have seen how people who experience self-pity may move from intense involvement in self-pity to a position where they get past feeling sorry for themselves.

Strauss, Fagerhaugh, Suczek, and Wiener (1985) have examined illness trajectories of the chronically ill; they have also examined the medical technology and medical work that go into the treatment of chronic illness. We summarize part of their findings below (see also Charmaz, 1991; Ellis, 1995). In using the term *illness trajectory,* Strauss et al. refer "not only [to] the physiological unfolding of a patient's disease but to the total *organization of work* done over that course, plus the *impact* on those involved with that work and its organization" (p. 8). For different chronic illnesses the trajectories will be different and will involve different medical personnel, treatments, experiences, and so on.

Illness trajectories can be routine or problematic, lingering or fast, and can occur in multiples involving several different treatments at the same time or in sequence. A heart patient, for example, may require immediate acute care and then be shifted to long-term care, where physical therapy and the like are required. Strauss et al. (1985, pp. 15-16) offer the example of a patient who had been hospitalized for the fourth time. She had been diagnosed as having lupus erythematosus. As a result of her lupus she now had pericarditis, pleuritis, cerebritis, and chronic obstructive lung disease caused by her lupus and heavy smoking, and as a result of the steroid treatments she was receiving she had gastric ulcers and Cushing's syndrome. This patient required several different types of treatment. She had a trajectory that was regarded by everyone (physicians, nurses, and herself) as problematic. She had several different medical and illness trajectories going on at the same time. She had multiple treatment managers who often became confused over their areas of responsibility. The services of several different medical and technical departments had to be used. It was difficult to predict treatment outcomes given all the different medical interventions that were going on simultaneously.

This case illustrates how multiple forms of chronic illness in the same patient create interactional and social organizational problems for both patient and staff. It suggests that control and contingencies, unforeseen events, scheduling problems, diagnostic projections, and therapeutic action all have to come together if treatment is to be accomplished. The chronically ill face special problems, not the least of which is understanding what all the treatments they receive mean.

A key problem for the chronically ill, especially those who are required to be treated by modern medical technology, lies in coordinating their illnesses and their bodies to machines.

Medical technology. Strauss and his associates (1985) have analyzed the machine work that goes on in hospitals. As any visitor to a modern hospital will quickly notice, machines are everywhere: X-ray and EKG machines, respiratory machines, TV screens monitoring the operations of machines, computers monitoring other machines. These machines present several problems, two of which are tending and monitoring; a third is teaching patients how to be compliant so that the machines can do their work on them.

Hospital staff members are now trained to tend, monitor, and maintain machines. When the machines break down, they have to be repaired; the safety of the machines has to be monitored, and the accuracy of the machines must be maintained.

Every machine used with patients requires connection to the patient's body. These connections differ from machine to machine. The problems with machine connection vary by the trajectory phase of the patient and the condition of the receiving part of the body. As Strauss et al. (1985, pp. 55-56) note, some machines go inside the body and others attach to the outside of the body; some must be connected for long periods of time and others are temporary; some machines cause pain and discomfort; and some are dangerous to use. These problems affect medical work, the treatment process, and the patient; there is always the danger that a patient will die while on a machine (Strauss et al., 1985, p. 58).

Chronic illness, technology, and hospital organization as sources of hazard. Many chronic illnesses, of course, are life-threatening. When the illness is coupled with the technology required to treat it, two sources of hazard are combined. For example, a person suffering from cancer is threatened both by the illness and by the old and new chemotherapeutic drugs used to control the disease (Strauss et al., 1985, p. 70). Similar processes are at work in open-heart and brain surgery, where surgical procedures and machines can cause life-threatening problems.

The organization of hospitals also creates problems concerning medical treatment of the chronically ill. Hospitals are generally quite decentralized in terms of ward functioning and work; this decentralization affects the safety of patients. Each ward is responsible for the functioning of its own machines; if there is a safety department, it often lacks the force to make sure its guidelines are carried out. This means that there are often only a few safety guidelines that are monitored. Strauss et al. (1985) offer an example of this problem. A researcher had been discussing a recent electrical blowout in the hospital with an environmental safety person:

> He had been discussing, with the dialysis staff, emergency plans for evacuating patients in case of disaster. When he found out it takes an hour to unhook the patients, he hit the ceiling. He kept mentioning during the interview twenty minutes for evacuation, like it was a magic number—the usual time required to get people out. He had been pushing the physician, he said, to come up with a plan so that patients can be unhooked as quickly as possible without endangering them. (p. 72)

This same person, when prompted by the researcher, revealed that he had no safety plans for unhooking patients from machines in the critical care areas of the hospital. Chronically ill people often appear to be in situations where they may die from their illnesses or from the technology created to treat those illnesses.

Sentimental work. An essential feature of chronic illness is that it impinges on the emotional life of the person. Crippling, deforming, and stigmatizing symptoms are sources of self-pity for patients. Accordingly, a great deal of medical work involves dealing with these negative emotional experiences. Strauss et al. (1985, pp. 129-150) call this sentimental work. There are several different types of sentimental work, including interactional work, trust work, composure work, biographical work, identity work, awareness context work, and rectification work.

Interactional work involves organizing treatment so that the patient is not handled like an inanimate object. Often patients are not treated as moral, individual beings. For example:

> When my daughter-in-law had that burned retina, they had a parade of thirty doctors come through, and all that they told her was that, "You're going to be presented in rounds." . . . So there was this army that walked through, but nobody looked at anything but the eye in the dark. (quoted in Strauss et al., 1985, p. 133)

Trust work takes place when staff members build a relationship with the patient that is caring and creates for the patient a belief that staff can be trusted. In *composure work,* staff help patients to maintain poise and self-control. This often involves getting to know patients and their biographies. This kind of *biographical work* blurs with *identity work,* in which medical staff make an effort to understand patients' personal identities. Such understandings also involve considerations of *awareness context work*—asking patients what they know about their situation at any given moment in time. *Rectification work* occurs when patients become upset about the treatment they are receiving; staff members attempt to rectify errors and soothe patients' feelings.

Chronic illness creates special problems for patients and medical personnel. The preceding discussion indicates how the social psychologist studies and analyzes just a few of these problems.

The Social Worlds of the Dying Child

Myra Bluebond-Langner (1978) has studied the private yet social worlds of the dying child. Her subjects were young children, ages 3 to 9, who were dying from leukemia. She examined how the children came to know they were dying, how and why they attempted to conceal this information from their parents and medical staff, and how these adults attempted to conceal from the children their awareness of the children's impending death.

Bluebond-Langner learned that young children learn to confront the death taboo in our society, the idea that one does not discuss impending death. She found that the dying children directly confronted their own and other children's death; they became preoccupied with death and disease imagery in play, art, and literature. They often sought out adults to discuss their own death, avoided talking about the future, and became concerned with getting things done immediately. She found that the children, contrary to many theories of child development, took an active part in the organization of their own lives. They were able to conceptualize death and its meanings. They were able to move from the world of living to the world of death with some ease. These young children confronted and dealt with the stages of dying that have been identified by Elisabeth Kübler-Ross (1969)—denial, anger, bargaining, depression, and acceptance. Often they did a better job at this than their parents.

Awareness of Death

Bluebond-Langner (1978) utilizes Glaser and Strauss's (1965) concept of awareness context as it relates to the dying trajectory (see Chapter 10). The *awareness context* refers to what a person in a situation knows about his or her own and the other's status in the context of their shared interaction. Glaser and Strauss identify four types of awareness contexts: closed, suspected, mutual pretense, and open awareness. In the *closed* context, related to the dying trajectory, the patient does not know of his or her impending death, even though everyone else does. In the *suspected* context, the patient suspects what the others know and tries to confirm or invalidate that suspicion. In the *mutual pretense* context, both parties (patient and family or staff) define the patient as dying but agree to act as if he or she were going to live. In the *open* awareness context, everyone is aware that the patient is going to die, and all parties act on this awareness relatively openly.

The awareness context affects the interaction that goes on among patient, staff, and family. For the children that Bluebond-Langner studied, the mutual pretense context was the dominant mode of interaction. Even when children tried to open up interactions and confront their death directly, their parents did not cooperate.

Stages of Dying Awareness

The leukemic children acquired factual information about themselves and their disease in five stages. Following the diagnosis of leukemia, these stages were (a) learning that this was a serious disease, (b) learning the names of drugs and their side-effects, (c) learning the purposes of treatment procedures, (d) experiencing the disease as a series of relapses and remissions minus death, and (e) experiencing the disease as a series of relapses and remissions that would lead to the child's death (Bluebond-Langner, 1978, p. 166).

Each of these stages was marked by more disease-related information. What was learned in one stage was necessary for moving to the next; however, in order to move from one stage to the next, the child needed specific disease experiences, such as nosebleeds and bone pain, to gather disease-related information. As the children moved through these stages, they related the information they had acquired to their specific experiences in the clinic, with various medications, and so on.

Changes in Self-Concept

As they moved through the five stages of acquisition of information, the children also passed through five different definitions of themselves. Bluebond-Langner (1978, p. 169) labels these as follows: Stage 1 is *well* (prior to diagnosis); Stage 2 is *seriously ill* (after diagnosis); Stage 3 is *seriously ill and getting better*; Stage 4 is *always ill and will never get better*; and Stage 5 is *dying* (terminally ill). The following dialogue illustrates how these children moved from Stage 4 to Stage 5 in terms of both information and self-conception:

> *Tom:* Jennifer died last night. I have the same thing. Don't I?
>
> *Nurse:* But they are going to give you different medicines.
>
> *Tom:* What happens if they run out? (Bluebond-Langner, 1978, p. 183)

Other children made statements like "You see, I'm dying"; "I'm not going to be here for your birthday"; and "I'm not going back to school" (Bluebond-Langner, 1978, p. 184).

We take up the topics of dying and death in greater detail in the next section. We have introduced this discussion of the private worlds of dying children at this point to indicate how children, as competent interactants, structure and give meaning to the pain and illnesses they experience when they are about to die.

The Social Worlds of the Old

Aging is a social process that is subject to different definitions. The establishment of age 65 as a significant milestone in the aging process was supported by biological criteria, given that for many years the average life expectancy for men in 13 European countries of Western culture was 65 (for women, the age was slightly higher; Cowgill, 1980; Havighurst, 1956). In recent years, life expectancy figures have increased somewhat. Chronological age is rather arbitrary, however, and some have proposed a social definition of aging that stresses instead reductions in social competence (Havighurst, 1956). Nonetheless, the age of 65 is commonly utilized by those enumerating the proportions of given populations that are old or aging. Most Western societies, in fact, employ this definition, as evidenced in most pension, health care, and social security programs (Schultz et al., 1974), although some countries vary from the standard of 65 years by a few years either way.

As of 1991, approximately 13% of the total population of the United States was age 65 or older. Other Western societies vary in the proportions of their populations in this age category: In Denmark, people age 65 and up make up 14% of the population; in Finland, they make up 10%; in Germany, 17%; in Sweden, 15%; and in the Soviet Union, 9%. These figures suggest that the social worlds of the old and the aging are sizable. In addition, we can expect these worlds to increase. When the post-World War II baby-boomer population becomes 65 and over, there will be a significant increase in the proportion of "aged" to "nonaged" people in the United States. By the year 2030, the ratio of the retired population (over 65) to working population (20-64) in the United States will change from 18% to 26%.

Attributes and Images of the Old

It has been suggested that an "old-age subculture" is emerging in the United States (Hochschild, 1973, pp. 24-25). This subculture, in part a reaction to the increasing stratification of American society along age-specific, work-related, and kinship lines, stresses a return to the values and ideologies of rural America at the beginning of the 20th century. The values of the small town and fond memories of an ethnically divided nation and earlier historic times and customs are seen as characteristic of this "subculture" (Hochschild, 1973, pp. 7-9). The old have formed this social world perspective in response to (a) pressures to retire by age 65, (b) increased leisure time as a result of early retirement or loss of family roles, and (c) a weakening of the family's functions as social welfare and educational agencies take over the family's responsibilities in the areas of health care, child supervision, and extended family support in the forms of financial, moral, and social assistance.

The elderly, it is argued, have been cut off from the mainstream of modern industrialized society (Cumming & Henry, 1961, pp. 14-23; Cumming, Henry, & Damianopoulos, 1961, pp. 210-218). They may become social and psychological isolates who have *disengaged* themselves from society. Freed (or cut off) from the interactions and demands of family and work, the old are thrown together and often forced to live in age-segregated residences, which may range from retirement villages to health care centers, from run-down hotels to the back wards of mental hospitals for the senile. This isolation from the "youthful" and gainfully employed sectors of society reinforces the construction of an age-based subculture or social world and further isolates the elderly from their familiar worlds of discourse, thought, and remembrance.

Disengagement Theory

A popular theory of aging has been set forth by Cumming and Henry (1961). Termed *disengagement theory,* it contains the following postulates:

1. Although individuals differ, the expectation of death is universal. Therefore a mutual severing of ties will take place between aging individuals and those others in their society who belong to their social groups.
2. Disengagement becomes a self-perpetuating process, for once bonds have been cut, the freedom from other bonds is thereby increased.
3. Because males occupy instrumental roles in American society and females occupy affective roles, their processes of disengagement will differ accordingly.
4. Disengagement may be initiated by the individual or by society, as when a male fails to perform adequately on the job.
5. When both the individual and society are ready for disengagement to occur, complete disengagement results. When society is ready and the individual is not, the result is usually disengagement.
6. Because disengagement results in the loss of central roles, personal crises will be produced for individuals if they cannot find new roles to fill.
7. Persons can ready themselves for disengagement if they perceive that death is near.

These postulates and a number of additional correlates suggest that elderly and aging individuals in American society often die socially before they die biologically.

Disengagement theory assumes that the growing isolation of the elderly person is a natural process, in part a consequence of the increasing "depersonalization" and industrialization of American society. Furthermore, it assumes that kinship ties cease to function as symbolic and moral links to the common worlds of family life. The theory does not account for the "nondisengaging" behaviors of certain groups and of certain individuals. Elderly rural Americans, for example, are still commonly absorbed into the fabric of the extended family. Furthermore, those persons who do not leave the labor market at age 65 often have been observed to lead healthy, involved, and politically influential lives into their late 80s. Both Charles de Gaulle and Winston Churchill were in their mid-80s when they died; Pablo Casals was 93, and Picasso was 86.

Disengagement theory, then, may apply only to special sectors or populations of the aged. In addition, it may apply only under specific social circumstances.

The Functions of Disengagement

We must recognize, however, that the disengagement of the aged in modern society, as Blauner (1968) observes, enhances "the continuous functioning of social institutions" (p. 352). It permits the changeover of personnel in an orderly manner, without the disruption that would occur if positions were filled only after persons worked to the end and died on the job. Blauner remarks on the chaos that followed the assassination of President Kennedy and suggests that most bureaucracies could not tolerate or function in the face of high mortality in the middle years of the adult work cycle.

Consistent with our social psychological perspective, we are inclined to argue that persons' attitudes toward aging will directly reflect the definitions they hold toward themselves as aging individuals. A theory of aging that ignores personal and social identities will be devoid of insights into the subjective elements of the aging process. As currently stated, disengagement theory tends to neglect the *interpersonal context* in which aging occurs. There is also an assumption that death represents an ugly and undesirable end to the life cycle. This view is contradicted by the beliefs of many individuals and social groups (Aries, 1974, p. 32).

If the interpersonal context of aging is considered, we would assume that like-situated persons who share similar worldviews and experiences would develop, over the course of time, a set of friendly, if not intimate, primary group relationships that would integrate them into a common community of discourse and interaction. If a newcomer finds him- or herself fitting into such a structure of social relationships, and if others accept that person, he or she will find, if not create, a niche. If the identities, social relationships, and *images* of self offered to individuals fit their ongoing conceptions of themselves, then they will not experience isolation or negative disengagement. In short, as Rosow (1967) and Hochschild (1973) have suggested, old people living in a community of peers are much less likely to disengage, to isolate or cut themselves off from society, or to feel that they have been so cut off.

We turn to a study of a community of the aged that was conducted by Hochschild (1973) among the residents of Merrill Court, a small apartment building for the elderly and the retired in the San Francisco Bay Area.

An Unexpected Community

The residents of Merrill Court were mostly rural-born, white, working-class, Anglo-Saxon Protestant, widowed females in their 60s. Only five of the residents were men, three of whom were widowed. The widows' husbands had been carpenters, construction workers, farmers, grocery clerks, and salesmen. Three-fourths of them had come to California in the early 1940s. These residents of Merrill Court had developed their own community based on close, almost "sisterly" bonds. The widows of Merrill Court exchanged cups of coffee, lunches, potted plants, kitchen utensils, and baked goods. They watched after one another's apartments and took phone calls for each other. They shared in common conversations, and their topics ranged over problems that confronted all of them: would Medicare pay for chiropractors, what were the visiting hours at various hospitals, which kinds of dentures are best, how much were TV repairs, and what were the latest developments in the daytime TV soap operas.

Merrill Court, Hochschild (1973) reports, "was a beehive of activity" (p. 38). There were weekly meetings of the Service Club, bowling schedules to be met, Bible-study classes to be attended, birthdays to organize for, crafts to be made out of discarded household items, and Christmas cards to be cut out for the Hillcrest Junior Women's Club.

The social arrangements of Merrill Court took on a life of their own. "They were designed, as if on purpose, to assure an ongoing community" (Hochschild, 1973, p. 47). The residents of Merrill Court felt that they were valued members of the local community. Delta, a club president who, like past presidents, had come from a small town, expressed this sense of belonging as follows:

> Since I've been president here, I feel we are part of [the town] just like the VFW and the Eagles. "Why do they come to us [referring to other organizations]?" some of the women ask. They come and say they want 50 favors to be made for the Mayor's conference. They come to us because they think we can do the job; they wouldn't come to us if they didn't think that. It's an honor. (quoted in Hochschild, 1973, p. 56)

The residents of Merrill Court had disengaged themselves from their earlier social worlds and social relationships. Within their own group, however, they produced an *unexpected community,* a social world unique in its customs, rituals, and routines. Hochschild's research provides an empirical challenge to disengagement theory and suggests that more ethnographies of the social worlds of the elderly are needed.

What, for example, do the aging worlds of the members of racial and ethnic minority groups in the United States look like? How do Native Americans, Japanese Americans, Spanish Americans, Greek Americans, and Hungarian Americans age and grow old in large metropolitan locales? How do the ill and poor age and carve out lives in diners, parks, run-down apartment houses, and cheap hotels? Recent research suggests that the average income of couples over age 65 is at or near the poverty level. The mental and physiological deteriorations of the body that accompany aging must be coupled in future ethnographies with studies of the elderly urban and rural poor. Such persons often lack access to proper medical care, a circumstance that increases the negative effects of aging.

Hochschild discovered a community of elderly people who were not isolated. It remains for future investigators to probe the worlds of such persons as the following elderly male:

> He lingers at the counter making talk with the waitress.
>
> "What'll it be today?"
>
> "Well, what do you have for me? You got some of that homemade potato soup? That's a good soup. We used to have that at home. Back in Michigan."
>
> "Anything else today?"
>
> "Coffee. My usual coffee. My mother won a prize at the county fair with her potato soup. She had a secret recipe."
>
> "And what else? Some dessert?"
>
> At a quarter of five, he is slowly eating his potato soup, his pie, and sipping his cup of coffee. He remarks:
>
> "I used to be a very busy person. I used to have plenty of friends." He lives at the Executive Hotel at $2.00 a day. He plays solitaire in his room and watches television in the downstairs lobby.
>
> "The Executive's alright," he says. "Now I just came here four years ago; but there are some older folks who *live* here." (Hochschild, 1973, pp. 137-138)

Social Involvement in the Social Worlds of the Elderly

David R. Unruh (1980, 1983) has criticized disengagement theory for its failure to consider a social worlds perspective in the study of the lives of older people. He notes that a variety of social worlds and subworlds of involvement exist for the elderly, and these are often ignored (Unruh, 1980, pp. 159-165). Examples of what he has in mind include the subworld of senior gleaners, the California Old Folks bicycling club, the worlds of ballroom dancing and bingo, and the social world of antique selling and gathering.

Each of these social worlds draws elderly persons into networks of communication and interaction. Each provides opportunities for members to try on new and multiple social and personal identities. Various types and levels of involvement in these worlds can be identified. Senior centers, for example, allow strangers to get involved in such new social worlds as art, dance, and music. Some elderly people act like tourists and become involved in new worlds out of curiosity and make few, if any, long-term commitments. Others become regulars and insiders to new worlds of involvement. Unruh (1980) quotes a 78-year-old bicyclist:

> I've brought a lot of guys into cycling, ya know. When they see the publicity I get, they say, "By gosh, I'm going to do that too! If that guy can do it, so can I." There are a lot of good racers out there who are twenty or thirty years younger than I who have seen me and got started in cycling. Some of them turned into very good racers and that makes me feel good. (p. 164)

This man is a regular and an insider in the world of cycling. The social worlds perspective that Unruh develops suggests that students of aging should examine the social, organizational, and interactional structures that bring the elderly together. A social worlds perspective alerts us to the multiple strands and lines of action that unite older people with others, including their age peers and others who share similar interests with them (Unruh, 1980, p. 165).

Living and Dying Behind Closed Doors

Fontana (1977) and Gubrium (1975) have both studied the social lives of elderly persons who live in nursing homes. Fontana employed a dramaturgical framework in his study of Sunny Hill Convalescent Center. The stage where this drama of life occurred consisted of a building with two wards, situated one below the other. The center was located on a 6-acre site in the middle of a small town. Rooms with two beds each were located on both sides of the corridors, with adjoining toilets between two rooms. Each ward had a large recreational lounge furnished with sofas, armchairs, other chairs, and a television set. Each also had a nursing station. At the end of each corridor was a large bathroom where aides washed patients. The lower ward had a small waiting hall for visitors.

The actors in this setting included the center staff, which consisted of an administrator, a bookkeeper, two janitors, a laundry person, the kitchen staff, and the nursing staff and aides. The rest of the cast consisted of the patients. Staff members classified patients into two categories: those who were "up and about," and those "in chairs," meaning those in wheelchairs. Patients were further classified as "feeders" and "nonfeeders": Nonfeeders were patients who could feed themselves; feeders had to be fed by staff.

The interactions that occurred in the center could be divided into several types: staff-to-patient, patient-to-staff, staff-to-staff, and patient-to-patient. The Cheshire Cat from *Alice in Wonderland* might have been a resident at Sunny Hill, for it captures, in the following lines, the approach to patients at this facility:

> "But I don't want to go among mad people," Alice remarked. "Oh, you can't help that," said the Cat: "We're all mad here. I'm mad, you're mad." "How do you know I'm mad?" said Alice. "You must be," said the Cat, "or you wouldn't have come here." (Lewis Carroll; quoted in Fontana, 1980, pp. 486-487)

Fontana characterizes staff-to-patient interaction, following Strauss and Glaser (1970), as "work-time." Work-time at the center was organized in terms of shift time. The day shift had the responsibility of getting patients up for breakfast, changing their bed linens, feeding them, bathing them, and taking them to lunch and back to their rooms after lunch. In addition, staff on the day shift had to give patients their medications. There was never enough time for staff to treat patients as human beings; they were treated as work objects. This meant that patients competed with one another for staff time. Patients existed on another time schedule, their own, and in that schedule they often tried to get personal attention from the staff; they would wave their hands or call to aides.

Many of the patients felt that they were prisoners. Fontana (1980) describes one patient:

> Mr. Anderson used to live in a boarding house. One day the people who managed the house told him that he had to go to the doctor for a checkup. He was taken to the center and has been there ever since. He feels that this is illegal, and that the doctor signed his release to the center because he is a good patient, ambulatory and quiet, and they wanted his money. He has written to his daughter about it but has received no reply. Mr. Anderson . . . feels as if he were in a prison. (pp. 492-493)

In many cases the patients Fontana studied felt that the only people they had to interact with were themselves.

Living and Dying at Murray Manor

Jaber F. Gubrium (1975, 1993) studied a nursing home that he calls Murray Manor. Part of his research involved examining how the clients in the nursing home spent their time. He identified a number of major time categories, including passing time, sitting around, keeping track of time, eating, walking, sleeping, watching, talking, ceremonials (e.g., church services), and therapy.

A great deal of time at Murray Manor was involved in what Gubrium calls bodywork—bathing, eating, walking, taking medications, sleeping, and bowel movements. A great deal of staff and patient talk concerned the bowels. Many patients were either constipated or had diarrhea or were incontinent; some had to have daily enemas. Complaints about the disgusting habits of certain patients were common—those who piddled on the floor, "crapped in others' rooms," or just couldn't keep clean (Gubrium, 1975, p. 186). One patient described this concern about bowels:

> I know it's funny sometimes when you think about all the talk that goes on here about it

> [bowels]. But ya talk and ache about your bowels all the time. I don't know why an eighty-two year-old woman has to be bothered with bowels. I'm so packed, if I don't have a movement, I'll blow up. I sit down and hit my stomach and it's hard. Ever since I came here, it's been bowel problems all the time—all that rice and noodles that we eat. (quoted in Gubrium, 1975, p. 186)

Gubrium (1993, p. 179) observes that there are few official roles or statuses in the nursing home (administrator, aide, nurse, dietitian, social workers, therapists). Residents are commonly classified into three categories based on the degree of care they require: personal, intermediate, and skilled. This structural picture does not convey the complexity of life in the nursing home. Different residents orient differently to the nursing home experience. Residency in the nursing home is shaped by the stories and biographies persons bring into the experience (Gubrium, 1993, p. 180). Biographically active persons articulate different horizons of meaning about this new place where they live. Some persons are worried to death, others see it as a new home, some use a religious framework (the Lord's will) to cope with it, some see it as a hotel or a home away from home, and more than a few are fatalistic—"It has come to this" (p. 53).

Dying and Death at Murray Manor

According to Gubrium (1975, p. 197), there were three worlds of dying and death at Murray Manor: those of the top staff, the floor staff, and the clientele. These worlds often clashed. Top staff (administrators) viewed death and dying as part of the routine work of floor personnel; they treated it as an administrative problem. Floor staff felt that the administrators treated the dying of clients as "funeral men" would.

All patients and residents defined their futures in terms of death (Gubrium, 1975, p. 198). The problem, for them, was when they would die. They all had "dying" self-conceptions, to use Bluebond-Langner's (1978) term. One resident spoke about his death:

> All I can think about is that God will call me someday. They'll take me out and bury me. I don't think nothin'. I take it day by day. I don't plan anything, because generally when you plan somethin', it never turns out that way anyway. So I don't try to think or make any plans whatsoever. I take it day by day and leave the rest in God's hands. (quoted in Gubrium, 1975, p. 198)

When patients and residents died, staff had to prepare them for removal from the center. This meant that the dead had to be bathed and dressed. Gubrium (1975) describes this process:

> Aides washed the body of the deceased, as if they were performing the usual bed-and-body work on living bedfast patients. For example, when an "alert" roommate is present on the other side of a pulled curtain, aides preparing the body refrain from talking about it in a depersonalized fashion, since this would signify to the roommate that it is lifeless. The dead patient is adjusted (face and body posture) to make him appear to be sleeping. His eyes are closed, his mouth shut, and his head turned to one side. The appearance of the "sleeping" dead and the sleeping living are strikingly similar. (p. 213)

Old age is a stage in the life cycle that nearly every individual enters (Quadagno, 1980). The social worlds of the old are diverse; they crosscut income, racial, ethnic, religious, sexual, occupational, and kinship boundaries. Entry into this world signals a confrontation with dying and death, which we discuss next.

Dying and Death

Every social structure must confront the biological and social realities that surround the eventual death of its members. Whether expected or accidental, involuntary or deliberate, death is a biological and existential fact of life that effects every human society. Death, an approaching reality for the elderly, is an obdurate factor of everyone's reality, however frequently dismissed. Death produces serious organizational, moral, occupational, political, religious, and kinship problems for humans. The statuses held and the functions previously performed by the dead person must be filled and carried on. Orderly transitions of power and leadership from the dead to the living must be organized. Affective obligations and duties previously met by the dead person must be transferred to other members of the community. The symbolic and sacred moral worth of the dead person must be established and either affirmed or denied. The bonds that tie the dead individual to the living, whether these be relatives, citizens of a nation, or coworkers and friends from the past, must also be symbolically signified. In short, all social structures organize ritual acts that recognize and take note of death and of the dead.

In recognizing the "passing on" of the dead (Sudnow, 1967), societies and social groups establish a moral and symbolic distance between the living and the dead. As Blauner (1968) suggests:

> The social distance between the living and the dead must be increased after death, so that the group first, and the most affected grievers later, can reestablish their normal activity without a paralyzing attachment to the corpse. (p. 357)

There are, however, efforts to maintain a symbolic link or social and historical relationship with the deceased person. The funeral and interment ceremony, while formally disposing of the deceased body, symbolically announce that the living have properly cared for the body, the self, and the reputation of the person who has died. Grave markers, flowers placed on graves, photographs of the deceased, printed announcements in newspapers commemorating the death of a father or mother, memorabilia such as treasured rings, watches, quilts, smoking pipes, books, coin collections, and other valued objects (often passed from generation to generation)—all serve to record the fact that the dead person still occupies a place in the social worlds of the living.

But before links to the dead can be established, the person's death must be a confirmed fact. A death, as we noted at the beginning of this chapter, must be socially produced.

Dying

David Sudnow (1967) investigated the place and production of death and dying in the social organization of hospitals. Such an investigation was warranted on at least two grounds: First, hospitals are the major settings for dying in our society, and second, little sociological attention has been given to the care and definition of the "terminally ill" or dying patient. Sudnow's concern was with an identification of the events, cues, and symptoms physicians utilize when they define a patient as "terminal." His interest was processual, for persons must first be defined as dying before their deaths can be certified. Sudnow notes:

> In certain medical circles there is considerable disagreement over the precise biological meaning of death; some argue that the cessation of cellular activity constitutes death, and others insist upon a more specific attention to properties of cellular multiplication. . . . Some persons argue that "dying" is a thing which becomes recognized once a deadly disease is located, i.e., that "dying" is a state wherein a person suffers from a disease that is nonreversible and is known to "produce death." (p. 65)

The location of a "death-causing disease" will not explain those deaths where no disease is discovered, such as death from a gunshot wound. The cessation of cellular activity also will not explain the cause of death, for it is only a "sign" at best, an operational definition of the fact that a "death" is in process.

These remarks suggest that disease categories and measures of cellular multiplication are not, in and of themselves, causes of death in any biological sense. They are social categories, or linguistic labels, that members of the medical community utilize when they formulate a diagnosis and prognosis of a patient who appears to be "dying." Such categories are predictive indicators that serve to make the *dying trajectory* of the terminally ill patient understandable (in medical and lay terms) and hence controllable.

Social Death, Clinical Death, and Biological Death

Considerations of this order led Sudnow (1967, p. 62) to propose that deaths occur within a social order that links the person not only to the medical order of the hospital, but also to the social worlds of kinship, work, aging, and illness. "Dying" provides a set of definitions that permit not only the patient but also the patient's kin and the hospital personnel to orient their actions to the future; that is, they can prepare for death's actual occurrence. By placing persons in the "dying" category, hospital personnel establish a way of attending to them (Sudnow, 1967, p. 75). This places an interpretive frame around the experiences of dying persons such that these experiences can be processed within the medical order of the hospital.

At County Hospital—one of two medical settings Sudnow studied—patients who were considered "dying" or "terminally ill" had their names posted on the "critical patients list." Morgue attendants would regularly consult this list so that they could make an estimate of the work load for the coming week. Physicians who were in need of particular organs for research projects were alerted to upcoming deaths, and nurses were encouraged to speak with members of these patients' families concerning the chances of getting permission to relinquish the patients' eyes, livers, or other organs for research.

At County Hospital, the Catholic chaplain would regularly check the critical patients list to determine which patients should be administered last rites. Many "posted patients" did not die, even after they had received last rites. The priest reported that "such cleansing [was] not permanent . . . and that upon readmission to the hospital one must, before he dies, receive last rites again; the first administration [was] no longer operative" (Sudnow, 1967, p. 73). In these senses, seriously ill "posted patients" can be regarded as candidates for autopsy *before* their death; that is, their medical death actually precedes their biological death.

It is now possible to distinguish three categories of death: *clinical death,* which signals the appearance of "death signs" upon physical examination; *biological death,* which is marked by the cessation of cellular activity; and *social death,* which occurs at that time when the patient is "treated essentially as a corpse, though perhaps still 'clinically' and 'biologically' alive" (Sudnow, 1967, p. 74). Socially dead persons are, for all practical, moral, and symbolic purposes, treated "as if" they are dead. Once persons have socially died, they can be treated as absent others whose affairs now become the sole concern of others. Their personal effects can be disposed of; their funeral ceremonies can be scheduled, their caskets picked out, and their burial plots paid for. Their insurance policies can be cashed, and survivors can apply for their retirement benefits.

Sudnow (1967, p. 77) gives an example of a "social death." A male patient was admitted to the emergency unit with a perforated duodenal ulcer. He was in critical condition for 6 days following his operation, and his wife was informed that his chances of survival were slim. She stopped visiting the hospital upon receipt of this information. The patient, however, began to show marked improvement and was released from the hospital after 2 weeks. He was readmitted the next day and died shortly thereafter of a severe coronary attack. Before he died, he told the following story concerning his experiences upon his return home. He discovered that his wife had removed all his clothing and his personal effects, and had made arrangements for his burial. He found his wife with another man, and she was not wearing her wedding ring. The patient reported that he then left his house, began to drink heavily, and suddenly suffered a heart attack.

If the *dying trajectory* of the terminally ill person were to be charted, it would appear that often (though not always) clinical death precedes social death, followed then by actual biological death. However, a person may be defined as socially dead even before a clinical diagnosis is made. Indeed, there are certain benefits to narrowing the temporal gaps that separate clinical, social, and biological death, not the least of which involve the fact that an inevitable process is brought to rapid conclusion, thereby lessening social and psychological grief. A rapid death reduces the ambiguities—interactional and personal—that surround the relationships between the living and the dead, and it permits the living to return to the routine demands of their everyday worlds. Morticians, furthermore, find that, in preparing the body for viewing, the best results are obtained "if the subject is embalmed before life is completely extinct—that is, before cellular death has occurred" (Mitford, 1963, p. 70). In the average case, this would mean within an hour after the heart has ceased beating. Such haste raises fears of live burial, fears that are allayed by embalming itself. The removal of blood from the body, which "prevents" infection and discoloration, "has made the chances of a live burial quite remote" (Mitford, 1963, p. 70).

Dying Trajectories

The dying careers of terminally ill persons have variable temporal shapes (Glaser & Strauss, 1965, p. 23). A dying trajectory may be short or long and lingering, or it may vacillate between periods of recovery and periods of "near" death. The social, clinical, and biological definitions that surround the dying career also shift and take on new meaning over time. If a patient's biological death lingers, his or her social death may be hastened. On the other hand, if a person's biological death is unexpected and perhaps instant (as in an accident), it may take days or weeks before his or her social death is actually realized.

A patient's dying career appears to involve a series of "critical junctures" (Glaser & Strauss, 1965, p. 13). First, the patient is defined as dying. Second, staff and family make preparations for the death. Third, death is defined as inevitable. The fourth juncture is the final descent into death, which entails the fifth juncture, the last hours; the sixth juncture, the death watch; and the seventh juncture, the death itself. At some point in this career, announcements may be made that the patient is dying, or that he or she is leaving one phase and entering another. After death, legal pronouncements must be made, and then the death is made public.

The Social Consequences of Death

Mourning

Death sets in motion a series of processes that serve to distinguish the living from the dead and thereby establish continuity in the life cycle. Perhaps death's most important consequence is the disruption of the relational worlds of the living, in particular those intimates who mourn the passing of the deceased (Gorer, 1965, p. 112).

On the basis of extensive research in Great Britain, Gorer (1965, p. 11) proposes that most adult mourners pass through three stages: a short period of shock, which usually lasts from the occurrence of the death to the time of the disposal of the body; a period of intense mourning accompanied by withdrawal from the external world, often linked with weight loss and lack of rest; and a final period of readjustment in which mourners return to their normal rounds of activity. Gorer (1965) observes:

> The first period of shock is . . . generally given social recognition. Kinsfolk gather around the mourners for the family gatherings, religious ceremonies and, often, ritual meals. . . . Once the funeral, and possibly the post-funeral meal, are finished, the ritual which might give support to the bereaved is finished too, and they are left to face the period of intense mourning without either sup-

> port or guidance. . . . The customs of Britain . . . prescribe usually in great detail the costume and behavior appropriate to mourners in the period of intense mourning after the funeral; they also typically impose an etiquette on all those who come in contact with the mourners; and usually designate the number of days, weeks, months or years that this behavior should be followed. (p. 112)

Mourning, although a social process and one that reflects each mourner's relationship to the deceased, is concomitantly a ritual act that is imposed upon the person by the social group. On this point, Durkheim (1947) argues:

> Mourning is not the spontaneous expression of individual emotions. . . . mourning is not a natural movement of private feelings wounded by cruel loss; it is a duty imposed by the group. One weeps, not simply because he is sad, but because he is forced to weep. It is a ritual attitude which he is forced to adopt . . . but which is, in a large measure, independent of his affective state. (p. 397)

Among mourners in contemporary American society, individuals pay the debt of mourning, in part, by purchasing floral arrangements, visiting the funeral home, and assisting in the preparation of post-funeral meals for the members of the deceased's immediate family. One's relationship to the deceased, and to the living members of the deceased's family, stands suspended until one or more of these ritual acts have been completed, or at least attempted.

For the immediate family, the purchase of the casket takes on some significance (Salomone, 1973); not only must a casket (or some suitable substitute) be purchased, but its cost is understood to define the moral worth of the deceased person (and perhaps of his or her remaining family). If a casket cannot be purchased, the funeral ceremony cannot be completed, and the mourners find themselves in the uneasy situation of still having to grieve. A 1979 strike involving four major vault manufacturers and Teamsters Union Local 786 in Cook County, Illinois, placed some 1,500 families in a situation where their funerals could not be promptly completed because of the unavailability of caskets. One woman remarked:

> It is hard enough to lose your mother, but this kind of thing just leaves you hanging—knowing the funeral is not completed. . . . Now we'll have to go through all of that grief again when we bury her. . . . At the time of the funeral, you are surrounded by relatives and friends. Now when we go out there [to the cemetery], it will just be us. (quoted in O'Connor, 1977, p. 5)

The obligatory character of mourning is well displayed in the death practices of the Kiowa Apache, as reported by Opler and Bittle (1967):

> Among the Kiowa Apache the reaction to a death was immediate and violent. Close relatives wailed, tore their clothes, and exposed their bodies without shame; some shaved the head, lacerated the body, and cut off a finger joint. . . . A widower went to great lengths to show his grief. Sometimes he requested relatives of his wife to gash his forehead or to cut off all his hair, and gave presents to the one who performed the service. (p. 473)

The Social Shaping of Grief

Lofland (1985) has examined the proposition that grief is a universal feature of human nature. She defines grief as "a response to the involuntary loss through death of a human being who is viewed as significant by the actor of reference" (p. 172). She argues that the data that would test the universality of the grief emotion are not available; this makes the universalistic hypothesis suspect. She further suggests that grief is shaped by such social factors as (a) the level of significance of the one who dies, (b) the definition of the situation surrounding the death, (c) the character of the self experiencing the death, and (d) the interactional setting in which the prior three features occur.

Lofland (1985) offers the following example. She quotes from Volkart's discussion of anthropologist M. W. Spiro's analysis of the Ifaluk people:

> In his study of the Ifaluk people, Spiro was puzzled by some features of bereavement behavior there. When a family member dies, the immediate survivors displayed considerable pain and distress, which behavior was in accordance with local custom. However, as soon as the funeral was over, the bereaved were able to laugh, smile and behave in general as if they had suffered no loss or injury at all. (p. 176)

Grief, then, is an emotion that follows death, but its shape, its meaning, the length of time it is expressed, and how it is expressed vary from one cultural and historical group to another. The character of grief, like that of mourning, is variable. The conditions that appear to produce grief are as follows: (a) The person is connected to a small number of highly significant others; (b) death is defined as personal annihilation and as unusual and tragic except among the aged (Lofland, 1985, p. 181); (c) persons take their emotional states seriously; and (d) there are interactional settings that provide the opportunity to contemplate and express the loss (Lofland, 1985, p. 181).

The Meanings of Death

As an event that disrupts social structures, death represents an elaborate ritual occurrence that forces the living to define and reestablish their own relational ties to one another. The paradoxical consequence of death, then, is that the movement of a member out of a social group becomes the occasion for affirming the group's very foundation and basis of existence. For without acknowledging—however ritualistically—the "passing on" of one of its members, the group as a collectivity runs the risk of having no one recognize its collective or individual death. The rituals of death, from this point of view, function in a self-serving manner for the group.

Death and its rituals reaffirm the social order. As a social process, death and dying represent the interplay, at the group level, of biological and social events. As we have shown, a biological death cannot occur until the occurrence of "social death" has been established. That social death often precedes biological death is a measure of humans' control over the termination of the life cycle of themselves and their fellows. Peter Freuchen's (1967) discussion of the problem of the aged in Eskimo society makes this point rather forcefully. He describes the social and then biological death of an elderly woman named Naterk:

> [Old Naterk called her son Mala.] "I am tired and I am old. You must build me a snow house because I shall go on a very long journey all alone." . . .
>
> Thus Mala built a house. . . . Then she crawled into the house built for her and quietly stretched out on the old skin. Soon Mala came. . . .
>
> He now took his knife, cut a block of snow and walled up the entrance with it. . . .
>
> There, then, the old woman reposed, waiting for death. . . .
>
> How hard it was to play dead. But Old Naterk was no longer to be reckoned among the living. To the others she had passed on; she was gone. . . .
>
> Life, surely, was much more wearisome than death. But the most wearisome thing of all was this slow transition from life to death. (pp. 178-181)

Medicine, McDonald's, and the Risk Society

Today we live in a risk society, a belief that the modern world has become increasingly uncertain, contingent, filled with risk and danger (Turner, 1997, p. xvii). Throughout the conservative decades of the 1980s and the 1990s there have been profound changes in systems of government, in the structure of the economy, and in the delivery of social services (Turner, 1997, p. xvii). The past two decades have seen an increase in the privatization of government services and the deregulation of key industries. At the same time, the globalization of the world economy has profoundly transformed the service industries. It has produced great growth in tourism and consumerism. It has also produced a renewed dependency on Third World labor markets. We life in an age of post-Fordist, conservative economic practices, with their logics of financial deregulation, new internal markets, competitive spending, and new cost-accounting schemes. These economic and cultural practices have destabilized long-standing notions in the democratic nations of central governments providing to their citizens social security and collective welfare and medical benefits (Turner, 1997, p. xvii).

All of the developments mentioned above have contributed to a global environment of political and economic uncertainty—an age of oil spills, new surveillance systems, rampant spread of sinister diseases (e.g., AIDS), misinformation campaigns, conspiracies, deterioration of food supplies, "mad cow" disease, and contaminated water supplies. "As the global economy develops into a culture of risk, the nation-state is forced to invest more and more in internal systems of governmentality" (Turner, 1997, p. xviii). A risk society based on deregulation requires more subtle forms of control and surveillance. Risk increases in the deregulated society. Central regulatory agencies no longer systematically monitor potential situations of economic, industrial, financial, and environmental risk; private industries can now put the entire culture, or an entire region and its population, at risk.

Contemporary societies, as Turner (1997, p. xviii) observes, are now structured by two contradictory processes: the growth of risk cultures and risk industries and the "McDonaldization" of society (Ritzer, 1993). Drawing on the fast-food industry, the term *McDonaldization* refers to the extension of production-line methods and strategies of rational managerialism to all sectors of society (Turner, 1997, p. xviii). The lures of McDonaldization are strong: It reduces risk, uncertainty, and unpredictability; "it is a response to risk uncertainty" (Turner, 1997, p. xviii). McDonaldization removes surprises from daily life and "extends the principles of instrumental rationality to production, distribution and consumption" (Turner, 1997, p. xviii). This model now applies to education, medicine, leisure, even consumerism, and "McDentists and McDoctors extend the principles of cheapness, standardization, and reliability to the health industry" (Turner, 1997, p. xviii).

As Turner notes, complex mixtures of the risk culture and the McDonaldization of services currently organize the welfare and health care systems in the United States. Paradoxically, the increase in generalized risks from the unregulated environment and from epidemics such as AIDS leads to greater unregulated societal surveillance. An age of increased health risks generates the need for more control from within the medical establishment. This is especially the case as medicine extends its arguments concerning positive lifestyles, preventive medicine, and greater personal responsibility. Of course, an increase in health risks justifies increased medical and police surveillance, intervention, and control.

CONCLUSION

The technologies of medical power create selves with medical bodies, dying bodies, sick bodies, and chronically ill bodies in great pain. The body is a material and social construction. Medical bodies are controlled by the medical regimes of any culture. The medicalization critique points to the limits and dangers of the medical model. Illness, aging, dying, and death are social and biological processes that find their meanings and interpretations both in the human body and in human social groups. They are discursive constructions. They are of concern to social psychologists because they are recurring events that all social structures and all groups must confront. Their meanings vary from group to group, from one historical moment to the next. The social worlds of the elderly have assumed a subculture flavor that emphasizes solidarity and mutual support. Death, whether clinical, biological, or social, is surrounded by a complex network of ritual acts that serve to establish important relationships between the living and the deceased. In a risk society, there are grave dangers associated with the increasing McDonaldization of medicine and health care.

SUGGESTED READINGS

Charmaz, K. (1991). *Good days, bad days: The self in chronic illness and time.* New Brunswick, NJ: Rutgers University Press. A very moving and carefully crafted study of how chronically ill persons organize their lives and their days.

Ellis, C. (1995). *Final negotiations: A study of love, loss and chronic illness.* Philadelphia: Temple University Press. An important experimental ethnography about how chronic illness can shape loving and dying in an intimate relationship.

Gubrium, J. F. (1993). *Speaking of life: Horizons of meaning for nursing home residents.* New York: Aldine de Gruyter. A powerful collection of first-person stories and interviews about what life means to residents of several Florida nursing homes.

STUDY QUESTIONS

1. How are medical bodies created?
2. What is the medicalization critique? How does it apply to the McDonaldization of medicine?
3. What is a risk society?
4. What are the linguistic and interactional foundations of chronic pain?
5. What is biological death?

Glossary

Addict	A person addicted to a drug and to a way of life.
Alcoholic	(a) A person who calls him- or herself an alcoholic, often (b) displaying an inability to abstain from alcohol for any continuous period of time and who, once drinking starts, is unable to control the amount he or she consumes.
Amnesia	An inability to remember past experiences. One form, *childhood amnesia,* refers to the dearth of recollections of childhood experiences.
Anthropomorphism	The projection of human traits onto things not human, such as lower animals.
Aphasia	The loss of the power or ability to use language; types include verbal, nominal, syntactic, and semantic. Recent research classifies aphasia in terms of *expressive* disorders (problems understanding and producing written and spoken speech) and *receptive* disorders (problems producing speech that is understandable to others).
Artificial intelligence theory	A cognitive social psychology that models human thinking after the inner workings and problem-solving activities of computers.
Atomism	The error of reducing a whole to the sum of its parts.
Attachment	An affectional bond that ties one person to another over an extended period of time.

Awareness context The total combination of what each interactant in a situation knows about the identity of the other and his or her own identity in the eyes of the other. Types are *open, closed, pretense,* and *suspicion.*

Base Marxist term referring to the underlying material, economic basis of social structure.

Career Involves three interrelated notions (a) a person's *objective* movement from one position to another through a social structure, (b) *subjective* changes in self-conception that accompany these movements, and (c) *moral* meanings of self that follow these objective and subjective changes.

Categorical attitude Consists of the following (a) things can be named, (b) things can be grouped and classified, and (c) by naming and classifying we create new possibilities of behavior.

Cause (a) *Scientific:* Antecedent processes that precede events and influence their occurrence. (b) *Commonsense:* Reasons everyday interactants give for their actions, also called accounts.

Childhood socialization Those interactional experiences that build human nature into the child.

Chronic illness (or pain) An illness or pain that often has no cure and hence is lifelong.

Chronological age The actual age of a person.

Code How a message or spoken utterance is organized—in terms of a formal logic, a computer program, a commonsense framework, and so on.

Cognitive social psychology A point of view that stresses rational, thinking processes and often tends to be experimental and statistical. Examples include artificial intelligence theories, role identity theories, exchange theory, and dramaturgical formulations.

Collective behavior Emergent, extrainstitutional forms of behavior, including the behavior of crowds, rumor, gossip, panic, fashion, fads, and collective protest.

Componential analysis The study and classification of the meanings, terms, cognitions, and perceptions utilized by a cultural group.

Conventional sign A term that derives its meaning from social consensus—for example, the American flag. *First-order sign:* A sign that operates for lower animals, such as the sound of a bell. *Second-order sign:* A sign that operates for humans and that is applied to visual and auditory data, often called a conventional sign.

Coping mechanism	A technique of self-defense; may include selective perception, the use of accounts, disclaimers, scapegoating, rationalization, projection, denial, detachment, and the use of privacy.
Criminal world	The social worlds of crime and criminals in a society, usually divided into three categories: conventional criminals, white-collar criminals, and racketeers; may also be classified in terms of amateurs and professionals.
Death	In modern Western societies, there are three meanings of death: *clinical, biological,* and *social.* Death is organized in terms of a dying trajectory that moves persons through these three categories. *Stages of acceptance* are denial, anger, bargaining, depression, acceptance.
Demoralization	A breakdown in group morale and collective group effort and the appearance of bickering, fighting, and factionalism.
Deviance	A definition conferred on behavior by others, often including a conception of behavior that departs from the "normal."
Disclaimer	A verbal device people use when they wish to ward off criticisms of something they are about to do or say.
Discourse	Extended speech or language behavior in any context; includes conversations between speakers and printed texts.
Disengagement theory	A popular theory of aging that assumes that as people age, they disengage from their normal social obligations and relationships.
Dream work	Transformation of the latent content of a dream into manifest meanings; also called secondary elaboration.
Dualistic error I	The belief that the mind and the body are separate entities.
Dualistic error II	The conceptualization of thinking as independent of the more overt forms of language behavior, including speech.
Egocentric utterance	Self-centered speech; contrasted with sociocentric speech, which merges speech with the perspectives of others.
Emotional associate	A person who, directly or indirectly, shares in an emotional experience.
Emotional situations	Situations in which emotions are recognized, defined, shared, and experienced.
Emotional understanding	Knowing, comprehending, and interpreting through emotional means—including sympathy and imagination—the intentions, feelings, and thoughts of another.
Emotionality	The process of being emotional; consists of self-feelings. There are four forms of emotional experience: *sensible feelings,* or sensations

such as pain; *feelings of the lived body,* such as sorrow; *intentional value feelings,* as when we feel anger at a mistake we have made; and *feelings of the self,* such as self-loathing or self-pride.

Energy principle A Freudian concept referring to the argument that energy cannot be destroyed or created.

Erotic imagery The internal flow of thought that accompanies sexual experience.

Ethnomethodology The study of how individuals create taken-for-granted meanings and understandings in social situations.

Family violence An interactional process that is self-destructive, involving physical and emotional abuse of family members.

Fixation process Addiction to a drug occurring when a person uses the drug to alleviate withdrawal distress. The person uses "fixes" or injections of the drug to alleviate the withdrawal distress.

Functional autonomy of motives Describes a situation in which a behavior first performed as a means to an end becomes an end in itself when the original purpose has disappeared.

Gender The cultural patterning of maleness and femaleness.

Gender belief system A society's beliefs about gender. In Western society, this belief system has six components: (a) belief in the natural differences between the sexes based on biology, (b) belief that the home is the woman's place, (c) belief in male patriarchy, (d) belief that men's and women's work are different, (e) belief that married heterosexual love is the only natural love, and (f) belief that women should be sexually and erotically attractive to men.

Gender code How gender is coded—or worked into selfhood—involving the learning of masculine and feminine identities in childhood.

Gender stratification system How men and women are located within the economic and prestige systems of a society.

Generalized other Mead's term referring to the organized community of attitudes to which the person responds in a social situation. Also called the third stage of self-development.

Genetic fallacy Confusion of the last event in a chronological series with the first event in the sequence; common in some versions of Freudian theory.

Homosexuality (a) *Scientific:* Wanting or having sexual relations with members of the same sex. (b) *Commonsense:* Holding the belief that one is the sort of person who has, or wants, sexual experiences with members of one's own sex.

Icon	A sign that represents something else—for example, the cross in Christianity.
Identity	How one is situated by others in a social situation in terms of social categories that are meaningful—father, husband, student, daughter, Mrs. Jones, and so on.
Identity transformation	The changes and transformations of self that can occur during a person's lifetime. One type, *alternation,* involves changes within the prescribed boundaries of the individual's social group—for example, movement from identification as a Methodist to a Lutheran. The other type, *conversion,* involves identity changes that embrace negative self-identities—for example, a Jew becoming a fundamentalist Christian.
Idiolect	The speech or language of a specific linguistic community or particular speaker.
Individual deviance	Deviance that does not have a cultural base; often called eccentric behavior.
Inner speech	Inner thought.
Interactional age	The amount of time a person spends interacting with a particular form of experience, like a game or television.
Interactional loss	The ceding of self-control to an interactional situation.
Interactional repertoire	Characteristic lines of action associated with a particular self or person.
Internal environment	The world of the body and its feelings and sensations, as contrasted to the external environment of the physical world. Both environments are mediated by the symbolic environment, which is based on language.
Interpersonal theory of psychiatry	Sullivan's theory, which is at odds with orthodox Freudian accounts of the self and development, draws heavily on symbolic interactionist concepts. It has seven stages of development: infancy, childhood, juvenile era, preadolescence, adolescence, late adolescence, and adulthood.
Interpretive social psychology	A point of view that stresses the emotional, interpretive, emergent, historical, and personal dimensions of human experience; symbolic interactionism is an example.
Inversion	The assumption of a female gender identity by a man or a male gender identity by a woman.

Kinesics The study of nonverbal behavior, including body gestures; includes the use of batons, ideographs, kinetographs, pictographs, and deictic, spatial, and rhythmic movements

Language A system of signs or words—organized by a set of rules called syntax—given meaning through semantics and including speech behavior itself and the institution of speaking, thinking, and using words within a society, group, or culture. Language's key properties are (a) duality, (b) productivity, (c) arbitrariness, (d) interchangeability, (e) specialization, (f) displacement, and (g) cultural transmission.

Linguistic emotional ritual Words, gestures, and phrases that acknowledge respect of others; includes words like *please* and *thank you*; important in the socializing of emotions in childhood.

Linguistic experience Sullivan asserts there are three modes of linguistic experience; these refer to the manner in which experience is registered and the degree to which inner elaboration is produced. These modes are (a) *prototaxic,* in which there is a minimum of inner elaboration; (b) *syntaxic,* in which there is maximum inner elaboration and this can be communicated to others (unlike the prototaxic); and (c) *parataxic,* in which experience is partially organized but there are elements of which the person is unaware.

Looking-glass self Our imagination of our appearance to others, the imagination of their judgment of our appearance, and some sort of self-feeling based on that judgment; Cooley's concept.

Love Caring as much about another person's life as one cares about one's own.

Media self (a) Images of self and identity offered through the mass media, and (b) the selves attached to celebrities in our culture who become "media" personalities.

Mesostructure Interactional processes that mediate between the world of immediate social interaction and larger institutional and organizational structures—for example, the war game played in the American military.

Metaphor Speaking of something as if it were something else—for example, describing a helicopter as if it were a hovering insect.

Metonymy Giving the name of one thing to another thing that is related to it—for example, giving the name of the French town Bordeaux to the wine produced there.

Mirror phase In Lacan's theory, a phase of self-development in which the infant first sees an image of him- or herself in the eyes and words of the other.

Motive The explanation a person gives for his or her actions; includes various styles (intimate, causal, consultative, formal, frozen) and types (in-order-to and because). The disclaimer is an example.

Myth Text from everyday life that hides or veils meaning; based on everyday phenomena (e.g., advertisements for fast-food chains).

Natural language The language of everyday speakers, as contrasted to *formal languages* (machine languages) such as FORTRAN and Pascal, which are based on symbol token systems and utilized in computer programming.

Natural sign The occurrence together of a term and what it relates to; for example, the sound of a siren and the passing of a fire engine.

Neologism New, made-up words, often used by young children. Neologisms can be used in a *declarative* or *manipulative* manner—that is, to draw attention to an object or to put an object to work for the child through the assistance of an adult.

Orientational other The significant other the person is most fully committed to, who has given the person his or her most crucial concepts and categories of self.

Perception How organisms respond to the stimuli picked up by their sense organs. Perception is selective and is organized by schemata.

Power Force applied to others to make them comply with one's will; often involves violence and death.

Pseudo-communication The use of the same words in different ways by speakers who are unaware of each other's meanings.

Psychosocial crisis A key concept in Erikson's theory of development; involves interpersonal crises concerning trust and mistrust, autonomy and doubt, intimacy and confusion, integrity and despair.

Rationalization (a) *Freudian*: Repression of painful experiences. (b) *Sociological:* The interpretation a person gives of his or her behavior in problematic situations.

Reductionism The analysis of human social behavior in terms of biological, neurological, or genetic processes.

Reference group Any group with which the person psychologically identifies; types include positive, negative, comparative, and normative.

Remembering The response to and interpretation of signs that relate to past experience, based on memory; it is a symbolic process.

Role (self) distance The placement of distance between one's situated identity and one's expressed feelings in the situation.

Schemata	Abstractions that organize information processing, based on group languages.
Selective inattention	The ignoring or misperceiving of things that would be damaging to the self or ego.
Self	A set of interpretations on a conceptual level that exercise a regulatory function over other responses and interpretations of the same organism at lower levels; also refers to how the person sees him- or herself as a subject and object in a social situation. The self is an organization of behavior imposed on the person by him- or herself and by others. It is an elusive process that haunts and is always in front of the person.
Self-awareness	Awareness of who one is in a social situation.
Self-control	A person's guidance, direction, and interpretation of his or her own lines of behavior.
Self-fulfilling prediction	Prediction of an outcome that leads a person to act in such a way as to make the belief come true. Also called self-fulfilling prophecy.
Selfhood	The state of being reflectively self-aware. Involves three stages: play, game, and generalized other (also termed preparatory, interactional, and participatory stages).
Self-negating prediction	Prediction of an outcome that leads a person to act in such a way as to disprove the prediction.
Self-system	The system or structure of defenses and reactions the person constructs to avoid anxieties. Consists of three components: (a) *good me* (self-acts the individual approves of), (b) *bad me* (self-acts the individual disapproves of and that produce anxiety), and (c) *not me* (acts that provoke deep anxiety and are disavowed and dissociated).
Semiology	The science that studies the life of signs within a society.
Sensorimotor intelligence	Piaget's term referring to the forms of intelligence displayed by young children prior to the acquisition of language; displayed through touch, sight, and movement.
Sentimental work	The organization of work in a hospital that is directed to the emotional life of the patient.
Sexual identity	Self-identifications involving sexuality and gender. There are three types of self-identities specific to gender and sexual conduct: (a) good sexual me, (b) bad sexual me, and (c) not sexual me.
Sign	A term (word) that is unmotivated and exact. A sign has two components: the *signifier*, or sound-image that is heard when a word is spo-

ken, and the *signified,* or the concept that is seen as lying behind the sound-image.

Sign system The organization of signs for any society or given group; organized in terms of *myths.* Examples include sign systems for food, the garment industry, and higher education.

Significant other A person who exerts influence over an individual's thoughts, emotions, actions, and languages of self.

Signification The process of using signs; also called signifying acts.

Small social group A network of one-, two-, and three-person social relationships organized around a framework of shared emotional and interactional experiences.

Social control How society—in the form of other individuals, language, and cultural and moral feelings—enters into the organization of individual conduct.

Social psychological imagination A perspective that attempts to grasp the larger historical context that shapes lives and group experience.

Social psychology The study of the interplay between lives and social structure, or biography and society.

Social relationship An ongoing interaction between two or more people based on shared understandings, languages, and activities. Types include (a) *interpersonal* (entered by the exchange of personal names), (b) *structural* (entered by the exchange of titles and the movement into an already existing position in a social structure, like an office), (c) *human* (relations based on shared, universal human characteristics, such as age, sex, race, and ethnicity), and (d) *larger public* (relations entered anonymously, as in the public).

Social world Groups of individuals bound together through networks of shared communication, common meanings, and shared experiences and activities—for example, the social world of the elderly.

Sociobiology A branch of evolutionary biology that studies the biological bases of all social behavior.

Sociolinguistics The study of the social organization of language behavior in social situations; includes discourse and conversational analysis.

Specious present Mead's term for merger of the past and the future in the present.

Speech act The production of a verbal utterance that is understandable to at least one other person.

Status passage	The movement of persons in and out of positions in a social structure.
Superstructure	Mental products in society formed and shaped by the base; includes ideology, consciousness, self, motive, and emotion.
Symbol	The ability of a sign to stand for something else; implies a relationship between thing and sign that is indirect. For example, the American flag means more than the United States.
Symbolic environment	The world of reality, based on language, that mediates between humans and the direct physical environment.
Symbolic interactionism	The social psychological point of view that studies the underlying symbolic, linguistic foundations of human interactional experience.
Techniques of neutralization	Symbolic devices (motives and accounts) used by persons so that they can continue a line of action that would otherwise cause guilt. Forms include (a) denial of harm, (b) denial of the victim, (c) attacking the accuser, and (d) invoking higher authorities.
Thomas's dictum	"If human beings define situations as real they are real in their consequences."
Trance logic	The ability of hyponotized subjects to tolerate and act on logical incongruities.
Universal singular	Sartre's term for the status each person's life has as both universal and unique.
Violence	The attempt to regain, through the use of force, something that has been lost by the self.
Voluntary behavior	A type of activity involving the internalization of language.
Zoomorphism	Explaining human behavior in terms of principles derived from the study of lower animals.

References

Aberle, D. F. (1966). *The peyote religion among the Navaho.* New York: Wenner-Gren Foundation for Anthropological Research.

Adler, P. (1953). *House is not a home.* New York: Holt, Rinehart & Winston.

Agar, M. H., & Hobbs, J. R. (1985). How to grow schemata out of interviews. In J. W. D. Dougherty (Ed.), *New directions in cognitive anthropology* (pp. 413-431). Urbana: University of Illinois Press.

Ainsworth, M. D. S. (1973). The development of infant-mother attachment. In B. M. Caldwell & H. N. Riciuti (Eds.), *Child development and social policy: Review of child development research* (Vol. 3). Chicago: University of Chicago Press.

Alcoholics Anonymous. (1953). *The twelve steps and the twelve traditions.* New York: Alcoholics Anonymous World Services.

Alcoholics Anonymous. (1976). *Alcoholics Anonymous.* New York: Alcoholics Anonymous World Services.

Alexander, F. (1952). Development of the fundamental concepts of psychoanalysis. In F. Alexander & H. Ross (Eds.), *Dynamic psychiatry* (pp. 3-34). Chicago: University of Chicago Press.

Allee, W. (1931). *Animal aggregations: A study in general sociology.* Chicago: University of Chicago Press.

Allee, W. (1951). *Cooperation among animals* (Rev. ed.). New York: Henry Schuman.

Allport, G. W. (1937). *Personality.* New York: Holt, Rinehart & Winston.

Allport, G. W. (1961). *Pattern and growth in personality.* New York: Holt, Rinehart & Winston.

Allport, G. W., & Postman, L. (1947). The basic psychology of rumor. In T. Newcomb & E. L. Hartley (Eds.), *Readings in social psychology* (pp. 547-558). New York: Holt, Rinehart & Winston.

Altheide, D. (1985). *Media power.* Beverly Hills, CA: Sage.

Althusser, L. (1969). *For Marx.* Harmondsworth: Penguin.

Althusser, L. (1971). *Lenin and philosophy and other essays.* New York: Monthly Review.

Anderson, E. (1990). *Streetwise: Race, class, and change in an urban community.* Chicago: University of Chicago Press.

Anderson, P. (1984). *In the tracks of historical materialism.* Chicago: University of Chicago Press.

Appadurai, A. (1990). Disjuncture and difference in the global cultural economy. *Public Culture, 2,* 1-24.

Appadurai, A. (1993). Patriotism and its future. *Public Culture, 5,* 411-429.

Appadurai, A. (1996). *Modernity at large: Cultural dimensions of globalization.* Minneapolis: University of Minnesota Press.

Argyle, M. (1969). *Social interactions.* Chicago: Aldine.

Aries, P. (1962). *Centuries of childhood.* New York: Random House.

Aries, P. (1974). *Western attitudes toward death: From the Middle Ages to the present.* Baltimore: Johns Hopkins University Press.

Asquith, P. J. (1984). The inevitability and utility of anthropomorphism in description of primate behavior. In R. Harré & V. Reynolds (Eds.), *The meaning of primate signals* (pp. 30-61). Cambridge: Cambridge University Press.

Athens, L. (1994). The self as soliloquy. *Sociological Quarterly, 35,* 521-532.

Athens, L. (1995). Dramatic self change. *Sociological Quarterly, 36,* 571-586.

Athens, L. (1998). Dominance, ghettos, and violent crime. *Sociological Quarterly, 39,* 478-493.

Ault, A. (1996). Ambiguous identity in an unambiguous sex/gender structure: The case of bisexual women. *Sociological Quarterly, 37,* 449-463.

Bain, R. (1936). The self- and other words of a child. *American Journal of Sociology, 41,* 767-775.

Bakhtin, M. M. (1986). *Speech genres and other late essays.* Austin: University of Texas Press.

Baldwin, J. M. (1987). *Social and ethical interpretations in mental development.* New York: Macmillan.

Balsamo, A. (1990). Rethinking ethnography: A work for the feminist imagination. In N. K. Denzin (Ed.), *Studies in symbolic interaction: A research annual* (Vol. 11, pp. 45-57). Greenwich, CT: JAI.

Balsamo, A. (1996). *Technologies of the gendered body: Reading cyborg women.* Durham, NC: Duke University Press.

Bar-Hillel, Y. (1960). The present status of automatic translation of languages. In F. L. Alt (Ed.), *Advances in computers* (Vol. 1, pp. 140-175). New York: Academic Press.

Barthes, R. (1967). *Elements of semiology.* New York: Hill & Wang. (Original work published 1964)

Barthes, R. (1972). *Mythologies.* New York: Hill & Wang. (Original work published 1957)

Barthes, R. (1985). *The grain of the voice: Interviews: 1962-1980.* New York: Hill & Wang.

Bartlett, F. C. (1932). *Remembering.* New York: Cambridge University Press.

Bateson, G. (1972). *Steps to an ecology of mind.* San Francisco: Chandler.

Bateson, G. (1979). *Mind and nature.* New York: Dutton.

Baudrillard, J. (1981). *For a critique of the political economy of the sign.* St. Louis, MO: Telos.

Baudrillard, J. (1983). *Simulations.* New York: Semiotext(e).

Bauman, B. (1995, February 4). The man who talked too much. *New York Times,* p. A15.

Beach, F. A. (1947). Evolutionary changes in the physiological control of mating behavior in mammals. *Psychological Review, 54,* 297-315.

Beach, F. A. (Ed.). (1965). *Sex and behavior.* New York: John Wiley.

Beauchamp, D. E. (1980). *Beyond alcoholism: Alcohol and public health policy.* Philadelphia: Temple University Press.

Becker, H. S. (1953). Becoming a marijuana user. *American Journal of Sociology, 59,* 235-252.

Becker, H. S. (1964). *The other side: Perspectives on deviance.* New York: Free Press.

Becker, H. S. (1967). History, culture, and subjective experience: An exploration of the social bases of drug-induced experiences. *Journal of Health and Social Behavior, 8,* 163-176.

Becker, H. S. (Ed.). (1973). *Outsiders: Studies in the sociology of deviance* (Rev. ed.). New York: Free Press.

Becker, H. S. (1986). *Doing things together.* Evanston, IL: Northwestern University Press.

Becker, H. S., Geer, B., & Hughes, E. (1968). *Making the grade: The academic side of college life.* New York: John Wiley.

Becker, H. S., & Strauss, A. L. (1956). Careers, personality and adult socialization. *American Journal of Sociology, 62,* 253-263.

Benedek, T. (1952). Personality development. In F. Alexander & H. Ross (Eds.), *Dynamic psychiatry* (pp. 63-113). Chicago: University of Chicago Press.

Benhabib, S. (1992). *Situating the self: Gender, community and postmodernism in contemporary ethics.* New York: Routledge.

Benjamin, J. (1981). The oedipal riddle: Authority, autonomy and the new narcissism. In J. P. Diggins & M. E. Kann (Eds.), *The problem of authority in America* (pp. 195-224). Philadelphia: Temple University Press.

Benson, P. (Ed.). (1993). *Anthropology and literature.* Urbana: University of Illinois Press.

Berger, P. L., & Kellner, H. (1964). Marriage and the construction of reality: An exercise in the microsociology of knowledge. *Diogenes, 46,* 1-23.

Berger, P. L., & Luckmann, T. (1967). *The social construction of reality: A treatise in the sociology of knowledge.* Garden City, NY: Doubleday.

Beringer, R. E., Hattaway, H., Jones, A., & Still, W. N., Jr. (1985). *Why the South lost the Civil War.* Athens: University of Georgia Press.

Berk, L. E. (1997). *Child development* (4th ed). Boston: Allyn & Bacon.

Bierens de Haan, J. (1929). *Animal psychology for biologists.* London: Hutchinson.

Birdwhistle, R. (1970). *Kinesics and context.* Philadelphia: University of Pennsylvania Press.

Birenbaum, A. (1970). On managing a courtesy stigma. *Journal of Health and Social Behavior, 11,* 196-206.

Blankenship, R. L. (1973). Organizational careers: An interactionist perspective. *Sociological Quarterly, 14,* 88-98.

Blasius, M., & Phelan, S. (Eds.). (1997). *We are everywhere: A historical sourcebook of gay and lesbian politics.* New York: Routledge.

Blauner, R. (1968). Death and social structure. In M. Truzzi (Ed.), *Sociology and everyday life* (pp. 346-367). Englewood Cliffs, NJ: Prentice Hall.

Bleier, R. (1984). *Science and gender: A critique of biology and its theories in women.* New York: Pergamon.

Blondel, C. (1928a). *La conscience morbide.* Paris: Librairie Félix Alcan.

Blondel, C. (1928b). *Introduction á la psychologie collective.* Paris: Librairie Armand, Colin.

Blondel, C. (1939). Les volitions. In G. Dumas (Ed.), *Nouveau traité de psychologie.* Paris: Librairie Félix Alcan.

Bluebond-Langner, M. (1978). *The private worlds of dying children.* Princeton, NJ: Princeton University Press.

Blum, A., & McHugh, P. (1971). The social ascription of motives. *American Sociological Review, 36,* 98-109.

Blumer, H. (1933). *Movies and conduct.* New York Macmillan.

Blumer, H. (1937). Social psychology. In E. P. Schmidt (Ed.), *Man and society* (pp. 144-198). New York: Prentice Hall.

Blumer, H. (1962). Society as symbolic interaction. In A. Rose (Ed.), *Human behavior and social processes* (pp. 179-192). Boston: Houghton Mifflin.

Blumer, H. (1969). *Symbolic interactionism.* Englewood Cliffs, NJ: Prentice Hall.

Blumer, H. (1978). Social unrest and collective protest. In N. K. Denzin (Ed.), *Studies in symbolic interaction: A research annual* (Vol. 1, pp. 1-54). Greenwich, CT: JAI.

Blumer, H. (1981). George Herbert Mead. In B. Rhea (Ed.), *The future of the sociological classics* (pp. 136-169). Boston: George Allen & Unwin.

Blumer, H. (1990). *Industrialization as an agent of social change* (D. R. Maines & T. J. Morrione, Eds.). New York: Aldine de Gruyter.

Blumstein, P., & Schwartz, P. (1983). *American couples.* New York: Basic Books.

Boden, D., & Zimmerman, D. H. (Eds.). (1991). *Talk and social structure: Studies in ethnomethodology and conversation analysis.* Cambridge: Polity.

Bordo, S. (1988). Anorexia nervosa: Psychopathology as the crystallization of culture. In I. Diamond & L. Quinby (Eds.), *Feminism and Foucault: Reflections on resistance* (pp. 87-117). Boston: Northeastern University Press.

Bossard, J. H. S., & Boll, E. S. (1960). *The sociology of child development* (3rd ed.). New York: Harper & Row.

Boster, J. S. (1985). Requiem for the omniscient informant: There's life in the old girl yet. In J. W. E. Dougherty (Ed.), *New directions in cognitive anthropology* (pp. 177-197). Urbana: University of Illinois Press.

Boswell, J. (1980). *Christianity, social tolerance, and homosexuality: Gay people in Western Europe from the beginning of the Christian era to the fourteenth century.* Chicago: University of Chicago Press.

Boutan, L. (1913). Le pseudo-language: Observations effectueés sur un anthropoide: Le gibbon. *Actes de la Société Linné de Bordeaux, 16,* 5-77.

Bowlby, J. (1953). *Child care and the growth of love.* Baltimore: Penguin.

Bowlby, J. (1980). *Attachment and loss: Vol. 3. Loss.* New York: Basic Books.

Bridges, K. (1931). *The social and emotional level of the preschool child.* London: Routledge & Kegan Paul.

Broderick, C. B. (1965). Social heterosexual relationships among urban Negroes and whites. *Journal of Marriage and the Family, 28,* 200-203.

Brooks-Gunn, J., & Lewis, M. (1982). Affective exchanges between normal and handicapped infants and their mothers. In T. Field & A. Fogel (Eds.), *Emotions and early interactions* (pp. 178-191). Hillsdale, NJ: Lawrence Erlbaum.

Brown, R. (1958). *Words and things.* New York: Free Press.

Brown, R. (1965). *Social psychology.* New York: Free Press.

Brown, R. (1970). *Psycholinguistics.* New York: Free Press.

Brown, R., & Lenneberg, E. (1954). A study in language and cognition. *Journal of Abnormal and Social Psychology, 49,* 454-462.

Brownlee, S. (1985, October). A riddle wrapped in a mystery. *Discover,* pp. 85-93.

Bruner, E. M. (1984). Experience and its expressions. In V. M. Turner & E. M. Bruner (Eds.), *The anthropology of experience* (pp. 3-30). Urbana: University of Illinois Press.

Bruner, J., & Oliver, R. (1963). The development of equivalence transformations in children. In J. Wright & J. Kagan (Eds.), *Basic cognitive processes in children.* Chicago: University of Chicago Press.

Brynner, W. (1929). *The jade mountain.* New York: Alfred A. Knopf.

Bullock, C. C. (1987). Interpretive lines of action of mentally retarded children in mainstreamed play settings. In N. K. Denzin (Ed.), *Studies in symbolic interaction: A research annual* (Vol. 8, pp. 76-94). Greenwich, CT: JAI.

Burke, K. (1935). *Permanence and change: An anatomy of purpose.* New York: New Republic.

Burr, A. R. (1934). *Alice James: Her brothers—her journal.* Cornwall, NY: Dodd, Mead.

Butler, J. (1990). *Gender trouble: Feminism and the subversion of identity.* New York: Routledge.

Butler, J. (1993a). *Bodies that matter: On the discursive limits of "sex."* London: Routledge.

Butler, J. (1993b). Imitation and gender insubordination [Extract]. In C. Lemert (Ed.), *Social theory: The multicultural and classic readings* (pp. 637-648). Boulder, CO: Westview.

Butler, J. (1997). *Excitable speech: A politics of the performative.* London: Routledge.

Cahill, S. (1986). Language practices and self definition: The case of gender identity acquisition. *Sociological Quarterly, 27,* 295-311.

Cahill, S. (1989). Fashioning males and females: Appearance management and the social reproduction of gender. *Symbolic Interaction, 12,* 281-298.

Cahill, S. (1994). And a child shall lead us? Children, gender, and perspectives by incongruity. In N. J. Herman & L. T. Reynolds (Eds.), *Symbolic interaction: An introduction to social psychology* (pp. 459-469). Dix Hills, NY: General Hall.

Cahman, W. J. (1968). The stigma of obesity. *Sociological Quarterly, 9,* 283-299.

Calhoun, C. (1994). Social theory and the politics of identity. In C. Calhoun (Ed.), *Social theory and the politics of identity* (pp. 9-36). Cambridge, MA: Blackwell.

Cameron, N., & Magaret, A. (1951). *Behavioral pathology.* Boston: Houghton Mifflin.

Campbell, D. T. (1975). On the conflicts between biological and social evolution and between psychology and moral tradition. *American Psychologist, 30,* 1103-1126.

Carey, J. W. (1989). *Communication as culture.* Boston: Unwin Hyman.

Carstairs, G. M. (1954). Daru and Bhang. *Quarterly Journal of Studies in Alcohol, 15,* 220-237.

Carvajal, D. (1995, February 6). Three words engulf Rutgers president. *New York Times,* p. A8.

Carver, R. (1981). The calm. In R. Carver, *What we talk about when we talk about love.* New York: Alfred A. Knopf.

Cassirer, E. (1944). *An essay on man.* New Haven, CT: Yale University Press.

Casson, R. W. (1983). Schemata in cognitive anthropology. In B. J. Siegel, A. R. Beals, & S. A. Tyler (Eds.), *Annual review of anthropology* (Vol. 12, pp. 429-462). Palo Alto, CA: Annual Reviews.

Charmaz, K. (1980). The social construction of self-pity in the chronically ill. In N. K. Denzin (Ed.), *Studies in symbolic interaction: A research annual* (Vol. 3, pp. 123-145). Greenwich, CT: JAI.

Charmaz, K. (1991). *Good days, bad days: The self in chronic illness and time.* New Brunswick, NJ: Rutgers University Press.

Chase, S. (1938). *The tyranny of words.* New York: Harcourt Brace.

Cheney, D. L. (1984). Category formation in varet monkeys. In R. Harré & V. Reynolds (Eds.), *The meaning of primate signals* (pp. 127-140). Cambridge: Cambridge University Press.

Chomsky, N. (1965). *Aspects of the theory of syntax.* Cambridge: MIT Press.

Cicourel, A. (1974). *Cognitive sociology.* New York: Free Press.

Clark, K., & Holquist, H. (1984). *Mikhail Bakhtin.* Cambridge, MA: Belknap.

Clarke, A. E., & Fujimura, J. H. (1992). What tools? Which jobs? Why right? In A. E. Clarke & J. H. Fujimura (Eds.), *The right tools for the job: At work in the twentieth-century life sciences* (pp. 3-44). Princeton, NJ: Princeton University Press.

Clough, P. T. (1992). *The end(s) of ethnography: From realism to social criticism.* Newbury Park, CA: Sage.

Clough, P. T. (1994). *Feminist thought: Desire, power and academic discourse.* Cambridge, MA: Blackwell.

Cockerham, W. (1978). *Medical sociology.* Englewood Cliffs, NJ: Prentice Hall.

Coles, R. (1972). *Erik H. Erikson.* Boston: Little, Brown.

Collins, P. H. (1990). *Black feminist thought: Knowledge, consciousness, and the politics of empowerment.* Boston: Unwin Hyman.

Collins, R. (1986). Is 1980s sociology in the doldrums? *American Journal of Sociology, 91,* 1336-1355.

Conn, J. H., & Kanner, L. (1947). Children's awareness of sex differences. *Journal of Child Psychiatry, 1,* 3-57.

Connell, R. W. (1987). *Gender and power.* Stanford, CA: Stanford University Press.

Conrad, P., & Schneider, J. H. (1992). *Deviance and medicalization: From badness to sickness* (Rev. ed.). Philadelphia: Temple University Press.

Cook-Gumperz, J. (1975). The child as practical reasoner. In M. Sanches & B. G. Blount (Eds.), *Sociocultural dimensions of language use* (pp. 45-67). New York: Academic Press.

Cooley, C. H. (1902). *Human nature and social order.* New York: Scribner.

Cooley, C. H. (1930). *Sociological theory and social research.* New York: Holt, Rinehart & Winston.

Cooley, C. H. (1956). *Social organization.* New York: Scribner/Free Press. (Original work published 1909)

Corey, D. W. (1951). *The homosexual in America.* Philadelphia: Chilton.

Corsaro, W. A. (1981). Friendship in the nursery school: School organization in a peer environment. In S. R. Asher & J. M. Gottman (Eds.), *The development of children's friendships* (pp. 207-241). Cambridge: Cambridge University Press.

Corsaro, W. A. (1996). Transitions in childhood: The promise of comparative, longitudinal ethnography. In R. J. Jessor, A. Colby, & R. Shweder (Eds.), *Ethnography and human development: Context and meaning in social inquiry* (pp. 419-457). Chicago: University of Chicago Press.

Coser, L. A. (1975). Presidential address: Two methods in search of a substance. *American Sociological Review, 40,* 691-700.

Cottrell, L., & Gallagher, R. (1941). Developments in social psychology, 1930-1940. *Sociometry Monographs, 1.*

Couch, C. J. (1984a). *Constructing civilizations.* Greenwich, CT: JAI.

Couch, C. J. (1984b). Symbolic interactionism and generic sociological principles. *Symbolic Interaction, 7,* 1-13.

Couch, C. J., Saxton, S. L., & Katovich, M. A. (Eds.). (1986). *Studies in symbolic interaction: The Iowa school.* Greenwich, CT: JAI.

Coulter, J. (1989). *Mind in action.* Atlantic Highlands, NJ: Humanities Press.

Coward, R., & Ellis, J. (1977). *Language and materialism: Developments in semiology and the theory of the subject.* London: Routledge & Kegan Paul.

Cowgill, D. O. (1980). The aging of populations and societies. In J. S. Quadagno (Ed.), *Aging the individual and society: Readings in social gerontology* (pp. 15-33). New York: St. Martin's.

Crain, W. (1992). *Theories of development: Concepts and applications* (3rd ed.). Englewood Cliffs, NJ: Prentice Hall.

Cumming, E., & Henry, W. E. (Eds.). (1961). *Growing old: The process of disengagement.* New York: Basic Books.

Cumming, E., Henry, W. E., & Damianopoulos, E. (1961). A formal statement of disengagement theory. In E. Cumming & W. E. Henry (Eds.), *Growing old: The process of disengagement* (pp. 210-227). New York: Basic Books.

Dale, E. (1954). *Audio visual methods in teaching* (Rev. ed.). New York: Holt, Rinehart & Winston.

Damon, W. (1977). *The social world of the child.* San Francisco: Jossey-Bass.

Damon, W. (1988). *The moral child: Nurturing children's natural moral growth.* New York: Free Press.

Davis, F. J., & Stivers, R. (Eds.). (1975). *The collective definition of deviance.* New York: Free Press.

Davis, K. (1937). The sociology of prostitution. *American Sociological Review, 2,* 744-755.

Davis, L. J. (1997). Introduction: The need for disability studies. In L. J. Davis (Ed.), *The disability studies reader* (pp. 1-6). New York: Routledge.

Davis, R. E. (1976). *Response to innovation: A study of popular argument.* New York: Arno.

de Beauvoir, S. (1952). *The second sex.* New York: Alfred A. Knopf.

de Certeau, M. (1984). *The practice of everyday life.* Berkeley: University of California Press.

Deegan, M. J. (1987). Symbolic interaction and the study of women: An introduction. In M. J. Deegan & M. R. Hill (Eds.), *Women and symbolic interaction* (pp. 3-18). Boston: Allen & Unwin.

Deegan, M. J., & Hill, M. R. (Eds.). (1987). *Women and symbolic interaction.* Boston: Allen & Unwin.

Degler, C. N. (1980). *At odds: Women and the family in America from the revolution to the present.* New York: Oxford University Press.

de Laguna, G. M. (1927). *Speech: Its functions and development.* New Haven, CT: Yale University Press.

Denzin, N. K. (1971). Children and their caretakers. *Transaction, 8,* 62-72.

Denzin, N. K. (1972). The genesis of self in early childhood. *Sociological Quarterly, 13,* 291-314.

Denzin, N. K. (1977). *Childhood socialization: Studies in the development of language, social behavior, and identity.* San Francisco: Jossey-Bass.

Denzin, N. K. (1982). The significant others of young children: Notes toward a phenomenology of childhood. In K. M. Borman (Ed.), *The social life of children in a changing society* (pp. 29-46). Hillsdale, NJ: Lawrence Erlbaum.

Denzin, N. K. (1984a). *On understanding emotion.* San Francisco: Jossey-Bass.

Denzin, N. K. (1984b). Retrieving the small social group. In N. K. Denzin (Ed.), *Studies in interaction* (Vol. 5, pp. 35-48). Greenwich, CT: JAI.

Denzin, N. K. (1984c). Toward a phenomenology of domestic, family violence. *American Journal of Sociology, 3,* 483-513.

Denzin, N. K. (1985). On the phenomenology of sexuality, desire and violence. *Current Perspectives in Social Theory, 6,* 39-56.

Denzin, N. K. (1987a). *The alcoholic self.* Newbury Park, CA: Sage.

Denzin, N. K. (1987b). *The recovering alcoholic.* Newbury Park, CA: Sage.

Denzin, N. K. (1987c). *Treating alcoholism.* Newbury Park, CA: Sage.

Denzin, N. K. (1989). *Interpretive interactionism.* Newbury Park, CA: Sage.

Denzin, N. K. (1991). *Images of postmodern society: Social theory and contemporary cinema.* London: Sage.

Denzin, N. K. (1992). *Symbolic interactionism and cultural studies.* London: Blackwell.

Denzin, N. K. (1995). *The cinematic society.* London: Sage.

Denzin, N. K. (1997). *Interpretive ethnography: Ethnographic practices for the 21st century.* Thousand Oaks, CA: Sage.

Derrida, J. (1972). Structure, sign and play in the discourse of the human sciences. In R. Macksey & E. Donato (Eds.), *The structuralist controversy: The language of criticism and the sciences of man* (pp. 247-265). Baltimore: Johns Hopkins University Press.

Derrida, J. (1981). *Positions* (A. Bass, Trans.). Chicago: University of Chicago Press.

DeVilliers, P., & DeVilliers, J. G. (1979). *Early language.* Cambridge, MA: Harvard University Press.

Dewey, J. (1922). *Human nature and conduct.* New York: Holt, Rinehart & Winston.

Dewey, J. (1925). *Experience and nature.* La Salle, IL: Open Court.

Dewey, J. (1934). *Art as experience.* New York: Minton, Balch.

Dewey, J. (1938). *Logic: The theory of inquiry.* New York: Holt, Rinehart & Winston.

Dewey, J., & Bentley, A. F. (1949). *Knowing and the known.* Beacon, NY: Beacon House.

Dewsbury, D. A. (1987). Animal sociobiology. In R. J. Corsini (Ed.), *Concise encyclopedia of psychology* (Abr. ed., pp. 66-68). New York: John Wiley.

Dilthey, W. (1976). *Selected writings* (H. P. Rickman, Ed. and Trans.). Cambridge: Cambridge University Press. (Original work published 1900)

Dobash, R. E., & Dobash, R. P. (1979). *Violence against wives: A case against the patriarchy.* New York: Free Press.

Dougherty, J. W. D. (Ed.). (1985). *Directions in cognitive anthropology.* Urbana: University of Illinois Press.

Dougherty, J. W. D., & Keller, C. M. (1985). Taskonomy: A practical approach to knowledge structures. In J. W. D. Dougherty (Ed.), *Directions in cognitive anthropology* (pp. 161-174). Urbana: University of Illinois Press.

Douglas, J. D. (Ed.). (1970). *Understanding everyday life.* Chicago: Aldine.

Douglas, J. D., Adler, P. A., Adler, P., Fontana, A., Freeman, C. R., & Kotarba, J. A. (1980). *Introduction to the sociologies of everyday life.* Boston: Allyn & Bacon.

Douglas, J. D., & Johnson, J. M. (Eds.). (1977). *Existential sociology.* New York: Cambridge University Press.

Du Bois, W. E. B. (1989). *The souls of black folk: Essays and sketches.* New York: Bantam. (Original work published 1903)

du Gay, P., Hall, S., Janes, L., Mackay, H., & Negus, K. (1997). *Doing cultural studies: The story of the Sony Walkman.* London: Sage.

Durkheim, E. (1947). *Elementary forms of religious life.* New York: Free Press.

Ebaugh, H. R. F. (1984). Leaving the convent: The experience of role exit and self-transformation. In J. A. Kotarba & A. Fontana (Eds.), *The existential self in society* (pp. 156-176). Chicago: University of Chicago Press.

Ebin, D. (Ed.). (1961). *The drug experience.* New York: Orion.

Edgerton, R. B. (1964). Pokot intersexuality: An East African example of the resolution of sexual incongruity. *American Anthropologist, 66,* 1288-1299.

Ehrmen, L., & Parsons, P. A. (1976). *The genetics of behavior.* Sunderland, MS: Sinauer.

Eibl-Eibesfeldt, I. (1970). *Ethology.* New York: Holt, Rinehart & Winston.

Ekman, P. (1970). Universal facial expressions of emotion. *California Mental Health Research Digest, 8,* 151-158.

Ekman, P. (1972). Universals and cultural differences in facial expression of emotions. In J. R. Cole (Ed.), *Nebraska Symposium on Motivation* (pp. 100-130). Lincoln: University of Nebraska Press.

Ekman, P. (1973). *Darwin and facial expression.* New York: Academic Press.

Ekman, P. (1980). Biological and cultural contributions to body and facial movement in the expression of emotion. In A. Rorty (Ed.), *Explaining emotions* (pp. 56-75). Berkeley: University of California Press.

Ekman, P., & Friesen, W. (1972). Hand movements. *Journal of Communication, 22,* 353-374.

Elkind, D. (1981). *The hurried child.* Reading, PA: Addison-Wesley.

Ellis, C. (1995). *Final negotiations: A study of love, loss and chronic illness.* Philadelphia: Temple University Press.

Epstein, S. (1994). A queer encounter: Sociology and the study of sexuality. *Sociological Theory, 12,* 188-202.

Ericsson, K., & Simon, H. A. (1984). *Protocol analysis: Verbal reports as data.* Cambridge: MIT Press.

Erikson, E. H. (1950). *Childhood and society.* New York: W. W. Norton.

Erikson, E. H. (1959). Identity and the life cycle. In G. S. Klein (Ed.), *Psychological issues.* New York: International Universities Press.

Erikson, E. H. (1962). *Young man Luther.* New York: W. W. Norton.

Erikson, E. H. (Ed.). (1965). *The challenge of youth.* Garden City, NY: Doubleday.

Erikson, E. H. (1969). *Gandhi's truth.* New York: W. W. Norton.

Erikson, K. (1965). *Wayward puritans.* New York: John Wiley.

Farberman, H. A. (1980). Fantasy in everyday life: Some aspects of the interaction between social psychology and political economy. *Symbolic Interaction, 3,* 9-22.

Faris, R. E. L. (1952). *Social psychology.* New York: Ronald.

Faulkner, R. R. (1973). Orchestra interaction: Some features of communication and authority in an artistic organization. *Sociological Quarterly, 14,* 147-157.

Feld, T. (1979). Differential behavioral and cardiac responses of 3-month-old infants to a mirror and peer. *Infant Behavior Development, 2,* 179-184.

Ferguson, C. A. (1964). Baby talk in six languages. *American Anthropologist, 66*(pt. 2), 103-114.

Fine, G. A. (1984). Humorous interaction and the social construction of meaning: Making sense in a jocular vein. In N. K. Denzin (Ed.), *Studies in symbolic interaction: A research annual* (Vol. 5, pp. 71-82). Greenwich, CT: JAI.

Fine, G. A., House, J. S., & Cook, K. S. (1995). Introduction. In K. S. Cook, G. A. Fine, & J. S. House (Eds.), *Sociological perspectives on social psychology* (pp. ix-xii). Boston: Allyn & Bacon.

Fine, G. A., & Leighton, L. F. (1993). Nocturnal omissions: Steps toward a sociology of dreams. *Symbolic Interaction, 16,* 95-104.

Finestone, H. (1957). Cats, kicks, and color. *Social Problems, 5,* 3-13.

Fischer, M. J. (1994). Autobiographical voices (1,2,3) and mosaic memory: Experimental sondages in the (post)modern world. In K. Ashley, L. Gilmore, & G. Peters (Eds.), *Autobiography and postmodernism* (pp. 79-129). Amherst: University of Massachusetts Press.

Flaherty, M. G. (1984). A formal approach to the study of amusement in social interaction. In N. K. Denzin (Ed.), *Studies in symbolic interaction: A research annual* (Vol. 5, pp. 49-67). Greenwich, CT: JAI.

Fontana, A. (1977). *The last frontier.* Beverly Hills, CA: Sage.

Fontana, A. (1980). Growing old between walls. In J. S. Quadagno (Ed.), *The individual and society: Readings in social gerontology* (pp. 482-499). New York: St. Martin's.

Foucault, M. (1972). *The archaeology of knowledge.* London: Tavistock.

Foucault, M. (1980a). *The history of sexuality: Vol. 1. An introduction.* New York: Pantheon.

Foucault, M. (1980b). *Power/knowledge: Selected interviews and other writings* (C. Gordon, Ed. and Trans.; L. Marshall, J. Mepham, & K. Soper, Trans.). New York: Pantheon.

Foucault, M. (1985). *The history of sexuality: Vol. 2.* New York: Vintage.

Frake, C. (1961). The diagnosis of disease among the Subanun of Mindanao. *American Anthropologist, 63,* 113-132.

Frake, C. (1962). Cultural ecology and ethnology. *American Anthropologist, 64,* 53-59.

Frank, A. (1990). Bringing bodies back in: A decade of review. *Theory, Culture & Society, 7,* 131-162.

Frank, L. K. (1966). Tactile communication. In A. G. Smith (Ed.), *Communication and culture* (pp. 199-208). New York: Holt, Rinehart & Winston.

Franklin, J. H. (1956). *From slavery to freedom: A history of American Negroes* (2nd ed.). New York: Alfred A. Knopf.

French, T. (1952). Dreams and rational behavior. In F. Alexander & H. Ross (Eds.), *Dynamic psychiatry* (pp. 35-39). Chicago: University of Chicago Press.

Freuchen, P. (1967). The problem of the aged in Eskimo society. In R. C. Owen, J. F. Deetz, & A. D. Fisher (Eds.), *The North American Indians: A sourcebook* (pp. 175-183). New York: Macmillan.

Freud, S. (1933). *New introductory lectures on psychoanalysis.* New York: W. W. Norton.

Freud, S. (1938). *The basic writings of Sigmund Freud* (A. A. Brill, Ed. and Trans.). New York: Random House.

Friedman, L. D. (1991). Celluloid palimpsests: An overview of ethnicity and the American film. In L. D. Friedman (Ed.), *Unspeakable images: Ethnicity and the American cinema* (pp. 11-35). Urbana: University of Illinois Press.

Gagnon, J. H., & Simon, W. (Eds.). (1967). *Sexual deviance.* New York: Harper & Row.

Gagnon, J. H., & Simon, W. (1970). Perspectives on the sexual scene. In J. H. Gagnon & W. Simon (Eds.), *The sexual scene* (pp. 1-21). Chicago: Aldine.

Gardiner, H. (1987). *The mind's new science: A history of the cognitive revolution.* New York: Basic Books.

Gardner, B., & Gardner, R. A. (1969). Teaching sign language to a chimpanzee. *Science, 165,* 664-672.

Gardner, C. B. (1995). *Passing by: Gender and public harassment.* Berkeley: University of California Press.

Garfinkel, H. (1956). Conditions of successful degradation ceremonies. *American Journal of Sociology, 61,* 420-424.

Garfinkel, H. (1967a). Passing and the managed achievement of sex status in an intersexed person: Part 1. In H. Garfinkel, *Studies in ethnomethodology* (pp. 116-185). Englewood Cliffs, NJ: Prentice Hall.

Garfinkel, H. (1967b). *Studies in ethnomethodology.* Englewood Cliffs, NJ: Prentice Hall.

Garfinkel, H. (1967c). What is ethnomethodology? In H. Garfinkel, *Studies in ethnomethodology.* Englewood Cliffs, NJ: Prentice Hall.

Garfinkel, H., Lynch, M., & Livingston, E. (1981). The work of a discovering science construed with material from the optically discovered pulsar. *Philosophy of the Social Sciences, 11,* 131-158.

Garfinkel, H., & Sacks, H. (1970). On formal structures of practical actions. In J. C. McKinney & E. A. Tiryakian (Eds.), *Theoretical sociology: Perspectives and developments* (pp. 119-151). New York: Appleton-Century-Crofts.

Geertz, C. (1995). *After the fact.* Cambridge, MA: Harvard University Press.

Gelles, R. J., & Cornell, C. P. (1985). *Intimate violence in families.* Beverly Hills, CA: Sage.

Gergen, K. J. (1973). Social psychology as history. *Journal of Personality and Social Psychology, 26,* 309-320.

Gergen, K. J. (1982). *Toward transformation in social knowledge.* New York: Springer-Verlag.

Gergen, K. J. (1991). *The saturated self: Dilemmas of identity in contemporary life.* New York: Basic Books.

Gergen, K. J., & Gergen, M. M. (Eds.). (1984). *Historical social psychology.* Hillsdale, NJ: Lawrence Erlbaum.

Gibbs, J. P., & Erickson, M. L. (1975). Major developments in the sociological study of deviance. *Annual Review of Sociology, 1,* 21-42.

Giddens, A. (1976). *New rules of sociological method: A positive critique of interpretative sociologies.* New York: Basic Books.

Giddens, A. (1981). *A contemporary critique of historical materialism: Vol. 1. Power, property and state.* Berkeley: University of California Press.

Giddens, A. (1984). *The constitution of society: Outline of the theory of structuration.* Berkeley: University of California Press.

Giddens, A. (1989). *Sociology.* Cambridge: Polity.

Giddens, A. (1990). *The consequences of modernity.* Cambridge: Polity.

Giddens, A. (1991). *Modernity and self-identity: Self and society in the late modern age.* Stanford, CA: Stanford University Press.

Gilligan, C. (1982). *In a different voice: Psychological theory and women's development.* Cambridge, MA: Harvard University Press.

Gilroy, P. (1996). British cultural studies and the pitfalls of identity. In H. A. Baker, Jr., M. Diawara, & R. H. Lindeborg (Eds.), *Black British cultural studies: A reader* (pp. 223-239). Chicago: University of Chicago Press.

Glaser, B. G., & Strauss, A. L. (1964). Awareness contexts and interaction. *American Sociological Review, 29,* 669-679.

Glaser, B. G., & Strauss, A. L. (1965). *Awareness of dying.* Chicago: Aldine.

Glaser, B. G., & Strauss, A. L. (1967). *The discovery of grounded theory: Strategies for qualitative research.* Chicago: Aldine.

Glaser, B. G., & Strauss, A. L. (1968). *Time for dying.* Chicago: Aldine.

Glaser, B. G., & Strauss, A. L. (1971). *Status passage.* Chicago: Aldine.

Goffman, E. (1955). On face-work: An analysis of ritual elements in social interaction. *Psychiatry, 18,* 213-231.

Goffman, E. (1956). The nature of deference and demeanor. *American Anthropologist, 58,* 473-502.

Goffman, E. (1959). *The presentation of self in everyday life.* Garden City, NY: Doubleday.

Goffman, E. (1961a). *Encounters.* Indianapolis: Bobbs-Merrill.

Goffman, E. (1961b). The moral career of the mental patient. In E. Goffman, *Asylums: Essays on the social situation of mental patients and other inmates* (pp. 128-169). Garden City, NY: Doubleday.

Goffman, E. (1963a). *Behavior in public places.* New York: Free Press.

Goffman, E. (1963b). *Stigma: Notes on the management of spoiled identity.* Englewood Cliffs, NJ: Prentice Hall.

Goffman, E. (1967). *Interaction ritual: Essays on face-to-face behavior.* Garden City, NY: Anchor.

Goffman, E. (1969). *Strategic interaction.* Philadelphia: University of Pennsylvania Press.

Goffman, E. (1971). *Relations in public.* New York: Basic Books.

Goffman, E. (1974). *Frame analysis.* New York: Harper & Row.

Goffman, E. (1981). *Forms of talk.* Philadelphia: University of Pennsylvania Press.

Goffman, E. (1983). The interaction order. *American Sociological Review, 48,* 1-17.

Gold, M. S. (1984). *800-COCAINE.* New York: Bantam.

Gold, R. (1952). Janitors versus tenants: A status income dilemma. *American Journal of Sociology, 57,* 486-493.

Goldstein, K. (1940). *Human nature in the light of psychopathology.* Cambridge, MA: Harvard University Press.

Goode, W. (1959). The theoretical importance of love. *American Sociological Review, 24,* 37-48.

Goodman, M. E. (1970). *The culture of childhood.* New York: Teachers College Press.

Goody, J., & Watt, I. (1972). The consequences of literacy. In P. P. Giglioli (Ed.), *Language and social context: Selected readings* (pp. 311-357). Baltimore: Penguin.

Gorer, G. (1965). *Death, grief and mourning in contemporary Britain.* London: Cressey.

Gove, W. R. (Ed.). (1980). *The labelling of deviance* (2nd ed.). Englewood Cliffs: NJ: Prentice Hall.

Gray, H. (1995). *Watching race: Television and the struggle for "blackness."* Minneapolis: University of Minnesota Press.

Green, A. I. (1998). Sex and the city [Letter to the editor]. *Lingua Franca, 8,* 88.

Greene, P. J., Morgan, C. J., & Barash, D. P. (1979). Sociobiology. In S. G. McNall (Ed.), *Theoretical perspectives in sociology* (pp. 414-430). New York: St. Martin's.

Griffin, J. (1962). *Black like me.* New York: Signet.

Grimshaw, A. D. (1981). Talk and social control. In M. Rosenberg & R. H. Turner (Eds.), *Social psychology: Sociological perspectives* (pp. 235-268). New York: Basic Books.

Gross, E., & Stone, G. P. (1964). Embarrassment and the analysis of role requirements. *American Journal of Sociology, 70,* 1-15.

Gubrium, J. F. (1975). *Living and dying at Murray Manor.* New York: St. Martin's.

Gubrium, J. F. (1986). The social preservation of mind: The Alzheimer's disease experience. *Symbolic Interaction, 9,* 37-51.

Gubrium, J. F. (1993). *Speaking of life: Horizons of meaning for nursing home residents.* New York: Aldine de Gruyter.

Gubrium, J. F., & Holstein, J. A. (1995). Individual agency, the ordinary, and postmodern life. *Sociological Quarterly, 36,* 555-570.

Guerrero, E. (1993). *Framing blackness: The African American image in film.* Philadelphia: Temple University Press.

Gusfield, J. R. (1967). Moral passage: The symbolic process in public designations of deviance. *Social Problems, 15,* 175-188.

Gusfield, J. R. (1992). Foreword. In P. Conrad & J. H. Schneider, *Deviance and medicalization: From badness to sickness* (pp. v-x). Philadelphia: Temple University Press.

Halbwachs, M. (1925). *Les cadres sociaux de la mémoire.* Paris: Librairie Félix Alcan.

Halbwachs, M. (1950). *La mémoire collective.* Paris: Presses Universitaires.

Hall, C. S. (1953). A cognitive theory of dream symbols. *Journal of General Psychology, 48,* 169-186.

Hall, C. S., & Lindzey, G. (1957). *Theories of personality.* New York: John Wiley.

Hall, S. (1980). Cultural studies: Two paradigms. *Media, Culture & Society, 2,* 57-72.

Hall, S. (1996a). Introduction. In S. Hall, D. Held, D. Hubert, & K. Thompson (Eds.), *Modernity: An introduction to modern societies* (pp. 3-18). Cambridge, MA: Blackwell.

Hall, S. (1996b). The West and the rest: Discourse and power. In S. Hall, D. Held, D. Hubert, & K. Thompson (Eds.), *Modernity: An introduction to modern societies* (pp. 184-228). Cambridge, MA: Blackwell.

Hall, S. (1996c). The question of cultural identity. In S. Hall, D. Held, D. Hubert, & K. Thompson (Eds.), *Modernity: An introduction to modern societies* (pp. 595-634). Cambridge, MA: Blackwell.

Hall, S. (1996d). What is this "black" in black popular culture? In D. Morley & K. Chen (Eds.), *Stuart Hall: Critical dialogues in cultural studies* (pp. 465-475). London: Routledge.

Hall, S. (1997). The work of representation. In S. Hall (Ed.), *Representation: Cultural representations and signifying practices* (pp. 13-64). London: Sage.

Hamilton, G. (1939). Changes in personality and psychosexuality with age. In E. V. Cowdry (Ed.), *Problems of aging: Biological and medical aspects* (pp. 459-482). Baltimore: Williams & Wilkins.

Haraway, D. J. (1989). *Primate visions: Gender, race, and nature in the world of modern science.* New York: Routledge.

Haraway, D. J. (1991). *Simians, cyborgs, and women: The reinvention of nature.* New York: Routledge.

Harman, L. D. (1986). Sign, symbol and metalanguage: Against the integration of semiotics and symbolic interaction. *Symbolic Interaction, 9,* 147-160.

Harré, R. (1982). Psychological dimensions. In P. F. Secord (Ed.), *Explaining human behavior: Consciousness, human action, and social structure* (pp. 93-114). Beverly Hills, CA: Sage.

Harré, R. (1992). The discursive creation of human psychology. *Symbolic Interaction, 15,* 515-527.

Harré, R. (1995). Discursive psychology. In J. A. Smith, R. Harré, & L. Van Langenhove (Eds.), *Rethinking psychology* (pp. 143-159). London: Sage.

Harré, R., & Reynolds, V. (Eds.). (1984). *The meaning of primate signals.* Cambridge: Cambridge University Press.

Harré, R., & Secord, P. (1972). *The explanation of social behaviour.* London: Blackwell.

Hartup, W. W. (1979). The social worlds of childhood. *American Psychologist, 34,* 944-950.

Haugeland, J. (1985). *Artificial intelligence: The very idea.* Cambridge: MIT Press.

Havighurst, R. (1956). *Psychological aspects of aging.* Washington, DC: American Psychological Association.

Hawkes, T. (1977). *Structuralism and semiotics.* Berkeley: University of California Press.

Hayes, C. (1926). *Essays on nationalism.* New York: Macmillan.

Hayes, C. (1951). *The ape in our house.* New York: Harper & Row.

Head, H. G. (1926). *Aphasia and kindred disorders of speech.* New York: Macmillan.

Healey, J. F. (1995). *Race, ethnicity, gender, and class.* Thousand Oaks, CA: Pine Forge.

Heap, J. L., & Roth, P. (1973). On phenomenological sociology. *American Sociological Review, 38,* 354-367.

Heidegger, M. (1962). *Being and time.* New York: Harper & Row. (Original work published 1927)

Heidegger, M. (1977). *Basic writings from Being and time (1927) to The task of thinking (1964).* New York: Harper & Row.

Henry, J. (1963). *Culture against man.* New York: Random House.

Heritage, J. (1984). *Garfinkel and ethnomethodology.* Cambridge: Polity.

Herrnstein, R. J., & Murray, C. (1994). *The bell curve: Intelligence and class structure in American life.* New York: Free Press.

Hess, R. D., & Handel, G. (1959). *Family worlds.* Chicago: University of Chicago Press.

Hewes, G. W. (1973). Primate communication and the gestural origin of language. *Current Anthropology, 14*(1-2), 5-12.

Hewitt, J. P. (1984). *Self and society: A symbolic interactionist social psychology* (3rd ed.). Boston: Allyn & Bacon.

Hewitt, J. P., & Stokes, R. (1975). Disclaimers. *American Sociological Review, 40,* 1-11.

Heyl, B. S. (1979). *The madam as entrepreneur: Career management in house prostitution.* New Brunswick, NJ: Transaction.

Hill, R., & Aldous, J. (1969). Socialization for marriage and parenthood. In D. Goslin (Ed.), *Handbook of socialization theory and research* (pp. 885-950). Chicago: Rand McNally.

Hiller, E. T. (1933). *Principles of sociology.* New York: Harper & Row.

Hite, S. (1976). *The Hite report: A nationwide study of female sexuality.* New York: Dell.

Hochschild, A. R. (1973). *The unexpected community.* Englewood Cliffs, NJ: Prentice Hall.

Hochschild, A. R. (1979). Emotion work, feeling rules, and social structure. *American Journal of Sociology, 85,* 551-575.

Hochschild, A. R. (1983). *The managed heart: Commercialization of human feeling.* Berkeley: University of California Press.

Hockett, C. F. (1965). *A course in modern linguistics.* New York: Macmillan.

Holland, D., & Reeves, J. R. (1994). Activity theory and the view from somewhere: Team perspectives on the intellectual work of programming. *Mind, Culture, and Activity, 1,* 8-24.

hooks, b. (1990). *Yearning: Race, gender, and cultural politics.* Boston: South End.

Horowitz, I. L., & Liebowitz, M. (1968). Social deviance and political marginality. *Social Problems, 15,* 280-296.

Horowitz, R. (1936). Spatial localization of the self. *Journal of Social Psychology, 6,* 379-387.

Horowitz, R. S. (1982). Adult delinquent gangs in a Chicano community. *Urban Life, 11,* 3-27.

Howley, J. A. (1998). *"I'm not dead yet": Gay male narratives in the age of AIDS.* Unpublished doctoral dissertation, University of Illinois, Champaign-Urbana, Department of Sociology.

Hughes, E. C. (1937). Institutional office and the person. *American Journal of Sociology, 43,* 404-413.

Hughes, E. C. (1958). *Men and their work.* New York: Free Press.

Hulett, J. E., Jr. (1964). Communication and social order: The search for a theory. *Audio-Visual Communication Review, 12,* 458-468.

Hulit, L. M., & Howard, M. R. (1997). *Born to talk: An introduction to speech and language development* (2nd ed.). Boston: Allyn & Bacon.

Humphreys, L. (1970). *Tearoom trade: Impersonal sex in public places.* Chicago: Aldine.

Humphreys, L. (1972). *Out of the closets: The sociology of homosexual liberation.* Englewood Cliffs, NJ: Prentice Hall.

Hunter, E. (1951). *Brainwashing in Red China.* New York: Vanguard.

Hymes, D. H. (1972). Toward ethnographies of communication: The analysis of communicative events. In P. P. Giglioli (Ed.), *Language and social context: Selected readings* (pp. 21-44). Baltimore: Penguin.

Ibanez-Gracia, T., & Rueda, L. I. (Eds.). (1997). *Critical social psychology.* London: Sage.

Icheiser, G. (1949). Misunderstandings in human relations. *American Journal of Sociology, 55*(pt. 2), 1-70.

Icheiser, G. (1970). *Appearances and realities: Misunderstandings in human relations.* San Francisco: Jossey-Bass.

Isaacs, S. S. (1933). *Social development in young children.* London: Routledge & Kegan Paul.

Ittelson, W., & Cantril, H. (1954). *Perception: A transactional approach.* Garden City, NY: Doubleday.

Jacobs, J. (1969). *The search for help: A study of the retarded child in the community.* New York: Brunner/Mazel.

Jakobson, R., & Morris, H. (1956). Two aspects of language and two aspects of aphasic disturbances. In R. Jakobson & H. Morris, *Fundamentals of language* (pp. 69-96). The Hague: Mouton.

James, A. (1964). *The diary of Alice James* (L. Edel, Ed.). New York: Dodd, Mead.

James, H. (1913). *A small boy and others.* London: Macmillan.

James, W. (1950). *The principles of psychology.* New York: Dover. (Original work published 1890)

Jay, M. (1988). Scopic regimes of modernity. In H. Foster (Ed.), *Vision and visuality* (pp. 3-23). Seattle: Bay.

Jellinek, E. M. (1962). Phases of alcohol addiction. In D. J. Pittman & C. R. Snyder (Eds.), *Society, culture, and drinking patterns* (pp. 356-368). New York: John Wiley.

Jennings, H. S. (1942). The transition from the individual to the social level. *Biological Symposia, 8,* 105-119.

Jersild, A. (1947). *Child psychology* (3rd ed.). Englewood Cliffs, NJ: Prentice Hall.

Joffe, C. (1971). Sex role socialization and the nursery school: As the twig is bent. *Journal of Marriage and the Family, 33,* 467-475.

Jordan, W. (1968). *White over black.* Chapel Hill: University of North Carolina Press.

Josselson, R., & Lieblich, A. (1993). *The narrative study of lives.* Newbury Park, CA: Sage.

Judd, C. H. (1926). *The psychology of social institutions.* New York: Macmillan.

Judd, C. H. (1939). *Educational psychology.* Boston: Houghton Mifflin.

Jung, C. G. (1953). *Collected works: Vol. 12. Psychology and alchemy.* Princeton, NJ: Princeton University Press.

Kadushin, A., & Martin, J. A. (1981). *Child abuse: An interactional event.* New York: Columbia University Press.

Kafka, F. (1952). *Selected short stories of Franz Kafka* (W. Muir & E. Muir, Trans.). New York: Random House.

Kando, T. J. (1972). Passing and stigma management: The case of the transsexual. *Sociological Quarterly, 13,* 475-483.

Kanter, R. (1972). *Communities and commitment.* Cambridge, MA: Harvard University Press.

Kazin, A. (1951). *A walker in the city.* New York: Harcourt Brace.

Keller, C. M., & Keller, J. D. (1996). *Cognition and tool use: The blacksmith at work.* New York: Cambridge University Press.

Kellogg, W. N. (1961). *Porpoises and sonar.* Chicago: University of Chicago Press.

Kellogg, W. N., & Kellogg, L. A. (1933). *The ape and the child.* New York: McGraw-Hill.

Kemper, T. D. (1978). *A social interactional theory of emotions.* New York: John Wiley.

Kincheloe, J. L., & Steinberg, S. R. (1994). Who said it can't happen here? In J. L. Kincheloe, S. R. Steinberg, & A. D. Gresson III (Eds.), *Measured lies:* The bell curve *examined* (pp. 3-47). New York: St. Martin's.

King, H., & Chambliss, W. J. (1972). *Box Man: A professional thief's journal* (W. J. Chambliss, Ed.). New York: Harper & Row.

King, J. E. (1987). Comparative psychology. In R. J. Corsini (Ed.), *Concise encyclopedia of psychology* (Abr. ed., pp. 222-224). New York: John Wiley.

Kinsey, A. C., Pomeroy, W. B., & Martin, C. E. (1948). *Sexual behavior in the human male.* Philadelphia: W. B. Saunders.

Kinsey, A. C., Pomeroy, W. B., Martin, C. E., & Gebhard, P. (1953). *Sexual behavior in the human female.* Philadelphia: W. B. Saunders.

Kitsuse, J. K. (1962). Societal reaction to deviant behavior: Problems of theory and method. *Social Problems, 9,* 247-257.

Kitsuse, J. K. (1975). Social problems and deviance: Some parallel issues. *Social Problems, 22,* 585-594.

Kitsuse, J. K., & Spector, M. (1973). Toward a sociology of social problems: Value judgments and social problems. *Social Problems, 20,* 407-419.

Kitzinger, C. (1987). *The social construction of lesbianism.* London: Sage.

Klaus, M. H., & Kennell, J. H. (1982). Parent-to-infant bonding. In J. Belsky (Ed.), *The beginning: Readings on infancy.* New York: Columbia University Press.

Klein, M. (1932). *The psychoanalysis of children.* London: Hogarth.

Klineberg, O. (1954). *Social psychology* (Rev. ed.). New York: Holt, Rinehart & Winston.

Kluckhohn, C., & Leighton, D. (1946). *The Navaho.* Cambridge, MA: Harvard University Press.

Kluckhohn, C., & Murray, H. A. (Eds.). (1948). *Personality in nature, society, and culture.* New York: Alfred A. Knopf.

Koch, H. L. (1954). Child psychology. *Annual Review of Psychology, 5,* 1-26.

Kohlberg, L. (1963a). The development of children's orientations toward a moral order: A sequence in the development of moral thought. *Vita Humana, 6,* 11-33.

Kohlberg, L. (1963b). Moral development and identification. In *National Society for the Study of Education 62nd yearbook.* Chicago: University of Chicago Press.

Kohlberg, L. (1966). Cognitive stages and preschool education. *Human Development, 9,* 5-7.

Kohlberg, L. (1969). Stage and sequence: The cognitive-developmental approach to socialization. In D. Goslin (Ed.), *Handbook of socialization theory and research* (pp. 180-213). Chicago: Rand McNally.

Kohlberg, L. (1971). From is to ought: How to commit the naturalistic fallacy and get away with it in the study of moral development. In T. Mischel (Ed.), *Cognitive development and epistemology* (pp. 79-83). New York: Academic Press.

Kohlberg, L. (1976). The study of moral development. In T. Lickona (Ed.), *Moral development and behavior* (pp. 102-136). New York: Holt, Rinehart & Winston.

Kohlberg, L. (1981). *The philosophy of moral development.* San Francisco: Harper & Row.

Köhler, W. (1926). *The mentality of apes.* New York: Harcourt Brace.

Kohut, H. (1977). *The restoration of self.* New York: International Universities Press.

Kolers, P. A. (1983). Perception and representation. In R. Rosenzweig & L. W. Porter (Eds.), *Annual review of psychology* (Vol. 34, pp. 129-166). Palo Alto, CA: Annual Reviews.

Kotarba, J. A. (1977). The chronic pain experience. In J. D. Douglas & J. M. Johnson (Eds.), *Existential sociology* (pp. 257-272). New York: Cambridge University Press.

Kotarba, J. A. (1984). A synthesis: The existential self in society. In J. A. Kotarba & A. Fontana (Eds.), *The existential self in society* (pp. 222-239). Chicago: University of Chicago Press.

Krieger, S. (1983). *The mirror dance: Identity in a women's community.* Philadelphia: Temple University Press.

Kronus, S. J. (1971). *The black middle class.* Columbus, OH: Charles E. Merrill.

Kübler-Ross, E. (1969). *On death and dying.* New York: Macmillan.

Kuhn, M. H. (1954a). Factors in personality: Sociocultural determinants as seen through the Amish. In F. L. K. Hsu (Ed.), *Aspects of culture and personality* (pp. 43-60). New York: Abelard-Schuman.

Kuhn, M. H. (1954b). Kinsey's view of human behavior. *Social Problems, 1,* 119-125.

Kuhn, M. H. (1960). Self-attitudes by age, sex, and professional training. *Sociological Quarterly, 1,* 39-55.

Kuhn, M. H. (1964). Major trends in symbolic interaction theory in the past twenty-five years. *Sociological Quarterly, 5,* 61-84.

Labov, W. (1968). *A study of the non-standard English of Negro and Puerto Rican speakers in New York City.* Washington, DC: U.S. Office of Education.

Lacan, J. A. (1977). *Écrits: A selection.* New York: W. W. Norton.

Laclau, E., & Mouffe, C. (1985). *Hegemony and socialist strategy: Towards a radical democratic politics.* London: Verso.

Langer, S. K. (1948). *Philosophy in a new key.* Baltimore: Penguin.

Largey, G., & Watson, D. (1972). The sociology of odors. *American Journal of Sociology, 77,* 1021-1034.

Lears, J. (1994, January 9). [Review of the book *Going out: The rise and fall of public amusements,* by D. Nasaw]. *New York Times Review of Books,* p. 29.

Leavitt, R. L. (1994). *Power and emotion in infant-toddler day care.* Albany: State University of New York Press.

Lee, D. (1954). Symbolization and value. In L. Byson et al. (Eds.), *Symbols and values: An initial study* (pp. 73-85). New York: Harper & Row.

Lefebvre, H. (1984). *Everyday life in the modern world.* New Brunswick, NJ: Transaction. (Original work published 1971)

Lemert, C. (1994). Dark thoughts about the self. In C. Calhoun (Ed.), *Social theory and the politics of identity* (pp. 100-129). Cambridge, MA: Blackwell.

Lemert, C. (1995). *Sociology after the crisis.* New York: Westview.

Lemert, E. M. (1962). Paranoia and the dynamics of exclusion. *Sociometry, 25,* 2-20.

Lengermann, P. M., & Wallace, R. A. (1985). *Gender in America: Social control and social change.* Englewood Cliffs, NJ: Prentice Hall.

Lerner, E. (1937). The problem of perspective in moral reasoning. *American Journal of Sociology, 30,* 249-269.

Lester, M. (1984). Self: Sociological portraits. In J. A. Kotarba & A. Fontana (Eds.), *The existential self in society* (pp. 18-68). Chicago: University of Chicago Press.

Lever, J. (1978). Sex differences in the complexity of children's play and games. *American Sociological Review, 43,* 471-483.

Lewis, M., & Michalson, L. (1983). *Children's emotions and moods.* New York: Plenum.

Lewis, M. M. (1936). *Infant speech.* New York: Harcourt Brace.

Lewis, M. M. (1948). *Language in society.* New York: Social Science Research Council.

Lewis, M. M. (1959). *How children learn to speak.* New York: Basic Books.

Lewontin, R. C., Rose, S., & Kamin, L. J. (1984). *Not in our genes: Biology, ideology and human nature.* New York: Pantheon.

Lieban, R. W. (1966). Sorcery, illness, and social control in a Philippine municipality. In W. R. Scott & E. H. Volkart (Eds.), *Medical care: Readings in the sociology of medical institutions* (pp. 222-232). New York: John Wiley.

Lifton, R. J. (1961). *Thought reform and the psychology of totalism.* New York: W. W. Norton.

Lilly, J. C. (1961). *Man and dolphin.* Garden City, NY: Doubleday.

Lindesmith, A. R. (1947). *Opiate addiction.* Bloomington, IN: Principia.

Lindesmith, A. R. (1965). *The addict and the law.* Bloomington: Indiana University Press.

Lindesmith, A. R. (1968). *Addiction and opiates.* Chicago: Aldine.

Lindesmith, A. R. (1975). A reply to McAuliffe and Gordon's "Test of Lindesmith's theory of addiction." *American Journal of Sociology, 81,* 147-153.

Lindesmith, A. R., & Strauss, A. L. (1949). *Social psychology.* New York: Dryden.

Linton, R. (1942). Age and sex categories. *American Sociological Review, 7,* 589-603.

Lippmann, W. (1922). *Public opinion.* New York: Harcourt Brace.

Livesay, J. (1989). Structuration theory and the unacknowledged conditions of action. *Theory, Culture & Society, 6,* 263-292.

Lofland, L. H. (1985). The social shaping of emotion: The case of grief. *Symbolic Interaction, 8,* 171-190.

Lorde, A. (1997). I am your sister: Black women organizing against sexualities. In M. Blasius & S. Phelan (Eds.), *We are everywhere: A historical sourcebook of gay and lesbian politics* (pp. 472-476). New York: Routledge.

Lorimer, F. (1929). *The growth of reason.* New York: Harcourt Brace.

Lowry, M. (1984). *Under the volcano.* New York: Harper & Row. (Original work published 1947)

Luckey, E. B., & Nass, G. D. (1969). A comparison of sexual attitudes and behavior in an international sample. *Journal of Marriage and the Family, 17,* 364-379.

Luker, K. (1975). *Taking chances: Abortion and the decision not to contracept.* Berkeley: University of California Press.

Luker, K. (1984). *Abortion and the politics of motherhood.* Berkeley: University of California Press.

Lupton, D. (1997). Foucault and the medicalisation critique. In A. Petersen & R. Bunton (Eds.), *Foucault, health and medicine* (pp. 94-112). London: Routledge.

Luria, A. R. (1928). The problem of the cultural behavior of the child. *Journal of Genetic Psychology, 35,* 493-504.

Luria, A. R. (1960). *The nature of human conflicts: An objective study of disorganization and control of human behavior.* New York: Grove.

Luria, A. R. (1972). *The man with a shattered world: The history of a brain wound.* New York: Basic Books.

Luria, A. R. (1976). *Cognitive development: Its cultural and social foundations* (M. Cole, Ed.; M. Lopez-Morillas & L. Solotaroff, Trans.). Cambridge, MA: Harvard University Press.

Luria, A. R., & Yudovich, F. (1959). *Speech and the development of mental process in the child: An experimental investigation.* London: Staples.

Lyman, S., & Scott, M. (1967). Territoriality: A neglected social dimension. *Social Problems, 15,* 236-249.

Lynch, R. (1982). Play, creativity and emotion. In N. K. Denzin (Ed.), *Studies in symbolic interaction: A research annual* (Vol. 4, pp. 45-62). Greenwich, CT: JAI.

Lyotard, J.-F. (1984). *The postmodern condition: A report on knowledge* (G. Bennington & B. Massumi, Trans.). Minneapolis: University of Minnesota Press. (Original work published 1979)

MacCannell, D. (1976). The past and future of symbolic interaction. *Semiotica, 16,* 99-114.

MacIver, R. (1942). *Social causation.* Boston: Ginn.

MacLeod, S. (1981). *The art of starvation.* London: Virago.

Maines, D. R. (1978). Bodies and selves: Notes on a fundamental dilemma in demography. In N. K. Denzin (Ed.), *Studies in symbolic interaction: A research annual* (Vol. 1, pp. 241-266). Greenwich, CT: JAI.

Maines, D., Sugrue, N. M., & Katovich, M. A. (1983). The sociological import of G. H. Mead's theory of the past. *American Sociological Review, 48,* 161-173.

Manis, J. G., & Meltzer, B. N. (Eds.). (1972). *Symbolic interaction: A reader in social psychology* (2nd ed.). Boston: Allyn & Bacon.

Mannheim, K. (1936). *Ideology and utopia.* New York: Harcourt Brace.

Manning, P. K. (1987). Structuralism and social psychology. In N. K. Denzin (Ed.), *Studies in symbolic interaction: A research annual* (Vol. 8, pp. 93-119). Greenwich, CT: JAI.

Manning, P. K., & Fabrega, H., Jr. (1973). The experience of self and body: Health and illness in the Chiapas highlands. In G. Psathas (Ed.), *Phenomenological sociology* (pp. 251-301). New York: John Wiley.

Markey, J. F. (1978). *The symbolic process and its integration in children: A study in social psychology.* Chicago: University of Chicago Press. (Original work published 1928)

Martin, G. B., & Clark, R. D. (1982). Distress crying in neonates: Species and peer specificity. *Developmental Psychology, 11,* 571-578.

Marx, K. (1983). From the eighteenth brumaire of Louis Bonaparte [1844]. In E. Kamenka (Ed.), *The portable Karl Marx* (pp. 287-323). New York: Penguin.

Masters, W., & Johnson, E. (1966). *Human sexual response.* Boston: Little, Brown.

Masters, W., & Johnson, E. (1968). *Human sexual inadequacy.* Boston: Little, Brown.

Maxwell, M. A. (1984). *The alcoholic experience: A close-up view for professionals.* New York: McGraw-Hill.

Maynard, D. W., & Whalen, M. R. (1995). Language, action and social interaction. In K. S. Cook, G. A. Fine, & J. S. House (Eds.), *Sociological perspectives on social psychology* (pp. 149-175). Boston: Allyn & Bacon.

McAuliffe, W. E., & Gordon, R. A. (1974). A test of Lindesmith's theory of addiction: The frequency of euphoria among long-term addicts. *American Journal of Sociology, 77,* 795-840.

McCall, G. J., & Simmons, J. L. (1966). *Identities and interactions.* New York: Free Press.

McKee, J. B. (1993). *Sociology and the race problem: The failure of a perspective.* Urbana: University of Illinois Press.

McNeill, D. (1966). The creation of language. *Discovery, 27,* 34-38.

Mead, G. H. (1929). The nature of the past. In J. Coss (Ed.), *Essays in honor of John Dewey* (pp. 16-34). New York: Henry Holt.

Mead, G. H. (1932). *The philosophy of the present.* LaSalle, IL: Open Court.

Mead, G. H. (1934). *Mind, self, and society: From the standpoint of a social behaviorist.* Chicago: University of Chicago Press.

Mead, G. H. (1936). *Movements of thought in the nineteenth century.* Chicago: University of Chicago Press.

Mead, G. H. (1938). *The philosophy of the act.* Chicago: University of Chicago Press.

Mead, M. (1955). Children and ritual in Bali. In M. Mead & M. Wolfenstein (Eds.), *Childhood in contemporary cultures* (pp. 67-87). Chicago: University of Chicago Press.

Meltzer, B. N. (1972). Mead's social psychology. In J. G. Manis & B. N. Meltzer (Eds.), *Symbolic interaction: A reader in social psychology* (2nd ed., pp. 4-22). Boston: Allyn & Bacon.

Mercer, J. R. (1973). *Labelling the mentally retarded.* Berkeley: University of California Press.

Mercer, K. (1990). Welcome to the jungle. In J. Rutherford (Ed.), *Identity* (pp. 28-43). London: Lawrence & Wishart.

Merleau-Ponty, M. (1962). *The phenomenology of perception.* London: Routledge & Kegan Paul.

Merleau-Ponty, M. (1963). *The structure of behavior.* Boston: Beacon.

Merleau-Ponty, M. (1968). *The primacy of perception.* Evanston, IL: Northwestern University Press.

Messinger, S. L., & Warren, C. A. B. (1984). The homosexual self and the organization of experience: The case of Kate White. In J. A. Kotarba & A. Fontana (Eds.), *The existential self in society* (pp. 196-206). Chicago: University of Chicago Press.

Metz, C. (1982). *The imaginary signifier: Psychoanalysis and the cinema.* Bloomington: Indiana University Press.

Miller, G., & Holstein, J. A. (1993). Reconsidering social constructionism. In J. A. Holstein & G. Miller (Eds.), *Reconsidering social constructionism* (pp. 5-23). New York: Aldine de Gruyter.

Miller, N. E., & Dollard, J. (1941). *Social learning and imitation.* New Haven, CT: Yale University Press.

Miller, P. J. (1996). Instantiating culture through discourse practices: Some personal reflections on socialization and how to study it. In R. J. Jessor, A. Colby, & R. Shweder (Eds.), *Ethnography and human development: Context and meaning in social inquiry* (pp. 183-204). Chicago: University of Chicago Press.

Mills, C. W. (1939). Language, logic, and culture. *American Sociological Review, 4,* 670-675.

Mills, C. W. (1940). Situated actions and culture. *American Sociological Review, 5,* 904-913.

Mills, C. W. (1956). *The power elite.* New York: Oxford University Press.

Mills, C. W. (1959). *The sociological imagination.* New York: Oxford University Press.

Mills, C. W. (1963). *Power, politics, and people: The collected essays of C. Wright Mills* (I. L. Horowitz, Ed.). New York: Ballantine.

Mitchell, J. (1983). Introduction: I. In J. Mitchell & J. Rose (Eds.), *Feminine sexuality: Jacques Lacan and the école Freudienne* (pp. 1-28). New York: Pantheon.

Mitford, J. (1963). *The American way of death.* New York: Simon & Schuster.

Mizruchi, E. M., & Perrucci, R. (1962). Norm qualities and differential effects of deviant behavior. *American Sociological Review, 27,* 391-399.

Morgan, L. (1894). *Introduction to comparative psychology.* New York: Young Scott.

Morris, C. (1946). *Signs, language, and behavior.* Englewood Cliffs, NJ: Prentice Hall.

Much, N. (1995). Cultural psychology. In J. A. Smith, R. Harré, & L. Van Langenhove (Eds.), *Rethinking psychology.* London: Sage.

Mullins, N. (1973). *Theories and theory groups in contemporary American sociology.* New York: Harper & Row.

Murphy, G., Murphy, L., & Newcomb, T. (1937). *Experimental social psychology.* New York: Harper & Row.

Murray, K. D. (1995). Narratology. In J. A. Smith, R. Harré, & L. Van Langenhove (Eds.), *Rethinking psychology.* London: Sage.

Murstein, B. (Ed.). (1971). *Theories of attraction and love.* Berlin: Springer-Verlag.

Musolf, G. R. (1996). Interactionism and the child: Cahill, Corsaro, and Denzin on childhood socialization. *Symbolic Interaction, 19,* 303-322.

Myrdal, G., with Sterner, R., & Rose, A. (1944). *An American dilemma: The Negro problem and modern democracy.* New York: Harper & Row.

Namaste, K. (1994). The politics of inside/out: Queer theory, poststructuralism, and a sociological approach to sexuality. *Sociological Theory, 12,* 220-231.

Nash, J. (1985). *Social psychology: Self and society.* St. Paul, MN: West.

Neubeck, G. (Ed.). (1969). *Extramarital relations.* Englewood Cliffs, NJ: Prentice Hall.

Newcomb, T., Turner, R., & Converse, P. (1965). *Social psychology.* New York: Holt, Rinehart & Winston.

Newton, E. (1972). *Mother Camp: Female impersonators in America.* Englewood Cliffs, NJ: Prentice Hall.

Nicolson, P. (1995). Feminism and psychology. In J. A. Smith, R. Harré, & L. Van Langenhove (Eds.), *Rethinking psychology.* London: Sage.

Noy, R. S., & Sharron, A. (1985). The indiscretion of Franz Kafka: The artist as a victim of child abuse. In N. K. Denzin (Ed.), *Studies in symbolic interaction: A research annual* (Vol. 6, pp. 261-287). Greenwich, CT: JAI.

Nurge, E. (1961). Etiology of illness in Guinhangdan. *American Anthropologist, 638,* 113-132.

O'Connor, P. J. (1977, July 23-24). Burial vault strike: A double dose of grief. *Chicago Daily News,* p. 5.

O'Grady, W., Dobrovolsky, M., & Aronoff, M. (1997). *Contemporary linguistics* (3rd ed.). New York: St. Martin's.

O'Neill, J. (1985). *Five bodies: The human shape of modern society.* Ithaca, NY: Cornell University Press.

Opie, I., & Opie, P. (1969). *Children's games in street and playground.* New York: Oxford University Press.

Opler, M. E., & Bittle, W. E. (1967). The death practices of the Kiowa Apache. In R. C. Owen, J. J. F. Deetz, & A. D. Fisher (Eds.), *The North American Indians: A sourcebook* (pp. 472-482). New York: Macmillan.

Packard, V. (1983). *Our endangered children.* Boston: Little, Brown.

Pannabecker, B. J., Emde, R. N., Johnson, W., Stenberc, C., & Davis, M. (1980). *Maternal perceptions of infant emotions from birth to eighteen months: A preliminary report.* Paper presented at the International Conference on Infant Studies, New Haven, CT.

Park, K. (1996). Use and abuse of race and culture: Black-Korean tension in America. *American Anthropologist, 98,* 492-499.

Parsons, T., & Platt, G. M. (1970). Age, social structure and socialization in higher education. *Sociology of Education, 43,* 1-37.

Parten, M. B. (1932). Social participation among preschool children. *Journal of Abnormal and Social Psychology, 27,* 263-269.

Patterson, N. (1985, April). Koko. *National Geographic, 95,* 400-409.

Pavlov, I. P. (1929). *Conditioned reflexes.* New York: Oxford University Press.

Pavlov, I. P. (1960). *Conditioned reflexes: An investigation of the physiological activity of the cerebral cortex.* New York: Dover.

Peirce, C. S. (1960). Elements of logic. In C. Hartshorne & P. Weiss (Eds.), *Collected papers of Charles Sanders Peirce* (Vol. 2). Cambridge, MA: Harvard University Press.

Perinbanayagam, R. S. (1982). *The karmic theater: Self, society, and astrology in Jaffna.* Amherst: University of Massachusetts Press.

Perinbanayagam, R. S. (1985). *Signifying acts.* Carbondale: Southern Illinois University Press.

Perinbanayagam, R. S. (1991). *Discursive acts.* New York: Aldine de Gruyter.

Persons, S. (1958). *American minds: A history of ideas.* New York: Holt.

Piaget, J. (1937). Principal factors determining intellectual evolution from childhood to adult life. In J. Piaget, *Factors determining human behavior.* Cambridge, MA: Harvard University Press.

Piaget, J. (1948). *The moral judgment of the child.* New York: Free Press.

Piaget, J. (1950). *The psychology of intelligence.* London: Routledge & Kegan Paul.

Piaget, J. (1951). *Play, dreams, and imitation in childhood.* New York: W. W. Norton.

Piaget, J. (1952a). *The child's conception of number.* New York: Humanities Press.

Piaget, J. (1952b). *The origins of intelligence in children.* New York: International Universities Press.

Piaget, J. (1952c). *Judgment and reasoning in the child.* New York: Humanities Press.

Piaget, J. (1954). *The construction of reality in the child.* New York: Basic Books.

Piaget, J. (1959). *The language and thought of the child.* New York: Humanities Press.

Piaget, J. (1960). *The child's conception of physical causality.* Paterson, NJ: Littlefield, Adams.

Piaget, J. (1967). *The child's conception of the world.* Totowa, NJ: Littlefield, Adams. (Original work published 1929)

Piaget, J. (1970). *Structuralism.* New York: Basic Books.

Piaget, J. (1983). *Intelligence and affectivity: Their relationship during child development.* Palo Alto, CA: Annual Reviews.

Pittinger, R. E., & Smith, H. L. (1967). A basis for some contributions of linguistics to psychiatry. *Psychiatry, 20,* 61-78.

Pizzey, E. (1974). *Scream quietly or the neighbors will hear.* Baltimore: Penguin.

Plummer, K. (1997). *Telling sexual stories.* London: Routledge.

Plummer, K. (1991). [Review of the books *Homosexuality, which homosexuality? Essays from the International Scientific Conference on Lesbian and Gay Studies,* edited by A. van Kooten Niekerk and T. van der Meer; *Homosexuality: A philosophical inquiry,* by M. Ruse; and *The construction of homosexuality,* by D. Greenberg]. *Theory, Culture & Society, 8,* 175-186.

Polsky, N. (1966). *Hustlers, beats, and others.* Chicago: Aldine.

Ponse, B. R. (1978). *Identities in the lesbian world.* New York: Greenwood.

Postman, N. (1982). *The disappearance of childhood.* New York: Laurel.

Power, M. B. (1985). The ritualization of emotional conduct in early childhood. In N. K. Denzin (Ed.), *Studies in symbolic interaction: A research annual* (Vol. 6, pp. 213-227). Greenwich, CT: JAI.

Premack, A. J., & Premack, D. (1972). Teaching language to an ape. *Scientific American, 227,* 92-99.

Preston, J. (1989). Prologue. In J. Preston (Ed.), *Personal dispatches: Writers confront AIDS* (pp. 1-12). New York: St. Martin's.

Price, S. (1993). *Media studies.* London: Pitman.

Psathas, G. (1995). *Conversation analysis: The study of talk-in-interaction.* Thousand Oaks, CA: Sage.

Quadagno, J. S. (Ed.). (1980). *Aging, the individual and society: Readings in social gerontology.* New York: St. Martin's.

Quiatt, D. (1984). Devious intentions of monkeys and apes. In R. Harré & V. Reynolds (Eds.), *The meaning of primate signals.* Cambridge: Cambridge University Press.

Ragland-Sullivan, E. (1986). *Jacques Lacan and the philosophy of psychoanalysis.* Urbana: University of Illinois Press.

Ray, R. B. (1985). *A certain tendency of the Hollywood cinema, 1930-1980.* Princeton, NJ: Princeton University Press.

Reeves, J. L., & Campbell, R. (1994). *Cracked coverage: Television news, the anti-cocaine crusade, and the Reagan legacy.* Durham, NC: Duke University Press.

Reiss, I. L. (1971). *The family system in America.* New York: Holt, Rinehart & Winston.

Reynolds, L. T. (1990). *Interactionism: Exposition and critique* (2nd ed.). Dix Hills, NY: General Hall.

Reynolds, V. (1980). *The biology of human action* (2nd ed.). San Francisco: W. H. Freeman.

Richardson, L. (1997). *Playing the field.* New Brunswick, NJ: Rutgers University Press.

Richardson, S. A. (1969). The effect of physical disability on the socialization of the child. In D. A. Goslin (Ed.), *Handbook of socialization theory and research* (pp. 1047-1064). Skokie, IL: Rand McNally.

Riley, J. W., Jr. (1983). Dying and the meanings of death: Sociological inquiries. *Annual Review of Sociology, 9,* 191-216.

Ritzer, G. (1993). *The McDonaldization of society: An investigation into the changing character of contemporary social life.* Newbury Park, CA: Pine Forge.

Roby, P. (1969). Politics and criminal law: Revision of the New York State penal law on prostitution. *Social Problems, 17,* 83-109.

Rose, J. (1983). Introduction: II. In J. Mitchell & J. Rose (Eds.), *Feminine sexuality: Jacques Lacan and the école Freudienne* (pp. 29-47). New York: Pantheon.

Rosow, I. (1967). *Social integration of the aged.* New York: Free Press.

Ross, H. L. (1971). Modes of adjustment of married homosexuals. *Social Problems, 18,* 385-393.

Rossi, A. S. (1965). Naming children in middle class families. *American Sociological Review, 30,* 499-513.

Rossi, A. S. (1984). Gender and parenthood. *American Sociological Review, 49,* 1-19.

Runyon, T. (1953). *In for life.* New York: W. W. Norton.

Sacks, O. (1985). *The man who mistook his wife for a hat and other clinical tales.* New York: Harper & Row.

Salomone, J. J. (1973). An empirical report on some controversial American funeral practices. *Sociological Symposium, 1,* 47-66.

Sandburg, C. (1943). Elephants are different to different people. In C. Sandburg, *Home front memo.* New York: Harcourt Brace.

Sanders, W. B. (1994). *Gangbangs and drive-bys: Grounded culture and juvenile gang violence.* New York: Aldine de Gruyter.

Sansom, W. (1955). *A contest of ladies.* London: Hogarth.

Sapir, E. (1942). Communication. In *Encyclopedia of the social sciences* (Vol. 2, pp. 78-81). New York: Macmillan.

Sapir, E. (1949). Time perspective in aboriginal American culture: A study in method. In D. G. Mandelbaum (Ed.), *Selected writings in language, culture, and personality.* Berkeley: University of California Press.

Sartre, J.-P. (1956). *Being and nothingness.* New York: Philosophical Library. (Original work published 1943)

Sartre, J.-P. (1976). *The critique of dialectical reason.* London: NLP. (Original work published 1960)

Sartre, J.-P. (1981). *The family idiot: Gustave Flaubert: Vol. 1. 1821-1857.* Chicago: University of Chicago Press.

Saukko, P. (1996). Anorexia nervosa: Rereading the stories that became me. In N. K. Denzin (Ed.), *Cul-*

tural studies: A research annual (Vol. 1, pp. 49-65). Greenwich, CT: JAI.

Saussure, F. de. (1959). *A course in general linguistics.* New York: McGraw-Hill.

Saxton, S. L., Jr., & Hall, P. M. (1987). Two social psychologies: New grounds for discussion. In N. K. Denzin (Ed.), *Studies in symbolic interaction: A research annual* (Vol. 8, pp. 43-67). Greenwich, CT: JAI.

Schachtel, E. (1947). On memory and childhood amnesia. *Psychiatry, 10,* 1-26.

Schachter, S., & Singer, J. E. (1962). Cognitive, social, and physiological determinants of emotional states. *Psychological Review, 69,* 379-399.

Schaffer, H. R. (1971). *The growth of sociability.* Baltimore: Penguin.

Scheff, T. J. (1979). *Catharsis in healing ritual and drama.* Berkeley: University of California Press.

Schein, E. I., Schneier, I., & Barker, C. H. (1961). *Coercive persuasion.* New York: W. W. Norton.

Schneirla, T. (1946). Problems in the biopsychology of social organization. *Journal of Abnormal and Social Psychology, 41,* 390-398.

Schneirla, T. (1949). Levels in the psychological capacities of animals. In R. Sellars (Ed.), *Philosophy for the future.* New York: Macmillan.

Schneirla, T. (1953a). Animal behavior and human relations. In M. Sherif & C. Sherif (Eds.), *Groups in harmony and tension.* New York: Harper & Row.

Schneirla, T. (1953b). The concept of levels in the study of social phenomena. In M. Sherif & C. Sherif (Eds.), *Groups in harmony and tension* (pp. 54-75). New York: Harper & Row.

Schultz, J., Carrin, G., Krupp, H., Peochke, M., Sclar, E., & Van Steenberge, J. (1974). *Providing adequate retirement income.* Waltham, MA: Brandeis University Press.

Schutz, A. (1962). *Collected papers: Vol. 1. The problem of social reality.* The Hague: Martinus Nijhoff.

Schutz, A. (1964). *Collected papers: Vol. 2. Studies in social theory.* The Hague: Martinus Nijhoff.

Schutz, A., & Luckmann, T. (1973). *The structures of the life world.* Evanston, IL: Northwestern University Press.

Schwartz, B. (1970). Notes on the sociology of sleep. *Sociological Quarterly, 11,* 485-499.

Schwartz, C. G., & Kahne, M. J. (1973). *Conflict and contradiction in psychiatry: The evolution of a professional sub-specialty.* Unpublished manuscript.

Schwartz, D., & Merten, G. (1967). The language of adolescence. *American Journal of Sociology, 72,* 453-468.

Schwartz, D., & Merten, G. (1971). Participant observation and the discovery of meaning. *Philosophy of Social Science, 1,* 290-295.

Scott, M. B., & Lyman, S. M. (1968). Accounts. *American Sociological Review, 33,* 46-62.

Scott, M. B., & Stanford, M. L. (1969). The socialization of blind children. In D. A. Goslin (Ed.), *Handbook of socialization theory and research* (pp. 1025-1045). Skokie, IL: Rand McNally.

Scott, R., & Lyman, S. M. (1970). *A sociology of the absurd.* New York: Appleton-Century-Crofts.

Scully, D. (1991). *Understanding sexual violence.* Newbury Park, CA: Sage.

Searle, J. R. (1970). *Speech acts.* New York: Cambridge University Press.

Secord, P. F. (Ed.). (1982). *Explaining human behavior: Consciousness, human action, and social structure.* Beverly Hills, CA: Sage.

Sedgwick, E. K. (1990). *Epistemology of the closet.* Berkeley: University of California Press.

Seidman, S. (1994). Queer theory/sociology: A dialogue [Symposium]. *Sociological Theory, 12,* 166-177.

Seigfried, C. H. (1996). *Pragmatism and feminism: Reweaving the social fabric.* Chicago: University of Chicago Press.

Selman, R. L. (1981). The child as a friendship philosopher. In S. R. Asher & J. M. Gottman (Eds.), *The development of children's friendships* (pp. 242-272). New York: Cambridge University Press.

Seward, G. H. (1946). *Sex and the social order.* New York: McGraw-Hill.

Seyfarth, R. (1984). What the vocalizations of monkeys mean to humans and what they mean to the monkeys themselves. In R. Harré & V. Reynolds (Eds.), *The meaning of primate signals* (pp. 38-64). Cambridge: Cambridge University Press.

Sherif, M., & Cantril, H. (1947). *The psychology of ego-involvement.* New York: John Wiley.

Shibutani, T. (1962). Reference groups and social control. In A. Rose (Ed.), *Human behavior and social process* (pp. 128-147). Boston: Houghton Mifflin.

Shibutani, T. (1966). *Improvised news: A sociological study of rumor.* Indianapolis: Bobbs-Merrill.

Shibutani, T. (1978). *The derelicts of Company K: A sociological study of demoralization.* Berkeley: University of California Press.

Shinn, M. W. (1891). Notes on the development of a child. *Education, 1,* 140-145.

Shotter, J. (1995). Dialogical psychology. In J. A. Smith, R. Harré, & L. Van Langenhove (Eds.), *Rethinking psychology* (pp. 160-178). London: Sage.

Shover, N. (1985). *Aging criminals.* Beverly Hills, CA: Sage.

Silverman, K. (1988). *The acoustic mirror: The female voice in psychoanalysis and cinema.* Bloomington: Indiana University Press.

Simmel, G. (1950). *The sociology of Georg Simmel* (K. Wolff, Trans.). New York: Free Press.

Simmel, G. (1953). *Conflict and the web of group affiliations* (R. Bendix & E. C. Hughes, Eds. and Trans.). New York: Free Press.

Singer, J. L. (1975). *The inner world of daydreaming.* New York: Harper & Row.

Skinner, B. F. (1953). *Science and human behavior.* New York: Macmillan.

Skolnick, A. S., & Skolnick, J. H. (Eds.). (1977). *Family in transition.* Boston: Little, Brown.

Smelser, N. (1963). *Theory of collective behavior.* New York: Free Press.

Smythe, D. (1994). The material reality under monopoly capitalism is that all non-sleeping time of most of the population is work time. In D. Smythe, *Counterclockwise: Perspectives on communication from Dallas Smythe* (T. Guback, Ed.; pp. 263-299). Boulder, CO: Westview.

Solomon, D. (1964). *LSD: The consciousness-expanding drug.* New York: Putnam.

Spector, M., & Kitsuse, J. (1987). *Constructing social problems.* New York: Aldine de Gruyter.

Stam, R. (1989). *Subversive pleasures: Bakhtin, cultural criticism, and film.* Baltimore: Johns Hopkins University Press.

Star, S. L. (1991). The sociology of the invisible: The primacy of work in the writings of Anselm Strauss. In D. R. Maines (Ed.), *Social organization and social process: Essays in honor of Anselm Strauss* (pp. 265-283). New York: Aldine de Gruyter.

Stebbins, R. A. (1970). Career: The subjective approach. *Sociological Quarterly, 11,* 32-49.

Stein, A., & Plummer, K. (1994). "I can't even think straight": "Queer" theory and the missing sexual revolution in sociology. *Sociological Theory, 12,* 178-187.

Stoller, R. S. (1967). [Appendix to Chapter 5]. In H. Garfinkel, *Studies in ethnomethodology.* Englewood Cliffs, NJ: Prentice Hall.

Stoller, R. S. (1979). *Sexual excitement: Dynamics of erotic life.* New York: Pantheon.

Stone, B. (1982). Saussure, Schutz and symbolic interactionism on the constitution and interpretation of signitive behavior. In N. K. Denzin (Ed.), *Studies in symbolic interaction: A research annual* (Vol. 4, pp. 91-106). Greenwich, CT: JAI.

Stone, G. P. (1962). Appearance and the self. In A. M. Rose (Ed.), *Human behavior and social process* (pp. 86-118). Boston: Houghton Mifflin.

Stone, G. P. (1981a). Appearance and the self: A slightly revised version. In G. P. Stone & H. A. Farberman (Eds.), *Social psychology through symbolic interaction* (2nd ed., pp. 187-202). New York: John Wiley.

Stone, G. P. (1981b). The circumstance and situation of social status. In G. P. Stone & H. A. Farberman (Eds.), *Social psychology through symbolic interaction* (2nd ed., pp. 3-41). New York: John Wiley.

Stone, G. P. (1984). Conceptual problems in small group research. In N. K. Denzin (Ed.), *Studies in symbolic interaction: A research annual* (Vol. 5, pp. 3-21). Greenwich, CT: JAI.

Strauss, A. L. (1952). The development and transformation of monetary meanings in the child. *American Sociological Review, 17,* 275-286.

Strauss, A. L. (1954). The development of conceptions of rules in children. *Child Development, 23,* 193-208.

Strauss, A. L. (1959). *Mirrors and masks.* Glencoe, IL: Free Press.

Strauss, A. L. (1977). Sociological theories of personality. In R. J. Corsini, (Ed.), *Current personality theories* (pp. 277-302). Itasca, IL: F. E. Peacock.

Strauss, A. L. (1993). *Continual permutations of action.* New York: Aldine de Gruyter.

Strauss, A. L., Fagerhaugh, S., Suczek, B., & Wiener, C. (1985). *The social organization of medical work.* Chicago: University of Chicago Press.

Strauss, A. L., & Glaser, B. G. (1970). *Anguish: A case history of a dying trajectory.* San Francisco: Sociology Press.

Sudnow, D. (1967). *Passing on: The social organization of dying.* Englewood Cliffs, NJ: Prentice Hall.

Sudnow, D. (Ed.). (1972). *Studies in social interaction.* New York: Free Press.

Sudnow, D. (1978). *Ways of the hand.* New York: Alfred A. Knopf.

Sudnow, D. (1979). *Talk's body.* New York: Alfred A. Knopf.

Sullivan, H. S. (1953). *The interpersonal theory of psychiatry.* New York: W. W. Norton.

Suransky, V. P. (1982). *The erosion of childhood.* Chicago: University of Chicago Press.

Sutherland, E. H. (1949). *White-collar crime.* New York: Holt, Rinehart & Winston.

Sutherland, E. H., & Cressey, D. (1966). *Principals of criminology* (7th ed.). Philadelphia: J. B. Lippincott.

Sykes, G. M., & Matza, D. (1959). Techniques of neutralization: A theory of delinquency. *American Sociological Review, 22,* 664-670.

Taine, H. (1877). Note on the acquisition of language by children and in the human species. *Mind, 2,* 251-256.

Tajfel, H. (1969). Social and cultural factors in perception. In G. Lindzey & E. Aronson (Eds.), *Handbook of social psychology: Vol. 3. The individual in a social context* (2nd ed., pp. 315-394). Reading, MA: Addison-Wesley.

Taylor, C. (1982). Consciousness. In P. F. Secord (Ed.), *Explaining human behavior: Consciousness, human action, and social structure* (pp. 38-51). Beverly Hills, CA: Sage.

Taylor, C. (1985). *Human agency and language: Philosophical papers.* Cambridge: Cambridge University Press.

Terrance, H. S. (1984). Language in apes. In R. Harré & V. Reynolds (Eds.), *The meaning of primate signals* (pp. 130-155). Cambridge: Cambridge University Press.

Thomas, W. I., & Thomas, D. S. (1928). *The child in America.* New York: Alfred A. Knopf.

Thomas, W. I., & Znaniecki, F. (1927). *The Polish peasant in Europe and America.* New York: Alfred A. Knopf.

Thorne, B., & Luria, Z. (1986). Sexuality and gender in children's daily worlds. *Social Problems, 33,* 176-190.

Traub, S. H., & Little, C. B. (Eds.). (1980). *Theories of deviance* (2nd ed.). Itasca, IL: F. E. Peacock.

Travisano, R. (1981). Alternation and conversion as qualitatively different transformations. In G. P. Stone & H. A. Farberman (Eds.), *Social psychology through symbolic interaction* (2nd ed., pp. 237-248). New York: John Wiley.

Treichler, P. A. (1987). AIDS, homophobia, and biomedical discourse: An epidemic of signification. *Cultural Studies, 1,* 263-305.

Trinh T. M. (1989). *Woman, native, other: Writing postcoloniality and feminism.* Bloomington: Indiana University Press.

Trinh T. M. (1991). *When the moon waxes red: Representation, gender, and cultural politics.* New York: Routledge.

Trinh T. M. (1992). *Framer framed.* New York: Routledge.

Trivers, R. (1971). The evolution of reciprocal altruism. *Quarterly Review of Biology, 46,* 35-57.

Turiel, E. (1975). The development of social concepts. In D. DePalma & J. Foley (Eds.), *Moral development* (pp. 150-176). Hillsdale, NJ: Lawrence Erlbaum.

Turner, B. (1984). *The body and society: Explorations in social theory.* Oxford: Basil Blackwell.

Turner, B. (1997). From governmentality to risk: Some reflections on Foucault's contribution to medical sociology. In A. Petersen & R. Bunton (Eds.), *Foucault, health and medicine* (pp. ix-xxi). London: Routledge.

Twain, M. (1976). Two ways of seeing a river [1897]. In B. DeVoto (Ed.), *The portable Mark Twain.* New York: Penguin.

Unruh, D. R. (1980). The social organization of older people: A social world perspective. In N. K. Denzin (Ed.), *Studies in symbolic interaction: A research annual* (Vol. 3, pp. 147-170). Greenwich, CT: JAI.

Unruh, D. R. (1983). *Invisible lives.* Beverly Hills, CA: Sage.

Van Gennep, A. (1960). *The rites of passage* (M. B. Visedom & G. L. Caffee, Trans.). Chicago: University of Chicago Press.

Vendryes, J. (1925). *Language.* New York: Alfred A. Knopf.

Vinacke, W. E. (1953). *The psychology of thinking.* New York: McGraw-Hill.

Vygotsky, L. S. (1939). Thought and speech. *Psychiatry, 2,* 29-52.

Vygotsky, L. S. (1962). *Thought and language* (E. Haufmann & G. Vakar, Eds. and Trans.). Cambridge: MIT Press.

Vygotsky, L. S. (1978). *Mind in society: The development of higher psychological processes* (M. Cole, V. John-Steiner, S. Scribner, & E. Souberman, Eds.). Cambridge, MA: Harvard University Press.

Wallace, P. M. (1984). Aphasia. In R. J. Corsini (Ed.), *Encyclopedia of psychology* (Vol. 1, p. 80). New York: John Wiley.

Wallace, R. A., & Wolf, A. (1986). *Contemporary sociological theory: Continuing the classical tradition* (2nd ed.). Englewood Cliffs, NJ: Prentice Hall.

Waller, W. (1930). *The old love and the new: Divorce and readjustment.* New York: Liveright.

Walshok, M. (1971). The emergence of middle-class deviant subcultures: The case of swingers. *Social Problems, 18,* 488-495.

Walstrom, M. (1996). "Mystory" of anorexia nervosa: New discourses for change and recovery. In N. K. Denzin (Ed.), *Cultural studies: A research annual* (Vol. 1, pp. 67-99). Greenwich, CT: JAI.

Warner, M. (1991). Fear of a queer planet. *Social Text, 9,* 3-17.

Warner, M. (Ed.). (1993). *Fear of a queer planet.* Minneapolis: University of Minnesota Press.

Warren, C. A. B. (1974). *Identity and community in the gay world.* New York: John Wiley.

Watson, J. D. (1968). *The double helix: A personal account of the discovery of the structure of DNA.* New York: Atheneum.

Weber, M. (1946). *From Max Weber: Essays in sociology* (H. Gerth & C. W. Mills, Eds.). New York: Oxford University Press.

Weinstein, E., & Deutschberger, P. (1963). Some dimensions of altercasting. *Sociometry, 26,* 454-466.

Werner, H., & Kaplan, B. (1963). *Symbol formation: An organismic-developmental approach to language and expression of thought.* New York: John Wiley.

West, C. (1984). *Routine complications: Troubles with talk between doctors and patients.* Bloomington: Indiana University Press.

West, C. (1989). *The American evasion of philosophy.* Madison: University of Wisconsin Press.

West, C., & Zimmerman, D. (1987). Doing gender. *Gender and Society, 1,* 125-151.

Westby, D. L. (1960). The career experience of the symphony musician. *Social Forces, 38,* 223-230.

Wiley, N. (1979). Notes on self genesis: From me to we to I. In N. K. Denzin (Ed.), *Studies in symbolic interaction: A research annual* (Vol. 2, pp. 87-107). Greenwich, CT: JAI.

Wiley, N. (1994). *The semiotic self.* Cambridge: Polity.

Wilson, E. O. (1975). *Sociobiology: The new synthesis.* Cambridge, MA: Belknap.

Wilson, R. (1998, February). Transgendered scholars defy convention. *Chronicle of Higher Education, 6,* A10-A12.

Winch, R. (1967). *Mate-selection: A study of complementary needs.* New York: Harper & Row.

Winn, M. (1983). *Children without childhood.* New York: Pantheon.

Wittgenstein, L. (1953). *Philosophical investigations.* Oxford: Basil Blackwell.

Wolfenstein, M. (1954). *Children's humor.* Glencoe, IL: Free Press.

Wolfenstein, M. (1955). French parents take their children to the park. In M. Mead & M. Wolfenstein (Eds.), *Childhood in contemporary cultures* (pp. 99-117). Chicago: University of Chicago Press.

Woolf, V. (1929). *A room of one's own.* London: Hogarth.

Yerkes, R. M. (1943). *Chimpanzees: A laboratory colony.* New Haven, CT: Yale University Press.

Yerkes, R. M., & Yerkes, A. W. (1945). *The great apes: A study of anthropoid life.* New Haven, CT: Yale University Press.

Young, M., & Willmott, P. (1957). *Family and kinship in East London.* London: Routledge & Kegan Paul.

Zelizer, V. A. (1985). *Pricing the priceless child: The changing social value of children.* New York: Basic Books.

Zigler, E. F., & Harter, S. (1969). The socialization of the mentally retarded. In D. A. Goslin (Ed.), *Handbook of socialization theory and research* (pp. 1065-1102). Skokie, IL: Rand McNally.

Zimmerman, D., & Wieder, L. (1970). Comment on Denzin. In J. D. Douglas (Ed.), *Understanding everyday life* (pp. 275-290). Chicago: Aldine.

Index